ECONOMIC SUBSTANCE AND TAX AVOIDANCE:

AN INTERNATIONAL PERSPECTIVE

Robert McMechan
LL.B., LL.M., Ph.D.

CARSWELL

Thomson Reuters Canada Limited

CE AND DISCLAIMER: All rights reserved. No part of this publication may be roduced, stored in a retrieval system, or transmitted, in any form or by any means, electronic, mechanical, photocopying, recording or otherwise, without the prior written consent of the publisher (Carswell).

Carswell and all persons involved in the preparation and sale of this publication disclaim any warranty as to accuracy or currency of the publication. This publication is provided on the understanding and basis that none of Carswell, the author/s or other persons involved in the creation of this publication shall be responsible for the accuracy or currency of the contents, or for the results of any action taken on the basis of the information contained in this publication, or for any errors or omissions contained herein.

No one involved in this publication is attempting herein to render legal, accounting or other professional advice. If legal advice or other expert assistance is required, the services of a competent professional should be sought. The analysis contained herein should in no way be construed as being either official or unofficial policy of any governmental body.

ISBN: 978-07798-5332-8

A cataloguing record for this publication is available from Library and Archives Canada.

Composition: Computer Composition of Canada LP

Printed in Canada by Thomson Reuters.

TELL US HOW WE'RE DOING
Scan the QR code to the right with your smartphone to send your comments regarding our products and services.
Free QR Code Readers are available from your mobile device app store.
You can also email us at carswell.feedback@thomsonreuters.com

THOMSON REUTERS

CARSWELL, A DIVISION OF THOMSON REUTERS CANADA LIMITED

One Corporate Plaza	Customer Relations
2075 Kennedy Road	Toronto 1-416-609-3800
Toronto, Ontario	Elsewhere in Canada/U.S. 1-800-387-5164
M1T 3V4	Fax 1-416-298-5082
	www.carswell.com
	E-mail www.carswell.com/email

For Allison

Foreword

Robert McMechan's thesis is that Canada should amend its tax legislation to incorporate an economic substance test. I think he's right. Not every reader will think that an economic substance test is necessary (at least at the outset); which is why they should read this book.

In aid of his argument, McMechan delineates the parameters of tax avoidance, examines the effects of unchecked abusive tax avoidance, reviews the available judicial doctrines and legislation and finds them wanting, explores the case law that grapples with the Canadian and U.S. avoidance legislation (or doctrine), traces the development of an economic substance doctrine, compares avoidance regimes in five other jurisdictions, explores the overlay of information reporting and penalty provisions, and ultimately uses all of that context to argue in favour of the integration of an economic substance test.

The book makes five contributions worth highlighting in this foreword. First, much has been written about Canada's general anti-avoidance rule and others have situated that legislative development in its historical context. For those who have not followed the evolution of that literature closely, McMechan presents a thoughtful overview of the work that has been done in the broad area of tax avoidance and abuse.

Second, the book provides a rich comparative review of the law. In coming to recommendations about the possible approaches to general avoidance in Canada, chapters explore the related law in the United States, South Africa, Australia, New Zealand, and the United Kingdom. On the specific issue of penalties, in addition to these jurisdictions, McMechan adds an exploration of the law in Quebec. While others have undertaken some of this comparative work, this book is detailed in its review of the law across five jurisdictions in addition to Canada, an impressive feat.

Third, one of the significant challenges of approaching tax avoidance as a topic is delineating the scope of the research and concept. McMechan has done a particularly remarkable job in this book of identifying appropriate cases and of describing those cases accurately and sensibly. Indeed, in a few instances, although I have taught most of these cases at some time or another, I felt I garnered new insights about them or understood them better after reading McMechan's review.

Fourth, McMechan employs an historical methodology. I suspect that tax policy makers and scholars will look back at the period between the mid 1990s and the mid 2010s as a period of massive, dynamic change in our legislative, policy, and possibly judicial approaches to tax avoidance on both the domestic and international levels. McMechan recounts the legislative history in each of the five jurisdictions he explores. It is what I would think of as "dynamic history," proximate in time, but historical nevertheless. Unfolding an historical narrative that reveals some of the key underlying concerns of the moment is complicated even with the benefit of a good deal of hindsight. The book does fine work here, too.

Fifth, the book provides a wonderful review of the different types of tax avoidance arrangements entered into by taxpayers. The section that reviews and summarizes these transactions – from sale and leaseback shelters to distressed asset debt shelters – is one of the clearest descriptions of these arrangements I have seen. This part of the book should serve as a terrific support to courses in tax law policy and design, and should help legislators, judges, and policy makers who want to clarify their thinking about the repercussions of ignoring McMechan's conclusions.

This is a book that bridges and compares approaches across six jurisdictions, assisting the reader to understand some of the global context in which the Canadian law is situate. It provides a doctrinal review of some of the case law that clarifies the reader's understanding of the underlying cases and assists the reader in framing the contours of the tax avoidance problem for policy makers and courts.

This book is a pleasure to read. It is thoughtfully crafted and McMechan's argument is extensively documented. It should be required reading for those of us with an interest in the ongoing sensibility of tax law policy and legislative design.

Kim Brooks
Dean
Weldon Professor of Law
Schulich School of Law
March 2012

Acknowledgements

I acknowledge with great appreciation, and thanks, the direction of Professor Neil Brooks in the research and writing of my PhD dissertation, which this book is based upon. Without his encouragement, kindness and invaluable insights, I would not have commenced, much less completed, the years of hard work that it involved. I also wish to thank Professors Jinyan Li, Lisa Philipps and Tim Edgar of Osgoode Hall Law School for their helpful comments and suggestions regarding early drafts of my dissertation. Former Chief Justice Bowman and David Sherman have also provided me with valuable feedback. I also greatly appreciate the contribution of Dean Kim Brooks in writing a Foreword. All of the shortcomings and views in this book are mine alone. In particular, my views as to the legislative amendments required for the successful application of GAAR in Canada should not be ascribed to anyone.

Table of Contents

Foreword v
Acknowledgements ix
Table of Cases xvii
Introduction 1

I	**Tax Minimization Versus Abusive Tax Avoidance** 29	
	What is tax avoidance? 31	
	Central role of economic consequences 33	
II	**Effects of Unchecked Abusive Tax Avoidance** 41	
	Detrimental effects on taxpayer compliance 42	
	Inequitable allocation of tax liabilities 45	
	Wasting of resources on uneconomic activity 47	
	Interference with government social and economic policies 48	
	Distortion of competition 54	
	Conclusion 54	
III	**A Case for Standards in Responding to Abusive Tax Avoidance** 57	
IV	**Limits of Judicial Doctrines in Canada** 71	
	Legal ineffectiveness 72	

	Substance versus form 73
	Sham..77
	Business purpose 79

V	**SCC's Treatment of Economic Substance** 83
	Legal form trumps economic substance in tax cases 84
	Mara Properties Ltd. v. R. 92
	Duha Printers (Western) Ltd. v. R. 95
	Shell Canada Ltd. v. R. 98
	SCC's rationale...................................107
	Prohibition against "judicial re-drafting"..........108
	Certainty and predictability 119
	Right to minimize taxes 125
	SCC's different approach in non-tax cases............127

VI	**U.S. Economic Substance Doctrine**................139
	Leading U.S. court cases 149
	Gregory v. Helvering 149
	Knetsch v. United States........................154
	Goldstein v. Commissioner......................155
	Frank Lyon v. United States 157
	An ordinary business exception? 160
	Legislatively intended benefits......................168
	Import of bona fide legal relationships...............169
	U.S. tax shelter cases 169
	Sale and leaseback ("SILO") shelters..............180
	Contingent instalment sale ("CINS") shelters 185
	Corporate-owned life insurance ("COLI") shelters . .192
	High-basis, low-value shelters 193
	Bond and option sales strategy ("BOSS") and
	son-of-BOSS ("SOB") shelters................195
	Distressed asset debt ("DAD") shelters 200
	U.S. economic substance doctrine codified 202
	For and against codification....................203
	U.S. Judicial Economic Substance Doctrine ("ESD"). . 206
	Budget proposal for fiscal year 2000 211
	Abusive Tax Shelter Shutdown Act of 1999 211

  Joint Committee Study / White Paper on Corporate
   Tax Shelters.................................212
  Budget Proposal for the Fiscal Year 2001 213
  Abusive Tax Shelter Shutdown Act of 2001 213
  Jumpstart Our Business Strength (JOBS) Act 2004...215
  Tax Reduction and Reform Act of 2007 216
  Budget Proposal for Fiscal Year 2010 216
  Codification at last 217

VII Economic Substance Under GAAR in Other Jurisdictions 229
 South Africa.................................229
  Historical GAAR 231
  2005 Discussion Paper on Tax Avoidance 236
  2006 GAAR amendments 237
  Arrangement.................................237
  Avoidance arrangement/Tax benefit...............238
  Impermissible avoidance arrangement............238
  Purpose of avoiding taxes......................239
  Objective versus subjective determination of purpose..241
  Abnormality requirement......................242
  Eleven factors: the draft legislation 243
  Lack of commercial substance 245
  Misuse or abuse of provisions 248
  Application to scheme as a whole or any part thereof..252
  Application in the alternative...................252
  Remedies under GAAR 253
  Notice requirement...........................253
  What has been accomplished 253
  Conclusion 255
 Australia....................................256
  Historical GAAR in Australia 259
  Part IVA...................................262
  Essential elements 263
  Tax benefit.................................264
  Scheme....................................266
  Dominant purpose 267

        Reconstruction provision 273
        Notice provision 274
        Provision of last resort 274
        What has been accomplished .275
        Conclusion 278
    New Zealand. 278
        Historical GAAR 283
        Section BG 1 — Essential Elements 285
            Arrangement 286
            Tax avoidance 286
            Tax avoidance arrangement 288
        Reconstruction provision 293
        Relationship of section BG 1 to other provisions. . . .294
        What has been accomplished .295
        Conclusion 299
    Other countries 300
    U.K. draft GAAR 300
        Historical anti-avoidance efforts 303
        HMRC's administrative position 307
        1997 Tax Law Review Committee Report 307
        1998 Inland Revenue Consultation Document. 309
        2009 Tax Law Review Committee Discussion Paper . . 310
        2011 Advisory Committee GAAR Study Group
            Report 310
        European Community concept of abusive practice
            or abuse of law 312
        Observations. 313
        Conclusion 313

VIII Reporting Requirements and Penalties 315
    Canada 317
        Reporting requirements 317
        Promoter penalties 320
        Proposed additional reporting requirements. 321
        Proposed additional penalty .323
        Observations. 324

Québec 325
    Mandatory disclosure regime/Understatement
        penalties. 326
    Observations. 326
United States. 327
    Reporting requirements 327
    Promoter penalty 329
    Penalties for failure to file returns and failure to
        maintain investor lists 330
    Penalties for false statements and gross valuation
        overstatements. 330
    Penalties for failure to disclose 331
    Penalties for understatement 331
    Strict liability understatement penalty 331
    Website advisories, standards of practice and
        settlement initiatives 336
    Enjoined conduct 337
    Observations. 337
Australia 337
    No reporting requirement. 338
    Shortfall penalties. 338
    Promoter penalties 339
    Tax alerts 340
    Observations. 341
New Zealand. 341
    No reporting requirement. 341
    Shortfall penalties. 342
    Promoter penalties 345
    Revenue alerts 346
    Observations. 346
South Africa 347
    Reporting requirements 347
    Reporting penalties. 350
    No shortfall penalties 350
    Observations. 350
U.K. 351
    Reporting requirements 351

	Promoter penalties 353
	Investor penalties 353
	Observations..................................353
	Conclusion 354

IX	**Case Studies**.....................................355
	Canada Trustco Mortgage Co. v. R..................357
	OSFC Holdings Ltd. v. R..........................364
	First appellate GAAR decision..................367
	Primary purpose issue 368
	Produits Forestiers Donohue Inc. c. R. 372
	Faraggi c. R.....................................376
	4145356 Canada Ltd. v. The Queen.................379

| X | **Conclusion**......................................387 |

XI	**Select Bibliography**.............................391
	Articles..391
	Books 422
	Conference Papers/Research Papers.................423
	Magazine and Newspaper Articles...................426
	Reports..427
	Websites 431

Appendix A Economic and Commercial Realities in Tax Cases...................................437
Reliance on economic realities in tax cases 437
Computation of Profit........................437
Employees versus Independent Contractors........438
Whether Business Exists 440
Fair Market Value Determinations...............441
Miscellaneous Instances......................441
Reliance on commercial realities in tax cases 443

Appendix B Tax Court GAAR Cases 455

Index...461

Table of Cases

1207192 Ontario Ltd. v. R. (2011), [2012] 1 C.T.C. 2085, 2011 D.T.C. 1301 (Eng.), 2011 CarswellNat 3414, 2011 CarswellNat 4609, 2011 CCI 383, 2011 TCC 383 (T.C.C. [General Procedure]), affirmed 2012 CarswellNat 3894, 2012 FCA 259 (F.C.A.) 107, 459

4145356 Canada Ltd. v. R., 2011 TCC 220, [2011] 4 C.T.C. 2207, 2011 D.T.C. 1171, 2011 CarswellNat 1238, 2011 CarswellNat 3711, 2011 CCI 220 (T.C.C. [General Procedure]) 76, 379, 381, 383

4145356 Canada Ltd. v. The Queen, see 4145356 Canada Ltd. v. R.

671122 Ontario Ltd. v. Sagaz Industries Canada Inc., [2001] 2 S.C.R. 983, [2001] 4 C.T.C. 139, 2001 CarswellOnt 3357, 2001 CarswellOnt 3358, 2001 SCC 59 (S.C.C.), reconsideration / rehearing refused 2001 CarswellOnt 4155, 2001 CarswellOnt 4156 (S.C.C.) 115, 438

722540 Ontario Inc. v. R. (2001), [2002] 1 C.T.C. 2872, 2002 D.T.C. 1307, 2001 CarswellNat 3015, 2001 CarswellNat 4883 (T.C.C. [General Procedure]), affirmed [2003] 3 C.T.C. 1, (*sub nom.* Novopharm Ltd. v. R.) 2003 D.T.C. 5195, 2003 CarswellNat 1350, 2003 CarswellNat 469, 2003 CAF 112, 2003 FCA 112 (Fed. C.A.), leave to appeal refused 2003 CarswellNat 4612, 2003 CarswellNat 4613 (S.C.C.) 446

74712 Alberta Ltd. v. Minister of National Revenue, [1997] 2 C.T.C. 30, (*sub nom.* 74712 Alberta Ltd. v. R.) 97 D.T.C. 5126, 1997 CarswellNat 18, 1997 CarswellNat 1569 (Fed. C.A.) 449

A.S.A. Investerings Partnership v. C.I.R., 201 F.3d 505 (D.C. Cir., 2000) 368

Accent Management Ltd. & Ors v. CIR (2005), 22 NZTC 19,027 (H.C.) 47, 281

ACM Partnership v. C.I.R., 157 F.3d 231 (3d Cir., 1998), cert. denied 526 U.S. 1017 (1999) 161, 186

Aessie v. R., [2004] 4 C.T.C. 2159, 2004 CarswellNat 7140, 2004 CarswellNat 1822, 2004 TCC 421 (T.C.C. [Informal Procedure]) 346

Air Canada v. British Columbia, [1989] 1 S.C.R. 1161, 1989 CarswellBC 706, 1989 CarswellBC 67 (S.C.C.) 7

Alexander v. Minister of National Revenue, [1969] C.T.C. 715, 70 D.T.C. 6006, 1969 CarswellNat 349, 1969 CarswellNat 332 (Can. Ex. Ct.) 439

Am. Elec Power, Inc. v. United States, 136 F. Supp.2d 762 (S.D. Ohio, 2001), affirmed 326 F.3d 737 (6th Cir., 2003). 140, 183

American Boat Co., LLC v. U.S., 583 F.3d 471 (7th Cir., 2009) 196

American Elec. Power Co., Inc. v. U.S., see *Am. Elec Power, Inc. v. United States*

Ampliscientifica Srl v. Ministero dell'Economia e delle Finanze (C-162/07), [2008] ECR I-4019, [2011] STC 566 312

Andrews v. Grand & Toy Alberta Ltd., [1978] 2 S.C.R. 229, 1978 CarswellAlta 214, 1978 CarswellAlta 295 (S.C.C.) 129

Angostura International Ltd. v. R., [1985] 2 C.T.C. 170, 85 D.T.C. 5384, 1985 CarswellNat 322 (Fed. T.D.) 444

Antle v. R. (2009), [2010] 4 C.T.C. 2327, 2009 D.T.C. 1305 (Eng.), 2009 CarswellNat 2792, 2009 CarswellNat 5470, 2009 CCI 465, 2009 TCC 465 (T.C.C. [General Procedure]), affirmed 2010 FCA 280, 2010 D.T.C. 5172 (Eng.), 2010 CarswellNat 3894, 2010 CarswellNat 4878, 2010 CAF 280 (F.C.A.), leave to appeal refused 2011 CarswellNat 5822, 2011 CarswellNat 5823 (S.C.C.), reconsideration / rehearing refused 2012 CarswellNat 172, 2012 CarswellNat 173 (S.C.C.), leave to appeal refused 2011 CarswellNat 1491, 2011 CarswellNat 1492 (S.C.C.), reconsideration / rehearing refused 2012 CarswellNat 183, 2012 CarswellNat 184 (S.C.C.) 356

Archambault v. Minister of National Revenue, [1988] 2 C.T.C. 2391, 88 D.T.C. 1722, *(sub nom.* Archambault c. M.N.R.) 88 D.T.C. 1714 (Fr.), 1988 CarswellNat 468 (T.C.C.) 438

ASA Investerings Partnership v. C.I.R., 201 F.3d 505 (D.C. Cir., 2000) 65, 188

Assurance-Vie Banque Nationale, cie d'assurance-vie c. R., [2006] G.S.T.C. 60, 2006 CarswellNat 3340, 2006 CarswellNat 1143, 2006 CAF 161, 2006 FCA 161 (F.C.A.) 63

Atlantic Coast Line R. Co. v. Phillips, 332 U.S. 168 (1947). . . . 190

Avis Immobilien GmbH v. R., *(sub nom.* Avis Immobilien G.M.B.H. v. R.) 97 D.T.C. 5002 (Fr.), 1996 CarswellNat 2529 (Fed. C.A.), leave to appeal refused (May 22, 1997), Doc. 25749 (S.C.C.) 442

AWG Leasing Trust et al v. United States, No. 1:07-cv-00857-JG (N.D. Ohio May 28, 2008), Doc 2008-11830; 2008 TNT 105-10 . . . 182

AWG Leasing Trust v. United States, 592 F.Supp.2d 953 (N.D. Ohio, 2008) 140

B.C.G.E.U., Re, [1988] 2 S.C.R. 214, 1988 CarswellBC 762, 1988 CarswellBC 363 (S.C.C.) 114

B.P. Australia Ltd. v. Commissioner of Taxation of Australia (1965), [1966] A.C. 224 (Australia P.C.) 84, 89

Bail Bonds by Marvin Nelson, Inc. v. Comm'r, 820 F.2d 1543 (9th Cir., 1987)..159

Bank of America Canada v. Mutual Trust Co., [2002] 2 S.C.R. 601, 2002 CarswellOnt 1114, 2002 CarswellOnt 1115, 2002 SCC 43 (S.C.C.)..129

Baxter v. R., [2007] 3 C.T.C. 211, (*sub nom.* R. v. Baxter) 2007 D.T.C. 5199 (Eng.), 2007 CarswellNat 2944, 2007 CarswellNat 962, 2007 CAF 172, 2007 FCA 172 (F.C.A.), leave to appeal refused 2007 CarswellNat 3625, 2007 CarswellNat 3626 (S.C.C.)........ 318

BB&T Corp. v. U.S., 523 F.3d 461 (4th Cir., 2008) 140

Becker v. Pettkus, [1980] 2 S.C.R. 834, 1980 CarswellOnt 299, 1980 CarswellOnt 644 (S.C.C.) 129

Ben Nevis Forestry v. CIR, (2009) 24 NZTC 23 (SC)... 127, 363, 382

Ben Nevis Forestry Ventures Ltd v. Commissioner of Inland Revenue, [2008] NZSC 115......................279, 281, 284, 408

Bernick v. R., [2004] 3 C.T.C. 191, 2004 D.T.C. 6409, 2004 CarswellNat 1394, 2004 CarswellNat 4653, 2004 CAF 191, 2004 FCA 191 (F.C.A.).............................438

Blier c. R. (2003), [2004] 2 C.T.C. 2392, 2003 D.T.C. 970, 2004 D.T.C. 2207, 2003 CarswellNat 4209, 2003 CarswellNat 2152, 2003 CCI 505, 2003 TCC 505 (T.C.C. [Informal Procedure]) 320

BNZ Investments Limited & ORS v. Commissioner of Inland Revenue (2009), 24 NZTC 23 (H.C.) 292, 382, 383

Boardman v. R. (1985), [1986] 1 C.T.C. 103, 85 D.T.C. 5628, 1985 CarswellNat 452 (Fed. T.D.).........................356

Bois Daaquam Inc. c. R. (2000), [2002] 1 C.T.C. 2650, (*sub nom.* Bois Daaquam Inc. v. R.) 2000 D.T.C. 2452 (Fr.), 2000 CarswellNat 1978, 2000 CarswellNat 3614 (T.C.C. [General Procedure])...442

Bonavia v. R., [2010] 6 C.T.C. 99, 2010 D.T.C. 5114 (Eng.), 2010 CarswellNat 3174, 2010 CarswellNat 1801, 2010 CAF 129, 2010 FCA 129 (F.C.A.). 77

Bow Valley Husky (Bermuda) Ltd. v. Saint John Shipbuilding Ltd., [1997] 3 S.C.R. 1210, 1997 CarswellNfld 207, 1997 CarswellNfld 208 (S.C.C.) 133

Bowater Power Co. v. Minister of National Revenue, [1971] C.T.C. 818, 71 D.T.C. 5469, 1971 CarswellNat 316, 1971 CarswellNat 369 (Fed. C.A.). 444

Bradford (City) v. Pickles, [1895] A.C. 587 (U.K. H.L.) 79

Bronfman Trust v. R., [1987] 1 S.C.R. 32, [1987] 1 C.T.C. 117, 87 D.T.C. 5059, 1987 CarswellNat 901, 1987 CarswellNat 335 (S.C.C.) 88-90, 104, 131, 440

Brouillette c. R., [2005] 4 C.T.C. 2013, (*sub nom.* Brouillette v. R.) 2005 D.T.C. 493 (Fr.), 2005 D.T.C. 1004 (Eng.), 2005 CarswellNat 742, 2005 CarswellNat 1767, 2005 CCI 203, 2005 TCC 203 (T.C.C. [General Procedure]) 457

Brown v. R. (2001), [2002] 1 C.T.C. 2451, 2001 D.T.C. 1094, 2001 CarswellNat 4803, 2001 CarswellNat 2574 (T.C.C. [General Procedure]), additional reasons (2001), [2002] 1 C.T.C. 2514, 2001 CarswellNat 2824 (T.C.C. [General Procedure]), additional reasons [2002] 2 C.T.C. 2338, 2002 D.T.C. 1385, 2002 CarswellNat 402, 2002 CarswellNat 5049 (T.C.C. [General Procedure]), additional reasons [2002] 2 C.T.C. 2840, 2002 D.T.C. 1925, 2002 CarswellNat 5531, 2002 CarswellNat 839 (T.C.C. [General Procedure]), affirmed [2003] 3 C.T.C. 351, 2003 D.T.C. 5298, 2003 CarswellNat 1071, 2003 CarswellNat 1852, 2003 CAF 192, 2003 FCA 192 (Fed. C.A.), leave to appeal refused 2004 CarswellNat 84, 2004 CarswellNat 85 (S.C.C.), reversed in part [2003] 3 C.T.C. 351, 2003 D.T.C. 5298, 2003 CarswellNat 1071, 2003 CarswellNat 1852, 2003 CAF 192, 2003 FCA 192 (Fed. C.A.) 448

Byram v. R., [1999] 2 C.T.C. 149, (*sub nom.* R. v. Byram) 99 D.T.C. 5117, 1999 CarswellNat 77, 1999 CarswellNat 4251 (Fed. C.A.) 452

C.I.R. v. Court Holding Co., 324 U.S. 331 (1945) 75

C.I.R. v. Newman, 159 F.2d 848 (2d Cr., 1947) 112

Cadbury Schweppes Plc v. IRC (C-196/04), [2006] ECR I-7995, [2006] STC 1908. 312

Canada Life Assurance Co. v. Canadian Imperial Bank of Commerce, [1979] 2 S.C.R. 669, 1979 CarswellOnt 163, 1979 CarswellOnt 687 (S.C.C.) 135

Canada Trustco Mortgage Co. v. R., [2003] 4 C.T.C. 2009, 2003 D.T.C. 587, 2003 CarswellNat 1299, 2003 CarswellNat 5460, 2003 CCI 215, 2003 TCC 215 (T.C.C. [General Procedure]), affirmed [2004] 2 C.T.C. 276, (*sub nom.* R. v. Canada Trustco Mortgage Co.) 2004 D.T.C. 6119, 2004 CarswellNat 305, 2004 CarswellNat 523, 2004 CAF 67, 2004 FCA 67 (F.C.A.), affirmed [2005] 5 C.T.C. 215, (*sub nom.* Canada Trustco Mortgage Co. v. Canada) 2005 D.T.C. 5523 (Eng.), (*sub nom.* Hypothèques Trustco Canada v. Canada) 2005 D.T.C. 5547 (Fr.), 2005 CarswellNat 3212, 2005 CarswellNat 3213, 2005 SCC 54 (S.C.C.) 104, 357

Canada Trustco Mortgage Corp. v. Port O'Call Hotel Inc., (*sub nom.* Alberta (Treasury Branches) v. Minister of National Revenue) [1996] 1 S.C.R. 963, (*sub nom.* Pigott Project Management Ltd. v. Land-Rock Resources Ltd.) [1996] 1 C.T.C. 395, (*sub nom.* R. v. Alberta Treasury Branches) 96 D.T.C. 6245, 1996 CarswellAlta 366, 1996 CarswellAlta 366F (S.C.C.). . . 91, 133

Canadian Council of Churches v. R., (*sub nom.* Canadian Council of Churches v. Canada (Minister of Employment & Immigration)) [1992] 1 S.C.R. 236, 1992 CarswellNat 650, 1992 CarswellNat 25 (S.C.C.) 114

Canadian Marconi Co. v. R., [1986] 2 C.T.C. 465, 86 D.T.C. 6526, 1986 CarswellNat 402, 1986 CarswellNat 740 (S.C.C.) 84

Canadian National Railway v. Norsk Pacific Steamship Co., [1992] 1 S.C.R. 1021, 1992 CarswellNat 168, 1992 CarswellNat 655 (S.C.C.), reconsideration / rehearing refused (July 23, 1992), Doc. 21838 (S.C.C.) 134

Canadian Pacific Ltd. v. R. (2000), [2001] 1 C.T.C. 2190, 2000 D.T.C. 2428, 2000 CarswellNat 2097, 2000 CarswellNat 4709 (T.C.C. [General Procedure]), affirmed (2001), [2002] 2 C.T.C. 197, *(sub nom.* R. v. Canadian Pacific Ltd.) 2002 D.T.C. 6742, 2001 CarswellNat 2916, 2001 CarswellNat 3155, 2001 FCA 398 (Fed. C.A.), reconsideration / rehearing refused [2002] 2 C.T.C. 150, 2002 CarswellNat 555, 2002 CarswellNat 5995, 2002 CAF 98, 2002 FCA 98 (Fed. C.A.) 78, 357, 399, 454

Canadian Propane Gas & Oil Ltd. v. Minister of National Revenue, [1972] C.T.C. 566, 73 D.T.C. 5019, 1972 CarswellNat 170 (Fed. T.D.)... 18

Canderel Ltd. v. R., (sub nom. Canderel Ltd. v. Canada) [1998] 1 S.C.R. 147, [1998] 2 C.T.C. 35, 98 D.T.C. 6100, 1998 CarswellNat 80, 1998 CarswellNat 81 (S.C.C.) 115

Canwest Broadcasting Ltd. v. R. (1995), *(sub nom.* Canwest Broadcasting Ltd. v. Canada) [1995] 2 C.T.C. 2780, 96 D.T.C. 1375, 1995 CarswellNat 598 (T.C.C.) 443, 447, 450

Carma Developers Ltd. v. R., [1996] 3 C.T.C. 2029, 96 D.T.C. 1798, 1996 CarswellNat 1479 (T.C.C.), affirmed (1996), [1997] 2 C.T.C. 150, (sub nom. R. v. Carma Developers Ltd.) 96 D.T.C. 6569, 1996 CarswellNat 1739 (Fed. C.A.)............... 74

Case V160 (1988), 88 ATC 1058 276

Cemco Investors, LLC v. U.S., 515 F.3d 749 (7th Cir., 2008), certiorari denied 129 S.Ct. 131 (2008) 141, 199, 419

Challenge Corporation Ltd v. Commissioner of Inland Revenue, [1986] 2 NZLR 555 (PC) 225, 280-282, 299, 399

Cheesemond v. R., [1995] 2 C.T.C. 2567, 1995 CarswellNat 533 (T.C.C.) 440, 447

Chernesky v. Minister of National Revenue, 2000 CarswellNat 4324, 2000 CarswellNat 4325, [2000] T.C.J. No. 704 (T.C.C. [Employment Insurance]) 439

CIR v. BNZ Investments, [2002] 1 NZLR 450 (C.A.) 120

CIR v. Challenge Corporation Ltd., see Commissioner of Inland Revenue v. Challenge Corp.

CIR v. Conhage, (1999) (4) SA 1149 (SCA) 233-237, 252

CIR v. King, 1947 (2) SA 196 (A) 231, 232

CIT Financial Ltd. v. R. (2003), [2004] 1 C.T.C. 2232, 2003 D.T.C. 1138, 2003 CarswellNat 2674, 2003 CarswellNat 5341, 2003 CCI 544, 2003 TCC 544 (T.C.C. [General Procedure]), reconsideration / rehearing refused (2003), [2004] 1 C.T.C. 2992, 2003 D.T.C. 1545, 2003 CarswellNat 3670, 2003 TCC 882 (T.C.C. [General Procedure]), affirmed [2004] 4 C.T.C. 9, 2004 D.T.C. 6573, 2004 CarswellNat 2845, 2004 CarswellNat 1478, 2004 CAF 201, 2004 FCA 201 (F.C.A.), leave to appeal refused 2004 CarswellNat 4370, 2004 CarswellNat 4371 (S.C.C.) 456

Clayton v. R. (2003), [2004] 1 C.T.C. 2265, 2003 CarswellNat 2707, 2003 CarswellNat 6643, 2003 CCI 640, 2003 TCC 640 (T.C.C. [Informal Procedure]) 319

Collins & Aikman Products Co. v. R., 2009 CarswellNat 1510, 2009 D.T.C. 1179 (Eng.), 2009 CarswellNat 6474, 2009 CCI 299, 2009 TCC 299 (T.C.C. [General Procedure]), affirmed (2010), [2011] 1 C.T.C. 250, 2010 D.T.C. 5164 (Eng.), 2010 CarswellNat 3613, 2010 CarswellNat 4574, 2010 CAF 251, 2010 FCA 251 (F.C.A.) 458

Coltec Industries, Inc. v. U.S., 454 F.3d 1340 (Fed. Cir., 2006), certiorari denied 127 S.Ct. 1261 (2007) . . . 4, 15, 110, 140-142, 189-191, 199, 402

Com Dev Ltd. v. R., [1999] 2 C.T.C. 2566, 99 D.T.C. 775, 1999 CarswellNat 425, 1999 CarswellNat 4026 (T.C.C.) 446

Commissioner of Inland Revenue v. Challenge Corp., [1987] A.C. 155 (U.K. H.L.). 35, 120, 306

Commissioner of Inland Revenue v. Gerard, [1974] 2 NZLR 279 284

Commonwealth Construction Co. v. R., [1984] C.T.C. 338, 84 D.T.C. 6420, 1984 CarswellNat 228 (Fed. C.A.) 12

Compania General de Tobacos de Filipinos v. Collector of Internal Revenue, 275 U.S. 87 (1904) 42

Consolidated Edison Co. of New York, Inc. v. U.S., 90 Fed.Cl. 228 (2009) 140, 166, 167, 219, 415

Consumers Distributing Co. v. Seiko Time Canada Ltd., [1984] 1 S.C.R. 583, 1984 CarswellOnt 869, 1984 CarswellOnt 801 (S.C.C.). . . 135

Continental Bank of Canada v. R., (*sub nom.* Continental Bank Leasing Corp. v. Canada) [1998] 2 S.C.R. 298, [1998] 4 C.T.C. 119, (*sub nom.* Continental Bank Leasing Corp. v. R.) 98 D.T.C. 6505, 1998 CarswellNat 1496, 1998 CarswellNat 1497 (S.C.C.). 72, 90, 91

Continental Lime Ltd. v. R., [1999] 3 C.T.C. 2525, 99 D.T.C. 1154, 1999 CarswellNat 1299 (T.C.C. [General Procedure]). 444

Contino v. Leonelli-Contino, [2005] 3 S.C.R. 217, 2005 CarswellOnt 6281, 2005 CarswellOnt 6282, 2005 SCC 63 (S.C.C.). 129

Cooper v. Minister of National Revenue, [1987] 1 C.T.C. 2287, 87 D.T.C. 194, 1987 CarswellNat 402 (T.C.C.), reversed (1988), [1989] 1 C.T.C. 66, 88 D.T.C. 6525, 1988 CarswellNat 478 (Fed. T.D.) 443

Copthorne Holdings Ltd. v. R. (2011), [2012] 2 C.T.C. 29, 2012 D.T.C. 5006 (Fr.), 2012 D.T.C. 5007 (Eng.), 2011 CarswellNat 5201, 2011 CarswellNat 5202, 2011 SCC 63 (S.C.C.) 16, 17, 24, 27

COT v. Ferera, 1976 (2) SA 653 (RAD), 656F-G; 38 SATC 66. . . 46

Côté (Succession de) c. R. (1995), *(sub nom.* Coté (Succession de) v. R.) [1996] 1 C.T.C. 2862, *(sub nom.* Côté Estate v. R.) 96 D.T.C. 2057, 1995 CarswellNat 1372, 1995 CarswellNat 1955 (T.C.C.).. 440

Cottage Sav. Ass'n v. C.I.R., 499 U.S. 554 (1991) 161, 162

Crestbrook Forest Industries Ltd. v. R., [1992] 2 C.T.C. 81, 92 D.T.C. 6412, 1992 CarswellNat 313 (Fed. T.D.), reversed *(sub nom.* Crestbrook Forest Industries Ltd. v. Canada) [1993] 2 C.T.C. 9, *(sub nom.* R. v. Crestbrook Forest Industries Ltd.) 93 D.T.C. 5186, 1993 CarswellNat 914, 1993 CarswellNat 1323 (Fed. C.A.), leave to appeal refused (1993), *(sub nom.* Crestbrook Forest Industries Ltd. v. Minister of National Revenue) 163 N.R. 320 (note) (S.C.C.)................................. 451

Cridland v. FCT (1977), 140 CLR 330 (High Court)......... 261

Curragh Inc. v. R. (1994), *(sub nom.* Curragh Inc. v. Canada) [1995] 1 C.T.C. 2163, 94 D.T.C. 1894, 1994 CarswellNat 1169 (T.C.C.).. 73

Dale v. R., [1997] 2 C.T.C. 286, 97 D.T.C. 5252, 1997 CarswellNat 2710, 1997 CarswellNat 391 (Fed. C.A.) 128

DCT v. Purcell (1921), 29 CLR 464 (High Court)........... 259

De Walden v. Inland Revenue Commissioners, [1942] 1 All E.R. 287 (Eng. C.A.)..................................... 123

Del Grande v. R. (1992), *(sub nom.* Del Grande v. Canada) [1993] 1 C.T.C. 2096, 93 D.T.C. 133, 1992 CarswellNat 1329 (T.C.C.) 441

Diggs v. C.I.R., 281 F.2d 326 (2d Cir., 1960) 15

Dionne c. R. (2001), [2003] 3 C.T.C. 2503, 2001 CarswellNat 2826, 2001 CarswellNat 3790 (T.C.C. [Informal Procedure]) 442

Dow Chemical Co. v. U.S., 435 F.3d 594 (6th Cir., 2006), certiorari denied, 549 U.S. 1205, 127 S.Ct. 1251 (2007)
.... 140, 192, 193, 407

Dow Chemical Co. v. U.S., 549 U.S. 1205, 127 S.Ct. 1251 (2007)
.... 80, 85, 95, 97, 392

Duha Printers (Western) Ltd. v. R., (*sub nom.* Duha Printers (Western) Ltd. v. Canada) [1998] 1 S.C.R. 795, [1998] 3 C.T.C. 303, 98 D.T.C. 6334, 1998 CarswellNat 750, 1998 CarswellNat 751 (S.C.C.)
.... 80, 85, 95, 97, 392

Duncan v. R., [2002] 4 C.T.C. 1, (*sub nom.* Water's Edge Village Estates (Phase II) Ltd. v. R.) 2002 D.T.C. 7172, 2002 CarswellNat 1621, 2002 CarswellNat 4557, (*sub nom.* Water's Edge Village Estates (Phase II) Ltd. v. Canada) 2002 FCA 291 (Fed. C.A.), leave to appeal refused 2003 CarswellNat 707, 2003 CarswellNat 708 (S.C.C.) 362

Dundas v. Minister of National Revenue, (*sub nom.* Dundas v. Canada) [1995] 1 C.T.C. 184, (*sub nom.* Dundas v. R.) 95 D.T.C. 5116, 1995 CarswellNat 269 (Fed. C.A.), leave to appeal refused (1995), 8 C.C.P.B. 224 (note) (S.C.C.) 451

Dunfield v. R., [2001] 4 C.T.C. 2518, 2001 D.T.C. 3774, 2001 CarswellNat 1802, 2001 CarswellNat 4860 (T.C.C. [Informal Procedure]) 64

Echo Bay Mines Ltd. v. R., (*sub nom.* Echo Bay Mines Ltd. v. Canada) [1992] 2 C.T.C. 182, 92 D.T.C. 6437, 1992 CarswellNat 611, 1992 CarswellNat 323 (Fed. T.D.) 452

Eisner v. Towne, 245 U.S. 418 (1918). 113

Elmiger v. Commissioner of Inland Revenue, [1966] NZLR 638 (SC)..175

Ensign Tankers (Leasing) Ltd. v. Stokes (Inspector of Taxes), (1992), [1992] 1 A.C. 655, [1992] 2 All E.R. 275......33, 36, 280, 292

Entré Computer Centers Inc. v. R. (1996), [1997] 1 C.T.C. 2291, 97 D.T.C. 846, 1996 CarswellNat 2204 (T.C.C.).........445

Entreprises Ludco ltée c. Canada (2001), (*sub nom.* Ludco Enterprises Ltd. v. Canada) [2001] 2 S.C.R. 1082, [2002] 1 C.T.C. 95, (*sub nom.* Ludco Enterprises Ltd. v. R.) 2001 D.T.C. 5505 (Eng.), 2001 D.T.C. 5518 (Fr.), 2001 CarswellNat 2017, 2001 CarswellNat 2018, 2001 SCC 62 (S.C.C.)...............59, 80, 85, 115, 310

Evans v. R. (2005), [2006] 2 C.T.C. 2009, 2005 D.T.C. 1762 (Eng.), 2005 CarswellNat 3887, 2005 CarswellNat 6512, 2005 CCI 684, 2005 TCC 684 (T.C.C. [General Procedure])....106, 457

F.A.S. Seafood Producers Ltd. v. R., [1998] 4 C.T.C. 2794, 98 D.T.C. 2034, 1998 CarswellNat 3574, 1998 CarswellNat 1477 (T.C.C.)...444

Faraggi c. R. (2007), [2008] 1 C.T.C. 2425, (*sub nom.* Faraggi v. R.) 2007 D.T.C. 911 (Fr.), (*sub nom.* 2530-1284 Québec Inc. v. R.) 2008 D.T.C. 3245 (Eng.), 2007 CarswellNat 1681, 2007 CarswellNat 1441, 2007 CCI 286, 2007 TCC 286 (T.C.C. [General Procedure]), affirmed (2008), [2009] 3 C.T.C. 77, 2009 D.T.C. 5023 (Eng.), 2008 CarswellNat 4465, 2008 CarswellNat 4466, 2008 FCA 398 (F.C.A.), leave to appeal refused 2009 CarswellNat 1152, 2009 CarswellNat 1153 (S.C.C.)...376, 378

FCT v. Consolidated Press Holdings (No. 1) (1999), 99 ATC 4945 (Full Federal Court) 269, 273

FCT v. Consolidated Press Holdings Ltd, [2001] HCA 32......271

FCT v. Hart (2004), 55 ATR 712 (High Court) 264, 266, 269

FCT v. Peabody (1993), 93 ATC 4104 (F.C.A.).........270, 273

FCT v. Peabody (1994), 94 ATC 4663 (High Court) 266

FCT v. Spotless (1996), 96 ATC 5201. 271

FCT v. Spotless Services Ltd. (1996), 186 C.L.R. 404 (Aust. High Court) 276

Federal Commissioner of Taxation v. Consolidated Press Holdings Ltd, 2001 ATC 4343 (Aust. High Court). 271

Federal Commissioner of Taxation v. Spotless Services Ltd. See FCT v. Spotless

Federal Commissioner of Taxation v. Spotless Services Ltd., [1996] HCA 34 (H.C. Australia). 388

Foresbec Inc. c. R. (2001), [2002] 2 C.T.C. 2683, (*sub nom.* Foresbec Inc. v. R.) 2002 D.T.C. 1786 (Eng.), 2001 D.T.C. 180 (Fr.), 2001 CarswellNat 53, 2001 CarswellNat 3136 (T.C.C. [General Procedure]), affirmed (2002), [2003] 3 C.T.C. 374, (*sub nom.* Foresbec Inc. v. R.) 2002 D.T.C. 7041 (Fr.), 2003 D.T.C. 5455, 2002 CarswellNat 3771, 2002 CarswellNat 1053, 2002 CAF 186, 2002 FCA 186 (Fed. C.A.). 77

Frank Lyon Co. v. U.S., 435 U.S. 561 (1978)
. . . . 157-159, 180, 181, 191

Fraser Milner Casgrain LLP v. Minister of National Revenue, [2002] 4 C.T.C. 210, 2002 D.T.C. 7310, 2002 CarswellNat 3332, 2002 CarswellNat 2261, 2002 CFPI 912, 2002 FCT 912 (Fed. T.D.)
. . . . 13, 21

Fraser River Pile & Dredge Ltd. v. Can-Dive Services Ltd., [1999] 3 S.C.R. 108, 1999 CarswellBC 1927, 1999 CarswellBC 1928 (S.C.C.). 133

Friedmann Equity Developments Inc. v. Final Note Ltd., [2000] 1 S.C.R. 842, 2000 CarswellOnt 2458, 2000 CarswellOnt 2459, 2000 SCC 34 (S.C.C.). 132

Furniss v. Dawson, [1984] A.C. 474 (U.K. H.L.) 126

Futuris Corporation Ltd v. Federal Commissioner of Taxation, [2010] FCA 935 (Aust. Fed. Ct.) 274

Gabie v. R. (1998), [1999] 1 C.T.C. 2352, 98 D.T.C. 2207, 1998 CarswellNat 2113, 1998 CarswellNat 3670 (T.C.C.) 451

Garron Family Trust (Trustee of) v. R. (2009), [2010] 2 C.T.C. 2346, (*sub nom.* Garron Family Trust v. R.) 2009 D.T.C. 1287 (Eng.), 2009 CarswellNat 2600, 2009 CarswellNat 5415, 2009 CCI 450, 2009 TCC 450 (T.C.C. [General Procedure]), affirmed (2010), [2011] 2 C.T.C. 7, (*sub nom.* St. Michael Trust Corp. (Trustee of) v. R.) 2010 D.T.C. 5189 (Eng.), 2010 CarswellNat 5521, 2010 CarswellNat 4259, 2010 CAF 309, 2010 FCA 309 (F.C.A.), affirmed [2012] 3 C.T.C. 265, (*sub nom.* St. Michael Trust Corp. v. R.) 2012 D.T.C. 5063 (Eng.), 2012 D.T.C. 5064 (Fr.), 2012 CarswellNat 953, 2012 CarswellNat 954, 2012 SCC 14 (S.C.C.) 115, 458

General Electric Capital Canada Inc. v. R. (2009), [2010] 2 C.T.C. 2187, 2010 D.T.C. 1007 (Eng.), 2009 CarswellNat 5603, 2009 CarswellNat 3961, 2009 CCI 563, 2009 TCC 563 (T.C.C. [General Procedure]), additional reasons 2010 D.T.C. 1353 (Eng.), 2010 CarswellNat 3787, 2010 TCC 490 (T.C.C. [General Procedure]), affirmed (2010), 2010 FCA 344, [2011] 2 C.T.C. 126, (sub nom. R. v. General Electric Capital Canada Inc.) 2011 D.T.C. 5011 (Eng.), 2010 CarswellNat 5760, 2010 CarswellNat 4858, 2010 CAF 344 (F.C.A.) 52, 69

Geransky v. R., [2001] 2 C.T.C. 2147, 2001 D.T.C. 243, 2001 CarswellNat 4666, 2001 CarswellNat 272 (T.C.C. [General Procedure])..... 456

Gibson Petroleum Co. v. R., [1997] 3 C.T.C. 2453, 97 D.T.C. 1420, 1997 CarswellNat 836 (T.C.C.) 451

Gilbert v. Commissioner of Internal Revenue, 248 F.2d 399 (2d Cir., 1957) 152

Gillette Canada Inc. v. R., [2001] 4 C.T.C. 2884, 2001 D.T.C. 895, 2001 CarswellNat 4871, 2001 CarswellNat 2256 (T.C.C. [General Procedure]), affirmed [2003] 3 C.T.C. 27, 2003 D.T.C. 5078, 2003 CarswellNat 54, 2003 CarswellNat 634, 2003 CAF 22, 2003 FCA 22 (Fed. C.A.) 74

GlaxoSmithKline Inc. v. R., 2008 D.T.C. 3957 (Eng.), 2008 CarswellNat 1666, 2008 CarswellNat 6307, 2008 CCI 324, 2008 TCC 324 (T.C.C. [General Procedure]), reversed [2010] 6 C.T.C. 220, 2010 D.T.C. 5124 (Eng.), 2010 CarswellNat 5563, 2010 CarswellNat 2409, 2010 CAF 201, 2010 FCA 201 (F.C.A.), affirmed 2012 CarswellNat 3880, 2012 CarswellNat 3881, 2012 SCC 52 (S.C.C.)..................... 52, 53, 75

Glenharrow Holdings Ltd v. CIR, [2008] NZSC 116 .... 279, 281, 289, 290, 297, 408

Global Equity Fund Ltd. v. R. (2011), [2012] 1 C.T.C. 2224, 2011 D.T.C. 1350 (Eng.), 2011 CarswellNat 4286, 2011 CarswellNat 6006, 2011 CCI 507, 2011 TCC 507 (T.C.C. [General Procedure]), reversed 2012 CarswellNat 4117, 2012 FCA 272 (F.C.A.) 107, 459

Goldstein v. Commissioner, 364 F.2d 734 (2d Cir., 1966), affirmed 385 U.S. 1005 (1967) 154-157

Goodyear Tire & Rubber Co. of Canada Ltd. v. T. Eaton Co., [1956] S.C.R. 610, 56 D.T.C. 1060, 1956 CarswellNat 247 (S.C.C.).... 14

Gordon v. R., [1996] 3 C.T.C. 2229, 96 D.T.C. 1554, 1996 CarswellNat 1530 (T.C.C.)............................... 132, 449, 450

Goren v. R., [1997] 3 C.T.C. 2025, 98 D.T.C. 1963, 1997 CarswellNat 616 (T.C.C.) 447

Gravel v. Minister of National Revenue, [1992] 1 C.T.C. 2521, 92 D.T.C. 1935, (*sub nom.* Gravel c. Ministre du Revenu national) 92 D.T.C. 1923, 1992 CarswellNat 284 (T.C.C.) 442

Gregory v. Commissioner, 27 B.T.A. 223 (B.T.A., 1932), reversed 69 F.2d 809 (2d Cir., 1934), affirmed 293 U.S. 465 (U.S., 1935) 143, 150

Gregory v. Helvering, 293 U.S. 465 (U.S. Sup. Ct.)
. . . . 15, 94, 97, 149, 150, 191, 304

Guarantee Co. of North America v. Gordon Capital Corp., [1999] 3 S.C.R. 423, 1999 CarswellOnt 3171, 1999 CarswellOnt 3172 (S.C.C.) 132

Gulf Canada Ltd. v. R., (*sub nom.* R. v. Gulf Canada Ltd.) [1992] 1 C.T.C. 183, 92 D.T.C. 6123, 1992 CarswellNat 225 (Fed. C.A.), leave to appeal refused (*sub nom.* Gulf Canada Ltd. v. Minister of National Revenue) 141 N.R. 393n, [1992] S.C.C.A. No. 102 (S.C.C.) 248

Haggarty c. R., [2003] 4 C.T.C. 2535, (*sub nom.* Haggarty v. R.) 2003 D.T.C. 899, 2003 D.T.C. 733, 2003 CarswellNat 1796, 2003 CarswellNat 1570, 2003 CCI 358, 2003 TCC 358 (T.C.C. [Informal Procedure]) 319

Halifax Plc, Leeds Permanent Development Services Ltd, County Wide Property Investments Ltd v. Commissioners of Customs and Excise (Case C–255/02), [2006] S.T.C. 919 312

Hallatt v. R. (2000), [2001] 1 C.T.C. 2626, 2001 D.T.C. 128, 2000 CarswellNat 3105 (T.C.C. [General Procedure]), affirmed [2004] 2 C.T.C. 313, 2004 D.T.C. 6176, 2004 CarswellNat 613, 2004 CarswellNat 7367, 2004 CAF 104, 2004 FCA 104 (F.C.A.) 448

Hallstrom's Propriety Ltd. v. Federal Commissioner of Taxation (1946), 72 C.L.R. 634 (Australia H.C.) 84

Hart v. FCT, 2002 ACT 4608 (FCA) 264, 266, 269, 270

Hickman Motors Ltd. v. R. (1997), [1997] 2 S.C.R. 336, [1998] 1 C.T.C. 213, 97 D.T.C. 5363, 1997 CarswellNat 3046, 1997 CarswellNat 3047 (S.C.C.) 80, 85, 92, 392

Hidden Valley Golf Resort Assn. v. R., (*sub nom.* Hidden Valley Golf Resort Assn. v. Canada) [1998] G.S.T.C. 95, 1998 CarswellNat 1590, 1998 CarswellNat 3861 (T.C.C.), reversed 2000 CarswellNat 1162, 2000 CarswellNat 4792 (Fed. C.A.). 446

Higgins v. Smith, 308 U.S. 473 (1940) 149

Hill v. R. (2002), [2003] 4 C.T.C. 2548, 2002 D.T.C. 1749, 2002 CarswellNat 5896, 2002 CarswellNat 946 (T.C.C. [General Procedure]) 456

Howe v. R. (2004), [2005] 1 C.T.C. 2243, 2004 D.T.C. 3619, 2004 CarswellNat 6779, 2004 CarswellNat 3821, 2004 CCI 719, 2004 TCC 719 (T.C.C. [General Procedure]). 457

Hunter v. R., [2001] 4 C.T.C. 2762, 2001 D.T.C. 907, 2001 CarswellNat 4876, 2001 CarswellNat 2076 (T.C.C. [Informal Procedure]) . . 64

Husky Oil Ltd. v. R. (1998), [1999] 4 C.T.C. 2691, 99 D.T.C. 308, 1998 CarswellNat 3553, 1998 CarswellNat 2588 (T.C.C.) 455

Imperial Drywall Contracting Ltd. v. R., (*sub nom.* Imperial Drywall Contracting Inc. v. Canada) [1997] G.S.T.C. 81, 1997 CarswellNat 1593 (T.C.C.) 445

Imperial Oil Ltd. v. R. (2002), [2003] 2 C.T.C. 2754, 2002 D.T.C. 1954, 2002 CarswellNat 5902, 2002 CarswellNat 1885 (T.C.C. [General Procedure]), affirmed [2004] 2 C.T.C. 190, (*sub nom.* R. v. Imperial Oil Ltd.) 2004 D.T.C. 6044, 2004 CarswellNat 104, 2004 CarswellNat 1936, 2004 CAF 36, 2004 FCA 36 (F.C.A.) 456

In re CM Holdings, Inc., 301 F.3d 96 (3d Cir., 2002). 140

Inco Ltd. v. R., [2007] 2 C.T.C. 2347, 2007 D.T.C. 357 (Eng.), 2007 CarswellNat 16, 2007 CarswellNat 6573, 2007 CCI 1, 2007 TCC 1 (T.C.C. [General Procedure]) 441

Industries S.L.M. Inc. c. Ministre du Revenu national (1995), (*sub nom.* Industries S.L.M. Inc. v. Minister of National Revenue) [1996] 2 C.T.C. 2572, 96 D.T.C. 3241, 1995 CarswellNat 1469, 1995 CarswellNat 2090 (T.C.C.), reversed in part (*sub nom.* Les Industries S.L.M. Inc. v. R.) 2000 D.T.C. 6648 (Fr.), 2000 CarswellNat 2416, 2000 CarswellNat 3299 (Fed. T.D.).... 442

Ingram v. Minister of National Revenue (1991), 91 D.T.C. 939, [1991] 2 C.T.C. 2259, 1991 CarswellNat 586 (T.C.C.) 73

Inland Revenue Commissioner v. Wattie, [1998] S.T.C. 1160 (N.Z. P.C.)... 88

Inland Revenue Commissioners v. Duke of Westminster (1935), [1936] A.C. 1, [1935] All E.R. 259 (U.K. H.L.)........ 85, 86

Inland Revenue Commissioners v. McGuckian, [1997] 3 All E.R. 817 (N.I. H.L.) 87, 304, 413

Inland Revenue Commissioners v. Willoughby, [1997] 4 All E.R. 65, 70 TC 57, [1997] S.T.C. 995 (U.K. H.L.) 33, 35, 281, 306

J.F. Newton Ltd. v. Thorne Riddell (1990), 91 D.T.C. 5276, [1991] 2 C.T.C. 91, 1990 CarswellBC 737 (B.C. S.C.) 63

Jabin Investments Ltd. v. R. (2001), [2002] 1 C.T.C. 2315, 2001 D.T.C. 1002, 2001 CarswellNat 4847, 2001 CarswellNat 2578 (T.C.C. [General Procedure]), affirmed (2002), [2003] 2 C.T.C. 25, 2003 D.T.C. 5027, 2002 CarswellNat 4346, 2002 CarswellNat 3689, 2002 CAF 520, 2002 FCA 520 (Fed. C.A.) 456

Jabs Construction Ltd. v. R., [1999] 3 C.T.C. 2556, 99 D.T.C. 729, 1999 CarswellNat 3970, 1999 CarswellNat 1210 (T.C.C. [General Procedure]).......................... 448, 455

Jade Trading LLC et al v. United States, No. 03-cv-2164 (Fed. Cir. Mar. 23, 2010)........................... 199, 397, 419

Jade Trading, LLC v. U.S., 80 Fed.Cl. 11 (2007) 140, 199, 397, 419

Jeffs v. R., (sub nom. Jeffs v. Canada) [1999] G.S.T.C. 48, 1999 CarswellNat 720, 1999 CarswellNat 4137 (T.C.C. [Informal Procedure]) 442

Jewett v. The Queen, 2020 D.T.C. 2796 (TCC) 452

Johns-Manville Canada Inc. v. R., [1985] 2 S.C.R. 46, [1985] 2 C.T.C. 111, 85 D.T.C. 5373, 1985 CarswellNat 313, 1985 CarswellNat 666 (S.C.C.) 84, 115

Johnston v. Minister of National Revenue, [1948] S.C.R. 486, [1948] C.T.C. 195, 3 D.T.C. 1182, 1948 CarswellNat 26 (S.C.C.) .. 15

Kenneth B.S. Robertson Ltd. v. Minister of National Revenue, [1944] C.T.C. 75, 2 D.T.C. 655, 1944 CarswellNat 31 (Can. Ex. Ct.) ... 12

King v. R., [2001] 1 C.T.C. 295, 2001 D.T.C. 5116, 2001 CarswellNat 59, 2001 CarswellNat 5129 (Fed. C.A.) 447, 449

Klamath Strategic Investment Fund ex rel. St. Croix Ventures v. U.S., 568 F.3d 537 (5th Cir., 2009)................ 140, 198

Klotz v. R., [2004] 2 C.T.C. 2892, 2004 D.T.C. 2236, 2004 CarswellNat 303, 2004 CarswellNat 7102, 2004 CCI 147, 2004 TCC 147 (T.C.C. [General Procedure]), affirmed [2005] 3 C.T.C. 78, 2005 D.T.C. 5279 (Eng.), 2005 CarswellNat 1169, 2005 CarswellNat 3787, 2005 CAF 158, 2005 FCA 158 (F.C.A.), leave to appeal refused 2006 CarswellNat 930, 2006 CarswellNat 931 (S.C.C.) 448

Knetsch v. United States, 364 U.S. 361 .... 123, 131, 154, 155, 159, 193, 394

Kowdrysh v. R., [2001] 2 C.T.C. 156, 2001 D.T.C. 5221, 2001 CarswellNat 379, 2001 CarswellNat 5139, 2001 CAF 34, 2001 FCA 34 (Fed. C.A.)................................ 449

Krashinsky v. R., [2010] 4 C.T.C. 2301, 2010 D.T.C. 1105 (Eng.), 2010 CarswellNat 475, 2010 TCC 78 (T.C.C. [Informal Procedure]) 63

Landrus v. R. (2008), [2009] 1 C.T.C. 2009, 2008 D.T.C. 3583 (Eng.), 2008 CarswellNat 1342, 2008 CarswellNat 5640, 2008 CCI 274, 2008 TCC 274 (T.C.C. [General Procedure]), affirmed [2009] 4 C.T.C. 189, (*sub nom.* R. v. Landrus) 2009 D.T.C. 5085 (Eng.), 2009 CarswellNat 919, 2009 CarswellNat 5074, 2009 CAF 113, 2009 FCA 113 (F.C.A.) 362, 370, 371, 393, 401, 458

Lipper v. R., [1979] C.T.C. 316, 79 D.T.C. 5246, 1979 CarswellNat 246 (Fed. T.D.) 438

Lipson v. R., [2006] 3 C.T.C. 2494, 2006 D.T.C. 2687 (Eng.), 2006 CarswellNat 6782, 2006 CarswellNat 982, 2006 CCI 148, 2006 TCC 148 (T.C.C. [General Procedure]), affirmed [2007] 3 C.T.C. 110, 2007 D.T.C. 5172, 2007 CarswellNat 640, 2007 CarswellNat 2257, 2007 CAF 113, 2007 FCA 113 (F.C.A.), affirmed [2009] 1 S.C.R. 3, [2009] 1 C.T.C. 314, 2009 D.T.C. 5015 (Eng.), 2009 D.T.C. 5016 (Fr.), 2009 CarswellNat 1, 2009 CarswellNat 2, 2009 SCC 1 (S.C.C.) 3, 7, 16, 106, 111, 130, 218, 457

London Drugs Ltd. v. Kuehne & Nagel International Ltd., [1992] 3 S.C.R. 299, 1992 CarswellBC 913, 1992 CarswellBC 315 (S.C.C.) 134

Long Term Capital Holdings v. U.S., 330 F.Supp.2d 122 (D. Conn., 2004), affirmed 150 Fed.Appx. 40 (2d Cir., 2005) ... 47, 194, 195

Loyens v. R., [2003] 3 C.T.C. 2381, 2003 D.T.C. 355, 2003 CarswellNat 904, 2003 CarswellNat 5277, 2003 CCI 214, 2003 TCC 214 (T.C.C. [General Procedure]) 456

Lutheran Life Insurance Society of Canada v. R. , 91 D.T.C. 5553, (*sub nom.* Lutheran Life Insurance Society of Canada v. Canada) [1991] 2 C.T.C. 284, 1991 CarswellNat 525 (Fed. T.D.) 72

MacKay v. R., [2007] 3 C.T.C. 2051, 2007 D.T.C. 425 (Eng.), 2007 CarswellNat 6154, 2007 CarswellNat 399, 2007 CCI 94, 2007 TCC 94 (T.C.C. [General Procedure]), reversed [2008] 4 C.T.C. 161, (*sub nom.* R. v. MacKay) 2008 D.T.C. 6238 (Eng.), 2008 CarswellNat 677, 2008 CarswellNat 2145, 2008 CAF 105, 2008 FCA 105 (F.C.A.), leave to appeal refused 2009 CarswellNat 19, 2009 CarswellNat 20 (S.C.C.), leave to appeal refused 2009 CarswellNat 21, 2009 CarswellNat 22 (S.C.C.), leave to appeal refused 2009 CarswellNat 23, 2009 CarswellNat 24 (S.C.C.), leave to appeal refused 2009 CarswellNat 29, 2009 CarswellNat 30 (S.C.C.), leave to appeal refused 2009 CarswellNat 25, 2009 CarswellNat 26 (S.C.C.), leave to appeal refused 2009 CarswellNat 27, 2009 CarswellNat 28 (S.C.C.), leave to appeal refused 2009 CarswellNat 31, 2009 CarswellNat 32 (S.C.C.), leave to appeal refused 2009 CarswellNat 33, 2009 CarswellNat 34 (S.C.C.), leave to appeal refused 2009 CarswellNat 35, 2009 CarswellNat 36 (S.C.C.), leave to appeal refused 2009 CarswellNat 37, 2009 CarswellNat 38 (S.C.C.), leave to appeal refused 2009 CarswellNat 39, 2009 CarswellNat 40 (S.C.C.), leave to appeal refused 2009 CarswellNat 41, 2009 CarswellNat 42 (S.C.C.) 458

Macklin v. R. (1992), (*sub nom.* Macklin v. Canada) [1993] 1 C.T.C. 21, 92 D.T.C. 6595, 1992 CarswellNat 448 (Fed. T.D.).... 449

MacMillan Bloedel Ltd. v. R., [1997] 3 C.T.C. 3012, 97 D.T.C. 1446, 1997 CarswellNat 1032 (T.C.C.), affirmed [1999] 3 C.T.C. 652, (*sub nom.* R. v. MacMillan Bloedel Ltd.) 99 D.T.C. 5454, 1999 CarswellNat 1183, 1999 CarswellNat 4227 (Fed. C.A.) ... 444

Makuz v. R., [2006] 5 C.T.C. 2332, 2006 D.T.C. 3201 (Eng.), 2006 CarswellNat 2002, 2006 CarswellNat 6481, 2006 CCI 263, 2006 TCC 263 (T.C.C. [General Procedure]), additional reasons (2006), [2007] 1 C.T.C. 2370, 2006 D.T.C. 3464 (Eng.), 2006 CarswellNat 3375 (T.C.C. [General Procedure]) 445

Mangin v. CIR, [1971] NZLR 591 (P.C.) 283, 289

Mangin v. Inland Revenue Commissioners, [1971] A.C. 739 (New Zealand P.C.)................................287, 289

Mara Properties Ltd. v. R., (*sub nom.* Mara Properties Ltd. v. Canada) [1993] 2 C.T.C. 3189, 93 D.T.C. 1449, 1993 CarswellNat 1168 (T.C.C.), reversed (*sub nom.* Mara Properties Ltd. v. Canada) [1995] 2 C.T.C. 86, (*sub nom.* R. v. Mara Properties Ltd.) 95 D.T.C. 5168, 1995 CarswellNat 665, 1995 CarswellNat 665F (Fed. C.A.), reversed (*sub nom.* R. v. Mara Properties Ltd.) [1996] 2 S.C.R. 161, [1996] 2 C.T.C. 54, 96 D.T.C. 6309, 1996 CarswellNat 584F, 1996 CarswellNat 868 (S.C.C.) 80

Maritime Life Assurance Co. v. R., 99 G.T.C. 3055, 1999 CarswellNat 8, 1999 CarswellNat 4136 (T.C.C.), affirmed 2000 G.T.C. 4157, 2000 CarswellNat 2166, 2000 CarswellNat 4811 (Fed. C.A.) 92-94, 101

Mark Resources Inc. v. R., (*sub nom.* Mark Resources Inc. v. Canada) [1993] 2 C.T.C. 2259, 93 D.T.C. 1004, 1993 CarswellNat 1001 (T.C.C.) 90

Markevich v. Canada, [2003] 1 S.C.R. 94, [2003] 2 C.T.C. 83, (*sub nom.* R. v. Markevich) 2003 D.T.C. 5185, 2003 CarswellNat 446, 2003 CarswellNat 447, 2003 SCC 9 (S.C.C.). . . . 114, 120

Marotta v. R., [1986] 1 C.T.C. 393, 86 D.T.C. 6192, 1986 CarswellNat 675, 1986 CarswellNat 248 (Fed. T.D.). 439

Mathew v. R., [2005] 2 S.C.R. 643, [2005] 5 C.T.C. 244, (*sub nom.* Mathew v. Canada) 2005 D.T.C. 5538 (Eng.), 2005 D.T.C. 5563 (Fr.), 2005 CarswellNat 3214, 2005 CarswellNat 3215, 2005 SCC 55 (S.C.C.) 95, 111, 130, 153, 365

McEwen Brothers Ltd. v. R., [1999] 3 C.T.C. 373, 99 D.T.C. 5326, 1999 CarswellNat 2846, 1999 CarswellNat 891 (Fed. C.A.) . . . 77

McGowen v. R., [2005] G.S.T.C. 109, 2005 CarswellNat 1450, 2005 CarswellNat 5374, 2005 CCI 353, 2005 TCC 353 (T.C.C. [General Procedure]). 446

McMullen v. R., [2007] 2 C.T.C. 2463, 2007 D.T.C. 286 (Eng.), 2007 CarswellNat 5923, 2007 CarswellNat 125, 2007 CCI 16, 2007 TCC 16 (T.C.C. [General Procedure]). 458

McNichol v. R., [1997] 2 C.T.C. 2088, 97 D.T.C. 111, 1997 CarswellNat 33 (T.C.C.) 78

Merck Frosst Canada Inc. v. Canada (Minister of National Health & Welfare), [1998] 2 S.C.R. 193, 1998 CarswellNat 1059, 1998 CarswellNat 1060 (S.C.C.) 53, 133, 426

MIL (Investments) S.A. v. R., [2006] 5 C.T.C. 2552, 2006 D.T.C. 3307 (Eng.), 2006 CarswellNat 6423, 2006 CarswellNat 2558, 2006 CCI 460, 2006 TCC 460 (T.C.C. [General Procedure]), affirmed [2007] 4 C.T.C. 235, 2007 D.T.C. 5437 (Eng.), 2007 CarswellNat 1719, 2007 CarswellNat 4139, 2007 CAF 236, 2007 FCA 236 (F.C.A.) 450, 457

Minister of National Revenue v. Leon, [1976] C.T.C. 532, 76 D.T.C. 6299, 1976 CarswellNat 229, 1976 CarswellNat 406 (Fed. C.A.) 77

Minister of National Revenue v. M.P. Drilling Ltd., [1976] C.T.C. 58, 76 D.T.C. 6028, 1976 CarswellNat 170 (Fed. C.A.).... 445, 447

Minister of National Revenue v. Taylor, [1956] C.T.C. 189, 56 D.T.C. 1125, 1956 CarswellNat 222 (Can. Ex. Ct.) 12

Minister of National Revenue v. Yonge-Eglinton Building Ltd., [1974] C.T.C. 209, 74 D.T.C. 6180, 1974 CarswellNat 152, 1974 CarswellNat 54F (Fed. C.A.) 73

Moloney v. R., (sub nom. Moloney v. Canada) [1989] 1 C.T.C. 213, 89 D.T.C. 5099, 1989 CarswellNat 201 (Fed. T.D.), affirmed [1992] 2 C.T.C. 227, 92 D.T.C. 6570, 1992 CarswellNat 328 (Fed. C.A.), leave to appeal refused 1993 CarswellNat 2467 (S.C.C.).... 440

Monarch Marking Systems Inc. v. Esselte Meto Ltd. (1983), [1984] 1 F.C. 641, 1983 CarswellNat 64F, 1983 CarswellNat 64 (Fed. T.D.) 451

National Trust Co. v. H & R Block Canada Inc., [2003] 3 S.C.R. 160, 2003 CarswellOnt 4443, 2003 CarswellOnt 4444, 2003 SCC 66 (S.C.C.) 132

NAV Canada c. Wilmington Trust Co., (*sub nom.* Canada 3000 Inc., Re) [2006] 1 S.C.R. 865, 2006 CarswellQue 4890, 2006 CarswellQue 4891, 2006 SCC 24 (S.C.C.).............132

Nelson v. R. (1997), [1998] 1 C.T.C. 2008, 97 D.T.C. 1253, 1997 CarswellNat 1297 (T.C.C.), affirmed 98 D.T.C. 6305, 1998 CarswellNat 618, 1998 CarswellNat 3901 (Fed. C.A.), leave to appeal refused (1999), (*sub nom.* Nelson v. Canada) 237 N.R. 398 (note) (S.C.C.)............................159, 439

Neuman v. Minister of National Revenue, [1998] 1 S.C.R. 770, [1998] 3 C.T.C. 177, (*sub nom.* Neuman v. R.) 98 D.T.C. 6297, 1998 CarswellNat 685, 1998 CarswellNat 686 (S.C.C.) 59, 61, 80, 85, 108

New Phoenix Sunrise Corp. v. C.I.R., 132 T.C. 161 (2009) 140

Newton v. Commissioner of Taxation of the Commonwealth of Australia, [1958] 2 All E.R. 759 (England P.C.)..........287

Newton v. F.C.T. (1958), 98 CLR 1 (P.C.) ...260, 261, 262, 272, 284

Nicole Rose Corp. v. C.I.R., 320 F.3d 282 (2d Cir., 2002).....140

No. 476 v. Minister of National Revenue, [1960] S.C.R. 902, [1960] C.T.C. 384, 60 D.T.C. 1270, 1960 CarswellNat 314 (S.C.C.) 115

Non-Marine Underwriters, Lloyd's London v. Scalera, [2000] 1 S.C.R. 551, 2000 CarswellBC 885, 2000 CarswellBC 886, 2000 SCC 24 (S.C.C.)..................................132

Northern Securities Co. v. U.S., 193 U.S. 197 (1904) 164

On-Guard Self-Storage Ltd. v. R., (*sub nom.* On-Guard Self-Storage Ltd. v. Canada) [1996] G.S.T.C. 9, 1996 CarswellNat 5 (T.C.C.), reversed 1996 CarswellNat 1999 (Fed. C.A.), leave to appeal refused (1997), (*sub nom.* Minister of National Revenue v. Sentinel Self-Storage Corp.) 222 N.R. 399 (S.C.C.).....446

On-Line Finance & Leasing Corp. v. R. (2010), [2011] 1 C.T.C. 2068, 2010 D.T.C. 1325 (Eng.), 2010 CarswellNat 3420, 2010 CarswellNat 5712, 2010 CCI 475, 2010 TCC 475 (T.C.C. [General Procedure]) 448

OSFC Holdings Ltd. v. R., [2001] 4 C.T.C. 82, 2001 D.T.C. 5471, 2001 CarswellNat 1967, 2001 CarswellNat 3521, 2001 CAF 260, 2001 FCA 260 (Fed. C.A.), leave to appeal refused 2002 CarswellNat 1388, 2002 CarswellNat 1389 (S.C.C.) 21, 364, 366-370, 458

Ovenstone v. SIR, (1980) (2) SA 731 (A) 241

Overs v. R., [2006] 3 C.T.C. 2255, 2006 D.T.C. 2192 (Eng.), 2006 CarswellNat 6793, 2006 CarswellNat 41, 2006 TCC 26 (T.C.C. [General Procedure]). 106, 457

P.S.A.C. v. United States Defense Department, (sub nom. Code Canadien du Travail, Re) [1992] 2 S.C.R. 50, 1992 CarswellNat 656, 1992 CarswellNat 1005 (S.C.C.) 134

Pacific Coast Coin Exchange of Canada v. Ontario (Securities Commission) (1997), [1978] 2 S.C.R. 112, 1977 CarswellOnt 50, 1977 CarswellOnt 469 (S.C.C.) 130

Palm Canyon X Investments, LLC v. Commissioner, T.C. Memo. 2009-288 140

Parfeniuk v. R., (sub nom. Parfeniuk v. Canada) [1996] G.S.T.C. 22, 1996 CarswellNat 639 (T.C.C.) 446

Peabody v. FCT (1993), 40 FCR 531 .... 269, 396

Pecore v. Pecore, [2007] 1 S.C.R. 795, 2007 CarswellOnt 2752, 2007 CarswellOnt 2753, 2007 SCC 17 (S.C.C.). 14

Penny and Hooper v. Commissioner of Inland Revenue, [2011] NZSC 96 .... 282, 285, 286, 290, 291, 295, 346

Peterson v. CIR, [2005] U.K.PC 17, 22 NZTC 19 .. 306, 363, 399, 420

Peterson v. CIR, [2006 3 NZLR 433 (P.C.)..........363, 399, 420

Peterson v. Commissioner of Inland Revenue, [2001] NZLR 316 (PC)...399, 420

Peterson v. Commissioner of Inland Revenue, [2005] UKPC 5 ....291, 292, 296

Placements Marcel Lapointe Inc. c. Ministre du Revenu national (1992), (*sub nom.* Placements Marcel Lapointe Inc. v. Minister of National Revenue) [1993] 1 C.T.C. 2506, 93 D.T.C. 809, 93 D.T.C. 821, 1992 CarswellNat 487, 1992 CarswellNat 500 (T.C.C.) 439

Placer Dome Canada Ltd. v. Ontario (Minister of Finance), [2006] 1 S.C.R. 715, 2006 D.T.C. 6532 (Eng.), 2006 CarswellOnt 3112, 2006 CarswellOnt 3113, 2006 SCC 20 (S.C.C.)........15, 111

Placer Dome Inc. v. R., (*sub nom.* Placer Dome Inc. v. Canada) [1992] 2 C.T.C. 99(sub nom. R. v. Placer Dome Inc.) 92 D.T.C. 6402, 1992 CarswellNat 316 (Fed. C.A.), leave to appeal refused 1993 CarswellNat 2484 (S.C.C.)...............443

Posno v. R., (*sub nom.* Posno v. Canada) [1989] 2 C.T.C. 234, 89 D.T.C. 5423, 1989 CarswellNat 294 (Fed. T.D.).........63

Potash v. Royal Trust Co., [1986] 2 S.C.R. 351, 1986 CarswellMan 353, 1986 CarswellMan 404 (S.C.C.)..................135

President's Choice Bank v. R., [2009] G.S.T.C. 60, 2009 CarswellNat 801, 2009 CarswellNat 6388, 2009 CCI 170, 2009 TCC 170 (T.C.C. [General Procedure]) 453

Pridecraft Pty Ltd v. Commissioner of Taxation, 2005 ATC 4001 ....257, 270

Produits Forestiers Donohue Inc. c. R. (2001), [2003] 1 C.T.C. 2010, *(sub nom.* Produits Forestiers Donohue Inc. v. R.) 2001 D.T.C. 586 (Fr.), *(sub nom.* Donohue Forest Products Inc. v. R.) 2001 D.T.C. 823 (Eng.), 2001 CarswellNat 1566, 2001 CarswellNat 1366 (T.C.C. [General Procedure]), affirmed (2002), [2003] 3 C.T.C. 160, *(sub nom.* R. v. Produits Forestiers Donohue Inc.) 2002 D.T.C. 7512 (Fr.), *(sub nom.* R. v. Donahue Forest Products Inc.) 2003 D.T.C. 5471, 2002 CarswellNat 3052, 2002 CarswellNat 4047, 2002 CAF 422, 2002 FCA 422 (Fed. C.A.)............ 372, 456

Prosperous Investments Ltd. v. Minister of National Revenue, [1992] 1 C.T.C. 2218, *(sub nom.* Ed Sinclair Construction & Supplies Ltd. v. Minister of National Revenue) 92 D.T.C. 1163, 1992 CarswellNat 257 (T.C.C.) 437

Québec (Commission des droits de la personne & des droits de la jeunesse) c. Montréal (Ville), [2000] 1 S.C.R. 665, 2000 CarswellQue 649, 2000 CarswellQue 650, 2000 SCC 27 (S.C.C.).. 14

Québec (Communauté urbaine) c. Notre-Dame de Bonsecours (Corp.) (1994), [1994] 3 S.C.R. 3, *(sub nom.* Notre-Dame de Bon-Secours (Corp.) v. Quebec (Communauté urbaine)) [1995] 1 C.T.C. 241, *(sub nom.* Corp. Notre-Dame de Bon-Secours c. Québec (Communauté urbaine)) 95 D.T.C. 5091 (Fr.), 95 D.T.C. 5017, 1994 CarswellQue 86, 1994 CarswellQue 115 (S.C.C.)....... 48

R. Bruce Graham Ltd. v. Minister of National Revenue, [1986] 1 C.T.C. 2326, 86 D.T.C. 1256, 1986 CarswellNat 294 (T.C.C.) 444

R. v. Capitol Life Insurance Co., [1986] 1 C.T.C. 388, 86 D.T.C. 6164, 1986 CarswellNat 672, 1986 CarswellNat 247 (Fed. C.A.) 451

R. v. Edwards, [1996] 1 S.C.R. 128, 1996 CarswellOnt 2126, 1996 CarswellOnt 1916 (S.C.C.)........................... 22

R. v. Fries, *(sub nom.* Fries v. R.) [1990] 2 C.T.C. 439, 90 D.T.C. 6662, 1990 CarswellNat 369, 1990 CarswellNat 740 (S.C.C.) 115

R. v. Grant, [2009] 2 S.C.R. 353, 2009 CarswellOnt 4104, 2009 CarswellOnt 4105, 2009 SCC 32 (S.C.C.) 22

R. v. Imperial General Properties Ltd., [1985] 2 C.T.C. 299, 85 D.T.C. 5500, 1985 CarswellNat 335, 1985 CarswellNat 667 (S.C.C.) 84

R. v. Malmo-Levine, [2003] 3 S.C.R. 571, 2003 CarswellBC 3133, 2003 CarswellBC 3134, 2003 SCC 74 (S.C.C.) 22

R. v. Mills (1999), 180 D.L.R. (4th) 1, 1999 CarswellAlta 1055, 1999 CarswellAlta 1056 (S.C.C.) 14

R. v. Seaboyer (1991), 7 C.R. (4th) 117, 1991 CarswellOnt 109, 1991 CarswellOnt 1022 (S.C.C.) 22

R. v. Shok, [1975] C.T.C. 162, 75 D.T.C. 5109, 1975 CarswellNat 149, 1975 CarswellNat 354 (Fed. T.D.) 18

Re: Clough Engineering and Deputy Commissioner of Taxation (1997), 35 ATR 1164. 270

Reference re Act to Amend Chapter 401 of the Revised Statutes, 1989, the Residential Tenancies Act, S.N.S. 1992, c. 31, (sub nom. Reference re Amendments to the Residential Tenancies Act) [1996] 1 S.C.R. 186, 1996 CarswellNS 166, 1996 CarswellNS 166F (S.C.C.) 133

Reid v. R., (sub nom. Reid v. Canada) [1993] 2 C.T.C. 3145, 95 D.T.C. 308, 1993 CarswellNat 1161 (T.C.C.) 450

Remai Estate v. R. (2008), [2009] 3 C.T.C. 2024, (sub nom. Remai v. R.) 2008 D.T.C. 4567 (Eng.), 2008 CarswellNat 2834, 2008 CarswellNat 5620, 2008 CCI 344, 2008 TCC 344 (T.C.C. [General Procedure]), affirmed (2009), [2010] 2 C.T.C. 120, (sub nom. R. v. Remai Estate) 2009 D.T.C. 5188 (Eng.), 2009 CarswellNat 5570, 2009 CarswellNat 3773, 2009 CAF 340, 2009 FCA 340 (F.C.A.). 458

Rice's Toyota World, Inc. v. C.I.R., 752 F.2d 89 (4th Cir., 1985) 159, 180

Rigid Box Co. v. Minister of National Revenue, [1991] 2 C.T.C. 2374, 91 D.T.C. 1173, 1991 CarswellNat 608 (T.C.C.) 444

RMM Canadian Enterprises Inc. v. R. (1997), [1998] 1 C.T.C. 2300, 97 D.T.C. 302, 1997 CarswellNat 400 (T.C.C.), additional reasons [1997] 3 C.T.C. 2103, 97 D.T.C. 420, 1997 CarswellNat 734 (T.C.C.) 78, 106, 107

Rogers v. U.S., 281 F.3d 1108 (10th Cir., 2002) 72, 271, 273, 274

Rousseau-Houle c. R., 2001 CarswellNat 1126, (*sub nom.* Rousseau-Houle v. R.) 2001 D.T.C. 250 (Fr.), 2006 D.T.C. 3181 (Eng.), 2001 CarswellNat 500 (T.C.C. [General Procedure]). 455

Roy v. Minister of National Revenue (1987), (*sub nom.* Roy v. M.N.R.) [1988] 1 C.T.C. 2361, 88 D.T.C. 1275 (Fr.), (*sub nom.* Roy c. M.R.N.) 88 D.T.C. 1278, 1987 CarswellNat 592 (T.C.C.) 440

Roynat Inc. v. Ja-Sha Trucking & Leasing Ltd., [1992] 2 C.T.C. 139, 1992 CarswellMan 217 (Man. C.A.) 63

Schimmens v. R., [1996] 3 C.T.C. 2132, 1996 CarswellNat 1505 (T.C.C.) 447

Schwartz v. R., (*sub nom.* Schwartz v. Canada) [1996] 1 S.C.R. 254, 96 D.T.C. 6103, 1996 CarswellNat 2940, 1996 CarswellNat 422F (S.C.C.) 115

Shell Canada Ltd. v. R., (*sub nom.* Shell Canada Ltd. v. Canada) [1999] 3 S.C.R. 622, [1999] 4 C.T.C. 313, 99 D.T.C. 5669 (Eng.), 99 D.T.C. 5682 (Fr.), 1999 CarswellNat 1808, 1999 CarswellNat 1809 (S.C.C.)
.... 59, 74, 80, 85, 90-92, 98, 104, 369, 377, 399, 417, 418

Shell Canada Ltd. v. R., [1997] 3 C.T.C. 2238, 97 D.T.C. 395, 1997 CarswellNat 401 (T.C.C.), reversed [1998] 2 C.T.C. 207, *(sub nom.* R. v. Shell Canada Ltd.) 98 D.T.C. 6177, 1998 CarswellNat 1643, 1998 CarswellNat 170 (Fed. C.A.), reversed 1999 CarswellNat 951, 1999 CarswellNat 952 (S.C.C.), additional reasons [1999] 3 S.C.R. 622, [1999] 4 C.T.C. 313, 99 D.T.C. 5669 (Eng.), 99 D.T.C. 5682 (Fr.), 1999 CarswellNat 1808, 1999 CarswellNat 1809 (S.C.C.) 100, 101, 399, 417, 418

Shepard v. British Columbia (Minister of Finance) (1978), 4 E.T.R. 268, 1978 CarswellBC 362 (B.C. S.C.), reversed 1980 CarswellBC 109 (B.C. C.A.) 64

Sherman v. R., 2008 D.T.C. 3069 (Eng.), 2008 CarswellNat 5309, 2008 CarswellNat 834, 2008 CCI 186, 2008 TCC 186 (T.C.C. [General Procedure]), affirmed 2009 D.T.C. 5042 (Eng.), 2009 CarswellNat 2110, 2009 CarswellNat 132, 2009 CAF 9, 2009 FCA 9 (F.C.A.) 452

Shore v. Minister of National Revenue, [1992] 1 C.T.C. 34, *(sub nom.* R. v. Shore) 92 D.T.C. 6059, 1992 CarswellNat 218 (Fed. T.D.) 449

Simpsons-Sears Ltd. v. New Brunswick (Provincial Secretary), [1978] 2 S.C.R. 869, [1978] C.T.C. 296, 78 D.T.C. 6242, 1978 CarswellNB 7, 1978 CarswellNB 8 (S.C.C.) 7

Singleton v. The Queen, see Singleton v. R.

Singleton v. R., [1996] 3 C.T.C. 2873, 96 D.T.C. 1850, 1996 CarswellNat 1816 (T.C.C.), reversed [1999] 3 C.T.C. 446, 99 D.T.C. 5362, 1999 CarswellNat 2949, 1999 CarswellNat 1009 (Fed. C.A.), affirmed (2001), *(sub nom.* Singleton v. Canada) [2001] 2 S.C.R. 1046, [2002] 1 C.T.C. 121, 2001 D.T.C. 5533 (Eng.), 2001 D.T.C. 5545 (Fr.), 2001 CarswellNat 2019, 2001 CarswellNat 2020, 2001 SCC 61 (S.C.C.)............................ 74, 75, 90, 103, 104

SIR v. Gallagher, (1978) (2) SA 463 (A) 241

SIR v. Geustyn, Forsyth and Joubert, 1971 (3) SA 567 (A) 232

SmithKline Beecham Animal Health Inc. v. R., [2002] 4 C.T.C. 93, 2002 CarswellNat 1244, 2002 CarswellNat 2201, 2002 FCA 229 (Fed. C.A.) 52

Sneyd v. R., [2000] G.S.T.C. 46, 2000 CarswellNat 3594, 2000 CarswellNat 1250 (Fed. C.A.) 52

Society of Composers, Authors & Music Publishers of Canada v. Canadian Assn. of Internet Providers (2004), 322 N.R. 306, 2004 CarswellNat 1919, 2004 CarswellNat 1920, 2004 SCC 45 (S.C.C.) 14

Sorochan v. Sorochan, [1986] 2 S.C.R. 38, 1986 CarswellAlta 714, 1986 CarswellAlta 143 (S.C.C.) 129

Southgate Master Fund LLC v. United States of America, No. 3:06-cv-2335-K (N.D. Tex., Aug 18, 2009), Doc 2009-18785, 2009 TNT 160-6 .... 200-202, 394

Stewart v. R., (*sub nom.* Stewart v. Canada) [2002] 2 S.C.R. 645, [2002] 3 C.T.C. 439, 2002 D.T.C. 6969 (Eng.), 2002 D.T.C. 6983 (Fr.), 2002 CarswellNat 1070, 2002 CarswellNat 1071, 2002 SCC 46 (S.C.C.) 12, 115

Stobie Creek Investment, LLC v. U.S., 82 Fed.Cl. 636 (2008) ... 140

Stubart Investments Ltd. v. R., [1984] 1 S.C.R. 536, [1984] C.T.C. 294, 84 D.T.C. 6305, 1984 CarswellNat 690, 1984 CarswellNat 222 (S.C.C.) 7, 60, 61, 73, 79, 80, 85, 87-89, 91, 131

Symes v. R. (1993), (*sub nom.* Symes v. Canada) [1993] 4 S.C.R. 695, [1994] 1 C.T.C. 40, 94 D.T.C. 6001, 1993 CarswellNat 1387, 1993 CarswellNat 1178 (S.C.C.) ... 7, 13, 114, 115, 120

Teleglobe Canada Inc. v. R., [2000] 4 C.T.C. 2448, 2000 D.T.C. 2493, 2000 CarswellNat 1973, 2000 CarswellNat 1974 (T.C.C. [General Procedure]), affirmed (2002), [2003] 1 C.T.C. 255, (*sub nom.* Teleglobe Inc. v. R.) 2002 D.T.C. 7517, 2002 CarswellNat 3053, 2002 CarswellNat 4797, 2002 CAF 408, 2002 FCA 408 (Fed. C.A.) 441

Tennant v. R., (*sub nom.* Tennant v. Minister of National Revenue) [1996] 1 S.C.R. 305, [1996] 1 C.T.C. 290, 96 D.T.C. 6121, 1996 CarswellNat 421F (S.C.C.)............ 89-91, 104, 108, 120

Thomson Newspapers Ltd. v. Canada (Director of Investigation & Research), [1990] 1 S.C.R. 425, 1990 CarswellOnt 991, 1990 CarswellOnt 92 (S.C.C.)............................ 134

Ticketnet Corp. v. R., [1999] 3 C.T.C. 564, 99 D.T.C. 5409, 1999 CarswellNat 1030, 1999 CarswellNat 4326 (Fed. T.D.), additional reasons 99 D.T.C. 5429, 1999 CarswellNat 1298 (Fed. T.D.) 445

Triad Gestco Ltd. v. R., [2011] 6 C.T.C. 2302, 2011 D.T.C. 1254 (Eng.), 2011 CarswellNat 4213, 2011 CarswellNat 2416, 2011 CCI 259, 2011 TCC 259 (T.C.C. [General Procedure]), affirmed 2012 CarswellNat 3853, 2012 FCA 258 (F.C.A.)..... 107, 458

United Parcel Service of America, Inc. v. C.I.R., 254 F.3d 1014 (11th Cir., 2001), cert. denied (2/20/07)............ 162, 172

United States v. Silk, 331 U.S. 704 (U.S. Sup. Ct., 1947)...... 440

Univar Canada Ltd. v. R. (2005), [2006] 1 C.T.C. 2308, 2005 D.T.C. 1478 (Eng.), 2005 CarswellNat 3594, 2005 TCC 723 (T.C.C. [General Procedure]).................................. 457

Vancouver Island Railway, An Act Respecting, Re, [1994] 2 S.C.R. 41, 1994 CarswellBC 188, 1994 CarswellBC 1239 (S.C.C.) 133, 134

Vancouver Society of Immigrant & Visible Minority Women v. Minister of National Revenue, [1999] 1 S.C.R. 10, [1999] 2 C.T.C. 1, 99 D.T.C. 5034, 1999 CarswellNat 18, 1999 CarswellNat 19 (S.C.C.)... 7

Vincent v. Commissioner of Taxation, 2002 ATC 4742 (Aust. Fed. Ct.) 273, 274

W.F. Botkin Construction Ltd. v. R., (*sub nom.* W.F. Botkin Construction Ltd. v. Canada) [1993] 1 C.T.C. 2765, 93 D.T.C. 448, 1993 CarswellNat 913 (T.C.C.) 450

W.T. Ramsay Ltd. v. Inland Revenue Commissioners (1981), [1982] A.C. 300, [1981] 2 W.L.R. 449 (U.K. H.L.)
.... 36, 87, 109, 304, 305

Ward v. Vancouver (City), 2010 CarswellBC 1947, 2010 CarswellBC 1948, 2010 SCC 27 (S.C.C.). 22

Web Press Graphics Ltd. v. Minister of National Revenue, 2006 G.T.C. 1151, 2006 CarswellNat 584, 2006 CarswellNat 1978, 2006 CF 358, 2006 FC 358 (F.C.). 452

Wells Fargo & Co. and Subsidiaries v. U.S., 91 Fed.Cl. 35 (2010)
.... 140, 361, 397, 421

Wells Fargo & Company and Subsidiaries v. United States, No. 06-628T, 2010 TNT 6-15 (Fed. Cl., 2010)
.... 182-184, 361, 397, 421

Wells Fargo & Company and Subsidiaries v. United States, No. 2010 5108 (Fed. Cir. April 15, 2011) 184, 397, 421

Western Securities Ltd. v. R., 97 D.T.C. 977, 1997 CarswellNat 56 (T.C.C.). 441

Wiebe Door Services Ltd. v. Minister of National Revenue, [1986] 2 C.T.C. 200, 87 D.T.C. 5025, 1986 CarswellNat 366, 1986 CarswellNat 699 (Fed. C.A.) 438

Winn-Dixie Stores, Inc. v. Comm'r, 113 T.C. 254 (U.S.Tax Ct., 1999), affirmed 254 F.3d 1313 (11th Cir., 2001) 140, 183, 192

Woolford Realty Co. v. Rose, 286 U.S. 319 (1932). 153

Wotherspoon v. Canadian Pacific Ltd., (*sub nom.* Wotherspoon v. Cdn. Pacific Ltd.) [1987] 1 S.C.R. 952, 1987 CarswellOnt 673, 1987 CarswellOnt 966 (S.C.C.) 128

WT Ramsay Ltd. v. Inland Revenue Commissioners, [1979] 1 W.L.R. 974 (C.A.). 36, 304

XCO Investments Ltd. v. R. (2005), [2006] 1 C.T.C. 2220, 2005 D.T.C. 1731 (Eng.), 2005 CarswellNat 3664, 2005 CarswellNat 4479, 2005 CCI 655, 2005 TCC 655 (T.C.C. [General Procedure]), affirmed [2007] 2 C.T.C. 243, 2007 D.T.C. 5146 (Eng.), 2007 CarswellNat 128, 2007 CarswellNat 1482, 2007 CAF 53, 2007 FCA 53 (F.C.A.). 18

Yosha v. C.I.R., 861 F.2d 494 (7th Cir., 1988). 118

Zupet v. Minister of National Revenue, 2005 TCC 89, 2005 CarswellNat 7352, 2005 CarswellNat 382, 2005 CCI 89 (T.C.C. [Employment Insurance]) 446

"Whoever hopes a faultless tax to see, hopes what ne'er was, is not and ne'er shall be."

– Alexander Pope

Introduction

There are judicial tools available, including a number of common law doctrines, for use by the courts in Canada in dealing with abusive tax avoidance; however, there is no route currently recognized in our courts for setting aside tax avoidance transactions on the ground that they are lacking in economic substance.[1] This stands in contrast with the position in the U.S.,[2] where its longstanding

---

[1] James Morgan, "Cross-Border Regulation of Tax Shelters: The Implied Economic Substance Doctrine", *Tax Notes International* 387-395 (Oct. 22, 2007), 395 (arguing that the development by national judiciaries of a body of precedent based on economic substance would provide a standard for multinational enterprises re tax avoidance).

[2] David P. Hariton, "When and How Should the Economic Substance Doctrine be Applied?", 60 *Tax Law Review* 29-56 (2006), 33-34 (the judicial economic substance doctrine is used to guard against the success of tax avoidance transactions engineered to result in tax benefits, where there is no risk of loss); Yoram Keinan, "The Many Faces of the Economic Substance's Two-Prong Test: Time For Reconciliation?", 1 *NYU Journal of Law and Business* 371-456 (2005), 387 (the economic substance doctrine, the substance over form or step transaction doctrines and statutory anti-abuse rules are the three major means that the IRS uses for disallowing tax benefits arising from tax-motivated transactions); Joseph Bankman, "The Tax Shelter Problem", 57 *National*

common law economic substance doctrine has recently been codified.[3] Also, as I show in this book, Canada is now out-of-step with Australia, New Zealand, South Africa and the European Court of Justice, regarding the role economic substance plays in tax avoidance cases.[4]

We require legislative amendments in Canada, to enable us to emulate the U.S. treatment of economic substance, and to bring us abreast with its treatment in Australia, New Zealand, South Africa, and by the European Court of Justice. This is because the Supreme Court has severely restricted the ability of the lower courts to rely upon findings as to economic substance in tax avoidance cases,[5] apart from for the limited purpose of determining whether transactions are an abuse or misuse of the provisions of the *Income Tax*

Tax Journal 925 (2004), 928 (the economic substance doctrine is a "blunt instrument", that works best in the most egregious cases, which is not applied in the face of clearly expressed legislative intent); Jeff Rector, "A Review of the Economic Substance Doctrine", vol. 10, no. 1 *Stanford Journal of Law, Business & Finance*, 173-190 (2004), 174 (the economic substance doctrine is "the Government's trump card" because where the legal form chosen technically complies with all of the statutory requirements for obtaining a deduction, tax benefits are denied when the transactions lack economic substance).

[3] H.R. 4872, 111th Cong., § 1409. Also see my discussion of the US position re economic substance in chapter VI.

[4] The position of economic substance vis-à- vis the GAARs in Australia, New Zealand and South Africa is examined in chapter VII. Also note that the illustrative draft GAAR that is presently being considered in the U.K. includes economic substance as an objective factor to be used in detecting abusive tax avoidance – see my examination of this point in chapter VII.

[5] David Bishop Debenham, "From the Revenue Rule to the Rule of the 'Revenuer': A Tale of Two Davids and Two Goliaths", (2008) vol. 56, no. 1 CTJ 1-66, 13 (commenting that the Supreme Court of Canada has taken a restrictive view of the common law doctrines that attempt to eliminate aggressive tax avoidance schemes, whereas the U.S. Supreme Court and lower courts have been receptive to common law doctrines designed to curb such schemes); also see: "Discussion Paper on Tax Avoidance", (Law Administration, South African Revenue Service, November 2005), 37 (stating that insofar as "robust judicial doctrines to counter abusive tax avoidance schemes" have been developed in the U.S. courts, but not in Canada "generally reflect(s) a willingness of the American courts to grapple with business and commercial realities in the tax arena.").

Act[6] in the last stage of analysis under GAAR in subsection 245(4) of the Act. In the Supreme Court's words, in its initial decision concerning the application of GAAR, a "lack of substance ... [has] no meaning in isolation from the proper interpretation of specific provisions of the *Income Tax Act*."[7]

The Supreme Court's position has been criticized by Canadian academics as an unfortunate and wrong limitation.[8] There is no justification for restricting examinations of economic substance to those circumstances where specific provisions of the *Income Tax Act* are being interpreted. Indeed, there are few provisions in the *Income Tax Act* for which an economic substance inquiry is even germane.[9] Moreover, determining whether transactions have economic

---

[6] RSC 1985, c. 1 (5th Supp.) as amended (hereinafter referred to as "the Act").

[7] *Canada Trustco Mortgage Co. v. R.*, [2005] 2 S.C.R. 601 (S.C.C.) at paras. 59 and 66; see also: *Lipson v. R.*, [2009] 1 C.T.C. 314 (S.C.C.) at para. 38, per LeBel J. ("Motivation, purpose and economic substance are relevant under s. 245(4) only to the extent that they establish whether the transaction frustrates the purpose of the relevant provisions (*Canada Trustco*, at paras. 57-60)").

[8] Benjamin Alarie, Sanjana Bhatia and David G. Duff, "Symposium on Tax Avoidance After Canada Trustco and Mathew: Summary of Proceedings" (2005) vol. 53, no. 4 CTJ 1010, per Professor Jinyan Li, 1016-18, 1024 (arguing that the Supreme Court's approach to economic substance under GAAR is too narrow. "Transactions lacking economic substance should be presumed to frustrate the legislative purpose of the Act, unless the transactions are clearly supported by the text, context, and purpose of specific provisions or the Act read as a whole"); Brian J. Arnold, "Confusion Worse Confounded – The Supreme Court's GAAR Decisions", (2006) vol. 54, no. 1 CTJ 167-209, 192, 208-209 (according to the Supreme Court of Canada, reference to the economic substance of transactions is warranted under ss. 245(4) of the *Income Tax Act* only if the relevant statutory provisions justify it. "The court has rendered the GAAR virtually meaningless by restricting the significance of economic substance." and "Without consideration of the economic substance of a transaction the GAAR will be ineffective"); Jinyan Li, "'Economic Substance': Legitimate Tax Minimization vs. Abusive Tax Avoidance", (2006) vol. 54, no. 1 C.T.J. 23-56, 27 (arguing that "consideration of economic substance is called for by Parliament through the enactment of the GAAR"; this is "consistent with the purposive approach to statutory interpretation"; it is "justified on theoretical grounds"; and, evaluation of economic substance is "the best method for balancing conflicting policy concerns in Canadian income tax law").

[9] Arnold, *supra* no. 8 at 192 (noting that very few provisions in the *Income Tax Act* refer to economic substance); also see Brian A. Felesky and Sandra E. Jack, "Is There Substance to 'Substance Over Form' in Canada?", (1992)

substance involves a factual inquiry,[10] which is not itself an aspect of statutory interpretation. Although Halpern and many others have argued that consideration of economic substance independently from the particular language of the taxing statute "risks venturing onto policy-making terrain usually reserved for the legislature",[11] I do not find this argument convincing, for reasons I explain in chapter V, in my review and evaluation of the Supreme Court of Canada's position regarding economic realities and substance. Rather, the nexus of economic substance with statutory interpretation is that a proper question for courts to be asking in tax avoidance cases is whether Parliament intended, when enacting the relevant tax legislation, that transactions without economic substance should give rise to tax benefits.[12] Unfortunately, however, the position of the

---

Conference Report (Toronto: Canadian Tax Foundation, 1993), 50:1-50:63, 50:45 (arguing that "The fact that only certain provisions of the Act specifically contemplate that the tax consequences of a transaction may not be consistent with the legal effect thereof is strong support for the proposition that the scheme of the Act does not provide for a general economic substance doctrine."); Nik Diksic, "Some Reflections on the Roles of Legal and Economic Substance in Tax Law', 2010 *Conference Report* (Toronto: Canadian Tax Foundation, 2011), 25:1-34 (suggesting that "the preferred share rules ... are a rare instance of prescriptive statutory provisions that are designed to effectively treat certain share investments as debt based on clearly articulated 'economic substance' principles.").

[10] Li, *supra* no. 8 at 34, 37, 44 (commenting that while the examination of economic substance is a factual determination which calls for the taxpayer's transaction to be assessed "with an eye to commercial and economic realities", "The economic substance analysis has a more natural fit with a purposive interpretation of the statute.").

[11] James S. Halpern, "Putting The Cart Before The Horse: Determining Economic Substance Independent of the Language of the Code", 30 *Virginia Tax Review* 327-338 (2010), 328-329 (also arguing with regard to the Federal Circuit's statement in *Coltec Industries Inc. v. United States* that "[T]he economic substance doctrine is merely a judicial tool for effectuating the Congressional purpose that, despite literal compliance with the statute, tax benefits not be afforded based on transactions lacking in economic substance.", "I agree but caution that difficulties in framing the relevant transaction and identifying the pertinent Congressional purposes may make the search for economic substance more problematic than it would at first appear.")

[12] See my discussion of the "self-defeating" theory of statutory interpretation in chapter VI.

Supreme Court as to the minor ancillary role of economic substance in tax avoidance cases precludes this inquiry.

My contention is that the general anti-avoidance rule ("GAAR") in section 245 of the *Income Tax Act*[13] should be amended, in order to bring clarity and consistency to this difficult area, to require that the economic substance of transactions must be considered as a relevant factual element in determining, for the purposes of GAAR, whether a transaction is an "avoidance transaction", and also in deciding whether the transaction results in a misuse of the relevant taxing provisions or an abuse of the Act when read as a whole.[14]

I also contend that GAAR should be amended to provide that transactions which are primarily entered into in order to secure tax benefits, and which are found not to have substantial[15] economic

---

[13] RSC 1985, c. 1 (5th Supp.) as amended (hereinafter referred to as "the Act")

[14] Judith Freedman, "Improving (Not Perfecting) Tax Legislation: Rules and Principles Revisited", vol. 6 *British Tax Review* 717-736 (2010), 728 (suggesting that a general anti-avoidance principle with a direction from the legislature that economic substance is a factor in the application of the principle would be acceptable as "a broad principle intended to underpin the entire tax system", and operative as "part of the architecture of the legislation"); see also: Brian J. Arnold, "The Canadian General Anti-Avoidance Rule", vol. 6 *British Tax Review* 541-556 (1995), 550 (warning, however, against the "real danger" that the interpretation of subsection 245(4) "will degenerate into an unprincipled, conclusory approach based on judges' views of the substance or economic reality of transactions.").

[15] Regarding the proposed requirement for "substantial economic consequences" in relation to the expected tax benefits see: Jasper L. Cummings, Jr., "Enforcement Responses to Intentional Tax Reduction, Including the Economic Substance Doctrine", *The Supreme Court's Federal Tax Jurisprudence*, American Bar Association Section of Taxation, 145-241 (2010), 232 (suggesting that "by using the term 'substantial' [in the codified economic substance doctrine] Congress intended to send a message that it will not be enough for taxpayers to prove a reasonable (much less a remote) possibility of some economic profit."); Bret Wells, "Economic Substance Doctrine: How Codification Changes Decided Cases", vol. 10, no. 6 *Florida Tax Review* 416-457 (2010), 435 (commenting that "the bifurcation authority set forth in section 7701(o)(5)(D) [of the codified economic substance doctrine] now calls into question the ability of a taxpayer to bootstrap a tax motivated step into an overall transaction unless the tax motivated step has a 'substantial' economic consequence when judged on a stand-alone basis."); Tony Swiderski and Alexey Manasuev, "The New

consequences for the taxpayer in relation to their expected tax benefits,[16] shall be presumed not to give rise to any tax benefits.

> US Statutory Economic Substance Doctrine: They Forgot the Important Parts – Has Everything or Nothing Changed?", 2010 *Conference Report* (Toronto: Canadian Tax Foundation, 2011), 18:1-31 (predicting that the codified economic substance doctrine in the U.S. "will tend to have greater application to a transaction that results in disproportionate tax benefits, such as tax attribute duplication, the allocation of income to a tax-indifferent party, the creation of a tax loss that is not supported by a corresponding economic loss, the affirmative use of technical tax rules to yield a result that was clearly not intended and the like."); Marie Saparie, "Codified Economic Substance Doctrine Still an Uncertain Area", 129 *Tax Notes* 30-31 (Oct. 4, 2010), 31 (referring to a tax practitioner suggesting that it is unclear what level of profit will be considered "substantial" compared with tax savings, but if pretax profit potential is less than 10 percent of tax savings there is a significant risk it will be considered insubstantial ,whereas "if the pretax profit potential is more than half the tax savings, ... that's pretty clearly substantial compared to the tax benefit", and it's "anybody's guess" where the courts and the IRS are going to draw the line between 10 percent and 50 percent); Rachel Anne Tooma, "Legislating Against Tax Avoidance", (Amsterdam: IBFD, 2008), 48 (suggesting that the economic substance doctrine has applied in the U.S. to disallow tax benefits "where there is a gross departure from sensible economic results and the fundamental tax principles underlying the Code"); Nöel B. Cunningham and James R. Repetti, "Textualism and Tax Shelters", 24 *Virginia Tax Review* 1-63 (2004), 23 (noting that under the economic substance doctrine before its codification "the courts will deny tax benefits if the purported pre-tax economic profit is insubstantial in relation to the value of the expected benefits from the transaction"); David A. Weisbach, "Ten Truths About Tax Shelters", vol. 55 *Tax Law Review* 215-254 (2001-2002), 228 (noting that some U.S. court cases have treated "transactions that yield a profit only minimally above zero ..., transactions that no sane person would enter into absent taxes, as having adequate tax potential."); Daniel N. Shaviro, "Economic Substance, Corporate Tax Shelters and the Compaq Case", 88 *Tax Notes* 221-244 (July 10, 2000), 243 (noting IRS Notice 98-5 requires the expected economic profit from a deal to be more than "insubstantial" compared to the foreign tax credits generated); Calvin H. Johnson, "H.R. ___, The Anti-skunk Works Corporate Tax Shelter Act of 1999", 84 *Tax Notes* 443-461 (July 19, 1999), 447 ("Having tax benefits greater than the entire cost of the transaction is the *reducio ad absurdum* for a transaction. Transactions with a cost less than the tax benefit have no economic meaning except for tax and no economic constraints except by the courts ripping away the tax benefits. Tax is not supposed to be a profit center. ... The closer that the cost is to the value of tax benefits and the farther the deducted amount is from true losses ... the more questionable the transaction becomes.").
>
> [16] Graeme Cooper and Clare Cunliffe, "Skinning the Tax Avoidance Cat", vol. 30 *Australian Tax Review* 26-38 (2001), 32-33 (suggesting that it would

That is to say, although the transactions have ostensibly given rise to a "tax benefit", it will be denied unless the taxpayer can show that the benefit was legislatively intended.[17]

These proposals are made for a number of reasons: (1) they represent a simple and modest incremental change to the existing GAAR provisions, rather than a radical overhaul – they can thus be easily implemented and should be palatable as legislative measures;[18] (2) they rely upon a conceptual foundation with which the courts and taxpayers are already familiar – the courts are very experienced with respect to the meaning of "substantial";[19] and, as I

---

be "by no means heroic" for courts to be able to identify the benefits that are "expected" to arise from a transaction).

[17] The statutory presumption is rebuttable – see the discussion of this point that follows. Also see: *Taxation of Private Corporations and Their Shareholders, 4th ed. (Toronto: Canadian Tax Foundation,* 2010), Paul Bleiwas and John Hutson (eds.), c. 16, V. GAAR, Canada's Answer to Tax Avoidance, B. Analysis of Section 245, 7. Misuse or Abuse, h. Selected Supreme Court of Canada Cases (commenting that "One question that continues to be troublesome is the statement in *Canada Trustco* that the burden is on the Minister to establish the existence of 'abusive tax avoidance'").

[18] John Prebble, "The US GAAR", Victoria University, Wellington NZ TaxProfBlog, May 25, 2010 (suggesting that "[O]nce the major philosophical decision has been taken and a GAAR is in place, most legislatures become willing to amend and improve it as litigation reveals loopholes or shortcomings.")

[19] The Tax Court of Canada *General Procedure Rules* contemplate determinations of questions of law, fact or mixed law and fact under Rule 58, and special cases under Rule 50, where the result would be a "substantial saving of costs" and Practice Note 18 speaks of "substantial indemnity costs" in the context of settlement offers. The Supreme Court of Canada also often uses the term "substantial" in a tax context, e.g.: *Lipson v. R.*, *(sub nom.* Lipson v. Canada) [2009] 1 S.C.R. 3 (S.C.C.) at para. 70 ("substantial block of stock"); *Air Canada v. British Columbia*, [1989] 1 S.C.R. 1161 (S.C.C.) at para. 96 ("substantial agreement"); *Symes v. R.*, *(sub nom.* Symes v. Canada) [1993] 4 S.C.R. 695 (S.C.C.) at para. 21 ("substantial objective"); *Stubart Investments Ltd. v. R.*, [1984] 1 S.C.R. 536 (S.C.C.) at para. 3 ("substantial losses"); *Simpsons-Sears Ltd. v. New Brunswick (Provincial Secretary)*, [1978] 2 S.C.R. 869 (S.C.C.) at para. 30 ("substantial number"); *Vancouver Society of Immigrant & Visible Minority Women v. Minister of National Revenue*, [1999] 1 S.C.R. 10 (S.C.C.) at para. 200 ("substantial effect"). There are also many instances where determinations as to the meaning of "substantial" have been made for *Income Tax Act* purposes; and, the courts have held that the term does not need to be expressed quantitatively or as a percentage – see the

show in this book, the courts are well-acquainted with finding, and often already make decisions by reference to, the perceived "economic realities" of transactions;[20] (3) they will send a signal to taxpayers that the government is serious about its efforts to curb abusive tax avoidance – this possibly having some beneficial deterrent tax effects;[21] (4) they leave considerable flexibility for the courts in judging whether transactions should be respected for tax purposes – this being imperfect, but preferable to the further proliferation of complex and difficult to apply technical tax rules, which are mostly designed after-the-fact, in an attempt to combat the abusive tax avoidance which has emerged;[22] (5) they should encourage the

---

cases under "Substantially – Substantially All", *Tax Court Practice* (Toronto: Carswell, 2013), Robert McMechan and Gordon Bourgard, c. 17.

[20] See Appendix A for examples of tax cases where the courts have made findings re economic realities.

[21] Benjamin Alarie, "Price Discrimination in Income Taxation: Defending Half-Hearted Anti-Avoidance", pp. 1-34, available at http://ssrn.com/abstract=1796284 (Mar. 26, 2001), 12 (suggesting that the "main point" of a general anti-avoidance rule is to "put taxpayers on notice in a formal way that the benefits they may claim based on literal adherence to the text of tax legislation and from respect for the formal legal substance of transactions may be elusive."); also see: Judith Freedman, "Defining Taxpayer Responsibility: In Support of a General Anti-Avoidance Principle", no. 4 *British Tax Review* 332-357 (2004), 333 (arguing in favour of a legislative anti-avoidance principle that "It is not the content of the provision which matters so much as the signposting that will be provided by it.").

[22] Weisbach, *supra* no. 15 at 229, 247 (arguing that "significantly increasing the strength of antitax avoidance doctrines" is a better approach than "making repeated amendments to complicated rules", as a rules-based system tends to be very complex whereas standards can be less complex); Craig Elliffe and Jess Cameron, "The Test for Tax Avoidance in New Zealand: A Judicial Sea Change", *New Zealand Business Law Quarterly* 440-460 (December 2010), 445 (explaining that under New Zealand's GAAR "The court will have no hesitation (and in fact, will find it necessary) to look through the legal form of the arrangements to the economic substance of the taxpayer's arrangements. There is more and more emphasis by the court being placed on this factor."; Craig Elliffe and Mark Keating, "Tax Avoidance – Still Waiting for Godot?", 23 *NZULR* 368-392 (June 2009), 369 (noting that under New Zealand's GAAR the courts have "continued development of the concept of commercial reality and economic burden, clearly articulating that in order to sustain deductions or claims for input tax, the taxpayer must evidence the payments were made in a commercially and economically realistic way."; Diksic, *supra* no. 9 at 25:1-34 (suggesting that "a qualified economic substance analysis" may

courts in Canada to disallow claims by taxpayers for tax benefits in circumstances where the taxpayers have not experienced any economic losses – this being the desirable result from both a fiscal and a tax policy vantage point, i.e. they should assist in stemming losses from tax revenues, which are badly needed by government, and also help to counter the other ill-effects of abusive tax avoidance;[23] (6) they will bring the tax anti-avoidance law in Canada within reasonable proximity of the tax anti-avoidance measures that are already in place in a number of other jurisdictions that are similar to Canada, including Australia, Hong Kong, Ireland, South Africa and the United States;[24] and (7) they will elevate GAAR to the position it was intended to occupy according to the explanatory Technical Notes from the Department of Finance accompanying the draft GAAR legislation, i.e. the provisions of the *Income Tax Act* "are intended to apply to transactions with real economic substance."[25]

It is not envisaged that making these amendments will dispense with the need to resort, on an ongoing basis, to the range of other anti-avoidance measures that are commonly used to combat abusive tax avoidance, including the enactment of specific anti-avoidance rules and the passage of retroactive legislation.[26] Indeed,

---

be an appropriate way to identify some tax avoidance transactions through a characterization exercise as opposed to via a statutory interpretation exercise)

[23] See my discussion of the effects of unchecked abusive tax avoidance in chapter II.

[24] See my examinations of the legislative anti-avoidance regimes in other jurisdictions in chapters VI and VII.

[25] Canada, Department of Finance, *Explanatory Notes to Legislation Relating to Income Tax* (Ottawa: Department of Finance, June 1988), clause 186 "Subsection 245(4) recognizes that the provisions of the Act are intended to apply to transactions with real economic substance, not to transactions intended to exploit, misuse or frustrate the act to avoid tax.") ; see also: David G. Duff, "The Supreme Court of Canada and the General Anti-Avoidance Rule", *Tax Avoidance in Canada After Canada Trustco and Mathew*, (Irwin Law: Toronto, 2007), c. 1, p. 36 (arguing that it follows from the above statement in the *Explanatory Notes* that "transactions that lack economic substance might reasonably be considered to result in an abuse having regard to the provisions of the ITA read as a whole.")

[26] Judith Freedman, "Analysis GAAR: challenging assumptions", www.taxjournal.com, Sept. 27, 2010, 12-14 (commenting that "No jurisdiction has yet

these proposed amendments to the GAAR will only have an impact on the most egregious tax avoidance transactions, where tax benefits are sought to be manufactured out of "thin air",[27] leaving the balance of the tax avoidance field to be dealt with as it is being currently.[28] However, legislating an economic substance component into GAAR should improve its effectiveness.[29]

This suggestion that GAAR should be amended to expressly incorporate an economic substance component is not a novel one.[30]

---

    developed a perfect solution to tax avoidance and none ever will."); also see: GAO-11-493, "Abusive Tax Avoidance Transactions", 1-55 (May 2011), 27 ("Because [abusive tax avoidance transactions] have been a long-standing, ever-changing, and often a hidden problem ... no set of actions taken by the IRS would completely eliminate the problem."); Tim Edgar, "Building a Better GAAR", vol. 27 *Virginia Tax Review* 833-905 (2008), 833-834, 871-872 (arguing the under-inclusiveness of GAAR in Canada can best be over-come through the use of a primary business purpose test which is tailored to apply differently in the identification of tax-attribute creation and tax-attribute trading transactions, as compared to tax-driven transactional substitutions which "should be addressed by the legislative and executive branches of government in discharging their policy making function" on account of concerns about "institutional competence" in the latter case); Tim Edgar, "Financial Instruments and the Tax Avoidance Lottery: A View from North America", vol. 6 *New Zealand Journal of Taxation Law and Policy* 63-102 (2000), 92 (suggesting that in the case of "synthetic" financial instruments that detailed legislative response is preferable to "reliance on broadly drawn purpose-based rules"); Johnson, *supra* no. 15 at 444 ("No single line of defense is sufficient. If a platoon wants to hold the perimeter against attack by overwhelming numbers, it needs to set up more than a single strand of barbed wire; it needs layer upon layer of defense. So too, defense of the corporate tax base and the self-reporting tax system requires a number of layers of defense.")

[27] The origin of the expression "thin air" is attributed to Shakespeare in *The Tempest* (1610).

[28] See the Table of GAAR Cases in Appendix B, showing that in those cases where the Tax Court of Canada has decided to date that the GAAR does not apply, the proposed amendments only impact on the type of scenarios dealt with in the case studies included in chapter IX of this paper. They will, of course, also impact on future scenarios.

[29] Graeme Cooper, "The Design and Structure of General Anti-Avoidance Regimes", *Bulletin for International Taxation* 26-32 (January 2009), 31 ("A solution does not need to remove 100% of the problems; 75% is still a worthy achievement.")

[30] See, for example, Judith Freedman, "Converging Tracks? Recent Developments in Canadian and U.K. Approaches to Tax Avoidance", (2005) vol. 53,

Larin and Doung have recently asserted, for example, that legislative adoption in our GAAR of the eight objective criteria expressed in the Australian GAAR would give the courts "the latitude required to apply the economic substance doctrine with the flexibility seen in the decisions in the U.S. courts", and it would also "reduce the risk of applying the [economic substance] doctrine with sole reference to the taxpayer's subjective intentions."[31] While I agree with the assertion that GAAR should be amended to bring economic substance fully into the tax avoidance arena, I do not agree with the balance of this analysis for at least two reasons. In the first place, our courts

---

no. 4 CTJ 1038-1046, 1046 (suggesting that amending legislation may be needed in Canada to open up the scope of judicial activity re GAAR); Arnold, *supra* no. 8 at 206, footnote 139 (suggesting GAAR should be amended to require the courts to consider the economic substance of a transaction in assessing whether a transaction is abusive under subsection 245(4), pointing out that the GAARS of Australia, Hong Kong and Ireland all require the courts to consider economic substance, among other factors, in determining whether a transaction is offensive. A GAAR amendment could specify circumstances in which a transaction would be considered to lack economic substance: "for example, if the transaction did not have any reasonable prospect of pre-tax profit at least equal to the amount of the expected tax benefit."); Aviv Pichhadze and Amir Pichhadze, "Economic Substance Doctrine: Time for a Legislative Response", 48 *Tax Notes International* 61 (Oct. 1, 2007), 65 (suggesting that for a GAAR to be of use in any country, it should expressly incorporate a general requirement of economic substance); Brian J. Arnold, *The Canadian Experience with General Anti-Avoidance Rule*, Beyond Boundaries *"Developing Approaches to Tax Avoidance and Task Risk Management"*, Judith Freedman (ed.), Oxford University, Centre for Business Taxation, 2008, p. 31 ("Amendments to the GAAR are necessary to eliminate the major deficiencies in the case law. In particular, the GAAR should be amended to require the courts to consider the economic substance of the transaction in question and should provide some guidance to the courts as to the meaning of economic substance."); see also: Finances Québec, Aggressive Tax Planning, Working Paper (Québec: Finances Québec, January 2009), 1-120, 90 (concluding that "Québec's *unilateral* addition of an economic substance test to the provisions of Québec's GAAR is not desirable", as it might be disruptive vis-à-vis the federal tax authorities, etc.)

[31] Gilles Larin and Robert Doung, "Effective Responses to Aggressive Tax Planning: What Canada Can Learn From Other Jurisdictions", Canadian Tax Paper No. 112 (2009), 35, 39 (also arguing that "the economic substance doctrine has enabled the US tax administration and the courts to deny tax benefits that, in our opinion, Canadian taxpayers could obtain notwithstanding the presence of the GAAR.")

have historically demonstrated that they are capable of fashioning their own application criteria, once they are on board conceptually.

In the realm of trading cases, for example, they have enumerated a variety of criteria for the purpose of evaluating whether a gain or loss is on account of income or capital, sometimes called the "badges of trade",[32] without the necessity of microscopic legislative intervention. There is little doubt that the judiciary will also be up to the task of enumerating the "badges of tax avoidance",[33] once GAAR is amended to bring it on board with the project. In this regard, nothing precludes the courts in Canada from looking to U.S. tax jurisprudence for possible inspiration.[34] Given the already Brobdingnagian[35] dimensions of our *Income Tax Act*, it is hard to argue that more tax legislation than necessary is a good thing. Professor Cooper has also noted that the identification of eight objective criteria has given rise to a number of interpretative problems for GAAR in Australia, including whether the list is exhaustive and whether they must all be satisfied in a given case.[36]

---

[32] A classic statement of several relevant criteria for determining whether a gain is from trading or on capital account was formulated by President Thorson in *Minister of National Revenue v. Taylor*, [1956] C.T.C. 189 (Can. Ex. Ct.); see also: *Stewart v. R.*, [2002] 3 C.T.C. 439 (S.C.C.) at para. 52, where "badges of trade" are discussed in the context of whether an activity bears sufficient indicia of commerciality to be considered to be a business for tax purposes.

[33] Dr. Justin Dabner, "The Spin of a Coin – In Search of a Workable GAAR", 3 *Journal of Australian Taxation* 232 (2000) (noting that the Australian Tax Office identified "badges of tax avoidance" following the High Court's decision in *Federal Commissioner of Taxation v. Spotless Services Ltd.*, [1996] HCA 34 (H.C. Australia), which upheld an assessment under GAAR).

[34] Note, for example, that the case law in Canada dealing with "quality of income" references the U.S. Supreme Court's decision in *Brown v. Helvering* – see *Kenneth B.S. Robertson Ltd. v. Minister of National Revenue*, [1944] C.T.C. 75 (Can. Ex. Ct.) at pp. 90-91, per Thorson J.; *Commonwealth Construction Co. v. R.*, [1984] C.T.C. 338 (Fed. C.A.) at paras. 21-22, per Urie. J.

[35] See Jonathan Swift, "Part II: A Voyage to Brobdingnag", *Gulliver's Travels* for an account of Gulliver's experiences amongst the Brobdingnagians.

[36] G. Cooper, "The emerging High Court jurisprudence on Part IVA", vol. 9, no. 5 *The Tax Specialist* 234-251 (June 2006).

Furthermore, I also find that the "risk" Larin and Duong have identified of courts applying the economic substance doctrine solely by reference to the taxpayer's subjective intentions to be over-stated.

The courts in Canada have not generally had difficulty to date in focusing their scrutiny on objective criteria in evaluating taxpayers' intentions and purposes,[37] and there is no good reason to suppose that they will do otherwise when they are faced with the necessity of evaluating the economic substance of transactions in GAAR cases. In this regard, the Federal Court has already held in *Fraser Milner Casgrain LLP v. Minister of National Revenue* that "in applying the purpose test [in subsection 245(3) of the *Income Tax Act*] the Court will look to *all* of the relevant facts and circumstances, determining intent at the time the transactions in question were carried out."[38] Amending GAAR to expressly include economic substance as one of the "relevant facts and circumstances" should thus be a sufficient measure.

The recommendation that transactions without economic substance be presumed to be a misuse of provisions of the *Income Tax Act*, or an abuse having regard to the provisions of the Act as a whole, has also been made before.[39] The courts already rely upon

---

[37] As Iacobucci J. explained in *Symes v. R.* (1993), (*sub nom.* Symes v. Canada) [1994] 1 C.T.C. 40 (S.C.C.) at para. 74: "As in other areas of law where purpose or intention behind actions is to be ascertained, it must not be supposed that in responding to this question [in a tax law context] courts will be guided only by a taxpayer's statements, *ex post facto* or otherwise, as to the subjective purpose …. Courts will, instead, look for objective manifestations of purpose, and purpose is ultimately a question of fact to be decided with due regard for all of the circumstances.") (my underlining emphasis – this highlights the fact that economic substance should be a reference point under subsection 245(3) of the *Income Tax Act*, in deciding whether a transaction was undertaken primarily for purposes other than to obtain a tax benefit).

[38] *Fraser Milner Casgrain LLP v. Minister of National Revenue*, [2002] 4 C.T.C. 210 (Fed. T.D.) at para. 30, per Dawson J (my italics emphasis); also see Bleiwas and Hutson, *supra* no. 17, c. 16, III. Specific Statutory Avoidance Tests, A. The Purpose Test (also suggesting that "to ascertain a taxpayer's subjective purpose, it is necessary to rely not only on the taxpayer's statement or testimony, but also on her conduct and other relevant facts and circumstances.")

[39] Li, *supra* no. 8 at 53 ("As a general proposition, unless the relevant provisions of the Act are intended to permit the enjoyment of a tax benefit resulting from a transaction that lacks economic substance, such a transaction should

many common law rebuttable presumptions that apply in taxation and other cases. Examples include presumptions that (a) Parliament does not intend its legislation to receive extraterritorial effect;[40] (b) statutes form a coherent whole;[41] (c) the legislature does not speak in vain;[42] (d) Parliament intends to enact constitutional legislation;[43] (e) the legislature does not intend to depart from the common law without expressing its intention to do so in clear and unequivocal terms; [44] and (f) where a transfer is made for no consideration the onus is on the transferee to demonstrate that a gift was intended by the transferor.[45] Given the fundamental nature of the point that tax benefits should ordinarily only arise in relation to transactions which have economic substance, unless there is a clearly expressed legislative intention to the contrary, it would behoove our courts to also invoke a presumption to this effect in tax cases. Indeed, the point is analogous to the case of a transferee receiving a gift for no consideration, as the notion that an expense or loss is deductible in the absence of economic outlay (i.e. receiving something for nothing) is worthy of Dr. Strangelove.[46] Since the courts in Canada have not to date decided that the absence of economic substance is an important factual indicator of abusive tax avoidance, the point needs to be made legislatively, and added to the multitude of interpretative presumptions that are already used in deciding cases.

---

be presumed to be abusive."); Duff, *supra* no. 25 at 36 (arguing that it follows from the Explanatory Notes to GAAR that transactions that lack economic substance might reasonably be considered to result in an abuse having regard to the provisions of the Act when read as a whole)

[40] *Society of Composers, Authors & Music Publishers of Canada v. Canadian Assn. of Internet Providers* (2004), 322 N.R. 306 (S.C.C.).

[41] *Québec (Commission des droits de la personne & des droits de la jeunesse) c. Montréal (Ville)*, [2000] 1 S.C.R. 665 (S.C.C.)

[42] *Ibid.*

[43] *R. v. Mills* (1999), 180 D.L.R. (4th) 1 (S.C.C.)

[44] *Goodyear Tire & Rubber Co. of Canada Ltd. v. T. Eaton Co.*, [1956] S.C.R. 610 (S.C.C.).

[45] *Pecore v. Pecore*, [2007] 1 S.C.R. 795 (S.C.C.) (this latter presumption seems most analogous to the circumstances where a taxpayer is seeking a tax benefit without having incurred any economic cost)

[46] "Dr. Strangelove" (1964), co-written by Stanley Kubrick and ex-RAF flight lieutenant Peter George, described by Roger Ebert as "arguably the best political satire of the century"–see http://www.webcitation.org/5QSnSWw4n

Where tax benefits are sought by taxpayers in respect of transactions which lack economic substance, it should be presumed that Parliament did not intend to grant such benefits, unless its intention to do so can be shown to have been expressed in clear and unequivocal terms. There is nothing sinister about requiring taxpayers to show that Parliament intended that the tax benefits would in any event be available, if it has been established that transactions for which tax benefits are claimed have no economic substance. Under the U.S. economic substance doctrine, it is the taxpayer who bears the burden of proving that a transaction has economic substance.[47] In the event that the Canada Revenue Agency assumed that a transaction had no factual economic substance, this burden of proof would also be on the taxpayer in Canada under the judicial assumptions doctrine.[48] In the U.S., it is also the taxpayer who has the burden of showing that Congress intended to give favourable tax treatment: "*Gregory v. Helvering* requires that a taxpayer carry an unusually heavy burden when he attempts to demonstrate that Congress intended to give favorable tax treatment to the kind of transaction that would never occur absent the motive of tax avoidance."[49] This state of affairs is supported by Professor Warren, who argues that the burden of persuasion should be on taxpayers to show that their transactions involve preferential tax provisions which have been explicitly justified on incentive grounds.[50]

---

[47] *Coltec Industries, Inc. v. U.S.*, 454 F.3d 1340 (Fed. Cir., 2006) at para. 57

[48] *Placer Dome Canada Ltd. v. Ontario (Minister of Finance)*, [2006] 1 S.C.R. 715 (S.C.C.) (the taxpayer bears the burden of establishing that the factual findings upon which the Minister based the assessment are wrong); *Johnston v. Minister of National Revenue*, [1948] S.C.R. 486 (S.C.C.) (the onus is on the taxpayer to demolish the basic fact on which taxation rests)

[49] *Coltec Industries, Inc. v. U.S.*, 454 F.3d 1340 (Fed. Cir., 2006) at para. 57, quoting from *Diggs v. C.I.R.*, 281 F.2d 326 (2d Cir., 1960) at para. 5

[50] Alvin C. Warren, Jr., "The Requirement of Economic Profit in Tax Motivated Transactions", 59 *Taxes – The Magazine* 985-992 (1981), 991-992 (also noting that a requirement of a pretax economic profit is not appropriate for transactions involving provisions specifically enacted by Congress as incentives); compare: Daniel Sandler, "The Minister's Burden of Proof Under GAAR", (2006) vol. 54, no. 1 CTJ 3-22, 13-14 (suggesting that "there is no doubt that the burden is (and should be) on the minister" to show misuse or abuse under subsection 245(4) of the Act)

However, the Supreme Court of Canada's decisions in tax avoidance cases display that it will not place an onus on taxpayers to show that transactions without economic substance were intended by Parliament to give rise to tax benefits. Indeed, the Court has already held in *Canada Trustco* that the burden is on the Crown to establish abusive tax avoidance.[51] Parliament should therefore enact this presumption.[52] There are many other instances of legislated presumptions throughout the law,[53] including those located in section 244 of the *Income Tax Act*.[54] Putting an onus on taxpayers to show that Parliament intended that tax benefits would be available in respect of transactions without economic substance would not significantly add to the workload already present for taxpayers in civil tax proceedings,

---

[51] *Canada Trustco Mortgage Co. v. R.*, [2005] 2 S.C.R. 601 (S.C.C.) at paras. 64-66; also see: *Lipson v. R.*, (*sub nom.* Lipson v. Canada) [2009] 1 S.C.R. 3 (S.C.C.) at para. 21, per LeBel J. ("the burden is on the Minister to prove, on the balance of probabilities, that the avoidance transaction results in abuse and misuse within the meaning of s. 245(4) [ITA]."); see also: *Copthorne Holdings Ltd. v. R.*, 2011 SCC 63 (S.C.C.) at para. 72, per Rothstein J. ("[T]he Minister must clearly demonstrate that the transaction is an abuse of the Act, and the benefit of the doubt is given to the taxpayer.")

[52] The Tax Law Review Committee in the U.K. set out an "illustrative GAAR" in 1997, which provided that "In the application of this rule, it shall be assumed that a tax-driven transaction is not a protected transaction unless the contrary is demonstrated." – see Tax Law Review Committee, Tax Avoidance, IFS Commentary no. 64, (http://www.ifs.org.U.K./comms/comm64.pdf)

[53] See, for example, s. 91(1)(b) *Securities Act*, R.S.O. 1990, c. S.5 (persons presumed to be acting jointly or in concert with an offeror); s. 253(2) *Canada Business Corporations Act*, R.S. 1985, c. C-44 (director named in notice presumed to be director); s. 8, *Children's Law Reform Act*, R.S.O. 1990, c. C.12 (presumption of paternity); s. 6(6) *Patented Medicines (Notice of Compliance) Regulations*, SOR/93-133 (presumption of infringement); s. 6.1 *Workers Compensation Act*, R.S.B.C. 1996, c. 492 (firefighter's occupational disease presumption); s. 34.1 *Copyright Act*, R.S. 1985, c. C-42 (presumption of infringement); s. 43(2) *Patent Act*, R.S. 1985, c. P-4 (presumption of validity); s. 95(2) *Bankruptcy and Insolvency Act*, R.S. 1985, c. B-3 (presumed preference); s. 192(2) *Highway Traffic Act*, R.S.O. c. H.8 (presumed consent of owner).

[54] See: subsection 244(5) – proof of service by mail; subsection 244(7) – proof of failure to comply; subsection 244(8) – proof of time of compliance; subsection 244(9) – proof of documents; subsection 244(10) – proof of no appeal; subsection 244(11) – authority of officials; subsection 244(14) – date of mailing; subsection 244(15) – date assessment made; subsection 244(19) – proof of non-receipt; and, subsection 244(21) – proof of filing return.

as the exercise of preparing to meet their onus would essentially involve developing the same legal argumentation that taxpayers would be required to develop in responding to the Minister. The enactment of this rebuttable presumption would arguably to some extent only be symbolic, as the matter of legislative intent is finally one that the courts need to decide in every case in any event, and the existence of the presumption would be unlikely to often have a direct bearing on the outcome.[55] However, it would at least have the potential to help move the yard sticks towards the desirable tax policy goal, given that the heightened awareness of the role of economic substance that it would bring to the judiciary should help contribute to the growth of economic substance as a matter to be taken seriously.

The Supreme Court of Canada's present position that a "'lack of substance' ... [has] no meaning in isolation from the proper interpretation of specific provisions of the *Income Tax Act*"[56] ignores the language of our GAAR, which mandates in subsection 245(3) that the determination vis-à-vis purpose shall be made on the basis of what "may reasonably be considered", and in subsection 245(4) that the determination vis-à-vis misuse or abuse shall be made on the same basis. This language "may reasonably be considered" entails an objective standard,[57] which in turn requires the consideration of *all* relevant factual circumstances, including economic substance.[58] There are many instances where courts are required to

---

[55] Cummings, *supra* no. 15 at 226 (arguing that it is incorrect to speak of a party having a burden of proof on an issue of law because "issues of law are reviewed *de novo*" and decided on the basis of "all relevant precedents")

[56] *Canada Trustco Mortgage Co. v. R.*, [2005] 2 S.C.R. 601 (S.C.C.) at paras. 59 and 66.

[57] Rosmarie Wertschek and James R. Wilson, "Shelter from the Storm: The Current State of the Tax Shelter Rules in Section 237.1", (2008) vol. 56, no. 2 *Canadian Tax Journal* 285-336 (noting that the phrase "can [or "may"] reasonably be considered" is used throughout the *Income Tax Act* to manifest an objective or reasonable standard)

[58] See the discussion of this point immediately below. See also: *Copthorne Holdings Ltd. v. The Queen*, *supra* no. 51 per Rothstein, J., at para. 59: "The determination of whether a transaction is undertaken primarily for a non-tax purpose and is therefore not an avoidance transaction is to be objectively considered, and must be based on all of the evidence available to the court (*Trustco*, at paras. 28-29)."

make findings as to reasonableness.[59] This occurs, for example, in regard to the limitation of reasonableness on the deduction of expenses found in section 67 of the *Income Tax Act*.[60]

As Cattanach J. stated, in the context of paragraph 20(6)(g) of the Act, "I should think that 'reasonable' … does not mean from the subjective point of view of the Minister alone or the appellant alone, but rather from the point of view of an objective observer with a knowledge of *all* of the pertinent facts."[61] Concerning what the pertinent facts are vis-à-vis reasonableness, a Tax Court decision holding that "economic reality" is "an important ingredient" in determining what is "reasonable" has been upheld by the Federal Court of Appeal.[62] As "reasonably" is an element in the definition of "avoidance transaction" under subsection 245(3) of the Act, it follows that "economic reality" should also be regarded as "an important ingredient" in GAAR cases. Professor Li has also made this point in regard to the misuse or abuse requirement in subsection 245(4).[63]

Since the U.S. has a long history of reliance upon economic substance as an effective barometer in tax avoidance cases, and is the country with which we have the closest business and economic ties, it is one jurisdiction to which we should look in considering the

---

[59] Jeremy Waldron, "Thoughtfulness and the Rule of Law", British Academy Lecture, Feb. 1, 2011, 1-20, 7 (value terms like "reasonableness" are enacted standards which are just as much part of the rule of law as "rules with their strict logic and numerical predicates." The Eighth Amendment to the U.S. Constitution has value terminology such as "excessiveness" which is no less truly law than the Article II rule that says the President must be 35 years old; see also: cases annotated under the heading "Reasonableness", McMechan and Bourgard, *supra* no. 19, c. 17.

[60] Section 67 *Income Tax Act*, R.S.C. 1985, c. 1 (5th Supp.) as amended.

[61] *Canadian Propane Gas & Oil Ltd. v. Minister of National Revenue* (1972), 73 D.T.C. 5019 (Fed. T.D.) at p. 5028; also see: *R. v. Shok* (1975), 75 D.T.C. 5109 (Fed. T.D.) at p. 5119 where the same interpretation of "reasonableness" was adopted.

[62] *XCO Investments Ltd. v. R.* (2005), [2006] 1 C.T.C. 2220 (T.C.C. [General Procedure]) at para. 35, affirmed [2007] 2 C.T.C. 243 (F.C.A.) at para. 26.

[63] Li, *supra* no. 8 at 35 (making this argument in the context of the reasonableness requirement in subsection 245(4) regarding misuse or abuse of the *Income Tax Act*).

importance of economic substance in tax avoidance cases.[64] In this regard, it is significant that the use by U.S. courts of a common law economic substance doctrine has resulted in the disallowance of billions of dollars of deductions in abusive tax avoidance cases.[65] It is also apparent that tax benefits which have been denied by courts under the economic substance doctrine in the U.S. are available to taxpayers in Canada, notwithstanding that we have a statutory GAAR.[66] This sort of anomaly can only contribute to the growth of Canada as a centre for abusive tax avoidance.

Transactions found by U.S. courts to lack economic substance are set aside for tax purposes, regardless of whether they are otherwise compliant with the provisions of the *Internal Revenue Code*, unless they fall into the realm of legislatively intended benefits. Whether transactions lack economic substance has generally been determined by U.S. courts by reference to whether (a) the only purpose for their implementation was to achieve a tax benefit – a subjective test; and (b) there has been any meaningful change in the economic position of the parties as a result of the transactions, apart from achieving a tax benefit – an objective test.[67] Under the recently codified U.S. economic substance doctrine, its similar tests are to be applied conjunctively, i.e. in order for a transaction to be recognized as having economic substance it must have had a substantial purpose (apart from Federal income tax effects) and it must

---

[64] It does not seem desirable to have a substantial difference in anti-avoidance laws with the U.S., given the ease with which the location of the transactions of commercial enterprises can now be manipulated and re-located.

[65] Joseph Bankman, "The Economic Substance Doctrine", 74 *Southern California Law Review* 5 (2000-2001), 6 ("[I]n a handful of cases decided within the past year, the economic substance doctrine has been used to deny tax benefits aggregating many billions of dollars.")

[66] See the comparison of the *Rice's Toyota* and *Canada Trustco* decisions in my first case study in chapter IX.

[67] Charlene D. Luke, "What Would Henry Simons Do:: Using An Ideal To Shape And Explain The Economic Substance Doctrine", 10 *Houston Business and Tax Law Journal* (forthcoming) (2010) (noting that pre-tax profit potential has been the most prevalent test under the objective prong, with "the overall riskiness of the transaction ... and the normalcy of the transaction in terms of the taxpayer's business" also being relied upon under this prong)

have changed the taxpayer's economic position in a meaningful way (apart from Federal income tax effects). Assuming a finding of no economic substance, the final inquiry is whether the tax benefits are nevertheless legislatively intended.

Subject to local adaptation, with a view to minimizing the degree of departure from our existing anti-avoidance tax law, my view is that the codified U.S. economic substance doctrine provides a pragmatic model for the treatment of economic substance in a tax avoidance context in Canada. I do not propose at present, however, that we legislatively incorporate any of the elements of the codified U.S. economic substance doctrine into GAAR which provide technical rules for the manner in which economic substance is to be measured.[68] This is because, once it is made clear to our courts that economic substance is a relevant and central factual element in the application of GAAR, the courts should be free to analyze and define the economic substance concept, by reference to their experience with reliance upon economic realities in other cases – consistency in the application of tax and other laws being a desirable end goal from the point of view of the welfare of the citizenry.[69] It is also because attempts to define economic substance by the application of technical rules will invariably lead to previously unknown and roguishly clever avenues that are designed to circumvent the definition.[70] Attempts to define economic substance by reference to some legislated level of pre-tax profit, for example, can always be thwarted by investors who are able to dedicate sufficiently large amounts of capital to produce

---

[68] Terrance O' Reilly, "Economics and Economic Substance", 9 *Florida Tax Review* 725-792 (2010), 769-770, 790 (arguing "the fact an investment has an after-tax profit but lacks a pretax profit is not a sensible test of economic substance or economic efficiency ... [because] the economic substance doctrine's distinction between pretax profit and after-tax profit is not sound as a matter of economic theory" ... and "no credible explanation of why a lack of pre-tax profit should matter has emerged."); Charlene D. Luke, "Risk, Return, and Objective Economic Substance", 27 *Virginia Tax Review* 783-831 (2008), 785 (suggesting exclusive use of pre-tax profit is "fundamentally flawed")

[69] See many examples of decisions in Appendix A that courts have made as to the "economic realities" in tax cases.

[70] Alan Gunn, "Tax Avoidance", 76 *Michigan Law Review* 733-767 (1978), 767 (suggesting "[T]he most successful tax legislation has been the most general.")

pre-tax profit which will satisfy the threshold, while simultaneously hedging away related economic risks.[71]

Furthermore, in the absence of detailed legislative directions as to how the amended provisions of GAAR should be applied, the courts will be free to rely upon our traditional advocacy system for input as to how best to proceed. In this regard, the Federal Court has already held, in the absence of detailed legislative provisions regarding the point, that in applying GAAR, "looking to what a party expected to receive from a transaction may be relevant, and a comparison of the amount of the estimated tax benefit to the estimated business earnings may be helpful."[72] The Federal Court of Appeal has also made a statement much to the same effect.[73]

There is also a further point that the courts are now accustomed to making determinations about a variety of economics/financial points, and they are doing this well without legislative direction as to how they must proceed. In the realms of valuations and transfer pricing, for example, the courts consider various approaches to the determination of value, most often with the benefit of hearing conflicting expert opinion evidence, which they evaluate and weigh. In these cases there has not been any need to legislate when a direct sales comparison method or a comparable uncontrolled price method must be utilized, and the results are not unimpressive.[74] De-

---

[71] Hariton, *supra* no. 2 at 47-50 (arguing instead that the test should be whether "the transactions, considered as a whole, ... could be viewed as lacking economic substance because the profit they generated was insignificant in relation to the tax benefits in question")

[72] *Fraser Milner Casgrain LLP v. Minister of National Revenue*, [2002] 4 C.T.C. 210 (Fed. T.D.) at para. 30, per Dawson J.

[73] *OSFC Holdings Ltd. v. R.*, [2001] 4 C.T.C. 82 (Fed. C.A.) at para. 58, leave to appeal refused 2002 CarswellNat 1388 (S.C.C.), per Rothstein JA: "I would stress that the primary purpose of a transaction will be determined on the facts of each case. In particular, a comparison of the amount of the estimated tax benefit to the estimated business earnings may not be determinative, especially where the estimates of each are close. Further, the nature of the business aspect of the transaction must be carefully considered. The business purpose being primary cannot be ruled out simply because the tax benefit is significant."

[74] There are many reported valuation cases and a growing number of transfer pricing cases in which the courts have received and weighed expert opinion

viation from this traditional manner of reaching tax outcomes under our advocacy system is not warranted, unless the courts show that they are unable to cope with this additional domain.

Leaving part of the definition of economic substance to the courts, after its foundation has been laid by amending GAAR, could also produce intangible benefits in that it will give the courts some degree of ownership of the concept, and thus perhaps a greater inclination towards its application than would be the case in the event of yet another round of complex *Income Tax Act* amendments. There is no doubt that the courts can take up the mantle of making rules for the definition and application of the concept, as they have already done, for example, in formulating rules for calculating income, and in distinguishing between income and capital. In this regard, the Supreme Court has also shown great dexterity in formulating the rules for the application of various Charter concepts.[75] Professor Freedman has also commented that English judges are "adept at handling jurisprudence from the European Court and under the *Human Rights Act*, both of which involve the application of principles."[76] It is also notable that the U.S. courts gave birth to and attended to the evolution of the economic substance concept for many decades, without legislative intervention. While there has been a pre-codification divergence of views amongst U.S. appellate courts as to how economic substance is ascertained and how the doctrine applies, Canada does not have to contend with eleven separate appellate circuit courts tending in different directions, and

---

concerning these and other methodologies. See, for examples, the cases annotated under "Expert evidence", McMechan and Bourgard, *supra* no. 19, c. 17.

[75] See, for example, *R. v. Seaboyer* (1991), 7 C.R. (4th) 117 (S.C.C.) – setting out the steps for an analysis under section 1 of the Charter; *R. v. Malmo-Levine*, [2003] 3 S.C.R. 571 (S.C.C.) – setting out the criteria that must be satisfied to constitute a principle of fundamental justice; *R. v. Edwards*, [1996] 1 S.C.R. 128 (S.C.C.) – setting out the principles relevant to whether there has been an unreasonable search or seizure; *Ward v. Vancouver (City)*, 2010 SCC 27 (S.C.C.) – setting out a four-part test for awarding damages under ss. 24(1); *R. v. Grant*, [2009] 2 S.C.R. 353 (S.C.C.) – setting out three lines of inquiry relative to the possibility of the application of ss. 24(2) of the Charter.

[76] Freedman, *supra* no. 26 at12-14.

should have less difficulty on this front, as appellate tax decisions are handled by one court of appeal and one supreme court.

There is also merit in leaving the work of defining the economic substance concept to the courts unencumbered, as legislating, for example, that they should proceed by considering whether "the present value[77] of the reasonably expected pre-tax profit" from the transaction is substantial in relation to "the present value of the expected net tax benefits" assumes a degree of sophistication that may not always be present,[78] and there are in any event attendant problems.[79] These are matters which can be left to expert opinion evidence at trial, thus giving the courts the opportunity to hear and weigh competing expert opinion, as they already do in many other cases.

---

[77] Larry R. Scott, "Sale-Leaseback v. Mere Financing: *Lyon*'s Roar And The Aftermath", no. 4 *University of Illinois Law Review* 1075-1104 (1982), 1098 (suggesting present value analysis is the most appropriate method for calculating the necessary amount of economic substance that transactions should have to be respected for tax purposes because it accounts for the time value of money. It is based on the theory that a sum of money today is worth more than the same sum of money received sometime in the future, because the money can be invested today and grow by reason of appreciation or the receipt of dividends or interest. Present value analysis thus allows a comparison, at a point in time, of the cash inflows and outflows from an investment. If an investor simply totals all costs and returns in determining the economic substance of a transaction the investor ignores the proposition that money received today is worth more than money received in the future).

[78] Edgar, "Building a Better GAAR", *supra* no. 26 at 834, 837, 841, 851, 871-873, 884, 897, 899, 902 (some anti-avoidance tasks are not within "the institutional competence of the judiciary")

[79] Monte A. Jackel, "Dawn of a New Era: Congress Codifies Economic Substance", 127 *Tax Notes* 289-308 (Apr. 19, 2010), 292 (observing that while reasonable expectation of pre-tax profit will be tested at the inception of the transaction, there are several outstanding questions including what discount rate to use in determining present value); Martin J. McMahon Jr., "Living With the Codified Economic Substance Doctrine", 128 *Tax Notes* 731-754 (Aug. 16, 2010), 740 (also commenting that "selection of the proper discount rate will be a problem in every case."); Brian J. Arnold, "The Land of the Free, the Home of the Brave, and the Economic Substance Doctrine", *The Arnold Report*, Jan. 17, 2011 (commenting that the newly-codified US REOP test in section 7701(o) of the Internal Revenue Code is "fraught with uncertainty" ,"when combined with the vagaries of present value analysis")

Nevertheless, that GAAR needs to be amended to provide guidance to the judiciary regarding the role of economic substance in tax avoidance cases is not in doubt. Justice Rothstein, who wrote the unanimous judgment of the Supreme Court of Canada in *Copthorne Holdings Ltd. v. R.*,[80] has spoken publicly about the judiciary's uncertainty regarding the role economic substance is to play in GAAR cases:

> How will we know when we are supposed to be looking at transactions or whether we are supposed to be cutting through the transactions and looking at economic substance? How will we know when economic substance is supposed to be the dominant test or whether there is going to be some kind of weighing involved, and how will we carry out that weighing? These are just a few of the questions that come to mind in thinking about how to deal with the question of economic substance.[81]

This judicial uncertainty highlights the need for legislative direction to the courts regarding the role of economic substance, relative to the matter of purpose.

The book is organized as follows. Chapter I is a discussion of tax minimization or planning versus abusive tax avoidance, highlighting the central role that economic consequences are understood to have in identifying abusive tax avoidance. Chapter II is an examination of the effects of unchecked abusive tax avoidance. I argue in chapter III in favour of the use of judicial doctrines, in addition to technical rules, in defending against abusive tax avoidance. In chapter IV, I analyze the existing judicial approaches to tax avoidance in Canada, and I explain their limitations vis-à-vis the concept of economic substance. In chapter V, I examine the treatment by the Supreme Court of Canada of economic substance in tax and non-tax cases, together with the treatment of its frequent companion commercial realities. I also argue in chapter V that the reasons

---

[80] *Supra* no. 51.
[81] Brian Arnold, Judith Freedman, Al Meghji, Mark Meredith, and Hon. Marshall Rothstein, "The Future of GAAR", 2005 *Conference Report* (Toronto: Canadian Tax Foundation, 2006), 4:1-4:16, at 4:12 -4:13 (Justice Rothstein speaking of economic substance in the context of GAAR)

given by the Supreme Court for declining to endorse the substantial importance of economic substance in tax avoidance cases do not stand up to scrutiny.

In chapter VI, I trace the development of a common law economic substance doctrine by the U.S. courts, and I review the extensive use of the doctrine in disallowing deductions in tax shelter cases. I also look at the decade-long efforts in the U.S. to codify its economic substance doctrine, which culminated in 2010, and I consider the argumentation in the U.S. regarding its pros and cons, suggesting that the U.S. experience highlights our shortcomings in Canada.

The GAAR regimes in South Africa, Australia and New Zealand are examined in chapter VII, together with the draft proposed GAAR in the U.K. In this chapter, I argue that Canada is out-of-step with these jurisdictions, and with the European Court of Justice, regarding the present treatment of economic substance in tax avoidance cases, and that our GAAR now requires amendments to rectify this situation.

In chapter VIII, I next examine the information reporting and penalty regimes in place in Canada, and in other jurisdictions, and I argue that while it is meritorious to proceed with the strengthened reporting regime that Canada is presently proposing, and that it is also desirable for there to be penalties associated with GAAR adjustments, the more fundamental problem is that our GAAR needs to be amended, to correct the Supreme Court's position relative to the role of economic substance in tax avoidance cases.

There are five Canadian case studies in chapter IX, in which I explore the role that economic substance has had to date in tax avoidance cases, and the impact on those cases of the economic substance amendments that I am proposing. I also argue in chapter IX that tax benefits are being allowed in Canada that are being denied elsewhere, because of non-recognition of the essential role of economic substance in tax avoidance cases.

My conclusion in chapter X is that utilization of an economic substance test is a fundamental necessity for the courts in tax avoidance cases; and that, given the present state of the law in Canada, GAAR should be amended to (1) impose a requirement that courts consider economic substance as a relevant fact in the subsection 245(3) and 245(4) analyses; and, also to (2) provide that transactions undertaken primarily for tax purposes, that are found by the courts not to possess substantial economic substance compared to their expected tax benefits, shall be presumed not to give rise to tax benefits, subject to contrary proof from the taxpayer.

A further introductory note is that the focus in this book is not upon criminal tax evasion, which involves the payment of less tax than a taxpayer is legally obligated to pay, and is usually accomplished by hiding income or information from tax authorities.[82] Typical examples of tax evasion include deliberate under-reporting by a cash business of its revenues, or the deliberate overstatement of expenses that have not been incurred. These types of activities are subject to prosecution as criminal offences. It has been noted elsewhere, however, that the traditional line between tax avoidance and tax evasion has been blurred somewhat, by the efforts made in some tax avoidance schemes to hide or disguise various aspects of the schemes in order to avoid detection or confuse revenue authorities.[83]

While discussions of tax avoidance, as opposed to tax evasion, are often premised on a notion that since it is not illegal, in the sense of inviting criminal law sanctions, it does not involve questions of morality, there is nevertheless a substantial argument that "the ideology underpinning tax avoidance is in direct conflict with

---

[82] OECD, *International Tax Terms for the Participants in the OECD Programme of Cooperation with Non-OECD Economies*; also see: Freedman, *supra* no. 21 at 351 (noting that the distinction between evasion and avoidance is more easily made than it is between different types of tax avoidance)

[83] "The Problem of Corporate Tax Shelters: Discussion, Analysis and Legislative Proposals", *supra* no. 83 at 16.

core democratic values."[84] I examine this suggestion in chapter V, together with the merits of the claims about the necessity for certainty in tax law matters, in conjunction with my analysis of the Supreme Court of Canada's position.

My final introductory point is to re-emphasize that the GAAR amendments I am proposing do not represent a sort of panacea for other existing ailments under the GAAR. There continue to be difficult and legitimate questions about how the existence and quantum of a "tax benefit" is to be determined and measured; and, concerning when a transaction falls within the realm of being an "avoidance transaction," having regard to whether it was an event which took place as part of what was in contemplation by reference to other transactions which form part of a series.

Moreover, the matter of whether there has been a misuse of statutory taxing provisions, or an abuse of those provisions when considered as a whole, is a perennial perplexing problem. This is well-illustrated by the Supreme Court's GAAR decision in *Copthorne Holdings Ltd. v. R.*,[85] where it found an abuse of a provision of the *Income Tax Act* dealing with paid-up capital in the context of vertical amalgamations, although a horizontal amalgamation took place.[86] In regard to the misuse or abuse problem, however, my proposed GAAR economic substance amendments will be a

---

[84] William B. Barker, "The Ideology of Tax Avoidance", vol. 40 Loyola *University Chicago Law Journal* 229-251 (2009), 232, 250-251 (arguing that "plain meaning" or literal interpretation of tax statutes which underlies tax avoidance amounts to a failure by jurists "to advance through tax a society that is committed to maintaining and enforcing substantive equality for its entire people.").

[85] *Supra* no. 51.

[86] Ed Kroft and Deborah Toaze, "Copthorne: Supreme Court of Canada's Latest Views on Statutory Interpretation and GAAR", CBA PracticeLink, http://www.cba.org/CBA/PracticeLink/02-12-BC/03.aspx (suggesting that "[t]he most troubling aspect" of the Supreme Court's analysis in *Copthorne* in relation to the contextual review in a GAAR analysis is understanding how the abuse of a provision is to be determined when there are "bright-line" tests in statutory provisions or when the text of a provision expressly provides for certain transactions to be exempted or caught).

contributor to the solution, in cases where the transactions in question are found to have been lacking in economic substance.

In the following chapter I distinguish between legitimate tax minimization activity, which is very often accomplished while engaging in transactions which have economic substance, and abusive tax avoidance activity,[87] which is often based on transactions without any economic substance.[88] In this latter regard, the Tax Law Review Committee Discussion Paper on tax avoidance, issued in the U.K. in 2009, makes the point that the most aggressive forms of tax avoidance are those where there is found to be little economic substance to the transactions.[89]

---

[87] Bleiwas and Hutson, *supra* no. 17, c.16, V. GAAR, Canada's Answer to Tax Avoidance, B. Analysis of Section 245, 7. Misuse or Abuse, i. Selected Cases Decided by Other Courts (commenting re abusive tax avoidance, "No court will admit or state openly that there is a strong subjective element in the determination of misuse or abuse. The term "smell test" has not officially become part of the Canadian judicial vocabulary, but like the elephant in the living room, it is indisputably there, whether anyone is willing to acknowledge its existence or not. Stewart J, of the US Supreme Court, famously said that while he could not define obscenity, he could recognize it when he saw it. The judicial view of misuse or abuse in tax avoidance is essentially the same. Unfortunately, the olfactory sense varies from judge to judge.")

[88] Pichhadze and Pichhadze, *supra* no. 30 at 61 ("As a general rule, an effective strategy for combating tax avoidance within an income tax system is to require that market transactions have an economic substance.", citing Victor Thuronyi (ed.), *Tax Law Design and Drafting*, Vol. 1 (Washington: IMF, 1996)).

[89] Tax Law Review Committee Discussion Paper No. 7, The Institute for Fiscal Studies, p. 40, para. 12.6

I

Tax Minimization Versus Abusive Tax Avoidance

In this chapter, I examine the boundary between acceptable tax planning or tax minimization and abusive tax avoidance, highlighting the fact that a characteristic of abusive tax avoidance is very often an absence of economic consequences or economic substance. This helps to show that the minimalist role given to economic substance by the Supreme Court of Canada in tax avoidance cases is not in keeping with a widespread recognition of its importance elsewhere.

Professor Chirelstein claims that the extent to which taxpayers should be able to minimize their tax obligations has consumed the tax community since the inception of income taxes.[90] Professor Freedman adds that "[i]t is inevitable that there will be fundamental tensions between the essential need of governments to raise revenue and the lack of desire of taxpayers to pay for this."[91] In recent times,

---

[90] Marvin A. Chirelstein, "Learned Hand's Contribution to the Law of Tax Avoidance", vol. 77, no. 3 *Yale Law Journal* 440-474 (1968), 440 (noting that tax minimization is generally accomplished by choosing one legal form rather than another as the basis for relationships or transactions).

[91] Freedman, *supra* no. 21 at 334.

however, according to Tanzi and Braithwaite, "fiscal termites"[92] and "moral termites"[93] have been eating away at the foundations of national tax systems. Prominent amongst these "termites" are increasingly aggressive and abusive tax avoidance schemes.[94] A working paper released by the Province of Québec in January 2009 has reported that aggressive tax planning is "a global phenomenon that constitutes a risk to the integrity of tax systems."[95]

---

[92] Vito Tanzi, "Globalization, Technological Developments, and the Work of Fiscal Termites", vol. 38, no. 1 Finance & Development (Washington DC: IMF, March 2001) (legal entities such as international business corporations and off-shore trusts "provide an impenetrable veil around particular [tax avoidance] transactions.")

[93] John Braithwaite, "Tax Systems in Crisis", *Markets in Vice: Markets in Virtue*, ch. 2, 24-25 (Oxford University Press: Sydney, 2005) ("moral termites" follow from the existence of Tanzi's "fiscal termites." They include wealthy national celebrities and sports stars who do not pay taxes commensurate with their incomes–or any taxes–on account of their resort to aggressive tax avoidance schemes).

[94] Chris Evans, "Barriers to Tax Avoidance: Recent Legislative and Judicial Developments in Common Law Jurisdictions", vol. 37, no. 1 *Hong Kong Law Journal* 103-136 (2007), 112 (tax avoidance activity has grown significantly in recent decades and is a worldwide concern).

[95] Aggressive Tax Planning Working Paper, *supra* no. 30 at 1.

WHAT IS TAX AVOIDANCE?

"Tax avoidance" does not have any specific limiting or definite meaning.[96] The term can potentially be applied to a wide range of tax minimization and tax avoidance strategies that lie along a spectrum.[97]

According to Professor Littlewood, "[t]hat tax avoidance is one of the slipperiest ideas in the whole of the law is notorious."[98] If I had collected only one dollar for every time I have come across the statement, during the course of my research for this book, that the definition of tax avoidance is unacceptably unclear, I would be considerably wealthier today. Nevertheless, for the purpose of giving context to the points about economic substance that I make in the book, it is important to begin with a definition of tax avoidance. In this regard, the OECD definition of tax avoidance is a good working definition: "the arrangement

---

[96] Barker, *supra* no. 84 at 229 ("Tax avoidance is a common term used in tax law and scholarship. Though the concept is sometimes explicitly used in statutes, it is more often an underlying premise for legislative, administrative, or judicial action targeting taxpayer conduct that is perceived to undermine fair and equitable taxation."); see also: Gunn, *supra* no. 70 at 733 footnote 3, 738, 759-760 (observing that tax laws are not uniquely subject to avoidance attempts, and contending that although the courts often assert that the tax consequences of a transaction do not depend upon whether the taxpayer was motivated by an intention to avoid taxes, this position is "seriously undermined" by the existence of a business purpose test. Furthermore, the description of transactions as "tax avoidance" omits addressing the real question as to why it is that the transactions are being taxed differently); Edgar, "Building a Better GAAR", *supra* no. 26 at 844 ("Used in its broadest (and perhaps most simplistic) sense, the term 'tax avoidance' refers to any change in behavior that occurs as a response to the change in price of particular activities, assets, or transactions occasioned by the imposition of tax."); Tooma, *supra* no. 15 at 12 (defining tax avoidance as "the legal exploitation of tax laws to one's own advantage", citing broad definitions by the Royal Commission on Taxation of Profits and Income (1955) and the Royal Commission on Taxation, Canada (1966)

[97] Evans, *supra* no. 94 at 134 (suggesting that despite the large numbers of tax avoidance cases heard by the courts, "The dividing line between acceptable tax mitigation and unacceptable tax avoidance remains as indistinct as ever.")

[98] Michael Littlewood, "The Privy Council and the Australasian anti-avoidance rules", vol. 2 *British Tax Review* 175-205 (2007), 175 (suggesting that although the idea of tax avoidance is "not susceptible to coherent explication" and that rules against it are "inescapably problematic", having a GAAR "might nonetheless be better than not having one")

of a taxpayer's affairs that is intended to reduce his tax liability and that although the arrangement could be strictly legal it is usually in contradiction with the intent of the law it purports to follow."[99]

According to Professor Krishna, the first known incidence of tax avoidance occurred 4000 years ago in Mesopotamia. A king who needed money for his army levied a tax on individuals who crossed a bridge over a river in order to farm on the other side. The citizens began swimming across the river to avoid the tax; however, the king made it a capital crime to swim across the river, thus putting an end to the tax avoidance.[100] While the penalty in the Mesopotamia case was severe, the citizens were simply carrying on their ordinary activity of farming, while adopting a route to their farms which minimized their taxes.[101] This type of tax planning or tax mitigation involves organizing one's affairs (or the structuring of transactions) so that they give rise to the minimum tax liability contemplated by the existing law.

---

[99] OECD, Centre for Tax Policy and Administration, *Glossary of Tax Terms*: http://www.oecd.org/document/29/0.3343en_2649_33933853_1_1_1_1.00.html
[100] Vern Krishna, "Please report your aggressive tax avoidance plans", *Financial Post*, April 15, 2010.
[101] Another benign form of tax mitigation took place in England in the 1600's, when people without sufficient wealth to pay the "window tax" bricked up the windows in their homes. This followed the repeal of the "hearth tax", which had been repealed on the basis that it was "not only a great oppression to the poorer sort, but a badge of slavery on the whole people"–see Bob Greene, "And you thought the IRS was heartless", *Chicago Tribune*, October 24, 1999; Geoff Harley, "Collecting Taxes", *Roles and Perspectives in the Law* (Victoria University Press, Wellington, N.Z.: 2002), 333 at 338.

CENTRAL ROLE OF ECONOMIC CONSEQUENCES

Tax mitigation[102] is not generally considered to be offensive,[103] as the taxpayer actually bears the economic consequences associated with obtaining the tax benefit: "The hallmark of tax mitigation ... is that the taxpayer takes advantage of a fiscally attractive option afforded to him by the legislation, and genuinely suffers the consequences that Parliament intended to be suffered by those taking advantage of the option."[104] Tax mitigation typically involves, for example, refraining from certain types of behaviour, such as crossing the bridge in Mesopotamia, smoking tobacco, drinking alcoholic beverages, and earning certain types of income.[105] Legitimate tax planning or tax mitigation in a modern context will include, for example, the decision as to whether or not to incorporate a business; the decision to "roll-over" assets to a company; and, the decision as to whether to acquire or lease equipment to be used in a business.

Unacceptable tax avoidance, by comparison, has been defined in the Final Report of the Review of Business Taxation in Australia as "a misuse of the law [that] is often driven by the exploitation of structural loopholes in the law to achieve tax outcomes that were not intended by Parliament but also includes the manipulation of the law

---

[102] Zoe Prebble and John Prebble, "The Morality of Tax Avoidance", 43 *Creighton Law Review* 693-746 (2010), 706 ("'Tax mitigation' is a label for a conclusion: that a scheme under examination that reduces tax is valid under relevant legislation (including relevant specific anti-avoidance rules), and not vulnerable to a GAAR, either statutory or judge-made. ... Nevertheless, it is a useful term, serving as a label for a concept that must be distinguished from avoidance. It does not tell us where the line between avoidance and acceptable reduction of tax is drawn, but it gives a name to the territory on the acceptable side of that line.")

[103] Lord Templeman explained in *Ensign Tankers (Leasing) Ltd. v. Stokes (Inspector of Taxes)*, [1992] 2 All E.R. 275 (U.K. H.L.) at pp. 285, 291 that the right to organize one's affairs to minimize taxes in accordance with the *Duke of Westminster* doctrine applies to tax mitigation but not to tax avoidance.

[104] *Inland Revenue Commissioners v. Willoughby*, [1997] 4 All E.R. 65 (U.K. H.L.) at p. 73, per Lord Nolan.

[105] Frans Vanistendael, "Legal Framework for Taxation", vol. 1 *Tax Law Design and Drafting*, ch. 2, p. 45 (Washington: IMF, 1996), Victor Thuronyi, ed. (stating that tax minimization is "perfectly legal" and is to be distinguished from tax evasion and tax avoidance).

and a focus on form and legal effect rather than substance."[106] Highlighting its difference with tax mitigation, Professor Graetz is quoted by the U.S. Treasury Department as having said that unacceptable tax avoidance can be described as "a deal done by very smart people that, absent tax considerations, would be very stupid."[107]

All tax systems have differences amongst their tax rules that give rise to the opportunities for tax avoidance. The differences exist on account of the different tax treatments extended to different types of income; the different taxation applicable to different kinds of taxpayers; and, tax benefits created to encourage certain activities.[108] In this regard, the New Zealand Report of the Committee of Experts on Tax Compliance identified three conditions that need to be present in order for tax avoidance to exist. These are "a difference between the effective marginal tax rates on economic income"; "ability to exploit differences in tax by converting high-tax activity into low-tax activity"; and, the high-tax income "must come back in a low-tax form."[109]

According to the Discussion Paper on Tax Avoidance released by the South African Revenue Service ("SARS") in 2005, tax avoidance is generally sought to be accomplished through one or a combination of these four goals: permanent elimination of tax liability; deferral or postponement of tax liability, with reliance on the concept of the time value of money for its effectiveness; recharacterization, involving conversion of the character of an item or transaction, such as from a highly taxed item like revenue to a tax exempt or less heavily taxed item like capital; and, shifting, as in income or profit shifting from a highly taxed entity to a less heavily taxed or exempt entity, as well as value shifting between assets.[110]

---

[106] "Final Report of the Review of Business Taxation, A Tax System Redesigned", (Canberra: Australian Government Printing Service, July 1999), s. 6.2(c).
[107] Professor Michael Graetz, quoted in "The Problem of Corporate Tax Shelters: Discussion, Analysis and Legislative Proposals", *supra* no. 83 at v.
[108] "Discussion Paper on Tax Avoidance", *supra* no. 5 at 17.
[109] Report of the Committee of Experts on Tax Compliance, "Tax Mitigation, Avoidance and Evasion", chapter 6 (Wellington: NZ Government Printer, 1999), para. 6.22.
[110] "Discussion Paper on Tax Avoidance", *supra* no. 5 at 16.

While the line between acceptable tax mitigation and unacceptable tax avoidance is not a bright one,[111] there has been a wide consensus that an absence of real economic consequences is an important indicator of the latter. Academics,[112] courts outside Canada, and governments have often identified lack of economic consequences to taxpayers as one of the principal features of unacceptable tax avoidance. Lord Nolan's words in *CIR v. Willoughby* highlight the essential role of economic consequences in making the distinction: "The hallmark of tax avoidance is that the taxpayer reduces his liability to tax without incurring the economic consequences that Parliament intended to be suffered by any taxpayer qualifying for such reduction in his tax liability."[113] Lord Templeman also described unacceptable tax avoidance in *CIR v. Challenge Corporation Ltd.* in these terms: "Income tax is avoided and a tax advantage is derived from an arrangement when the taxpayer reduces his liability to tax without involving him in the loss or expenditure which entitles him to that reduction. The taxpayer engaged in tax avoidance does not reduce his income or suffer a loss or incur an expenditure but nevertheless obtains a reduction in his liability to tax as if he had."[114]

---

[111] Prebble and Prebble, *supra* no. 102 at 708-709 (arguing that "boundary uncertainty" is not fatal to a discussion of tax avoidance: "even if we are uncertain whether euthanasia or failure to take an acceptable risk to save human life amount to murder, we can be sure that some instances of killing are murder and that some are not. ... It seems that we know tax avoidance when we see it, but we have to see it to know it."); Freedman, *supra* no. 21 at 345 (noting that in this context clear lines "may in any event be an impossibility.")

[112] Calvin H. Johnson, "What's a Tax Shelter?", 68 *Tax Notes* 879-883 (Aug. 15, 1995), 883 (noting, however, that "Tax professors do not constitute a constituency.")

[113] *Inland Revenue Commissioners v. Willoughby*, [1997] 4 All E.R. 65 (U.K. H.L.) at p. 73.

[114] *Inland Revenue Commissioner v. Challenge Corp.*, [1987] A.C. 155 (U.K. H.L.) at p. 168; see also: Tracey Bowler, "Countering Tax Avoidance in the U.K.: Which Way Forward?", Tax Law Review Committee, The Institute for Fiscal Studies, TLRC Discussion Paper No. 7, 1-168 (Feb. 2009), 11-12 (noting that "even this appealing definition would soon be seen to be incapable of fully encapsulating all the nuances of what is and is not tax avoidance. An exemption from tax (and therefore taking steps to fall within it) may not depend upon any expenditure. An example of this problem arises in relation to income-shifting. In cases of income-shifting, one person shifts income that would otherwise be theirs to another person who can benefit from a reduced

The House of Lords later cited this statement with approval in *Ensign Tankers (Leasing) Ltd. v. Stokes (Inspector of Taxes)*.[115] Lord Goff added in his minority decision:

> [T]here is a fundamental difference between tax mitigation and unacceptable tax avoidance. ... These are cases in which the taxpayer takes advantage of the law to plan his affairs so as to minimise the incidence of tax. Unacceptable tax avoidance typically involves the creation of complex artificial structures by which, as though by the wave of a magic wand, the taxpayer conjures out of the air a loss, or a gain, or expenditures, or whatever it may be, which otherwise would never have existed. These structures are designed to achieve an adventitious tax benefit for the taxpayer, and in truth are no more than raids on the public funds at the expense of the general body of taxpayers, and as such are unacceptable.[116]

Again highlighting the importance of economic consequences, Lord Templeman also penned this description of unacceptable tax avoidance in *W.T. Ramsay Limited v. IRC*: "The facts ... demonstrate yet another circular game in which the taxpayer and a few hired performers act out a play; nothing happens save that the Houdini taxpayer appears to escape from the manacles of tax."[117]

Following the *Ramsay* decision, Canadian tax writers observed that in the United Kingdom, unlike in Canada, when the tax statute contemplates that a taxpayer will be entitled to a tax result if an expenditure is incurred or a loss is suffered, the contemplated result will only follow so long as the taxpayer has actually been involved in the expenditure or loss.[118] Tax writers have also noted, in relation

---

rate of tax on the income. The classic example of this arises in the context of husbands and wives owning a company between them and shifting income from the more highly taxed spouse to the other who pays a lower rate of tax.")

[115] *Ensign Tankers (Leasing) Ltd. v. Stokes (Inspector of Taxes)*, [1992] 2 All E.R. 275 (U.K. H.L.) at p. 290, per Lord Templeman for Lords Keith, Brandon and Jauncey.

[116] *Ensign Tankers (Leasing) Ltd. v. Stokes (Inspector of Taxes)*, [1992] S.T.C. 226 (U.K. H.L.) at p. 244.

[117] *WT Ramsay Ltd. v. Inland Revenue Commissioners*, [1979] 1 W.L.R. 974 (C.A.) at p. 978.

[118] J. Scott Wilkie and Heather Kerr, "Common Links Among Jurisdictions: Informing The GAAR Through Comparative Analysis", 1997 *Conference*

to recent court decisions in New Zealand, that "in expenditure related tax avoidance cases, the test of whether the economic burden is actually shouldered by the taxpayer is fundamental to the tax avoidance test, regardless of the legal form."[119]

The U.S. Department of the Treasury, in its report "The Problem of Corporate Tax Shelters," identified lack of economic substance as one of the most important characteristics common to most corporate tax shelters. According to the report, there are no significant economic consequences for parties to most tax shelter transactions, as a result of the utilization of hedges and circular cash flows, etc., apart from the tax benefits which they claim.[120] The SARS Discussion Paper on Tax Avoidance also identified lack of economic substance, usually resulting from pre-arranged circular or self-cancelling arrangements, as one of the most important characteristics of abusive tax avoidance schemes.[121] According to the Discussion Paper, in many tax avoidance schemes the taxpayer purports to make a substantial investment, which is largely an illusion. Through various devices, the taxpayer remains insulated from virtually all economic risk, while creating a carefully crafted impression to the contrary. Since abusive tax avoidance schemes typically involve little or no economic risk, they also typically offer little or no opportunity for pre-tax gain. Rather, the "return" to the "investor" takes the form of the significant tax benefits to be obtained. In many cases, the pre-tax profit is less than the transaction fees and costs, and in some cases, the transactions even

---

Report (Toronto: Canadian Tax Foundation, 1998), 34:1-30 at 34:12 (the House of Lords arrived at this position in considering the relieving provisions in respect of the anti-avoidance rule in section 739 of the *Income and Corporation Taxes Act 1988*. The anti-avoidance section would not be applied where it could be shown that avoiding liability to taxation was not one of the purposes for which the transactions were effected).

[119] Elliffe and Cameron, *supra* no. 22 at 451 (arguing that when courts focus on factors indicative of tax avoidance, it enables them to identify transactions in which statutory provisions are not being used in the way Parliament intended them to be used.).

[120] "The Problem of Corporate Tax Shelters: Discussion, Analysis and Legislative Proposals", *supra* no. 83 at v.

[121] "Discussion Paper on Tax Avoidance", *supra* no. 5 at 19-20.

produce pre-tax losses.[122] The Province of Québec Working Paper on Aggressive Tax Planning, released in 2009, has also reported that "[e]xcept for the resulting tax benefits, the economic justification of an [aggressive tax planning] scheme is generally limited and may even be totally non-existent."[123]

In the academic realm, Professor A.C. Warren of Harvard Law School has said that "tax arbitrage", which involves manipulation and exploitation of differences and inconsistencies in the tax system in order to generate tax savings, where the anticipated tax benefit exceeds the transaction costs, is "generally used to describe transactions that involve tax advantages, but no other financial consequences, for the taxpayer."[124] Professor Uph suggests that "[t]he crucial difference between tax planning and tax avoidance is that tax planning involves a real cost over and above that of acquiring the scheme/advice."[125] Professor Luke argues that the Haig-Simons income concept is useful in framing the economic substance doctrine, and that it follows from a Haig-Simons driven analysis that "a tax base reduction would only result to the extent of actual economic loss."[126] In Canada, Professor Li has noted that "[i]n many GAAR cases, the taxpayer's aim was to create a tax benefit in the form of a loss, expense or exclusion from gross income that has no economic corollary but is simply the consequence of taking advantage of the tax rules. Other than the transac-

---

[122] *Ibid.*
[123] Aggressive Tax Planning Working Paper, *supra* no. 30 at 4.
[124] AC Warren, Jr., "Financial Contract Innovation and Income Tax Policy", 107 *Harvard Law Review* 460-492 (1993), 471 (noting that "tax arbitrage" is a term used to describe the manipulation and exploitation of differences and inconsistencies in the tax system in order to generate tax savings, where the anticipated tax benefit exceeds the transaction costs).
[125] David Uph, "Avoidance Policies – A New Conceptual Framework", Working Paper 09/22, Oxford Centre University Centre for Business Taxation 1-31 (2009), 5, footnote 6.
[126] Luke, *supra* no. 67 (noting that the definition authored by Henry Simons is "most famous": "Personal income may be defined as the algebraic sum of (1) the market value of rights exercised in consumption and (2) the change in the value of the store of property rights between the beginning and end of the period in question. In other words, it is merely the result obtained by adding consumption during the period to 'wealth' at the end of the period and then subtracting 'wealth' at the beginning")

tion costs, the taxpayer really had little to lose."[127] Professor Edgar also suggests that "[i]n most instances, the effectiveness of a tax-avoidance transaction depends on the significance of the legal form of the relevant arrangements necessary to attract a tax treatment that is inconsistent with the underlying economics."[128] In this regard, Professor Arnold has argued that while the Supreme Court has insisted on strict adherence to the legal form of transactions in tax avoidance cases and consistently rejected any reference to economic realities,[129] "a court could decide that a taxation statute applies only to the economic or commercial substance of what a taxpayer does."[130]

Despite this impressive congregation of voices, emphasizing the important role of economic consequences in identifying

---

[127] Li, *supra* no. 8 at 44 (arguing that economic substance analysis offers the best standard for drawing the line between legitimate tax planning and abusive tax avoidance).

[128] Tim Edgar, "Some Lessons from the Saga of Weak-Currency Borrowings", (2000) vol. 48, no. 1 CTJ 1-34, 13-14 (making the point that while "The Supreme Court of Canada decision in *Shell* is just the latest in a line of avoidance cases that cite 'commercial reality' as a supposed basis for respecting the legal form adopted by taxpayers for tax-planning purposes ... the alternative to this approach characterizes transactions based on perceptions of economic substance and applies the relevant provisions of the Act to that perceived substance. [However] it is probably accurate to say that a lack of well-defined criteria for the application of a characterization approach based on economic substance underlies a distaste of Canadian tax practitioners and many judges for this approach."); Edgar, "Financial Instruments and the Tax Avoidance Lottery: A View from North America", *supra* no. 26 at 64 (suggesting that in general terms the substantive issues related to U.S. tax shelters "continue to revolve around the integrity of legal form as a basis for the application of income tax legislation, and in particular, the bounds within which legal form can defensibly be ignored in favour of perceptions of economic substance as the proper basis for taxation.")

[129] Brian J. Arnold, "The Long, Slow, Steady Demise of the General Anti-Avoidance Rule", (2004) vol. 52, no. 2 CTJ 488-511, 492 (thus forcing Parliament to enact the general anti-avoidance rule against abusive tax avoidance); Arnold, *supra* no. 8 at 198 ("An appreciation of the economic substance of the transactions is essential, in my view, to any assessment of the propriety of the transactions for tax purposes.")

[130] Brian J. Arnold, "Reflections on the Relationship Between Statutory Interpretation and Tax Avoidance", (2001) vol. 49, no. 1 C.T.J. 1-39, 34, footnote 20 (following this approach, the formal legal validity of transactions can be ignored for tax purposes if they are lacking in economic or commercial substance).

unacceptable tax avoidance (not to mention the views of the many proponents of the U.S. economic substance doctrine that are canvassed in chapter VI), the courts in Canada are only now officially examining economic substance in tax avoidance cases in the limited context of interpreting specific provisions of tax legislation when considering GAAR.

Lack of economic substance is widely understood by courts in other countries, foreign governments, and by academics to be a primary indicator of abusive tax avoidance; but, our Supreme Court has severely limited the role of economic substance in tax avoidance cases in Canada. I next study what the results are thought to be of unchecked abusive tax avoidance.

II

Effects of Unchecked Abusive Tax Avoidance

Whether there is significant unchecked abusive tax avoidance in Canada is not in doubt. The Government of Canada has recently said, in soliciting comments on its proposals for strengthening information reporting requirements in relation to tax avoidance transactions,[131] that it is aware aggressive tax avoidance has an impact on the tax system.[132] While the legislation as proposed would very likely assist the Canada Revenue Agency in identifying potentially abusive transactions, it is substantially less vigorous than the reporting and penalty regime that has recently been strengthened in the U.S. The proposed penalty in Canada is much less severe than in the U.S., and unlike in Canada, the U.S. is no longer recognizing a due diligence defence.[133]

---

[131] See the discussion of the proposals in chapter VIII.
[132] See Backgrounder: 2010-043–*Government of Canada Seeks Public Input on Proposals To Require Information Reporting of Tax Avoidance Transactions*, Ottawa, May 7, 2010.
[133] See my review of the information reporting and penalty regimes in several jurisdictions in chapter VIII.

The more fundamental issue, however, is that unless the courts in Canada begin considering economic substance, in the manner that U.S. courts have done for decades, it will matter little whether the Agency can identify abusive transactions, as abusive tax avoidance will continue to succeed in the courts. Reliance on the Government's proposed new information reporting requirements alone will not solve the tax avoidance quagmire the Supreme Court of Canada has created, by not giving appropriate recognition to the role of economic substance.

The further point, which I examine below, is that the effect of abusive tax avoidance is more dramatic and far-reaching than the loss of revenues required by governments for spending on health, education, law enforcement, public works, national defence, old age security benefits, international relief, anti-poverty and environmental measures, and the plethora of other government priorities.[134]

DETRIMENTAL EFFECTS ON TAXPAYER COMPLIANCE

One of the main ill-results of unchecked abusive tax avoidance is the detrimental effect that it has on overall taxpayer compliance.[135]

---

[134] Justice Oliver Wendell Holmes of the Supreme Court of the United States, in dissent in *Compania General de Tobacos de Filipinos v. Collector of Internal Revenue*, 275 U.S. 87 (1904) at p. 100 famously wrote: "Taxes are what we pay for civilized society."; see also: David A. Dodge, "A New and More Coherent Approach to Tax Avoidance", (1988) 36 CTJ 1-78, 3-4 (noting the Carter Commission's identification of loss of revenue to government, unfair shifting of taxation burdens, wasting of resources and "deterioration of tax morality" as ill-effects of aggressive avoidance); J.W. Neville, "Macro-Economic Effects of Tax Avoidance", Working Paper No. 44, Centre for Applied Economic Research, University of New South Wales 1-11(March 1983) (suggesting that the amount of uncollected revenue due to tax avoidance has implications for the level of other taxes, government expenditures and the deficit size)

[135] Allen D. Madison, "Rationalizing Tax Law By Breaking The Addiction to Economic Substance", 47 *Idaho Law Review* 1-37 (2011), 20 ("When it appears that one taxpayer has abused the tax laws, other taxpayers do not want to feel like chumps."); Prebble and Prebble, *supra* no. 102 at 724 (citing Jørn Henrik Petersen for the proposition that "If others seem not to be complying with social duties, such as the duty not to freeload ... then from a self-interested, game-theoretical point of view, there is little incentive for an individual

According to a Staff of U.S. Joint Committee on Internal Revenue Taxation report, "[w]hen the great majority of taxpayers perceive that a few wealthy taxpayers escape tax almost completely in return for making investments that may not even be sensible from an economic standpoint, it becomes hard to convince them that the tax system is fair and progressive. The resulting disrespect for law and reduced compliance therewith may entail a hidden revenue loss which is far in excess of the loss measured by the deductions claimed by those who participate in tax shelters."[136] This concern has also been noted in a Treasury Department White Paper on tax shelters in the U.S.;[137] and, it has also been echoed by private sector groups such as the New York Bar Association: "The constant promotion of these frequently artificial transactions breeds significant disrespect for the tax system, encouraging responsible corporate taxpayers to expect this type of activity to be the norm, and to follow the lead of other taxpayers who have engaged in tax advantaged transactions."[138] In the modern context of Enron, fear has been expressed by Treasury Department officials that the view that corporations can avoid tax liabilities by participating in "tax-engineered transactions" may cause a "race to the bottom," with long term adverse consequences for the U.S. tax system.[139] David P. Hariton, a leading commentator in the U.S. on

---

to comply."); Joshua D. Blank, "What's Wrong with Shaming Corporate Tax Abuse", vol. 62 *Tax Law Review* 539-589 (2009), 542 ("As reciprocity theory hypothesizes, actors may reduce their own contributions towards public good if they begin to feel like 'chumps' for complying while others do not."; Aggressive Tax Planning Working Paper , *supra* no. 30 at 21 (noting that transfer of tax burden fosters feelings of unfairness and injustice which threaten taxpayer compliance).

[136] Staff of Joint Committee on Internal Revenue Taxation, 94th Cong., Overview of Tax Shelters (1975) quoted by Zachary Nahass, "Codifying the Economic Substance Doctrine: A Proposal on the Doorstep of Usefulness", 58 *Admin. L. Rev.* 247-268 (2006), 250, footnote 9.

[137] "The Problem of Corporate Tax Shelters", *supra* no. 83 at iv; *Tax Notes Today* (July 1, 1999), TaxBase, TA Doc. No. 1999-22641, P 38.

[138] Statement of Harold R. Handler, on behalf of the Tax Section, New York State Bar Association, before the Committee on Finance (27 April 1999) at p. 2, quoted in "The Problem of Corporate Tax Shelters – Discussion, Analysis and Legislative Proposals", *supra* no. 83 at 3.

[139] The Problem of Corporate Tax Shelters – Discussion, Analysis and Legislative Proposals", *supra* no. 83 at 3.

the economic substance doctrine, has suggested that an increasingly inequitable allocation of tax liabilities, that results from permitting tax benefits claimed in relation to transactions that have only been undertaken in order to achieve those tax benefits, causes taxpayers to lose confidence in the self-assessment system of determining tax liabilities.[140] This loss of confidence by taxpayers "give[s] rise to a vicious circle: as confidence falls, members of the public become less likely voluntarily to comply with tax laws."[141]

Empirical evidence, derived from laboratory experiments, also exists to support the view that "people tend to contribute to public goods when they perceive that others contribute."[142] A related point is that belief the tax system is unfair can lead people to rationalize "cheating".[143]

---

[140] Hariton, *supra* no. 2 at 33 (arguing that there must be a rule that permits tax benefits to be disallowed on the basis that permitting the results of transactions to stand undermines the tax system–the economic substance doctrine performs this role in the U.S.); see also: Jonathan Shaw, Joel Slemrod and John Whiting, "Administration and Compliance", *Dimensions of Tax Design: The Mirrlees Review*, Oxford University Press, 2010, pp. 1100-1162, 1127 (concluding that tax authorities "should be careful not to alienate taxpayers and thereby reduce the extent to which they comply out of a sense of duty").

[141] Prebble and Prebble, *supra* no. 102 at 726 (citing Michael O'Grady, Revenue Commissioner, address at KPMG Tax Conference: Acceptable Limits of Tax Planning: A Revenue Perspective (Nov. 7, 2003))

[142] Leandra Lederman, "The Interplay Between Norms and Enforcement in Tax Compliance", vol. 64, no. 6 *Ohio State Law Journal* 1453-1514 (2003), 1461 (referring to Dan M. Kahan, "The Logic of Reciprocity: Trust, Collective Action, and Law", 102 *Michigan Law Review* 71-103 (2003), 72-74 ("[I]ndividuals who lack faith in their peers can be expected to resist contributing to public goods. ... "[P]ublic-goods experiments" "have consistently shown that the willingness of individuals to make costly contributions to collective goods is highly conditional on their perception that others are willing to do so. Empirical studies of real-world behavior corroborate this finding.")

[143] James Andreoni, Brian Erard and Jonathan Feinstein, "Tax Compliance", vol. XXXVI *Journal of Economic Literature* 818-860 (June 1998), 851-852 (noting that "adding moral and social dynamics to models of tax compliance is as yet a largely undeveloped area of research.") It has also been reported that there is some evidence that aggressive tax planners are more likely than the general public to consider that the taxation burden they bear is unfair relative to the government benefits they receive – see Tooma, *supra* no. 15 at 16 (citing K. Murphy, "An examination of taxpayers' attitudes towards

INEQUITABLE ALLOCATION OF TAX LIABILITIES

The inequitable allocation of tax liabilities is a further ill-result of unchecked abusive tax avoidance, i.e. it causes an unfair and disproportionate share of the tax burden on those who can least afford it.[144] In this regard, the Final Report of the Review of Business Taxation in Australia described an effect of tax avoidance on the equity and fairness of a tax system as the creation of "a form of subsidy from those paying their fair share of tax according to the intention of the law to those shirking their similar obligations."[145] This concern has also been noted elsewhere and termed "the free rider problem."[146] This is a longstanding problem, which President Roosevelt once addressed in Congress: "All [methods of tax avoidance] are alike in that they are definitely contrary to the spirit of the law. All are alike in that they represent a determined effort on the part of those who use them to dodge the payment of taxes which Congress based on ability to pay. All are alike in that failure to pay results in shifting the tax load to the shoulders of those less able to pay."[147] This complaint about the problem that unchecked abu-

---

the Australian tax system: Findings from a survey of tax scheme avoiders", *Australian Tax Forum* 18(2) (2003), 209-242 and survey findings by Dr. IG Wallschhtsky in Sept. 1984)

[144] Arnold, *supra* no. 8 at 169 (arguing that tax avoidance benefits wealthy individuals and large corporations disproportionately, at the expense of taxpayers who cannot engage in tax avoidance, such as employees); Barker, *supra* no. 84 at 239 (noting that the majority of dutiful taxpayers end up assuming a larger portion of the costs of government than do the avoiders and evaders); Andreoni, Erard and Feinstein, *supra* no. 143 at 818 (commenting that if the wealthy can systematically pay a smaller "share of their taxes than can the poor, then the effective tax system will be less equitable than the legislated one.")

[145] "Final Report of the Review of Business Taxation, A Tax System Redesigned", *supra* no. 106 at s. 6.2(c).

[146] J. Waincymer, "The Australian Tax Avoidance Experience and Responses: A Critical Review*", Tax Avoidance and the Rule of Law*, (Amsterdam: IBFD Publications, 1997), 256; David P. Hariton, "Sorting Out The Tangle of Economic Substance", 52 *Tax Lawyer* 235 (1999), 237-274 (larger tax benefits accrue to [and therefore greater distortion is caused by] larger taxpayers able and amenable to entering into costly tax avoidance transactions).

[147] President Roosevelt's Message to Congress on Tax Evasion and Avoidance (June 17, 1937), reprinted in U.S. Revenue Acts 1909-1950, 20 The Laws, Legislative Histories and Administrative Documents 2 (Bernard D. Reams ed., 1979).

sive tax avoidance causes in relation to the distribution of the tax burden has also been expressed in strong terms by a South African judge: "I endorse the opinion expressed that the avoidance of tax is an evil. Not only does it mean that a taxpayer escapes the obligation of making his proper contribution to the fiscus, but the effect must necessarily be to cast an additional burden on taxpayers who, imbued with a greater sense of civic responsibility, make no attempt to escape or, lacking the financial means to obtain the advice and set up the necessary avoidance machinery, fail to do so."[148]

This point of view has not been endorsed by the Supreme Court of Canada, which has instead repeatedly chosen to support the right of taxpayers to be able to rely upon technical tax law provisions to organize their affairs in order to minimize their taxes payable. However, as Professor Arnold has noted, the principle that everyone should pay his or her fair share of tax, this principle being "consistent with equity, basic morality and good citizenship", would be an attractive alternative principle on which our taxation system could be based.[149] Professor Duff also suggests, having regard to the loss of respect for the integrity of the tax system and the legal system more generally, and other factors set out below, that there is a serious question as to whether a "right" of taxpayers to arrange their affairs solely to minimize tax, absent a statutory provision, should be recognized at all, as it involves sanctioning conduct that has been deliberately designed to defeat the law.[150] I defer the balance of my

---

[148] *COT v. Ferera*, 1976 (2) SA 653, 656F-G; 38 SATC 66 at p. 70 [SATC] per MacDonald JP.

[149] Arnold, *supra* no. 130 at 6 (this principle is to be contrasted with the statement by Lord Tomlin in the House of Lords in the *Duke of Westminster* case which is often quoted by the courts in Canada: "Every man is entitled if he can to order his affairs so as that the tax attaching under the appropriate Acts is less than it otherwise would be."); see also: Tooma, *supra* no. 15 at 33 (citing findings by the Asprey Committee reported by M. McKerchar, The Impact of Complexity Upon Tax Compliance: A study of Australian Personal Taxpayers (Australian Tax Research Foundation, Research Study 39, Sydney (2003), 15 that "equity, simplicity and efficiency" are the most important values for a tax system)

[150] David G. Duff, "Justice Iacobbuci and the 'Golden and Straight Metwand' of Canadian Tax Law", (2007) 57 *University of Toronto Law Journal* 525-579, 574-75 (also noting the substantial costs of tax avoidance in terms of lost

discussion of this point to chapter V, where I examine the Supreme Court of Canada's position regarding certainty, etc.

WASTING OF RESOURCES ON UNECONOMIC ACTIVITY

Another problem abusive tax avoidance causes is that efforts related to it involve wasting significant resources, both in the private and government sectors, on uneconomic activity. The New Zealand GAAR case of *Accent Management Ltd & Ors v. CIR*, where seventeen expert witnesses testified, provides a striking example of how resources are unproductively consumed by the necessity of litigating tax avoidance cases on a case-by-case basis.[151] According to a former Deputy Chief of Staff of the U.S. Joint Committee on Taxation, "[y]ou can't [over] estimate how many of America's greatest minds are being devoted to what economists would all say is totally useless economic activity."[152] *Long Term Capital Holdings v. U.S.*,[153] a case where an artificial loss was cloned, sold twice, and deducted by two groups of taxpayers provides a good illustration of this point. A designer of the tax shelter, found by the Second Circuit Court of Appeals to lack economic substance, was Canadian-born financial economist Myron S. Scholes,[154] a Nobel Prize winner in economics and author of *Taxes and Business Strategy:*

---

revenue and the inefficiency of devoting resources to tax avoidance arrangements. In Professor Duff's view the explanation for the present unsatisfactory state-of-affairs in Canada "turns on the early antipathy exhibited by English and Canadian courts towards taxes, which were regarded as encroachments on private property.")

[151] *Accent Management Ltd. & Ors v. CIR* (2005), 22 NZTC 19,027 (H.C.); also see: Blank, *supra* no. 135 at 542 (noting that tax litigation places a significant drain on government resources and also increases the risk of government high-profile losses)

[152] "The Problem of Corporate Tax Shelters: Discussion, Analysis and Legislative Proposals", *supra* no. 83 at iv-v.

[153] 330 F.Supp.2d 122 (D. Conn., 2004), affirmed 150 Fed.Appx. 40 (2d Cir., 2005).

[154] Alvin C. Warren, Jr., "Understanding Long Term Capital", 106 *Tax Notes* 681-696 (Feb. 7, 2005), 687 (observing that the trial court judge rejected testimony of Dr. Scholes as unsupported, farfetched and contrived to show expected profitability and objective economic substance, rather than serious economic analysis).

A Planning Approach, a text for students used in courses all over North America.[155]

A related objection is that "impermissible tax avoidance creates significant deadweight losses for the economy by distorting trade and investment flows. In particular, avoidance schemes often involve a re- or misallocation of resources from productive investments to activities that are, at best, marginally profitable on a pre-tax-basis. These distortions reduce economic activity and impede growth."[156] Slemrod also makes the argument that the high costs of tax planning put society in a losing position, as no value is created by abusive tax avoidance and it results in transferring resources away from other taxpayers and beneficiaries of government programs.[157]

INTERFERENCE WITH GOVERNMENT SOCIAL AND ECONOMIC POLICIES

One of the problems with the Supreme Court of Canada's position is that although it has acknowledged that the *Income Tax Act* is today an instrument for implementing economic and social policy, as well as a revenue raising device,[158] its position on economic substance in tax avoidance cases thwarts government economic and social policy, as well as revenue-raising objectives. This is because upholding tax avoidance transactions, without regard to their economic substance, deprives government of tax revenues required to fund its economic and social policy objectives. The extent of this revenue deprivation is difficult to assess; but, in a U.S. context,

---

[155] Burgess J.W. Raby and William L. Raby, "Practitioner Advice as a Defense Against Penalties", 109 *Tax Notes* 329-334 (Oct. 17, 2005), 329 (also noting that the appeals court upheld the trial judge's finding that the taxpayer had not placed reasonable reliance upon professional advice and so could not rely on a good-faith reasonable-cause exception to penalties)
[156] "Discussion Paper on Tax Avoidance", *supra* no. 5 at 12.
[157] Joel Slemrod, "The Economics of Corporate Tax Selfishness", Working Paper 10858, National Bureau of Economic Research, 1-37 (2004), 25.
[158] *Québec (Communauté urbaine) c. Notre-Dame de Bonsecours (Corp.)*, [1994] 3 S.C.R. 3 (S.C.C.) at para. 34.

Professor Bankman has reported that the CINS tax shelter marketed by Merrill Lynch gave one taxpayer a deduction of approximately $100 million and another a deduction of over $400 million, while the leading COLI tax shelter case involved tax savings of over $1 billion for a single taxpayer.[159] This suggests that large dollar amounts are very likely also at stake in Canadian tax avoidance cases,[160] as the proliferation of abusive tax avoidance schemes is not much affected by national boundaries.[161]

According to Slemrod and Yitzhaki, no one has attempted to calculate the aggregate avoidance "tax gap," although there are certainly estimates that the gap is large.[162] The manipulation of tax

---

[159] Joseph Bankman, "Modeling the Tax Shelter World", 55 *Tax Law Review* 455-464 (2002), 463 (noting that a single shelter used by the optimal number of participants could cost the government many billions of dollars).

[160] David G Duff, "Tax Avoidance in the 21st Century", Australian Business Tax Reform in Retrospect and Prospect 477-501 (2009), 486 (reporting that federal administrative efforts to counteract aggressive tax planning were estimated to yield $1.4 billion in additional identified taxes for a single taxation year: Canada Revenue Agency, 2006-2007 Canada Revenue Agency Annual Report, p. 59).

[161] "Discussion Paper on Tax Avoidance" *supra* no. 5 at 9 (pointing out that tax avoidance schemes now migrate quickly from country to country because of advances in computer and telecommunications technology); also see: Alarie, *supra* no. 21 at 18-19 ("When creative tax planners devise a new unanticipated scheme that manages to avoid tax under plausible interpretations of current income tax law, it is reasonable to expect these innovations to spread relatively quickly within the tax planning community ....").

[162] Joel Slemrod and Shlomo Yitzhaki, "Tax Avoidance, Evasion, and Administration", Working Paper 7473, National Bureau of Economic Research, 1-76 (2000), 31; Slemrod, *supra* no. 157 at 5 ("Several studies have documented a large and growing gap between the book income reported on public corporations' financial statements and the tax income of corporations, which remains even after eliminating what arises from known differences in the accounting procedures used for book and tax income."); Prem Sikka and Mark P. Hampton, "The Role of Accountancy Firms in Tax Avoidance: Some Evidence and Issues", 29 *Accounting Forum* 325 (2009) (referring to estimates that Britain may be losing more than £100 billion of tax revenues owing to tax avoidance each year); Prebble and Prebble, *supra* no. 102 at 725 (quoting Tax Justice Network figures that revenue lost in the U.K. to tax avoidance "runs to tens of billions of pounds every year" and reports that "The United States tax avoidance boom of the 1990s was estimated to cost the federal government billions of dollars in lost tax revenue."); Tooma, *supra* no. 15 at 24 (citing estimates

laws through the creation of transactions with little or no economic substance is nevertheless said to severely undermine the ability of government to set and implement economic and social policy, because of the diversion of resources from their intended targets.[163] In this regard, Professor Avi-Yonah has argued that one of the harmful effects arising from the avoidance of corporate taxes is the corresponding reduction of the "social safety net."[164]

It has also been suggested that tax avoidance, in the Australian context, interfered with intended government tax reforms because of revenue shortfalls.[165] Professor Weisbach's related point is that "[t]hose who tax plan are not in some way more deserving of lower taxes than those who do not. There is no reason why we would want to distribute money toward shelterers."[166] This point is quite vivid, when one considers it, for example, in the context of world poverty.[167]

According to the G8 Muskoka Accountability Report released on June 20, 2010, spending on the G8's commitments to global issues,

---

from K. Murphy, "Procedural Justice and the Australian Tax Office: A study of scheme investors", *Centre for Tax Integrity Working Paper No. 35* (2002) Canberra: The Australian National University, that $4 billion in tax revenue was lost with 42,000 Australians becoming involved in aggressive tax avoidance schemes in the 1990s); Neville, *supra* no. 134 (suggesting a revenue loss in Australia through tax avoidance in the order of three billion dollars annually)

[163] "Discussion Paper on Tax Avoidance", *supra* no. 5 at 14.
[164] Reuven S. Avi-Yonah, "Globalization, Tax Competition, And the Fiscal Crisis of the Welfare State", 113 *Harvard Law Review* 1573-1676 (2000), 1578 (arguing that there is substantial need for a social safety net because globalization has led to income inequality and lack of job security).
[165] Waincymer, *supra* no. 146 at 257; see also: Neville, *supra* no. 134 (arguing that the belief wage earners have that businesses are not paying their fair share of taxes leads to immoderation in wage demands, with a resulting impact on employment and on inflation)
[166] Weisbach, *supra* no. 15 at 223 ("[T]ax planning can be analogized to an externality. Those who tax plan impose costs on those who do not in the form of higher taxes. The person who engages in the tax planning does not take that external cost into account, nor is it reflected through the price system.")
[167] On July 12, 2011 United Nations Secretary General Ban Ki-moon called for urgent support to respond to the crisis in the Horn of Africa, where more than 11 million people are in need of life-saving assistance as they face the worst drought in decades–see http://www.un.org/apps/news/story.asp?NewsID=39016&Cr=horn+of+africa&Cr1=

including international assistance, economic development, health, food security, and peace and security, has already fallen about $10 billion short in aid previously pledged to the world's poor.[168] Permitting tax revenues to be kept in the coffers of aggressive "free-rider" taxpayers will not be helpful in allowing governments to combat this problem. A similar point is that Studin advocates the rapid growth of Canada's population to 100 million, so that Canada becomes "a serious force to be reckoned with" in terms of strategic power in the world community. He anticipates that this will require increased national wealth and tax base, to enable Canada to mobilize very significant quanta of money in order to properly lead in international conventions – non-military and military alike, in development, intelligence, reconstruction, war and peace-making.[169] Regardless of whether Studin's goal of achieving this growth through accelerated immigration materializes, it remains inevitable that Canada will continue to increase in size.[170] This, in turn, speaks to a need for Government to take intelligent steps to protect its tax revenues.[171] Given the resources which are and will continue to be required to fund essential spending by Canada's governments, it would be enormously

---

[168] Juliet O'Neill, "G8 countries fall $10B short of aid commitments: report", Canwest News Service, June 20, 2010.

[169] Ian MacLeod, "Push Canadian population to 100 million, scholar argues", *Ottawa Citizen*, June 12, 2010.

[170] The United Nations projects a population for Canada of 44 to 50 million by 2050 and Statistics Canada projects populations in Canada as high as 47.6 million by 2036 and 63.7 million by 2060 – see "The 2010 Revision", United Nations, Department of Economic and Social Affairs, Population Division; Population Estimates and Projections Section, and Population Projections for Canada, Provinces and Territories 2009 to 2036, Table 7-1, Components of population growth, high-growth scenario – Canada, 2009/2010 to 2060/2061, Ministry of Industry (June 2010).

[171] The OECD notes in "The Global Forum on Transparency and Exchange of Information for Tax Purposes: A Background Information Brief" (March 16, 2001), http://www.oecd.org/dataoecd/32/43757434.pdf, page 4: "Tax avoidance and tax evasion threaten government revenues throughout the world. In many developed countries the sums run into billions of Euros and developing countries lose vital revenue through tax evasion. This translates into fewer resources for infrastructure and affects the standard of living for all in both developed and developing countries."

short-sighted for Parliament to permit tax avoidance to continue to thrive by not strengthening the present GAAR.

Relative to depriving governments of important tax revenues, another objection to the Supreme Court's position that the economic realities of transactions are not relevant in tax cases, absent sham or a statutory provision to the contrary,[172] is that it is problematic in the growing and important area of transfer pricing. Section 247 of the *Income Tax Act* requires that non-arm's length parties carry out their transactions in accordance with arm's length terms and conditions. Courts have recognized that arm's length prices are to be determined in accordance with the OECD Guidelines on Transfer Pricing.[173] The OECD Guidelines, in turn, recognize that legal ownership may not be consistent with economic reality, in the context of transactions between related parties. With respect to intangibles, the Guidelines rely primarily on an analysis of the functions and risks assumed by the respective parties in the controlled transaction in order to determine whether, in economic substance, there has been a transfer of the intangible.[174]

---

[172] See my examination of this point in chapter V.

[173] *SmithKline Beecham Animal Health Inc. v. R.*, [2002] 4 C.T.C. 93 (Fed. C.A.) at para. 8; *GlaxoSmithKline Inc. v. R.*, 2008 D.T.C. 3957 (Eng.) (T.C.C. [General Procedure]) at paras. 59-60, reversed [2010] 6 C.T.C. 220 (F.C.A.), affirmed 2012 CarswellNat 3880 (S.C.C.), judgment reserved January 13, 2012; *General Electric Capital Canada Inc. v. R.*, [2010] 2 C.T.C. 2187 (T.C.C. [General Procedure]), additional reasons 2010 D.T.C. 1353 (Eng.) (T.C.C. [General Procedure]), affirmed 2010 FCA 344 (F.C.A.).

[174] James R. Mogle, "The Future of International Transfer Pricing: Practical and Policy Opportunities Unique to Intellectual Property, Economic Substance, and Entrepreneurial Risk in the Allocation of Intangible Income", 10 *George Mason Law Review* 925-950 (2002), 928, 931 ("[T]he [OECD] guidelines tend to emphasize the importance of economic ownership over legal ownership, particularly in situations involving marketing intangibles. Moreover, the Guidelines also recognize that for 'legitimate business reasons,' related parties may structure their inter-company transactions in a manner that unrelated companies would not contemplate. In that event, the allocation of income attributable to intangibles based on the principles of economic ownership under the OECD Guidelines seems more appropriate than allocation based on legal title.")

There is therefore a large potential for tension between the Supreme Court's position regarding the need to uphold *bona fide* legal relationships, versus the need for analysis of economic substance, for the purpose of determining ownership under the OECD Guidelines. Transfer pricing litigation is still in its infancy in Canada, relative to the experience in the U.S., and only one transfer pricing case has been heard to date by the Supreme Court.[175] It will be a conundrum, however, when eventually faced with the application of the OECD Guidelines in the context of s. 247 of the Act (which does not allude to economic substance), for the Court to be faced with the central role of economic substance.[176] This is not an insubstantial problem, as estimates of the size of I.R.S. claims in the U.S. re the transfer of intangibles to low tax jurisdictions have been in the tens of billions of dollars for several corporations.[177]

From Canada's perspective, as long ago as 2001 the Canada Revenue Agency had made transfer pricing reassessments of over $300 million,[178] and the *Globe and Mail* reported in October 2006 that the Agency was seeking $2 billion from Merck Frosst in relation to its transfer of profits from the sale of an asthma treatment developed in Canada to Barbados.[179] Cases of this kind will require a determination of whether there has been a transfer of intangibles to tax havens, having regard to the economic substance of the transactions, regardless of the formal legal relationships.

---

[175] Judgment was released by the Supreme Court in *GlaxoSmithKline Inc. v. The Queen* on October 18, 2012, which was well after the manuscript for this edition of my book was completed. Suffice it to say at this late juncture, that my point is diminished somewhat by the fact that in *GlaxoSmithKline,* the Supreme Court essentially ignored the taxpayer's legal relationships (in odd contrast with its position in tax avoidance cases) and favoured an analysis based upon "economic and business reality." See 2012 CarswellNat 3880 (S.C.C.).

[176] Diksic, *supra* no. 9 at 25:1-34 (commenting that the OECD Guidelines also call for recognition of the actual transactions undertaken in all but "exceptional circumstances" in discussing whether the transfer pricing rules in section 247 of the Act will be interpreted as "statutory recognition of economic substance.")

[177] Glenn R. Simpson, "A New Twist in Tax Avoidance: Firms Send Best Ideas Abroad", *Wall Street Journal* (June 24, 2002).

[178] Report of the Auditor General of Canada – December 2002, c. 4, para. 4.22.

[179] "Revenue Canada seeks $2 billion from Merck Frosst", *Globe & Mail* (October 19, 2006)

This goes to show that if Canada hopes to attract its fair share of revenues from global businesses, it should not stray too far from the model that is used by other OECD countries. As many other OECD countries are treating economic substance as a central factor in determining whether there has been abusive tax avoidance, this is another reason for Canada to follow suit.

DISTORTION OF COMPETITION

There is also a further point that businesses that gain tax savings through abusive tax avoidance arrangements have a competitive advantage over other businesses that do not. Professor Pagone explains that this occurs, in part, because funds employed in the ventures that have engaged in such tax avoidance arrangements are not gained from sources that have "the same rigours and constraints" as funds from conventional sourcing. Thus funds can be obtained at lower costs than would otherwise be available, putting competitors at a disadvantage.[180]

CONCLUSION

It will be apparent from my examination of the ill-effects of unchecked abusive tax avoidance in this chapter that a failure by government to take the appropriate measures to contend with it is an inexcusable lapse in governance and foresight. Having said that, the question becomes what measures are best-suited for the task of containing abusive avoidance.

In the next chapter, I consider whether unacceptable tax avoidance is best dealt with by the creation of more technical tax rules, or by the application of judicial standards, or by some combination of the two. My conclusion is that the proliferation of more technical

---

[180] GT Pagone, "Part IVA: The General Anti-Avoidance Provisions in Australian Law", vol. 27, no. 3 *Melbourne University Law Review* 770 (2003), 799 (arguing that there is unfair competition where others in the same marketplace do not gain the same tax savings)

rules deepens the quagmire, whereas the application of standards by the judiciary, when also applying technical rules, is a not-perfect, but a more palatable and workable solution, than reliance upon technical rules alone. I also note that the adoption of ever-more technical rules, as a response to abusive tax avoidance, in any event seriously challenges the tax administration's capacity to cope.[181]

---

[181] Johnson, *supra* no. 15 at 444 (noting in a US context that "IRS agents are undertrained, undermotivated, and stretched too thin. ... The IRS does not pay enough, in honor or dollars, to attract recruits who can understand the tax system that Congress has adopted. The disparity between well paid private tax lawyers and accountants and poorly paid, poorly motivated IRS agents is even worse for older agents. The IRS has trouble retaining its best. The IRS is understaffed with respect to the most important transactions, compared with the talent and resources devoted to the other side. The IRS cannot compete with the big corporations in the warfare of full-scale litigation."); see also: Genevieve Loutinsky, "Gladwellian Taxation: Deterring Tax Abuse Through General Anti-Avoidance Rules", vol. 19, no. 2 *Temple Political & Civil Rights Law Review* 101-135 (Spring 2010), 131 (suggesting that there are probably only a few hundred tax specialists in the United States who can deal with the issues involved in highly sophisticated avoidance transactions on a timely basis)

III

A Case for Standards in Responding to Abusive Tax Avoidance

One of the planks behind the Supreme Court of Canada's position that it should not adopt an interpretative approach which plays any role in discouraging abusive tax avoidance is that such matters are best left to the legislature. This is a highly debatable point which I examine here.

There is a wide consensus in the tax community that there must be limits to the notion that taxpayers should be free to structure their affairs as they choose – otherwise, taxes would be too easy to avoid.[182] Even passionate opponents of interference with the claimed right of taxpayers to structure their transactions so as to enable them to minimize their taxes acknowledge that some forms of tax avoidance, although short of criminal evasion, are not appropriate.[183]

---

[182] Keinan, *supra* no. 2 at 387 (noting tension between the need of taxpayers to be able to plan their affairs by reference to existing law and the ability of tax administrations to curb abusive tax avoidance)

[183] Daniel J. Glassman, "'It's Not A Lie If You Believe It': Tax Shelters and the Economic Substance Doctrine", 58 *Florida Law Review* 665-711 (2006),

Although the Canadian Government has indicated that it wishes to strengthen reporting requirements for tax avoidance transactions, a strengthened information reporting system will not accomplish much, unless it is coupled with an effective way of disallowing tax benefits arising from abusive tax avoidance.[184] This raises the question of whether it is technical rules, judicial standards,[185] or a combination of the two, that provides the most effective defence against abusive tax avoidance.[186]

The matter of whether a tax system is better served by rules or standards does have serious advocates on both sides;[187] however, it is

---

669 (acknowledging that there is a "line between aggressive, yet permissible, tax planning and improper, and *sometimes* criminal, tax evasion"[my emphasis]); Jason Quinn, "Being Punished for Obeying the Rules: Corporate Tax Planning and the Overly Broad Economic Substance Doctrine", 15 *George Mason Law Review* 1041-1080 (2008), 1073 (suggesting "egregious disregard for the intended results of the Internal Revenue Code" should be dealt with by the economic substance doctrine)

[184] See, for example, David A. Weisbach, "The Failure to Disclose as an Approach to Tax Shelters", 54 *SMU Law Review* 73-82 (2001), 82 (arguing disclosure requirements and penalties alone will not overcome aggressive tax planning and there must be "strong anti-shelter doctrines." The matter of how balance should be struck between the courts and the legislature in terms of how these strong anti-shelter doctrines are best structured needs to be studied)

[185] Freedman, *supra* no. 14 at 729-730 (noting that the use of principles "is not intended to imply any introduction of morality into tax law. ... The debate at its most fundamental is how best to convey and give effect to the intention of Parliament." Also citing an illustration by Andrei Marmor re ordering a restaurant meal, e.g. If we begin to add specific instructions to the waiter as to how the meal is to be delivered, it may come without some unspecified (but reasonable to assume) ingredients such as sauce: "This is precisely what happens with tax law drafting at present.")

[186] David A. Weisbach, "Corporate Tax Avoidance", John M. Olin Program in Law and Economics Working Paper no. 202 (Chicago: University of Chicago Law School, January 2004), 11 (stating that a rule can be defined as a law which is given content before individuals act, whereas a standard is given content *ex post* after individuals act)

[187] Joseph Bankman, "The Business Purpose Doctrine and the Sociology of Tax", 54 *SMU Law Review* 149-157 (2001), 154-157 (noting a split amongst academics on the perennial issue of rules versus substance in tax jurisprudence); see also: Louis Kaplow, "Rules Versus Standards: An Economic Analysis", vol. 42 *DukeLaw Journal* 557-629 (1992), 621 (noting, among other matters: "The central factor influencing the desirability of rules and standards is the

not enough to simply state, as the Supreme Court of Canada has done in *Neuman* and other cases,[188] that a rules-based approach is the better approach in tax avoidance cases.[189] Erecting limits against tax avoidance based strictly on technical rules is subject to the objection that the rules must become increasingly narrow, defensive and complex,[190]

---

frequency with which a law will govern conduct. If conduct will be frequent, the additional costs of designing rules – which are borne once – are likely to be exceeded by the savings realized each time the rule is applied. ... If behavior subject to the law is infrequent, however, standards are likely to be preferable.")

[188] See also: *Entreprises Ludco ltée c. Canada*, (*sub nom.* Ludco Enterprises Ltd. v. Canada) [2001] 2 S.C.R. 1082 (S.C.C.) at para. 39, per Iacobucci, J.: "[G]iven that the *Income Tax Act* has many specific anti-avoidance provisions and rules, it follows that courts should not be quick to embellish provisions of the Act in response to concerns about tax avoidance when it is open to Parliament to be precise and specific with respect to any mischief to be prevented"; *Shell Canada Ltd. v. R.*, (*sub nom.* Shell Canada Ltd. v. Canada) [1999] 3 S.C.R. 622 (S.C.C.) at para. 45, per McLachlin J.: "[A]bsent a specific provision to the contrary, it is not the courts' role to prevent taxpayers from relying on the sophisticated structure of their transactions, arranged in such a way that the particular provisions of the Act are met, on the basis that it would be inequitable to those taxpayers who have chosen to structure their transactions that way. ... The courts' role is to interpret and apply the Act as it was adopted by Parliament.")

[189] Morgan, *supra* no. 1 at 392 (arguing that a judicial anti avoidance regime is more effective than one based on statutory regulation because the judicial regime diminishes opportunities for more avoidance); Bleiwas and Hutson, *supra* no. 17, c. 16, V. GAAR: Canada's Answer to Tax Avoidance, A. Introduction (articulating a distinction between "abusive tax avoidance" and "legitimate commercial and family transactions" "in legislative language is virtually impossible"); compare: John Tiley, "Judicial Anti-Avoidance Doctrines: The US Alternatives", *British Tax Review* 180-197 (1987), 180, 188 (suggesting that the "United States Courts have been much more willing than United Kingdom Courts to develop some general tax jurisprudence or overriding principle that can be plucked from the sky to solve problems", but "they can be extremely difficult to grasp and at times simply lack intellectual credibility")

[190] Luke, *supra* no. 67 (arguing that "the necessity of relying on rough justice becomes more apparent" when one considers the "nitty-gritty reality" of complex rules); John Braithwaite, "Making Tax Law More Certain: A Theory", Working Paper No. 44, Centre for Tax System Integrity, The Australian National University (December 2002) (noting that ordinary people cannot make any sense out of much of tax law, and even experts can't have coherent conversations about it without researching the points)

in order to contend with the creativity and ingenuity of tax professionals dedicated to finding ever-more tax avoidance opportunities.[191]

Also, according to the OECD, increasingly complex tax laws increase the administrative costs and the compliance burdens upon both taxpayers and government.[192] Furthermore, the creation of more technical rules to fight tax avoidance simply invites further tax avoidance, as the new limits provide new foundation for arguments that tax benefits are justified, given novel and strict interpretations of the new rules. This means that a purely technical rules-based defence against abusive tax avoidance is inefficient, because resort to incremental reform of tax laws contributes to an indefinite continuation of the same problem. Where government identifies tax avoidance that it considers inappropriate and moves to prevent it through a change in the law, taxpayers may still consider that the after-tax return from the desired outcome is greater than the costs necessary to achieve that outcome subsequent to the change, and respond by attempting to circumvent the change in the law. The government eventually discovers and responds to these efforts, and the "tax avoidance game" continues.[193]

The Supreme Court of Canada at one time appeared to be sensitive to this reality, when it announced a set of interpretative guidelines in *Stubart*, said to be aimed at reducing "the action and reaction endlessly produced by complex, specific tax measures aimed at sophisticated business practices, and the inevitable,

---

[191] Chris Evans, "Containing Tax Avoidance: Anti-Avoidance Strategies", [2008] *University of New South Wales Faculty of Law Research Series* 40, p. 24 (arguing that simplicity has a critical role in responding to tax avoidance)

[192] OECD, "Harmful Tax Competition: An Emerging Global Issue", (Paris: OECD, 1998), para. 30.

[193] George K. Yin, "Getting Serious About Corporate Tax Shelters: Taking A Lesson From History", 54 *SMU Law Review* 209-237 (2001), 216 (referencing the legislative steps taken in the 1970s and 1980s which did not curb U.S. tax shelter activity as evidence of this phenomenon). Note that there are also huge resources devoted by tax practitioners who are not involved in aggressive tax avoidance planning, in learning and understanding the new technical rules in order to advise their clients. This, of course, also results in huge costs being borne by clients.

professionally-guided and equally specialized taxpayer reaction."[194] However, the *Stubart* interpretative guidelines have basically been ignored by the courts, and the Supreme Court itself emphasized, only four years after releasing its interpretative guidelines, that it should "not be quick to embellish" anti-avoidance provisions "when it is open for the legislator to be precise and specific with respect to any mischief to be avoided."[195]

Professors Chirelstein and Zelenak, among others, have said that in their views the "always-one-step-behind" nature of a strictly rules-based approach means it can never be an adequate response to the proliferation of tax avoidance.[196] Professor Arnold adds that the lengthy time it takes to make tax law amendments, and the reality that the passage of such amendments is subject to Parliament's agenda, both militate against the courts not playing an active role in tax avoidance cases.[197]

Stephen Bowman has also commented that detailed legislative provisions invite the courts to conclude that treatment of the subject is exhaustive, so the legislation does not mean to say anything that it omits. Legislatures respond with more legislation intended to plug gaps exposed by restrictive interpretations by the courts. The

---

[194] *Stubart Investments Ltd. v. R.*, [1984] 1 S.C.R. 536 (S.C.C.) at para. 66.
[195] *Neuman v. Minister of National Revenue*, [1998] 1 S.C.R. 770 (S.C.C.) at para. 63.
[196] Marvin A. Chirelstein and Lawrence Zelenak, "Tax Shelters and the Search for a Silver Bullet", vol. 105, no. 6 *Columbia Law Review* 1939-1966 (2005), 1951 (arguing there needs to be a "silver bullet" that stands ready to defeat particular tax avoidance schemes before they take place and "that would leave little to judicial discretion").
[197] Arnold, *supra* no. 130 at 27 (arguing that the Supreme Court of Canada has taken "an antiquated approach to its role in the tax system", by declining to assist in controlling tax avoidance, and that "it is largely responsible for the flourishing of tax-avoidance schemes to the detriment of most taxpayers"); see also: *Study into the Role of Tax Intermediaries*, Paris: OECD, 2008, http://www.oecd.org/28/34/39882938.pdf, p. 5 (noting that the concern of tax administrations associated with the unintended and unexpected tax revenue consequences of aggressive tax planning "is exacerbated by the often lengthy period between the time schemes are created and sold and the time revenue bodies discover them and remedial legislation is enacted.")

result is that over time the interpretation of increasingly wide areas of tax law must be left to specialists who are able to devote substantial time and energy to understanding the provisions.[198] As Scarborough has noted, "[p]iecemeal reforms, each designed to make the tax system more neutral and to reduce tax avoidance, have created inconsistencies that themselves distort taxpayer behaviour and create tax avoidance opportunities."[199]

The problem of growing complexity associated with the ongoing creation of technical tax laws to combat unacceptable tax avoidance is not one that can be much over-stated.[200] In Canada, we have seen the federal Department of Finance announce a veritable blizzard

---

[198] Stephen W. Bowman, "Interpretation of Tax Legislation: The Evolution of Purposive Analysis", (1995), vol. 43, no. 5 CTJ 1167-89, 1183-84 ("[T]he consistently restrictive approach to legislation adopted by the Anglo-Canadian courts historically has contributed to a detailed and complex style of legislative drafting .... By virtue of the courts' focusing solely on the statutory language and applying restrictive general rules, the dice may have been loaded against one side or the other (but usually against the tax authority.)"); see also: Justin Dabner, "There are Too Many Witchdoctors in Our Tax Courts: Is There a Better Way?", vol. 15, no. 1 *Revenue Law Journal* 36-48 (2005), 37 "[T]he law is dying. It has pneumonia. It is drowning in its own detail. Every day it becomes more complex and perplexing. It is now well beyond the understanding of the average citizen and even some tax academics.")

[199] RH Scarborough, "Different Rules for Different Layers and Products: The Patchwork Taxation of Derivatives", 72 *Taxes* 1031-1049 (1994), 1044 (noting that these inconsistencies include circumstances where two sides of the same transaction are subject to different tax rules, and also where "economically similar derivatives [are] taxed in different ways.")

[200] See the view of the House of Commons Standing Committee on Finance and Economic Affairs recorded in the Report on the White Paper on Tax Reform (Stage 1), Ottawa, Queen's Printer, November 1987, p. 122: "The inability of government to effectively stop tax leakage under the current rules is amply demonstrated by the constant stream of press releases announcing new rules to close loopholes which are emerging with ever greater frequency as tax law becomes more and more complex."; see also: Dodge, *supra* no. 134 at 4 ("[R]ecent years have seen a profusion of sophisticated tax-motivated strategies involving various technical provisions of the Act. One only has to go through the list of press releases issued by the Department of Finance in the last two years to find evidence of this increased use of complex tax avoidance schemes."); Judith Freedman, "A GANTIP: Was it really such a bad idea?", *The Tax Journal* 8-10 (April 2009), 10 (noting that the Institute of Chartered Accountants of Scotland has "warmed to the idea of a GAAR in view of the

of technical tax legislation in an attempt to combat tax avoidance, including the at-risk rules, limited recourse debt rules, rules relating to gifting arrangements, non-resident trust rules and foreign investment entity rules. In spite of these technical measures, it cannot reasonably be supposed that the existing number of aggressive tax avoidance transactions has been measurably diminished,[201] whereas the comprehensibility of large sections of the *Income Tax Act* has been dramatically diminished. It is more than a little ironic, then, that while the judiciary in Canada often complains about the complexity of tax legislation,[202] it has contributed substantially to the problem, by declining to apply judicial standards to abusive tax avoidance.

---

volume of recent legislation. ... A [general anti-avoidance principle could ... simplify our tax law and cut down on the need for new provisions.")

[201] Vern Krishna, Tax Avoidance: The General Anti-Avoidance Rule, (Toronto: Carswell, 1990), p. 21, § 38 (noting the "frenzy" of legislative activity aimed at combating tax avoidance schemes, "but just as the legislature blocked one avenue of fiscal escape, innovative tax planners burrowed another hole in the statutory patchwork.")

[202] See for some, among many, fine examples of complaints by judges about the interpretative difficulties caused by the complexity of taxation laws: *J.F. Newton Ltd. v. Thorne Riddell* (1990), 91 D.T.C. 5276 (B.C. S.C.) at p. 5282 (in reference to subsection 55(2) ITA: "It surpasses my imagination that anyone considers language such as this to be capable of an intelligent understanding, or that such language is thought to be capable of application to events in real life, such as the sale of a business."); *Posno v. R.*, (*sub nom.* Posno v. Canada) [1989] 2 C.T.C. 234 (Fed. T.D.) (in reference to leasing property rules in the *Income Tax Regulations*: "The foregoing passages may not be the worst examples of circuitous obscurity in the income tax legislation but they are worthy contenders."); *Assurance-Vie Banque Nationale, cie d'assurance-vie c. R.*, [2006] G.S.T.C. 60 (F.C.A.) (in determining whether supplies of financial services were exempted or zero-rated under the *Excise Tax Act* the court stated: "It was an understatement on the part of the Tax Court of Canada when it said ... that the wording of the legislation in question was not crystal clear. ... Where and how is one to find the guiding light that will enable to find an exit to what, in interpretative terms, is a real labyrinth?"); *Sneyd v. R.*, [2000] G.S.T.C. 46 (Fed. C.A.) (considering an application for a rebate under the *Excise Tax Act* the Court commented on the legislation as "a model of ambiguity created by a maze of definitions"); *Krashinsky v. R.*, [2010] 4 C.T.C. 2301 (T.C.C. [Informal Procedure]) (stating that the fact that senior capable family lawyers would not have an item on their checklist of items to cover off in a separation agreement "is an unfortunate comment on the complexity of our taxation laws"); *Roynat Inc. v. Ja-Sha Trucking & Leasing Ltd.*, [1992] 2 C.T.C. 139 (Man. C.A.) (considering priority claims under the *Income Tax Act* "The resolution of the issue

A further problem, which is said to be quite visible from the experience in the U.S. in the 1970s and 1980s, is that it has proven to be extremely difficult to "clean out the underbrush of unnecessary tax laws once their time has passed."[203] It is also widely-recognized that rule-makers can never fully anticipate, much less draft technical rules to contend with, all of the possible combinations and permutations of legal relationships, transactions and tax provisions that will be employed in the next generations of aggressive tax avoidance plans.[204] The Carter Commission, amongst others, has warned that "drafters cannot foresee all the possible avoidance transactions and

> raised on the appeal is not as simple as its statement. This is due, at least in part, to the language of the legislation. It might have come from Lewis Carroll's world of Alice and Humpty Dumpty where words mean anything you please and concepts are impenetrable."); *Shepard v. British Columbia (Minister of Finance)* (1978), 4 E.T.R. 268 (B.C. S.C.), reversed 1980 CarswellBC 109 (B.C. C.A.) (interpreting the *Succession Duty Act* (B.C.): "I found the language of the legislation to be almost impenetrable. To some it may have a certain sense of order when viewed from afar but when one has to descend into the unpleasant task of analyzing the detail the words of the statute seem to run off in different directions all at the same time."); *Dunfield v. R.*, [2001] 4 C.T.C. 2518 (T.C.C. [Informal Procedure]) (regarding a claim for a deduction in relation to payment of child support "The legislation in this area of tax law was, before the 1997 amendments, complex and bewildering to those unfortunately clutched by its talons. Now it is almost incomprehensible. *Planned* legislative abstruseness could not have ascended the Olympian heights scaled by both the substantive and implementing provisions respecting the income inclusion and deduction of maintenance payments. ... Thousands of taxpayers are affected by this maze of legislative pitfalls. ... What chance do they have of making any sense of these provisions when lawyers and judges are driven to the wall in their attempts to understand and apply them? The agonies of domestic combatant strife are debilitating and depressing. No one in that position needs a torpefying journey through this legislative labyrinth."); *Hunter v. R.*, [2001] 4 C.T.C. 2762 (T.C.C. [Informal Procedure]) ("[T]he provisions of the Act in this area [marital breakdown, spousal and child support] affect a large number of taxpayers .... Yet the provisions of the Act in this area are among the most complex in Canadian legislation. Indeed, even the professionals probably find the provisions of the Act in this area at best ambiguous and at worst incomprehensible. It is surely not too much to expect that our legislative draftspersons express themselves simply, clearly and unambiguously.").

[203] Yin, *supra* no. 193 at 217 (arguing that "something more [than particular *ad hoc* legislative responses] is needed if the shelter dragon is to be slain").
[204] See, for example, Hariton, *supra* no. 2 at 33 (arguing that governments cannot rely solely upon objective rules to disallow tax benefits arising from tax

... specific rules might create roadmaps for new tax planning."[205] The D.C. Circuit Court of Appeals expressed a similar view in *ASA Investerings Partnership*: "the smartest drafters of legislation and regulation cannot be expected to anticipate every device."[206]

According to Professor Cooper, no country has succeeded or is likely to succeed in framing tax laws in such a way that it is clear how the tax liability will be calculated on any conceivable set of facts.[207] Professor Gunn comments that "many tax rules have proved unsatisfactory in practice because they were made with an incomplete recognition of the measures people would take in response."[208] Professor Arnold also observes that the Supreme Court of Canada, unlike the House of Lords, has not addressed itself to these difficulties that a legislature experiences in trying to amend tax legislation to keep up with complex tax avoidance schemes.[209]

In light of these realities, it is essential that courts apply judicial standards, in addition to technical tax rules, in order to prevent tax legislation from being undermined by abusive tax avoidance.[210] Professor Vanistendael says that the application of standards by the judiciary merely reflects "the common law tradition of legal analysis in which common sense plays an important role in the interpretation of facts and rules."[211] Hariton's analysis is to the same effect:

---

shelter transactions as taxpayers will always be in a position to discover exceptions to technical tax rules)

[205] Report of the Royal Commission on Taxation, volume 3 (Ottawa, Queen's Printer, 1966), 554-556.
[206] 201 F.3d 505 (D.C. Cir., 2000) at p. 513.
[207] Cooper, GS, "Conflicts, Challenges and Choices – The Rule of Law and Anti-Avoidance Rules", *Tax Avoidance and the Rule of Law*, (Amsterdam: IBFD Publications, 1997), 13.
[208] Gunn, *supra* no. 70 at 765.
[209] Arnold, *supra* no. 130 at 27 (arguing that the Supreme Court "simply says, in effect, 'It's not our job to control tax avoidance and the reason is that we've said so many times in the past.'")
[210] Braithwaite, *supra* no. 190 (arguing that tax law requires the approach of combining principles with rules more than other areas of the law)
[211] F. Vanistendael, "Judicial Interpretation and the Role of Anti-Abuse Provisions in the Tax Law", *Tax Avoidance and the Rule of Law*, (Amsterdam: IBFD Publications, 1997), 144.

"A few words set out in a statute cannot possibly serve to govern an entire world of complex business transactions (just as a few words of due process set out in a Constitutional amendment cannot serve to govern an entire world of social transactions) ... in the absence of an active and flexible application of those words to specific cases. Interpretation and application are the very heart of the law. Anyone who eschews them does not understand the practice of law."[212]

Professor Weisbach also argues that a combination of rules and standards that can override the rules where their strict application does not produce appropriate results is the most cost-effective way to implement tax law: "Overriding standards allows rules to cover most common situations without the complexity that would come from ensuring perfect application in all cases. The question is the appropriate strength of those standards, not whether standards of this type have a place in the tax law."[213] To the extent that it is not apparent to the judiciary what standards should be applied, this can be remedied by incorporating the appropriate standards in anti-avoidance legislation. In Canada's case, this can at least partly be accomplished by ensuring an economic substance ingredient in GAAR, by making the amendments that I am proposing.

Professor Isenbergh, who opposes using judicial doctrines in tax cases, has argued that the notion courts have an important function in preventing tax avoidance through the use of judicial doctrines, because technical tax laws cannot possibly catch all of the forms of transactions used by taxpayers to reduce taxes, is a "myth" that is "easily dispelled." The support he cites for his position is that it hard for him to think of a single case "that has ever permanently

---

[212] Hariton, *supra* no. 2 at 56 (arguing that courts are "implementing" rather than "abrogating the authority of Congress" by applying the economic substance doctrine to tax avoidance transactions).
[213] Weisbach, *supra* no. 184 at 79; Weisbach, *supra* no. 186 at 14 ("The standards-based approach ... avoids the complexity of a purely rules-based approach. A mix of rules and over-riding standards minimizes the overall cost of promulgating the tax law. We should expect the law to take this approach, as it does, mixing a set of detailed rules with over-riding standards."); also see: Rector, *supra* no. 2 at 173 (arguing that there must be some principle-based limits that can be used to disallow transactions that create unintended tax benefits)

staunched any fissure in the congressional dyke."[214] However, whether judicial doctrines have ever provided a "permanent fix" for leaky tax laws is not a proper measure of their merits, as even a temporary staunching of the loss of revenues from the government's coffers can be extremely valuable.

Professor Isenbergh's statement was made in 1982, and it predated the era of multi-billion dollar tax shelter transactions. The fact that the economic substance doctrine has been relied upon so extensively by U.S. courts, in cases involving sale and leaseback ("SILO"), contingent instalment sale ("CINS"), corporate owned life insurance ("COLI"), bond and option sales strategy ("BOSS"), and other mass-marketed tax shelter products (see chapter VI, re the application of the common law economic substance doctrine in U.S. tax shelter cases), speaks volumes as to its usefulness. The more apt contemporary view of Professors Shaviro and Weisbach, in light of the experience in the U.S. with tax shelters, is that the use of black letter rules alone, unsupported by judicial doctrines "could lead to the elimination of wholesale swathes of corporate income tax liability."[215]

Professor Isenbergh also argued against the use of judicial doctrines on the basis that he considered that they owed their existence to "the psychological vanity of judges." His thesis was that there is "little glory" in "the painstaking process of examining transactions and statutes to determine whether they concord," whereas "society ... has always looked to courts for strokes of penmanship," and judges therefore resort to judicial doctrines "to cut through, rather than unravel, the Gordian knot." His related thesis was that judges

---

[214] Joseph Isenbergh, "Musings on Form and Substance in Taxation", 49 *University of Chicago Law Review* 859-884 (1982), 880 (arguing that none of the cases where judicial doctrines were used overcame the necessity of amending the law).

[215] Daniel N. Shaviro & David A. Weisbach, "The Fifth Circuit Gets it Wrong in Compaq v. Commissioner", 94 *Tax Notes* 511-518, (Jan. 28, 2002), 511 (although also arguing that the courts frequently do not "understand the doctrines they are applying").

have "the desire not to look naïve", and their judgments "display the tone of one who wants very much not to be taken in."[216]

This is an unhappy view of the judiciary, that does not allow room for the obvious possibility that judges are at least sometimes motivated by their desire to see that tax legislation is not undermined by excessive allegiance to a technical reading of words, that is itself often suspect. One might also fairly question whether there is really any "glory" to be obtained through the resort to judicial doctrines in tax avoidance cases, given the limited extent of the community's knowledge about the existence, much less the content, of the judiciary's decisions in tax cases. As to Professor Isenbergh's point about judges resorting to judicial doctrines because they do not wish to look naive, it might as fairly be suggested that judges who do not use judicial doctrines in tax avoidance cases are governed by a desire not to be seen by members of the business community and the tax profession as capitulating to the evil forces of taxation. As there is no empirical support for either claim, they are of little value, and would not be worthy of mention if not for Professor Isenbergh's stature.[217]

Another criticism of the use of judicial doctrines in tax cases is that they have been said to be used only to justify decisions in favour of government. However a quantitative assessment by Professor Schneider of the use of judicial doctrines in federal tax cases

---

[216] Isenbergh, *supra* no. 214 at 882 ("Little attention is drawn to those [judges] who hew narrowly to technical rules").

[217] Robert Thornton Smith, "Business Purpose: The Assault Upon The Citadel", 53 *Tax Lawyer* 1-34 (1999), 2 (Professor Isenbergh is described by Smith as "perhaps the harshest critic of the economic substance doctrine"); see also: Weisbach, *supra* no. 15 at 219 (in response to Isenbergh's comment that "there is no natural law of reverse triangular mergers", in arguing for literal interpretation of tax statutes, Smith says that "It simply does not follow that because Congress is creating formal requirements for a particular treatment that it cannot restrict the treatment in any way it chooses, including restricting them on the basis of business purpose, motive, economic substance, or whether the documents are written in Egyptian hieroglyphics. Congress could add to the list of requirements for reverse triangular mergers any of the doctrines Isenbergh disparaged.")

decided by trial courts in the U.S. shows that the assumption underlying this criticism is incorrect, and that judicial doctrines are actually asserted by taxpayers in many cases, and are applied by the judiciary for the benefit of taxpayers.[218]

Nevertheless, one advantage of judicial doctrines is that they can help to somewhat level the playing field between government and large corporations. In major tax avoidance disputes, where very significant amounts of money are involved, governments are invariably outgunned, as large corporate taxpayers are in a position "to hire ten times as many people and pay them each ten times as much."[219] This phenomenon is well-illustrated recently in Canada, where the government was represented by three (3) counsel and the taxpayer tendered its bill of costs for the services of seventy-seven (77) counsel, in a single case heard by the Tax Court of Canada.[220] In the face of this sort of uneven playing field, judicial doctrines can provide an attractive avenue for government counsel to argue against abusive tax avoidance by enabling attacks on the relatively-straightforward basis that the legislature could not have intended to sanction transactions with no reason for existing other than to obtain tax benefits.[221]

---

[218] Daniel M. Schneider, "Use of Judicial Doctrines in Federal Tax Cases Decided By Trial Courts, 1993-2006: A Quantitative Assessment", 57 *Cleveland State Law Review* 35-75 (2009), 70 (observing that there should be more empirical research done concerning the use of judicial doctrines in tax so a greater understanding can be gained as to how they are used)

[219] Hariton, *supra* no. 2 at 33 (arguing that for this and other reasons "there must be a rule that allows the [Internal Revenue] Service to disallow tax benefits not on technical grounds, but rather because the transaction is a tax shelter and allowing the result to stand would therefore undermine the tax system and ultimately prevent the Service from collecting any revenue at all.")

[220] *General Electric Capital Canada Inc. v. R.*, 2010 TCC 490 (T.C.C. [General Procedure]).

[221] Gerald W. Miller, Jr., "Corporate Tax Shelters and Economic Substance: An Analysis of the Problem and its Common Law Solution", 34 *Texas Tech Law Review* 1015-1069 (2003), 1027 (stating that the U.S. economic substance doctrine enables government counsel to argue that Congress "surely" could not have intended to endorse tax shelter transactions without economic substance which have been engineered entirely on the basis that they will achieve tax benefits.)

MacKnight has also noted, quoting the words of an American legislator, that fairness requires that there must be room for judgment in the application of technical tax rules: "General principles are often better than detailed rules. All too often, detailed rules result in the worst of both worlds – they suffocate the many taxpayers who try to do what's right, or provide a road map for the few with larceny in their hearts."[222]

Given all of the above, it is apparent that judicial doctrines, coupled with technical tax rules, are essential in defending against the tax system being undermined by abusive tax avoidance. In the next chapter I examine the common law judicial doctrines in Canada that have historically been applied in a tax avoidance context and I explain why they are deficient vis-à-vis the important realm of economic substance.

---

[222] Robin J. MacKnight, "Cabbages and Soda: A Skeptic's Review of Tax Shelters", 1993 *Conference Report* (Toronto: Canadian Tax Foundation, 1994) 50:1-50, 50:29-30, quoting Memorandum from Fred Goldberg et al to All Employees of the office of Chief Counsel, All Employees of the Office of Tax Policy, and All Assistants to the Commissioner (May 1, 1992), cited in John A. Miller, "Indeterminacy, Complexity, and Fairness: Justifying Rule Simplification in the Law of Taxation", 69 *Washington Law Review* 1-78 (1993), 4, footnote 14.

IV

Limits of Judicial Doctrines in Canada

Given my conclusion that the application of judicial doctrines is vital in the realm of efforts to counter abusive tax avoidance, it is important to examine the judicial doctrines that are now in place in Canada in order to determine their breadth. I undertake the examination in this chapter and I conclude that our present judicial doctrines are inadequate to contend with abusive tax avoidance transactions without economic substance.

The courts in Canada are now using limited non-statutory approaches in determining the legitimacy of transactions in tax avoidance cases.[223] These include assessing whether transactions are legally effective, having regard to their degree of completeness; identifying the actual as opposed to the nominal transaction under

---

[223] Debenham, *supra* note 5 at 13; see also: Johnson, *supra* no. 15 at 445 (speaking of non-statutory approaches in a U.S. context: "There is a judge-made common law of tax, which has a number of equitable or antiabuse doctrines. ... The court-made equitable doctrines such as substance over form, sham transaction, and step transaction give the law a vigor that helps the law defend against aggressive misinterpretations of the statute to avoid tax.")

the common law doctrine of substance versus form; and, setting aside transactions on the basis that they have been misrepresented by the taxpayer, with a view to deceiving the tax collector as to their real nature, and are hence contrary to the common law doctrine of sham.[224] These limited approaches are not broad enough to counter the serious problems caused by the proliferation of transactions, without economic substance, which have been created by sophisticated tax planning, primarily in order to obtain tax benefits.[225]

LEGAL INEFFECTIVENESS

Transactions are sometimes, but not invariably, held by the courts to be legally ineffective, and set aside for tax purposes, when there has been a failure to comply with legal formalities: "[I]t is necessary to examine the documents outlining the transaction to determine whether the parties have satisfied the legal requirements of creating the legal entity it sought to create."[226] For example, the Tax Court found that a $35 million loan with a 49 page loan agreement

---

[224] Schneider, *supra* no. 218 at 63 (there is also a not-as-frequently utilized step transaction common law doctrine in the U.S., which does not have a counterpart in Canada) also see: Bleiwas and Hutson, *supra* no. 17, c. 16, IV. Judicial Anti-Avoidance Doctrines, B. Judicial Doctrines (setting out business purpose test, sham, incomplete versus illegal transactions, agency, piercing the corporate veil, step transactions, abuse of law, object and spirit, and substance over form as rules that have been developed by the courts re tax avoidance. Also noting that the step transaction doctrine has only been expressly raised once in a court case in Canada and that the Minister's arguments were dismissed – see *Lutheran Life Insurance Society of Canada v. R.* (1991), 91 D.T.C. 5553 (Fed. T.D.)); several commentators have also noted that the differences between anti-avoidance common law doctrines are not large – in a U.S. context the Court stated in *Rogers v. U.S.*, 281 F.3d 1108 (10th Cir., 2002) at p. 115 "It is evident that the distinctions among the judicial standards which may be used in *ex post facto* challenges to particular tax results – such as substance over form, substantive sham/economic substance, and business purpose are not vast."

[225] Arnold, *supra* no. 8 at 168 (Canadian courts have rarely used judicial anti-avoidance doctrines to prevent abusive tax avoidance); Li, *supra* no. 8 at 45 (arguing, for example, that a transaction that is legally effective and not a sham in a legal sense may nevertheless be an economic or a substantive sham)

[226] *Continental Bank of Canada v. R.*, (*sub nom.* Continental Bank Leasing Corp. v. Canada) [1998] 2 S.C.R. 298 (S.C.C.) at para. 21.

had not been assigned when there was no formal document such as a director's resolution or an executed transfer.[227] By comparison, a sale of a business and its related assets has been held by the Supreme Court of Canada to be legally effective, although the vendor continued to hold the only licence for the operation of the business after its sale, and a trial court had found that the assets would be re-conveyed to the vendor after the purchaser's tax losses had been utilized.[228] However, regardless of how consistently the legal effectiveness approach is applied by the courts, it does not address the problem I have identified, as transactions found to be legally effective should still be ignored for tax purposes when they are lacking in economic substance. This has been the case in the U.S. for decades – see my examination of this point in chapter VI.

SUBSTANCE VERSUS FORM

A transaction can be re-characterized by the courts under the common law substance over form doctrine[229] when the legal description given to the transaction does not accord with its substance, e.g. calling a payment "interest" did not give it that legal character, when the payment was really a commitment fee.[230] The

---

[227] *Curragh Inc. v. R.* (1994), (*sub nom.* Curragh Inc. v. Canada) [1995] 1 C.T.C. 2163 (T.C.C.); (Also see cases annotated under "Incomplete Transactions", McMechan and Bourgard, *supra* no. 19, c. 17.

[228] *Stubart Investments Ltd. v. R.*, [1984] C.T.C. 294 (S.C.C.); also see: Bleiwas and Hutson, *supra* no. 17, c. 16, IV. Judicial Anti-Avoidance Doctrines, 3. Incomplete Versus Illegal Transactions (suggesting that sometimes even an incomplete transaction may be recognized for tax purposes, citing *Ingram v. Minister of National Revenue* (1991), 91 D.T.C. 939 (T.C.C.) for the proposition).

[229] Bleiwas and Hutson, *supra* no. 17, c. 16, IV. Judicial Anti-Avoidance Doctrines, B. Judicial Doctrines, 9. Substance Over Form (suggesting that the substance over form doctrine "is possibly the most difficult anti-avoidance rule to define" and referring to Lord Russell's reasons for judgment in *Duke of Westminster* for the meaning of "substance": "If all that is meant by the doctrine [of substance over form] is that having once ascertained the legal rights of the parties you may disregard mere nomenclature and decide the question of taxability or non-taxability in accordance with the legal rights, then well and good.")

[230] *Minister of National Revenue v. Yonge-Eglinton Building Ltd.*, [1974] C.T.C. 209 (Fed. C.A.).

rationale for this substance over form approach is that a taxpayer should not be able to alter the essential nature of a transaction for income tax purposes, by giving it a different name.[231] Chief Justice Rip of the Tax Court of Canada has described the doctrine in these terms: "Calling a horse a dog does not make the horse a dog."[232] Under the substance over form approach, transactions are not disregarded for tax purposes. Rather, having regard to the characteristics which the transaction possesses, the courts are able to determine the result for tax purposes according to what transaction has actually occurred, regardless of what the parties have called it. To give another example, if a document is described as a lease (under which the payments will generally be deductible on a current basis for tax purposes), whereas the terms are such that by the time of the final payment the economic life of the asset has expired, the transaction can properly be regarded as a sale for tax purposes (under which the payments are not currently deductible as expenses, as they are considered to be instalments of the purchase price). It is worth noting, however, that the matter of whether the form or the substance of a transaction will be regarded by the courts as prevailing for tax purposes is not always obvious.

In a number of important tax cases, the Crown's submissions that taxation should be imposed by reference to the substance rather than the legal form of the transactions has been rejected by the Supreme Court, mainly upon the basis that the legal relationships entered into by taxpayers must be respected in tax cases, except in the event of sham or when there is a statutory provision to the contrary.[233] In the words of Major J., writing for the majority in *Singleton v. The Queen*, it was the "shuffle of cheques" in the transaction

---

[231] See, for example, *Carma Developers Ltd. v. R.*, [1996] 3 C.T.C. 2029 (T.C.C.), affirmed (1996), [1997] 2 C.T.C. 150 (Fed. C.A.).

[232] *Gillette Canada Inc. v. R.*, [2001] 4 C.T.C. 2884 (T.C.C. [General Procedure]) at para. 25, affirmed [2003] 3 C.T.C. 27 (Fed. C.A.) (Also see cases under "Substance versus Form", McMechan and Bourgard, *supra* no. 19, c. 17.

[233] See, for example, *Shell Canada Ltd. v. R.*, (*sub nom.* Shell Canada Ltd. v. Canada) [1999] 3 S.C.R. 622 (S.C.C.) at para. 39, per McLachlin J.: "[A]bsent a specific provision of the Act to the contrary or a finding that they are a sham, the taxpayer's legal relationships must be respected in tax cases."

by the taxpayer which defined the legal relationship that had to be given effect.[234] By contrast, in the Federal Court of Appeal's first substantive (not interlocutory) decision in a transfer pricing case, which involved the sale of the pharmaceutical active ingredient ranitidine under a supply agreement with an entity that could only supply ranitidine, and which itself owned no intangibles, it held that the "business reality" of the purchaser's participation in a multinational group of companies had to be taken into account in determining the arm's length price for the sale of the ranitidine by the entity.[235]

This is peculiar, as for the most part Canadian courts say, subject to whether the transaction has been correctly characterized, that once a taxpayer has chosen the form of a transaction it is unable to maintain for tax purposes that a different legal relationship exists which is more consistent with the business realities.[236] In this respect the Canadian substance versus form doctrine differs from substance versus form's application in the U.S., where taxpayers are sometimes permitted to repudiate the form of transactions they have chosen when they can show that form conflicts with economic reality.[237]

---

[234] *Singleton v. R.*, (*sub nom.* Singleton v. Canada) [2001] 2 S.C.R. 1046 (S.C.C.) at para. 32, per Major. J.

[235] *GlaxoSmithKline Inc. v. R.*, [2010] 6 C.T.C. 220 (F.C.A.), affirmed 2012 CarswellNat 3880 (S.C.C.). Judgment in the appeal was released by the Supreme Court of Canada on October 18, 2012, which was well after the manuscript for this edition of my book was completed.

[236] The courts have consistently held that nomenclature does not govern, and that it is the legal (not economic) substance of the taxpayer's arrangements that must be given effect to for tax purposes. See the cases annotated under "Substance versus Form", McMechan and Bourgard, *supra* no. 19, c. 17.

[237] Ray Knight and Lee Knight, "Substance Over Form: The Cornerstone of Our Tax System or a Lethal Weapon in the IRS'S Arsenal?", 8 *Akron Tax Journal* 91 (1991), 103-105 (noting that both the IRS and taxpayers can invoke the substance versus form doctrine in the U.S. although the matters of when the doctrine will apply and in whose favour are difficult to predict); Bleiwas and Hutson, *supra* no. 17, c. 16, B. Judicial Doctrines, 9. Substance Over Form (suggesting that the US Supreme Court's decision in *C.I.R. v. Court Holding Co.*, 324 U.S. 331 (1945) can on a broad reading be interpreted as saying that "the means employed to transfer a legal title" cannot by themselves govern

However, variations in the scope, and inconsistency in the application of the substance versus form doctrine, are not what renders it inadequate as a response to transactions without economic substance that have been entered into primarily in order to secure tax benefits.[238] The important limitation of the substance over form doctrine, as it is employed in Canada, is that it only permits the legal re-characterization of transactions when the transactions have not been correctly described, whereas transactions which have been correctly characterized but lack economic substance should be entirely disregarded for tax purposes, as they have been for decades under the U.S. judiciary's economic substance doctrine. This is the appropriate tax result as, if it is possible to deprive the treasury of revenues by implementing transactions without economic consequences, which have been engineered to create deductions, taxation will be "optional" for taxpayers who are well enough off to engage in sophisticated tax avoidance arrangements.[239]

---

the tax consequences of a sale, and that this is the opposite of the position taken by Lord Russell in *Duke of Westminster*); Richard M. Lipton, "Going to Trial is No Guarantee of Success in A Silo Case if Non-Tax Purpose is Lacking", *Journal of Taxation* 205-212 (April 2010), 209 (noting that under the U.S. version of the substance versus form doctrine "The Court makes its determinations by reference to the substance of transactions rather than their form. The forms, titles, and labels placed on the transaction do not control; the court looks at the objective economic realities of the transaction.")

[238] Julie Cassidy, "The holy grail: The search for the optimal gaar", vol. 129, no. 4 *South African Law Journal* 740-779 (2009), footnote 24 (citing the SARS Tax Avoidance Interim Response re proposed amendments to section 103 of the *Income Tax Act*, as indicating that the common law substance over form doctrine was inadequate to combat many tax avoidance schemes because the underlying legal agreements are generally found to be technically valid)

[239] See, for example, the assessment of the impact of foreign tax credit generator transactions in the case study in chapter IX involving *4145356 Canada Ltd. v. R.*, 2011 TCC 220 (T.C.C. [General Procedure]): "FTC generators – if they work – can be scaled up to wipe out almost any amount of ... tax liability, assuming a willing foreign counterparty."–Thomas D. Greenaway, "International Tax Arbitrage: A Frozen Debate Thaws", 126 *Tax Notes* 631-639 (Feb. 1, 2010), 637, footnote 44

SHAM

Transactions are occasionally entirely disregarded for tax purposes by the courts in Canada under the common law doctrine of sham; however, sham requires proof of deceit by the taxpayer,[240] and it is not often employed for this reason.[241] An example of a sham is where the taxpayer was found to have created misleading documents, to attempt to convince the Minister that the rights and obligations were different from those which the parties intended to create, in circumstances where a purported consulting agreement was never intended to be acted upon and the payments pursuant to the arrangement were payments for the purchase of shares, rather than for services.[242] As a sham will not be found to exist in the absence of proof of deceit by the taxpayer, and deceit is very difficult to establish, the Crown has often argued unsuccessfully for the application of the sham doctrine.[243] In any event, transactions entered into primarily for the purpose of obtaining tax benefits, which have no economic substance but do not involve arrangements calculated to deceive the Minister, are not ignored for tax purposes under the sham doctrine.[244] This means that sham is also an inadequate response to transactions without economic substance which have been created in order to secure tax benefits.

---

[240] *Bonavia v. R.*, [2010] 6 C.T.C. 99 (F.C.A.) at para. 7 (the application of the common law doctrine of sham is restricted to circumstances where it is the taxpayer who has deceived the Minister of Revenue)

[241] Keith Kendall, "The Structural Approach to Tax Avoidance in Australia", vol. 9, no. 5 *The Tax Specialist* 290-298 (2006), 294 (noting that because of the generally sophisticated nature of tax planning, most arrangements are not so blatant that they are considered to be a sham)

[242] *Foresbec Inc. c. R.* (2001), [2002] 2 C.T.C. 2683 (T.C.C. [General Procedure]), affirmed (2002), [2003] 3 C.T.C. 374 (Fed. C.A.)

[243] See cases annotated under "Sham", McMechan and Bourgard, *supra* no. 19. c. 17.

[244] *McEwen Brothers Ltd. v. R.*, [1999] 3 C.T.C. 373 (Fed. C.A.) (holding that a transaction which lacks any purpose other than the attainment of a tax benefit is not a sham, in the absence of the element of deceit) (Note also, however, the existence of a no longer authoritative line of case law to the effect that "If the agreement or transaction lacks a *bona fide* business purpose, it is a sham." – *Minister of National Revenue v. Leon*, [1976] C.T.C. 532 (Fed. C.A.) at para. 20, per Heald J)

Both the substance versus form and sham doctrines involve the courts ultimately taxing a different transaction than the transaction represented by the taxpayer. The economic substance doctrine, however, is not concerned with whether what has actually occurred is different from the manner in which the transaction has been represented to others. In this regard, it is important to understand that an economic substance test does not involve re-characterizing transactions that have occurred, i.e. there is no body of law that mandates recognition of what has been called "economic substance over legal form."[245] Rather, under the economic substance doctrine, the identity of the transactions is not challenged; but, notwithstanding their identity, the transactions can be disregarded for tax purposes, if the tests under the economic substance doctrine are not met.[246] And, this is subject to the caveat that even transactions without economic substance will be upheld for tax purposes, when the tax benefits were legislatively intended. According to Professor Arnold, this point that an economic substance test does not involve the re-characterization of a transaction's legal form has not been universally well-understood.[247] This has been apparent in some GAAR decisions, where government arguments based on economic substance have been rejected on the basis that they depended upon re-characterization.[248]

---

[245] Arnold, *supra* no. 130 at 34, footnote 16 (noting that Lord Atkin's dissent in the *Duke of Westminster* case did not turn upon re-characterizing the transactions according to a doctrine of economic substance over legal form).

[246] Luke, *supra* no. 68 at 790 (the court determines whether the transaction should be ignored for tax purposes even though it factually took place)

[247] Arnold, *supra* no. 129 (noting, however, that in the Tax Court's decisions in *McNichol v. R.*, [1997] 2 C.T.C. 2088 (T.C.C.) and *RMM Canadian Enterprises Inc. v. R.* (1997), [1998] 1 C.T.C. 2300 (T.C.C.), additional reasons [1997] 3 C.T.C. 2103 (T.C.C.) the economic substance of the transactions was considered in the subsection 245(4) ITA analysis, in concluding that the statutory scheme had been abused)

[248] Arnold, *supra* no. 8 at 167, 172 (referring to the finding in *Canadian Pacific Ltd. v. R.* (2001), [2002] 2 C.T.C. 197 (Fed. C.A.) at para. 30, reconsideration / rehearing refused [2002] 2 C.T.C. 150 (Fed. C.A.) that accepting an argument that a weak-currency borrowing through a series of swap contracts was in economic substance a borrowing in Canadian currency would entail re-characterizing payments of interest as principal)

BUSINESS PURPOSE

The courts in Canada, unlike in a number of other jurisdictions, do not employ a common law business purpose test,[249] because of the Supreme Court's decision in *Stubart Investments Limited v. The Queen*.[250] This has been partly addressed through the enactment of GAAR, by way of the requirement in subsection 245(3) of the Act for the determination of whether it may reasonably be considered that a transaction has been undertaken or arranged primarily for *bona fide* purposes other than to obtain a tax benefit, in the definition of "avoidance transaction."[251]

Nevertheless, in a GAAR context the absence of a primary non-tax business purpose, by itself, will not result in the denial of tax benefits, although the transactions entered into lacked economic substance.[252] Moreover, the Supreme Court has held repeatedly that

---

[249] Weisbach, *supra* no. 15 at 252 (arguing "[T]here are good reasons to base anti-avoidance doctrines on motive or intent. There is a difference between somebody engaging in a transaction for purely business reasons that happen to have fantastic tax consequences and somebody entering into the transaction solely to limit taxes. In the former case, where the taxpayer enters into the transaction for business reasons, there is no economic distortion caused by taxes – while the person pays low taxes, behavior is not distorted by this prospect. In the latter case, where the motive is taxes, behavior is distorted, and there are real economic costs. The two cases are different precisely because of mental states.")

[250] *Stubart Investments Ltd. v. R.*, [1984] C.T.C. 294 (S.C.C.) at para. 23: ("[T]he law in Canada as regards the right of a taxpayer to order his affairs so as to reduce his tax liability without breaching any express term in the statute ... is found in *Bradford (City) v. Pickles*, [1895] A.C. 587 (U.K. H.L.) where it was stated: 'If it was a lawful act, however ill the motive might be, he had a right to do it.'").

[251] "Avoidance transaction" is defined in subsec. 245(3) of the *Income Tax Act* as "any transaction that, but for this section, would result, directly or indirectly, in a tax benefit, unless the transaction may reasonably be considered to have been undertaken or arranged primarily for *bona fide* purposes other than to obtain the tax benefit."

[252] *Canada Trustco Mortgage Co. v. R.*, [2005] 5 C.T.C. 215 (S.C.C.) at para. 17 ("The application of the GAAR involves three steps. The first step is to determine whether there is a 'tax benefit' arising from a 'transaction' under s. 245(1) and (2). The second step is to determine whether the transaction is an avoidance transaction under s. 245(3), in the sense of not being 'arranged

transactions entered into without any purpose other than to obtain a tax benefit must be respected for tax purposes.[253] For example, the creation of a company and declaration of dividends to a non-participating spouse, for the sole purpose of splitting income from the taxpayer's business with the spouse, has been upheld for tax purposes.[254] Similarly, the structuring of a complex set of transactions with a view to surrendering fleeting "control" of a company in order to facilitate a sale of non-capital losses to an otherwise arm's-length taxpayer has been upheld by the Court.[255]

Given the limited reach of these few judicial approaches in Canada, and of our GAAR as interpreted by the Supreme Court, there is a large gap in the present defences against abusive tax avoidance, because the courts are not able to set aside transactions that have been entered into primarily for the purpose of obtaining tax benefits because they lack economic substance.

As I have explained in chapter II, this state of affairs gives rise to a number of problems that are associated with unchecked abusive tax avoidance including (1) loss of confidence in the fairness of the taxation system, with a resulting less than favourable climate for compliance; (2) an inordinate and disproportionate share

---

primarily for *bona fide* purposes other than to obtain the tax benefit'. The third step is to determine whether the avoidance transaction is abusive under s. 245(4). All three requirements must be fulfilled before the GAAR can be applied to deny a tax benefit."

[253] *Entreprises Ludco ltée c. Canada* (2001), [2002] 1 C.T.C. 95 (S.C.C.) at para. 39 ("[A]bsent a provision to the contrary, taxpayers are entitled to arrange their affairs for the sole purpose of achieving a favourable position regarding taxation; also see: *Stubart*, *supra* at p. 540 *per* Wilson J., and at p. 557 *per* Estey J.; *Hickman Motors Ltd. v. R.*, [1997] 2 S.C.R. 336 (S.C.C.) at para. 8, *per* McLachlin J.; *Duha Printers (Western) Ltd. v. R.*, (*sub nom.* Duha Printers (Western) Ltd. v. Canada) [1998] 1 S.C.R. 795 (S.C.C.) at para. 88, *per* Iacobucci J.; *Neuman*, *supra*, at para. 63, *per* Iacobucci J.; *Shell Canada Ltd.*, *supra*, at para. 46, *per* McLachlin J.")

[254] *Neuman v. Minister of National Revenue*, [1998] 3 C.T.C. 177 (S.C.C.); also see: Brian J. Arnold, "Canada's Top Court Approves Income-Splitting Scheme", *International Tax News* 1829-1831 (June 15, 1988).

[255] *Mara Properties Ltd. v. R.*, [1996] 2 C.T.C. 54 (S.C.C.). The Supreme Court's decision in *Mara Properties* is reviewed in chapter V; see also: cases annotated under "Tax Planning", McMechan and Bourgard, *supra* no. 19, c. 17.

of taxation burdens by those, such as lower income salaried workers, who are not positioned to benefit from structured tax avoidance arrangements; (3) loss of the tax revenues that are required by governments to fund essential spending in important areas such as education, defence, health care, international aid, old age security and public works, to name a few; and huge compliance costs due to the resulting complexity of the *ad hoc* technical fixes.[256]

In the next chapter I examine the repeated preference of the Supreme Court of Canada for reliance on technical rules as the method of dealing with abusive tax avoidance, and I argue that its position has not been well thought-out, nor advanced on the basis of any principled analysis.

---

[256] See the examination of the effects of unchecked abusive tax avoidance in chapter II.

V

SCC's Treatment of Economic Substance

In this chapter I examine the Supreme Court of Canada's historical treatment of economic substance, and I note that it has been inconsistent; plus, I argue that the reasons relied upon by the Supreme Court for its refusal to endorse economic substance as an important indicator of abusive tax avoidance do not stand up to serious scrutiny.

The Supreme Court's treatment of economic substance or realities (and commercial realities) in tax cases has followed a very winding road. A major premise behind the concept of economic substance is the belief that legal substance on its own is not invariably the appropriate platform upon which to base taxation.[257] In this regard, the Supreme Court occasionally found in times past that legal form did not govern the result in tax cases. Estey J. wrote

---

[257] Freedman, *supra* no. 21 at 343 (noting a tax system has to be founded on legal reality rather than economic reality, "because that is the only practicable and operable way to construct a tax system. ... Legal reality may often be trying to reflect some sort of commercial or economic reality but it will not achieve this in every case.").

in 1985, for example, for a majority of the Court in *R. v. Imperial General Properties Ltd.*, when considering a control issue under the *Income Tax Act*, that "the court is not limited to a highly technical and narrow interpretation of the legal rights attached to the shares of a corporation."[258] Similarly, in *Johns-Manville Canada Inc. v. R.*[259] the Court quoted with approval from *B.P. Australia Ltd. v. Commissioner of Taxation of Australia*,[260] where Lord Pearce stated that the distinction between capital outlays and current expenses "depends on what the expenditure is calculated to effect from a practical and business point of view rather than upon the juristic classification of legal rights ...."[261] The Supreme Court also held in *Canadian Marconi Co. v. R.* that interest earned on short-term securities was income from business, rather than income from property, as the commercial reality was that the taxpayer was compelled to enter into the investment business, rather than the broadcasting or electronic manufacturing business, because of a forced sale of its broadcasting division by the C.R.T.C.[262] These cases represent instances where legal form alone did not dictate results.

LEGAL FORM TRUMPS ECONOMIC SUBSTANCE IN TAX CASES

More recently, however, the Supreme Court's position in tax avoidance cases has been that legal form and legal relationships are of paramount importance. Professor Philipps says the Court's approach to characterizing transactions has been to apply a "doctrine of form over substance", which means "transactions are to be characterized for tax purposes according to their legal form rather than their commercial or economic substance."[263] Moreover, the

---

[258] [1985] 2 C.T.C. 299 (S.C.C.) at para. 11.
[259] [1985] 2 S.C.R. 46 (S.C.C.).
[260] (1965), [1966] A.C. 224 (Australia P.C.).
[261] *Hallstrom's Propriety Ltd. v. Federal Commissioner of Taxation* (1946), 72 C.L.R. 634 at p. 648, per Dixon J..
[262] [1986] 2 C.T.C. 465 (S.C.C.) at para. 12.
[263] Lisa Philipps, "The Supreme Court of Canada's Tax Jurisprudence: What's Wrong with the Rule of Law?", 79 *Canadian Bar Review* 120-144 (2000),

statement by Lord Tomlin in the *Duke of Westminster* case that "[e]very man is entitled if he can to order his affairs so as that the tax attaching under the appropriate Acts is less than it otherwise would be."[264] has frequently been relied upon by the Court as a reason for upholding legal relationships in tax cases.[265] The Court's position has been that respecting taxpayers' legal relationships, regardless of whether they have economic substance, is an essential corollary of its position that "taxpayers are entitled to arrange their affairs for the sole purpose of achieving a favourable position regarding taxation."[266]

The Court's position in this regard is very different from that of the courts in the U.S., as transactions governed by legal relationships which are valid in the U.S. are nevertheless disregarded if they are also found not to have enough economic substance to be

---

126 (the Court's position is closely related to the traditional rule as to the necessity for the strict construction of taxation statutes. Although the strict construction approach to statutory interpretation has been replaced by the modern approach to statutory interpretation "its legacy remains strong")

[264] *Inland Revenue Commissioners v. Duke of Westminster* (1935), [1936] A.C. 1 (U.K. H.L.) at p. 19; also see: Shaw, Slemrod and Whiting, *supra* no. 140 at 1152 (commenting with reference to the *Duke of Westminster* case: "there is undoubtedly room for the view that the U.K.'s tax system, with its reliance on legal 'form' rather than on economic or financial 'substance', is particularly open to avoidance.")

[265] Arnold, *supra* no. 130 at 13-15 (the Supreme Court of Canada repeatedly endorses the *Duke of Westminster* principle as "a matter of blind belief, an article of faith", without analyzing "the principle, its origins and rationale, or its appropriateness as part of the Canadian tax system 65 years after it was enunciated by the House of Lords.")

[266] Lisa T. Wong, "Goodbye 'Economic Realities', Hello 'Legal Substance'", (2001) vol. 49, no. 6 CTJ 1571-1575 (the Supreme Court has repeatedly taken this position in *Stubart Investments Ltd. v. R.*, [1984] 1 S.C.R. 536 (S.C.C.) at para. 71, per Wilson J.; *Hickman Motors Ltd. v. R.*, [1997] 2 S.C.R. 336 (S.C.C.) at para. 8, per McLachlin J.; *Duha Printers (Western) Ltd. v. R.*, (*sub nom.* Duha Printers (Western) Ltd. v. Canada) [1998] 1 S.C.R. 795 (S.C.C.) at para. 87, per Iacobucci J.; *Neuman v. Minister of National Revenue*, [1998] 1 S.C.R. 770 (S.C.C.) at para. 63, per Iacobucci J.; *Shell Canada Ltd. v. R.*, (*sub nom.* Shell Canada Ltd. v. Canada) [1999] 3 S.C.R. 622 (S.C.C.) at para. 46, per McLachlin J.; *Entreprises Ludco ltée c. Canada*, (*sub nom.* Ludco Enterprises Ltd. v. Canada) [2001] 2 S.C.R. 1082 (S.C.C.)) at para. 39, per Iacobucci J.)

respected for tax purposes, unless their tax results clearly concord with congressional intent.

Since the *Duke of Westminster* case has figured so prominently in the Supreme Court's reasoning regarding the courts not having an active role to play in opposition to unacceptable tax avoidance, the facts of the case are worth reviewing. The Duke wanted to deduct wages and salaries he was paying to his servants, in order to avoid surtaxes. British law did not permit such deductions, but it did allow taxpayers to deduct "annuities" and other "annual payments." The Duke therefore entered into agreements with his servants under which he would pay them an annuity for the period of seven years or their joint lives, whichever was shorter. Although the payments made under the agreements were equivalent to the salaries that were being paid to the servants before the new annuity arrangements were struck, and the servants formally agreed that they would not seek payment of additional amounts for salary,[267] the annuity payments were purportedly unrelated to the servants' services.[268] Remarkably, the House of Lords, with Lord Atkin dissenting, held that the legal form of the annuity arrangements could not be ignored and permitted the deduction of the annuity payments to the servants, allowing the Duke's appeal.[269]

---

[267] Duff, *supra* no. 150 at 528 (noting that the deed of covenant that the Duke entered into was intended to convert non-deductible payments for services to his gardener into deductible "annual payments" under the U.K *Income Tax Act, 1918*. The deed contained a provision stating that the gardener was not expected to claim payment for his services so long as the payments he received under the deed equaled the salary he'd been receiving.)

[268] Assaf Likhovski, "The Duke and The Lady: Helvering v. Gregory and The History of Tax Avoidance Adjudication", 25 *Cardozo Law Review* 953-1018 (2004), 963 (noting that the annuity payments to the servants were "supposedly unrelated to the services they were providing' and also that "the Duke case has been the cornerstone of a narrow, literal, pro-taxpayer approach" to tax avoidance which dominated until the 1960's)

[269] *Inland Revenue Commissioners v. Duke of Westminster*, [1935] All E.R. 259 (U.K. H.L.) at p. 265, per Lord Atkin dissenting on the basis that the substance of the transaction was that the Duke was paying his employees remuneration; see also: Arnold, *supra* no. 130 at 5-6 (suggesting that the annuities arrangement was arguably a sham, as the servants formally agreed not to seek payment of the wages owing to them. Moreover, the *Duke of Westminster*

However, the House of Lords also held many years later in *W.T. Ramsay Ltd. v. Inland Revenue Commissioners* that the *Duke of Westminster* principle does not apply to tax avoidance.[270] This important qualification vis-à-vis tax avoidance was later stated again by the House of Lords in *Inland Revenue Commissioners v. McGuckian*: "While Lord Tomlin's observations in the *Duke of Westminster's* case still point to a material consideration, namely the general liberty of the citizen to arrange his financial affairs as he thinks fit, they have ceased to be canonical as to the consequences of a tax avoidance scheme."[271]

Following the House of Lords decision in *Ramsay*, senior tax practitioners in Canada considered that "[w]hile the Duke may not be dead, he has been wounded",[272] and they viewed *Ramsay* as a "potentially significant departure" from the *Duke of Westminster*.[273] Despite this, and until 2005 in the first of its decisions under GAAR in which the Supreme Court conceded that the *Duke* principle "may be attenuated" in Canada,[274] it continued to steadfastly pledge its allegiance to the *Duke* of *Westminster* principle. This position of the

---

decision is based on the principle of strict construction of taxing statutes, which holds that taxpayers are not subject to tax unless they fall within the literal words of the statute. However, the Supreme Court's adoption in the *Stubart* case of a modern day non-literalist approach to interpreting taxing statues should have called the continuing applicability of the principle stated in the *Duke of Westminster* case into question.)

[270] *W.T. Ramsay Ltd. v. Inland Revenue Commissioners*, [1981] 2 W.L.R. 449 (U.K. H.L.) at p. 459, per Lord Wilberforce.

[271] *Inland Revenue Commissioners v. McGuckian*, [1997] 3 All E.R. 817 (N.I. H.L.) at p. 825, per Lord Steyn.

[272] Tom McDonnell, "Business Purpose Test – Whither the Duke's Case?", (1981) vol. 29, no. 2 C.T.J. 184-192, 188 (noting "the obvious difference [of effective tax planning arrangements upheld by the House of Lords] with the *Ramsay* type of case was the absence of a series of inherently artificial transactions which, when taken together, had no real economic substance.")

[273] David A. Ward and Maurice C. Cullity, "Abuse of Rights and the Business Purpose Test as Applied to Taxing Statutes", (1981) vol. 29, no. 4 C.T.J. 451-475, 464 (noting "apart from the tax benefits that the taxpayer hoped to achieve [in *Ramsay*], the economic position of the taxpayer remained unchanged.")

[274] *Canada Trustco Mortgage Co. v. R.*, [2005] 5 C.T.C. 215 (S.C.C.) at para. 13.

Supreme Court of Canada has been said by Professor Arnold to be in "startling contrast" with that of the House of Lords.[275]

The historical evolution of the Supreme Court's position on the role of economic and commercial realities in tax cases is unusual, to say the least. Although in 1984, in *Stubart Investments Ltd. v. R.*, it emphasized the importance of the *Duke of Westminster* principle,[276] the Court stated three years later in *Bronfman Trust v. R.* that reliance on commercial and economic realities, rather than juristic classification of form, was a "laudable trend."[277] The Supreme Court's decision in *Bronfman Trust* is the high-water mark in terms of its endorsement of the importance of examining commercial and economic realities in tax cases,[278] although Felesky and Jacks have argued that, considered in context, the Court was really only commenting on the relevance of commercial and economic realities for the limited purpose of determining subjective income earning purpose.[279] Nevertheless, in the

---

[275] See Arnold, *supra* no. 130 at 26 (the House of Lords decisions "grapple with the appropriate role for a court in dealing with tax avoidance schemes" whereas the Supreme Court of Canada "simply states, without analysis, that the role of the courts is simply to interpret and apply the law and not to prevent taxpayers from engaging in tax-avoidance schemes").

[276] [1984] 1 S.C.R. 536 (S.C.C.) at paras. 23 and 71.

[277] [1987] 1 S.C.R. 32 (S.C.C.) at para. 40.

[278] Diksic, *supra* no. 9 at 25:1-34 (suggesting that the Supreme Court's decisions in *Bronfman Trust v. The Queen* and *McClurg v. M.N.R.* "represented somewhat of a high point for economic substance in Canadian jurisprudence."; see also: Duff, *supra* no. 150 at 538-540 ("[T]he Supreme Court of Canada's decision in *Bronfman Trust* ... stands out for its explicit disapproval of the traditional Anglo-Canadian approach, according to which tax consequences should depend on the legal form of transactions and relationships regardless of their commercial or economic reality.")

[279] Felesky and Jack, *supra* no. 9 at 50:33 (commenting that it is perplexing that after endorsing a broad look into commercial and economic realities, the Court took a strict approach in interpreting para. 20(1)(c) of the Act); see also: Bleiwas and Hutson, *supra* no. 17, c. 16, B. Judicial Doctrines, 9. Substance Over Form, b. Substance over Form in Canada ("it appears that the majority [in *Bronfman Trust*] is saying that as long as the form of the transaction (that is, the true legal rights and obligations of the parties as determined by non-tax law) is valid, the form determines the economic and commercial realities of the transaction." Also arguing, however, that in *Inland Revenue Commissioner v. Wattie*, [1998] S.T.C. 1160 (N.Z. P.C.) the Supreme Court's position has been

Supreme Court's decision in 1996 in *Tennant v. R.*,[280] the taxpayer was permitted to deduct the amount of interest payable on a loan for $1 million, although he had exchanged the original investment for one with a value of only $1,000. The Supreme Court reasoned that although at the time of assessment the taxpayer was only using $1,000 for the purposes of earning income from property, the "economic reality" of the situation was that he had originally borrowed $1 million for the purpose of investment.[281] Here the legal form of the transaction did not govern the result.

In writing the *Tennant* decision, Iacobucci J. referred, with approval, to Professor Krishna's complaint that earlier lower court rulings about interest deductibility ending where a related source of income ceased to exist "... may be logical from a technical source perspective but [they do] little to promote the commercial and economic substance of the transactions."[282] Iacobucci J. also wrote that "[a]s Dickson C.J. stated in *Bronfman Trust* ..., the courts should strive to focus on the economic realities of a transaction rather than juristic classifications."[283] Iacobucci J. also quoted, with approval, Dickson C.J.'s comments in *Bronfman Trust*, concerning reliance upon commercial and economic realities:

> I acknowledge ... that just as there has been a recent trend away from strict construction of taxation statutes (see *Stubart Investments Ltd. v. The Queen*, [1984] 1 S.C.R. 536 at 573-79: and *The Queen v. Golden*, [1986] 1 S.C.R. 209 at 214-15); so too has the recent trend in tax cases been towards attempting to ascertain the true commercial and practical nature of the taxpayer's transactions. There has been, in this country and elsewhere, a movement away from tests based on the form of transactions and towards tests based on what Lord Pearce has referred to as a "common sense appreciation of all the guiding features" of the events in question: *B.P. Australia Ltd. v. Commissioner of Taxation of Australia*, [1966] A.C. 224 at 264, [1965] 3 All E.R. 209 at 218 (P.C.). ...

---

said to be "out of step with the rest of Commonwealth", but "the simple fact remains that the ... position is based on common sense and principle.").

[280] (*sub nom.* Tennant v. Minister of National Revenue) [1996] 1 C.T.C. 290 (S.C.C.).
[281] *Ibid.* at para. 31.
[282] *Ibid.* at para. 32.
[283] *Ibid.* at para. 31.

This is, I believe, a laudable trend provided it is consistent with the text and purposes of the taxation statute. Assessment of taxpayers' transactions with an eye to commercial and economic realities, rather than juristic classification of form, may help to avoid the inequity of tax liability being dependent upon the taxpayer's sophistication at manipulating a sequence of events to achieve a patina of compliance with the apparent prerequisites for a tax deduction.[284]

As Justice Le Bel subsequently wrote for the minority in *Singleton v. The Queen*, "[i]n a long history of cases at this Court, from *Bronfman Trust v. R.*, [1987] 1 S.C.R. 32 (S.C.C.), through *Tennant v. R.*, (*sub nom.* Tennant v. Minister of National Revenue) [1996] 1 S.C.R. 305 (S.C.C.), as well as in a number of important cases in the courts below such as *Mark Resources Inc. v. R.* (1993), 93 D.T.C. 1004 (T.C.C.), it had come to be accepted as part of the jurisprudence that, in tax cases, courts should look to the economic realities of the situation and not merely to the legal technique adopted by the taxpayer."[285]

Nevertheless, although the Court had endorsed the "laudable trend" towards "attempting to ascertain the true commercial and practical nature of the taxpayer's transactions", it later held in *Shell Canada Ltd. v. R.*, very shortly after its decision in *Tennant* approving *Bronfman*:

This Court has repeatedly held that courts must be sensitive to the economic realities of a particular transaction, rather than being bound to what first appears to be its legal form: *Bronfman Trust, supra*, at pp. 52-53, *per* Dickson C.J.; *Tennant, supra*, at para. 26, per Iacobucci J. But there are at least two *caveats* to this rule. First, this Court has never held that the economic realities of a situation can be used to recharacterize a taxpayer's *bona fide* legal relationships. To the contrary, we have held that, absent a specific provision of the Act to the contrary or a finding that they are a sham, the taxpayer's legal relationships must be respected in tax cases. Recharacterization is only permissible if the label attached by the taxpayer to the particular transaction does not properly reflect its actual legal effect: *Continental Bank of Canada v. R.*, [1998] 2 S.C.R. 298 (S.C.C.) at para. 21, *per* Bastarache J.

---

[284] *Ibid.* at para. 31.
[285] [2002] 1 C.T.C. 121 (S.C.C.) at p. 135, per Le Bel J..

Second, it is well established in this Court's tax jurisprudence that a searching inquiry for either the 'economic realities' of a particular transaction or the general object and spirit of the provision at issue can never supplant a court's duty to apply an unambiguous provision of the Act to a taxpayer's transaction. Where the provision at issue is clear and unambiguous, its terms must simply be applied: *Continental Bank of Canada, supra*, at para. 51, *per* Bastarache J.; *Tennant, supra*, at para. 16, per Iacobucci J.; *Antosko v. Minister of National Revenue*, [1994] 2 S.C.R. 312 (S.C.C.) at pp. 326-27 and 330, per Iacobucci J.; *Friesen v. R.*, [1995] 3 S.C.R. 103 (S.C.C.) at para. 11, per Major J; *Canada Trustco Mortgage Corp. v. Port O'Call Hotel Inc.*, [1996] 1 S.C.R. 963 (S.C.C.) at para. 15, per Cory J.[286]

This statement that taxpayer's legal relationships must be respected in tax cases, absent a specific provision of the Act to the contrary or a finding of sham, was a substantial departure from the Court's earlier position as to the importance of commercial and economic realities in tax cases. This observation is highlighted by the fact that there are few "specific provision[s] of the Act to the contrary",[287] and because determining that a sham exists requires hard-to-find proof that the taxpayer has deliberately constructed the form of a transaction so as to create a false impression in order to mislead the Minister.[288] Professor Arnold has said that the *Shell* decision "eviscerated" the Court's earlier decisions, amounting to a total rejection of any role for economic realities in applying tax legislation other than GAAR.[289] Professor Duff's view is that the *Shell* decision was an affirmation by the Supreme Court of the traditional Anglo-Canadian approach to tax avoidance: "the tax consequences

---

[286] (*sub nom.* Shell Canada Ltd. v. Canada) [1999] 3 S.C.R. 622 (S.C.C.) at paras. 39-40.

[287] Felesky and Jack, *supra* no. 9 at 50:45 (arguing that the fact only certain provisions of the *Income Tax Act* specifically contemplate that the consequences of a transaction may not be consistent with the legal effect thereof is strong support for the proposition that the scheme of the Act does not provide for a general economic substance doctrine).

[288] *Stubart Investments Ltd. v. R.*, [1984] 1 S.C.R. 536 (S.C.C.) at paras. 50-51.

[289] Arnold, *supra* no. 130 at 19, 21 ("[I]f economic realities cannot be used to recharacterize legal relationships except where the label attached to the relationship is inappropriate, then the legal substance of a transaction governs and there is no role at all for economic realities.")

of a particular transaction or arrangement are to be based on its legal character rather than its economic or commercial substance."[290]

The *Shell* decision was the culmination of a series of tax avoidance cases decided by the Supreme Court in which abusive tax avoidance schemes were upheld, without regard for the absence of economic substance from the transactions. Some examples of these cases follow.

Mara Properties Ltd. v. R.[291]

Mara Properties Ltd. v. R. was a "blatant tax-avoidance case"[292] which involved aggressive arm's length trading in tax losses.[293] The Appellant's counsel had stated at trial: "Now let's be clear, Your Honour. We make no bones about the fact that this was an entirely tax-motivated transaction. We make no bones about the fact that

---

[290] David G. Duff, "Weak-Currency Borrowings and the General Anti-Avoidance Rule in Canada: From Shell Canada to Canadian Pacific", *I.B.F.D. Bulletin* 233-240 (June 2001), 235-236 (noting that the traditional Anglo-Canadian approach to tax avoidance coupled with a "plain meaning" approach to statutory interpretation is to emphasize the legal character of transactions and arrangements rather than commercial or economic substance)

[291] *Mara Properties Ltd. v. R.*, (*sub nom.* R. v. Mara Properties Ltd.) [1996] 2 S.C.R. 161 (S.C.C.)

[292] Al Meghji and Gerald Grenon, "An Analysis of Recent Avoidance Cases", 1996 *Conference Report* (Toronto: Canadian Tax Foundation, 1997), 66:1-54, 66:2-3, 66:12 ("[T]he outcome in tax-avoidance cases seems often to turn as much upon the individual judge's views about the role of the judiciary in resolving such disputes as it does upon the legislation. ... The Supreme Court ... allowed the taxpayer to deduct a loss in a blatant tax-avoidance case ...."); Brian J. Arnold, "Canada's Supreme Court Holds for Taxpayer in Hickman Motors", 15 *Tax Notes International* 337 (Aug. 4, 1997)(stating "[T]he *Mara Properties* case involved another blatant tax-avoidance transaction.")

[293] Judith M. Woods, "Recent Jurisprudence", 1993 *Conference Report* (Toronto: Canadian Tax Foundation, 1994) 48:1-22, 48:13 (noting that although Revenue Canada has administratively blessed loss utilization within a related corporate group the same cannot be said of the "sale" of losses to an unrelated party); Kent Davison, "Avoidance, Evasion and the Problem Client", 1998 *Conference Report* (Toronto: Canadian Tax Foundation, 1999), 7:1-20, 7:10 (stating that *Mara Properties* is "one of the better examples of an aggressive filing position").

there was no reasonable expectation of profit in property where we acquired it at noon and sold it by dusk for a loss of four and a half million dollars."[294]

The taxpayer had acquired all of the shares of an unrelated corporation – Fraserview – in 1982 for $69,998, prior to the enactment in 1987 of the stop-loss rules designed to prevent the transfer of losses between unrelated corporations. At the time, the only asset of Fraserview was real estate with a cost of $7.577 million and a fair market value of $3 million. Immediately after the acquisition, Fraserview was wound up and the taxpayer acquired the real estate at a deemed cost under subsection 88(1) of the Act equal to $7.577 million, i.e. the cost of the property to Fraserview.[295] The taxpayer transferred the real estate to the shareholder of Fraserview for its fair market value of $3 million in a pre-arranged sale, and deducted a loss on the sale of $4.433 million in its 1982 taxation year.

The taxpayer would only be entitled to deduct the loss as a business loss if it held the property as inventory, and the question in the tax appeal was whether the character of property held by a subsidiary flows through to its parent corporation on a winding-up of the subsidiary on a rollover basis under subsection 88(1) of the Act. The Supreme Court permitted the deduction of the loss, by simply stating that it adopted the conclusion of the Tax Court and the dissenting judge in the Court of Appeal, without giving reasons for finding that the property retained its character as inventory. It is therefore unclear whether the Supreme Court permitted the deduction of the loss on the basis that the property retained its character as inventory on the facts, or by virtue of the application of the rules

---

[294] *Mara Properties Ltd. v. R.*, (*sub nom.* Mara Properties Ltd. v. Canada) [1993] 2 C.T.C. 3189 (T.C.C.) at para. 9, reversed 1995 CarswellNat 665 (Fed. C.A.), reversed 1996 CarswellNat 868 (S.C.C.).

[295] Woods, *supra* no. 293 at 48:13 (noting Fraserview had approximately $4.6 million of debt inherited by the taxpayer on the winding-up; however, the taxpayer took care of this problem by arranging for the purchase of the debt by a friendly party for a nominal amount prior to the winding-up. While the taxpayer later paid the debt in full the payment was presumably made to a corporation owned by the taxpayer's shareholders.)

in subsection 88(1).[296] In any event, the Court gave its decision without any reference to the economic substance of what had occurred, although the transaction was entirely tax-motivated and the taxpayer had incurred a sizeable economic loss.

The transaction fails under the subjective business purpose prong of the U.S. economic substance doctrine, because the taxpayer admitted its only purpose was to acquire Fraserview's non-capital loss. The tax savings of approximately $2.3 million[297] were the only reason for the transaction. The transaction also fails the objective economic substance prong of the economic substance doctrine as the taxpayer netted no proceeds from the sale of the land and it paid out $4.6 million in order to retire debt that it also acquired from Fraserview on the winding-up.[298]

As to legislative intent it can easily be concluded, by analogy to Judge Hand's reasoning in *Gregory v. Helvering*,[299] that Parliament did not intend that subsection 88(1) could be utilized to transfer losses between arm's length parties in circumstances which were lacking in commercial and economic reality. As the Supreme Court stated only that "the property retained its character as inventory in the hands of the appellant", without any further elaboration, it did not address whether the tax benefit could have been legislatively intended. I contend that in circumstances such as these, it should be up to the taxpayer to show that Parliament intended to extend tax benefits to transactions with no non-tax business purpose and without any economic substance.

---

[296] *Mara Properties Ltd. v. R.*, (*sub nom.* R. v. Mara Properties Ltd.) [1996] 2 S.C.R. 161 (S.C.C.) at para. 1; Meghji and Grenon, *supra* no. 292 at 66:12 (noting that "Unfortunately, the court's brief reasons raise almost as many questions as they answer.")

[297] Woods, *supra* no. 293 at 48:13 (noting the taxpayer "benefited entirely from the tax savings of approximately $2.3 million" and "did actually suffer an economic loss on the series of transactions")

[298] *Ibid.* at 48:13-14 (suggesting the taxpayer's actions in paying off the lossco's debts acquired on the winding up made commercial sense to its shareholders, but not to the taxpayer itself).

[299] See the discussion of *Gregory v. Helvering* in chapter VI.

Duha Printers (Western) Ltd. v. R.[300]

Duha was yet another "remarkable taxpayer victory"[301] in the Supreme Court, which involved the purchase of non-capital losses from an unrelated third party, by way of a complicated set of transactions through which the third party was paid an amount equal to 7.5 percent of its accumulated non-capital losses.[302]

Duha was a profitable company that carried on a printing business. Outdoor was an inactive company with accumulated non-capital losses that had formerly carried on a business of retailing recreational vehicles. A plan was developed to enable Duha to utilize Outdoor's accumulated losses, by purportedly conferring "control" of Duha on Outdoor's parent at the time of an amalgamation between Outdoor and Duha.[303]

The general policy of the Act is to prohibit the transfer of losses between taxpayers, subject to specific exceptions,[304] one of which is relevant here. Subsection 111(5) denies the flow-through of non-capital losses of a corporation that undergoes a corporate change of control; however, if the person who acquired control was "related" to the corporation it was acquiring, the loss transfer prohibition in subsection 111(5) does not apply by virtue of subsection 256(7).

---

[300] (*sub nom.* Duha Printers (Western) Ltd. v. Canada) [1998] 1 S.C.R. 795 (S.C.C.).

[301] Robert Couzin, "Some Reflections on Corporate Control", (2005) vol. 53, no. 2 CTJ 305-332, 310 (suggesting Justice Iacobucci's caveat in *Duha Printers* that the concept of *de jure control* "is really an attempt to ascertain who is in effective control of the corporation" could have led to an inquiry into substance, but also noting that "It is often difficult to reconcile broad judicial statements of principle with their application, even in the case in which they are enunciated, and *Duha Printers* may be such a case.")

[302] T.E. McDonnell, "Who's in control here?, Current Cases" (1997), vol. 45, no. 1 C.T.J. 114 , 115 (noting that one half of the purchase price was paid on closing and the balance was only payable when the new voting shares were redeemed).

[303] Norman Loveland, "Recent Cases of Interest", 1997 *Conference Report* (Toronto: Canadian Tax Foundation, 1998) 22:1-23, 22:29 (stating that formal voting control of Duha was "purportedly conferred" on the lossco's parent through the purchase for $2,000 of a new class of voting preferred shares of Duha, at a time when Duha was worth approximately $600,000).

[304] *Mathew v. R.*, [2005] 2 S.C.R. 643 (S.C.C.) at para. 49.

Duha therefore undertook a complex set of transactions in order to be "related" to Outdoor, by purportedly surrendering "control" of itself to Outdoor's parent, at the time of an arranged amalgamation between Outdoor and Duha. This was done by having Duha temporarily issue 2,000 class C voting shares to Outdoor's parent for $2,000, which gave the parent 56 percent of the voting shares of Duha. At the time, Duha's shares were worth $600,000. The Duha family did not actually give up control of its profitable company for $2,000, although it yielded ostensible *de jure* voting control to Outdoor's parent. The Duha family's interests were protected by entering into a shareholder's agreement with the new shareholders, whereby the majority of directors would always be Duha shareholders or their nominees; no new shares could be issued, and no transfers of shares could take place without the consent of all of the shareholders; and, the Class C voting shares would be redeemed within a short period. The transactions included the purchase by Duha for $34,599 of a receivable in the amount of $441,253 owing by Outdoor to its parent. The terms of the purchase were that one half of the purchase price was payable on closing, and the other one half was payable when the Class C voting shares were redeemed. This occurred when the shares were redeemed by Duha for $2,000, eleven months after they were issued for $2,000.

The Supreme Court found in favour of the loss-purchase scheme, on the basis of its reasoning that the meaning of "control" for the purposes of subsection 111(5) of the Act is *de jure* control.[305] While, as Couzin has suggested, the Court could have decided that *de jure* control had not passed, having regard to the substance of the matter,[306] it can also be seen that the transactions would not have passed scrutiny if an economic substance analysis had applied.

Duha would not survive the subjective business purpose prong of the U.S. economic substance test, as there was no purpose for the

---

[305] Couzin, *supra* no. 301 at 320 (commenting that "It may seem strange that restrictions in the constating documents regarding who may be elected to the board are irrelevant to legal control.")
[306] See footnote 298.

transactions, other than the tax benefits sought by the acquisition of the tax losses of an unrelated party.[307] There was similarly no objective economic substance to the transactions, as the issuance and redemption of the Class C voting shares was merely a device used to achieve fleeting ostensible *de jure* control. The purchase of a receivable owing by the inactive company (for an amount equal to 7.5 percent of its losses) did not represent a meaningful change in Duha's economic position, as it amounted to nothing more than the agreed upon payment by Duha for acquiring Outdoor's losses.

No analysis was done by the courts in *Duha* of the economic substance of what had occurred; and, the Supreme Court held that it was entirely open to the parties to use the "technicalities of revenue law" to achieve the purchase of losses.[308] The Court did not address the question, however, as to whether the legislature intended the exception to the general prohibition against loss transfers between arm's length parties to be available, where it is plain that the passage of "control" was merely a device used to access the exception. As Professor Arnold has written, "[c]an anyone really believe that the owners of a corporation worth about C $600,000 would transfer effective control of the corporation to someone for C $2,000?"[309]

Bearing in mind Judge Hand's analysis in *Gregory v. Helvering*, to the effect that although the transactions undertaken in the case were real, they did not qualify for the exemption in the taxing statute because they "were no part of the conduct of the business of either or both companies", it could as easily be concluded here that Parliament

---

[307] McDonnell, *supra* no. 302 (stating there was no business purpose for the transaction involved in the scheme other than making the losses of Outdoor available to Duha. After the transaction Outdoor's parent had a new class of preferred shares that ostensibly gave it voting control over Duha).

[308] *Duha Printers (Western) Ltd. v. R.*, (*sub nom.* Duha Printers (Western) Ltd. v. Canada) [1998] 1 S.C.R. 795 (S.C.C.) at para. 88.

[309] Brian J. Arnold, "Canada's Supreme Court Rules on Duha Printers: The Triumph of Plain Meaning", 17 *Tax Notes International* 8 (July 6, 1998)(stating "The transaction at issue in the case was a blatant loss utilization scheme"); see also: Arnold, *supra* no. 130 at 14,19 (stating *Duha* was a "blatant artificial loss-trading scheme" and the "transaction hardly has an air of commercial reality about it.")

did not intend the exception to the general prohibition against loss transfers to apply to artificially manufactured transactions.

Interestingly, the Supreme Court's decision in *Duha* has been relied upon for the proposition that the distinction as between "tax mitigation" and "tax avoidance" does *not* rest in Canada upon whether deductions or losses for tax purposes have corresponding economic outlays or losses.[310] Accepting this observation as correct, it speaks loudly of the need for legislation to be adopted in Canada, which very clearly spells out that economic substance is a relevant factor in determining whether there has been an avoidance transaction which crosses the boundary.

Shell Canada Ltd. v. R.[311]

Using an "ingenious series of transactions"[312] involving a "Kiwi loan" and hedging transactions, pursuant to a "weak currency borrowing"[313] strategy proposed by Goldman Sachs &

---

[310] Bleiwas and Hutson, *supra* no. 17, c. 16, IV. Judicial Anti-Avoidance Doctrines, A. What is Tax Avoidance? (quoting the Supreme Court's statements to the effect that taxpayers are entitled to take advantage of provisions of the *Income Tax Act* even where transactions are solely motivated by the minimization of tax)

[311] *Shell Canada Ltd. v. R.*, (*sub nom.* Shell Canada Ltd. v. Canada) [1999] 3 S.C.R. 622 (S.C.C.)

[312] Richard B. Thomas, "Tax Avoidance with a Little Help from Downunder – Shell Canada Limited v. The Queen, Current Cases", (1997) vol. 45, no. 2 CTJ 295-96 (noting Shell wanted to raise $100 million in U.S. funds to be used in its business and that the market rate of U.S. borrowing was 9.1 percent; however, because of the financial conditions in New Zealand at the time, the market interest rate for New Zealand borrowing was 15.4 percent.)

[313] Duff, *supra* no. 290 at 234 (explaining that a weak currency borrowing refers to the series of transactions in which funds are borrowed in a currency with a relatively high interest rate, converted into a currency with a lower interest rate, and repaid pursuant to forward contracts that lock in the foreign exchange gains attributable to the expected depreciation in the first currency. Although borrowing in one currency is economically equivalent to borrowing in another, taxpayers can obtain significant tax advantages through weak currency borrowings because of the application of conventional tax rules. Interest is deductible in the year it is paid or payable during the term of a loan, whereas foreign exchange gains are recognized only on the payment of

Co.[314] that was designed to inflate deductible interest expense on a US$100,000,000 borrowing,[315] Shell succeeded in deducting interest at the NZ rate of 15 percent, although the U.S. market rate was nine percent and it effectively reduced its cost of borrowing to the lower rate.[316]

The Supreme Court's decision upholding Shell's interest deduction has been described by Professor Edgar as "outrageous."[317] The Court's willingness to tolerate such aggressive tax avoidance schemes has also been said by Hayward to give rise to significant

---

principal and are half taxable. This asymmetry produces tax advantages for weak currency borrowings as compared to domestic borrowings.); see also: Tim Edgar, "Financial Instruments and the Tax Avoidance Lottery: A View from North America", *supra* no. 26 at 74 (explaining that some Canadian companies used weak currency borrowings as a financing technique in the late 1980s/early 1990s).

[314] Goldman Sachs & Co. was paid a commission of NZ$1,125,000 for this strategy. See Douglas J. Forer, "Recent Tax Cases and Legislative Proposals", 1998 *Prairie Provinces Tax Conference*, (Toronto: Canadian Tax Foundation, 1998), 15:1-30, 5:3 (explaining that Goldman Sachs & Co. was a "player" in the heady corporate financing days of the late 1980's when "junk bonds" and leveraged buyouts were the norm).

[315] Paul D. Hayward, "Income Trusts: A 'Tax-Efficient' Product or the Product of Tax Inefficiency?", (2002) vol. 5 CTJ 1529-1569, 1554 (stating that Shell was able to predict with reasonable certainty that the increased expense of borrowing New Zealand currency would be effectively cancelled by the capital gain to be earned since the principal of US $100 million would return a greater number of New Zealand dollars at the maturity date than had been initially borrowed. The risks associated with foreign exchange fluctuations had therefore been hedged.)

[316] Bleiwas and Hutson, *supra* no. 17, c. 16, IV. Judicial Anti-Avoidance Doctrines, A. What is Tax Avoidance? (noting that "Shell was able to reduce its effective borrowing costs to the amount that it would have been if the borrowing had taken place in US dollars. ... The Supreme Court of Canada held not only that the interest on the NZ dollars was deductible, notwithstanding that the rate was over six percentage points higher than it would have been had the money been borrowed in US dollars, but also the gain [realized when debenture agreements and a forward exchange contract closed on the same day] was on capital account.")

[317] Tim Edgar, "Lisa Philipps, 'The Supreme Court of Canada's Tax Jurisprudence: What's Wrong with the Rule of Law', Current Tax Reading" (2000), vol. 48, no. 6 CTJ 1975-1976, 1976 (arguing the Supreme Court has refused to accept any significant role in controlling tax avoidance).

tax policy concerns in the areas of efficiency, neutrality, tax fairness and simplicity.[318]

Stripped to their essentials, the facts were that in 1988 Shell borrowed New Zealand dollars equal to U.S. $100 million, for a five year term, at the prevailing market rate of 15 percent for New Zealand dollar loans. The New Zealand dollars were immediately converted to U.S. dollars that were used in Shell's business. Simultaneous hedging transactions were entered into so that the U.S. dollar cost of the loan repayment required in 1993 was fixed. The rate for a U.S. dollar loan on similar terms would have been nine percent. The hedging transactions resulted in a predetermined capital gain that reduced Shell's net financing costs to approximately nine percent.[319]

The trial judge found that Shell did not carry on business in New Zealand, and that it had no intention of using New Zealand dollars in its business. The trial judge also found that if Shell had directly borrowed the U.S. dollars that it required in its business, the interest rate would have been 9 percent; and, also that the purpose of borrowing New Zealand dollars and entering into the hedging transactions was to secure the US$ at the lowest attainable after-tax cost.[320] Shell itself recognized, in an inter-office memo, that the net interest expense of the borrowing should be calculated by amortizing the gain realized on retirement of the loan over the period of

---

[318] Paul D. Hayward, "Monetization, Realization, and Statutory Interpretation", (2003) vol. 51, no. 5 CTJ 1761-1824, 1763, 1767-68 (arguing that the Supreme Court's recent jurisprudence "has created highly fertile conditions" for exploitation of the Canadian tax system's "distinctions in the treatment of equivalent financial positions").

[319] Karen R. Sharlow, "Recent Developments – Deductibility of Fines and Penalties", 1998 *British Columbia Tax Conference* (Vancouver: Canadian Tax Foundation, 1998), 18A:1-11, 18A:2 (noting that Shell anticipated that the 15 percent interest would be fully deductible, while the hedging transaction would yield a capital gain that would result in no tax liability because of available net capital losses).

[320] *Shell Canada Ltd. v. R.*, [1997] 3 C.T.C. 2238 (T.C.C.) at para. 15, per Christie A.C.J., reversed 1998 CarswellNat 1643 (Fed. C.A.), reversed 1999 CarswellNat 951 (S.C.C.), additional reasons 1999 CarswellNat 1808 (S.C.C.).

the borrowing, "since the discount arises as a function of the high nominal interest rate."[321]

The trial judge nevertheless found that although the transactions might be regarded as "convoluted," nothing before him enabled the conclusion that the interest deductions sought by Shell were "not in accordance with normal business practice."[322] Citing the Supreme Court's decision in *Mara Properties* as authority for the proposition that transactions entered into solely for the purpose of reducing tax will be respected for tax purposes, the trial judge upheld Shell's claim for the inflated interest deduction. The Federal Court of Appeal disagreed with the trial judge, finding that the 15 percent interest paid by Shell "was not the true interest rate. If it were, Shell would not have paid it."[323] Looking at the transactions in their entirety, which involved taking account of the pre-determined gain realized on the retirement of the New Zealand dollar loan, the Court of Appeal concluded that the "interest" on the borrowed money did not exceed 9 percent. In doing so, the Court held that it was "looking realistically at the substance of the situation."[324]

The Supreme Court was aware that Shell had effectively only paid the rate that it would have paid for a US$ borrowing: "[B]y agreeing to buy NZ$ in the future at the lower forward exchange rate, Shell not only was able to 'hedge' its exposure to the market fluctuation of the NZ$, but was also able to effectively bring the rate of interest it was paying for the NZ$ down to approximately

---

[321] *Shell Canada Ltd. v. R.*, [1998] 2 C.T.C. 207 (Fed. C.A.) at para. 50, and fn. 46, reversed 1999 CarswellNat 951 (S.C.C.), additional reasons 1999 CarswellNat 1808 (S.C.C.).

[322] *Supra* no. 318 at para. 31. Brian Arnold has noted, however, that weak-currency borrowings are only common because of their tax benefits – see "Supreme Court of Canada Approves Blatant Tax-Avoidance Scheme", 19 *Tax Notes International* 1813-21 (Nov. 8, 1999), 1819.

[323] *Supra* no. 319 at para. 48.

[324] *Ibid.* at para. 53. *Shell* has thus been described as embodying "the classic confrontation between legal substance and economic substance"– see Richard B. Thomas, "Shellshocked! The Queen v. Shell Canada Limited, Current Cases", (1998) vol. 46, no. 2 CTJ 357-376, 358.

the rate of interest it would have had to pay for US$."[325] Nevertheless, the Supreme Court declined to consider the economic reality of the matter, holding that *bona fide* legal relationships must be respected, absent sham or a statutory provision to the contrary. The Court's refusal to consider the economic realities gave rise to totally inappropriate tax results.[326]

The New Zealand $ borrowing and its associated hedging transactions would not survive scrutiny under either of the two prongs of the U.S. economic substance doctrine. As the only purpose for borrowing in New Zealand $ was to secure an increased tax deduction, the subjective business purpose prong of the doctrine is not met. Objective economic substance is also missing, as the borrowing of New Zealand $ and the associated hedging involved a series of "convoluted" transactions that were only inserted to inflate the interest deduction, which did not result in any meaningful change in the taxpayer's economic position when considered apart from their tax effects.[327] As to whether the economic substance doctrine would be "relevant" in *Shell* within the meaning of the U.S. codification of the doctrine, the question to be asked is whether Parliament intended that taxpayers would be able to secure inflated interest deductions by entering into "convoluted" transactions without economic risk. While the Supreme Court reasoned in *Shell* that the transactions were not contrary to the object and spirit of the interest deduction provision, because its purpose is "to encourage the accumulation of capital which would produce taxable income,"[328] this avoided the question of whether Parliament intended that taxpayers should benefit from inflated interest deductions by manufacturing circumstances without any economic

---

[325] *Supra* no. 309 at para. 5.
[326] Edgar, "Some Lessons from the Saga of Weak-Currency Borrowings", *supra* no. 128 at 15-16 (making the point that tax avoidance cases such as the weak-currency borrowing in *Shell* highlight the weaknesses in the underlying structure of an income tax system based on legal form and variations in that form as proxies for economic income and changes in economic income).
[327] Arnold, *supra* no. 130 at 32 (arguing that on any practical, realistic view of the weak-currency borrowing in Shell, the taxpayer did nothing more than borrow US dollars for use in its business).
[328] *Supra* no. 309 at para. 57.

risk.[329] Again, by reference to Judge Hand's reasoning in *Helvering v. Gregory*, Parliament could not have intended that taxpayers would gain the benefit of a tax deduction by engaging in a set of artificial maneuveres that were not "undertaken for reasons germane to the conduct of the venture in hand, [but rather] as an ephemeral incident, egregious to its prosecution." [330]

Following its decision in *Shell*, the Court dismissed this finding in the Tax Court in *Singleton* by Bowman, J. [later C.J.], which he made in the course of denying an interest deduction: "[T]he true economic purpose for which ... borrowed money was used was the purchase of a house, not the enhancement of the firm's income earning potential by a contribution of capital."[331] Major J., writing for the majority, held that the legal form of the transactions determined their tax consequences: "The Tax Court Judge found that the purpose in using the money was to purchase a house and that this purpose could not be altered by the 'shuffle of cheques' that occurred on October 27, 1988. I respectfully disagree. It is this 'shuffle' of cheques that defines the legal relationship which must be given effect."[332]

Le Bel J., writing for the minority, was of the view that ousting an examination of economic realities while holding for the priority of *bona fide* legal relationships "... simply turns one difficult normative question into another. Rather than asking what the economic realities are, McLachlin J. says that we should ask whether the legal relations created by the taxpayer were *bona fide*. This, of course, still requires courts to look beyond the legal instruments used by the taxpayer. It limits such inquiries to those cases where the legal relations were not created *bona fide*, for instance where transactions

---

[329] Arnold, *supra* no. 322 at 1818 ("For tax planners, the champagne corks must be popping. The Supreme Court is giving them carte blanche to pillage the tax system without much opposition from Revenue Canada or the courts, both of whom must follow the dictates of the Supreme Court.")
[330] 69 F.2d 809 (2d Cir., 1934) at p. 811.
[331] [1996] 3 C.T.C. 2873 (T.C.C.) at 2878-79, per Bowman J., reversed 1999 CarswellNat 2949 (Fed. C.A.), affirmed 2001 CarswellNat 2019 (S.C.C.).
[332] (*sub nom.* Singleton v. Canada) [2001] 2 S.C.R. 1046 (S.C.C.) at para. 32.

simply amount to window dressing ...".[333] Nevertheless, the majority's decision in *Singleton* was an affirmation of the Court's post-*Bronfman* and post-*Tennant* position in *Shell* that *bona fide* legal relationships must be respected in terms of the tax consequences which flow from them, regardless of the economic or commercial realities, in the absence of a sham or a specific statutory provision to the contrary.[334]

The Court's most recent forays into the realm of economic substance in tax cases have occurred in its GAAR decisions. The Court reasoned in *Canada Trustco Mortgage Co. v. R.* that "certainty" and "predictability" tax policy concerns outweighed the government's argument that a capital cost allowance deduction should be denied because the taxpayer was not economically at risk for the cost on which the claimed deduction was based.[335] As already noted, although the Supreme Court said in *Canada Trustco* that the economic substance of transactions may be relevant in the GAAR analysis, it also held that "this expression [economic substance] has little meaning in isolation from the proper interpretation of specific provisions of the Act."[336] The Court's position in this regard has been critically assailed on the basis that it is "too narrow"[337] and also because it renders any reference to economic substance in the context of GAAR as "virtually meaningless."[338]

---

[333] (*sub nom.* Singleton v. Canada) [2001] 2 S.C.R. 1046 (S.C.C.) at para. 52.
[334] (*sub nom.* Shell Canada Ltd. v. Canada) [1999] 3 S.C.R. 622 (S.C.C.) at para. 39.
[335] [2005] 2 S.C.R. 601 (S.C.C.) at para. 75; see also: Weisbach, *supra* no. 15 at 248 (noting "Tax lawyers tend to exaggerate the extent of uncertainty created by standards" and that the assumption that uncertainty is more important in tax law than tort law has not been proved.)
[336] *Canada Trustco Mortgage Co. v. R.*, [2005] 2 S.C.R. 601 (S.C.C.) at para. 59.
[337] "Symposium on Tax Avoidance After Canada Trustco and Mathew: Summary of Proceedings", *supra* no. 8 per Professor Li, 1016-18, 1024 (the relevance of economic substance follows from "a textual, contextual and purposive analysis" of GAAR. "[T]ransactions lacking economic substance should be presumed to frustrate the legislative purpose of the [*Income Tax*] *Act*, unless the transactions are clearly supported by the text, context, and purpose of specific provisions or the Act read as a whole.")
[338] Arnold, *supra* no. 8 at 192 (noting that very few provisions in the *Income Tax Act* refer to economic substance, and even in the rare cases where they do, the

The Technical Notes issued by the Department of Finance with the introduction of GAAR stated that the provisions of the *Income Tax Act* are intended to apply to transactions with real economic substance, and not to transactions intended to exploit, misuse or frustrate the Act to avoid tax.[339] While Technical Notes are not determinative of legislative purpose[340] they have been held to be entitled to weight in statutory interpretation,[341] and nothing in the Technical Notes with respect to GAAR warrants limiting the examination of whether transactions have economic substance to circumstances where "the proper interpretation of specific provisions of the Act" is in question. The courts in the U.S., which for decades have been determining whether transactions have enough economic substance to be respected for tax purposes, do not limit the inquiry into economic substance in this fashion. Rather, the matters of whether the subjective and the objective branches of the economic substance doctrine have been satisfied are addressed by U.S. courts, separately from their interpretation of statutory provisions. In the event transactions are found not to have economic substance in the U.S., they are ignored for tax purposes, unless the taxpayer is able to show that the benefits are legislatively intended.

In concluding this section of chapter V, I also raise a point suggested by Singer and Vardy, i.e. that despite the Supreme Court of Canada's statements as to the limited role of economic substance in tax avoidance cases, Tax Court decisions in some GAAR cases do in fact turn upon economic substance determinations:

> In *Canada Trustco*, the Supreme Court cautioned that whether transactions were motivated by any economic, commercial, family, or other non-tax

---

Supreme Court's position is that absence of economic substance or a lack of business purpose is not sufficient in itself to justify a finding that the transaction is abusive).

[339] *Explanatory Notes*, *supra* no. 25 at clause 186.

[340] See annotations under "Explanatory or Technical Notes, Interpretation of Tax Statutes", McMechan and Bourgard, *supra* no. 19, c. 18 (Technical Notes are entitled to weight in statutory interpretation).

[341] *Canada Trustco Mortgage Co. v. R.*, [2005] 2 S.C.R. 601 (S.C.C.) at para. 15 (The *Explanatory Notes to Legislation Relating to Income Tax* (June 1988) are an aid to interpretation).

purpose may form one part of the factual context to be considered, but this is insufficient by itself to establish abusive tax avoidance. Artificiality, or the lack of economic substance or commerciality, was not in itself enough to consider a transaction to be abusive. In fact, an examination of the recent Tax Court cases leads to a sense that artificiality, or lack of economic substance, can be a decisive or determining factor in certain GAAR cases. The different results in various surplus strips, such as *Evans*,[342] *RMM*[343] and *McNichol*,[344] can only be explained with regard to the degree of economic substance characteristic of one arrangement as opposed to another. Similarly, the different outcomes of various interspousal property transfers, such as *Overs*[345] and *Lipson*,[346] can only be readily rationalized having regard to economic substance or lack thereof. As the Supreme Court noted in *Canada Trustco*, the determination of whether the GAAR applies involves factual decisions. The recent Tax Court decisions demonstrate that important facts such as artificiality, or lack of economic substance, cannot be ignored.[347]

As already noted above, Professor Arnold agrees that early GAAR cases had this feature of reliance upon the economic substance of transactions, in determining whether misuse or abuse

---

[342] *Evans v. R.* (2005), [2006] 2 C.T.C. 2009 (T.C.C. [General Procedure]) (decided after SCC *Canada Trustco* decision).
[343] *RMM Canadian Enterprises Inc. v. R.* (1997), [1998] 1 C.T.C. 2300 (T.C.C.), additional reasons 1997 CarswellNat 734 (T.C.C.).
[344] *McNichol v. R.*, [1997] 2 C.T.C. 2088 (T.C.C.).
[345] *Overs v. R.*, [2006] 3 C.T.C. 2255 (T.C.C. [General Procedure]).
[346] *Lipson v. R.*, [2006] 3 C.T.C. 2494 (T.C.C. [General Procedure]), affirmed [2007] 3 C.T.C. 110 (F.C.A.), affirmed [2009] 1 S.C.R. 3 (S.C.C.) at paras. 38-39 (the Supreme Court confirmed its position in *Canada Trustco* that economic substance is only relevant under subsection 245(4) to the extent that it establishes whether the transaction frustrates the purpose of particular statutory provisions).
[347] Livia Singer and Marilyn Vardy, "The Supreme Court's GAAR Decisions: Change or Chimera?", *Tax Avoidance in Canada After Canada Trustco and Mathew*, (Irwin Law: Toronto, 2007), c.4, 137. Support for this approach in the interpretation of GAAR can also be found in Chief Justice Bowman's decision in *Lipson v. R.*, [2006] 3 C.T.C. 2494 (T.C.C. [General Procedure]), at paras. 29-32, affirmed 2007 CarswellNat 640 (F.C.A.), affirmed 2009 CarswellNat 1 (S.C.C.), where he found that "a number of factors may have to be considered and assigned their appropriate weight in the circumstances, and that the *Lipson* scheme had "no underpinning of commerciality."

existed, in the last stage of analysis under subsection 245(4) of the *Income Tax Act*.[348]

SCC'S RATIONALE

Professor Duff has concluded that the Supreme Court's approach to tax law shifted under the leadership of Justice Iacobucci, away from the emphasis of the late 1970s to early 1990s on the purpose of the relevant legislation and the economic or commercial reality of transactions, toward an emphasis on the statutory text and the legal form of transactions. He suggests that this shift was attributable to a conception of the rule of law that emphasized judicial restraint, legal certainty and individual liberty.[349] It is difficult to see, however, how the Court's view of the importance of judicial

---

[348] Arnold, *supra* no. 129 (noting that in the Tax Court's decisions in *McNichol v. R.*, [1997] 2 C.T.C. 2088 (T.C.C.) and *RMM Canadian Enterprises Inc. v. R.* (1997), [1998] 1 C.T.C. 2300 (T.C.C.), additional reasons 1997 CarswellNat 734 (T.C.C.) the economic substance of the transactions was considered in the subsection 245(4) ITA analysis, in concluding that the statutory scheme had been abused). Note also that the Tax Court decisions in *Triad Gestco Ltd. v. R.*, [2011] 6 C.T.C. 2302 (T.C.C. [General Procedure]), affirmed 2012 CarswellNat 3853 (F.C.A.) and *1207192 Ontario Ltd. v. R.* (2011), [2012] 1 C.T.C. 2085 (T.C.C. [General Procedure]), affirmed 2012 CarswellNat 3894 (F.C.A.) both relied upon the absence of economic substance in finding that GAAR applied, whereas in *Global Equity Fund Ltd. v. R.* (2011), [2012] 1 C.T.C. 2225 (T.C.C. [General Procedure]), reversed 2012 CarswellNat 4117 (F.C.A.) GAAR was not applied by the Tax Court, although the loss in issue was "created from a shuffle of paper" and "no real economic loss" took place. The Federal Court of Appeal reversed the Tax Court decision on the basis that although it is not necessary for there to be an actual economic loss as a prerequisite to the deduction of a business loss, "there must, at the very least, be an air of economic or business reality associated with that loss." This suggests to me that a legislative amendment should be welcome. Also see Brian J. Arnold, The Arnold Report, The GAAR Trilogy, Feb. 14, 2013.

[349] Duff, *supra* no. 150 at 526 ("During his years at the Supreme Court of Canada, Justice Iacobucci dominated Canadian income tax law as no other member of the Court before him ever did. More importantly, Justice Iacobucci's tax judgments effected a fundamental shift in the Supreme Court of Canada's approach to Canadian income tax law – away from the emphasis of the late 1970's to the early 1990's on the purpose of the relevant legislation and the economic or commercial reality of transactions toward an emphasis on the

restraint, legal certainty and individual liberty could have caused it to make a 180 degree turn in its assessment of the value of an economic and commercial realities approach in tax cases, in the thirty-nine month period between its decisions in *Tennant* and *Shell*.

However, Professor Duff's conclusion that a shift occurred is certainly borne out by reference to the history outlined above of the Court's uneven treatment of economic and commercial realities. Although the Court's reasons for its shift have not been transparently addressed by it, its judgments have often referred to the three considerations identified by Professor Duff: (1) the necessity for judges to defer in tax avoidance matters to Parliament and not engage in "judicial re-drafting"; (2) the necessity in tax law for certainty and predictability; and (3) the right of taxpayers to arrange their affairs in order to minimize their taxes, absent a statutory provision to the contrary. My position is that these three considerations do not justify the Court's position that the economic substance of transactions has at most only minimal relevance in a tax avoidance context.

Prohibition against "judicial re-drafting"

One of the principal reasons for the Court's position is reflected in the statement by Iacobucci J. in *Neuman v. M.N.R.* that "[t]he *ITA* has many specific anti-avoidance provisions and rules governing the treatment of non-arm's length transactions. We should not be quick to embellish the provision at issue here when it is open for the legislator to be precise and specific with respect to any mischief to be avoided."[350] The first problem with this perspective is that it rests upon a wrong assumption, i.e. that making tax decisions partly by reference to the economic substance of transactions amounts to anything other than a principled approach in interpreting and

---

statutory text and the legal form of transactions characteristic of traditional Anglo-Canadian tax jurisprudence.")

[350] *Neuman v. Minister of National Revenue*, [1998] 1 S.C.R. 770 (S.C.C.) at para. 63.

applying tax legislation.[351] Professor Arnold has suggested that it is not inconceivable that courts might view their role as assisting Parliament in carrying out its clear intention to prevent abusive tax avoidance.[352] In this regard, Smith has argued that the economic substance doctrine reflects a purposive approach to statutory interpretation under which statutory provisions must be interpreted in light of an ascribed purpose.[353] Professor Bankman similarly posits that the economic substance doctrine resembles "a substantive canon of interpretation; it has been part of the tax law for so long that it is accepted by jurists [in the U.S.] who would otherwise hew more closely to a textual reading of the applicable statute."[354] Sheppard agrees, and says that "[t]he economic substance doctrine is ... a doctrine of statutory interpretation that says the taxpayer is not entitled to the benefit of the statute that it seeks to abuse, even if it has a technical argument for the result. That is the way Judge Learned Hand decided *Gregory*."[355] O'Neill's analysis is to the same effect: "[A]n analysis of the key [U.S.] court cases applying the doctrine

---

[351] Lord Wilberforce put this point nicely in *W.T. Ramsay Ltd. v. Inland Revenue Commissioners* (1981), [1982] A.C. 300 (U.K. H.L.) when he said it would be "an excess of judicial abstinence" for the judiciary to decline to address tax avoidance schemes which do not possess economic reality.

[352] Arnold, *supra* no. 129 at 491-492 ("[A]busive tax avoidance ... undermines the fairness and integrity of the tax system.")

[353] Smith, *supra* no. 217 at 3-4 (suggesting that Judge Hand's decision in *Gregory* "arguably could have been decided on the purpose there ascribed to the reorganization provisions, without reliance on what subsequently has been attributed to the business purpose, or economic substance, doctrine.")

[354] Bankman, *supra* no. 65 at 11 ("The federal income tax is, and always has been, based on statute. The economic substance doctrine, like other common law tax doctrines, can thus perhaps best be thought of as a method of statutory interpretation. A related, though somewhat stronger, claim is that the legislature assumes that long-standing common law doctrines such as economic substance will be used to interpret the statutes it enacts. Under this claim, the doctrines have been implicitly adopted as part of the statute – at least where the statute does not indicate otherwise.")

[355] Lee Sheppard, "Economic Substance Abuse", 89 *Tax Notes* 1095-1100 (Nov. 27, 2000), 1099-1100 (also suggesting however that "Throwing the economic substance doctrine at anything that moves ... risks cheapening the economic substance doctrine, even if it does win cases. ... The economic substance doctrine is not a freestanding all-purpose answer to everything the IRS does not like.")

demonstrates that when applied correctly, it is no more than a doctrine of purposeful statutory construction, necessary to invalidate the tax benefits from those transactions that might meet the letter of the law but thwart the law's intended purpose and the statute's framework."[356] These views are all consistent with the Federal Circuit Court of Appeals' decision in *Coltec Industries, Inc.* that "the economic substance doctrine is not unlike other canons of construction that are employed in circumstances where the literal terms of a statute can undermine the ultimate purpose of the statute."[357] In other words, consideration of whether the legislature intended that tax benefits should be permitted to rise from transactions without economic consequences does not "embellish" the statute, but merely interprets it.

My contention is that the judiciary deciding that tax legislation should not give rise to tax benefits where nothing of economic substance has occurred is essentially not different from the judiciary deciding that tax legislation should not give rise to tax benefits where the transactions in question are a sham.[358] In both instances, an intention is being ascribed by the judiciary to the legislature as to when tax benefits are permissible. As the courts have no difficulty with the notion that sham transactions should not be given effect for tax purposes, it is only a short hop to the not dissimilar position that transactions without economic substance should not be given effect for tax purposes. While a court's inquiry into economic substance is a factual inquiry, deciding whether transactions without any economic

---

[356] Sandra O'Neill, "Let's Try Again: Reformulating the Economic Substance Doctrine", *Tax Notes* 1053-1062, (Dec. 1, 2008), 1053-1054 (stating that although it is argued by others that the economic substance doctrine is "jurisprudentially unjustifiable", "the historical articulation of the economic substance doctrine demonstrates that, at its essence, the doctrine is one of purposeful statutory interpretation.")

[357] *Coltec Industries, Inc. v. U.S.*, 454 F.3d 1340 (Fed. Cir., 2006) at p. 1354, certiorari denied 127 S.Ct. 1261 (2007).

[358] Luke, *supra* no. 68 at 788 (the objective prong of the economic substance doctrine is closely related to the sham doctrine); Luke, *supra* no. 67 (noting that "If the transaction fails application of the [economic substance doctrine], the transaction is treated as a substantive sham – that is, as though it did not occur in the first place. Codification of the ... doctrine does not change this approach.")

substance should be given effect for tax purposes involves ascertaining the legislature's intention – something the courts do routinely.

This book will is not a treatise on the correct approach to statutory interpretation, as the subject has been superbly dealt with elsewhere.[359] However, as the Supreme Court has acknowledged that in interpreting all legislation, including tax legislation, the intention of the legislature must be determined by considering the text, context and purpose of the provisions at issue,[360] there is no good reason for it to have refused to consider whether Parliament intends that tax benefits should be permitted to arise from transactions without economic substance.[361]

An argument sometimes made in defence of the Court's refusal to look to economic substance in tax avoidance cases is that the "plain meaning" of words must be respected.[362] However, the sug-

---

[359] See, for example, Stephen Bowman, "Interpretation of Tax Legislation: The Evolution of Purposive Analysis", *supra* no. 198; Kerry Harnish, "Interpreting the Income Tax Act: Purpose v. Plain Meaning and the Effect of Uncertainty in the Tax Law", (1996) 35 *Alberta Law Review* 687-725; Neil Brooks, "The Responsibility of Judges in Interpreting Tax Legislation", *Tax Avoidance and the Rule of Law* (Amsterdam: IBFD Publications, 1997), 93-129; Brian J. Arnold, "Statutory Interpretation: Some Thoughts on Plain Meaning", 1998 Conference Report (Toronto: Canadian Tax Foundation, 1999), 6:1-36; David G. Duff, "Interpreting the Income Tax Act-Chapter 1: Interpretive Doctrines" (1999), vol. 47, no. 3 CTJ 464-533 and "...- Chapter 2: Towards a Pragmatic Approach", (1999) vol. 47, no. 4 CTJ 741-98; Lisa Philipps, "The Supreme Court of Canada's Tax Jurisprudence: What's Wrong with the Rule of Law?", *supra* no. 263; Arnold, "Reflections on the Relationship Between Statutory Interpretation and Tax Avoidance", *supra* no. 130; Brian J. Arnold, "Policy Forum: The Supreme Court and the Interpretation of Tax Statutes—Again", (2006), vol. 54, no. 3 CTJ, 677-684; Duff, "Justice Iacobbuci and the 'Golden and Straight Metwand' of Canadian Tax Law", *supra* no. 150.

[360] See, for example: *Lipson v. R.*, (*sub nom.* Lipson v. Canada) [2009] 1 S.C.R. 3 (S.C.C.) at para. 26; *Mathew v. R.*, [2005] 2 S.C.R. 643 (S.C.C.) at para. 42; *Placer Dome Canada Ltd. v. Ontario (Minister of Finance)*, [2006] 1 S.C.R. 715 (S.C.C.) at paras. 21-23.

[361] Arnold, *supra* no. 130 at 21 (suggesting "It is ... fair to ask why the role of Canadian courts is so restricted with respect to tax avoidance, especially when the role of courts in other countries is not.")

[362] Guy Fortin, "Economic Reality Versus Legal Reality", 1996 *Conference Report* (Toronto: Canadian Tax Foundation, 1997) 5:1-39, 5:6 with comments

gestion that there is a "plain meaning" in tax legislation has little to commend it. As Professor Johnson says:

> It is sometimes assumed by the formalistic school of interpretation that the tax law must be clear and simple and that the taxpayer must benefit, and government must suffer, from any ambiguities or misinterpretations of the tax law. That attitude, however, sets unrealistically high standards of perfection for the language for the tax law, which no human product can meet. Tax law is not and never can be a perfect machine that will run by itself to defeat all the aggressive tax plans that would make the tax system worse. When the words are assaulted so energetically with so many resources, the English language and human understanding can never reach the level of perfection that the formalistic school expects. ... Loopholes can be created in any human tax system unless the system is defended and repaired. Shelters take razor-thin fissures of no material concern and turn them into gaping holes in the tax base. ... Given the imperfections of a human Congress and a human-drafted code, judges and administrators who interpret law need to construe the law with good sense and wisdom.[363]

Professor Arnold also argues that all language is ambiguous, "apart from the context in which the words are used and the purpose for which they are used."[364] Professor Gunn illustrates the point with an example of how a "plain meaning" is itself uncertain,

---

by Bruce R. Sinclair, 5:20 ("If the courts were to rely strictly on an 'economic reality' test in focusing on the economic and commercial result of a transaction, the judge might then 'overreach' or deviate from the plain meaning of the words with the risk of assuming at times the role of the law maker."; see also *C.I.R. v. Newman*, 159 F.2d 848 (2d Cr., 1947) at pp. 850-851 (Hand, J. dissenting) for the judicial proposition that plain meaning advocates cite: "Over and over again courts have said that there is nothing sinister in so arranging one's affairs as to keep taxes as low as possible. Everybody does so, rich or poor and all do right, for nobody owes any public duty to pay more than the law demands: taxes are enforced exactions, not voluntary contributions. To demand more in the name of morals is cant."; but see: Prebble and Prebble, *supra* no. 102 for the argument that the fundamental assumptions behind this point-of-view are all mistaken.)

[363] Johnson, *supra* no. 15 at 445.
[364] Arnold, *supra* no. 130 at 12 ("[A] court should refuse to permit vague unexpressed notions of tax policy to trump the clear meaning of the words. ... The difficulty is that the Supreme Court [of Canada] too readily dodges difficult issues of interpretation by finding – mistakenly in my view – that the words used in specific provisions are clear and unambiguous.")

where a statutory provision is sought to be applied in circumstances where it seems obvious that the legislature would have considered that it did not.[365] He therefore reasons that "[t]he reason for a rule must be understood if we hope to apply the rule sensibly in close cases."[366]

This difficulty with giving the words of a taxation statute their "plain meaning" was expressed long ago by Justice Oliver Wendell Holmes: "A word is not a crystal, transparent and unchanged, it is the skin of a living thought and may vary greatly in color and content according to the circumstances and the time in which it is used."[367] Smith also argues that the assumption "plain meaning" better reflects legislative intent than purposive interpretation misses the point that literal words are rarely conclusive of their scope. He adds that a "plain meaning" approach to statutory interpretation mistakenly assumes that the legislature is omniscient.[368]

According to Professor Barker, amongst others, the platform on which tax avoidance invariably relies is this strict or literal interpretation by the judiciary, which is "nurtured by the ideology of liberty."[369] Professor Brooks says this ideology seems to owe its

---

[365] Alan Gunn, "The Use and Misuse of Anti-Abuse Rules: Lessons from The Partnership Abuse Regulations", 54 *SMU Law Review* 159-176 (2001), 160-161 (a statute establishing a speeding limit which does not apply to an ambulance transporting an injured person to a hospital would literally apply where the injured person had a sore finger, although the literal reading seems ridiculous).

[366] Gunn, *supra* no. 70 at 760.

[367] *Towne v. Eisner*, 245 U.S. 418 (1918) at p. 425.

[368] Smith, *supra* no. 217 at 14-15 and 20 (One of the more "glaring problems" with a "plain meaning" approach to statutory interpretation is that "it assumes congressional omniscience in anticipating all issues." "The ... claim that literalism in interpretation is appropriate because a principled approach inherently represents an aesthetic response to controversial issues is self-refuting. It asserts an objectivity (correctness) for its own conclusions, which it denies to the principled interpretive approach. The fallacy of the assertion lies in the failure to realize that literalism itself must be justified and that justification can only be made by reference to reasons or principles.")

[369] Barker, *supra* no. 84 at 231 ("A legal method based on strict or literal interpretation is the prop that sustains tax avoidance. It, in turn, is nurtured by the ideology of liberty. ... [T]he ideology underpinning tax avoidance is in direct

origin to the treatment of tax law by judges as "an unjustified interference with private property" with a corresponding view that tax avoidance should be tolerated "since taxpayers are only acting to protect what is rightfully theirs."[370] This is an unhappy premise for a taxation law system in a country where, as the Supreme Court has said, "[t]he rule of law is ... recognized as a corner stone of our democratic form of government."[371] Firstly, as Professor Duff has argued, a legal system which sanctions transactions that are deliberately designed and carried out to defeat tax laws is itself undermining the rule of law.[372] Secondly, while the Supreme Court has noted the importance of horizontal and vertical equities to the fairness of the Canadian tax system,[373] its ongoing toleration of abusive tax avoidance has the effect of frustrating these policy goals.[374]

---

conflict with core democratic values. This ideology leads to a moral perspective that supports a right to avoid over a duty to pay a fair share of taxes. In a democratic society that values taxation in accordance with fairness, that moral perspective is wrong."); compare: Nabil Orow, "Policy Considerations", *General Anti-Avoidance Rules – A Comparative International Analysis* (Bristol: Jordan Publishing, 2000), c. 8 (arguing that "Whilst it may be going too far to suggest the presence of GAAR in taxation legislation is contrary to the rule of law, it is reasonable to conclude that the existence of GAAR in taxation legislation undermines and diminishes the many principles which combine to form the ideal of the rule of law.").

[370] Brooks, *supra* no. 359 at 97 ("This is fundamentally and profoundly the wrong way to view tax law.").

[371] *Canadian Council of Churches v. R.*, (*sub nom.* Canadian Council of Churches v. Canada (Minister of Employment & Immigration)) [1992] 1 S.C.R. 236 (S.C.C.) at para. 32; Also see: *B.C.G.E.U., Re*, [1988] 2 S.C.R. 214 (S.C.C.) at para. 30 ("the rule of law is the very foundation of the Charter").

[372] Duff, *supra* no. 150 at 575; Also see Mark P. Gergen, "The Common Knowledge of Tax Abuse", 54 *SMU Law Review* 131-147 (2001), 135-136.

[373] See *Symes v. R.*, (*sub nom.* Symes v. Canada) [1993] 4 S.C.R. 695 (S.C.C.) at para. 78; *Markevich v. Canada*, [2003] 1 S.C.R. 94 (S.C.C.) at para. 18. Horizontal equity is generally defined as meaning "similarly situated taxpayers should receive similar tax treatment, e.g. taxpayers who earn the same amount of income or capital should be accorded equal treatment." Vertical equity is generally defined as meaning "differently situated taxpayers should be treated differently, i.e. taxpayers with more income and/or capital should pay more tax." – OECD, *International Tax Terms for the Participants in the OECD Programme of Cooperation with Non-OECD Economies.*

[374] Martin J. McMahon, Jr., "Random Thoughts On Applying Judicial Doctrines To Interpret The Internal Revenue Code", 54 *SMU Law Review* 195-208

Relative to Justice Iacobucci's suggestion that "the promulgation of new rules of tax law must be left to Parliament",[375] the judiciary in Canada regularly grapples with a host of complex and fundamental taxation questions, in areas where the legislature has not made rules, and where there are gaps in existing tax legislation. Examples of this ongoing judicial work include the establishment of guidelines and rules for the determination of (a) whether a source of income exists;[376] (b) whether amounts received by taxpayers represent income from a source or are windfalls;[377] (c) whether receipts have the quality of income or capital;[378] (d) the manner in which profit is to be computed;[379] (e) how capital outlays and current expenses are distinguished;[380] (f) determining whether a taxpayer is engaged as an employee or as an independent contractor;[381] and, (g) determining the residence of corporations and trusts.[382] Given this high level of engagement by the judiciary in so many thresh-

---

(2001), 196 (if taxpayers are free to manipulate the rules defining "taxable income" to cause it to diverge from their economic income in ways not contemplated by Congress in writing the statutory rules, then the purpose of the statute will be frustrated)

[375] *Entreprises Ludco ltée c. Canada*, [2001] 2 S.C.R. 1082 (SCC) at para. 38; *Canderel Ltd. v. R.*, (*sub nom.* Canderel Ltd. v. Canada) [1998] 1 S.C.R. 147 (S.C.C.) at para. 41.

[376] See *Stewart v. R.*, (*sub nom.* Stewart v. Canada) [2002] 2 S.C.R. 645 (S.C.C.).

[377] *Schwartz v. R.*, (*sub nom.* Schwartz v. Canada) [1996] 1 S.C.R. 254 (S.C.C.). See also: *R. v. Fries*, [1990] 2 C.T.C. 439 (S.C.C.) (the Court found that strike pay was not income from a source on the basis that "the benefit of the doubt must go to the taxpayers." There is no rule to this effect in the *Income Tax Act*.)

[378] *No. 476 v. Minister of National Revenue*, [1960] S.C.R. 902 (S.C.C.).

[379] *Symes v. R.*, (*sub nom.* Symes v. Canada) [1993] 4 S.C.R. 695 (S.C.C.).

[380] *Johns-Manville Canada Inc. v. R.*, [1985] 2 C.T.C. 111 (S.C.C.).

[381] *671122 Ontario Ltd. v. Sagaz Industries Canada Inc.*, [2001] 2 S.C.R. 983 (S.C.C.), reconsideration/rehearing refused 2001 CarswellOnt 4155 (S.C.C.). (This decision was made in a tort law context, but it has been very widely applied by lower courts in making the same distinction in tax cases.)

[382] *Garron Family Trust (Trustee of) v. R.*, [2010] 2 C.T.C. 2346 (T.C.C. [General Procedure]) at p. 2369, per Woods J., affirmed (2010), [2011] 2 C.T.C. 7 (F.C.A.), affirmed 2012 SCC 14 (S.C.C.) ("The development of a test of trust residence in Canada has been left by Parliament to the courts. If courts decide to develop a totally different test of residence for trusts than they have for corporations, there should be good reasons for doing so. I am not satisfied that there are good reasons.")

old taxation questions, it seems likely that Parliament has chosen to leave such questions to the judiciary to resolve, as it is better situated to develop criteria that can be applied flexibly to an array of individual cases.

Although Felesky and Jacks have argued that there is less justification for an economic substance test in Canada because of the enactment of GAAR,[383] this misses the points that the judiciary has long played a role in developing tax law with Parliament's acquiescence;[384] and, that the judiciary, in deciding whether Parliament intended that transactions without economic substance would give rise to tax benefits that are used to shelter unrelated income, would simply be carrying out its task of statutory interpretation.

A further point, made by Professor Weisbach, is that emphasis on statutory interpretation in tax avoidance cases is in any event partly a "red herring", as "the appropriate focus is on the actual content of the law, whether it comes from congressional enactments alone, or some combination of Congress, the Executive Branch, and the courts."[385] From this perspective, it is illogical to assume away judicial doctrines, but most of the time there is an inappropriate focus on statutory interpretation alone, as there was in *Shell*.

---

[383] Felesky and Jack, *supra* no. 9 at 50:46 (arguing that because broader general anti-avoidance provisions have been enacted in Canada with the introduction of GAAR, there should be even less justification for Canadian courts to develop an economic substance doctrine).

[384] Gergen, *supra* no. 372 at 135 ("The courts and the Treasury have long played a significant role in making tax law, with Congress' acquiescence. Transactions that run afoul of the standards of tax motive and economic substance usually exploit technical details of tax law on which Congress says little and probably cares less.")

[385] Weisbach, *supra* no. 15 at 219-220, 240 (suggesting that "the administrative costs of significantly expanding anti-shelter doctrines, such as the economic substance doctrine, would be low. It would be relatively cheap to identify a vastly broader class of tax-motivated transactions and disallow the benefits. To avoid taxes with a vastly expanded economic substance or other anti-avoidance doctrine, taxpayers would have to significantly alter their behavior to avoid tax. My guess is that most would be unwilling to do so, particularly if any revenue from reducing shelters were used to lower tax rates.")

The Supreme Court's position that dealing with tax avoidance is best left to Parliament also ignores the point, previously considered in chapter III, that legislatures cannot anticipate and legislate with regard to all of the possible transactions that taxpayers may eventually engage in for tax avoidance purposes. In the word of Professor Gunn, "[t]he most important practical advantage in thinking about tax avoidance may be that someone who does so will understand the hopelessness of trying to deal in advance with complicated problems by laying down mechanical rules. The world in which a law will operate may not be the same as the lawmaker imagined, for people change their behavior in response to the law. Any sensible body of law must be in large part retroactive and therefore made by the courts."[386] Because of this limitation, courts need the ability to respond to tax avoidance schemes which, however brilliantly conceived and executed to conform with technical tax law requirements, sometimes cry out for the tax benefits to be denied by judges on the basis of "the simple man's reaction: Don't be silly!"[387] The related argument that legislative supremacy is at stake in the matter of whether the judiciary should assume an active role vis-à-vis tax avoidance is described by Professor Gergen as "frivolous." He suggests that the real principle at stake has to do with respect for the rule of law.[388]

---

[386] Gunn, *supra* no. 70 at 767 (also arguing that "the judge knows better than the legislator the facts to which his law will apply, and the most successful tax legislation has been the most general.").

[387] P. Millet, QC, "Artificial Tax Avoidance: The English and American Approach", 6 *British Tax Review* 327-339 (1986), 334 ("*Duke of Westminster* gave rise to two allied and dangerous myths: (i) that in tax cases, to an extent unknown in other areas of law, form prevails over substance; and (ii) that the substance of a transaction, and the only thing to be regarded, is its legal effect. ... [F]or nearly 50 years ... tax became an intellectual game of chess between the Revenue and taxpayer's advisers. ... Tax cases called for ... an abstract, sophisticated analysis of language of the statute, wholly divorced from practical or commercial considerations.").

[388] Gergen, *supra* no. 372 at 135-136 ("the objection is that ... these decisions [based on judicial standards] are arbitrary and non-transparent. ... But application of the standards is not arbitrary in the sense of being random.").

The claim that it is the legislature rather than judges who must address abusive tax avoidance is also said by Professor Duff to ignore the reality that courts have a "comparative institutional advantage" in the matter, as they are not confined, as legislatures for the most part practically are, to making complex after-the-fact amendments; have demonstrated the capacity for making decisions in tax cases on principled bases; and are usually independent from parochial and monetary influences.[389]

Judge Posner, a leading U.S. jurist in tax and other cases, who has been said to have more representation in tax casebooks than any other sitting judge,[390] defends the role of judges in closing loopholes created inadvertently by the tax code on the basis that the approach does not disregard congressional intent or involve overreaching.[391] Professor Johnson argues that "[o]ur tax law tradition, in fact, rests on an assumption that courts will sometimes act as courts of equity

---

[389] Duff, *supra* no. 150 at 578 ("Parliament itself recognized this comparative institutional advantage when it enacted the GAAR in 1988. That Justice Iacobucci did not recognize this comparative institutional advantage may, in part, reflect the characteristic humility for which he is so well known. It may also reflect a more optimistic assessment regarding the institutional abilities of the legislative and executive branches of the federal government. Above all, though, I expect that it reflected his deep conviction in a conception of the rule of law that emphasized judicial restraint, legal certainty and individual liberty.")

[390] Adam Chodorow, "Economic Analysis in Judicial Decision Making – An Assessment Based on Judge Posner's Tax Decisions", vol. 25, no. 1 *Virginia Tax Review* 67-127 (2005), 71-73 ("Judge Posner's academic writings demonstrate a keen understanding of tax policy and the economic considerations underlying taxation. His articles on diverse issues are routinely cited in tax articles. Since becoming a judge, he has written over sixty opinions covering tax matters, covering a wide range of topics, including capitalization, the economic substance doctrine, personal versus business consumption, and reasonable compensation. These cases reveal a deep understanding of the policy issues underlying the tax laws.")

[391] Smith, *supra* no. 217 at 10 (Judge Posner responded to Professor Isenbergh's criticisms of the use of judicial doctrines in tax cases with these points in his decision in *Yosha v. C.I.R.*, 861 F.2d 494 (7th Cir., 1988) at pp. 497-498: "There is no rule against taking advantage of opportunities created by Congress or the Treasury Department for beating taxes ... Many transactions are largely or even entirely motivated by the desire to obtain a tax advantage. But there is a doctrine that a transaction utterly devoid of economic substance will not be allowed to confer such an advantage.")

to prevent absurdity and abuse."[392] Smith also argues that purposive interpretation is essential, relative to the maintenance of equality of treatment of members of the community, and that it provides the best assurance of "legitimacy", in the sense that it requires that reasons be provided which it is reasonable to believe taxpayers and governments would endorse.[393]

Certainty and predictability

Claims as to a necessity for certainty and predictability for taxpayers stand at the centre of the arguments conventionally launched against the use of judicial doctrines in combating abusive tax avoidance.[394] For instance, the Supreme Court of Canada declined to act upon the fact that the taxpayer was not economically at risk in *Canada Trustco*, on the basis that "[t]his would offend the goal of the Act to provide sufficient certainty and predictability to permit taxpayers to intelligently order their affairs."[395] For this reason, the Court considered that the taxpayer's "cost" was $120 million for capital cost allowance purposes, rather than the zero amount for which the taxpayer was actually at risk.

---

[392] Johnson, *supra* no. 15 at 445 (also noting that Congress has praised the courts for "a commendable tendency to look through the mere form of a transaction to its substance" – House Rep. No. 704, 73 Cong., 2d Sess. 13 (1934)

[393] Smith, *supra* no. 217 at 17 ("A claim of legitimacy can be presented to anyone over whom power is exercised to justify to him the exercise of such power, assuming that each is reasonable and shares the over-arching aim of a fair system of cooperation. So understood, legitimacy is premised on and promotes equal concern and respect for each person.")

[394] See, for example, Richard B. Thomas, "Management Companies – Business Purpose Test", (1983) vol. 31, no. 2 CTJ 236-238, 236 ("The so-called business purpose test has created great uncertainty in our income tax law.") Also see: Ward and Cullity, *supra* no. 273 at 473 ("The introduction of the business purpose test would inevitably create a significant degree of uncertainty and unpredictability in the application of Canadian income tax law. ... As a legal principle, the business purpose test has nothing to commend it. It is merely a formula that, lacking any precise content, is available when, at the instigation of Revenue Canada, the court in its judgment concludes that Parliament has failed to legislate effectively.")

[395] [2005] 5 C.T.C. 215 (S.C.C.) at para. 75

However, judiciaries elsewhere have acknowledged that while certainty and predictability are important, they are not absolute values.[396] Avery Jones has argued that "massive increases in the volume and detail of tax legislation have not enhanced legal certainty; rather they have achieved the reverse."[397] Professor Arnold has also noted that proponents of the need for certainty and predictability in taxation law matters often merely state their value, without regard to other tax policy goals such as "fairness, neutrality and raising revenues".[398] What the Supreme Court has done is endorse the paramountcy of the value of certainty and predictability, even for aggressive taxpayers who seek tax benefits by entering into transactions, without economic substance, that have been manufactured to secure tax benefits, without weighing this value against the other important central values which our tax system is built upon, e.g. horizontal and vertical equities.[399]

While there is much to be said for the rule-of-law point that society should not be governed by laws that are arbitrary,[400] the

---

[396] *CIR v. BNZ Investments*, [2002] 1 NZLR 450 (C.A.) at p. 403 per Richardson, P.; *Commissioner of Inland Revenue v. Challenge Corp.*, [1987] A.C. 155 (U.K. H.L.) at p. 167 per Lord Templeman.

[397] Judith Freedman, Geoffrey Loomer and John Vella, "Corporate Tax Risk and Tax Avoidance: New Approaches", no. 1 *British Tax Review* 74-116 (2009), 101 (also referring to Professor Richard Vann's description of the disease of "tax rule madness" that prevails in the United Kingdom and other Anglo-Saxon countries)

[398] Arnold, *supra* no. 130 at 27 ("Certainty is undoubtedly an important objective for any tax system. But it is not the only goal, and it is not necessarily the pre-eminent goal. Fairness, neutrality and raising revenues are also important objectives that sometimes trump certainty. Moreover, the arguments advanced in favour of certainty and the predictions about the dire consequences that will result if the courts pursue purposive interpretation or create judicial anti-avoidance doctrines are exaggerated and lack credibility.")

[399] See *Symes v. R.* (1993), (*sub nom.* Symes v. Canada) [1994] 1 C.T.C. 40 (S.C.C.) at para. 78 ("[h]orizontal equity merely requires that "equals be treated equally, with the term "equals" referring to equality of ability to pay" and "vertical equity merely requires that the incidence of the tax burden should be more heavily borne by the rich than the poor"; *Markevich v. Canada*, [2003] 2 C.T.C. 83 (S.C.C.) at para. 18 ("the principles of horizontal and vertical equity ... should in part govern the ITA")

[400] Franz Kafka's "The Trial", first published in 1925, makes this point vividly.

required degree of certainty is a relative matter. We survive quite nicely as a society, with non-tax laws that have questionable boundaries. We are required by legislation to drive safely, and also precluded from impaired driving, without much clamour from the public about the inherent uncertainty of these notions. Three decades ago, as a junior prosecutor in Winnipeg, I assisted in successfully prosecuting the Venus Theatre for exhibiting films that had been alleged to be obscene, by reference to legislation which spoke of "undue exploitation", which at the time was measured by reference to vague "community standards".[401]

It is not apparent why taxation law requires a higher degree of certainty than these non-tax laws,[402] especially when one takes into mind the point that taxation laws, unlike most other laws, are often enacted with "distributional consequences" in mind.[403] It is also fair to doubt whether the proverbial "man on the Clapham omnibus" (or farmer on a tractor in Saskatchewan) would find transactions without any economic substance, that have only been engineered to secure tax benefits, any less offensive than obscene films or unsafe driving. In any event, and as Professor Duff argues, the need for certainty does not preclude examining tax legislation in accordance with its purpose.[404] Professor Li also notes that certainty is

---

[401] Bret Boyce, "Obscenity and Community Standards", vol. 33, *Yale Journal of International Law* 299-368 (2008), 325 & ff (suggesting that the community standards test has been replaced with a harm-based test, and noting that the Supreme Court has upheld the obscenity law as a reasonable limit on freedom of speech under s. 1 of the *Charter*)

[402] Rebecca Prebble and John Prebble, "Does the Use of General Anti-Avoidance Rules to Combat Tax Avoidance Breach Principles of the Rule of Law?", *Critical Tax Conference*, Saint Louis University School of Law Center for International and Comparative Law 1-25 (April 9 & 10, 2010), 9 (noting that criticism of general anti-avoidance rules because it is uncertain what situations they will apply in subjects them to a higher standard than that which is demanded of law in general)

[403] Brooks, *supra* no. 359 at 97

[404] Duff, *supra* no. 150 at 574-575 ("[W]here taxpayers engage in transactions that are deliberately designed to and carried out to defeat the object and spirit or purpose of the relevant legislation, the certainty and predictability on which they rely is not that of the law itself (assuming that its object and purpose is reasonably determinable), but of an alleged principle that they

in any event a relative concept, absolute certainty being impossible to achieve.[405] Professor Weisbach further argues that the assumption uncertainty is a strong argument against judicial doctrines is false, as the literature about the effects of uncertainty in tax law and other areas of law shows that it does not have uniformly good or bad results.[406]

Moreover, Professor McMahon suggests that the root cause of uncertainty and unpredictability in tax cases is usually attributable to aggressive tax avoidance by taxpayers:

> who seek to apply a wide variety of provisions of the code and regulations in contexts in which they were never intended to be applied to produce results they were never intended to produce. The level of predictability is not unmanageable in the vast bulk of cases involving transactions in the

---

are entitled to arrange their affairs solely to minimize taxes that they would otherwise be required to pay."); see also: F.A. Hayek, "Law, Legislation and Liberty: Volume I – Rules and Order", (University of Chicago Press, 1983) (arguing judicial decisions are more predictable if the judge thinks through the underlying issues even when the conclusions are not supported by the letter of the law)

[405] Li, *supra* no. 8 at 41 ("Absolute certainty is impossible because taxes are imposed on real business transactions, which cannot always be predicted by Parliament. [T]he Act requires line drawing in respect of fundamental questions, such as whether an economic receipt is from a 'source' or a 'windfall' and whether it is on income or capital account. ... [B]ecause the nature of economic analysis is flexible, there are naturally alternative formulations of the economic substance test and different conclusions may be drawn from similar facts. That does not mean, however, that the economic substance analysis is inherently 'uncertain' or 'unpredictable'. It would be unfortunate if Canadian courts refused to look at economic substance for the sake of promoting 'certainty' and 'predictability.'")

[406] Weisbach, *supra* no. 184 at 81 ("There is a lot of literature about the effects of uncertainty in tax law and in other areas of the law. The general thrust is that uncertainty does not have uniformly bad or good effects and that we should have no presumption that reducing uncertainty ... is a good thing. ... We cannot say that uncertainty is necessarily bad and cannot say that we should not impose significant uncertainty if it is needed to implement strong anti-shelter doctrines."); David A. Weisbach, "An Economic Analysis of Anti-Tax Avoidance Doctrines", John M. Olin Law & Economics Working Paper No. 99 (2d series), 1-41 (2002), 25 (arguing by reference to the large level of uncertainty in tort law cases that "it is not clear why the need for certainty in tax law would be greater than in any other area.")

ordinary course of the taxpayer's business. Unpredictability abounds and is inevitable, however, in cases involving transactions outside the ordinary course of business, especially transactions designed specifically to produce tax losses vastly disproportionate to before-tax losses and transaction costs.[407]

Put in another way, in the words of Lord Greene, "[i]t scarcely lies in the mouth of the taxpayer who plays with fire to complain of burnt fingers."[408] Professor Blum also argues, quoting from Surrey & Warren, *Federal Income Taxation* (1960 ed.), that some uncertainty can be beneficial for tax systems:

> Any uncertainty or puzzlement stemming from the Court's opinion [in *Knetsch*] need not be a cause for regret. Just as judicial unfriendliness to tax maneuvering may be in under our tax system, judicial vagueness may also have a place in coping with the avoidance problem. There is force to the point that the 'combination of the existence of a rule permitting transactions to be disregarded but uncertainty as to when the rule will be applied has an *in terrorem* effect that dampens the enthusiasm of some would-be tax manipulators but permits others to take a chance where little is at risk if the scheme fails.' Such a result might in some areas be preferable to an ever-growing crop of detailed statutory enactments tailored to specific minimization schemes. It is even possible that the judicial technique which produces that result is, as asserted by leading commentators, 'essential to our tax system as it now stands.'[409]

---

[407] M. McMahon, Jr., "Economic Substance, Purposive Activity, and Corporate Tax Shelters", 94 *Tax Notes* 1017-1026 (Feb. 25, 2002), 1018.

[408] *De Walden v. Inland Revenue Commissioners*, [1942] 1 All E.R. 287 (Eng. C.A.) at p. 289.

[409] Walter J. Blum, "Knetsch v. United States: A Pronouncement on Tax Avoidance", Taxes – *The Tax Magazine*, 296-312 (1962), 312. See also: Bleiwas and Hutson, *supra* no. 17, c. 16, V. GAAR, Canada's Answer to Tax Avoidance, B. Analysis of Section 245, 7. Misuse or Abuse, i. Selected Cases Decided by Other Courts (suggesting that "The principal influence of GAAR is not seen in the cases that have been decided, but in the matters that did not get to court. It acts as a deterrent, hanging like the sword of Damocles over the head of every tax adviser. It is an unseen presence in every tax-planning transaction."); Diksic, *supra* no. 9 at 25:1-34 (arguing "Except in extreme cases, tax law should not have as its goal the creation of uncertainty in order to discourage undesirable conduct.")

While acknowledging that certainty and predictability have a central role in the various formulations of the rule of law,[410] Professor Waldron also says that "though practitioners will often join in the demand for certainty and predictability, they know very well that anything approaching 'mechanical jurisprudence' is out of the question. Law is an exceedingly demanding discipline intellectually, and the idea that it could consist in the thoughtless administration of a set of operationalized rules with determinate meanings and clear fields of application is of course a travesty."[411]

A full discussion of the rule of law is beyond the scope of this book, however Professor Duff has also made the case that interpreting tax provisions in accordance with their purpose does not violate the rule-of-law principles of certainty and predictability.[412] Professor Freedman adds that "[w]hile it is a fundamental requirement of the rule of law that people should be able to use the law as a guide, it is not essential that the guide dictates an outcome in every case", citing TA Endicott.[413] Professor Waldron also says that "reasoning" (the verb) is an essential aspect of what it means to be ruled by law.[414]

---

[410] Waldron, *supra* no. 59 at 3 "There is a tradition of trying to capture the essence of the Rule of Law in a laundry list of principles: Dicey had three, John Rawls four, Cass Sunstein came up with seven, Lon Fuller had eight, Joseph Raz eight, John Finnis eight, Lord Bingham eight in his excellent book on the Rule of Law. (I don't know why eight is the magic number: but it's a slightly different eight in each case); Robert Summers holds the record, I think, with eighteen Rule of Law Principles.")

[411] *Ibid.* at 6, 10-14 (also arguing that, in any event, our legal system is partly founded on argumentation with its attendant loss of certainty. Even those who clamour for the alleged certainty and predictability of a rule-based legal system would have to acknowledge that they would dispute the unjust or irregular application of detrimental legal requirements.)

[412] Duff, *supra* no. 150 at 577 (noting this depends upon an assumption that the purposes of the relevant provisions are "reasonably determinable" by courts and taxpayers).

[413] Freedman, *supra* no. 200 at 9-10; Freedman, *supra* no. 21 at 346 (arguing that "some uncertainty at the border line is a price worth paying" in order to avoid "the production of ever more rules" which "simply encourages avoidance", provided that there is sufficient certainty for "the broadly compliant majority" to establish how their behaviour will be treated for tax purposes.)

[414] Waldron, *supra* no. 59.

Right to minimize taxes

The Supreme Court of Canada has repeatedly endorsed the *Duke of Westminster* notion that taxpayers are entitled to take legal steps to minimize their taxes, as part of its rationale for declining to take an active role in helping to halt the proliferation of abusive tax avoidance. This is simply the assertion of a value, however, rather than a reasoned justification for the position.

Professor Weisbach has argued that the "right" of taxpayers to arrange their affairs to minimize taxes just involves the assertion of a conclusion:[415]

> If the right were based on a source more profound than a mere statute, modifying it might be more troublesome. We would not want to limit fundamental rights or values. But the right cannot be found in any such source. For example, there is no right to engage in tax planning in the Constitution or any other foundational documents of our society. And the right to alter behavior to minimize taxes is not a basic principle of moral philosophy. Tax planning does not, for example, rank with the freedom of thought, speech, association, religion or other principles supported by moral philosophers. ... To summarize, no moral or philosophical basis for the right to tax plan has yet been articulated. There is no constitutional right. There is not even an explicit statutory right. There is, in short, no basis for a right to tax plan other than statements made up out of thin air by a few judges using questionable theories of statutory interpretation."[416]

---

[415] Weisbach, *supra* no. 406 at 5, 23-24 (also arguing that stronger anti-avoidance doctrines "reduce the elasticity of taxable income" and that a strictly rules based anti-avoidance regime is more costly and less efficient than "a mixed regime where we try to gain the benefits of rules for frequent transactions while limiting complexity through the use of standards."); McMahon Jr., *supra* no. 79 at 750 ("Demands for certainty regarding the scope of the application of an antiabuse doctrine ... lose weight when one recognizes that there really is no fundamental right to plan a transaction specifically for the purpose of reducing taxes.")

[416] Weisbach, *supra* no. 15 at 221 (arguing that there is no social benefit to tax planning and that it is "worse than worthless" as it is like polluting, in that it "imposes costs on neighbors" and "should be eliminated if possible, subject only to the cost of doing so.")

Proponents of the existence of a right to minimize taxation counter Weisbach's propositions with claims as to a deeper set of liberty rights to own and deal with private property without arbitrary interference by the state. These claims, in turn, are responded to by Professor Brooks and others with the argument that there is no basis for privileging the policies that underlie the rules of property and contract law, over the policies that underlie tax law rules which are often formulated with "distributional consequences" in mind, whereas property and contract laws "were often fashioned to favour the wealthy and the powerful."[417] While I will not lay claim to definitively resolving this debate between its philosophical opponents, I will say that it is not obvious why the Supreme Court would come down squarely in the corner of the libertarians.[418]

In summary, there is little to commend the Supreme Court's position, subsequent to its decision in *Tennant*, vis-à-vis the role of economic substance in tax avoidance cases. In Lord Roskill's words, "the ghost of the Duke of Westminster and of his transaction has haunted the administration of this branch of the law for far too long."[419] Elsewhere there has been judicial recognition that the right of taxpayers to organize their affairs must be balanced against other rights and obligations:

> [S]ince the House of Lords was obliged to consider the highly beneficial arrangements which were able to be made in 1930 on behalf of the Duke of Westminster, there has been a growing awareness by the legislature and the Courts alike that ingenious legal devices contrived to enable individual taxpayers to minimise or avoid their tax liabilities are often not merely sterile or unproductive in themselves (except perhaps in respect of their tax

---

[417] Brooks, *supra* no. 359 at 97. Note also that property rights are not protected by the *Charter of Rights and Freedoms,* suggesting that the right to maintain property does not sit on an equal footing with equality rights, etc.

[418] Prebble and Prebble, *supra* no. 402 (evaluating statutory general anti-avoidance rules by reference to the versions of the rule of law advanced by Dacey, Rawls, Hayek, Raz and Fuller, and arguing that although they conflict with the certainty requirement of rule of law they are justified, as tax avoidance "corrupts the rule of law by exploiting it")

[419] *Furniss (Inspector of Taxes) v. Dawson*, [1984] A.C. 474 (U.K. H.L.) at p. 515.

advantages for the taxpayer concerned), but that they have social consequences which are contrary to the public interest."[420]

The Supreme Court of Canada needs to arrive at a similar understanding to that of the Supreme Court of New Zealand, which it displayed in *Ben Nevis Forestry v. CIR*, in interpreting the New Zealand GAAR.[421] This approach has been applied with great results by the lower courts in New Zealand in relation to the foreign tax credit generator schemes – which have thus far been upheld in Canada – see the discussion of this in my case study in chapter IX.

In order for our courts in Canada to arrive at a similar station, this requires an amendment to GAAR, to provide the courts with guidance as to the relevance of economic substance in tax avoidance cases. This can be accomplished, as with the anti-tax avoidance legislation in other jurisdictions, by stipulating economic substance as one of the considerations that must be taken into account in deciding whether to permit tax benefits.[422]

SCC'S DIFFERENT APPROACH IN NON-TAX CASES

Although there have been many judicial pronouncements in Canada, following the Supreme Court's decision in *Shell*, as to the limited role that the economic substance of transactions now has in tax cases, judges do regularly make determinations, in both tax and non-tax cases, based upon their appreciations of the economic realities.[423] These determinations invariably do not involve the application of a judicial economic substance doctrine *per se*, in the manner that the U.S. courts have employed the doctrine in tax avoidance cases. However, the prevalence of such economic realities deter-

---

[420] *Elmiger v. CIR*, [1966] NZLR 638 (SC) at p. 686, per Woodhouse, J.
[421] *Ben Nevis Forestry v. CIR*, (2009) NZTC 23 at paras. 108-109, interpreting sections BG1 and GA 1, *Income Tax Act 2007* – see the review of this case and of the New Zealand GAAR in chapter VII – GAAR in other jurisdictions.
[422] See the review of anti-avoidance legislation in other countries in chapter VII – GAAR in other jurisdictions.
[423] See many examples of this in relation to tax cases that are included in Appendix A.

minations shows that the Supreme Court is mistaken in saying that economic realities have no role in tax cases where transactions are *bona fide*, absent sham or statutory provisions to the contrary. Furthermore, it is instructive to look at the Supreme Court's own reliance upon its appraisal of economic and commercial realities in many non-tax cases.

Tax law is a species of law which at a fundamental level calls for the same handling by the courts as all other laws.[424] Furthermore, non-tax cases enjoy a degree of kinship with tax cases,[425] as income tax consequences are generally determined by applying the rules of the taxing statute to the legal relationships which exist according to the governing private laws of each province.[426] This suggests that the economic realities of transactions should not be treated differently under income tax law than under other types of law. However, while the Supreme Court has given economic realities an extremely limited role in tax cases, it places major reliance upon economic realities in non-tax cases, in making a wide variety of legal determinations:

>   (a) interpreting the language of a lease by a railway company, of properties that it disposed of as they became surplus lands, had to accord with the economic reality of the period of the lease;[427]

---

[424] Smith, *supra* no. 217 at 17 ("At the deepest levels, there is no persuasive reason to distinguish tax law from other law"); Michael Livingston, "Practical Reason, 'Purposivism', and the Interpretation of Tax Statutes", 51 *Tax Law Review* 677-724 (1996), 679 ("Tax law, to paraphrase an old joke, is still law; it's just that there is so much more of it.")

[425] Matias Milet, "Permanent Establishments Through Related Corporations Under the OECD Model Treaty", (2007) vol. 55, no. 2 CTJ, 289-330, 302 (Non-tax decisions concerning legal personality, for example, echo the language used in tax avoidance cases).

[426] *Dale v. R.*, [1997] 2 C.T.C. 286 (Fed. C.A.) at para. 13, per Robertson J.A.: "In determining whether a legal transaction will be recognized for tax purposes one must turn to the law as found in the jurisdiction in which the transaction is consummated."

[427] *Wotherspoon v. Canadian Pacific Ltd.*, (*sub nom.* Wotherspoon v. Cdn. Pacific Ltd.) [1987] 1 S.C.R. 952 (S.C.C.) at para. 72.

(b) *economic reality* could not be ignored in determining whether an assessment of damages should be upheld in a negligence action for personal injury resulting from a traffic accident;[428]

(c) failure to recognize that *economic realities* giving rise to the law governing ownership of property did not remain static, where a common law wife sought a one-half interest in lands to which she had contributed through her labour and earnings, would amount to law being an exercise of naked power, rather than an instrument of social justice;[429]

(d) in deciding whether a court has jurisdiction to order payment of compound pre- and post-judgment interest, it was noted that the common law now incorporates the *economic reality* of compound interest, because it is commonplace in a variety of settings;[430]

(e) the *economic realities* of a marital relationship were taken into account, in awarding an interest in farmland on the basis of a constructive trust to a common law wife who had contributed labour to preserving and maintaining a farm, where her spouse owned the farm when their cohabitation had first commenced;[431]

(f) ensuring a fair level of child support under the *Federal Child Support Guidelines* is held to require an approach which allows sufficient flexibility to see that the *economic reality* and particular circumstances of each family are properly accounted for;[432] and

---

[428] *Andrews v. Grand & Toy Alberta Ltd.*, [1978] 2 S.C.R. 229 (S.C.C.) at para. 72.
[429] *Becker v. Pettkus*, [1980] 2 S.C.R. 834 (S.C.C.) per annotation of James G. McLeod, Faculty of Law, University of Western Ontario.
[430] *Bank of America Canada v. Mutual Trust Co.*, [2002] 2 S.C.R. 601 (S.C.C.) at para. 44.
[431] *Sorochan v. Sorochan*, [1986] 2 S.C.R. 38 (S.C.C.) per annotation of James G. McLeod, Faculty of Law, University of Western Ontario.
[432] *Contino v. Leonelli-Contino*, [2005] 3 S.C.R. 217 (S.C.C.) at para. 27.

(g) the term "*security*" in the Ontario *Securities Act* could not be given its literal meaning, as doing so would bring within the scope of the Act innumerable transactions which have no public aspect, and amount to not construing it in the context of the *economic realities*.[433]

These are largely instances where the court is adjudicating disputes between private citizens. Nevertheless, it is perplexing to see the Supreme Court relegate economic realities to a distant corner in tax cases, when they are given such a significant role in non-tax cases. While it is sometimes argued that taxation laws should be read more strictly than laws which govern legal relations between the general citizenry, as taxation laws involve the government exacting property from citizens as tax revenues, this argument reflects a philosophical position that is not universally held.[434] Plus, despite its pronouncements to the contrary about the point[435] it is manifest that "the [Supreme] Court continues to treat tax statutes as different from and more threatening than other kinds of legislation".[436] Given the position of the Court that the proper approach to statutory interpretation is the same for provisions of the *Income Tax Act* as for those of any other statute,[437] the uneven treatment of economic

---

[433] *Pacific Coast Coin Exchange of Canada v. Ontario (Securities Commission)* (1977), [1978] 2 S.C.R. 112 (S.C.C.) at para. 43.

[434] Brooks, *supra* no. 359 at 97 (arguing that the treatment of tax law by judges as an unjustified interference with private property "is fundamentally and profoundly the wrong way to view tax law.")

[435] *Lipson v. R.*, (*sub nom.* Lipson v. Canada) [2009] 1 S.C.R. 3 (S.C.C.) at para. 26 (the approach to statutory interpretation is the same for provisions of the *Income Tax Act* as for those of any other statute); *Mathew v. R.*, [2005] 2 S.C.R. 643 (S.C.C.) at para. 42 (there is an abiding principle of interpretation to determine the intention of the legislator by considering the text, context and purpose of the provisions at issue which applies to the *Income Tax Act* and the GAAR as much as to any other legislation).

[436] Philipps, *supra* no. 263 at142 (arguing the Supreme Court has not assumed "its appropriate and much needed role as a collaborator with Parliament in the elaboration of a fair, efficient and administrable tax system").

[437] Professor Arnold has argued that the Supreme Court's statements in its GAAR decisions are inconsistent with respect to the interpretation of tax statutes as compared with all other statutes – see Arnold, *supra* no. 8 at 175.

realities by the Court as between tax and non-tax cases does not inspire confidence.[438]

Notions of "economic substance" and "commercial substance" are sometimes married, as they were in the U.S. Supreme Court's decision in *Knetsch v. U.S.*, where the majority highlighted the District Court's finding that the transactions had "no commercial economic substance".[439] Diksic has suggested that the term "economic substance ... seeks to identify the underlying economic or commercial elements of a transaction."[440] Professor Li has also noted that an economic substance standard "is an objective test based on the commercial reality of the business world."[441] Although "commercial realities" and "economic realities" do not necessarily describe the same subject matter, they both relate to a state of affairs that exists, regardless of the legal form of the relevant transactions. Commercial and economic realities are also often referred to in the same breath. The Supreme Court's decision in *Bronfman* spoke of the assessment of taxpayer's transactions, "with an eye to commercial and economic realities, rather than juristic classification of form."[442] As the Court referred to commercial and economic realities in this generalization, and the Court's later admonishment in *Shell* was that the economic realities are largely irrelevant in tax cases because *bona fide* legal relationships must be upheld unless

---

[438] Li, *supra* no. 8 at 32-33 (noting that it is "puzzling" that the Supreme Court remained wedded to a formalistic construction of taxpayers' transactions in tax cases after its adoption of the "modern rule" of statutory interpretation in *Stubart Investments Ltd. v. R.*, [1984] 1 S.C.R. 536 (S.C.C.) at para. 60 and its pronouncement regarding the demise of the strict interpretation rule for the construction of taxation statutes).

[439] 364 U.S. 361 (1960) at p. 364.

[440] Diksic, *supra* no. 9 at 25:1-34

[441] Li, *supra* no. 8 at 42-43 (arguing that this "ensures ordinary business transactions are not affected by the GAAR." "In most cases, commercial reality is defined by the legal rights and obligations the taxpayers have created in private law. Thus, the legal form and substance of the transactions are controlling. In other words, in ordinary business and commercial transactions, economic substance is consistent with legal substance. In tax shelters and other structures that are designed solely to achieve tax savings, legal substance and economic substance are divorced.")

[442] *Bronfman Trust v. R.*, [1987] 1 C.T.C. 117 (S.C.C.) at para. 49.

there is a sham or a statutory provision to the contrary, it is surprising to find the degree of reliance by the Court upon its findings as to commercial realties in non-tax cases:

(a) the *commercial reality* of the marketplace was held to be an important part of the context, in deciding who was liable for the financial loss when an airline collapsed leaving bills for airport charges and air navigation charges;[443]

(b) when a bulk sale has been declared void for failure to comply with the Ontario *Bulk Sales Act*, *commercial realities* must be considered in interpreting the buyer's duty to account;[444]

(c) the Court declined to change the established common law rule that an undisclosed principal cannot be sued on a contract executed by his or her agent when that contract is executed under seal ("the sealed contract rule"), without evidence that the rule is inconsistent with *commercial reality*;[445]

(d) *commercial reality* was an important factor in deciding whether an insurance company had a duty to defend the holder of a homeowner's insurance policy against a sexual assault suit;[446]

(e) *commercial reality* was relied upon as the best indicator of contractual intention in determining whether a limitation period survived a wrongful rescission of contract;[447]

---

[443] *NAV Canada c. Wilmington Trust Co.*, (*sub nom.* Canada 3000 Inc., Re) [2006] 1 S.C.R. 865 (S.C.C.) at para. 38.
[444] *National Trust Co. v. H & R Block Canada Inc.*, [2003] 3 S.C.R. 160 (S.C.C.) at para. 29.
[445] *Friedmann Equity Developments Inc. v. Final Note Ltd.*, [2000] 1 S.C.R. 842 (S.C.C.) at para. 14.
[446] *Non-Marine Underwriters, Lloyd's London v. Scalera*, [2000] 1 S.C.R. 551 (S.C.C.) at para. 71.
[447] *Guarantee Co. of North America v. Gordon Capital Corp.*, [1999] 3 S.C.R. 423 (S.C.C.) at paras. 61-62.

(f) relaxing the doctrine of privity of contract was justified on *commercial reality* grounds, where an admitted tortfeasor claimed immunity from the payment of an award of damages arising from the sinking of a barge, in a subrogated action by the underwriters of the barge owner's insurance policy;[448]

(g) it was held that it would be somewhat out of step with *commercial reality*, considering the nature of the pharmaceutical industry, to find that a date of assessment was the 46th day following the issuance of a notice of allegation by a generic drug company;[449]

(h) the test for recovery of damages for contractual relational economic loss needs to be flexible enough to meet the complexities of *commercial reality*;[450]

(i) the *commercial reality* as to a bank's holding of a security interest in a receivable helped determine whether lending institutions were secured creditors under the *Income Tax Act* and *Excise Tax Act*;[451]

(j) the *commercial realities* of urban living were held to be relevant to the determination of the constitutionality of provisions of the Nova Scotia *Residential Tenancies Act* pertaining to the adjudication of residential tenancy disputes by provincial appointees;[452]

(k) demanding continued operation of uneconomic passenger rail services on Vancouver Island, in the absence of

---

[448] *Fraser River Pile & Dredge Ltd. v. Can-Dive Services Ltd.*, [1999] 3 S.C.R. 108 (S.C.C.) at para. 41.

[449] *Merck Frosst Canada Inc. v. Canada (Minister of National Health & Welfare)*, [1998] 2 S.C.R. 193 (S.C.C.) at para. 32.

[450] *Bow Valley Husky (Bermuda) Ltd. v. Saint John Shipbuilding Ltd.*, [1997] 3 S.C.R. 1210 (S.C.C.) at para. 50.

[451] *Canada Trustco Mortgage Corp. v. Port O'Call Hotel Inc.*, (*sub nom.* Alberta (Treasury Branches) v. Minister of National Revenue) [1996] 1 S.C.R. 963 (S.C.C.) at para. 24.

[452] *Reference re Act to Amend Chapter 401 of the Revised Statutes, 1989, the Residential Tenancies Act, S.N.S. 1992, c. 31*, (*sub nom.* Reference re Amendments to the Residential Tenancies Act) [1996] 1 S.C.R. 186 (S.C.C.) at para. 49.

subsidy support, would be to deny the *commercial reality* of the situation;[453]

(l) *commercial reality* and common sense required that employees benefit from limitation of liability clauses, in contracts between their employer and a third party, despite the doctrine of privity;[454]

(m) state immunity under the international law doctrine of sovereign immunity has been refined to reflect *commercial reality*, by recognizing a distinction between a foreign government's public acts (*jure imperii*) and private acts (*jure gestionis*);[455]

(n) the test for recovery of economic loss, where a person who contracts for the use of property sues a person who damages that property for losses resulting from his or her inability to use the property during the period of repair, needs to be flexible enough to meet the complexities of *commercial reality*;[456]

(o) LaForest J. held that that courts cannot be oblivious to *commercial realities*, in determining the level of expectation of privacy that a company has under section 8 of the Canadian *Charter of Rights and Freedoms*, where a requirement for the production of documents under section 17 of the *Combines Investigation Act* was challenged as unreasonable seizure;[457]

(p) section 10 of the federal *Interest Act* was enacted in light of the commercial practices of the day, but that did not

---

[453] *Vancouver Island Railway, An Act Respecting, Re*, [1994] 2 S.C.R. 41 (S.C.C.) at para. 162.

[454] *London Drugs Ltd. v. Kuehne & Nagel International Ltd.*, [1992] 3 S.C.R. 299 (S.C.C.) at para. 47.

[455] *P.S.A.C. v. United States Defense Department*, (*sub nom.* Code Canadien du Travail, Re) [1992] 2 S.C.R. 50 (S.C.C.) at para. 86.

[456] *Canadian National Railway v. Norsk Pacific Steamship Co.*, [1992] 1 S.C.R. 1021 (S.C.C.), reconsideration / rehearing refused (July 23, 1992), Doc. 21838 (S.C.C.) at para. 77.

[457] *Thomson Newspapers Ltd. v. Canada (Director of Investigation & Research)*, [1990] 1 S.C.R. 425 (S.C.C.) at para. 173.

preclude the Court from giving it an interpretation consonant with a later *commercial reality*, where such interpretation was equally compatible with the legislative language;[458]

(q) the role played by the tort of passing off in the common law has expanded to take into account the changing *commercial realities* in the present-day community;[459] and

(r) determining the final impact of a loss resulting from forgery of cheques turned upon interpreting a provision of the *Bills of Exchange Act* in a manner reflecting *commercial realities* which the statute was designed to serve.[460]

Professor Edgar has made the point, in a tax law context, that while the lack of well-defined criteria for the determination of economic substance may underlie the apparent distaste of Canadian tax practitioners and judges for characterization based on economic substance, the content of "commercial reality" is also elusive.[461] Nevertheless, since regular determinations of the commercial and economic realities or substance of transactions do take place, and they do obviously have a significant role in judicial decisions in non-tax cases, the limitation placed by the Supreme Court on the role of economic realities in tax cases appears inconsistent with the treatment of such realities in non-tax cases. It thus seems possible that the Court's position as to the relative insignificance of economic realities in tax avoidance cases may be the product of its unstated antagonism towards income taxation,[462] rather than because of its stated considerations.

---

[458] *Potash v. Royal Trust Co.*, [1986] 2 S.C.R. 351 (S.C.C.) at para. 34.
[459] *Consumers Distributing Co. v. Seiko Time Canada Ltd.*, [1984] 1 S.C.R. 583 (S.C.C.) at para. 24.
[460] *Canada Life Assurance Co. v. Canadian Imperial Bank of Commerce*, [1979] 2 S.C.R. 669 (S.C.C.) at para. 9.
[461] Edgar, "Some Lessons from the Saga of Weak-Currency Borrowings", *supra* no. 128 at 14 (arguing that commercial realities have been advanced by the Supreme Court in *Shell* and other cases as a supposed basis for recognizing the legal form of transactions adopted by taxpayers for tax planning purposes)
[462] Stephen Bowman, *supra* no. 198 at 1173-1174 (arguing that the historical antipathy of courts to tax legislation accounts for the evolution and persistence

In this regard, I consider that the Supreme Court of Canada's limitation on the role of economic substance in tax avoidance cases has been a colossal misstep by it in carrying out its role as final arbiter in the matter of when Parliament intends that tax benefits should be available.[463] Just as the Supreme Court decides whether receipts which are economic gains should be treated as income for the purposes of the *Income Tax Act*, it is for the Court to decide whether putative outlays without economic losses should give rise to deductions for the purposes of the Act. My view is also that the relegation by the Court of economic substance to a tiny corner in tax avoidance cases is inconsistent with its substantial reliance upon economic and commercial realities in a wide variety of non-tax cases, suggesting that the Court is operating with an odd double standard.

The most likely explanation I can offer, for the Supreme Court's fairly routine reliance upon findings as to the economic

---

of the literalist approach to statutory interpretation, notwithstanding the mischief rule in the *Interpretation Act* requiring a purpose approach); Barker, *supra* no. 84 at 233 and 251 ("Frustrating ... social and legislative goals is the fact that many persons with significant means do not pay a fair share of taxes consistent with the values of income taxation. One reason for this is a common judicial antagonism to the values of income taxation."); Brooks, *supra* no. 359 at 97 (arguing judges wrongly assume taxation is an unnatural form of government intervention in taxpayers' lives whereas tax laws, unlike property and contract laws, are formulated with "distributional consequences" in mind and are arguably more defensible than property and contract laws).

[463] Graeme S. Cooper, "International Experience with General Anti-Avoidance Rules", 54 *SMU Law Review* 83 (2001), 120 (noting the enactment of GAAR in Canada was a reaction to the perception that judicial doctrines were unlikely to evolve into a sufficiently robust rule against improper tax avoidance); Arnold, *supra* no. 130 at 31 (arguing that a general anti-avoidance rule would not be necessary if the Canadian courts had applied a more purposive interpretation to the *Income Tax Act*); Edgar, "Some Lessons from the Saga of Weak-Currency Borrowings", *supra* no. 128 at 24-26 (commenting that although the premise behind judicial interpretive activism as a route to combat abusive tax avoidance is sound, there are problems which undermine its potential effectiveness, including serious questions about the ability of courts to produce reasonable and timely results in areas as complex as the taxation of financial instruments. The Supreme Court's decision in *Shell* is said to highlight this problem.)

realities and commercial realities of transactions in non-tax cases, is that courts generally do not make or endorse factual findings, without consideration of *all* of the relevant facts. This approach obviously has much to commend it; and, the approach should not be any different in tax avoidance cases.[464] However, by virtue of the Supreme Court essentially ruling out economic substance as a relevant factual consideration in tax avoidance cases, there has been a departure from the prevailing common-sense judicial standard. This is a calamitous development, because the presence or absence of economic substance is a principal indicator of whether or not there has been abusive tax avoidance, which should be front and centre amongst all of the factual circumstances to be examined when the courts are deciding tax avoidance cases.

This discovery of the extent to which the Supreme Court does rely upon economic and commercial realities in non-tax cases suggests that the strict limits placed by the Court on the relevance of economic substance in tax avoidance cases are questionable. Given this, it is instructive to look to the judiciary's treatment of economic substance in the U.S., where economic substance has been front and centre in tax avoidance cases for many decades.

---

[464] Brian J. Arnold, "A comparison of statutory general anti-avoidance rules and judicial general anti-avoidance doctrines as a means of controlling tax avoidance: Which his better? (What Would John Tiley think?)", Comparative Perspectives on Revenue Law: Essays in Honour of John Tiley, Cambridge University Press (ed. John Avery Jones, Peter Harris and David Oliver), footnote 28 (noting general agreement with John Tiley "that the facts come first in tax avoidance cases", but "characterisation of the facts and the interpretation of the legislation are more integrated than separate in the analytical process. Judges do not interpret legislation in the abstract; they confront questions concerning the application of the legislation to a particular transaction or set of facts.") (My own view of the process is that judges very often (1) hear the evidence; (2) decide the outcome; and (3) make factual and legal findings accordingly. There are nevertheless also instances, depending on the sitting judge(s), where outcomes follow from precedent(s)).

VI

U.S. Economic Substance Doctrine

Although the Supreme Court of Canada has clung very steadfastly to its notion that the tax policy reflected in *Duke of Westminster* style reasoning is a proper cornerstone for its resolution of tax disputes, the situation has been much different in the United States. In this chapter I examine the origins, evolution and application of the common law (now codified) economic substance doctrine in tax avoidance cases in the U.S., and note its sharp contrast with the treatment of economic substance by the Supreme Court in tax avoidance cases in Canada.

The evolution of the common law economic substance doctrine in the U.S., and the extent to which it has been applied by the courts in the U.S., is strong evidence that there has been and continues to be a considerable gap in the defences against abusive tax avoidance in Canada. For decades, the U.S. has had a common law economic substance doctrine under which tax benefits are denied, where economic substance is found to be lacking, unless the benefits are found to be legislatively intended.[465] Although there have been a number of differences amongst U.S. courts as to how the doctrine is to be applied, it was said long before its codification to be "solidly entrenched, without the slightest suggestion in judicial opinions that it is ill-founded."[466]

The Tax Court, the Court of Federal Claims and each of the Court of Appeal Circuit Courts in the U.S. have all disallowed tax benefits by applying the common law economic substance

---

[465] Cummings, *supra* no. 15 at 156 (suggesting that the lack of guidance from Congress or the Treasury concerning "tax specific doctrines" such as the economic substance doctrine may reflect that "they are content to allow the courts to perform a role that is peculiar to American courts, of exercising more flexibility in solving statutory problems", with the caveat, however, that this view "is speculative and provides no logical basis of authority for the doctrines.")

[466] Smith, *supra* no. 217 at 1 (arguing that the economic substance doctrine is justified under a principled approach to statutory interpretation); McMahon Jr., *supra* no. 79 at 735 (noting that the economic substance doctrine has been applied by the courts many times over the past fifteen or so years to deny tax benefits whereas "the taxpayer has prevailed in only a few outlier cases." Cases where the doctrine has been applied include *Klamath Strategic Investment Fund ex rel. St. Croix Ventures v. U.S.*, 568 F.3d 537 (5th Cir., 2009); *BB&T Corp. v. U.S.*, 523 F.3d 461 (4th Cir., 2008), *Doc 2008-9547, 2008 TNT 84-15*; *Coltec*, 454 F.3d 1340; *Dow Chemical Co. v. U.S.*, 435 F.3d 594 (6th Cir., 2006), *Doc 2006-1308, 2006 TNT 15-11*, cert. denied, 549 U.S. 1205 (2007); *American Elec. Power Co., Inc. v. U.S.*, 326 F.3d 737 (6th Cir., 2003), *Doc 2003-10647, 2003 TNT 82-11*; *Nicole Rose Corp. v. C.I.R.*, 320 F.3d 282 (2d Cir., 2002), *Doc 2002-27525, 2002 TNT 243-14*; *In re CM Holdings, Inc.*, 301 F.3d 96 (3d Cir., 2002), *Doc 2002-19191, 2002 TNT 161-10*; *Winn-Dixie Stores, Inc. v. Commissioner*, 254 F.3d 1313 (11th Cir., 2001), *Doc 2001-18038, 2001 TNT 127-6*; *ACM*, 157 F.3d 231 (3d Cir., 1998); *New Phoenix Sunrise Corp. v. C.I.R.*, 132 T.C. 161 (2009); *Palm Canyon X Investments, LLC v. Commissioner*, T.C. Memo. 2009-288, *Doc 2009-27494, 2009 TNT 239-11*; *Wells Fargo & Co. and Subsidiaries v. U.S.*, 91 Fed.Cl. 35 (2010), *Doc 2010-540, 2010 TNT 6-15*; *Consolidated Edison Co. of New York, Inc. v. U.S.*, 90 Fed.Cl. 228 (2009), *Doc 2009-23332, 2009 TNT 203-7*; *Stobie Creek Investment, LLC v. U.S.*, 82 Fed. Cl. 636 (2008), *Doc 2008-5274, 2008 TNT 49-13*, affirmed 2010 WL 2331155 (Fed. Cir., 2010), *Doc 2010-12971, 2010 TNT 113-15*; *Jade Trading, LLC v. U.S.*, 80 Fed.Cl. 11 (2007), *Doc 2007-28072, 2007 TNT 248-5*, reconsideration denied, 81 Fed. Cl. 173 (2008), affirmed 598 F.3d 1372 (Fed. Cir., 2010), *Doc 2010-6335, 2010 TNT 56-10*; *Altria*, 105 A.F.T.R.2d 2010-1419; and *AWG Leasing Trust v. United States*, 592 F.Supp.2d 953 (N.D. Ohio, 2008), *Doc 2008-11830, 2008 TNT 105-10*).

doctrine.[467] The Federal Circuit has upheld the constitutionality of the economic substance doctrine, although the doctrine disallows tax benefits that the language of the *Internal Revenue Code* would otherwise allow.[468] The doctrine has also been approved by the U.S. Supreme Court, which in 2007-2008 declined to grant certiorari from three Court of Appeal decisions that denied tax benefits on the basis that the taxpayers' transactions lacked economic substance.[469]

The Federal Circuit Court of Appeals described the basis for the economic substance doctrine in *Coltec* in these terms:

> The economic substance doctrine represents a judicial effort to enforce the statutory purpose of the tax code. From its inception, the economic substance doctrine has been used to prevent taxpayers from subverting the legislative purpose of the tax code by engaging in transactions that are fictitious or lack economic reality simply to reap a tax benefit. In this regard, the economic substance doctrine is not unlike other canons of construction that are employed in circumstances where the literal terms of a statute can undermine the ultimate purpose of the statute – See, e.g., *Wisc. Dep't of Revenue v. William Wrigley, Jr., Co.*, 505 U.S. 214, 230 (1992) (noting that the maxim *de minimis non curat lex* – that 'the law cares not for trifles' or extremely minor transgressions – 'is part of the established background of legal principles against which all enactments are adopted'); *United States v. Native Vill. Of Unalakleet*, 411 F.2d 1255, 1258 (Ct. Cl. 1969) ('[W]e may at times construe a statute contrary to its 'plain language' if a literal interpretation makes a discrimination for which no rational ground can be suggested.')

* * *

---

[467] Paul L.B. McKenny, "Economic Substance Doctrine – Not Just for Shelters Anymore", (2008) ABATAX-CLE 0913048.
[468] Gray Jennings, "Economic Substance and the Taxpayer's Purpose", 127 *Tax Notes* 535-545 (May 3, 2010), 536 (arguing that the economic substance doctrine should "be based on the idea that Congress intends that steps a taxpayer undertakes that contribute to realizing a nontax objective have economic substance.").
[469] *Coltec Industries, Inc. v. United States*, 454 F.3d 1340 (Fed. Cir. 2006), vacating and remanding 62 Fed. Cl. 716 (2004) (slip opinion at 123-124, 128); cert. denied, 127 S. Ct. 1261 (Mem.) (2007). *Dow Chem. Co. v.United States*, 435 F.3d 594 (6th Cir. 2006), cert. denied, 549 U.S. 1205 (2007) *Cemco Investors, LLC v. United States*, 515 F.3d 749 (7th Cir.), certiorari denied, 129 S. Ct. 131 (2008).

> [T]he economic substance doctrine is merely a judicial tool for effectuating the underlying Congressional purpose that, despite literal compliance with the statute, tax benefits not be afforded based on transactions lacking in economic substance.[470]

The economic substance doctrine is said to be attractive to judges, because it is "a positive rule of law of their own making." It generally uses the same two factual tests for subjective purpose and objective economic substance, with which judges "gradually can become conversant and comfortable", and which they find "more accessible than the tax law as written."[471] Judges in the U.S. are said to have increasingly relied on the economic substance doctrine as a substitute for technical analysis of transactions.[472]

The harshest critics of the economic substance doctrine, who advocate with what sometimes resembles a religious fervour the necessity for taxpayers to be able to rely on the letter of the law, maintain that it is not appropriate for a judge to disregard the clear language of a taxation statute.[473] Professor Isenbergh, for example, praised Judge Sternhagen's opinion in the Board of Tax Appeals decision (later overturned) in *Gregory*, as the "clearest and most defensible statement I have yet encountered on the subject of form

---

[470] *Coltec Industries, Inc. v. U.S.*, 454 F.3d 1340 (Fed. Cir., 2006) at p. 1354.

[471] Jasper L. Cummings, Jr., "The New Normal: Economic Substance Doctrine First", 126 *Tax Notes* 521-530 (Jan. 25, 2010), 521 (arguing that this "is a terrible result for the tax system because it subverts the statutory and regulatory rules and standard fact-finding process that can reach the same results.")

[472] Jeremiah Coder, "Living With GAAR Lite?", 127 *Tax Notes* 1187-1190 (June 14, 2010), 1188 (arguing that since the economic substance doctrine has been codified it seems more like a GAAR; however, there are concerns that the taxing authority will not see the codified doctrine as a last-resort measure. The application of a GAAR is a serious matter, meant to be "a last-resort measure, used only after specific anti-avoidance rules have failed.")

[473] Hariton, *supra* no. 146 at 238 ("[M]ore cynically, [tax practitioners] recognize that results based to the maximum extent on the unadulterated application of objective rules tend to aggrandize both the power and the pocketbook of the tax practitioner. Most practitioners believe, however, that there is a need for some sort of balancing between rules and standards and that a judicious sprinkling of standards throughout a fundamentally objective set of statutes and regulations is a beneficial palliative.")

and substance in taxation:"[474] "a statute so meticulously drafted must be interpreted as a literal expression of the taxing policy and leaves only the small interstices for judicial consideration."[475] This opinion assumed, however, the rightness of its own conclusion, i.e. that literalism is appropriate, because it produces a more reliable result than a principled interpretive approach.[476] Moreover, as I have previously argued, the suggestion that there is a "plain meaning" in tax legislation has little to commend it. Hence this criticism of the economic substance doctrine, on the basis that judges have no business substituting their views for the words of the legislature, does not deliver a knock-out punch.

Further opposition to reliance upon the economic substance doctrine is based on the claim that those who design transactions that fall within technical provisions of the law must be entitled to rely on the rules of the game that existed at the start of the game, and applying the economic substance doctrine amounts to judges unfairly "changing the rules of the game."[477] This view has, however, been eloquently replied to by Professor McMahon, who considers that the use of judicial doctrines to defeat egregious transactions such as abusive tax avoidance shelters is warranted:

> because they treat tax law as law—an effort to determine the "right" result—rather than as a high-stakes game in which taxpayers bet transaction

---

[474] Isenbergh, *supra* no. 214 at 883-884 ("[I]f *Gregory* had gone the other way (and all that entails had ensued), we would now have a more readily fathomable demarcation between the respective spheres of statutory provisions and judicial intuition.").

[475] *Gregory v. Commissioner*, 27 B.T.A. 223 (B.T.A., 1932) at p. 225, reversed 69 F.2d 809 (2d Cir., 1934), affirmed 293 U.S. 465 (1935).

[476] Smith, *supra* no. 217 at 20 ("The ... claim that literalism in interpretation is appropriate because a principled approach inherently represents an aesthetic response to controversial issues is self-refuting. It asserts an objectivity (correctness) for its own conclusions, which it denies to the principled interpretive approach. The fallacy of the assertion lies in the failure to realize that literalism itself must be justified and that justification can only be made by reference to reasons or principles.").

[477] See, for example, Glassman, *supra* no. 183 at 670 ("Abandoning the economic substance doctrine ... would ... prevent the government from changing the rules after the [tax avoidance] game has been played.").

costs against their ability to find and exploit anomalies in the Code and regulations. As law, the Code and regulations should serve a purpose. Broadly speaking, that purpose is to divide the cost of the public goods among taxpayers relative to their incomes according to a predetermined formula, the rate schedules. This purpose is served by rules defining the "taxable income" to which the rate schedules will be applied. If taxpayers are free to manipulate the rules defining "taxable income" to cause it to diverge from their economic income in ways not contemplated by Congress in writing the statutory rules, then the purpose of the statute will be frustrated.[478]

A fairer criticism of the economic substance doctrine is that judicial inconsistency in its application has resulted in uncertainty. According to this complaint, the variance in judicial interpretation "verges on incoherence"[479] and taxpayers are left with little practical guidance in structuring their transactions.[480] Problems with the certainty argument have already been examined in chapter V, in reviewing the Supreme Court of Canada's treatment of economic realities and economic substance in tax cases. Rector has also suggested, in any event, that differences amongst the courts as to how the economic doctrine applies may be inconsequential, as they have not been determinative of results. In this regard, he points out that different Circuit courts came to the same results in the COLI, CINS and other tax shelter cases, although they were applying the economic substance doctrine differently.[481]

---

[478] McMahon, Jr., *supra* no. 374 at 196 ("This sort of thinking is common, although it is not universally accepted, among tax academicians. It is quite out of vogue, however, with much of the practicing bar.")

[479] David Mattingly, "Empty Forms: Applying the Assignment-of-Income Doctrine to Contingent Liability Tax Shelters", 94 *Georgetown Law Journal* 1993-2027 (2006), 2008 ("[T]he breadth and flexibility of the economic substance doctrine convey significant power. But the cost of such power is a variance in judicial interpretation that verges on incoherence.")

[480] Timothy R. Hicks, "Government Victories Using The Economic Substance Doctrine: A Changing of the Tide in Tax Practice?", 38 *Cumberland Law Review* 101-138 (2007), 119 ("[U]npredictability leaves taxpayers with little practical guidance in structuring transactions and further opens the door for the government to argue taxpayer abuse when it does not like the results of a tax advantaged transaction.")

[481] Rector, *supra* no. 2 at 186-187 ("There are not enough suitable cases to adequately test whether inter-circuit difference of application [in relation to the economic substance doctrine] matter. To the very limited degree that it is

Another response to the claim that inconsistency in the application of the economic substance doctrine has resulted in intolerable uncertainty relates to the fact that either judicial doctrines, or statutory anti-avoidance provisions, or some combination of the two must in any event be available, in order to prevent abusive tax avoidance from occurring on a massive scale. Since statutory anti-avoidance provisions are "plagued by almost all of the same ambiguities that ... make the application of the economic substance doctrine difficult,"[482] there is no likelihood that their existence results in any greater certainty than occurs in the case of judicial doctrines.[483] There must always, for example, be exceptions for transactions that are consistent with legislative intent, and whether this exception is available, in a particular case, will always by necessity be in the domain of the judiciary.

While the judiciary's inconsistency in its application of the economic substance doctrine has been criticized, the doctrine has often also been lauded for its flexibility. Several authors have defended the doctrine on the basis that it provides more effective protection against abusive tax avoidance than an inelastic rigid rule could provide, because of its flexibility.[484] In this respect, the fluidity of the

---

possible to observe, it seems that the differences are not outcome determinative."); also see McMahon Jr., *supra* no. 79 at 735 (noting "none of the courts applying the disjunctive test ever upheld the tax benefits of a transaction on the grounds that one of the two prongs but not the other had been satisfied; when one has been found absent, the other has also been found lacking, and when one has been found to be present, the other has also been found to be present."); Wells, *supra* no. 15 at 416-417 (also suggesting that "[I]t is unclear whether these divergent formulations of the economic substance doctrine resulted in any actual conflict in the decided cases.").

[482] Bankman, *supra* no. 2 at 934 (Many legislative proposals to deal with the U.S. tax shelter problem "like the more ambitious proposals to reform the economic substance doctrine, cannot avoid many of the ambiguities that make present law difficult to apply.").

[483] Compare: Tooma, *supra* no. 15 at 294 (the conclusion in her PhD thesis, Australian School of Taxation, Faculty of Law, University of New South Wales is "there may be greater certainty where a statutory GAAR exists, with safeguards to ensure that it is appropriately administered.").

[484] See, for example, Dennis J. Ventry Jr., "Save the Economic Substance Doctrine from Congress", 118 *Tax Notes* 1405-1412 (Mar. 31, 2008), 1405-06

economic substance doctrine has been praised by virtue of the fact that "it can be applied to the vast variety of tax avoidance transactions which exist in today's complex business world."[485]

The claim has also been made that U.S. courts have shown "uncommonly good judgment and common sense" in distinguishing between real transactions and tax shelters. This is said to be due to the fact that the distinction is not "narrowly based on a single test, such as a formulaic minimum return requirement, but rather

---

("Despite the antishelter success of the judicially created economic substance doctrine, Congress is preparing to straitjacket the doctrine by codifying it under the Internal Revenue Code. Codification is a *terrible* idea. Reducing the doctrine to an inelastic administrative rule would sap its power and lead to more rather than less abuse, by providing clever tax planners an opportunity to occupy and manipulate the statutory line between permissible and impermissible behavior. The power of the doctrine lies in its ability to adapt to new and unforeseen tax planning strategies. Malleable standards are particularly important in the context of tax law, where the law itself is often ambiguous and where application of fact to law contains countless outcomes, such that determining the 'right' answer is an inherently uncertain proposition. A rigid rule would provide opportunity rather than certainty, and it would foster overaggressive tax planning. The economic substance doctrine often acts as the last line of defense against abusive tax avoidance, and its facts and circumstances analysis is better left in the hands of judges than legislative drafters."); Robert Willens, "'Economic Substance' Doctrine Denies Tax Benefits", 118 *Tax Notes* 537-540 (Jan. 28, 2008), 540; ("[Court decisions seem] to firmly establish the judicially established economic substance doctrine as an important check on the tax avoidance activities who seek to achieve their goals by engaging in transactions that, are for the most part, devoid of profit potential (apart from the sought-after tax benefits). With this doctrine firmly ensconced, one wonders why the flexibility the courts have shown in applying it should be sacrificed for the rigidity that a legislative effort to 'codify' the doctrine would almost certainly entail."); Bernard Wolfman, "Why Economic Substance is Better Left Uncodified", 104 *Tax Notes* 445 (Jul. 26, 2004), 445 ("[The economic substance doctrine] ... would lose ... strength ... if ... reduced to a rigid or formulaic legislative Rx. The purpose of the doctrine and its application over time have served our tax system well. The doctrine has assured us that neither the government nor practitioners will succeed in their roles if they are excessively literal and mechanical in their reading of the statute ....")

[485] Miller, Jr., *supra* no. 221 at 1069 ("[T]he better view would suggest allowing the economic substance doctrine to remain a part of the common law or risk robbing the doctrine of the flexibility that gives it strength ....")

the entirety of the transaction, including the way it was created and sold, the involvement of extraneous (usually tax-exempt) parties, shifting allocations, the involvement of tax-indifferent parties and the presence of unusual contrived steps."[486]

Another criticism of the economic substance doctrine has been that its boundaries are easily manipulated. With respect to the objective prong of the doctrine, the U.S. courts have generally looked to a pre-tax rate of return, although there is no answer under the existing case law to the question of "[w]hat rate of return is high enough,?" because no tax shelter case has involved a positive return after transaction costs.[487] The problem with specifying a minimum rate of return is that it can be "readily sidestepped by taxpayers who invest in higher-yielding risky assets and then hedge out of the related risks in ways that could not readily be identified with the relevant transaction."[488] For this reason, Hariton concludes that the question which should be asked is whether the transaction gives rise to any unique economic risk that is significant in relation to the tax benefits claimed, rather than whether the transaction gives rise to any profit, or to any particular rate of profit, before moving to the more difficult question of whether the tax benefits claimed are in keeping with Congressional intent.[489] The codified version of the economic substance doctrine now in place in the U.S. takes an approach similar to Hariton's, with its requirement that there must have been a "meaningful" change in the taxpayer's economic

---

[486] Peter C. Canellos, "Tax Practitioner's Perspective on Substance, Form and Business Purpose in Structuring Business Transactions and in Tax Shelters", 54 *SMU Law Review* 47-72 (2001), 51-53 (arguing that real transactions are intended to make money by increasing revenues or reducing expenses, whereas tax shelters exist principally to generate tax benefits where economic risk has been largely eliminated through a "choreographed series of steps.").

[487] Bankman, *supra* no. 5 at 23-25 (commenting that in many of the tax shelter cases that have been litigated, the taxpayers had not placed any of their money at risk, and were receiving negative returns after transaction costs)

[488] Hariton, *supra* no. 2 at 48-49.

[489] *Ibid.* at 55 ("A balance must ... be struck between the importance of having objective results and the importance of having equitable results that are reasonably consistent with the intent of the relevant statutes.").

position, apart from Federal income tax effects – see the discussion of the codified economic substance doctrine in this chapter.

Regarding the subjective business purpose prong of the economic substance doctrine, it has been suggested that since the courts look for objective indicia of intent, such as contemporaneous documents and evidence of meetings, etc., this leads to the creation of false or misleading documents that evidence ostensible non-tax motives.[490] As Professor Freedman has noted, "engagement in an avoidance scheme can encourage taxpayers to be economical with the truth."[491] This criticism of the economic substance doctrine, on the ground that its subjective business purpose prong may turn on the self-serving testimony of taxpayers many years after-the-fact; plus, on the ground that a requirement for subjective business purpose can be satisfied even by unreasonably held expectations of profit,[492] also leads Hariton to conclude that subjective business purpose has no useful role in the application of the economic substance doctrine in the U.S.[493] Professor Lederman, who thinks the economic substance doctrine is a "terrible tool," as it is too disconnected from the essential inquiry of whether the claimed tax result is abusive or is consistent with the intent of the applicable legislative provisions, agrees that given the focus of the doctrine on

---

[490] Bankman, *supra* no. 65 at 27-28 ("Promoters supply corporations with reams of paper on the ostensible business benefits of a particular shelter; the corporation approves the purchase in meetings whose notes stress such benefits – all for a shelter that in truth is purchased only for its tax benefits.").

[491] Freedman, *supra* no. 21 at 349.

[492] This was explained in the U.S. White Paper on the problem of corporate tax shelters released in 1999 – see chapter VI.

[493] Hariton, *supra* no. 2 at 53 ("[T]he legitimacy of purported tax benefits should not turn on the self-serving testimony of principal actors many years after the fact. But its more fundamental flaw is that business purpose does not require the taxpayer to take on any economic risk. ... If all that is required of a tax shelter is that it be tacked onto a borrowing or onto an investment of capital, we shall never see the end of shelters. But if taxpayers are at least required to take on unique economic risk that is substantial in relation to the tax benefits they claim, we shall see relatively few shelters, for no one seems willing to lose real money just to claim questionable tax benefits. When one gets to the bottom of the facts in one of these shelter cases, one invariably discovers that all of the significant economic risks have been hedged away.").

business purpose and whether there was a prospect of pre-tax profit, it is easily manipulated by taxpayers.[494] Nevertheless, the codified economic doctrine includes a subjective business purpose and an objective economic substance test – see my later discussion of these points in this chapter.

LEADING U.S. COURT CASES

The following cases display the evolution of the economic substance doctrine in the U.S. in response to tax avoidance concerns. No counterpart to this evolution has occurred in Canada, and that is a substantial contributor in favour of my argument for amendments to our GAAR.

Gregory v. Helvering

The U.S. Supreme Court decision in 1935 in *Gregory v. Helvering*,[495] which upheld a non-literal interpretation of tax law, and allowed for the examination of the substance in addition to the legal form of transactions, is generally recognized as a forefather

---

[494] Leandra Lederman, "W(h)ither Economic Substance?", 95 *Iowa Law Review* 389-444 (2010), 442-443 ("Although courts often use the current economic substance doctrine to reach appropriate outcomes – disallowance of tax benefits claimed in abusive transactions – the doctrine has evolved into one that asks the wrong questions and is easily manipulated. It can be applied to uphold claimed tax benefits where the taxpayer can provide a plausible business purpose, even if the transaction is abusive. It can also uphold transactions that yield a small amount of pre-tax profit – or the prospect of pre-tax profit – even if that profit is less than what would be obtained from other equally risky investments, and even if the deal makes economic sense only because of the tax benefits. ... In addition, the business purpose prong of the doctrine yields results that differ depending on whether an abusive tax strategy, including a tax arbitrage transaction, is incorporated into a business. Conceptually and economically, the two situations are no different, and neither should be upheld.")

[495] 293 U.S. 465 (1935). The Supreme Court explained in *Higgins v. Smith*, 308 U.S. 473 (1940) at p. 476 "[if] the *Gregory* case is viewed as a precedent for the disregard of a transfer of assets without a business purpose ... it gives support to the natural conclusion that transactions, which do not vary control or change the flow of economic benefits, are to be dismissed from consideration.")

of the modern economic substance doctrine.[496] Mrs. Gregory was planning to sell stock, held by a company that she owned, to an unrelated purchaser. At the time, corporate-level tax could be avoided by having the company distribute the stock up to the shareholder, and having the shareholder sell the stock to the buyer.[497] However, Mrs. Gregory's tax planners attempted to structure the distribution of the stock to her by means of a tax-free reorganization. The route chosen was for Mrs. Gregory's company to first contribute the stock to a newly-formed subsidiary, and then have the newly-formed subsidiary distribute its stock to Mrs. Gregory in a liquidation. The stock of the liquidated company was then sold to the third party. As the distribution of the subsidiary's stock to Mrs. Gregory was not treated by her as a taxable dividend, because it technically qualified as a tax-free reorganization under the *Revenue Act of 1928*, this allowed use of part of the basis in her company's stock to offset the gain from the subsequent sale. Under this scenario, the amount of shareholder-level gain recognized by Mrs. Gregory was substantially less than it would have been if the stock eventually sold had been distributed directly to her without involving a re-organization.[498] The Commissioner sought to tax the sale of shares to the third party on the basis that would have prevailed, if not for the reorganization. However, Judge Sternhagen of the Board of Tax Appeals found that the distribution of shares fit within the statutory definition of a tax-free "reorganization", and allowed Mrs. Gregory's appeal while delivering this *obiter* which is a favourite of literalists: "a statute so meticulously drafted must be interpreted as a literal expression of the taxing policy and leaves only the small interstices for judicial consideration."[499]

In reversing Judge Sternhagen's decision, Judge Learned Hand did not have any objection to the elimination of the corporate-level

---

[496] Nahass, *supra* no. 136 at 255 (stating *Gregory v. Helvering* is generally cited as the genesis of the economic substance doctrine).
[497] Hariton, *supra* no. 2 at 41 (commenting that the reason for the two-step structuring was to avoid the corporate-level tax that otherwise would have been imposed on the sale).
[498] *Ibid.* at 43.
[499] *Gregory v. Commissioner*, 27 B.T.A. 223 (1932) at p. 225.

tax: "Anyone may so arrange his affairs that his taxes shall be as low as possible; he is not bound to choose that pattern which will best pay the Treasury; there is not even a patriotic duty to increase one's taxes."[500] Nevertheless, and although Judge Hand accepted that Mrs. Gregory had achieved technical compliance with the taxation statute, he held that the reorganization provision was only intended to apply to transactions "undertaken for reasons germane to the conduct of the venture in hand, not as an ephemeral incident, egregious to its prosecution. To dodge the shareholder's taxes is not one of the transactions contemplated as corporate 'reorganizations'... All these steps were real, and their only defect was that they were not what the statute means by a 'reorganization', because the transactions were no part of the conduct of the business of either or both companies ..."[501]

The crucial element of Judge Hand's approach was his rejection of a literal meaning of the term "reorganization", on the basis that "the meaning of a sentence may be more than that of the separate words, as a melody is more than the notes, and no degree of particularity can ever obviate recourse to the setting in which all appear, and which all collectively create."[502] The correctness and wisdom of Judge Hand's reasoning have long been debated; however, his decision was an important part of the foundation for the "business purpose" test in the U.S. Judge Hand's decision is said to have "left echoes in every corner of the tax law."[503]

The U.S. Supreme Court concurred with Judge Hand's reasoning for siding with the Commissioner, on the basis of its identical conclusion that what really occurred was "an operation having no business or corporate purpose."[504] The Supreme Court also wrote, with a *Duke of Westminster*-like tone that "the legal right of the taxpayer to decrease the amount of what otherwise would be his

---

[500] 69 F.2d 809 (2d Cir., 1934) at p. 810.
[501] *Ibid.* at 811.
[502] *Ibid.*
[503] Isenbergh, *supra* no. 214 at 867 (also stating that Learned Hand was writing for a panel of judges of great intellectual prestige.).
[504] 293 U.S. 465 (1935) at pp. 469-70, affirmed 69 F.2d 809 (2d Cir., 1934).

taxes, or all together to avoid them, by means which the law permits, cannot be doubted."[505] Thus, although the Supreme Courts of Canada and the U.S. have shared a similar tax leaning, as regards recognizing a right of taxpayers to organize their affairs so as to minimize taxes, the U.S. Supreme Court has stood apart in terms of its willingness to invoke a business purpose test in the face of what it considers to be unacceptable tax avoidance. The point appears to be that, in qualifying the right of taxpayers to take steps to reduce their taxes, "by means which the law permits", the U.S. Supreme Court recognizes that transactions designed to withstand scrutiny on a literal reading of the law may still be outside the realm of what "the law permits" in a tax avoidance context.

The rejection of literalism by Learned Hand and by the U.S. Supreme Court in *Gregory* "was apparently to limit tax avoidance to those situations where the tax objective sought by the taxpayer were not in plain opposition to those sought by Congress, at least as a judge might reasonably conceive of the latter."[506] Part of the foundation for this approach to statutory interpretation was explained by Judge Hand in *Gilbert v. Commissioner of Internal Revenue*. In this regard, transactions which are motivated solely by tax considerations should be disregarded "for we cannot suppose that it was part of the purpose of the act to provide an escape from the liabilities that it sought to impose."[507] This is an expression of what is sometimes referred to as the "self-defeating" theory of statutory interpretation.[508] Under this theory, courts should not presume that Parliament intended to allow taxpayers to defeat its intention with transactions which do not appreciably affect their beneficial

---

[505] 293 US 465 (1935) at p. 469.
[506] Chirelstein, *supra* no. 90 at 472-473 (noting the statutory definition of reorganization was supplemented by business purpose.)
[507] 248 F.2d 399 (2d Cir., 1957) at p. 411, per Hand J. dissenting.
[508] Tooma, *supra* no. 15 at 47 (suggesting that "The underlying rationale of the Economic Substance Doctrine is the Self-Defeating Rationale."); see also: Morgan, *supra* no 1 at 394 (suggesting that there is an implied economic substance doctrine in the common law if the judiciary accepts the corollary argument that it is not to interpret the law in a way that would be self-defeating)

interests, when considered apart from taxes.[509] Justice Cardozo would have had this notion in mind, when he wrote many decades ago, that "[t]he mind rebels against the notion that Congress ... was willing to foster an opportunity for juggling so facile and so obvious ... To such an attempt the reaction of an impartial mind is little short of instinctive that the deduction is unreasonable."[510]

The departure from literalism in the *Gregory* era occurred when the U.S. was facing unacceptable losses of revenue from tax avoidance, while confronted with the problems of the Great Depression. Tax avoidance had become a politically charged subject that involved leading industrialists, bankers and even a former Secretary of the Treasury.[511] The "tax trial of the century," involving charges against Andrew Mellon, formerly the Secretary of the Treasury, was major news during the period that the *Gregory* trial was under adjudication. In the year prior to *Gregory*, tax avoidance was so visible that even the Church took up the issue. The effects of the Depression, coupled with the work of a Senate Committee which revealed that the super-rich were exploiting ways to reduce their taxes, made

---

[509] Smith, *supra* no. 217 at 4-5 (commenting that the self-defeating theory of statutory interpretation is the implicit rationale of the business purpose requirement.); Li, *supra* no. 8 at 39 (arguing that the self-defeating approach requires an economic analysis of transactions and that it is both clearly expressed in the Department of Finance Technical Notes which accompanied GAAR and recognized by the Supreme Court in its *Mathew* decision [2005 SCC 55 (S.C.C.) at para. 62] where it held that "the only reasonable conclusion is that the series of transactions frustrated Parliament's purpose of confining the transfer of losses such as these to a non-arm's length partnership.").

[510] *Woolford Realty Co. v. Rose*, 286 U.S. 319 (1932) at p. 330.

[511] Likhovski, *supra* no. 268 at 955 and 957-958 ("Tax avoidance is ... one of the few areas of tax law which captures the attention of the general public because it involves highly contested and moral issues. ... [A] major factor that led [Judge] Hand to decide as he did was the political context in which the case was decided. Because of his general political convictions, Hand was pre-disposed to an anti-taxpayer position on tax avoidance and this pre-disposition was augmented by the fact that tax avoidance by the wealthy had become a subject of intense political debate at the precise time that *Helvering v. Gregory* was decided. In the months and weeks prior to the decision, newspapers were filled with reports about the tax avoidance tricks practiced by a group of leading industrialists and bankers, chief among whom was Andrew Mellon, former Secretary of the Treasury.").

tax avoidance such a politically charged subject that President Roosevelt conducted a lengthy campaign against "economic royalists". According to Professor Likhovski, these circumstances are an important part of the back-drop for the non-literalist approach to statutory interpretation adopted in *Gregory*.[512]

Knetsch v. United States

The Supreme Court's decision in 1960 in *Knetsch v. U.S.*[513] was a further step towards the establishment of the economic substance doctrine in the U.S. The *Knetsch* case, and the subsequent *Goldstein* case (see below), both involved transactions that were guaranteed to be cash flow negative, before the expected savings of the federal income tax, and that were isolated from the taxpayers' other activities.[514] Mr. Knetsch borrowed from an insurance company at an interest rate of 3 ½ percent, to finance a purchase from the same company of savings bonds paying 2 ½ percent. The transactions were structured so that the net result was that interest deductions were accelerated, while income was postponed and ordinary income was converted into capital gain.[515]

While the Supreme Court ultimately disallowed the interest deductions, on the ground that the loans from the insurance company were a façade, it also reasoned "it is patent that there was nothing of substance to be realized by Knetsch from this transaction beyond

---

[512] *Ibid.* at 1001 ("In the spring of 1935, the President finally started to exploit the huge symbolic capital of the [tax avoidance] issue in a deliberate and consistent manner (as *Time* magazine observed, 'tax dodging tycoons are a juicy copy'). Roosevelt began a two-year long presidential campaign against tax avoidance by the 'economic royalists'. The campaign culminated in the 1937 *Revenue Act*, an act explicitly directed at plugging various well-publicized (if economically insignificant) abuses of the tax code.")

[513] 364 U.S. 361 (1960).

[514] Jennings, *supra* no. 468 at 538 (suggesting that the emphasis of the economic substance doctrine should be shifted away from an objective review of the economics of transactions to whether the taxpayer's subjective purpose was to realize a nontax objective.)

[515] Blum, *supra* no. 409 at 297 (The full details and figures in the complicated transaction are reproduced in footnote 8.)

a tax deduction",[516] although all of the literal requirements for the claimed tax deduction were met. This emphasis by the Court on the importance of nothing of substance having occurred beyond a tax deduction helped to pave the way for recognition of the economic substance doctrine. Professor Blum has commented on the decision in *Knetsch*:

> [I]n our [U.S.] income tax system, the courts have exercised a major role in coping with the inventiveness of advisers who seek to shape transactions along lines that, they hope, will minimize tax liabilities while disturbing the economic position of their clients as little as possible.
>
> * * * * * *
>
> [T]he [U.S. Supreme] Court is not sympathetic to novel tax-reduction plans. There is nothing new in this. Through the years the Court has seldom been favorably disposed towards taxpayers who try to overexploit dispensations in the income tax law by arranging their affairs in uncommon ways. Perhaps this skeptical view of cunning conduct has set a healthy keynote for the whole judiciary; for it may be that a negative judicial attitude toward tax avoidance is most fitting under a tax system that attaches different tax consequences to alternative ways of arranging one's affairs.[517]

It will by now be apparent that the Supreme Court of Canada has not shared this "negative judicial attitude toward tax avoidance". Given its minimization of the role of economic substance under GAAR, the legislature in Canada needs to step up, to revise its position.

Goldstein v. Commissioner

The decision in 1966, of the Court of Appeals for the Second Circuit in *Goldstein v. Commissioner*,[518] established that even though transactions are found to be real and cannot be invalidated as façades or shams, deductions can still be disallowed where there was no non-tax business purpose for the transactions, and the

---

[516] 364 U.S. 361 (1960) at p. 366.
[517] Blum, *supra* no. 409 at 300.
[518] 364 F.2d 734 (2d Cir., 1966), affirmed 385 U.S. 1005 (1967).

transactions did not cause any meaningful change in the taxpayer's position, when considered apart from their tax benefits.

Mrs. Goldstein was a seventy year old woman living with her husband on a pension of $780 per year. She won an Irish sweepstakes prize of $140,000 in 1958; however, the highest marginal income tax rate at the time was 91 percent. With the benefit of tax planning advice from her accountant son, Mrs. Goldstein attempted to achieve income averaging and deferral by obtaining loans with prepaid interest charged at the rate of 4 percent, which were used to acquire bonds paying an interest rate of 1½ percent. On the assumption that the prepaid interest was deductible, Mrs. Goldstein would be ahead financially on account of her tax savings, despite the impossibility of making a profit on her "investment" in the bonds. The Tax Court disallowed the deductions on the ground that the transactions were shams. The Second Circuit did not agree with the sham characterization, but it disallowed the deductions as it found no non-tax business purpose and a lack of economic substance. The transactions were held to have "[no] purpose, substance or utility apart from their anticipated tax consequences".[519]

The *Goldstein* decision illustrates that even where legal relationships are accepted as *bona fide*, transactions will still be analyzed in the U.S. courts to determine whether they have sufficient economic substance to be respected for tax purposes.[520] The ultimate basis for the decision in the *Goldstein* case was a judicial inference that Congress never intended that taxpayers should be able to "zero out" their incomes by entering into offsetting borrowings and loans and prepaying interest on the former,[521] although the transactions were structurally sound.

---

[519] *Ibid.* at 740.
[520] Miller, Jr., *supra* no. 221 at 1038 (suggesting that an important lesson to take from *Goldstein* is that when business transactions are *bona fide*, as were Mrs. Goldstein's, such transactions should be recognized as legitimate, and then analyzed to determine if they are imbued with sufficient economic substance to be respected for tax purposes).
[521] Hariton, *supra* no. 146 at 249 (commenting that the economic substance doctrine applied to the transactions as Mrs. Goldstein entered into them for no

This position in *Goldstein* is to be contrasted with the Supreme Court of Canada's position in *Shell* to the effect that *bona fide* legal relationships must be respected in tax cases absent sham or a statutory provision to the contrary.

Frank Lyon v. United States

In 1978, the U.S. Supreme Court laid the balance of the foundation for the modern day economic substance doctrine, with its two subjective business purpose and objective economic substance prongs, in *Frank Lyon Co. v. U.S.*[522] The Worthen Bank had the objective of building a new building, but it would not have been able to gain approval from government authorities to invest the substantial amount in banking premises that the building would cost, and so it entered into a sale-leaseback transaction. As the building was built, Worthen sold it to Frank Lyon for a price not to exceed $7,640,000 and leased it back. Frank Lyon obtained a 25 year mortgage for $7,140,000 and invested cash of $500,000. Worthen's annual rent for the first 25 years of the building lease matched the mortgage payments. The building cost over $10 million to build. Worthen had a series of options to repurchase the building at various specified amounts plus assumption of the remaining mortgage. If an option was exercised in the first 25 years, Frank Lyon would receive $500,000 and 6 percent interest.

---

reason other than to offset her income from the Irish Sweepstakes, and they did not meaningfully change her economic position. The court was therefore entitled to ask whether the resulting deductions were within the scope of what Congress intended when it enacted an interest deduction under section 163(a) of *the Internal Revenue Code*); Jennings, *supra* no. 468 at 538-539 (observing that the court imposed a non-statutory requirement in *Goldstein* that it said was applicable because Congress intended that an interest deduction be available only for "purposive activity"); Gunn, *supra* no. 70 (arguing that the fact the transaction was unlikely to produce a nontax profit did not by itself justify denying the interest deduction and that the requirement that Mrs. Goldstein had to have a non-tax purpose is inconsistent with the frequent proposition that intent to reduce taxes is irrelevant.)

[522] 435 U.S. 561 (1978).

The tax issue was whether Frank Lyon was entitled to depreciation and other deductions as owner of the building, although it was in the economic position of being a lender, while Worthen enjoyed the economic equivalent of ownership. Frank Lyon had a downside risk in the event that Worthen became insolvent, as it remained liable on the mortgage. However, the security for Frank Lyon's position included the building that cost more than $10 million to build, plus the land it was on and a parking facility. In these circumstances, Frank Lyon was in the same risk position that a lender would face.[523]

The Supreme Court concluded that the sale and leaseback transaction was a *bona fide* legal relationship, but ruled that it would only be upheld for tax purposes if a tax-independent business purpose existed, and the transaction had economic reality apart from tax considerations.[524] The passage in the Supreme Court's decision, that is credited as the basis for the modern economic substance doctrine, is "where ... there is a genuine multiple-party transaction with economic substance which is compelled or encouraged by business or regulatory realities, is imbued with tax-independent considerations, and is not shaped solely by tax-avoidance features that have meaningless labels attached, the Government should honor the allocation of rights and duties effectuated by the parties."[525]

The Supreme Court's finding that Frank Lyon was entitled to the deductions, as the transactions had economic substance, has been criticized on the basis that it proceeded on the basis of a misunderstanding of the economics of the transaction, including mistaken reasoning that the depreciation deductions would cost the Treasury the same amount if either Frank Lyon or Worthen deducted them (Worthen did not need depreciation deductions to reduce

---

[523] Lederman, *supra* no. 494 at 411 (noting that the claimed tax benefits explain why Frank Lyon accepted a below-market return on its $500,000 investment).
[524] Miller, Jr., *supra* no. 221 at 1038 (noting that the *Frank Lyon* decision established the two-pronged subjective and objective inquiries to be made when analyzing economic substance); McMahon Jr., *supra* no. 79 at 735 (noting however that it is unclear whether the Court's test is be conjunctive or disjunctive).
[525] 435 U.S. 561 (1978) at pp. 583-84.

its taxable income).[526] Another criticism of the decision is that it condoned what was essentially a sale of depreciation deductions, which technically are not transferable, whereas Congress could not have intended this result.[527] Nevertheless, the *Frank Lyon* decision is widely credited with establishing the common law two-prong test for determining whether a transaction should be disregarded for tax purposes: "has the taxpayer shown that it had a business purpose for engaging in the transaction other than tax avoidance [and] has the taxpayer shown that the transaction had economic substance beyond the creation of the tax benefits?"[528]

The business purpose prong of the economic substance doctrine focuses on the motives of the taxpayer for entering into the transaction, while the objective substance prong involves an objective analysis of the taxpayer's economic position before and after the transaction.[529] These two prongs have been a feature of most of

---

[526] Bernard Wolfman, "The Supreme Court in the Lyon's Den: A Failure of Judicial Process", 66 *Cornell Law Review* 1075-1102 (1981), 1075-1076 ("The court's decision and opinion manifest an understanding that is questionable at best. ... [T]he story of this case casts some doubt on the adversary system itself as a reliable vehicle for attaining justice in tax disputes and for producing sound and authoritative interpretations of the Internal Revenue Code"); David A. Weisbach, "The Failure of Disclosure As An Approach to Tax Shelters", 54 *SMU Law Review* 73-82 (2001), 75 ("[T]he bottom line was that in virtually no event would the purported owner of the property recover anything more than its original investment plus six percent interest, and in virtually no event would the purported owner lose money. The purported owner of the property had no involvement in the transaction other than as a lender, but through fictions believed by the court, was able to cast itself as an owner. ... [T]he court was completely fooled by the arrangement."); Gunn, *supra* no. 70 at 747 footnote 44 (commenting that the court addressed the correct question in determining whether the taxpayer who held title to the building was in economic reality also the owner of the building, "whatever one may think of its answer.")

[527] Lederman, *supra* no. 494 at 414 (arguing that the Supreme Court erred in *Frank Lyon*, unlike in *Gregory* and *Knetsch*, by failing to consider Congress's intent).

[528] *Bail Bonds by Marvin Nelson, Inc. v. Comm'r*, 820 F.2d 1543 (9th Cir., 1987) at p. 1549; *Rice's Toyota World Inc.*, 752 F.2d 89 (4th Cir., 1985) at pp. 91-95.

[529] Keinan, *supra* no. 2 at 393-94 (noting that the courts have been divided on how to apply the two-prong test, with some courts considering it to be conjunctive and others to be disjunctive, while some courts give the prongs unequal weight, and some courts apply both tests as part of a "unitary" analysis).

the versions of the economic substance doctrine applied by courts in the U.S., and they have been maintained as part of the codified economic substance doctrine.

AN ORDINARY BUSINESS EXCEPTION?

A threshold question in deciding when to apply the economic substance doctrine is what transactions are to be lumped together and measured for economic substance.[530] In theory, the greater the number of transactions linked together, the greater the likelihood of finding some non-tax effect. In this regard, the courts in the U.S have shown a willingness to lump transactions together that are connected to ordinary business operations, whereas the elements in tax shelters are more likely to be viewed discretely.[531] This is reflected in the much-quoted phrase coined by Professor Gergen: "[Y]ou can pick up tax gold if you find it in the street while going about your business, but you cannot go hunting for it."[532] A common thread in the corporate tax shelter cases, where the economic substance doctrine has been applied, is that the transactions have been outside the ordinary course of the taxpayer's business.[533] The

---

[530] This is similar to the question of what amounts to a "series of transactions" under Canada's GAAR – see Brian J. Arnold, *The Arnold Report*, Canadian Tax Foundation, Posting 007 (Jan. 17, 2011) (commenting that the matter of what amounts to a series of transactions has been "reasonably handled in Canada" by the courts.)

[531] Bankman, *supra* no. 65 at15 ("In theory, by expanding or contracting the number of related events, a decision maker could reach virtually any result it wanted under the doctrine."); also see: Prebble and Prebble, *supra* no. 102 at 699 (suggesting that "If one can argue that a tax-reducing effect is a natural incident of certain economic activity, it is less likely that the authorities will stigmatize that effect as avoidance."); David P. Hariton, vol. 63 *Tax Lawyer* 1-42 (Fall 2009) (noting that "any tax-motivated financial structure can be made to look like a tax shelter by defining the transaction as consisting solely of the relevant tax-motivated steps).

[532] Gergen, *supra* no. 372 at140 (arguing that it is abusive to enter into transactions with little or no economic substance with the goal from the start of creating an artificial loss).

[533] McMahon, Jr., *supra* no. 374 at 206 noting that almost without exception, corporate tax shelters which have been found to be lacking economic

existence of an ordinary course of business exception to the economic substance doctrine is said to be illustrated by *Cottage Sav. Ass'n v. C.I.R.*,[534] where the taxpayer had a substantial investment that it had acquired at an earlier time in the course of its ordinary business operations, and which later declined in economic value by over $2 million. Where the taxpayer exchanged the investment for one of equivalent value and claimed a loss for tax purposes, the court declined to apply the economic substance doctrine, as the new investment represented a set of "legally distinct entitlements," and the loss had arisen in the course of ordinary business operations.[535]

The decision in *Cottage Savings* is often contrasted with the decision in *ACM Partnership v. C.I.R.*,[536] where although the transactions also gave rise to a set of legally distinct entitlements, they were disregarded partly because they were found to have arisen

---

substance "did not even have any semblance of a contribution to any business activity or objective that the taxpayer may have had apart from tax planning. They were, as Mr. Canellos properly observes, merely 'loss generating shelters'."); see also: Lipton, *supra* no. 237 at 212 (noting that "the courts will allow taxpayers to obtain tax advantages when structuring legitimate business transactions but will exercise heightened scrutiny whenever the court believes that the taxpayer entered into the transaction to obtain tax benefits and not much else."; Swiderski and Manasuev, *supra* no. 15 at 18:1-31 (suggesting the codified U.S. economic substance doctrine is likely to be applied to "transactions that possess both a high level of tax minimization motivation and a palpable remoteness to the taxpayer's business-proper."); Luke, *supra* no. 67 (noting "there appears to be a reluctance [by courts] to treat transactions as economic shams if they have a direct link to day-to-day operations and/or involve seemingly neutral third parties.")

[534] 499 U.S. 554 (1991).
[535] Wells, *supra* no. 15 at 436-437 (suggesting that strong arguments can be made that the economic substance doctrine would not be "relevant" in this case, within the meaning of newly-enacted section 7701(o), as "the taxpayer had already suffered an economic loss that had not been recognized for financial or tax reporting purposes.")
[536] 157 F.3d 231 (3rd Cir., 1998) at p. 250, cert. denied 526 U.S. 1017 (1999) (the Court found "only a fleeting and economically inconsequential investment in and offsetting divestment from [the] notes" so that the transactions left the taxpayer "in the same position it had occupied before engaging in the offsetting acquisition and disposition of those notes.")

from a fleeting inconsequential investment.[537] Although *Cottage Savings* is often cited by the tax bar as a case illustrating circumstances in which the economic substance doctrine should not be applied, Professor Weisbach disagrees: "*Cottage Savings* did not involve a real transaction. Absolutely nothing happened except for tax. The economics of the *ACM* transaction, an admitted shelter, swamp those of *Cottage Savings*. In fact, it would be difficult to imagine arranging a transaction so that less actually happens. And there was no point to the deal other than to raid the Treasury. The business purpose was precisely zero, not even one-tenth of one percent. These transactions were also marketed widely. All the shelter factors except the use of accommodation parties (which were not necessary) are present."[538] Nevertheless, the *Cottage Savings* case does illustrate the reluctance of the courts to set aside transactions which relate to the taxpayer's ordinary business.

Another example of a court said to be observing an ordinary course of business exception to the application of the economic substance doctrine is *United Parcel Service of America, Inc. v. C.I.R.*[539] The *UPS* case involved a business with an existing income stream that was restructured for tax purposes, rather than "a cookie-cutter transaction designed to create a loss unrelated to UPS's core business of shipping packages."[540]

---

[537] Weisbach, *supra* no. 15 at 238 ("In *ACM*-type transactions, taxpayers use an enormously complex off-shore partnership to do essentially nothing while creating tax losses. The trick involved a misallocation of basis when property is sold for a contingent payment to be made in the future. Under the rules in effect at the time, basis was over-allocated to late payments and under-allocated to early payments, effectively creating up-front gain with an offsetting loss later on. The offshore partnership, usually located in a Caribbean tax haven, allowed the gain to be allocated to a domestic company to use against its taxable income. The transaction was structured so that as little as possible happened, primarily through the use of financial instruments that hedged out all the risk and ensured that the money merely went in a circle.")

[538] Weisbach, *supra* no. 526 at 75 ("Courts regularly allow taxpayers to claim benefits from transactions ... that have little business purpose, no real economics, are marketed as shelters and have extraneous parties or steps. *Cottage Savings*, a favorite of the tax bar, is a good example.")

[539] 254 F.3d 1014 (11th Cir., 2001), cert. denied (2/20/07).

[540] *Ibid.* at 1016.

UPS was operating a very profitable parcel insurance business. It sought to avoid U.S. tax on these profits by transferring them to an offshore affiliate. An unrelated third party was engaged as the insurer and earned premiums from parcel insurance customers in exchange for providing the insurance. However, the third party was simultaneously required to transfer the premiums to a UPS offshore affiliate, in exchange for its assumption of the insurance risk.[541]

In framing the facts for the business purpose question, the Eleventh Circuit took account of both the restructuring transaction and the insurance business that existed before the restructuring: "[T]here was a real business that served the genuine need for customers to enjoy loss coverage and for UPS to lower its liability exposure."[542] The Tax Court and the minority in the Court of Appeal came to a different result, by limiting their examinations to the restructuring.[543] The Tax Court focused on the reinsurance contract to a UPS affiliate (concluding there was no objective economic substance to the transaction, as the obligations effectively cancelled each other out).[544]

Although the taxpayer succeeded on appeal, the case was remanded to the lower court to consider other theories on which the transactions could be attacked, e.g. under the common law doctrines of attribution of income and substance versus form, and under s. 482 of the *Internal Revenue Code*. The outcome of the referral back to the lower court is unknown as the case was ultimately settled.[545]

Hariton thinks the Commissioner's attempt to frame the transaction narrowly was properly rejected in *UPS*, as the transaction involved the operation of a highly profitable parcel insurance business,

---

[541] *Ibid.*
[542] *Ibid.* at 1020.
[543] Rector, *supra* no. 2 at 184-185 (arguing that courts often frame the facts of a case in a way that enables them to reach the result that they want to reach).
[544] *Ibid.* at 185 (noting that by limiting the examination of the facts to the restructuring it was easy to conclude that there were no non-tax considerations).
[545] Hariton, *supra* no. 2 at 45 (saying that although the outcome of the case is unknown the court's description of the facts suggests that UPS may have lost the case on grounds which did not involve the economic substance doctrine).

and it was not appropriate to separate out the structural aspects of the business designed to avoid tax.[546] However, not all reaction to the taxpayer success in *UPS* has been positive.[547] Professor Lederman argues that the critical question in the *UPS* case should have been whether the result claimed was consistent with Congress's intent. In her view, a link with a taxpayer's business should not make any difference in deciding whether a claimed tax result is upheld. Lederman thinks Congress likely did not intend that the exception from taxation of amounts earned by overseas corporations would also apply to amounts earned in the U.S. by a domestic corporation that directed the proceeds to an overseas corporation with the same owners.[548]

While Lederman's claim has clear merit, transactions that are apparently related to ordinary business transactions have obviously been favourably treated by judges in the U.S. under the economic substance doctrine. Hariton supports this approach, as his concern is that if the economic substance doctrine is sought to be applied too broadly, it will lose its effectiveness. This represents recognition that judges will generally not set aside transactions which they regard as inoffensive. In the words of Oliver Wendell Holmes Jr., "hard cases make bad law."[549]

The judiciary's unofficial fashioning of a kind of ordinary business exception in the application of the economic substance doctrine

---

[546] *Ibid.* (arguing that the transactions should not be framed too narrowly as it is inappropriate to apply the economic substance doctrine too broadly).

[547] Weisbach, *supra* no. 526 at 77-78 (noting that "good practitioners from respected firms, not just tax practitioners crawling out from under rocks" have been giving strong opinions in favour of deals which are "junk").

[548] Lederman, *supra* no. 494 at 432 (arguing that whether tax benefits should be disallowed should not depend on whether they are "bundled in business garb"); but compare: McMahon Jr., *supra* no. 79 at 738 (arguing that "the Eleventh Circuit's analysis makes sense, both before and after the codification of the economic substance doctrine. Even if the transaction was entirely tax motivated, it had economic substance as that doctrine has historically been applied. ... There was simply no identifiable transaction or series of transactions that lacked economic substance.")

[549] *Northern Securities Co. v. U.S.*, 193 U.S. 197 (1904) at pp. 400-401, per Justice Holmes dissenting. The complete statement was "Great cases, like hard cases, make bad law."

in the U.S. is quite likely a reflection of the inevitable, given the tendency of courts to look to whether transactions appear offensive. However, even accepting Professor Bankman's point that having an ordinary business exception is sound tax policy,[550] questions remain as to what will be found to constitute ordinary business operations, and how closely tax-motivated transactions must be tied to ordinary business operations in order to qualify for the favourable treatment.[551]

There are no easy answers to these questions; however, Professor Bankman predicts that courts are more likely to link transactions that arise out of "regular business operations," than they are to link tax-motivated transactions carried out in separate "investments."[552] Since transactions undertaken in the course of utilizing tax shelter products do not ordinarily occur in the course of a taxpayer's business operations, their economic effects are likely to be judged in isolation, rather than being linked with business transactions.[553] Although an ordinary business exception gives rise to the possibility that the same transactions will be treated differently in different circumstances, Professor Bankman argues that these results can be justified on pragmatic grounds. This is because a rule that allows taxpayers to take advantage of loopholes that naturally occur in the course of business operations will be limited by the number of "naturally present" loopholes, whereas "[a] rule that allows taxpayers not only to take advantage of loopholes but to manufacture circumstances in which they arise would be ruinous to the fisc."[554]

---

[550] See discussion below.
[551] Bankman, *supra* no. 65 at 17-18 (questioning what the result would be if a taxpayer with ordinary business operations engaged in a tax-motivated transaction as part of an investment that was not part of any business).
[552] *Ibid.* at 18 (suggesting also however that this is subject to the caveat that "there is obviously no single right answer").
[553] Jeremiah Coder, "Will Economic Substance Be Worth It?", 127 *Tax Notes* 16-19 (Apr. 5, 2010), 19 (suggesting that the closer a transaction is to the core of a taxpayer's business, the harder it will be for the IRS to challenge the transaction on economic substance grounds).
[554] Bankman, *supra* no. 65 at18 (arguing that in the latter case the tax shelter industry would be able to eliminate most corporate income).

Professor Bankman also argues that an ordinary course of business exception is defensible on efficiency grounds. This is because the high costs associated with the manufacture of circumstances required by tax shelters can be avoided if taxpayers are only allowed to exploit drafting errors that come up in the ordinary course of business: "It may be both efficient and politically desirable to allow taxpayers to interpret the law literally when operating in the normal course of business. Providing taxpayers with greater tax certitude in planning *bona fide* business transactions is a clear benefit."[555]

A caveat on the wisdom of an ordinary business exception is that it assumes it is impossible, or at least extremely difficult, for taxpayers to change their behaviour and manufacture shelter opportunities while staying within their ordinary course of business. Nevertheless, Professor Bankman thinks that the ordinary business exception is supportable, as although companies are willing to take aggressive tax positions on transactions done for non-tax reasons, and are willing to pay for tax shelters that do not involve business risk, they do not generally engage in risky enterprises for tax benefits. This suggests to him that recognizing an ordinary business exception, if strictly enforced and buttressed by enforcement / penalties "would significantly limit revenue loss to the federal coffers."[556]

The existence of an unofficial ordinary business exception to the economic substance doctrine is also supported by Shakow, who argues by reference to the Federal Claims Court decision in *Consolidated Edison Co. of New York, Inc. v. U.S.*[557] that although the practice "may not be fully satisfying intellectually", it appears that courts will except even generic tax transactions brought to the taxpayer's attention from the application of the economic substance

---

[555] Bankman, *supra* no. 2 at 928-929 (arguing that only tax-motivated transactions unconnected to profit-making enterprises should be subject to the full range of anti-tax-shelter defences).

[556] Bankman, *supra* no. 65 at 20 (suggesting that only targeting marketed tax shelters with the economic substance doctrine reduces social waste).

[557] 90 Fed.Cl. 228 (2009).

doctrine, when "the actual investment [was] related more or less directly to the taxpayer's business."[558]

Codification of the economic substance doctrine in the U.S. has not directly spoken to the existence of an ordinary business exception; however, section 7701(o)(1) says that the economic substance doctrine only applies where it is "relevant." This effectively leaves the matter of whether the doctrine applies to transactions undertaken in the course of ordinary business operations in the hands of judges. In this regard, the Joint Committee on Taxation has said that codification is not intended to alter the tax treatment of certain basic transactions that are respected under longstanding judicial and administrative practices; and, it has provided an "angel list" of transactions.

The section 7701(o)(1) silent approach as to whether there is an ordinary business exception regarding the application of the economic substance doctrine has a good deal to commend it, as it leaves the application of the doctrine in a flexible state; it does not risk the possibility of creating a safe-harbour for transactions that are dressed-up so they can appear to have occurred as part of regular business operations; and, it avoids the problems that have been identified as being associated with the creation of ever more technical provisions to fight abusive tax avoidance.[559] Concern has been expressed by Jackel, however, that although the economic substance doctrine has been codified, the entire body of case law involving the doctrine concerns tax shelter types of transactions, and this body of law does not provide any guidance whatsoever regarding the application of the doctrine to common business transactions.[560] Nevertheless, given the U.S. tax administration's assurances that the codified doctrine is not meant to alter the tax treatment of basic transactions that have

---

[558] David J. Shakow, "*Consolidated Edison* Turns on the Lights", 126 *Tax Notes* 625-630 (Feb. 1, 2010), 630.
[559] See the discussion of this point in chapter III.
[560] Monte A. Jackel, "Jackel Urges Comment on Economic Substance Doctrine", 127 *Tax Notes* 1398 (June 21, 2010) (suggesting that the integrity of the tax system is at risk because the IRS and the Treasury are not providing urgently required guidance as to how the codified economic substance doctrine is to be applied).

historically been respected, and the judiciary's ability to control overly-enthusiastic application of the codified doctrine by the IRS, the level of uncertainty that exists is small relative to the problems the codified economic substance doctrine is addressing.

LEGISLATIVELY INTENDED BENEFITS

Professor Weisbach notes that "the government sometimes enacts explicit incentives, such as the tax-exemption for state and local bonds or investment tax credits. Taxpayers are supposed to take these incentives into account, so anti-avoidance doctrines must take congressional intent regarding these incentives into account as well. Legislative intent is probably a necessary element in any anti-avoidance doctrines and, in fact, may be the predominant element."[561] Transactions clearly supported by legislation will therefore be upheld by the courts, regardless of whether they meet the economic substance test.[562] Another example of a congressionally intended benefit that would not be susceptible to an economic substance attack is the deduction of qualified mortgage interest by home owners.[563] Although transactions clearly supported by legislation, but lacking in economic substance, are not to be disregarded for tax purposes, Hariton has commented that when courts apply the economic substance doctrine they very often do not even undertake an analysis of whether the claimed tax results are reasonably consistent with congressional intent.[564] This may be so, however, because the cases in which the

---

[561] Weisbach, *supra* no. 406 at 33.
[562] Keinan, *supra* no. 2 at 388 (pointing out that "litigation involving the economic substance doctrine frequently involves disputes over the text, intent and purpose of the relevant statute.")
[563] LU.K.e, *supra* no. 68 at 792-793 (arguing that "congressionally-sanctioned tax benefits obtained through standard channels should not be scrutinized under objective economic substance").
[564] Hariton, *supra* no. 2 at 37 ("The hardest job a court has in the case of a tax-motivated transaction that lacks business purpose and economic substance is determining whether the purported tax results of the transaction are reasonably consistent with congressional intent. But very often, the court never reaches the analysis"); also see Lederman, *supra* no. 494 at 392 (arguing that "courts

doctrine has been applied are so egregious that the question of legislative intent seemed an academic one.

In any event, while it is clear that the economic substance doctrine is not to be used to disallow tax benefits which are claimed in a manner which is consistent with legislative intent, there will continue to be difficulty "identifying those provisions and specific transactions that deserve immunization under that standard."[565]

IMPORT OF BONA FIDE LEGAL RELATIONSHIPS

The judiciary in the U.S. has not had difficulty with a conceptual framework which allows for the evaluation of the economic substance of transactions, for the purpose of determining whether they should be respected for tax purposes, independently from the matter of whether transactions are governed by legal relationships which are *bona fide*. The separation of these questions in the U.S. contrasts with the fundamentally different approach of the Supreme Court of Canada, as per its decision in *Shell v. The Queen*, described in chapter V. The U.S. approach is the more desirable and effective, as regardless of whether legal relationships have been validly established, the courts should be in a position to consider whether it is appropriate to approve tax benefits, in circumstances where transactions without economic substance have been engineered.

U.S. TAX SHELTER CASES

The prevalence and effectiveness of the use of the common law economic substance doctrine in combating abusive tax avoidance associated with the use of corporate tax shelters in the U.S.[566]

---

generally do not perform this vital inquiry today, even when claimed tax benefits do not comport with the underlying economics of the transaction").

[565] McMahon Jr., *supra* no. 79 at 748.
[566] GAO-11-493, "Abusive Tax Avoidance Transactions", 1-55 (May 2011), 3 (noting that tax shelters such as the 401(k) retirement plan are legitimate to the extent they take advantage of provision in the Tax Code to avoid tax

is one of the major planks in support of my argument that amendments are required to GAAR to situate economic substance as an important indicator of unacceptable tax avoidance.

Part of the backdrop for an examination of use of the economic substance doctrine in the U.S. against tax shelters is that the "thriving industry of hustling corporate tax shelters" was the subject of a cover story in 1998 in *Forbes* magazine.[567] *Forbes* quoted a partner in a major accounting firm, who described the development and highly selective marketing of strategies for tax avoidance, that could save their purchasers from tens of millions to hundreds of millions of dollars at the expense of other U.S. taxpayers.[568] An IRS contractor has estimated the tax revenue loss from abusive tax shelters in 1999 to be between $14.5 and $18.4 billion.[569]

Aggressive tax avoidance had become so pervasive by 2001 that *Forbes* magazine suggested taxpayers were "chumps" if they were not involved in tax avoidance schemes.[570] A survey of tax professionals retained by medium-sized corporations showed that 70

---

whereas abusive tax shelters occur when they are designed to confer tax benefits that Congress did not intend); Johnson, *supra* no. 112 at 881, 883 ("The point of [a] tax shelter is to report the couple of hundred dollar tax loss, without losing the couple of hundred. ... My favorite definition of a tax shelter is that it is an investment that is worth more after than before tax."); Joshua D. Blank, "Overcoming Overdisclosure: Toward Tax Shelter Detection" 56 *UCLA Law Review* 1629-1690 (2009), 1635 ("An abusive tax shelter is a tax strategy that produces amazing tax benefits that Congress never envisioned, but that seem to flow, at least on a strict constructionist reading, from the text of the Internal Revenue Code."; Canellos, *supra* no. 486 at 52 ("tax shelters bear a relationship to real transactions analogous to the relationship between money laundering and banking.")

[567] Johnson, *supra* no. 15 at 443-444 (noting that "When even Forbes ... convey[s] the idea of deep and sinister plots by promoters of corporate tax shelters, we know that there is something ugly at the center of our tax system and that Congress is going to have to do something about it.")

[568] Janet Novack and Laura Saunders, "The Hustling of X Rated Shelters", *Forbes*, Dec. 14, 1998, 203.

[569] Slemrod, *supra* no. 157 at 5 (this estimate was based on IRS and Compustat data and surveys of IRS field offices. Other estimates based on familiarity with the industry, but not quantitative analysis, have been similar.)

[570] Janet Novack, "Are You A Chump?", *Forbes*, Mar. 5, 2001, 122.

percent had been asked by clients to look into tax shelters and 55 percent had been approached by tax shelter promoters.[571] In 2003, the US Government Accountability Office (GAO) reported IRS estimates that several hundred thousand participants were likely engaged in abusive tax avoidance schemes, and that abusive tax shelters totalled tens of billions of dollars of potential tax losses over a decade.[572] The IRS estimated that about 1 million tax returns and 11,000 to 15,000 promoters were involved in abusive tax avoidance transactions in the 2004 taxation year.[573]

Professor Slemrod notes that corporate tax departments have been increasingly looked to as profit centres, and that effective tax rates, rather than accuracy, are the single most important factor used to evaluate the tax department's performance. Since there has also been a widely held view, with a long tradition, that tax avoidance does not raise issues of ethics or virtue, and in any event the exceedingly complex nature of tax law and the corresponding availability of alternative interpretations "undoubtedly facilitates ethical rationalizations of positions taken," it is unsurprising that "tax shelters cost the government a large and growing amount of revenue."[574]

According to Jeffrey Owens, former Director of the OECD Centre for Tax Policy and Administration, one of the key characteristics of tax shelters is that they have little or no economic substance.[575] Tax

---

[571] Joel Slemrod and Varsha Venkatesh, "The Income Tax Compliance Costs of Large and Mid-Sized Businesses", *Report to the Internal Revenue Service Large and Mid-Size Business Division*, Washington, D.C., September 2002.

[572] GAO, Internal Revenue Service: Challenges Remain in Combating Abusive Tax Schemes, GAO-04-50 (Washington D.C.: Nov. 19, 2003) and GAO-04-10T (Washington, D.C.: Oct. 21, 2003).

[573] Internal Revenue Service, Forecasting Potential Abusive Tax Avoidance Transaction Promoters and Participants (June 2006).

[574] Slemrod, *supra* no. 157 at 4-15 (offering an economics perspective on corporate tax reporting behaviour).

[575] Jeffrey Owens, Director of OECD Centre for Tax Policy and Administration, "Abusive Tax Shelters: Weapons of Tax Destruction?", 40 *Tax Notes International* 873-876 (Dec. 5, 2005), 874 (also noting that "tax shelters typically test the limits of domestic tax laws and therefore prompt questions under economic substance, sham, or business purpose doctrines."); Hariton, *supra* no. 2 at 34 (arguing that "what makes a transaction a 'tax shelter' is not the mere fact that

shelters are entered into on account of the efforts of the tax shelter industry, comprised largely of banks, finance firms, multinational accounting firms and law firms that are devoted to the development, marketing and sale of increasingly complex and sophisticated tax "products."[576] These products or tax shelters typically involve the use of circular or offsetting flows of cash and property, special purpose entities or other accommodating parties, and often complex financial instruments.[577] Tax avoidance is of course not confined to circumstances where tax shelters are employed, and as already noted there has been a debate in the U.S. about whether unique one-off structures utilized in the course of the taxpayer's business operations, e.g. as in *United Parcel Service of America, Inc. v. C.I.R.*[578] (as opposed to mass-marketed tax shelter "products" that are unrelated to the business) should be disregarded under the economic substance doctrine.[579] However, the economic substance doctrine has largely been used in the U.S. to combat abusive tax shelters.[580]

Tax shelters are said to have contributed substantially to the problem of decreasing tax revenues in the U.S., where two-thirds of companies paid no federal income taxes on their profits between 1996 and 2000.[581] For the year 2000, 94 percent of all companies

---

tax is avoided. It is the fact that tax is avoided by entering into a completely unrelated financial transaction that does not result in any economic loss.")

[576] Johnson, *supra* no. 15 at 444 (suggesting that "A corporation with a big economic gain that wants cash and no tax will be inundated, at the asking, with proposals for avoiding tax from the competing skunk works operations.")

[577] "Discussion Paper on Tax Avoidance", *supra* no. 5 at 1.

[578] 254 F.3d 1014 (11th Cir., 2001).

[579] See, for example, Lederman's position that the only proper question is whether the result sought is consistent with congressional intent in "W(h)ither Economic Substance?", *supra* no. 494 at 444 and compare the justifications offered by Bankman, *supra* no. 5, for an ordinary business exception to the application of the economic substance doctrine.

[580] Bankman, *supra* no. 65 at 6 ("the economic substance doctrine has played a particularly important role in the government's fight against corporate tax shelters ... and in a handful of cases ... has been used to deny tax benefits aggregating to many billions of dollars").

[581] Christian Aid, 2005, "The shirts off their backs: How tax policies fleece the poor", Christian Aid Briefing Paper, p. 15; available at http://www.christinaaid.org.U.K..indepth/509tax/ ("In the U.S., 60 per cent of corporations with

paid income taxes of less than 5 percent of the profits they reported for financial accounting purposes, although the statutory rate applicable to most companies in the U.S. was 35 percent.[582] Former IRS Chief Counsel Donald Korb reported in 2005 that "[o]ne of the most serious problems that the IRS has had to face over the last 10 years is the proliferation of abusive tax shelters."[583] Former U.S. Treasury Secretary Lawrence Summers also cited tax shelters as the most significant problem in administering the Internal Revenue Code, adding that tax shelters have drained several billion dollars from the treasury on an annual basis.[584] Professor Bankman estimated in 2004 that tax shelters cost the U.S. treasury ten billion dollars a year.[585]

Another ill-result of the tax shelter phenomenon is the pressure on corporations to keep their effective tax rates low, and in line with rates reported by their competitors, by resorting to transactions in which the tax treatment varies from the financial accounting treatment.[586] This has been described as "the race to the bottom," and

---

at least US $250 million in assets reported no federal tax liability for any of the years between 1996 and 2000.").

[582] United States, "Comparison of the Reported Tax Liabilities of Foreign and U.S. Controlled Corporations", 1996-2000 (Washington, D.C.: U.S. General Accounting Office, 2004); "Discussion Paper on Tax Avoidance", *supra* no. 5 at 7.

[583] Donald Korb, "The Economic Substance Doctrine in the Current Tax Shelter Environment", Jan. 25, 2005, *Doc. 2005-1540, 2005 TNT 16-22* (suggesting that although the IRS and tax practitioners may not always agree on whether a particular transaction is abusive, there is a consensus among responsible tax practitioners that "tax shelter transactions that are used by taxpayers to inappropriately avoid paying taxes" must be challenged by the IRS.).

[584] Ryan J. Donmoyer, "Debate Over Tax Shelters Dominates Finance Hearing", *Tax Notes Today*, Mar. 8, 2000, Tax Base TA Doc. No. 2000-7054 (quoting Treasury Secretary Lawrence H. Summers); Christopher Bergin et al, Summers Delivers Sharp Words on Corporate Tax Shelters", 89 *Tax Notes* 991-994 (Nov. 20, 2000), 991 (quoting Treasury Secretary Summers as saying that in the Treasury's informed judgment the estimated 10 year revenue loss of tens of billions of dollars on account of abusive corporate tax shelters represents "just the tip of the iceberg").

[585] Bankman, *supra* no. 2 at 933 (arguing that the tax shelter battle is worth waging as shelters significantly reduce tax revenues).

[586] "Discussion Paper on Tax Avoidance", *supra* no. 5 at 23.

involves corporations holding a view that they can avoid their legal tax liabilities by engaging in tax-engineered transactions. According to the U.S. Treasury Department this view, if unabated, could have long-term consequences to the voluntary tax system far more significant than the short-term revenue losses caused by the tax shelter industry.[587] In the case of Enron Corporation, for example, which reported financial statement net income of $2.3 billion but tax losses of $3 billion, for the period 1996 through 1999, its tax department was a profit center for the company. This involved Enron engaging in large structured tax avoidance transactions. In most of the transactions the origin of the financial accounting benefits was the reduction in federal income tax that the transaction was anticipated to provide currently or in the future.[588] From 1995, until filing for bankruptcy in 2001, Enron paid $88 million in fees to advisors and promoters of transactions structured to avoid taxes. The promoters of these tax avoidance transactions included well-known entities such as Arthur Anderson, Bankers Trust, Chase Manhattan, Deloitte & Touche and the Deutsche Bank.[589]

In tax shelter projects known as Projects Tanya, Valor, Steele and Cochise, Enron's structured transactions were relied on to duplicate losses (i.e. deduct the same loss twice) with respect to a single economic loss. A second strategy, in Projects Tomas, Condor, Teresa, Tammy I and Tammy II, was to shift tax basis from a non-depreciable asset to a depreciable asset, with little or no economic outlay.[590] The

---

[587] "The Problem of Corporate Tax Shelters – Discussion, Analysis and Legislative Proposals", *supra* no. 83 at iv, 3.

[588] Report of Investigation of Enron Corporation and Related Entities Regarding Federal Tax and Compensation Issues, and Policy Recommendations, Staff of the Joint Committee on Taxation, February 2003, Vol. I, 6-8.

[589] *Ibid.* at 9. Deutsche Bank agreed to pay $553 million and admitted to criminal wrongdoing in relation to tax shelter deals that it sold to customers between 1996 and 2002. KPMG had earlier agreed to pay $456 million – "Deutsche Bank Settles Tax Shelter Case for $553 Million", *NY Times*, December 21, 2010; A civil suit was filed in Manhattan federal court on June 15, 2011 under forfeiture rules invoked against the bank as part of the settlement "U.S. files anticipated tax case against Deutsche Bank", Thomson Reuters News & Insight, June 15, 2011.

[590] *Ibid.* at 8.

first recommendation made by the Staff of the Joint Committee on Taxation in its Report in 2003 on Enron was that "[s]tronger measures (e.g. the imposition of substantial, punitive penalties) are necessary to increase the costs to taxpayers of engaging in transactions that lack a non-tax business purpose or economic substance."[591]

Tax shelter schemes are often "mind-numbingly complex" and "it can often require months of painstaking work simply to piece them together."[592] Furthermore, there are endless ways that shelter promoters can package and repackage the basic elements of the schemes, often involving multiple circular cash flows and tax indifferent parties. Professor Bankman quotes a tax shelter promoter as having said "[y]ou can have the greatest shelter in the world, and clients won't pay for it if it is too simple. I've rejected a lot of great ideas for that reason."[593] The reasons for such complexity in tax shelters have been identified by SARS as a requirement that certain formalistic steps be completed in order to be able to claim the desired tax result; insertion of extra steps to prop up a claim of business purpose; camouflage put in place to prevent detection by revenue authorities; and, the ostensible justification for tax professionals to charge higher fees.[594]

The manner in which professional fees have been charged in the tax shelter industry also contributes to fuelling its growth. Under contingent fee billing arrangements (also known as "value billing") the size of the professional fee eventually paid relates to the size of the tax benefits successfully obtained. For example, the fee charged to the purchaser might be equal to 30 percent of the tax

---

[591] *Ibid.* at 17; Johnson, *supra* no. 15 at 453 (Tax shelters "are hard to diagnose. Commonly even for the shallowest shelters, consisting of nothing but paper, it is difficult to diagnose what were the errors that made the shelter possible or to explain why the nonsense differs from other transactions that do not cross the line.").

[592] "Discussion Paper on Tax Avoidance", *supra* no. 5 at 21, 53.

[593] Joseph Bankman, "The New Market in Corporate Tax Shelters", 83 *Tax Notes* 1775-1795 (June 21, 1999), 1781 ("Promoters attempt to avoid this problem ... by designing shelters that require hard-to-locate accommodation parties, such as zero-bracket foreign taxpayers").

[594] "Discussion Paper on Tax Avoidance", *supra* no. 5 at 22.

benefits successfully generated.[595] Since the purchaser's exposure to transaction fees is limited in this manner, this encourages the proliferation of abusive tax shelter activity.

As to the relevance of this discussion of tax shelters in Canada, SARS has made the point that tax avoidance schemes developed in one country now migrate to others almost immediately, on account of the large advances in computer and telecommunications technology in recent times.[596] While the tax shelters examined in this Part were sold in the U.S., it would be exceedingly naïve to think that pre-packaged tax shelters have not been a significant part of the tax landscape in Canada, although they have not attracted as much attention here as they have in the U.S., where tax shelters have been scrutinized extensively.[597] Canada introduced rules for registration and reporting information concerning tax shelters in 1987 as part of its effort to combat tax avoidance.[598] According to MacKnight, in his paper "Cabbages and Soda: A Skeptic's Review of Tax Shelters", many taxpayers in Canada have accepted the risks of tax shelters and participated in vigorously promoted tax shelters in order to reduce their tax bills.[599] MacKnight also says "[a]lmost by definition, a tax shelter involves an investment that would not otherwise be made, or at least not made in the form presented to tax shelter investors, without the tax benefits the investor hopes to obtain."[600] MacKnight's examples of tax shelters marketed in Canada include transactions involving computer software, films, nursing homes, recreational vehicles and yachts. In a follow-up by MacKnight on tax shelters, in his paper "Prophecies and Soda: Evolving and Surviving Tax Shelters" he concluded that "tax shelters are a

---

[595] *Ibid.* at 12, 25.
[596] *Ibid.* at 9.
[597] GAO-11-493, "Abusive Tax Avoidance Transactions", 1-55 (May 2011), 9-10 (noting that abusive tax avoidance transactions "have become more sophisticated and international in scope ... with promoters changing the countries and mechanics of their promotions")
[598] Department of Finance Canada, *Tax Reform 1987*, note 39, p. 131-132.
[599] MacKnight, *supra* no. 222 at 50:2 (aggressive promotion now seems a hallmark of tax shelters).
[600] *Ibid.* at 50:4-5.

permanent fixture in our tax landscape."[601] The Province of Québec Working Paper on Aggressive Tax Planning also identifies "off-the-shelf tax product" as a substantial contributor to the recently vigorous growth of aggressive tax planning schemes, noting that tax revenue lost to the public treasury amounts to hundreds of millions of dollars.[602]

According to the OECD's Centre for Tax Policy and Administration, the experience in many countries, including Canada, shows that mass-marketed tax shelter schemes have moved down-market from very large corporations and wealthy individuals to medium-size enterprises and middle-income taxpayers.[603] Anecdotal evidence also suggests Canada has not been trailing in terms of the adoption of strategies designed to avoid taxes. A *MacLean's* magazine 1995 cover story reported that the movement of billions of dollars offshore to tax havens was taking place in highly questionable schemes from a tax law perspective.[604] Given recognition that the tax shelter phenomenon is at least as serious a threat as transfer pricing to the tax bases of OECD countries, including Canada,[605]

---

[601] Robin J. MacKnight, "Prophecies and Soda: Evolving and Surviving Tax Shelters", 95 *Conference Report* 14:1-14:17 (Toronto: Canadian Tax Foundation, 1996), 14:17 (suggesting that some tax shelters should not survive challenges by Revenue Canada whereas others are valid investments. In any case, purchasers of tax shelters should undertake reasonable due diligence as to their viability).

[602] Aggressive Tax Planning Working Paper, *supra* no. 30 at 8-11, 22 (noting development of communications technologies and electronic finance, introduction of innovative financial products and global integration of national economies as important exogenous factors fuelling aggressive tax planning, with an attractive risk/reward ratio and emerging marketing of highly specialized "tax products" as two endogenous factors that are also important in this regard)

[603] Owens, *supra* no. 575 at 874 (arguing that taxpayers' confidence in the integrity of tax systems will be eroded if governments do not respond successfully to mass-market tax schemes).

[604] Stevie Cameron, "Offshore Billions: Canadians are finding new ways to hide their money from the tax man", *Maclean's* (9 October 1995), 54.

[605] Lawrence B. Gibbs, "Constancy and Change in Our Federal Tax System", 2008 Erwin L. Griswold Lecture Before the American College of Tax Counsel, vol. 61, no. 3 *Tax Lawyer* 673-703, 686 (remarks attributed to Jeffrey Owens, Director of the Centre for Tax Policy and Administration, Organization for Economic Co-operation and Development).

a Joint International Tax Shelter Information Center was established in 2005 by a Memorandum of Understanding between Australia, Canada, the UK and the U.S., to help identify abusive tax avoidance. This is said to have already produced "real results", as in the identification of a cross-border tax scheme in 2006 involving hundreds of taxpayers and tens of millions of dollars.[606] The Canada Revenue Agency's 2006-2007 annual report to Parliament stated that it had issued about 14,600 reassessments during the year related to $1.4 billion in additional revenues, due in part to its focus on tax shelter planning schemes.[607]

The Province of Québec released an Information Bulletin in October 2009 re Fighting Aggressive Tax Planning stating that "[t]he phenomenon of aggressive tax planning (ATP) is of major concern to Québec tax authorities. ATP threatens Québec's tax base and attacks the integrity and fairness of the tax system. The revenue lost to the government because of ATP must sooner or later be collected from other Québec taxpayers, which violates the long-established principle that each must pay their fair share of taxes."[608] The focus of these new measures announced by Québec to fight aggressive tax planning is on the creation of mandatory disclosure requirements and penalties. However, while detection of tax avoidance schemes is an important part of the efforts to combat abusive tax avoidance, detection will be of little value[609] unless the courts in Canada are required to con-

---

[606] Canada Revenue Agency News Release, "Abusive tax schemes tackled by international tax administrations", May 23, 2007, Ottawa, Ontario; see also: Shaw, Slemrod and Whiting, *supra* no. 140 at 1152, describing the establishment of JITSIC between Australia, the U.K., the US, Canada and Japan as a "significant step forward" in sharing information between governments in order to identify abusive tax avoidance arrangements).

[607] Canada Revenue Agency, 2006-2007 Canada Revenue Agency Annual Report, p. 59.

[608] Finances Québec, "Fighting Aggressive Tax Planning", Information Bulletin 2009-5, October 15, 2009, available at www.finances.gouv.qc.ca.

[609] Weisbach, *supra* no. 15 at 225-230 (arguing that disclosure requirements for transactions that meet specified criteria "leads to constant legal change to eliminate the shelter de jour. It makes the law less stable and more complex. This means more work for tax lawyers and accountants. They can command high fees for interpreting the latest changes and even higher fees for structuring new shelters that avoid the changed rules. Disclosure is not a sufficient

sider economic substance in determining whether transactions will be respected for tax purposes, as the U.S. courts have now done for decades.

An examination follows of a number of U.S. cases, involving several high-profile tax shelters, which were successfully attacked by the IRS under the economic substance doctrine. These are cases where, in the words of the Supreme Court of Canada, "bona fide legal relationships" existed; however, the transactions were ignored for tax purposes because they were found to be lacking in economic substance. These cases help to illustrate, because of the enormous impact the economic substance doctrine has had in curbing abusive tax avoidance in the U.S., that our GAAR needs to be amended to introduce a requirement that economic substance must be considered by the courts as part of the big picture in tax avoidance cases.

The review of the U.S. treatment of sale and leaseback shelters which follows is of particular importance, as the transactions in these cases were ignored by U.S. courts for tax purposes on the basis that they lacked economic substance, whereas in its first decision under GAAR the Supreme Court of Canada upheld a sale and leaseback transaction in *Canada Trustco Mortgage Co. v. R.*, by virtue of its ill-considered holding that lack of substance has "no meaning in isolation from the proper interpretation of specific provisions of the Income Tax Act."[610]

---

answer to the problem."); Blank, *supra* no. 566 at 1632-1633 (also arguing that an "overdisclosure response [which is said to be a 'natural reaction from conservative, cautious taxpayers and advisors'] poses serious threats to tax administration" as the effort required from the government to audit the overdisclosure response can hinder "investigations of truly abusive transactions. ... For aggressive taxpayers and advisors – those that push the envelope by claiming the riskiest tax positions – over disclosure becomes an attractive strategy for avoiding IRS detection of abusive tax planning. By reporting a multitude of nonabusive transactions along with their most questionable tax positions, aggressive taxpayers and advisors may believe they will escape high penalties for nondisclosure without increasing the likelihood that the IRS will detect and challenge their abusive transactions.").

[610] *Canada Trustco Mortgage Co. v. R.*, [2005] 2 S.C.R. 601 (S.C.C.) at para. 59. Also see the case study in chapter IX.

Sale and leaseback ("SILO") shelters

The Court of Appeals for the Fourth Circuit disallowed accelerated depreciation and interest expense deductions in *Rice's Toyota World, Inc. v. C.I.R.*,[611] which had been claimed in relation to a sale and leaseback transaction. In disallowing the deductions, the Court interpreted the Supreme Court's decision in *Frank Lyon* as having established a disjunctive two-prong economic substance test. This approach to the economic substance doctrine has been called "taxpayer-friendly", as the government must show that the corporation had no business purpose for the transaction and also that the transaction had no objective economic substance.[612]

The taxpayer was an auto dealership that had purchased a used computer from a leasing company, and subsequently leased it back to the company under terms which made it impossible for the dealership to make a pre-tax profit. The dealership had entered into the transaction to enable it to claim accelerated depreciation and interest deductions which made the transaction profitable on an after-tax basis.[613] The Fourth Circuit (as some other U.S. courts have also done) used the term "sham" in describing the economic substance doctrine: "To treat a transaction as a sham, the court must find that the taxpayer was motivated by no business purpose other than obtaining tax benefits ... and that the transaction has no economic substance because no reasonable possibility of a profit exists."[614] The Court then disallowed the deductions sought for depreciation and interest payments on nonrecourse debt, on the basis of its findings that the transaction was motivated by no business purpose other than obtaining tax benefits and

---

[611] 752 F.2d 89 (4th Cir., 1985).
[612] Nahass, *supra* no. 136 at 259 (noting that under the Fourth Circuit's "taxpayer-friendly" version of the economic substance doctrine the government must prove that the taxpayer had no non-tax business purpose and that the transaction lacked economic substance).
[613] Keinan, *supra* no. 2 at 381 (noting that the taxpayer paid $1,455,227, including non-recourse financing totaling $1,205,227 payable over eight years, to purchase a used computer from a financing company which it immediately leased back to the financing company under an eight year lease with rents calculated so the taxpayer had a pre-tax cash flow of $10,000 per year).
[614] 752 F.2d 89 (4th Cir., 1985).

that the transaction had no objective economic substance because no reasonable possibility of a profit existed. Although the Court used the term "sham" to describe what had occurred, it was not applying the common law doctrine of sham, as we know it in Canada, with its element of deceit.

The Fourth Circuit's decision has been criticized on the basis that it relied upon a profit test as the measuring stick for economic substance, based on a misreading of the Supreme Court's *Frank Lyon* decision, whereas a profit test creates an asylum for tax shelters, which can always derive some profit even though they are lacking in economic substance.[615] The Fourth Circuit has nevertheless also been credited for its "innovative approach" in *Rice's Toyota*, in using the economic substance doctrine to combat the adverse impact that the "crisis levels" of tax shelter disputes and litigation had been having in the U.S. on its self-assessment tax system.[616]

While the facts of the *Rice's Toyota* case seem relatively benign, in terms of the amount of tax leakage potentially involved, the transactions represent the proverbial tip of a tax shelter iceberg. Sale-in, lease out or SILO tax shelters, which follow a similar M.O. to the transactions in *Rice's Toyota*, have been known in the tax world since 2003.[617] In SILO shelters property is typically

---

[615] Miller, Jr., *supra* no. 221 at 1062-64 (suggesting that the Fourth Circuit Court of Appeals mistakenly employed a profit test, although "virtually any economic substance test would have invalidated the transaction", because it "fit squarely against the transaction at issue." According to Miller, the correct approach would be to determine whether "the taxpayer's economic position was sufficiently changed because the transaction produced substantial economic consequences, not an anemic profit that appears *de minimis* against the transaction's benefits.")

[616] Mortimer Caplin, "Tax Shelter Disputes and Litigation With The Internal Revenue Service – 1987 Style", 6 *Virginia Tax Review* 709-750 (1986-1987), 710-711, footnote 7 (noting that in 1987 over 43,000 of the Tax Court's approximately 84,000 cases were tax shelter cases, representing an estimated $2 billion in assessed deficiencies).

[617] Peter Glicklich and Angela M. Eiref, "New US International Tax Legislation May be the Most Significant Since 1986", Selected US Tax Developments, (2004) vol. 52 no. 4 CTJ 1259-1284, 1274 (noting that the American *Jobs Creation Act* 2004 added substantial limitations on the ability of US

purchased from a municipality and leased back to the municipality. The tax benefit sought for the purchaser is a depreciation deduction that the municipality cannot use, because it is tax exempt.[618] Professor Bankman estimates that SILO tax shelters were responsible by 2004 for transferring hundreds of billions of dollars of deductions for depreciation from tax indifferent municipalities to for-profit corporations.[619]

In *AWG Leasing Trust et al v. United States*,[620] the District Court considered the purchase of a German energy facility in 1999, with a simultaneous leaseback and an option to repurchase the facility for a fixed price in 2024. For the years 1999 through 2003, the AWG trust claimed $88 million in tax deductions resulting from the transaction. The Court agreed with the IRS that the deductions were not allowable, noting that the transaction had "minimal substance apart from tax benefits."[621] The Court of Federal Claims also found in *Wells Fargo & Co. v. United States*[622] that SILO transactions lacked economic substance, as they provided no reasonable possibility of profit, absent a claim for tax deductions, and they were

---

taxpayers to engage in "sale-in, lease-out" transactions for transactions entered into after the effective date of the legislation)

[618] Bankman, *supra* no. 2 at 932 (also noting in 2004 that SILO shelters were too new to have generated any cases, and that SILOs were tax-motivated transactions unrelated to the taxpayer's prior business operations, that seemed inconsistent with Congressional intent, which threatened to substantially reduce government revenues).

[619] *Ibid.* (noting there is some evidence to this effect although the public record is incomplete); also see: Robert W. Wood and Steven E. Hollingworth, "SILOs and LILOs Demystified", 129 *Tax Notes* 195-205 (Oct. 11, 2010), 196 (stating that "before the congressional crackdown on most SILOs entered into after March 12, 2004 U.S. taxpayers were involved in at least 400 SILO transactions, claiming tax deductions of more than $35 billion.")

[620] No. 1:07-cv-00857 (N.D. Ohio May 28, 2008), Doc 2008-11830; 2008 TNT 105-10.

[621] Jeremiah Coder, "IRS Wins Third Sale-Leaseback Case and Penalties", 119 *Tax Notes* 909-910 (June 2, 2008), 910 (suggesting that it is hard to avoid the economic substance and substance over form doctrines in SILO cases when the court finds that there is no real chance the purchase option will be exercised at the end of the head lease).

[622] *Wells Fargo & Company and Subsidiaries v. United States*, No. 06-628T, 2010 TNT 6-15 (Fed. Cl., 2010).

not supported by any nontax business purpose.[623] Wells Fargo had claimed $115 million in deductions for depreciation, interest and transaction costs from 26 leveraged lease transactions in its 2002 taxation year. The transactions involved an arrangement in which enough collateral was deposited to pay off the borrower's debt – this is sometimes called "economic defeasance." The tax-exempt entities which facilitated the transactions for a fee, generally equal to 4 to 8 percent of the transaction's value, continue to "use, operate, and maintain the property during the lease term in the same manner as before."[624] The Wells Fargo argument that the SILO transactions were structured to comply with and take advantage of the "front-loading" of income under FAS 13[625] was rejected as a "bootstrap argument", on the basis that "[the taxpayer's] intended use of the cash flows generated by the [transaction] is irrelevant to the subjective prong of the economic substance analysis. If a legitimate business purpose for the use of the tax savings 'were sufficient to breathe substance into a transaction whose only purpose is to reduce taxes, [then] every sham tax-shelter device might succeed.'"[626] Regarding the finding as to lack of objective economic substance, fixed purchase option and early buyout clauses in the transactions essentially gave Wells Fargo a fixed minimum return and eliminated all risk. The circular flow of funds meant none of the money was actually used to purchase or build the assets involved in the transactions:

---

[623] Jeremiah Coder, "Wells Fargo Loses $115 Million SILO Refund Suit", 126 *Tax Notes* 293-295 (Jan. 18, 2010) (pointing out that $115 million in tax refunds from participation in 26 SILO transactions were denied under the economic substance and substance over form doctrines).

[624] Robert W. Wood, "What Wells Fargo Brings to the SILO/LILO Debate", 131 *Tax Notes* 1389-1393 (June 27, 2011), 1389-1391 (also noting that the valuation of SILO property had been boosted to increase deductions).

[625] The Statement of Financial Accounting Standards No. 13 establishes standards of financial accounting and reporting for leases by lessees and lessors.

[626] *Wells Fargo & Company and Subsidiaries v. United States*, No. 06-628T, 2010 TNT 6-15 (Fed. Cl., 2010) at p. 68, quoting *Am. Elec Power, Inc. v. United States*, 136 F. Supp.2d 762 (S.D. Ohio, 2001) at pp. 791-92, affirmed 326 F.3d 737 (6th Cir., 2003) and *Winn-Dixie Stores, Inc. v. Comm'r*, 113 T.C. 254 (1999) at p. 287, affirmed 254 F.3d 1313 (11th Cir., 2001).

> Although well-disguised in a sea of paper and complexity, the SILO transactions essentially amount to Wells Fargo's purchase of tax benefits for a fee from a tax-exempt entity that cannot use the deductions. The transactions are designed to minimize risk and assure a desired outcome to Wells Fargo, regardless of how the value of the property may fluctuate during the term of the transactions. Indeed, nothing of any substance changes in the tax-exempt entity's operation and ownership of the assets. The only money that changes hands is Wells Fargo's up-front fee to the tax-exempt entity, and Wells Fargo's payments to those who have participated in or created the intricate agreements. The equity and debt 'loop' transactions simply are offsetting accounting entries not involving actual payments, or pools of money eventually returned to the original holder. If the Court were to approve of these SILO schemes, the big losers would be the Internal Revenue Service ("IRS"), deprived of millions in taxes rightfully due from a financial giant, and the taxpaying public, forced to bear the burden of the taxes avoided by Wells Fargo.[627]

The Court found that despite reliance on attorneys, appraisers and lenders, to give the transactions apparent legitimacy, "[t]he heart of these transactions is that Wells Fargo paid a fee to tax-exempt entities to acquire valuable tax deductions that the tax-exempt entities could not use."[628] An appeal to the Court of Appeals was dismissed under the U.S. substance-over-form doctrine, by virtue of which the tax consequences of a transaction are determined based on the underlying substance of the transaction rather than its legal form. It was held to be virtually certain that the tax-exempt entities would exercise their repurchase options and reacquire the assets at the end of their leases, and the transactions were held to be "purely circular transactions that elevate form over substance."[629] Since Wells Fargo never acquired the benefits and burdens of ownership in the leased assets, it was not entitled to the depreciation and interest deductions.

---

[627] *Wells Fargo & Company and Subsidiaries v. United States*, No. 06-628T, 2010 TNT 6-15 (Fed. Cl., 2010) at p. 4.
[628] *Ibid.* at 62.
[629] *Wells Fargo & Company and Subsidiaries v. United States*, No. 2010 5108 (Fed. Cir. April 15, 2011).

A variation of SILO shelters is the lease-in, lease-out (LILO) shelter, which involved leasing arrangements in which corporations leased assets such as sewer and transportation systems from owners without a tax liability, and immediately leased them back to their original owners.[630]

Contingent instalment sale ("CINS") shelters

Contingent instalment sale or CINS tax shelters, which were marketed by the investment banking firm Merrill Lynch in the late 1980's, are another example of a tax-indifferent party being paid a fee to absorb taxable income.[631] The shelters were designed to generate capital losses, by a pre-arranged series of transactions affected through partnerships, each involving a corporation seeking a loss, an investment bank and an offshore bank.[632] The shelters were structured and promoted on the basis of a perceived flaw in regulations governing the timing of the recognition of a gain from an instalment sale.

A partnership was formed with the foreign "investor" contributing capital to the partnership, which purchased high-grade corporate bonds and sold them in exchange for a large fixed payment, plus small contingent payments in subsequent taxable years. The large gain in the year of sale, which arose because a *pro rata* portion of the basis of the instalment obligation was allocated to the initial

---

[630] GAO-11-493, "Abusive Tax Avoidance Transactions", 1-55 (May 2011), 3 (LILOs are given as an example of tax shelters designed to confer tax benefits that Congress did not intend. A LILO shelter "involved complex purported leasing arrangements in which corporations supposedly leased large assets, such as sewer systems, from owners without a tax liability and immediately leased them back to original owners in an attempt to delay income recognition for tax purposes for many years.")
[631] Miller, Jr., *supra* no. 221 at1021 (noting that tax-indifferent parties that are paid fees are generally foreign persons or tax-exempt organizations that are not subject to federal taxation)
[632] Canellos, *supra* no. 486 at 65-66 (noting that all CINS tax shelters have failed in court and that U.S. judges appear to have accepted that the strain on the tax system would be unbearable if uneconomic transactions were upheld because they fell within the wording of technical tax rules)

payment under the regulation in question, was allocated to the foreign partner. The foreign partner served as an accommodation party for a fee as it was not taxable on the gain. Later years' losses were allocated to the U.S. partner to be used to offset otherwise taxable gains from the sale of other property. The parties to the transaction did not stand to gain or bear the risk of any economic loss, and the U.S. partner bore the costs of the transaction.[633]

The Court of Appeals for the Third Circuit disallowed tax losses in *ACM Partnership v. C.I.R.*,[634] which involved an early version of the CINS tax shelter transactions, that had been manufactured through a series of transactions undertaken in an attempt to reduce the tax on a $104 million capital gain realized in an unrelated transaction. The Third Circuit disallowed the tax loss by applying the economic substance doctrine, which it described in the following terms: "The inquiry into whether the taxpayer's transactions had sufficient economic substance to be respected for tax purposes turns on both the 'objective economic substance of the transactions' and the 'subjective business motivation' behind them. ... However, these distinct aspects of the economic sham inquiry do not constitute discrete prongs of a 'rigid two-step analysis', but rather represent related factors both of which inform the analysis of whether the transaction had sufficient substance, apart from its tax consequences, to be respected for tax purposes ...".[635]

The finding that the transactions had no objective economic substance was arrived at by applying a present value analysis. The Court concluded that the investments acquired in implementing the shelter's pre-ordained steps were "economically inconsequential" and "economically disadvantageous".[636]

---

[633] Hariton, *supra* no. 146 at 263 (commenting that CINS tax shelter developers attempted to "fashion a transaction which would take the form of a sale of property in exchange for contingent payments without saddling the parties with its economic substance.").

[634] 157 F.3d 231 (3d Cir., 1998), cert. denied 526 U.S. 1017 (1999).

[635] *Ibid.* at 247.

[636] Lawrence Zelenak, "Codifying Anti-Avoidance Doctrines and Controlling Corporate Tax Shelters", 54 *SMU Law Review* 177-193 (2001), 179-80

One commentator says the *ACM* case shows that a transaction that is isolated from the taxpayer's other activities, and that is to evolve over just a few days, will usually not have pre-tax profit because the recovery of the costs of executing the transaction over a few days requires a rate of return on invested capital that is higher than that which is usually available.[637] The *ACM* decision has been criticized on the basis that, by separating the transaction steps that resulted in the gains and losses and finding that they lacked economic substance, considered apart from the transaction as a whole, the Third Circuit endorsed an approach under which the economic substance doctrine could apply to tax motivated steps taken as part of a legitimate business transaction. The criticism is that if the economic substance doctrine is applied too broadly, this "will serve only to deprive the doctrine of any coherent meaning and thereby render it useless, much in the way that a flashlight pointed at everything is in effect pointed at nothing."[638]

According to Hariton, the better approach would have been to find that, as the tax losses claimed were vastly out of proportion to the investment income generated and were used to offset tax on unrelated income, the use of a tax-motivated structure to obtain a tax loss in the absence of any economic loss was inconsistent with congressional intent.[639] The result in *ACM* has nevertheless been applauded, on the basis that the case involved an instance of a tax-

---

(pointing out that the finding the transactions lacked economic substance was made in spite of the fact that there were real investments of capital and economic returns in the form of interest).

[637] Jennings, *supra* no. 468 at 541 (stating that the transactions were "guaranteed to be cash flow negative before the effect of any tax savings" and hence "could have no credible nontax objective.").

[638] Hariton, *supra* no. 2 at 30-31 (arguing that the economic substance doctrine should apply to "transactions that, when considered as a whole, serve primarily to generate net losses, deductions or credits that can be used to eliminate the tax that otherwise would be imposed on unrelated income.").

[639] *Ibid.* at 55-56 (although taxpayers need to be able to rely on objective rules, there are substantive objectives for the rules: "Congress does have an interest in seeing that taxes are equitably imposed on taxpayers, and that includes both horizontal and vertical equity. And Congress does not wish to encourage replicable and economically meaningless tax-motivated transactions that serve to undermine that equity while enriching tax-shelter promoters.").

payer attempting to take advantage of highly technical tax rules to produce an artificial capital loss.[640]

The *ACM* decision has been described in Canada as showing that the US approach to identifying abusive tax avoidance is that of applying the technical tax rules to what remains when one ignores transaction steps having no separate independent economic or commercial significance.[641] This is obviously not the approach of judges in Canada. The *ACM* case also helps to illustrate the wasting of government resources that can be caused by tax avoidance. Reports indicate that the IRS spent more than $2 million in litigating the *ACM* case alone.[642]

The Court of Appeals for the D.C. Circuit also disallowed tax losses claimed in *ASA Investerings Partnership v. C.I.R.*,[643] which involved another version of a CINS tax shelter under which the taxpayer equity-funded the transaction, by purchasing a note which it held for several years. It was impossible to say that the transaction lacked any profit potential, as the taxpayer earned $3.6 million from its net investment after transaction costs; however, the profit generated was insignificant in relation to the $300 million of losses claimed.[644] Reported transaction costs of $24,783,800 were approximately 26.5 percent of the $93,500,000 of purported tax savings.[645]

---

[640] Gergen, *supra* no. 372 at 135 (arguing that the shelter transaction in *ACM* illustrates the need to use judicial standards to combat abusive tax avoidance).

[641] Wilkie and Kerr, *supra* no. 118 at 34:16 (suggesting that "the US approach to identifying tax avoidance [under the economic substance doctrine] ... might be usefully thought of as simply another method of determining the 'real' transaction." This is what exists after ignoring steps without "economic or commercial significance.")

[642] "Discussion Paper on Tax Avoidance", *supra* no. 5 at 42, footnote 151.

[643] 201 F.3d 505 (D.C. Cir., 2000).

[644] Hariton, *supra* no. 2 at 49-50 (arguing that although it was impossible to assert that the transaction lacked profit potential the economic substance doctrine should still apply because the profit was insignificant in relation to the tax benefits).

[645] Miller, Jr., *supra* no. 221 at 1019-1023 (observing that high transaction costs are characteristic of corporate tax shelters, together with the use of tax arbitrage, inconsistent financial accounting and tax treatment, the presence of tax-indifferent parties, and exceedingly complex transactions).

The Court held that there are no substantial differences between the business purpose doctrine and the economic substance doctrine, because they both permit the Commissioner to look beyond the form of a transaction to discover its substance.[646] On this basis, the failure of the taxpayer to show any legitimate business purpose for entering into the partnership apart from the tax benefit was held to render the transaction invalid for tax purposes.[647]

The Court of Appeals for the Federal Circuit also disallowed tax losses generated in a CINS tax shelter in *Coltec Industries, Inc. v. U.S.*[648] The Supreme Court denied certiorari in the case on February 20, 2007.[649] In this case, the Federal Circuit traced the history of the development of the economic substance in the U.S., and explained the policy reasons relied upon by the judiciary in developing the doctrine. An examination of the history of and the reasons for the development of the economic substance doctrine by the judiciary in the U.S. is located elsewhere in this chapter; however, it is fair to say that the *Coltec* decision is the *magnum opus* on the subject.

The taxpayer contributed a variety of assets (stock, cash, rights from future litigation and a promissory note), together with contingent liabilities related to asbestos claims, to a dormant subsidiary in exchange for newly issued stock. The estimated value of the note and the estimated amount of the liabilities were each $375 million. The tax plan turned upon a provision in the *Internal Revenue Code* that did not require the basis of the stock of the subsidiary to be reduced to reflect the contingent liabilities the subsidiary had assumed. This meant the subsidiary had a built-in loss that could be

---

[646] Rector, *supra* no. 2 at 182 (saying that the D.C. Circuit Court has taken a "flexible approach" to the economic substance doctrine by deciding that it is not substantially different from the business purpose doctrine because both doctrines permit the courts to look beyond the form of transactions).

[647] Nahass, *supra* no. 136 at 259 (noting that the D.C. Circuit has not ruled whether a transaction with a valid business purpose but no economic substance would be upheld).

[648] 454 F.3d 1340 (Fed. Cir., 2006).

[649] 127 S.Ct. 1261 (2007).

recognized upon disposition and used to offset the capital gains realized in an unrelated transaction.[650] Shortly after the contribution of assets and contingent liabilities to the subsidiary, the newly issued stock was sold to two unrelated banks for $500,000. After the sale, the taxpayer continued to own 93 percent of the subsidiary's stock. In its consolidated tax return for the year, it reported a capital loss of about $378.7 million on the sale of the subsidiary's stock ($500,000 less $375 million note and $4.2 million of other property contributed to the subsidiary). The loss was not recognized for "book purposes" and it was not reported in the financial statements.[651]

The Court of Federal Claims had allowed the deduction of the loss claimed, and in doing so quoted from *Atlantic Coast Line R. Co. v. Phillips*,[652] which in turn had quoted from Justices Holmes and Learned Hand: "As to the astuteness of taxpayers in ordering their affairs so as to minimize their taxes we have said that 'the very meaning of a line in the law is that you intentionally may go as close to it as you can if you do not pass it.' This is so because [there is no] 'public duty to pay more than the law demands: taxes are enforced exactions, not voluntary contributions.'"[653] The Federal Circuit, however, considered the government's economic substance argument and found that the transaction had no substance apart from tax benefits.

It also held that the economic substance test is conjunctive: "[w]hile the doctrine may well also apply if the taxpayer's sole subjective motivation is tax avoidance even if the transaction has economic substance, a lack of economic substance is sufficient to disqualify the transaction without proof that the taxpayer's sole motive is tax avoidance."[654] The Federal Circuit's decision was viewed

---

[650] Hicks, *supra* no. 480 at 120 (noting that the transactions were entered into on the recommendation of the now defunct Arthur Anderson LLP and were undertaken to shield a capital gain of $240.9 million arising from the sale of one of Coltec's businesses, through the filing of a consolidated tax return)
[651] Hariton, *supra* no. 2 at 29, footnote 1 (arguing that the Federal Circuit applied the economic substance doctrine "so broadly that it failed to provide taxpayers with any meaningful guidance").
[652] 332 U.S. 168 (1947).
[653] 332 U.S. 168 (1947) at pp. 172-173 (quoted in *Coltec Indus.*, 62 Fed. Cl. at 718).
[654] 454 F.3d 1340 (Fed. Cir., 2006) at p. 1353.

as a departure from the flexible two prong economic substance test, because of its emphasis on objective factors.[655]

The Court considered the transaction step that gave rise to the deduction, rather than the transaction as a whole, in applying the economic substance doctrine.[656] Once again, the approach of dissecting the transaction to examine only the economic substance of the tax-motivated portion has been criticized, on the basis that it has the potential to effectively rescind the taxpayers' legal right to minimize their tax liability,[657] contrary to earlier Supreme Court authorities requiring that the transaction must be examined as a whole.[658] A further criticism is that the Court did not determine whether the transactions were within the ambit of congressional intent as it did not focus on the relevant tax benefits.[659] Nevertheless, the *Coltec* decision stands as the best modern-day judicial statement as to the rationale for the economic substance doctrine.

---

[655] Hicks, *supra* no. 480 at 123-124 (pointing out differences amongst the Circuit Courts in their application of the economic substance doctrine).

[656] Leland I. Gardner, "An Elephant in the Room: Double Deductions and the Economic Substance Doctrine in Coltec Industries, Inc. v. United States", vol. 60, no. 2 *Tax Lawyer* 519-532 (2007), 528 (suggesting a more balanced approach would be for the court to have considered the transaction's broader context, e.g. whether the transaction arose in the taxpayer's normal course of business).

[657] Hicks, *supra* no. 480 at 125 (arguing that not concentrating on the transaction as a whole when applying the economic substance doctrine gives the power to the IRS to vitiate all tax planning); Swiderski and Manasuev, *supra* no. 15 at 18:1-31 ("the contentious lesson of *Coltec* regarding the subjective business purpose test is that the transaction to be analyzed under the economic substance sham review is limited to the one that gives rise to the tax benefit. … *Coltec* underscores the importance (and oftentimes the difficulty) of proving an objective business purpose to a skeptical audience. … The Court noted that 'there is a material difference between structuring a real transaction in a particular way to obtain a tax benefit (which is perfectly permissible) and creating a transaction, without a business purpose, in order to create a tax benefit (which is impermissible)'.")

[658] *Gregory v. Helvering*, 293 U.S. 465 (1935) at p. 479 (analyzing 'the whole transaction'); *Frank Lyon Co. v. U.S.*, 435 U.S. 561 (1978) at pp. 581-83 (analyzing the totality of the transaction and identifying factors relevant to the inquiry).

[659] Hariton, *supra* no. 2 at 39-40 (suggesting that congressional intent should have been the focus of the inquiry because the taxpayer really did expect to suffer substantial losses from its asbestos liabilities and may have only been trying to deduct the losses sooner rather than later).

Corporate-owned life insurance ("COLI") shelters

The Eleventh Circuit Court of Appeals found in *Winn-Dixie Stores, Inc. v. C.I.R.*[660] that transactions involving corporate-owned life insurance had no business purpose and no economic substance. Winn-Dixie had entered into a COLI group plan covering approximately 36,000 of its employees. The decision to shift from its existing "key-person" COLI program of individual policies, which covered only 65 managers, was made pursuant to a proposal that emphasized "[the] tax arbitrage created when deductible policy loan interest is paid to finance non-taxable policy gains."[661] The proposal indicated that Winn-Dixie would incur a pre-tax loss totalling $755 million for its 1993-2052 years; but, as the result of total projected income tax savings of more than $3 billion, it would realize increased after-tax earnings of more than $2.2 billion for the same period.[662] In disallowing the interest deductions and fees related to the policies, the Eleventh Circuit held that "[A] transaction is not entitled to tax respect if it lacks economic effects or substance other than the generation of tax benefits, or if the transaction serves no business purpose."[663] The Eleventh Circuit's version of the economic substance doctrine has also been labelled a "government-friendly" approach, as under it the taxpayer must show that a transaction has both a non-tax business purpose and objective economic substance.[664]

The Sixth Circuit Court of Appeals also relied on the economic substance doctrine in *Dow Chemical Co. v. U.S.*,[665] to disallow deductions claimed in a COLI tax shelter. The U.S. Supreme Court denied certiorari in the case on Feb. 20, 2007.[666] Dow had purchased COLI

---

[660] 254 F.3d 1313 (11th Cir., 2001).
[661] Memorandum from Wiedmann & Johnson proposing Winn-Dixie purchase a "broad-based COLI pool."
[662] 113 T.C. 254 (1999) (the projected tax savings were attributable to the anticipated tax deductions for policy loan interest and fees).
[663] 254 F.3d 1313 (11th Cir., 2001) at p. 1316.
[664] Nahass, *supra* no. 136 at 258 (emphasizing that the manner in which the economic substance doctrine is applied differs as between Circuit Courts)
[665] 435 F.3d 594 (6th Cir., 2006).
[666] 549 U.S. 1205, 127 S.Ct. 1251 (2007).

policies on the lives of more than 21,000 employees. Dow claimed deductions totalling over $33 million for interest paid on loans used to pay the COLI premiums and for fees related to the policies, which the IRS disallowed.[667] The majority for the Sixth Circuit held that it was unnecessary for it to discuss subjective motivation, as the COLI policies did not have "any practicable economic effects other than the creation of income tax losses."[668] The decision has been criticized on the basis that the Sixth Circuit interpreted the Supreme Court's decision in *Knetsch*[669] in a manner that it had never been interpreted before, by holding that, as a matter of law, future profits contingent on taxpayer action are an appropriate component in judging economic substance only when they "comport" with the taxpayer's actual past conduct related to the transaction in question.[670] The *Dow* decision has also been referred to as "further proof of the old saying that 'bad facts make bad law.'"[671]

High-basis, low-value shelters

High-basis, low-value tax shelters involve a profitable domestic corporation, its subsidiary, and a foreign party not subject to U.S. tax, which is located in a jurisdiction that does not tax gain or allow for deduction for a loss on investment assets. The foreign party holds property with a high basis and low value, which it contributes to the subsidiary and receives non-voting preferred stock

---

[667] Richard M. Lipton, "What Will Be The Long-Term Impact of the Sixth Circuit's Divided Decision in Dow Chemical?", 104 *Journal of Taxation* 332-337 (2006), 332 (noting that the COLI plans were projected to generate negative pre-tax cash flows for 17-18 years before generating positive cash flows contingent on Dow contributing large amounts of cash to the plans)

[668] 435 F.3d 596 (6th Cir., 2006) at para. 33.

[669] 364 U.S. 361 (1960).

[670] Lipton, *supra* no. 667 at 333-34 (arguing that the majority interpretation of *Knetsch* was created "out of thin air" and that it erroneously treated the District Court's factual finding that Dow intended to infuse large amounts of cash into the COLI plans as a legal finding that it was capable of overturning on appeal)

[671] *Ibid.* at 337 (arguing that the government should have conceded that the District Court's decision was based on factual findings and argued on appeal that the findings were clearly erroneous, instead of creating new legal arguments by giving an overly-broad interpretation to the *Knetsch* decision).

in exchange. The technical claim for the operation of the shelter is that the subsidiary obtains the high basis that the foreign party had in the property before the transfer, and after the property is sold to an accommodating third party, the loss is used to shelter the income of the parent.[672] In *Long Term Capital Holdings v. U.S.*[673] high-basis low-value preferred stock owned by the foreign party had been created in an earlier tax shelter transaction involving lease-stripping.[674] The stock was sold to Merrill Lynch for about $1 million, triggering over $106 million in losses.[675] The District Court held that the prevailing standard in the Second Circuit regarding the application of the economic substance doctrine is a unitary test, under which both subjective business purpose and objective economic substance may be relevant.[676] The Court rejected the argument that a meaningful change in the parties' economic position was enough to give the transaction economic substance, and applied a cost-benefit analysis in determining that the taxpayer had no realistic expectation of economic profit from the transaction considering the transaction costs.[677] The Court also found no business purpose for the transaction, partly because the complexity of the transaction was far greater than necessary to accomplish its stated purpose, and because

---

[672] Bankman, *supra* no. 2 at 926 (noting that a variation of this shelter was used by Enron)

[673] 330 F.Supp.2d 122 (D. Conn., 2004), affirmed 150 Fed.Appx. 40 (2d Cir., 2005).

[674] Lee A. Sheppard, "LTCM Case: What They Won't Do For Money, Chapter 2", 104 *Tax Notes* 1006 -1013 (Sept. 6, 2004) ("Lease stripping involves insertion of an American corporate tax shelter customer into the existing leveraged lease circle of payments as putative temporary owner of a leasehold interest so it can have the tax benefit of prepaid rent deductions. ... The goal was that only rent deductions, but not the associated rental income, would flow through to the American customer.")

[675] Jeffrey H. Paravano and Melinda L. Reynolds, "Tax Shelters: Evaluating Recent Developments", 895 Practising Law Institute Tax Law and Estate Planning Course Handbook Series, *Tax Law and Practice* (2005), 965 (the District Court upheld the denial of $106 million in claimed capital losses and also imposed $16 million in penalties).

[676] 330 F.Supp.2d 122 (D. Conn., 2004) at p. 171, fn. 68.

[677] Yoram Keinan, "It is Time for The Supreme Court to Voice its Opinion on Economic Substance", 7 *Houston Business and Tax Law Journal* 93-137 (2006), 103-104 (observing that the courts have several different approaches to the objective prong of the economic substance doctrine)

it was purchased as a tax shelter product.[678] It also applied a step transaction analysis to support its decision to disallow the deduction of losses.[679] The taxpayer only challenged the application of the step transaction doctrine and the imposition of penalties on appeal, which the Second Circuit dismissed.[680]

The District Court decision in *Long Term Capital* has also been criticized by Hariton, because it made the matter of whether the amount of interest income exceeded transaction costs the basis for its decision, rather than relying on the fact that the amount of losses claimed vastly exceeded the net interest income generated from the capital invested in the transaction.[681]

Bond and option sales strategy ("BOSS") and son-of-BOSS ("SOB") shelters

Originally this tax shelter was sold by PricewaterhouseCoopers under the name of Bond and Option Strategy, or "BOSS". Later versions were known as "son-of-BOSS" or "SOB".[682] There are

---

[678] Keinan, *supra* no. 2 at 422 (the court found that despite the parties' efforts to prove a business purpose of earning fees the transaction was not carried out in a way that showed the taxpayer had any motive other than to obtain tax benefits).

[679] 330 F.Supp.2d 122 (D.Conn., 2004) at p. 159.

[680] 150 Fed.Appx. 40 (2d Cir., 2005)

[681] Hariton, *supra* no. 2 at 51 (arguing that the decision should have turned on whether a few hundred thousand dollars of investment income was significant in relation to the hundreds of millions of dollars of tax losses being claimed)

[682] Miniority Staff of S. Permanent Subcomm. On Investigations for the Comm. on Gov't Affairs, 108th Cong., U.S. Tax Shelter Industry: The Role of Accountants, Lawyers and Financial Professionals 1-129 (2003), 8 (stating that many professional firms sold abusive tax shelters which denied the U.S. Treasury billions of dollars in revenues); Kathleen DeLaney Thomas, "The Case Against A Strict Liability Economic Substance Penalty", vol. 13:2 *University of Pennsylvania Journal of Business Law* 445-496 (2011), 476 ("The Son-of-BOSS shelter has multiple variations, all of which revolve around creating an artificially high basis in a partnership interest and subsequently disposing of that interest at a loss. ... As in all Son-of-BOSS transactions, the ultimate result for the taxpayer [is] a tax loss with only nominal economic outlay.")

a large number of SOB cases:[683] "The courts are positively lousy with son-of-BOSS cases these days."[684] Thousands of taxpayers purchased these shelters, claiming tax losses in the many billions of dollars.[685] According to the Court of Appeals for the Seventh Circuit in *American Boat Co., LLC v. U.S.*:

> A Son of BOSS shelter may take many forms, but common to them all is the transfer to a partnership of assets laden with significant liabilities. The liabilities are typically obligations to purchase securities, meaning they are not fixed at the time of the transaction. The transfer therefore permits a partner to inflate his basis in the partnership by the value of the contributed asset, while ignoring the corresponding liability. ... The goal of the shelter is to eventually create a large, but not out-of-pocket, loss on a partner's individual tax return. This may occur when the partnership dissolves or sells an over-inflated asset. In turn, this artificial loss may offset actual – and otherwise taxable – gains, thereby sheltering them from Uncle Sam.[686]

According to the United States Senate Permanent Subcommittee on Investigations, the BLIPS shelter (from the SOB family) functioned as a "loss generator", meaning it generated large paper losses that the purchaser of the product then used to offset other income, and shelter it from taxation. The BLIPS shelter is described as having generated hundreds of millions of dollars in phony paper losses for taxpayers, using a series of complex, orchestrated transactions involving shell corporations, structured finance, purported multi-million dollar loans and deliberately obscure investments. According to a document made public by the Subcommittee on Investigations, that was obtained from KMPG, "[in the case of BLIPS] a key objective is for the tax loss associated with the investment

---

[683] Monte A. Jackel and Robert J. Crnkovich, "Son-of-BOSS Revisited", 123 *Tax Notes* 1481-1485 (June 22, 2009), 1485 (arguing that inconsistent court results suggest that SOB cases should be resolved "other than through the imperfect process of continued litigation.")

[684] Lee A. Sheppard, "Recent Shelter Cases: The Right Result for the Wrong Reasons", 126 *Tax Notes* 421-428 (Jan. 25, 2010), 427-428 (arguing economic substance was originally devised to apply to individual cases and that the Tax Court should not be criticized for basing decisions on economic substance rather than on narrower grounds such as invalidating the taxpayer's partnership)

[685] IR-2005-37, March 24, 2005.

[686] 583 F.3d 471 (7th Cir., 2009) at pp. 472-473.

structure to offset/shelter the taxpayer's other, unrelated, economic profits."[687] The success of the BLIPS shelter depended upon establishing a partnership with a foreign corporation, and undertaking a number of transactions necessary to the scheme, with the ultimate question being whether an obligation to pay nominal interest was a true "liability" of a partnership.[688] One commentator has said that the ingenuity of the sponsor of these shelters was put to the test, because under some statutes it had to argue for recognition of the liability, whereas under others just the opposite.[689]

According to an indictment filed by the U.S. government against several tax professionals, the BLIPS tax shelter was marketed and sold in 1999 and 2000 and generated at least $5.1 billion in tax losses.[690] The government alleged, in a bill of particulars in its criminal proceedings, that BLIPS was designed to be a short-term tax shelter program terminating before year-end, virtually always within 67 days. The government also alleged that there was no realistic possibility of making a reasonable pre-tax profit, and no purpose for purported borrowing except to generate a tax loss.[691] In relation to

---

[687] Minority Staff of Senate Permanent Subcommittee on Investigations for the Comm. on Government Affairs, 108th Cong., U.S. Tax Shelter Industry: The Role of Accountants, Lawyers and Financial Professionals (2003), 6.

[688] Lee A. Sheppard, "KPMG: Has the Prosecution Overcharged the Crime?", 112 *Tax Notes* 405-416 (July 31, 2006) (explaining the complicated series of steps in BLIPS transactions based on opinion letters assuming a 7 year investment plan where customers were in and out of the deals in a few months so they could claim shelter losses in the same year as their capital gains)

[689] Alvin D. Lurie, "I Know Crane and BOSS isn't Crane (An Historical Perspective)", 86 *Tax Notes* 1932-1941 (Mar. 27, 2000), 1932 (arguing that the reasoning in support of BOSS shelters is based on a gross misreading of case law combined with an ingeniously selected set of steps that would be admirable if not destructive of tax policy).

[690] Sheryl Stratton, "KPMG Shelter Civil and Criminal Proceedings – Parallel No More?", 109 *Tax Notes* 297-298 (Oct. 17, 2005) (noting the *Wall Street Journal* criticized the government for prosecuting KPMG officials in relation to the promotion of tax shelters, alleging that the proceedings had "an Alice-in-Wonderland quality; the accused are on trial for promoting a fraudulent tax shelter that has never been proved to be fraudulent in the first place.")

[691] Sheryl Stratton, "DOJ Alleges Fraud in Design, Marketing of KPMG Tax Shelters", 111 *Tax Notes* 541-542 (May 1, 2006) (noting the government alleged fraud against 18 tax professionals re the design and approval of tax

BLIPS, and three other tax shelters called FLIP, OPIS and SOS,[692] KPMG entered into a deferred prosecution agreement with the U.S. government in 2005, under which it admitted to criminal wrongdoing and agreed to pay $456 million in fines, restitution and penalties. KPMG's admission was that it designed, marketed and implemented tax shelters, which generated at least $11 billion in phony tax losses.[693] According to an internal KPMG e-mail the FLIP product that it marketed and sold was a potential "tax disaster". In order to generate the claimed tax benefits, a purchaser of the "product" had to buy a stock warrant in a Cayman Island company that "was really illusory and stood out more like a sore thumb, since no one in his right mind would pay such an exorbitant price for such a warrant."[694]

The principal tax shelter at issue in *Klamath Strategic Investment Fund ex rel. St. Croix Ventures v. U.S.*[695] was the bond linked issue premium structure, or BLIPS, a son-of-BOSS transaction.[696] The Court of Appeals for the Fifth Circuit found in *Klamath* that the transactions did not survive the economic substance doctrine. The Fifth Circuit adopted the majority view of the other Circuits that there is a conjunctive test under the economic substance doctrine. The Court also wrote that "[t]he effect of disregarding a transaction

---

shelters in which the fraudulent aspects of transactions were concealed and misrepresented in opinion letters.)

[692] Foreign Leveraged Investment Program (FLIP); Offshore Portfolio Investment Strategy (OPIS); Short Options Strategy (SOS).
[693] IR-83, Aug. 29, 2005.
[694] "U.S. Tax Shelter Industry: The Role of Accountants, Lawyers and Financial Professionals – Four KPMG Case Studies: FLIP, OPIS, BLIPS and SC2", Report by the Minority Staff of the Permanent Subcommittee on Investigations, Committee on Government Affairs, US Senate 1-129 (2003), 44; see also: Jasper L. Cummings, Jr., "Economic Substance Doctrine Felonies", 131 *Tax Notes* 977-984 (May 30, 2011), 977-978 (noting that a law firm attorney was convicted of tax evasion along with two KPMG employees in relation to advice re the BLIPS structure)
[695] 568 F.3d 537 (5th Cir., 2009).
[696] Jeremiah Coder, "Fifth Circuit Adopts Majority View of Economic Substance Doctrine", 123 *Tax Notes* 969-971 (May 25, 2009) (noting that the taxpayer claimed losses arising from inflated tax basis calculations where loan transactions had purported 7 year terms but it was not contemplated that the transaction would exceed 60 days)

for lack of economic substance is that, for taxation purposes, the transaction is viewed to have never occurred at all."[697]

The Federal Court of Claims also relied on the economic substance doctrine in *Jade Trading, LLC v. U.S.*,[698] to disallow losses claimed in relation to the disposition of partnership interests in which high basis had been created using euro call options. The Court held that although the transactions complied literally with the terms of the *Internal Revenue Code*, they lacked economic substance, having regard to the five general economic substance principles outlined by the Federal Circuit in *Coltec Industries, Inc.*: "1 The law does not permit the taxpayer to reap tax benefits from a transaction that lacks economic reality. 2 The taxpayer bears the burden of proving that the transaction has economic substance. 3 The economic substance of a transaction must be viewed objectively. 4 The only transaction to be analyzed is the one that gave rise to the alleged tax benefit. 5 Arrangements with subsidiaries that do not affect the economic interests of independent third parties deserve particularly close scrutiny."[699] The Federal Circuit Court of Appeals upheld the Claims Court finding that the transactions lacked economic substance.[700]

The Court of Appeals for the Seventh Circuit also found in *Cemco Investors, LLC v. U.S.* that a son-of-BOSS transaction lacked economic substance, noting that "[a] transaction with an out-of-pocket cost of $6,000 and no risk beyond that expense, while generating a tax loss of $3.6 million, is the sort of thing that the Internal Revenue

---

[697] 568 F.3d 537 (5th Cir., 2009) at p. 549.
[698] 80 Fed.Cl. 11 (2007).
[699] Robert S. Walton and Jenny A. Austin, "Jade Trading and Cemco Investors: Economic Substance Governs in Son-of-Boss", 108 *Journal of Taxation* 300-306 (2008), 302-303 (noting that following *Coltec* the court considered that the question was not whether the partnership had the potential to earn pre-tax profits but rather whether the single spread transaction that gave rise to the tax benefits had the ability to earn pre-tax profits).
[700] *Jade Trading LLC et al v. United States*, No. 03-cv-2164 (Fed. Cir. Mar. 23, 2010), *Doc. 2010-6335, 2010 TNT 56-10*; Jeremiah Coder, "Federal Circuit Overturns Penalty Determination in Jade Trading", 126 *Tax Notes* 1568 (Mar. 29, 2010) (pointing out that the Federal Circuit overturned the section 6226 penalty on jurisdictional grounds).

Service frowns on."[701] The economic substance doctrine has also been relied upon by the IRS in disallowing losses claimed in relation to a son-of-BOSS shelter marketed by Ernst & Young under the name Currency Options Bring Rewards or COBRA. The government's position that COBRA transactions should be disregarding as having no economic substance is presently before the Federal Claims Court in *Murfam Farms LLC et al v. United States*.[702]

Distressed asset debt ("DAD") shelters

The U.S. District Court held in *Southgate Master Fund LLC v. United States of America*[703] that Texas billionaire Andrew Beal's $1.1 billion tax loss on investments in Chinese debt was properly disallowed by the IRS. Beal's $1.1 billion in claimed tax losses, which involved an estimated economic loss of about $10 million, were based upon transactions undertaken in conjunction with a distressed asset debt or "DAD" shelter. In a DAD shelter, a foreign company that isn't subject to U.S. taxes sells debt with built-in losses to U.S. partnerships at a fraction of its face value. The partnership's investors then claim loss deductions for the full face value of the debt to offset income earned from other sources.[704] In 2002, 2003 and 2004 Beal applied tax losses from Chinese non-performing loans (NPLs) acquired from China Cinda, a government-run asset management company whose purpose was to take poorly performing loans or NPLs off the books of China's banking system and facilitate the resolution of those loans through sales

---

[701] 515 F.3d 749 (7th Cir., 2008) at p. 751, certiorari denied 129 Ct. 131 (2008) (SCC).
[702] Sam Young, "Son-of-BOSS Ruling May Be Only a Temporary Setback for IRS", 124 *Tax Notes* 518-520 (Aug. 10, 2009) (noting that although the taxpayer was granted partial summary judgment based on the court's finding that a regulation was invalid as retroactively applied the government could proceed on economic substance grounds)
[703] No. 3:06-cv-2335-K (N.D. Tex., Aug 18, 2009), Doc 2009-18785, 2009 TNT 160-6.
[704] Ryan J. Donnoyer, "Andrew Beal Denied $1.1 Billion Tax-Shelter Loss by U.S. Judge", *Bloomberg*, August 21, 2009.

to foreign investors.[705] Southgate was a limited liability company formed in 2002, which received the NPL portfolio owned by China Cinda through a U.S. subsidiary of China Cinda known as Eastgate. The tax basis in Southgate was the face value of the NPL portfolio, which was approximately $1.4 billion. Through a wholly-owned LLC, Beal purchased 90 percent of Eastgate's 99 percent share of Southgate for approximately $19.4 million. The result of the transaction was that 89 percent of the built-in losses were allocated to Beal. Loans were sold by Southgate in 2002, and in subsequent years, for a fraction of their face value. Southgate realized losses of approximately $295 million in 2002, and similar losses in subsequent years.[706]

Beal's ability to deduct these losses for tax purposes was limited to his basis in Southgate, which was approximately the price paid for Eastgate's share of Southgate, plus a placement fee paid in conjunction with the transactions, which was a total of about $29 million. Beal therefore engaged in a "basis build" repurchase ("repo") transaction, by contributing $180 million in Ginnie Mae securities to Southgate, that secured a $162 million loan to US PaineWebber. The effect of these transactions was that Beal's capital account balance was increased by about $19 million, but his basis in Southgate increased by about $180 million in 2002. Similar transactions also took place in 2003 and 2004.

The District Court held that although Southgate's claimed loss appeared to fall within the literal terms of the statute, the transaction that created the high basis in the stock lacked economic substance, and it was therefore disregarded for tax purposes: "Objectively, the [repo]

---

[705] Alex Brill, "Dear DAD: Southgate and the American Jobs Creation Act", 126 *Tax Notes* 505-511 (Jan. 25, 2010), 505 (noting that in DAD transactions partnerships are used to transfer distressed assets from tax indifferent foreign parties to a domestic taxpayer who benefits from the built-in loss in the foreign party's asset by using the tax losses to offset other income).
[706] No. 3:06-cv-2335-K (N.D. Tex., Aug 18, 2009), Doc 2009-18785, 2009 TNT 160-6, para. 175 (the amount of loss triggered for Southgate in each year was dictated by Beal's "past practice" of sheltering most of his expected income for the tax year).

transaction lacks economic substance because Southgate did not have a reasonable possibility of profit from it, despite the opportunity for profit from the original NPL transaction. ... Subjectively, Plaintiff at trial did not establish any valid business purpose for this 'basis-build' transaction other than the tax benefits obtained by Beal. The proffered reasons for the deal read like afterthoughts designed to disguise the true purpose".[707] The ruling in *Southgate* is the first on the DAD shelter and has ramifications for dozens of other cases where the IRS is contesting billions of dollars in claimed tax losses, many of which are linked to the purchase of Brazilian debt.[708] The disallowance of Southgate's losses has been appealed to the Fifth Circuit.[709]

This extraordinary extent to which the economic substance doctrine has been used to deny deductions in abusive tax avoidance cases in the U.S. is compelling evidence that economic substance should also be front and centre in the adjudication of tax avoidance cases in Canada. In these U.S. cases, although the legal relationships have all been validly structured, the tax benefits have been denied, because the transactions lacked economic substance. This could not have happened in Canada, under the present state of our law. A further point is that, as judges in the U.S. have regularly assessed the economic substance of transactions, in order to decide whether they should be upheld, one should suppose that judges in Canada are no less capable.

U.S. ECONOMIC SUBSTANCE DOCTRINE CODIFIED

The codification of the economic substance doctrine in the U.S. is further evidence that our GAAR should be amended in Canada, to require courts to consider the economic substance of transactions, to a greater extent under GAAR. Prior to its decade-long efforts to

---

[707] *Ibid.* at 133.
[708] *Supra* no. 704.
[709] Brill, *supra* no. 705 (noting that DAD transactions entered into after October 22, 2004, similar to the one entered into by Beal, were effectively disallowed by the *American Jobs Creation Act* through a provision disallowing deductions from partnership loss transfers)

codify the economic substance doctrine, Congress had taken action against the "monstrous" tax shelter problem in the U.S., with the enactment of the *Tax Reform Act* of 1976.[710] This legislation attempted for the first time to limit tax deductions in transactions that involved no risk or loss to the taxpayer.[711] Subsequently, there were many attempts to codify the economic substance doctrine, all unsuccessful until the passage of the *Health Care and Education Reconciliation Act* of 2010.[712] As to why it took so long for the U.S. to codify its common law economic substance doctrine, Professor Prebble says that America has been able to manage without a statutory GAAR, because its courts have taken a more substantive, less formalistic, approach to statutory interpretation than other common law countries.[713]

For and against codification

During the years that efforts towards codification of the economic substance doctrine were underway, there was ongoing extensive debate in the U.S. about whether codification would be meritorious. The main claims by proponents of codification of the doctrine were that the Circuit Courts' inconsistent rulings were detrimental, as they did not provide a basis upon which to evaluate the tax implications of business transactions;[714] and, that the legislature's guidance was therefore needed, on when and how to apply the doctrine, in order to assist the IRS and taxpayers, and in order to avoid expensive tax litigation cases with uncertain outcomes.[715]

---

[710] Caplin, *supra* no. 616 at 713, 750 (following extensive congressional hearings in 1974 and 1975, tax shelters involving motion pictures, certain kinds of farming, equipment leasing, and oil and gas resources were targeted under new "at-risk" rules and a number of other anti-avoidance measures were adopted to limit deductions)

[711] Nahass, *supra* no. 136 at footnote 1 (the *Tax Reform Act of 1976* was Congress' response to the increasing problem of tax shelters and was the first attempt to limit deductions on transactions with no risk of loss)

[712] P.L. No. 111-152. The President signed the bill into law on March 30, 2010.

[713] Prebble, *supra* no. 18.

[714] Pichhadze and Pichhadze, *supra* no. 30 at 65; Nahass, *supra* no. 136 at 248; Rector, *supra* no. 2 at 189.

[715] *Supra* no. 711 at 248.

Further claims in favour of codification were that courts may take a statute more seriously than doctrine embodied only in case law;[716] codification would provide a "more salient warning" of a vigilant approach against tax shelters;[717] and, codification would send a strong message to the courts and ensure that the doctrine is not weakened or overturned by the Supreme Court.[718]

Opponents of codification claimed that the flexibility the courts have shown in applying the economic substance doctrine is an important source of its strength.[719] The IRS opposed codification on the basis that Congress should "leave well enough alone".[720] Opponents of codification also pointed out that a codified rule would continue to be a more-or-less vague standard.[721] Other opponents of codification said that turning the doctrine into a statute could cause its application by courts to be over-inclusive, with the undesirable effect of chilling legitimate business transactions.[722] A rigid rule could also foster overly-aggressive tax planning,[723] as well as

---

[716] Zelenak, *supra* no. 636 at 179-180.
[717] McMahon, Jr., *supra* no. 374 at 207-208.
[718] Rector, *supra* no. 2 at 189.
[719] O'Neill, *supra* no. 356 at 1061-1062; Willens, *supra* no. 484 at 540; Miller, Jr., *supra* no. 221 at 1067-1069; Wolfman, *supra* no. 484 at 445).
[720] Sheryl Stratton, "IRS, Tax Bar Urge Congress to Leave Economic Substance Alone", 114 *Tax Notes* 814-815 Feb. 26, 2007), 814 (citing an interview with IRS Chief Counsel Donald Korb); Allen Kenney, "Korb Speculates on Codification of Economic Substance Doctrine", 105 *Tax Notes* 932 (Nov. 15, 2004) (noting IRS Chief Counsel Donald Korb's concern that court losses could revive efforts re codification of the economic substance doctrine)
[721] Zelenak, *supra* no. 636 at 185-186 (arguing that under codification there would still be "great latitude for judicial interpretation"); Coder, *supra* no. 472 at 1189-1190 (Professor Steve Johnson of the University of Nevada says many countries have had a pattern of inconsistency in applying their GAARs, and a case can be made that enactment of a statutory GAAR has not really reduced the level of judicial unpredictability).
[722] Ellen P. Aprill, "Tax Shelters, Tax Law, and Morality: Codifying Judicial Doctrines", 54 *SMU Law Review* 9-35 (2001), 34 (noting however that some proponents of codifying the doctrine consider that it is under-inclusive).
[723] Ventry Jr., *supra* no. 484 at 1406 (arguing that a "rigid rule" would encourage tax avoidance whereas "The economic substance doctrine often acts as the last line of defense against abusive tax avoidance, and its facts and circumstances analysis is better left in the hands of judges than legislative drafters.")

its overly-aggressive application by the IRS.[724] More fundamentally, opponents of codification pointed to a long history of failed attempts to resolve leaky tax laws with more laws.[725] In this regard, as Professor Ginsberg famously warned,"[e]very stick crafted to beat on the head of a taxpayer will metamorphose sooner or later into a large green snake and bite the Commissioner on the hind part."[726]

Nevertheless, codification was seen by Congress to be attractive, because it was considered to have the potential to be a large revenue raiser.[727] The House of Representatives voted in November 2009 to codify the economic substance doctrine as a $5.7 billion offset in the *Affordable Health Care for America Act* (H.R. 3962), and the Senate voted in March 2010 to approve a tax extenders bill (H.R. 4213) that included a similar $5.5 billion offset.[728] Although the suggestion has been made that, in the event of fundamental tax reform, the new legislation should be scrapped and replaced with a statutory GAAR that

---

[724] Canellos, *supra* no. 486 at 71 (arguing that the risk is too great where "the IRS could unilaterally determine the substance of a transaction"); Cummings, Jr., *supra* no. 471 at 530 (arguing that even where Congress only codifies the tests and not the applicability of the economic substance doctrine, it will still put its imprimatur on the doctrine and further embolden its use).

[725] Steven A. Bank, "Codifying Judicial Doctrines: No Cure For Rules But More Rules", 54 *SMU Law Review* 37-45 (2001), 41 ("Rules have begat more rules with little effect on tax avoidance").

[726] Martin D. Ginsburg, "Making Tax Law Through the Judicial Process", 70 *A.B.A. Journal* 74 (March 1984), 76.

[727] Allen Kenny, "Korb Speculates on Codification of Economic Substance Doctrine", 105 *Tax Notes* 932 (Nov. 15, 2004), 932 (citing remarks by IRS Chief Counsel Donald Korb at a conference co-sponsored by the San Jose State University and Tax Executives Institute); see also: Jerome B. Libin, "Congress Should Address Tax Avoidance Head-On: The Internal Revenue Code Needs A GAAR", 30 *Virginia Tax Review* 339-353 (2010), 346 (suggesting that the fact Congress needed the revenue offset in the bill it was enacting was the primary impetus behind the "Clarification of Economic Substance Doctrine" in the *Health Care and Education Reconciliation Act* of 2010); Thomas, *supra* no. 682 at 467 (pointing out that revenue estimates for codification of the economic substance doctrine were $16 billion over 10 years in 2005 and $7 billion over 10 years in 2009, dropping to $4.5 billion over 10 years in 2010).

[728] Coder, *supra* no. 553 at 17 (stating that a proposal in the 109th Congress to codify the doctrine was estimated to raise around $17 billion over 10 years. In 2007 the JCT's estimate was $10 billion. By 2010 the estimate had declined to $4.5 billion).

"would have more of an impact on aggressive tax planning than codification of economic substance is likely to have,"[729] there has been wide support for the economic substance doctrine in the U.S.[730]

However, the body of opinion amongst commentators about the merits of codification of the economic substance doctrine has been divided. In the non-scientific sampling presented below, twenty-three of thirty authors expressed support for the economic substance doctrine, fifteen opposed codification, five expressed no opinion, and two opposed codification because in their views structural tax reforms are the only viable route for combating abusive tax avoidance.

U.S. JUDICIAL ECONOMIC SUBSTANCE DOCTRINE ("ESD")

Author	ESD Needed	Codify ESD	Reason for position
Aprill, Ellen P. Loyola Law School	Yes	Yes	Codifying would empower IRS and Treasury[731]
Bank, Steven A. UCLA School of Law	Yes	No	Rules have little effect on tax avoidance[732]

---

[729] Jerome B. Libin, "Congress Should Address Tax Avoidance Head-On: The Internal Revenue Code Needs A GAAR", 30 *Virginia Tax Review* 339-353 (2010), 351-352 (also arguing in favour of the proposition that "A GAAR could simply provide that the favorable tax consequences of a particular transaction would be realized only if the taxpayer were able to establish that tax avoidance was not the primary reason for the transaction.")

[730] Note also, however, the recently expressed "minority position" that the economic substance doctrine "is bad for tax law" as it "is somewhat like throwing hand grenades at ants that have infiltrated a house. It kills the ants, but it does serious damage to the house and the legitimate inhabitants." This point-of-view, in turn, is founded upon the premise that "the ability to ascertain the law in advance is paramount", without adoption of its competing values examined in the review of certainty in chapter V, or the point that the economic substance doctrine has only been applied by the courts to egregious tax shelters. This critic nevertheless concedes that "Perhaps incorporating the doctrine into the Internal Revenue Code has given the doctrine legitimacy.": see Madison, *supra* no. 135 at 3-7, 20 (arguing that a "risk requirement" would be superior, without providing a recommendation as to how it should be imposed).

[731] Aprill, *supra* no. 722 at 32.

[732] Bank, *supra* no. 725 at 41.

Author	ESD Needed	Codify ESD	Reason for position
Bankman, Joseph Stanford Law School	Yes	No	Rule would be plagued by ambiguities[733]
Canellos, Peter C Attorney, New York	Yes	No	Courts have shown uncommonly good judgment and statutory definition would create problems[734]
Cummings, Jasper L. Jr. Attorney, Raleigh, NC	No	NP	Creates uncertainty; no proper origins[735]
Gergen, Mark P., Berkeley Law School	Yes	NP	Standards required against technical exploitation[736]
Glassman, Daniel J. Attorney, Florida	No	No	Tax liability should depend on plain meaning of objective rules[737]
Grewal, Amandeep S. Attorney, Washington	No	No	Inappropriate to disregard statutory language[738]
Hariton, David P. Attorney, New York	Yes	Yes	Courts implementing not abrogating will of Congress but the courts' decisions "are all over the map"[739]
Isenbergh, Joseph University of Chicago	No	No	Statutes meticulously drafted should be interpreted as literal expressions of taxing policy[740]
Keinan, Yoram University of Michigan	Yes	Yes	Two-prong objective and subjective test should be collapsed into single, flexible, objective standard[741]

---

[733] Bankman, *supra* no. 2 at 925.
[734] Canellos, *supra* no. 486 at 51-52 and 71.
[735] Cummings, *supra* no. 15 at 145-241.
[736] Gergen, *supra* no. 372 at 131.
[737] Glassman, *supra* no. 183 at 670.
[738] Amandeep S. Grewal, "Economic Substance and the Supreme Court", *Tax Notes* 969 (Sept. 10, 2007), 987.
[739] David P. Hariton, "How to Fix Economic Substance", *Tax Notes*, 539 (Apr. 28, 2003), 542.
[740] Isenbergh, *supra* no. 214 at 879.
[741] Keinan, *supra* no. 2 at 454.

Author	ESD Needed	Codify ESD	Reason for position
Korb, Donald IRS Chief Counsel	Yes	No	Doctrine has been "a very useful tool" and codifying wouldn't provide additional tax administration tools[742]
Lederman, Leandra Indiana University	No	No	ESD is "a terrible tool" for distinguishing abusive transactions. Focus instead on legislative intent[743]
Luke, Charlene D. Florida State University	Yes	NP	Exclusive use of pre-tax profit to find objective economic substance is fundamentally flawed[744]
McMahon Jr., Martin J. University of Florida	Yes	Yes	Required to deter economically inefficient transactions; courts do not apply doctrine vigilantly[745]
Miller, Gerald W. Texas Tech Law Review	Yes	No	Keep discretionary nature of common law doctrine[746]
Nahass, Zachary Attorney, Washington	Yes	Yes	Establish uniform system of analysis to enable better planning for taxpayers and a stronger tool for IRS[747]
O'Neill, Sandra F. Attorney, Boston	Yes	No	Appellate courts generally apply doctrine correctly so defer to courts to avoid creating additional confusion[748]

---

[742] Crystal Tandon, "Economic Substance Codification Would Create More Problems Than It Solves, Says Korb", *Tax Notes* 777 (Feb. 18, 2008), 777.
[743] Lederman, *supra* no. 494.
[744] Luke, *supra* no. 68 at 792.
[745] McMahon Jr., *supra* no. 407 at 1018.
[746] Miller, Jr., *supra* no. 221 at 1069.
[747] Nahass, *supra* no. 136 at 268.
[748] O'Neill, *supra* no. 356 at 1061-62.

Author	ESD Needed	Codify ESD	Reason for position
New York State Bar Tax Section	Yes	No	Courts generally reach the right tax policy result; codification would create uncertainty[749]
Pichhadze, Aviv & Amir, York University & LSE*	Yes	Yes	Introduce consistency and predictability instead of having many different tests develop in the case law[750]
Shaviro, Daniel New York University	Yes	Yes	Strong substantive anti-abuse rules needed to require business purpose and economic substance[751]
Sheppard, Lee A. Tax Analysts	Yes	Yes	Strong language which does not merely restate case law is required to combat abusive tax avoidance[752]
Smith, Robert Thornton Attorney, New York	Yes	NP	Constructive purposive interpretation is required for a community that is committed to equal citizenship[753]
Thompson Jr, Samuel C. UCLA School of Law	Yes	Yes	Codifying will deter business people from pursuing transactions without any economic substance[754]
Ventry Jr., Dennis J. American University	Yes	No	Inelastic rule would sap doctrine's power and lead to more and not fewer abusive tax transactions[755]

[749] New York State Bar Association, Tax Section, "NYSBA Objects to Codification of Economic Substance Provisions", *Tax Notes* 1324 (June 2, 2003), 1324.
[750] Pichhadze and Pichhadze, supra no. 30 at 65.
[751] Shaviro and Weisbach, *supra* no. 215 at 517.
[752] Lee A. Sheppard, "Erroneous Application of the Economic Substance Doctrine", *Tax Notes* 259 (Jan. 14, 2008), 269.
[753] Smith, *supra* no. 217 at 16.
[754] Samuel C. Thompson Jr., "Despite Widespread Opposition, Congress Should Codify the ESD", *Tax Notes* 781 (Feb. 13, 2006), 785.
[755] Ventry Jr., *supra* no. 484 at 1405-06.

Author	ESD Needed	Codify ESD	Reason for position
Weisbach, David A. University of Chicago	Yes	Yes	Courts are often quite literal in interpreting tax laws and often arrive at "silly results" in deciding cases[756]
Willens, Robert Columbia University	Yes	No	Flexibility courts have shown in applying doctrine should not be sacrificed for rigidity by codifying[757]
Wolfman, Bernard Harvard Law School	Yes	NP	Doctrine has served U.S. tax system well over time[758]
Yin, George K. University of Virginia	No	No	Neither judicial doctrine nor codified provision is best solution. Structural tax reform is needed[759]
Zelenak, Lawrence Duke University	Yes	No	Might act as a brake on judicial abandonment of doctrine but substantive tax reform is required[760]

* London School of Economics. "NP" means no position expressed re codification in the article.

Thus, while the body of opinion about whether to codify the economic substance doctrine has been divided in the U.S., there has been wide support for the economic substance doctrine. This is powerful evidence that economic substance should occupy a much more substantial position in tax avoidance in Canada, than it does under the present version of our GAAR.

Key developments along the road to economic substance codification are described below.

---

[756] Weisbach, *supra* no. 184 at 76-77.
[757] Willens, *supra* no. 484 at 541.
[758] Wolfman, *supra* no. 484 at 445.
[759] Yin, *supra* no. 193 at 230.
[760] Zelenak, *supra* no. 636 at 182.

Budget proposal for fiscal year 2000

The Clinton Administration included "novel and far-reaching" corporate tax shelter provisions in its Budget Proposal submitted to Congress on February 1, 1999.[761] Under these proposals, the concept of a "tax avoidance transaction" was defined as "any transaction in which the reasonably expected pre-tax profit (determined on a present value basis, after taking into account foreign taxes as expenses and transaction costs) of the transaction is insignificant relative to the reasonably expected net tax benefits (i.e. tax benefits in excess of the tax liability arising from the transaction, determined on a present value basis) of such transaction."[762]

The Committee on Finance held hearings on the proposals, at which the American Bar Association ("ABA"), American Institute of Certified Public Accountants ("AICPA") and the New York State Bar Association ("NYSBA") made representations. Only the ABA supported codification, and it suggested that the economic substance doctrine be codified in its existing form, without the feature of the present value examination.[763] The objection by the NYSBA to codification was that it would disallow legitimate tax benefits in some circumstances.[764]

Abusive Tax Shelter Shutdown Act of 1999

Congressman Doggett introduced a bill in the House of Representatives in June 1999, which was intended to curb tax abuses "by disallowing tax benefits claimed to arise from transactions without

---

[761] Smith, *supra* no. 217 at 24-25 (pointing out a number of problems with the present value comparison making the proposed approach problematic).
[762] Department of the Treasury, General Explanations of the Administration's Revenue Proposals (February 1999), 95-104.
[763] Keinan, *supra* no. 2 at 444-445 and footnote 327 (the ABA suggested the economic substance doctrine only be codified in the way it then applied under the common law economic substance doctrine).
[764] Robert H. Scarborough, NYSB Tax Section Concerned About Codifying Substance Doctrine, 88 *Tax Notes* 752-753 (Aug. 7, 2000), 752 (the NYSBA also suggested the focus be on potential rather than expected pretax profit).

substantial economic substance".[765] This proposed legislation reflected the A.B.A.'s comments on the corporate tax shelter provisions submitted to Congress in February 1999. Taxpayers' subjective motives would not be taken into account,[766] and transactions which would be set aside were those in which the transaction did not change the taxpayer's economic position in a meaningful way (apart from Federal income tax consequences), and in which the present value of the reasonably expected income from the transaction was not substantial in relation to the present value of the tax benefits claimed.[767]

Joint Committee Study / White Paper on Corporate Tax Shelters

The Joint Committee on Taxation released a study in July 1999, calling for "a heightened economic substance requirement" in dealing with tax avoidance.[768] The Department of the Treasury also released a White Paper on the tax shelter problem in July 1999. According to the White Paper, a subjective test would likely prove inadequate, since corporations exist to make profit and would be presumed to satisfy a potential for profit test, even when expectations of profit were unreasonable. The White Paper reasoned that permitting corporations to enter into transactions with unreasonable expectations of profit would permit corporations to enter into transactions solely for tax benefits.[769]

---

[765] H.R. 2255, 106th Cong., 1st Session (June 17, 1999).

[766] Keinan, *supra* no. 2 at 403-404, 445 (the Treasury and the Joint Committee on Taxation released reports on tax shelters in 1999 which suggested subjective purpose not be taken into account).

[767] *Abusive Tax Shelter Shutdown Act* of 1999, subsec. 3(2), introduced in House of Representatives on June 17, 1999 (the understatement penalty was also to be increased in respect of the transactions that were to be affected).

[768] Joint Committee on Taxation, "Study of Present-Law Penalty and Interest Provisions as Required by Section 3801 of the Internal Revenue Service Restructuring and Reform Act of 1998 (including Provisions Relating to Corporate Tax Shelters)", JCS-3-99.

[769] "The Problem of Corporate Tax Shelters: Discussion, Analysis and Legislative Proposals", *supra* no. 83 at 160-161.

Budget Proposal for the Fiscal Year 2001

Under the 2001 Budget Proposals released in February 2000, the step of defining a "tax avoidance transaction" was abandoned in favour of codifying the economic substance doctrine under a "coherent standard" to be derived from existing case law.[770] Under this approach, tax benefits would be disallowed where they were not "clearly contemplated" by the applicable Code provision and the transaction lacked economic substance. The previously proposed quantitative test for whether a transaction had economic substance was retained (i.e. a determination was to be made using a present value analysis as to whether a transaction lacked economic substance, in the sense that the reasonably expected pre-tax profit was insignificant relative to the reasonably expected net tax benefits).[771]

Abusive Tax Shelter Shutdown Act of 2001

This proposed legislation contained a two prong analysis, under which a transaction had economic substance only if it changed the taxpayer's economic position in a meaningful way (apart from Federal income tax effects), and "the taxpayer has a substantial nontax purpose for entering into such transaction and the transaction is a reasonable means of accomplishing such purpose."[772] The proposed legislation treated foreign taxes as an expense in calculating pre-tax profits for taxpayers relying on a profit motive to show economic substance. This was in response to two cases lost by the government, in which taxpayers convinced the courts that their profit motive should be tested by looking to pre-foreign-tax income in schemes designed to capture the benefit of withholding taxes imposed in respect of dividends on stocks. The taxpayers had become

---

[770] General Explanations of the Administration's Fiscal Year 2001 Revenue Proposals, Department of the Treasury February 2000 at 124-126, http://www.treas.gov/offices/tax-policy/library/gfnbk00.pdf
[771] Zelenak, *supra* no. 636 at 178-179 and footnote 10 re 2001 Revenue proposals at 124, 126 (also arguing that codifying abuse as a distinct anti-avoidance measure would not include an economic substance component).
[772] H.R. 2250, 107th Cong. (1st Sess. 2001).

record owners for a very brief period of time of stock interests in foreign countries in order to receive their dividends. Because of receiving the dividends, the taxpayers claimed entitlement to credits for foreign taxes withheld from the dividend payments. The transactions were attractive to the taxpayers, because the price of the stock they purchased was determined by owners who could not use the credits.[773] The Government had argued that the transactions should be ignored, because the taxpayers had anticipated a post-foreign-tax loss. The investments had made economic profits before taxes, but lost money if the foreign taxes were treated as expenses.[774]

Several further attempts to codify the economic substance doctrine followed along these lines, including in the *American Competitiveness and Corporate Accountability Act of 2002*.[775] This version of the proposed codification of the economic substance doctrine did not address the issue of legislatively intended benefits, and its "government-friendly" two prong analysis was applauded by some, on the basis that it would signal lower tolerance for abuse of tax rules.[776]

---

[773] George K. Yin, "The Problem of Corporate Tax Shelters: Uncertain Dimensions, Unwise Approaches", 55 *Tax Law Review* 405-426 (2002), 407-408 (the taxpayer successfully contended that in order to make a pretax determination, all taxes including the foreign taxes paid in the transaction should be disregarded, and the foreign taxes therefore should not be treated as an expense).

[774] James M. Peaslee, "Creditable Foreign Taxes and the Economic Substance Profit Test", 114 *Tax Notes* 443-451 (Jan. 29, 2007), 444, footnote 6 (describing the cases of *IES Industries, Inc. v. United States* and *Compaq Computer Corp. v. Commissioner* as having "awful facts from the taxpayer's perspective as a litigant. The transactions were unrelated to the taxpayer's business, involved very little risk, and had been flogged by a promoter. A significant part of the government's argument was that the transactions lacked a nontax motive, because the taxpayer anticipated a post-foreign-tax loss. The taxpayers convinced the courts that their profit motive should be tested by looking to pre-foreign-tax income (which conformed to taxable income for a taxpayer claiming FTCs.)")

[775] H.R. 5095, 107th Cong. (2d Sess. 2002).

[776] Rector, *supra* no. 2 at 188-189 (also arguing that taxpayers would no longer need to wonder about what standard applied when tax planning and that codification ensures the doctrine would not be weakened by the Supreme Court)

Jumpstart Our Business Strength (JOBS) Act 2004

Under this proposed legislation,[777] the "government-friendly" version of the economic substance doctrine requiring that transactions would have to satisfy both the subjective business purpose and objective economic substance prongs of the doctrine was maintained; however, the language of the legislation was permissive, leaving the courts with a great deal of discretion. The proposed standard would only apply if a court determined the economic substance doctrine was "relevant" for the disputed transaction.[778]

Section 7701(n)(1)(B) provided that a transaction would have economic substance only if it changed the taxpayer's economic position in a meaningful way (apart from Federal tax effects), the taxpayer had a substantial nontax purpose for entering into the transaction, and the transaction was a reasonable means of accomplishing such purpose. The section also provided that where a taxpayer was relying on potential for profit to prove economic substance, it could only be taken into account if the present value of the reasonably expected pre-tax profit from the transaction was substantial in relation to the present value of the expected net tax benefits that would be allowed if the transaction were respected.[779] Fees, transaction expenses and foreign taxes were to be treated as expenses in determining pre-tax profit.[780]

---

[777] S. 1637, 108th Cong. (1st Sess. 2003).

[778] Nahass, *supra* no. 136 at 263 (saying that the proposal would give rise to some uniformity in the application of the economic substance doctrine)(Section 701 of the CARE Act of 2003, S. 476. 108th Cong. (passed by the Senate on April 9, 2003 and subsequently tabled) and section 101 of *Tax Shelter Transparency Enforcement Act of 2003*, S. 1937 (introduced in the Senate by Senator Baucus with the statement "It is inexcusable that Congress has not passed a single piece of tax shelter legislation to shut down ... abusive tax practices.", Committee on Finance Press Release, Nov. 24, 2003).

[779] Li, *supra* no. 8 at 46, footnote 86 ("The rationale for this test was that it would show whether the taxpayer had placed money at risk. This was important, as in many U.S. tax shelter cases taxpayers had negative returns after transaction costs and had hedged away upside and downside risks.").

[780] The ensuing *American Jobs Creation* Act, Pub. L. No. 108-357, 118 Stat. 1418 was signed by the President in 2004 without codification of the economic substance doctrine. This proposed version of the codification also

Tax Reduction and Reform Act of 2007

Comprehensive tax reform was proposed in 2007 by House and Ways Committee Chair Charles Rangel in H.R. 3970.[781] Section 3501 of the Rangel Bill continued to provide that, in the case of any transaction to which the economic substance doctrine was found to be relevant, transactions would only be treated as having economic substance if both the subjective business purpose and objective economic substance prongs of the doctrine are established; however, it no longer contained a requirement that a transaction be a reasonable means of accomplishing the substantial nontax purpose.[782] H.R. 3970 has been described as the simplest and shortest version of the attempts to codify the economic substance doctrine, addressing many of the criticisms that were made of prior versions.[783]

Budget Proposal for Fiscal Year 2010

The proposed codification contemplated by President Obama's 2010 Budget Proposals was the same version proposed in H.R. 3970. The mandatory 40 percent penalty in section 3502 for non-disclosed transactions was criticized as "strict and draconian ... [and it] threatens the very doctrine it seeks to strengthen."[784] Others, however, recommended that civil penalties for understatement of income should run as high as 75 percent of the tax due, in order

---

appeared in the *Highway Reauthorization and Excise Tax Simplification Act of 2005,* S. 1230, 109th Cong. (2005) and in the *Nonitemizer Real Property Tax Deduction Act of 2006*, S. 3738, 109th Cong. (2006).

[781] H.R. 3970, 110th Cong. (1st Sess. 2007).

[782] Lee A. Sheppard, "Behind the Economic Substance Codification Provision", 117 *Tax Notes* 205-206 (Oct. 15, 2007), 206 (although the proposal no longer included a requirement that the chosen transaction would have to be "a reasonable means of accomplishing" a non-tax purpose, it required that the business purpose be "substantial").

[783] David S. Miller, "An Alternative to Codification of the Economic Substance Doctrine", 123 *Tax Notes* 747-753 (May 11, 2009), 748 (stating that each of the prior proposals were different and they were all "roundly criticized")

[784] *Ibid* at 748 (arguing that the economic substance doctrine would be diluted by the mandatory penalties because for less aggressive transactions judges would be inclined to find economic substance where it did not exist)

to help combat the "perfect plague" caused over the past decade by marketing of tax shelters by leading accounting and investment banking firms.[785]

Another criticism of this proposed codification is that it maintained mandatory deduction of foreign taxes as expenses, in cases where pre-tax profits were to be relied on to show economic substance. The complaints against this measure were that there are transactions where taxpayers should be allowed credits for payments of foreign taxes, which do not pass a profit test if the taxes are treated as expenses, and that it conflicted with an existing legislative provision.[786]

Codification at last

The President's signing into law of the *Health Care and Education Reconciliation Act of 2010* on March 30, 2010 brought with it codification of the economic substance doctrine and a strict liability penalty for its violation, effective for transactions entered into after March 30, 2010.[787] The codification of the doctrine in section 7701(o) of the *Internal Revenue Code* (titled "Codification of Economic Substance Doctrine"), described by Professor Arnold as "a curious combination of case law and legislation,"[788] has been

---

[785] Chirelstein and Zelenak, *supra* no. 196 at 1939-40 ("The marketing of tax shelters by leading accounting and investment banking firms has developed into a perfect plague over the past decade. The aim in every case is to create a tax benefit in the form of a loss, expense, or exclusion from gross income that has no economic corollary but is simply the consequence, or the hoped-for-consequence, of rule manipulation. It is beyond doubt that such manipulations are contrary to congressional intent, but that perception has not always been conclusive or even probative in cases that have arisen.").

[786] Peaslee, *supra* no. 774 at 443 (arguing that an across-the-board requirement to treat foreign expenses as expenses for the purposes of the economic substance doctrine would require a calculation different from the complex system already in place for calculation of profits from transactions within specified "baskets" to justify credits under section 904).

[787] H.R. 4872, 111th Cong., § 1409.

[788] Arnold, *supra* no. 79 (also noting "The US rule is not as broadly applicable as the Canadian GAAR because its application to individuals is limited to

forecast to have a profound effect on taxpayer transactions for years to come, although section 7701(o)(5) provides that the determination of whether the economic substance doctrine is relevant to a transaction shall continue to be made in the same manner as if the codification had never taken place. This provision could be taken to imply that whether the economic substance doctrine is applicable to transactions is straightforward, but judges will continue to have the difficult task of making this determination on a case-by-case basis. The key reference point in making this determination will be whether the realization of the tax benefits of the transaction is consistent with the Congressional purpose or plan that the tax benefits were designed by Congress to effectuate.[789]

Newly-enacted section 7701(o) of the Internal Revenue Code stipulates the tests to be applied under the economic substance doctrine. In the case of any transaction where the doctrine is found by a court to be relevant, the transaction shall be treated as having economic substance only if (A) the transaction changes in a meaningful way[790] (apart from Federal income tax effects) the taxpayer's economic position, and (B) the taxpayer has a substantial[791] purpose

---

transactions in connection with a trade or business or an income-earning activity. It is not clear how broadly or narrowly the connection test will be interpreted. Arguably, for example, the US rule might not have applied to the transactions in the *Lipson* case." – see section 7701(o)(5)(B))

[789] Staff of Joint Committee on Taxation, "Technical Explanation of the Revenue Provisions of the Reconciliation Act of 2010, As Amended, In Combination with the Patient Protection and Affordable Care Act", JCX-18-10 (Mar. 21, 2010) 152, footnote 344 (stating that the economic substance doctrine is relevant unless the tax benefits are consistent with all applicable provisions of the Internal Revenue Code and the purpose of such provisions)

[790] McMahon Jr., *supra* no. 79 at (noting that the "meaningful" standard differs from the possibility of profit test applied in most of the economic substance cases and is meant to recognize that "taxpayers often undertake transactions related to their businesses (in contrast to investments unrelated to their core businesses, such as sale-in, lease-out and lease-in, lease out investments by financial institutions) that do not in isolation produce an identifiable profit stream – for example, reorganizations of subsidiary corporations.")

[791] *Ibid.* at 739, 741 (stating the "substantial" requirement is consistent with the analysis in the case law concerning economic substance and a barrier to claiming tax benefits where the tax benefits are "vastly disproportionate"

(apart from Federal income tax effects) for entering into such transaction. This is the "government-friendly" conjunctive version of the economic substance doctrine that a number of the Circuit Courts had previously adopted. The taxpayer is not required to establish the pre-tax profit of a transaction to prove that it has economic substance;[792] however, section 7701(o) provides that where the potential for the profit of a transaction is relied upon for the purpose of determining whether the requirements of the economic substance doctrine are met, the transaction will only be respected for tax purposes where the present value of the reasonably expected pre-tax profit[793] from the transaction is substantial in relation to the present value of the expected net tax benefits.[794] In calculating pre-tax profits, fees and other transaction costs are taken into account as expenses.[795] Whether foreign taxes are deducted in calculating pre-tax profits is to be governed by regulations, whereas several prior codification proposals mandatorily treated foreign taxes as an expense in computing pre-tax profit.[796] According to Treasury counsel, the

---

to nontax benefits, but "The $64,000 question is, of course, the meaning of 'substantial'.")

[792] McMahon Jr., *supra* no. 79 at 732 (noting however that "the statute does not explain what, other than profit potential, can satisfy its requirements.")

[793] Jackel, *supra* no. 79 at 292 (stating that reasonable expectation of pre-tax profit will be tested at the inception of the transaction but that there are several outstanding questions including what discount rate to use in determining pre-tax profit and the meaning of "substantial", etc.)

[794] Wells, *supra* no. 15 at 425-426 (commenting that the requirement to use net present value concepts overturns *Consolidated Edison Co. of New York, Inc. v. U.S.*, 90 Fed.Cl. 228 (2009) which rejected net present value analysis in applying the economic substance doctrine, and also suggesting that the comparative analysis called for "appears to increase the required showing on the part of the taxpayer of the level of non-tax benefits beyond what has generally been required under existing case law." "Section 7701(o) does not simply allow a transaction to withstand attack even though it has business purpose or some positive profit level. Instead, the economic consequences must be substantial in comparison to the tax benefits.")

[795] Coder, *supra* no. 553 at 18 (stating that this feature of the codification could turn a seemingly profitable shelter into one that doesn't even give rise to expected profits exceeding a riskless rate of return)

[796] Jackel, *supra* no. 79 at 293 (noting that the Treasury and IRS are required to provide guidance on treatment of foreign taxes as expenses); McMahon Jr., *supra* no. 79 at 740 (suggesting that in any event "the courts can conclude

current lack of regulations under this provision is not to be interpreted to mean that the government sees no cases in which foreign taxes should be deducted as expenses, as the present litigation regarding the point must be taken into account.[797]

Section 7701(o) also provides that achieving a financial accounting benefit shall not be taken into account in determining whether a transaction has a substantial non-federal-income-tax-effect if the origin of such financial accounting benefit is a reduction of the federal income tax. The reason for this rule is that if reduction of federal tax was the origin of the accounting treatment and the accounting treatment could be relied on in applying the economic substance test, the test would become circular.[798] Similarly, state or local income tax savings that are related to federal income tax effects cannot provide a profit potential or a business purpose.[799]

Regarding the threshold question of when the economic substance doctrine is relevant, section 7701(o) provides that the determination is to be made in the same manner as if the new provision had never been enacted.[800] According to a former tax legislative

---

that they are free to take foreign taxes into account as expenses under their inherent power to apply the economic substance doctrine as it has long existed as judicial interpretive doctrine.")

[797] Jeremiah Coder, "Economic Substance Guidance Will Have Limited Scope", 127 *Tax Notes* 1423-1424 (June 28, 2010), 1423 (quoting Treasury Deputy Legislative Counsel Byron Christensen speaking at the Second Annual Tax Controversy Forum sponsored by the New York University School of Continuing and Professional Studies).

[798] Jackel, *supra* no. 79 at 292-293 (stating that guidance is required from Treasury and the IRS regarding when the origin of the accounting benefit is federal tax reduction); McMahon Jr., *supra* no. 79 at 741 (suggesting that this provision probably has its origins in the Enron scandal where expected tax benefits were recorded on the financial statements as producing income).

[799] McMahon Jr., *supra* no. 79 at 740 (suggesting that a key factor re whether state or local income tax effect will be treated as related to a federal income tax effect is whether the state or local tax base differs from the federal tax base.)

[800] *Ibid.* at 737, 742 (arguing that the IRS and the courts should regard this provision as "extraordinarily important. It reflects a congressional intent that the codification of the economic substance doctrine should not result in its application in circumstances in which the courts have not applied the doctrine. ... [T]he enactment of section 7701(o) should not be treated as now imposing a

counsel at the Treasury, "[d]etermining what transactions are caught up by the statute and which ones are not affected because they are consistent with congressional intent will be a major undertaking, without necessarily any satisfactory conclusions."[801] Regarding the use of the word "relevant" in the codification, Hariton says that "I have never seen such a vague word at the fulcrum of a statute."[802] Hariton argues that if the term is broadly construed, there are an endless number of transactions subject to the doctrine, so the government needs to follow a narrow definition of relevancy.[803]

Section 7701(o)(5)(D) provides that the term "transaction" includes a series of transactions;[804] however, the matter of how it will

---

business purpose requirement on transactions that heretofore have produced allowable losses or deductions without regard to whether there was a business purpose for the transaction.", citing non-recognition of gains for like-kind exchanges of property as a classic example. Also noting in this regard: "Historically, the economic substance doctrine has been applied almost exclusively to deny (1) artificial loss deductions generated by artificial basis; (2) attempts to double dip, that is, claim two loss deductions when there had been only a single economic loss; (3) artificial losses generated by a mismatch of deductions and exempt income; and (4) timing manipulations involving cumulative circular cash flows with deductions front-end-loaded and income back-end-loaded. The economic substance doctrine has not been applied to deny loss deductions in transactions that closed out a real investment and represented a real loss of a real investment.")

[801] Coder, *supra* no. 553 at 17 (quoting Michael J. Desmond who also stated that in theory the IRS could issue an "angel list" of transactions not considered to be in contravention of the provision).

[802] Jeremiah Coder, "Alexander Addresses Determination of Economic Substance Relevance", 127 *Tax Notes* 1076-1077 (June 7, 2010), 1077 (Hariton says practitioners need to frame the question by asking whether Congress intended the benefits); also see: Thomas A. Cullinan and Shane A. Lord, "Economic Substance Doctrine: Unconstitutionally Vague?", 130 *Tax Notes* 700-705 (Feb. 7, 2011), 703-705 (suggesting the codified economic substance doctrine could be unconstitutional under the void-for-vagueness doctrine because of uncertainty about how the "relevancy" determination is to be made and concerns about arbitrary and discriminatory enforcement)

[803] Coder, *ibid.* at 1077 (citing Bryan C. Skarlatos of Kostelanetz & Fink LLP saying that in the past few years there has been a tendency by the IRS to assert economic substance or lack of business purpose in audits.)

[804] Arnold, *supra* no. 79 (noting "What constitutes a series of transactions is a critical concept. If transactions that prepare the table cannot be linked to the transactions in which the feast is consumed, the rule can easily be avoided

be determined whether transactions were entered into after March 30, 2010, so section 7701 is applicable to them, is also left to the courts to determine. Professor Wells forecasts that section 7701(o)(5)(D) "is likely to have a significant impact on how a transaction will be framed under the economic substance doctrine" in that it "seeks to make clear that the government has the ability to disaggregate transactions and to test each transactional step individually."[805]

The "reasonable means" test, which had been a feature of the version of the codification proposed in 2001, has not been included in section 7701(o). Nevertheless, in determining whether a transaction will be treated as having a "substantial" non-federal-income-tax purpose, whether the manner of effecting the objective bears a reasonable relationship to the objective will continue to be an important factor.[806] Open questions under the new legislation include what constitutes a "meaningful change" in the taxpayer's economic position;[807] what discount rate should be used in arriving at present values; how it is to be determined whether the pre-tax profit is "substantial"; which – if any – foreign taxes will be treated as expenses in calculating pre-tax profits; how a "transaction" is to be framed

---

through careful planning. ...The definition of a transaction to include a series, coupled with the legislative history, makes it clear that the economic substance doctrine can apply to a single transaction, a series of transactions as a whole, and a transaction that is part of a series. This makes sense because otherwise it would just be too easy to insert purely tax-motivated steps into a series of transactions that, as a whole, is clearly legitimate (for example an arm's length sale of a business or a business financing.)"

[805] Wells, *supra* no. 15 at 421-423 (commenting that the section resolves a conflict re whether the doctrine is applied on an overall basis or to each separate step individually); see also: Technical Explanation of the Revenue Provisions of the 'Reconciliation Act' of 2010, As Amended, in Combination With the 'Patient Protection and Affordable Care Act', *supra* no. 789 at 153 (stating that the court has the ability "to bifurcate a transaction in which independent activities with non-tax objectives are combined with an unrelated item having only tax-avoidance objectives in order to disallow those tax-motivated objectives.")

[806] Jackel, *supra* no. 79 at 294 (stating that the facts and circumstances of individual cases will be critical in this determination).

[807] *Ibid.* at 296 (suggesting that depending on how the term is defined and applied, the codified doctrine could lead to results that would not have occurred under pre-section 7701(o) law).

for the purposes of applying the doctrine; and, when the economic substance doctrine remains inapplicable because "the realization of the tax benefits is consistent with Congressional purpose or plan that the tax benefits were designed by Congress to effectuate."[808]

This set of fundamental questions leaves the economic substance doctrine, for a large part, in the same condition it was in prior to its codification.[809] An important difference, however, is that there is now a standard requirement that where pre-tax profits are being relied upon to satisfy the requirements of the doctrine, present value determinations must be made, and there must be a balancing of reasonably expected pre-tax profits in relation to the expected net tax benefits from the transaction.[810] The matter of whether the doctrine has conjunctive or disjunctive tests has also been clarified. Thus, one result of codification should be that there will be a harmonization of standards across jurisdictions.[811]

Prior proposals to codify the economic substance doctrine had expressly provided that the statutory version "shall not be construed as altering or supplanting any other rule of law, and the requirements of this subsection shall be construed as being in addition to any such other rule of law."[812] This provision has not been included in the codified doctrine; however, it is not expected that judicial doctrines such as step transaction, substance over form and business

---

[808] Technical Explanation of the Revenue Provisions of the 'Reconciliation Act' of 2010, As Amended, in Combination With the 'Patient Protection and Affordable Care Act', *supra* no. 789 at 152, n. 344.
[809] McMahon Jr., *supra* no. 79 at 731 (arguing that "the new substantive rules merely provide a gloss on the historic judicial economic substance doctrine")
[810] Jackel, *supra* no. 79 at 296 (discussing this point under heading "A. Law Hasn't Changed").
[811] Deloitte, "Codification of the Economic Substance Doctrine: What Does It Mean for Your Company?", webcast on April 27, 2010.
[812] *Supra* no 810 at 291, footnote 5 (noting however that the Joint Committee on Taxation health care report retains this language in its explanation of the new law).

purpose have been displaced[813] and the Joint Committee on Taxation report supports this view.[814]

Tax practitioners have expressed concern that the codified doctrine might be applied to normal business transactions that historically were not targeted by the IRS for lacking economic substance,[815] although the IRS associate chief counsel has said that while some change to the economic substance doctrine is contemplated, he does not think that the change is "going to be that radical".[816] In this regard, the Technical Explanation issued by the Joint Committee on Taxation on March 21, 2010 states that codification is not intended to alter the tax treatment of certain basic transactions that, under longstanding judicial and administrative practices are respected, merely because the choice between meaningful economic alternatives is largely or entirely based on comparative tax advantages. Examples given of these basic transactions are the choice between capitalizing a business with debt or equity; a U.S. person's choice between utilizing a foreign corporation or a domestic corporation to make a foreign investment; the choice to enter a transaction or series of transactions that constitute a corporate organization or reorganization under subchapter C (§§ 351-368 IRC); and the choice to use a related-party entity in a transaction, provided that the arm's length standard of section 482 IRC and other applicable concepts are satisfied.[817] According to Treasury Counsel, there is no

---

[813] McMahon Jr., *supra* no. 79 at 732 (arguing that it is "completely unrealistic" to think that these doctrines are displaced)

[814] "Technical Explanation of the Revenue Provisions of the Reconciliation Act of 2010, As Amended, in Combination With the Patient Protection and Affordable Care Act", *supra* no. 789 at 152.

[815] Coder, *supra* no. 553 at 18 (citing Philip Karter's argument that codification is the wrong congressional response to perceived tax abuse)

[816] Amy S. Elliott, "Alexander Downplays Effect of Economic Substance Doctrine", 126 *Tax Notes* 1309-1311 (Mar. 15, 2010), 1309 (citing remarks by William Alexander at a Federal Bar Association Tax Law Conference)

[817] Technical Explanation of the Revenue Provisions of the 'Reconciliation Act' of 2010, As Amended, in Combination With the 'Patient Protection and Affordable Care Act', *supra* no. 789 at 152-153.

expectation of expanding this "so-called angel list" contained in the Joint Committee's Technical Explanation.[818]

Jackel says section 7701(o) "will have a profound effect on taxpayer transactions for years to come."[819] Viewed by Professor Prebble from New Zealand:

[S]ection 7701(o) is a true GAAR, but it is GAAR with extra bite, in that sec. 7701(1) and (2) contain rules that sharpen its focus. The most important is a relative benefits rule, which strikes down a transaction where the economic profit is not 'substantial' in relation to its net tax benefits. This rule shares its philosophy of economic substance with a test to determine whether a GAAR applies that Lord Templeman enunciated in the Privy Council in London in *Challenge Corporation Ltd. v. Commissioner of Inland Revenue*, [1986] 2 NZLR 513, 561 line 41. His Lordship said that the GAAR 'does not apply to tax mitigation [this is, a reduction of tax] where the taxpayer obtains a tax advantage by reducing his income or by incurring expenditure in circumstances in which the taxing statute affords a reduction in tax liability. ... [S]ec. 7701(o) is a true GAAR that will be a powerful weapon in the hands of the Commissioner.[820]

---

[818] Coder, *supra* no. 797 at 1424 (citing remarks by Treasury Deputy Legislative Counsel Byron Christensen speaking at a Tax Controversy Forum sponsored by the New York University School of Continuing and Professional Studies); McMahon Jr., *supra* no. 79 at 746, 759 (also suggesting that the promulgation of a further angel list "is undesirable and unlikely to occur. ... Treasury and the IRS simply cannot anticipate the new transactions that would be devised by the army of hard-working mavens who will plumb the depths of the angel list searching for anomalies around which new tax shelters can be designed.")

[819] Jackel, *supra* no. 79 at 298 (stating guidance from Treasury and the IRS is necessary in a number of areas so the new law can be applied with minimal disruption to taxpayers and advisers who are planning and implementing transactions); also see: Wells, *supra* no. 15 at 452-453 (claiming "[S]ection 7701(o) ... does significantly alter the landscape. ... [It] provides the government with more latitude to argue against the plain meaning of its own regulations and the plain meaning of statutory provisions when the plain meaning ... creates an unintended consequence. ... [A]lthough new section 7701(o) does not fix all mistakes, taken as a whole [it] enhances the government's arguments with respect to the application of the economic substance doctrine. ... [N]ew section 7701(o) may serve to further dampen aggressive tax planning. ")

[820] Prebble, *supra* no. 18.

Professor McMahon, on the other hand, has referred to the codification as "[o]ld wine in a new bottle."[821] The Tax Section of the American Bar Association has nevertheless called for Treasury and the Internal Revenue Service "to provide prompt guidance so that taxpayers and their advisors will know how the legislation is to be applied."[822] Calling for such guidance to be issued in the form of binding regulations, the key claim behind the need for guidance is that "[a]n open-ended rule permitting a broad override of the substantive rules in the Code would lead to greater uncertainty in implementation of tax law."[823]

My conclusions that standards as well as rules are required for the effective administration of tax law, and that the perennial call by practitioners and Supreme Court of Canada judges for predictability and certainty vastly overstates their importance, have already been disclosed in this book. My conclusions are if anything fortified by inspection of the expansive list of subjects about which the American Bar Association Tax Section claims that binding published guidance and agreement is required from the government: (1) when the economic substance doctrine will be "relevant"; (2) a "framework" within which, among other things, the facts and circumstances pertaining to whether the transaction at issue had economic substance would not be considered, if at all, until after a determination was made that the claimed tax treatment did not comply with the substantive taxing provisions and was inconsistent with the underlying Congressional intent; (3) the factors to be considered in determining whether the facts and circumstances indicate that the economic substance doctrine is relevant; (4) the definition of "economic substance doctrine"; (5) the definition of "transaction"; (6) the meaning of "meaningful way", "economic position" and "substantial purpose"; (7) when State and local tax benefits will

---

[821] McMahon Jr., *supra* no. 79 at 752 (arguing that "except for the new penalty provisions, the codification of the economic substance doctrine really should not change legal analysis or outcomes very much.")

[822] Executive Summary, Request for Guidance on Implementation of Economic Substance Legislation, American Bar Association Tax Section, January 18, 2011.

[823] Request for Guidance on Implementation of Economic Substance Legislation, American Bar Association Tax Section, January 18, 2011, p. 12.

be "related" to Federal tax benefits; (8) the definition of "pre-tax profit"; (9) the meaning of "reasonably expected"; (10) a safe harbour for discount rates; (11) the meaning of "substantial" in the pre-tax profit context; (11) the meaning of "any similar rule of law"; and (12) new procedures to ensure certainty.[824]

While the American Bar Association Tax Section can hardly be accused of going under-board, in its enthusiasm for binding published guidance from the government, no mention is made in its treatise of the likelihood that such detailed published guidance would provide a roadmap to ambitious tax planners for the invention of new tax avoidance arrangements.[825]

Perhaps this is owing to the view that, in the words of Louis Eisenstein, "the [American Bar] Association "is a venerable organization from which very little should be expected."[826] The view of Professor McMahon, which I share, is that "[d]etailed regulations implementing codification of the business purpose and economic substance doctrines would create their own ambiguities, uncertainty, and loopholes. A complicated, comprehensive codification of the antiabuse rules inevitably would create their own ambiguities, uncertainty and loopholes. ... Thus, it is preferable to avoid detailed regulations implementing the legislation."[827]

---

[824] Request for Guidance on Implementation of Economic Substance Legislation, American Bar Association Tax Section, January 18, 2011, 1-51; see also: Joseph DiSciullo, "Guidance Issued on Codification of Economic Substance Doctrine", 128 *Tax Notes* 1237-1239 (Sept. 20, 2010), 1237 (noting that the IRS has issued Notice 2010-62 stating that it will continue to rely on relevant case law under the common law economic substance doctrine and that the case law will continue to develop)

[825] Instead, the American Bar Association Tax Section has rather neatly claimed that such publication will result in "furthering its intended deterrent effect" – see Executive Summary, p. 4.

[826] Louis Eisenstein, *The Ideologies of Taxation,* (New York, Ronald Press Company, 1961), 15, 210 ("One of the major achievements of the [American Bar] Association is that it enables tax lawyers to serve in several capacities without fear of embarrassment.")

[827] McMahon Jr., *supra* no. 79 at 753.

A further point is that the common law economic substance doctrine has been chugging along in the U.S. for decades, without detailed explanations from the tax administration, and the world has not come to an end. Section 7701(o)(5)(C) provides that "[t]he determination of whether the economic substance doctrine is relevant to the transaction shall be made in the same manner as if this subsection had never been enacted." This means that the courts will continue to be free to decide whether or not to apply the doctrine, having regard to all of the developing case law. The points the American Bar Association Tax Section seeks concessions about are matters that fall naturally within the realm of advocacy, and they can fairly be tested before the courts.[828] This point would be less powerful, were it not for the fact that tax professionals clamouring for certainty via binding published guidance include the same folks who are pushing at the margins. Regarding the Tax Section's certainty argument, and again in the apt words of Eisenstein, "[i]f an argument is repeated enough, it soon becomes a respectable doctrine."[829]

Given the prominence that economic substance has had in the United States for decades in pointing to the boundary between acceptable tax planning and abusive tax avoidance, it is hard to argue that giving economic substance a more central role in tax avoidance cases in Canada would be the beginning of the end. I also show in the next chapter that the GAAR regimes in other jurisdictions similar to Canada operate upon the basis of recognition that economic substance has central importance in the detection and minimization of abusive tax avoidance.

---

[828] Amy S. Elliott, "Courts Will Interpret Economic Substance: McMahon Says", 129 *Tax Notes* 391-392 (Oct. 25, 2010), 391 (quoting Treasury officer Emily McMahon as stating at a New York University program that it would be inappropriate for Treasury to spell out what transactions are subject to the codified economic substance doctrine and what terms in the statute mean as the questions involve decisions that courts will make).

[829] Eisenstein, *supra* no. 826 at 130. Also see chapter V for my review of the merits of the arguments concerning certainty.

VII

Economic Substance Under GAAR in Other Jurisdictions

While Canada's GAAR does not presently spell out that economic substance must be considered in determining whether abusive tax avoidance has occurred, this is not the case in other jurisdictions including South Africa and Australia. By comparison, the GAAR in New Zealand does not expressly allude to economic substance as a mandatory reference point; however, the Supreme Court of New Zealand has taken a radically different position in its interpretation of New Zealand's GAAR vis-à-vis economic substance than the Supreme Court of Canada has taken in its interpretation of GAAR.

SOUTH AFRICA

The proliferation of abusive tax avoidance arrangements has been an increasingly problematic phenomenon in South Africa, over the past several decades. In South Africa's case, the root causes of this difficulty have been ascribed to its growing participation in the global economy after the collapse of Apartheid, changes in financial markets including the emergence of different types of complex financial instruments and the recent explosion in information technology.[830]

South Africa's most recent efforts in attempting to counter abusive tax avoidance have emphasized the central role of economic substance. In this regard, the SARS Discussion Paper on Tax Avoidance released in 2005 identified lack of economic substance first amongst a set of common characteristics which exist in the most abusive avoidance schemes.[831] Draft GAAR amendments released following the Discussion Paper listed "the form and economic substance of the arrangement, or any step therein or part thereof" first amongst a non-exclusive list of factors to be considered in determining "abnormality."[832]

Although SARS stated in its Discussion Paper that it considered impermissible tax avoidance to be "artificial or contrived arrangements, with little or no economic impact upon the taxpayer, that are usually designed to manipulate or exploit perceived 'loopholes" in the tax laws in order to achieve results that conflict or defeat the intention of Parliament", fear was expressed by a South African tax commentator that the draft GAAR legislation was so wide in scope that it would affect ordinary business transactions and capture arrangements "where there is economic substance and a genuine outflow of funds."[833] All of this reflects an understanding

---

[830] Ed Liptak, "Battling with Boundaries: The South African GAAR Experience", Freedman, J. (ed.) *Beyond Boundaries*, United Kingdom, Oxford University Centre for Business Taxation, 2008, chapter 3, p. 23 (also suggesting that the historical tax compliance environment in South Africa has been extremely poor and that practitioner attitudes coupled with the absence of academic debate have been contributors to the problem).

[831] Discussion Paper on Tax Avoidance", *supra* no. 5 at 19.

[832] See the following discussion of this point under the Abnormality Requirement section of this chapter.

[833] Ernest Mazansky, "A New GAAR for South Africa – The Duke of Westminster is Struck a Blow", 60 *Bulletin for International Taxation* 124-132 (2006), 131-132 (also suggesting however that if SARS seeks to apply GAAR too broadly "the courts have a quaint habit of restoring balance to a situation").

in South Africa that economic substance is a key reference point in detecting unacceptable tax avoidance.

The ensuing GAAR amendments made in 2006 introduced the "lack of commercial substance" concept, which is said to have had its origins in the economic substance doctrine prevalent in many Western countries.[834] The SARS Draft Comprehensive Guide to the General Anti-Avoidance Rule released in December 2010 also states that the U.S. economic substance doctrine is now to some extent introduced into South Africa's anti-avoidance measures.[835] These points all highlight the central importance of economic substance under South Africa's GAAR.

Historical GAAR

South Africa's first general anti-avoidance rule was located in section 90 of its *Income Tax Act* (No. 31 of 1941). This rule stated that when SARS was satisfied that a transaction or operation had been entered into or carried out for the purpose of avoiding or reducing liability for tax, the tax would be determined as if the transaction or operation had not been entered into or carried out. There was also a rebuttable presumption that if it was proved that the transaction or operation resulted in the avoidance or reduction of tax, the purpose was the avoidance or reduction. This provision was "particularly emasculated by the decision [of Watermeyer CJ] in *CIR v. King*,"[836] which held that the legislature could not have

---

[834] EB Broomberg, "Then and now–V", 22 *Tax Planning Corporate and Personal* 52 (2008) (suggesting that the commercial substance test in new subsection 80C(1) is an articulation of the economic substance doctrine); see also: Cassidy, *supra* no. 238 at 771 (suggesting that the general rule as to lack of commercial substance in South Africa's amended GAAR addresses the fact that abusive tax avoidance schemes often "insulate the taxpayer from all economic risk").

[835] Draft Comprehensive Guide to the General Anti-Avoidance Rule, (Legal and Policy Division, South African Revenue Service, December 2010), 4 (referring to the commercial substance test in section 80C read with the purpose requirement. Comments on the contents of the draft guide were invited from the public by February 2011.

[836] *Supra* no 834, Cassidy at footnote 25; *CIR v. King*, 1947 (2) SA 196 (A).

intended that the provision would apply in circumstances where the taxpayer deliberately took steps to prevent income from accruing, and that the disposal of an asset was not a transaction or operation within the meaning of section 90. Section 90 was subsequently amended to clarify that an alienation of property was a "transaction" and to add a requirement that SARS had to be of the view that "abnormalities" existed. This latter amendment had its origins in the statement by Schreiner JA, in a minority concurring judgment in *CIR v. King* with reference to section 90 of the *Income Tax Act*, that it was "designed to meet the Commissioner's objections to the creation of abnormal or unnatural situations, to the detriment of the *fiscus*".[837] This statement was the genesis of an "abnormality requirement" in South Africa's GAAR which continues to exist in its modern-day GAAR.

Several further amendments were also made to South Africa's GAAR, before its eventual replacement in 2006. Prior to the amendments made in 1996, the four requirements for the GAAR's application under subsection 103(1) of the *Income Tax Act* (No. 58 of 1962) were that (a) there had to be a "transaction, operation or scheme"; (b) the transaction, operation or scheme had to have the effect of avoiding, postponing or reducing the liability for taxes; (c) the transaction, operation or scheme had to have been entered into or carried out solely or mainly for the purpose of avoiding, postponing or reducing liability for taxes; and (d) the transaction, operation or scheme had to have been entered into or carried out in a manner not normally employed or it had to have created rights or obligations which would not normally be created between person's dealing at arm's length in similar circumstances (this is known as the abnormality requirement).[838]

---

[837] Mazansky, *supra* no. 833 at 124-125 (noting that section 90 was amended considerably as a result of the decision in *CIR v. King* although it took the legislature about 12 years to react)

[838] *SIR v. Geustyn, Forsyth and Joubert*, 1971 (3) SA 567 (A) confirmed that all four elements had to be present for subsection 103(1) to be applied successfully. See also: Mazansky, *supra* no. 837 at 125 (noting that when the four requirements were met SARS could determine the taxes payable on the basis

Under the amendments to the GAAR made in 1996, the concept of avoidance, postponement or reduction of liability for tax was collapsed into the term "tax benefit"; plus, the abnormality requirement was refined so that (a) in the context of business, the test was whether the transaction, operation or scheme was entered into or carried out in a manner which would not normally be employed for *bona fide* business purposes, other than for the obtaining of a tax benefit; and (b) in a non-business context the test was whether the transaction, operation or scheme was entered into or carried out by means or in a manner which would not normally be employed in the particular circumstances.[839] Also, as an alternative to (a) and (b), subsection 103(1) would have application where the transaction, operation or scheme created rights and obligations which would not normally be created in the transaction, operation or scheme between parties that were dealing at arm's length.[840]

Before the 1996 amendments to the abnormality requirement could be tested in the courts, the Supreme Court of Appeal dealt a devastating blow to other provisions of subsection 103(1)[841] in *CIR v. Conhage*.[842] In the *Conhage* case the taxpayer had entered into a

---

of an assumption that the transaction, operation or scheme had never been entered into or carried out, subject to rights of appeal)

[839] Clauses 103(1)(b)(i)(aa) and (bb) *Income Tax Act* (No. 58 of 1962)

[840] Mazansky, *supra* no. 837 at 125 (describing the 1996 amendments to the abnormality requirement)

[841] Liptak, *supra* no. 830, c. 3, 23 (noting that the abnormality requirement was the "Achilles Heel" of GAAR, which Parliament sought to remedy by passing amendments in 1996; however, before the amendments were tested in the courts the Supreme Court of Appeal made a decision [*CIR v. Conhage*] regarding other provisions of GAAR which "effectively emasculated the legislation")

[842] (1999) (4) SA 1149 (SCA). It has nevertheless been suggested that the result under the subsequent amendments to GAAR would be no different than it was under subsection 103(1) – see Dave Meyerowitz. "What Does The New Section 80A Add To Our Law", vol. 57 *The Taxpayer* 64-67 (2008), 65 (suggesting that *Conhage* would not have been decided differently under section 80A as the essence of the transaction was a commercial lending); Dave Meyerowitz, "General Anti-Avoidance Rule", vol. 56, no. 3 *The Taxpayer* 41-42 (Mar. 2007), 42 (also arguing that essentially the same facts would be taken account of by a court under the amended abnormality requirement in section 80A as were taken account of under subsection 103(3)); see also: Mazansky, *supra* no.

Economic Substance Under GAAR in Other Jurisdictions

sale and lease-back agreement with a bank, rather than a conventional loan, in the process of funding its business operations. Although the taxpayer had been able to borrow funds from the bank, it sold a plant used in its business to the bank in return for funds it required in its business, and then leased the plant from the bank as it still required it in its business. The plant was sold to the bank for a large capital profit, at a time when capital gains were not taxed in South Africa, and the lease payments, which were based on the cost of the plant to the bank, were claimed as deductions.[843]

SARS claimed that the taxpayer's sole or main purpose for the transactions was to reduce its liability for tax and disallowed the deduction of the rent paid under the lease, relying upon subsection 103(1). The Supreme Court of Appeal held, however, that even if the sale and leaseback transaction was selected by the taxpayer solely on account of its tax benefits, the fact could not be ignored that, if the taxpayer had not needed capital, there would have been no transaction at all. Under this line of reasoning, it did not matter whether the taxpayer's sole purpose for entering into the particular transaction was to achieve tax benefits, as the main purpose of the transaction was to obtain capital.[844] Tax planners are said to have subsequently placed great reliance on the *Conhage* decision as a defence against the application of subsection 103(1) of the Act.[845]

---

837 at 127 (describing the *Conhage* decision as "if not the final nail, certainly a large nail in the coffin of the GAAR")

[843] Ernest Mazansky, "The Duke of Westminster Still Lives in South Africa (But is Very Careful When He Crosses the Road)", 59 *Bulletin for International Fiscal Documentation* 116-120 (March 2005), 120 (suggesting that subsection 103(1) would not apply to transactions which result in the lowest amount of tax being payable, "even if the method one chooses is somewhat unusual and not straightforward", provided it could be established that the sole or main reason for the transaction was not to obtain a tax benefit)

[844] Dave Meyerowitz, "Tax Avoidance Legislation", vol. 54, no. 4 *The Taxpayer* 61-64 (April 2005), 64 (arguing that both an abnormal arrangement and a purpose which is solely or mainly tax avoidance must exist as requirements of an anti-avoidance provision in order not to negate the legitimate use of the other provisions of the *Income Tax Act*)

[845] Mazansky, *supra* no. 843 at 119-120 (also noting that subsection 103(1) could only be invoked by SARS where it was unable to attack a transaction on other grounds); see also: Mazansky, *supra* no. 937 at 127 (suggesting that

A further point related to the loss of confidence by SARS in its ability to successfully litigate tax avoidance cases under subsection 103(1) was that the onus was on SARS to show that a transaction had been entered into in an abnormal manner. Since many tax avoidance arrangements contained elements consistent with *bona fide* non-tax motivated business arrangements, it was difficult to prove abnormality.[846] Also, as Professor Cassidy has noted, "[i]f normality is the only objective criterion for testing tax avoidance schemes, if a transaction is widely used for tax avoidance, it could obtain the status of normality. The result would be to leave open the 'everyone's doing it' defence."[847]

According to South Africa's Minister of Finance on November 3, 2005, "[w]hat we can't accommodate is a rule which is intended to limit avoidance that is so abused and tatty with wear."[848] SARS therefore set about to attempt to overcome adverse court decisions such as *Conhage*, and weaknesses it perceived in subsection 103(1) which had been criticized on the basis that it was "based on antiquated notions of legal form, rather than economic substance and subjective intent."[849] The first step in this process was the release of a Discussion Paper on Tax Avoidance.[850]

---

the failures of SARS in its attempts to apply subsection 103(1) may have been because "it persisted in attacking schemes which, in the main, were commercially or family driven even though they had tax benefits, rather than confining itself to attacking the blatant schemes.")

[846] David Pickup, "In Relation to General Anti-Avoidance Provisions: A Comparative Study of the Legal Frameworks Used by Different Countries to Protect Their Tax Revenues", Freedman, J. (ed.) *Beyond Boundaries*, United Kingdom, Oxford University Centre for Business Taxation, 2008, chapter 2, p. 14 (also suggesting that when a particular scheme is being widely used it may be problematic for SARS to attempt to characterize it as abnormal)

[847] Cassidy, *supra* no. 238 at 771(suggesting this is the reason for the introduction of the alternative "tainted element" test in clause 80A(a)(ii) of the present GAAR regarding arrangements lacking in commercial substance in whole or in part)

[848] See Keith Engel, Chief Director, Tax Legislation – National Treasury, "The GAAR proposal: A National Treasury Perspective", slide 3.

[849] Meyerowitz, "Tax Avoidance Legislation", *supra* no. 844, cited by Cassidy, *supra* no. 238, footnote 24.

[850] Discussion Paper on Tax Avoidance", *supra* no. 5

2005 Discussion Paper on Tax Avoidance

The Discussion Paper released by SARS in 2005 has been lauded as having been an effective vehicle for the provocation of a constructive wide-ranging discussion in South Africa amongst practitioners, members of the public, Parliamentarians and international experts regarding the impact of abusive tax avoidance and the means by which to combat abusive tax avoidance.[851]

Amongst other topics, the Discussion Paper described the most common characteristics of abusive tax avoidance schemes, which it identified as: (a) lack of economic substance; (b) use of tax-indifferent accommodating parties or special purpose entities; (c) unnecessary steps and complexity; (d) inconsistent treatment for tax and financial accounting purposes; (e) high transaction costs; and (f) fee variation clause and contingent fee arrangements.[852] The key problems it highlighted vis-à-vis subsection 103(1) were that (a) it had not proven to be effective as a deterrent against abusive avoidance schemes; (b) the abnormality requirement was being easily circumvented by the manufacture of plausible sounding business arrangements; and (c) the purpose requirement had been interpreted by the courts to involve a subjective test; plus, the "sole or main" aspect of the purpose requirement was problematic in its application as a result of the *Conhage* decision and its implication that a commercial purpose such as raising capital was sufficient to avoid the GAAR's application.[853]

---

[851] Meyerowitz, *supra* no. 842 at 41 (noting that "SARS commendably issued a discussion paper which ranged widely by way of citations from commentators, judgments and legislation in other jurisdictions."); Mazansky, *supra* no. 837 at 127-128 (noting that the Discussion Paper was a well-researched document dealing with problems involving anti-avoidance in general and the content and operation of the GAARS elsewhere; see also: Tim Edgar, Current Tax Reading, South African Revenue Service, *Discussion Paper on Tax Avoidance and Section 103 of the Income Tax Act, 1962, (Act no. 58 of 1961)*, (2006) vol. 54, no. 2 C.T.J. 551-553, (noting that the paper contains a worthwhile account of the common elements of anti-avoidance transactions and a review of the development of anti-avoidance law in South Africa)

[852] Discussion Paper on Tax Avoidance", *supra* no. 5 at 19-24

[853] *Ibid.* at 41-44.

2006 GAAR amendments

The ensuing amendments to the GAAR under the *Revenue Laws Amendment Act* of 2006 deleted the general anti-avoidance rule in subsection 103(1) and substituted sections 80A to 80L in Part II A of the *Income Tax Act*. The amendments were made after SARS received and took account of critical suggestions in relation to points it made in the Discussion Paper it released in 2005.[854] This version of the GAAR, which remains in place today, has been heavily criticized by South African tax commentators for its introduction of vague concepts and their attendant uncertainty, coupled with its complex and dense drafting.[855]

Arrangement

Under the proposed amendments, an "arrangement" was a transaction, operation or scheme and included the alienation of property. The final version retained this feature in the GAAR and also provided that it includes an agreement or understanding, whether enforceable or not, including all the effects or parts thereof.[856] This latter provision was included to overcome the *Conhage* decision, which had held that if the overall scheme was not tax-driven, the separate elements of it could not be attacked under the

---

[854] *Ibid.* at 19-25; see also: Meyerowitz, *supra* no. 842 at 41 (suggesting that lack of unanimity in South Africa as to what constitutes impermissible tax avoidance exists because "there is an inherent contradiction between specific provisions in terms of which things are allowable and general provisions which negate what the former allows.").

[855] See, for example, Dave Meyerowitz, vol. 57 *The Taxpayer* 64-67 (April 2008), 67 (arguing that the "relative simplicity" of former subsection 103(1) was superior to "the new style of overwritten and excessively complex provisions which serve little additional purpose"); Billy Joubert, "Legislative Restraint and The Problem of Over-Compensation", *Accountancy South Africa* (May 2010) (commenting that the general anti-avoidance rule is an example of legislative over-reaction: "It's long and complex and coma-inducing."); Justin Liebenberg, "General anti-avoidance rule", vol. 1 *the tax line* 1-10 (May 2007), 10 (the GAAR provisions are "exceptionally complex").

[856] Cassidy, *supra* no. 238 at 752 (suggesting that the definition of the term "arrangement" has much to commend it in that it eliminates the need for precision in identifying the factual arrangement to which the GAAR is to be applied).

GAAR, even if they were solely tax-driven.[857] Its enactment is said to have been useful, because it obliges the precise identification of to what it is that the GAAR is sought to be applied.[858] SARS has historically been successful with respect to whether there has been a transaction, operation or scheme.[859]

Avoidance arrangement/Tax benefit

The 1996 GAAR amendments had introduced the concept of "tax benefits". "Avoidance arrangement" is defined by section 80L in the final version of GAAR to mean any arrangement that results in a tax benefit. "Tax benefit" is defined in section 80L as including any avoidance, postponement or reduction of any liability for tax, which is very similar to its former definition.[860] This in turn is said to leave an existing question unresolved, in that there are situations where the application of a but-for test does not work, and some unknown standard of comparison is afoot.[861]

Impermissible avoidance arrangement

Section 80A of the final version of GAAR maintained the four traditional elements for the application of GAAR that had been located in subsection 103(1), as well as expanding the abnormality requirement and adding two alternatives to the abnormality

---

[857] Ernest Mazansky, "South Africa's New General Anti-Avoidance Rule – The Final GAAR", 31 *Bulletin for International Taxation* 159-167 (2007), 161 (noting that separate steps can now be targeted under the GAAR)

[858] EB Broomberg, "Then and Now–II", 21 *Tax Planning Corporate and Personal* 131-133 (2007), 131 (suggesting this may reduce the risk of misunderstandings that can lead to taxpayers losing their appeals when GAAR is applied)

[859] *Ibid.* at 131 (noting that there do not appear to be any cases where it has been suggested that no transaction, operation or scheme took place)

[860] Cassidy, *supra* no. 238 at 745 (noting that although the definitions of "avoidance arrangement" and "tax benefit" are stated to be non-exhaustive, the point may be academic as the "definitions are extremely comprehensive." The definition of "tax benefit" is also lauded as inclusionary and expansive giving the notion a broader scope than in Australia's GAAR)

[861] *Supra* no. 858 at 132 (suggesting that an unknown standard of comparison must be used in some instances to determine whether a tax benefit exists)

requirement.[862] The two new elements added as alternatives to abnormality were: (a) in a business context the absence of "commercial substance" to the arrangement; or (b) in any context, when the arrangement would directly or indirectly result in the misuse or abuse of provisions of the Act.[863]

Collectively, the three alternative branches of section 80A, denoting when an avoidance arrangement is an impermissible avoidance arrangement, are known as the "tainted elements".[864] An "impermissible tax avoidance arrangement" is thus defined in section 80A as an avoidance arrangement that meets the requirements of the section.[865] This introduction of the concept of "impermissible tax avoidance" was not universally acclaimed by South African tax advisors.[866]

Purpose of avoiding taxes

Prominent amongst the criticisms of the proposed changes to the GAAR was Meyerowitz's claim that an abnormal arrangement, and a purpose which is solely or mainly tax avoidance, should both be prerequisites for the application of a general anti-avoidance rule.[867] The

---

[862] See the discussion of this point in the Abnormality Requirement section below.
[863] Mazansky, *supra* no. 857 at 162 (noting this was the first adoption of the misuse or abuse concept in South Africa and that court decisions from European jurisdictions and Canada will be relevant in developing it)
[864] Explanatory Memorandum, Revenue Laws Amendment Bill 2006, (2006), note 28, at 62.
[865] *Supra* no. 863 at 161 (describing the definition of "impermissible avoidance arrangement" as "the core of the new GAAR which ... recognizes that avoidance arrangements are perfectly legitimate and unassailable as long as they do not qualify as being impermissible")
[866] Peter Surtees, "The Year in Review–South Africa", 41 *Tax Notes International* 99-101 (Jan. 9, 2006), 100 ("Presumably that [impermissible tax avoidance] means something on the right side of evasion but not honest enough for SARS. With respect, you cannot be a little dishonest; if an arrangement makes no commercial sense, SARS should take the taxpayer to court or change the Act to prevent perceived abuse. Labeling tax planning, however ingenious or complex, something reprehensible despite it being within the law, is risible. It is, however, a favorite ploy of tax authorities throughout the world.")
[867] Dave Meyerowitz, "Some Musings on the Meaning of Tax Avoidance", vol. 55, no. 4 *The Taxpayer* 62-64 (Apr. 2006), 63 (suggesting that otherwise "the

draft amendments proposed for discussion envisaged that it would be sufficient for the GAAR's application if avoidance of taxes was "one of the main purposes" of the transactions. However, the final version contemplates that the GAAR will only apply where the purpose of the transactions is "solely or mainly" to avoid tax.[868] The proposed amendment to trigger the application of the GAAR, when one of the main purposes was the obtaining of a tax benefit, had been criticized on the basis that it should be expected that transactions will be executed in the way that it is most tax efficient, whenever they may be entered into in more than one way. Thus the proposed "one of the main purposes" standard had been objected to on the basis that SARS could potentially argue in every case that the GAAR applied because reducing tax was a main purpose.[869]

The proposed amendments also provided that if SARS proved that the arrangement resulted in a tax benefit it would be presumed, unless the contrary was proved by the taxpayer, that its purpose was to obtain the tax benefit.[870] Under section 80G of the final GAAR, an avoidance arrangement is presumed to have been entered into or carried out for the sole or main purpose of obtaining a tax benefit, unless the taxpayer proves that, reasonably considered in light of

---

door is open to regarding all efforts to reduce tax liability as something 'unpatriotic and immoral'.")

[868] Meyerowitz, *supra* no. 842 at 42 (arguing that the draft amendments would have had the effect of stultifying "the use by a taxpayer of specific provision A which would have saved the tax payable had he used specific provision B, the taxpayer having the choice of using one or the other.")

[869] Dave Meyerowitz, "What Is Tax Avoidance?", vol. 54, no. 11 *The Taxpayer* 201-206 (Nov. 2005), 205 (noting "mainly" meant "dominant" under present law, and arguing that any standard less than "mainly" would create uncertainty and be "a clear recipe for disputes between SARS and taxpayers and likely to inhibit taxpayers from exercising their rights to order their affairs according to the provisions of the Act without the abuse of any of them.")

[870] Mazansky, *supra* no. 833 at 130; see also: Emil Brincker, "The Purpose Requirement of the General Anti-Avoidance Provision in South African Fiscal Law", vol. 2001, no. 1 *Journal of South African Law* 158-168, 160 (suggesting that the historical onus of proof in this regard under subsection 103(4) was "a formidable rebuttable presumption that arises to the extent that the transaction may have the effect of avoiding or reducing a liability for income tax, which is not easily discharged.")

the relevant facts and circumstances, obtaining a tax benefit was not the sole or main purpose.[871]

Under subsection 103(1), South African courts held that the time for testing the sole or main purpose is when the arrangement is implemented.[872] Part IIA does not address this question.

Objective versus subjective determination of purpose

The draft amendments to the GAAR also contemplated that purpose was to be objectively determined.[873] However, the final version of GAAR does not contain an express reference to objective determination of purpose. This is thought to have resulted in the retention of the subjective approach to determination of purpose which existed under subsection 103(1),[874] with the proviso that the relevant facts and circumstances are to be used as aids in testing the taxpayer's claim that avoiding taxes was not the sole or main purpose.[875] This is said to be consistent with the longstanding practice of the courts in South Africa of holding that the *ipse dixit* of a

---

[871] Cassidy, *supra* no. 238 at 763-764 (suggesting that it is unclear who bears the burden of proof under the balance of the GAAR)

[872] *Ovenstone v. SIR*, (1980) (2) SA 731 (A)

[873] Dave Meyerowitz, "Tax Avoidance", vol. 55, no. 3 *The Taxpayer* 49-52 (Mar. 2006), 51-53 (arguing that the formulation of an objective purpose test coupled with the presumption re abnormality under the proposed amendments would have effectively eliminated the right of taxpayers to legal tax mitigation); Meyerowitz, *supra* no. 842 at 42 (also arguing that these provisions would have "rendered it almost, if not entirely, impossible for taxpayers to discharge the onus that tax avoidance was not one of the main purposes.")

[874] See *SIR v. Gallagher*, (1978) (2) SA 463 (A) per Corbett JA at p. 471D: "If the subjective approach be adopted (as it must) then it is obvious that of prime importance in determining the purpose of the scheme would be the evidence of the respondent, the progenitor of the scheme, as to why it was carried out."; see also: Cassidy, *supra* no. 238 at 766 (noting however that although the words "determined objectively" were deleted from the final GAAR, subsection 80G(1) provides that the applicable standard in proving purpose is "reasonably considered in light of the facts and circumstances")

[875] Dave Meyerowitz, "Tax Avoidance Editorial", vol. 55, no. 10 *The Taxpayer* 181 (October 2006) (suggesting that the court will consider whether the taxpayer's stated purpose will be accepted by it having regard to the facts set out in section 80C which indicate a lack of commercial substance)

taxpayer must be consistent with all of the surrounding facts and circumstances.[876]

Since section 80A and section 80G have been drafted such that it is the avoidance arrangement's sole or main purpose, rather than the taxpayer's that is to be identified, questions have been raised as to how a construct that is not a thinking entity can have a purpose and how its purpose can be established.[877] This is one of very many questions that will need to be resolved in the courts.[878]

Abnormality requirement

Subsection 103(1) had as one of its elements a requirement that the impugned transaction, operation or scheme had to have been entered into or carried out in a manner not normally employed for business purposes, other than in obtaining a tax benefit – the abnormality requirement. [879] The SARS Discussion Paper cited difficulties with the abnormality requirement, i.e. that the world is not easily divided into arrangements for carrying out *bona fide* business transactions versus those for advancing impermissible tax avoidance schemes; plus, aggressive tax planners manage to manufacture various plausible sounding business arrangements, including lease-in/lease-out and sale and buy back schemes, which are really designed in order to

---

[876] Mazansky, *supra* no. 857 at 161 (noting that the final version of the GAAR retained the rebuttable presumption of purpose from subsection 103(1) but also required that purpose be examined in light of the relevant facts and circumstances, i.e. an objective standard); Broomberg, *supra* no. 858 at 132-133 (suggesting there has been a "profound change" in the onus of proof relating to the GAAR as the onus was on SARS to prove the presence of all of the requirements under subsection 103(1) whereas it now appears the onus is on the taxpayer to prove one of the elements is missing)

[877] Cassidy, *supra* no. 238 at 768 (suggesting the question remains unresolved re how purpose will be attributed to an arrangement)

[878] Numerous questions re the application and interpretation of the final GAAR are noted throughout this section.

[879] Meyerowitz, *supra* no. 873 at 49 (arguing that "if a general tax avoidance section were to be introduced without an abnormality requirement, it would follow that any transaction which had the effect of avoiding tax and where the taxpayer had as his or her sole or main purpose the obtaining of a tax benefit, would stand to be set aside.")

achieve tax benefits. The proposed draft amended version of GAAR therefore contained numerous provisions designed to point to abnormality, the presence of any one of which would give rise to a presumption of abnormality. The final GAAR does not contain this presumption.[880] This is said to suggest that SARS bears the burden of proving abnormality under section 80A.[881]

Eleven factors: the draft legislation

For the purpose of ascertaining the normality of a business arrangement it was proposed that the relevant facts and circumstances to be considered included, but were not limited to, the following:

(a) the form and economic substance of the arrangement, or any step therein or part thereof;

(b) the time at which the arrangement, or any step therein or part thereof, was entered into and the length of the period during which the arrangement, step or part was carried out;

(c) the result in relation to the operation of this Act which would, but for the application of this section, have been achieved by the arrangement;

(d) any circular flow of cash or assets between or among parties to the arrangement;

(e) the participation of any tax indifferent party in that arrangement;

(f) the inclusion of steps or transactions that offset or cancel each other, without a substantial effect upon the economic position of the parties;

(g) the inconsistent treatment of any items or amounts for tax purposes by parties to the arrangement (such as the

---

[880] Mazansky, *supra* no. 857 at 161 (noting that there was substantial opposition to the presumption of abnormality and that it did not carry forward into the final legislation)

[881] Cassidy, *supra* no. 238 at 769 (noting there is no specific onus of proof under section 80C and stating the position is unclear)

treatment of a payment as a deductible interest expense by the payer and as an exempt dividend by the recipient);

(h) a failure by any parties to the arrangement to deal at arm's length (without having regard to whether the parties are connected persons in relation to each other), including paying more than market value for any assets or service involved in that arrangement;

(i) the lack of any change in the financial position of any person resulting from that arrangement;

(j) the absence of a reasonable expectation of pre-tax profit in connection with the arrangement; or

(k) the value of the tax benefit that would have resulted from the arrangement, but for the application of this section, exceeds the amount of pre-tax profit reasonably expected in connection with that arrangement.[882]

These factors were designed to assist a court in determining whether the arrangement was an ordinary commercial dealing or rather one employed to obtain a tax benefit.[883] In this regard, it was also proposed that where any of the factors set forth in paragraphs (d) through (k) inclusive were found to exist it would be presumed, until the contrary was proved, that the arrangement or any step therein or part thereof was entered into or carried out by means or in a manner which would not normally be employed for *bona fide* purposes (other than in obtaining a tax benefit).

According to criticism by Meyerowitz, the factors articulated in the draft were "too broad and sweep in what may be termed to

---

[882] Mazansky, *supra* no. 833 at 129 (noting some of these indicia are used in Australia's GAAR – section 177D *Income Tax Assessment Act* 1936 – for concluding that a scheme was entered into to obtain a tax benefit)

[883] Meyerowitz, *supra* no. 873 at 50-51 (arguing that "the factors may well complicate the enquiry" and also that "they may have no real effect upon the outcome" because an impugned transaction needs to be compared to a transaction that would normally be entered into by a party in the context of business, as it was in the only decision dealing with the existing section 103 abnormality requirement)

be ordinary commercial arrangements."[884] It was further submitted that a circular flow of cash or assets was very common, "without in any way being sinister" and that the wide definition of "tax indifferent party" could be over-reaching.[885] In the version of GAAR enacted, the above "abnormality factors" were reduced from eleven to five.[886]

Lack of commercial substance

The introduction of the "lack of commercial substance" concept gave rise to the most substantial changes and new concepts in the GAAR.[887] The condition is defined in section 80C to occur where an avoidance arrangement would result in a significant tax benefit for a party (but for the GAAR), but does not have a significant effect upon either the business risks or net cash flows of that party, apart from any effect attributable to the tax benefit that would be obtained but for the provisions of the GAAR.[888] This is said by Broomberg to be

---

[884] Meyerowitz, *supra* no. 869 at 203-205 (arguing that the onus should be on SARS to satisfy a court that the facts indicate abnormality, rather than on the taxpayer to show normality, because "SARS, with all its experience behind it, is better able to explain why the facts result in abnormality than a taxpayer may be able to explain, without the aid and cost of expert evidence, why what he did was normally employed for *bona fide* business purposes, other than obtaining a tax benefit.").

[885] Mazansky, *supra* no. 857 at 160-161 (noting that SARS was not unsympathetic to these concerns).

[886] Johnathan Rickman, "Government Revises Proposed Antiavoidance Legislation", 43 *Tax Notes International* 1049 (Sept. 25, 2006) (noting that the proposed legislation to strengthen anti-avoidance rules was revised following the receipt of public comments with the number of initially proposed "abnormality factors" being scaled back and the related presumption of abnormality being eliminated).

[887] Draft Comprehensive Guide to the General Anti-Avoidance Rule, *supra* no. 835 at 26 (noting that generally speaking commercial substance will be lacking where there is a disproportionate relationship between the actual economic expenditure or loss incurred by a party and the value of the tax benefit that would have been obtained by that party but for the provisions of the GAAR; or, where a loss claimed for tax purposes significantly exceeds any reduction in the taxpayer's net worth).

[888] Cassidy, *supra* no. 238 at 771 (noting the courts will need to address how substantial the impact must be to be "significant"); see also: Draft Comprehensive

an articulation of the economic substance doctrine, whether of statutory or judicial origin, which exists in Western countries.[889]

Subsection 80C(2) then also stipulates that characteristics of an avoidance arrangement that are indicative of a lack of commercial substance include, but are not limited to:

(a) the legal substance or effect of the avoidance arrangement as a whole is inconsistent with, or differs significantly from, the legal form of its individual steps; or

(b) the inclusion or presence of –

  (i) round trip financing as described in section 80D; or

  (ii) an accommodating or tax-indifferent party as described in section 80E; or

  (iii) elements that have the effect of offsetting or cancelling each other.[890]

Substantial and lengthy definitions are provided in sections 80D and 80E of "round trip financing" and "accommodating or tax-indifferent" parties. The legal substance concept in paragraph 80C(2)(a) and the offsetting or cancelling concept in subparagraph 80C(2)(b)(iii) are said to be concepts imported into South African law from decisions in the US and the UK.[891]

Guide to the General Anti-Avoidance Rule, *supra* no. 835 at 18-19 (suggesting that in determining whether a significant tax benefit exists the focus is upon the magnitude of the tax benefit vis-à-vis the actual economic expenditure or loss that was incurred).

[889] Broomberg, *supra* no. 834 (suggesting that this is "a self-contained test, and is also a black and white issue").

[890] Meyerowitz, *supra* no. 842 at 42 (arguing that the detailed provisions regarding abnormality are "both vague and widely framed" and also that insofar as the provisions are relevant "a Court could and would have legitimately taken them into account under section 103.")

[891] Cassidy, *supra* no. 238 at 772 (stating that the U.K. "doctrine of fiscal nullity", which applies where a step with no commercial purpose other than tax avoidance has been inserted into a preordained composite transaction or series of transactions, is being introduced in subsection 80C(2)).

Broomberg argues that this construction of section 80C results in "a provision that is at war with itself, and by-pass surgery is urgently needed ... It is to be doubted, in short, whether any judicial sense can be made of these two subsections [80C(1) and (2)] when read together, though each could have stood on their own."[892] Furthermore, the test in paragraph 80C(2)(a) is also said to be confusing, as it invites a comparison of the legal substance or effect of an arrangement with the legal form of its individual steps, whereas the comparison to be expected is between economic or commercial effects of an arrangement and its legal effects.[893] Moreover, the element of round trip financing relating to funds transferred between or among the parties, specified in paragraph 80(D)(1)(a), has been described by Broomberg as too broad to serve any useful purpose.[894]

Mazansky has also complained that the "lack of commercial substance" aspect of the new GAAR introduces "very broad and even vague, concepts," causing "large areas of uncertainty."[895] The definitions in sections 80D and 80E are complex. Professor Cassidy has also suggested that the language of section 80E with respect to accommodating or tax-indifferent parties give rises to interpretational questions that could result in limiting the discretion of SARS in their treatment.[896]

Nevertheless, Professor Cassidy also thinks "there is greater surety of legislative impact when the courts are directed to make

---

[892] Broomberg, *supra* no. 834 at 51 (arguing that there is a standalone test under subsection 80C(1) which defines whether commercial substance exists whereas the facts and circumstances approach suggested under subsection 80C(2) implies that it means something different).

[893] EB Broomberg, "Then and now – VI", 22 *Tax Planning Corporate and Personal* 74-75 (2008), 74 (suggesting that the test that would have been consistent with the object of the exercise, i.e. determining whether commercial substance exists, is whether the economic effect of an avoidance arrangement as a whole is inconsistent with or differs significantly from the legal effect of its steps).

[894] *Ibid.* at 75 (arguing that this occurs under almost every commercial contract and it is not an indicator of a lack of commercial substance).

[895] Mazansky, *supra* no. 857 at 162-163 (suggesting that it "will take years, if not decades" for the courts to properly define the various unfamiliar and new concepts).

[896] Cassidy, *supra* no. 238 at 757-758 (although suggesting that this may be desirable in terms of promoting the goal of certainty).

a finding on particular 'badges of tax avoidance', rather than simply leaving them to be one of the many considerations to be taken into account when determining the issue of purpose.[897] This point is fairly debatable, and there is also room for the competing view that the more detailed the GAAR legislation, the less likely it is to be applied correctly and the more likely the courts are to be unsympathetic to assessments made under it.[898]

Misuse or abuse of provisions

The draft GAAR amendments also set out that "impermissible tax avoidance" exists where transactions "would frustrate the purpose of any provision of this Act", whereas under the final version of the GAAR it exists under subparagraph 80A(c)(ii) where transactions "would result directly or indirectly in the misuse or abuse of the provisions of this Act".[899] This provision was intended as an

---

[897] Cassidy, *supra* no. 238 at 774 (my own view after thirty years of tax litigation experience is that the more detailed the legislation the less likely tax officials are to apply it correctly and the more likely the courts are to be unsympathetic to it).

[898] I am not offering an empirical foundation for this view, although it is a subject that I consider worthy of study. Anecdotally, I can offer the experience of a three day hearing in the Federal Court of Appeal, dealing with the very detailed legislation concerning the calculation of the depletion base and the concept of "taxable production profits." When the only appellate justice who actively participated in the hearing stated that he was having some difficulty following a particular point, one of the other two justices remarked that "If that's how he feels imagine how I feel." The third justice at the hearing was silent throughout–*Gulf Canada Ltd. v. R.*, (*sub nom.* R. v. Gulf Canada Ltd.). [1992] 1 C.T.C. 183 (Fed. C.A.), leave to appeal refused (1992), (*sub nom.* Gulf Canada Ltd. v. Minister of National Revenue) 141 N.R. 393n (S.C.C.)

[899] Meyerowitz, *supra* no. 842 at 42 (noting that the final formulation is said by the Explanatory Memorandum to the Bill to have had its origins in Canadian and certain European jurisdictions); Linda van Schalkwyk and Bernard Geldennuys, "Section 80A(c)(ii) of the Income Tax Act and the scope of Part IIA: the big boom – Part II", *Accountancy South Africa* (October 2009) (arguing that establishing whether misuse or abuse of a provision has occurred is a much wider inquiry than whether the purpose of a provision has been frustrated and suggesting that introducing misuse or abuse as one of the tainted elements, rather than as a limitation clause as the Katz Commission recommended, could result in the courts finding that the ambit of Part IIA is too wide, thus leading to a narrow and restricted interpretation that "frustrate[s] the fiscus").

addition to and a fortification of the established concept of "abnormality" which existed in section 103.[900] Under this construction of the GAAR, "misuse or abuse" is one of the alternate "tainted elements" used to identify "impermissible tax avoidance" rather than an overriding exemption provision.[901]

According to SARS, subparagraph 80A(c)(ii) was introduced because of the discovery that section 103 "deviated from international best practice as [it] did not have a test or requirement based on the purpose of the underlying tax laws. In order to redress this shortcoming, the revised proposals would introduce a new Statutory Purpose Element aimed at schemes that would frustrate the purpose of any provisions of the [Income Tax] Act, including the provisions of the new Part IIA itself."[902] Also according to SARS, the introduction of the new statutory purpose element in the GAAR was intended to reinforce an emerging trend in the courts towards the modern approach to interpreting taxation statutes which requires a contextual and purposive rather than a literalist interpretation.[903]

The predominant criticism of this new provision by South African tax commentators has been that it is either ineffectual as it adds nothing to the existing common law, or else it is "incredibly far-reaching: [i]f the provision is seen as somehow *adding* something to the common law (which, it could be argued in the circumstances, must be presumed)."[904] With respect to the proposition that subpara-

---

[900] Chris Cilliers, "The Proposed Section 80A(c)(ii) of the Income Tax Act: Should It Be Enacted?", vol. 55, no. 10 *The Taxpayer* 182-187 (October 2006), 183 (arguing that if the provision is interpreted as adding something to the existing law, "the inevitable conclusion is that it would effectively outlaw virtually all attempts at tax avoidance" and would be "one of the most draconian provisions imaginable").

[901] Cassidy, *supra* no. 238 at 760-763 (suggesting that it may have been preferable to construct the misuse or abuse feature as an exempting provision).

[902] *Revised Proposals*, September 15, 2006, 15-16.

[903] *Ibid.*

[904] Cilliers, *supra* no. 900 at 183 (arguing that GAAR does not need a provision like section 80A(c)(ii) as "The rest of the GAAR is robust enough to survive without it."); Meyerowitz, *supra* no. 842 at 42 (suggesting that the analysis by Cilliers of the weaknesses of the proposed draft formulation of subparagraph 80A(c)(ii) is equally applicable to the final version of the provision).

graph 80A(c)(ii) adds nothing to the existing law, it is argued that a "purposive" or "contextual" approach to statutory interpretation is already called for under South African law when there is ambiguity in a provision and so a further call for identification of misuse or abuse is redundant.[905] The reasoning in support of the proposition that the provision may be "incredibly far-reaching" is that if the statutory purpose element in subparagraph 80A(c)(ii) is seen as adding something to the already existing modern contextual and purposive approach to interpretation, it must be supposed that it will lead to the purported discovery of purposes which are not otherwise apparent, using a conventional approach to statutory interpretation, i.e. the provision calls for the courts to look for "some inner or spiritual meaning within the legislation that would not become apparent on a normal purposive approach."[906] This in turn is said to be unacceptable, because it would undermine the rule of law by introducing an intolerable level of uncertainty into the interpretation of tax legislation.[907]

Subparagraph 80A(c)(ii) has been described as "the heart of section 80A", as it applies both "in the context of business" and also "in a context other than business."[908] The misuse or abuse concept in subparagraph 80(A)(c)(ii) had first surfaced in the Third Interim Report of the Commission of Inquiry into certain aspects of the Tax Structure of South Africa, 1995 (the Katz Commission). Because of concern expressed to the Katz Commission that mere reliance upon tax incentive provisions could be offside the normality requirement

---

[905] David Clegg, "Use it or abuse it", 21 *Tax Planning* 38 (2007) (arguing that "the misuse or abuse provision of s. 80A(c)(ii) does no more than set out in statute law the interpretive rules of the South African common law)

[906] *Ibid.* (arguing that if subparagraph 80A(c)(ii) envisages that some overriding purposive investigation is to be done there is no way to go about it and that the attendant risk is that "a court will be left wallowing in a sea of confusion")

[907] Cilliers, *supra* no. 900 at 185-186 (also suggesting that there is in any event no way of discerning a statutory purpose other than via the route utilized by courts under the modern approach to statutory interpretation)

[908] Chris Cilliers, "Thou shalt not peep at thy neighbour's wife: Section 80A(c)(ii) of the Income Tax Act and the Abuse of Rights", vol. 57 *The Taxpayer* 85-92 (May 2008), 85-86 (suggesting subparagraph 80A(c)(ii) should be deleted because the question is not whether a provision has been misused but its true scope in the first place)

and thus give rise to the application of section 103(1) of the Act, it examined the limitation in subsection 245(4) of the Canadian *Income Tax Act*, i.e. that even where a transaction results in a tax benefit and it has been primarily carried out for tax purposes, the general anti-avoidance provision will not apply to the transaction where it may reasonably be considered that it would not result in a misuse of the provisions of the Act or an abuse having regard to the provisions of the Act read as a whole. However, when subsection 103(1) of the Act was amended in 1996, the Katz Commission recommendation that a limitation similar to subsection 245(4) be implemented was not adopted.

Nevertheless, a decade later the SARS Discussion Paper referred again to subsection 245(4) of the Canadian *Income Tax Act* and this led to the formulation of the version of subparagraph 80A(c)(ii) recited above.[909] The provision has been labeled as "potentially dangerous"[910] and Meyerowitz argues that the inclusion of misuse or abuse under subparagraph 80A(c)(ii) as an alternative test for abnormality is wrong-headed, as there can be no basis for finding misuse or abuse of a provision of the Act, once the other requirements of section 80A have been met.[911]

---

[909] Linda van Schalkwyk and Bernard Geldenhuys, "Section 80A(c)(ii) of the Income Tax Act and the scope of Part II A: the big boom part I", *Accountancy South Africa* 30-31 (October 2009) (arguing that although it is inherent to a general anti-avoidance rule that it be of wide scope, because "government suffers from the first mover disadvantage: it lays out rules, which are then analyzed and parsed by taxpayers", formulating a general anti-avoidance rule too widely is undesirable because it violates the need for taxpayers to be able to determine taxes payable with certainty).

[910] Peter Surtees, "The Year in Review – South Africa", 44 *Tax Notes International* 1106 (Dec. 25, 2006) (also suggesting that the "Impermissible tax avoidance arrangements" title to Part IIA is "somewhat threatening" and that there will be continued challenges by taxpayers to the amended anti-avoidance provisions); see also: Cilliers, *supra* no. 908 at 109-110 (arguing that it is impossible to say with any certainty what subparagraph 80A(c)(ii) means, and that it amounts to being confronted with an "invisible yardstick, a stealthful nocturnal assassin").

[911] Meyerowitz, *supra* no. 842 at 66 (arguing that once a *bona fide* business purpose has been established under subparagraph 80A(c)(i), commercial

Application to scheme as a whole or any part thereof

Also, as set out above, one of the results of the *Conhage* decision was that if the sole or main purpose of the entire scheme was to obtain something other than a tax benefit, the GAAR could not be applied to steps in the scheme the sole purpose of which was tax avoidance.[912] The draft GAAR amendments made it clear that it could be applied to the scheme as a whole or any step therein or part thereof.[913] Section 80H of the final GAAR provides that it may be applied to steps in or parts of an arrangement.[914]

Application in the alternative

As there were conflicting decisions in the courts as to whether subsection 103(1) could be applied in the alternative to some other basis for disallowance, it was proposed to amend the GAAR to clarify that it can be applied in the alternative.[915] In the final GAAR, section 80I provides that it may be applied in the alternative or in addition to any other basis for raising an assessment.

---

substance is found to exist under section 80C and the normality tests have been met there can't be misuse or abuse)

[912] Mazanksy, *supra* no. 857 at 160 (explaining that the *Conhage* decision had "essentially denied the application of the GAAR to any inserted step or part of a composite transaction, even though the inserted step or part was solely tax-motivated, as long as the entire transaction was commercially motivated, i.e. not motivated by tax reasons")

[913] Mazansky, *supra* no. 833 at 129 (suggesting this to be the most important change to GAAR proposed by SARS in its Discussion Paper)

[914] Cassidy, *supra* no. 238 at 749 (noting that subsection 80G(2) compliments this provision by providing that the purpose of a step in or part of an avoidance arrangement may be different from a purpose attributable to the avoidance arrangement as a whole)

[915] Mazansky, *supra* no. 833 at 129-130 (referring to the philosophy behind the contention to the contrary)

Remedies under GAAR

Section 80B gives SARS a broad range of powers in determining the tax consequences of impermissible avoidance arrangements. These include (a) disregarding, combining or re-characterizing any steps or parts thereof; (b) disregarding any accommodating or tax-indifferent parties; (c) deeming persons who are connected to be one and the same; (d) reallocating any gross income, receipts, accruals and expenditures of a capital nature; (e) re-characterizing any gross income, receipts, accruals and expenditures of a capital nature; and (f) treating the impermissible avoidance arrangement as if it had not been entered into or carried out, etc.[916]

Notice requirement

SARS must give notice to taxpayers under section 80J of its intention to apply the GAAR, together with an explanation of the reasons for its proposed application. The taxpayer has 60 days from the date of the notice to respond to SARS, which then has a further 180 days to make its decision. As in any instance where a detailed legislative regime is created, new questions have arisen, including whether SARS is "bound" by the arrangement described in its notice.[917]

What has been accomplished

The amendments to GAAR are said to have had the effect of curbing abusive tax planning.[918] The post-2006 experience is also

---

[916] Cassidy, *supra* no. 238 at 745 (noting that section 80B contrasts with its predecessor section 103 in that SARS is no longer confined to "neutralising any tax benefit" in determining the tax consequences of impermissible avoidance).

[917] Cassidy, *supra* no. 238 at 752-753 (also querying whether the SARS notice can state multiple alternatives and raising the matter of procedural fairness vis-à-vis how the courts can apply the GAAR after the notice process has been exhausted).

[918] Dave Meyerowitz, "Aggressive Tax Planning", vol. 56, no. 2 *The Taxpayer* 37-38 (Feb. 2007), 37.

said to have been "generally positive" with a diminished interest in arrangements involving the indicia of a lack of commercial substance.[919] This may in part be attributable to an advance tax ruling system modified to permit taxpayers to obtain greater guidance and certainty from SARS as to what amounts to impermissible tax avoidance.[920] It has also been suggested that although taxpayer compliance has improved, this is unlikely to have anything to do with South Africa's "verbose GAAR", but rather has occurred because SARS is now much more effective than the revenue authorities used to be in South Africa.[921]

In any event, the revised version of the GAAR has not yet been tested in the courts, and a large number of interpretational issues have been identified as outstanding.[922] In this regard, Broomberg has opined that the new GAAR contains features "difficult enough to apparently confound the most formidable minds":

> Because detailed and complex legislation tends to drive out broad and simple rules, the inexorable process is beginning to pose a threat in South Africa, which is suffering from a life-threatening shortage of the skills required to manage even the older, broader provisions of the Income Tax Act. ... A typical illustration of the problem is to be found in the new general anti-avoidance rule in South Africa, which has replaced the old section 103(1) of the Income Tax Act. In place of a single subsection, the 12 new sections 80A to 80L, covering many pages, is an eclectic compilation of anti-avoidance measures garnered from around the globe, including Britain. These have all be superimposed on the two old and simple tests for a tax-avoidance scheme, viz. a main purpose to avoid tax and the presence of abnormal

---

[919] Liptak, *supra* no. 830, c. 3, 27 (also suggesting that it is an open question as to whether the amended GAAR increases or decreases uncertainty "for the majority of taxpayers who do not seek to push the envelope")

[920] Discussion Paper on Tax Avoidance", *supra* no. 5 at 47

[921] Joubert, *supra* no. 855 (arguing that "people get scared when laws are actually enforced" and that changes to the law "only makes a difference if you think you might get caught")

[922] Professor Cassidy, for example, has raised a number of questions which are mentioned throughout this chapter; see also: Theresa Calvert, "An analysis of the 2006 amendments to the General Anti-Avoidance Rules: A case law approach", unpublished dissertation (North-West University: 2011), p. 5 (stating that "the 2006 amendments to GAAR have not been applied on a practical basis to existing case law")

features. ... It is difficult to avoid the conclusion that the approach adopted in this new enactment in South Africa is excessively harsh, and may, accordingly, be restrictively interpreted by the courts.[923]

Cilliers has also argued that legislative borrowing from foreign legal systems has created "unpredictable and potentially dangerous circumstances."[924] Tooma has more optimistically suggested, however, that the listing of prescribed factors to be used by courts in determining whether a transaction is abnormal may result in providing increased certainty for taxpayers.[925]

Conclusion

While it remains to be seen whether the legislative labyrinth adopted in South Africa will be an effective way to combat abusive tax avoidance, there is no doubt that economic substance is front and centre amongst the factors to be considered in determining whether its GAAR applies.

The general test under subsection 80C(1) for the determination of whether commercial substance is lacking is whether an avoidance arrangement would result in a significant tax benefit for a party (but for the GAAR), but it does not have a significant effect upon either the business risks or the cash flows of that party, apart from any effect attributable to the tax benefit being claimed. This is the adoption of an economic substance test from jurisdictions outside South Africa.[926]

Since the Supreme Court of Canada has all but ruled out economic substance as a relevant factor in determining whether abusive

---

[923] E.B. Broomberg, "The legacy of U.K. tax law in South Africa", vol. 3 *British Tax Review* 291-303 (2008), 301-302 (admitting however that "the blame for the proliferation of prolix tax legislation cannot be attributed solely or even mainly to Britain").

[924] Cilliers, *supra* no. 908 at 107-109 (arguing 80A(c)(ii) is impermissibly vague).

[925] Tooma, *supra* no. 15 at 225-226 (arguing in her PhD dissertation that there may be greater certainty where a statutory GAAR exists with safeguards to ensure it is appropriately administered).

[926] Broomberg, *supra* no. 834 (suggesting that the test leads to quantifiable results which show whether an arrangement is an impermissible avoidance arrangement).

tax avoidance has occurred in Canada, whereas economic substance is understood in South Africa (and elsewhere) to be an important test for abusive tax avoidance, my claim is that Parliament must amend our present GAAR to expressly incorporate an economic substance test. However, this can and should be done in a much simpler fashion than is the case under South Africa's GAAR regime. In Canada's case, adding a provision that economic substance must be considered, amongst other factors, in determining whether (a) an avoidance transaction has occurred; and (b) there has been an abuse of provisions of the Act or an abuse of the Act as a whole, should be sufficient to head our judiciary in the right direction. Part of the reason for this optimism relates to the performance of the courts in New Zealand.[927]

AUSTRALIA

For the past three decades, economic substance has been one of several legislated objective criterion, which must be examined under Australia's GAAR.[928] In this regard, the Australian Tax Office (ATO) also defines "aggressive tax planning" as "the use of transactions or arrangements that have little or no economic substance and that are created predominantly to obtain a tax benefit that is not intended by law",[929] placing economic substance front and centre amongst several points to be examined in identifying abusive tax avoidance. The ATO also identifies transactions which generate "tax benefits unrelated to the economic substance of a commercial activity", as a "red flag" or "warning light" as to the existence of aggressive tax planning.[930]

---

[927] See the section in this chapter concerning the GAAR in New Zealand.
[928] Explanatory Memorandum, Income Tax Laws Amendment Bill (No. 2) 1981, pp. 10-11 (explaining that regard must be had to a specified set of considerations, including any change in the financial position of the taxpayer or connected persons, in determining whether the requisite degree of purpose exists for the GAAR to be applied)
[929] Cited in Evans, *supra* no. 191 at 16.
[930] Kevin Fitzpatrick, "The Australian Taxation Office's approaches to Aggressive Tax Planning", Centre for Tax System Integrity, Third International Research Conference Responsive Regulation: International Perspectives in Taxation: Canberra 24 and 25 July 2003, p. 6

The economic reality or substance of transactions is seen by Australian courts as an important factual reference point in determining "purpose." In carrying out its statutory GAAR mandate, the High Court of Australia has identified the absence of any substantial change in the taxpayer's financial position, in circumstances where a several million dollar tax benefit was obtained, while parting with only a few hundred thousand dollars, as suggesting that the dominant purpose of the scheme in question was to obtain a tax benefit.[931]

This state of affairs in the Australian courts contrasts sharply with our situation in Canada, where the Supreme Court has essentially ruled out reliance upon examination of the economic substance of transactions as a valid approach in determining whether there has been abusive tax avoidance, by holding that lack of substance has "no meaning in isolation from the proper interpretation of specific provisions of the *Income Tax Act*."[932] Relative to this point, it has recently been suggested in Canada, by Larin and Duong, that Australia's GAAR illustrates the usefulness of legislatively defining objective parameters based on economic substance, in opposing abusive tax avoidance.[933] I agree with this insight, given our Supreme Court's refusal to endorse an examination of the economic substance of transactions in tax avoidance cases, in large contrast with, for example, the position of the Supreme Court of New Zealand.[934]

By way of background, a tax avoidance industry is reported to have historically flourished in Australia, partly on account of a grossly disproportionate growth in tax collections relative to wages beginning in the 1950's,[935] outright antagonism by the judiciary to

---

[931] See *Pridecraft Pty Ltd v. Commissioner of Taxation*, 2005 ATC 4001 per Sackville J at p. 91, with Sundberg J and Ryan J concurring
[932] *Canada Trustco Mortgage Co. v. R.*, [2005] 2 S.C.R. 601 (S.C.C.) at para. 59
[933] Larin and Duong, "Australia General Anti-Avoidance Rule", *supra* no. 31 at 32
[934] See the discussion of the cases under New Zealand's GAAR in this chapter.
[935] Lidia Xynas, "Tax Planning, Avoidance and Evasion in Australia 1970-2010: The Regulatory Responses and Taxpayer Compliance", vol. 20, issue 1 *Revenue Law Journal* 1-37 (2010), 6-7 (stating that the disproportionate increase in tax liability contributed to a substantial appetite amongst taxpayers for artificial vehicles to reduce tax)

taxation,[936] the heavy promotion of abusive tax avoidance schemes by tax advisers and "a timid revenue authority."[937]

However, in the face of public criticism of government for failing to take steps to curtain gross abuse of the tax system, coupled with scorn directed at the High Court for upholding nefarious tax schemes, in 1981 a new GAAR regime was proposed to replace the existing GAAR regime.[938] This occurred at a time when the attitude of the public towards tax avoidance had changed to disapproval, prompted by a realization that wage earners were carrying most of the tax burden.[939]

A key aspect of the new GAAR regime introduced in 1981 was its focus on objective factors, including economic substance, in the determination of purpose.[940] This has proven to be about the least controversial and least problematic aspect of the new GAAR; and, the sky has not fallen in Australia, on account of the statutory inclusion of economic substance as an objective factor. Indeed, shortly after the introduction of the new GAAR, Professor Pederick noted "it seems clear that the High Court and other courts of Australia

---

[936] Pickup, *supra* no. 846 (Chief Justice Sir Garfield Barwick is said to have subjected Australia's previous GAAR to "judicial castration"); see also: Waincymer, *supra* no. 146 at 256 (noting that "when tax avoidance became virtually sanctioned by the High Court [in Australia] in the 1970's, tax avoidance packages reached epidemic proportions.")

[937] Evans, *supra* no. 94 at 109 (referring to reasons for the explosion of tax avoidance and evasion identified by A. Frieberg in "Ripples from the Bottom of the Harbour: Some Social Ramifications of Taxation Fraud", 12 *Criminal Law Journal* 136-192 (1998), 137

[938] Maurice Cashmere, "A GAAR for the United Kingdom? The Australian Experience", no. 2 *British Tax Review* 125-159 (2008), 133 (noting also that questions were raised about the government not adopting recommendations about re-drafting the existing GAAR provision made to it in 1975 by the Asprey Committee, which had been commissioned by the government to report on reforming the tax system)

[939] Julie Cassidy, vol. 11, issue 1 "Part IVA – A Toothless Tiger?", *Revenue Law Journal* 1-27 (2001), 2 (noting that the Australian public previously viewed tax avoidance as praiseworthy because of concern re government spending)

[940] Morgan, *supra* no 1 at 389 (noting that the economic substance doctrine is integrated into the GAAR regime and that the economic realities of transactions can be taken into account under Australia's GAAR)

have now come to an appreciation that technical schemes, however elegant, that have no real economic substance are not entitled to recognition in the real world of taxation", in presenting to the Victorian Chapter of the Taxation Institute of Australia.[941] This observation cannot be made even today regarding the courts in Canada, where obsession with legal form and the *Duke of Westminster* case have been in the forefront.[942]

Historical GAAR in Australia

Section 53 of the *Income Tax Assessment Act 1915* contained a GAAR adopted from a similar provision that applied in New Zealand. In 1936 this provision, in substantially the same form, became section 260 of the *Income Tax Assessment Act 1936*. Section 260 made contracts, agreements or arrangements void against the Commissioner that had the purpose or effect of, directly or indirectly, altering the incidence of tax, relieving any person from liability to pay tax; or, defeating, evading or avoiding any liability imposed on any person by the ITAA 1936.[943]

Despite its broad terms, it became apparent during the early days of section 260's existence that it would not be given a broad application, as the courts considered that if it were given a literal interpretation it would apply to virtually every transaction that had the effect of reducing tax.[944] In the 1950's, the application of section

---

[941] Willard Pederick, "Fair and Square Taxation for Australia", *Taxation in Australia* 570 (Dec 1984), 587-588 (also suggesting that "a Parliamentary declaration that, in evaluating contrived and insubstantial arrangements, it is the economic substance that is to determine tax liabilities would help illuminate the path of reason and a fundamental purpose of a taxing statute")

[942] See the discussion of this point in chapter V.

[943] Section 260, *Income Tax Assessment Act 1936*; see also: Cashmere, *supra* no. 938 at 129 (noting that it was not necessary for any purpose to avoid tax to exist for section 260 to apply)

[944] Cashmere, *ibid.* at 130 (citing the case of *DCT v. Purcell* (1921), 29 CLR 464 (High Court) at p. 470 in which the Chief Justice of the High Court noted that if the section were construed literally it would extend to every transaction which had the effect of reducing the income of any taxpayer)

260 became subject to Lord Denning's predication test, which was enunciated in a Privy Council decision on an appeal from Australia's High Court:

> In order to bring the arrangement within the section you must be able to predicate – by looking at the overt acts by which it was implemented – that it was implemented in that particular way so as to avoid tax. If you cannot so predicate, but have to acknowledge that the transactions are capable of explanation by reference to ordinary business or family dealing, without necessarily being labelled as a means to avoid tax, then the arrangement does not come within the section.[945]

Nevertheless, even where arrangements were subsequently not "capable of explanation by reference to ordinary business or family dealing", and were obviously designed to reduce tax, section 260 was often still held by the courts not to apply.[946] This is said by Cashmere to have been because the specific provisions of the ITAA 1936, which excluded amounts from income or increased allowable deductions, had to be given recognition by the courts, despite the apparently broad sweep of section 260.[947] This recognition led to the emergence of the "choice principle", under which section 260 had no application if the taxpayer was found to be choosing between alternatives under the ITAA 1936. The rationale for the principle was explained as follows:

> ... it proceeds on the footing that the taxpayer is entitled to create a situation by entry into a transaction which will attract tax consequences for which the Act makes specific provision and the validity of the transaction is not affected by s260 merely because the tax consequences which it attracts

---

[945] *Newton v. F.C.T.* (1958), 98 CLR 1 (P.C.) at p. 8
[946] Maurice Cashmere, "Towards an appropriate interpretative approach to Australia's general tax avoidance rule – Part IVA", 35 *Australian Tax Review* 231-247 (June 2006), 232-233 (noting that under section 260 a taxpayer could adopt almost any course of conduct, although it was undertaken to obtain a tax advantage, so long as the course was open on a literal reading of the legislation)
[947] Cashmere, *supra* no. 938 at 131 (suggesting that the substantive provisions of the ITAA 1936 which benefitted taxpayers created a dilemma vis-à-vis the broad terms of section 260)

are advantageous to the taxpayer and he enters into the transaction deliberately with a view to gaining that advantage.[948]

Again according to Cashmere, the choice principle developed over time into an over-riding principle, under which the courts found that almost any actions, although contrived and undertaken in order to secure a perceived tax advantage, did not offend section 260: "The extension of the choice principle ... ushered in a regime of optional tax for those who were able to exploit the system."[949]

A further problem with section 260 was that it only made arrangements void as against the Commissioner, rather than permitting the substitution of a different arrangement in relation to which tax could be imposed.[950] Thus, despite the enormous potential breadth of section 260's application, it eventually came to have almost no application.[951] The upshot of these problems was that the government set about in 1981 to overcome section 260's apparent structural problems, by announcing proposed amendments against tax avoidance arrangements which were "blatant, artificial or contrived."[952] The government also sought to restore an interpretative approach to the GAAR, akin to the position elucidated by Lord Denning in the *Newton* case,[953] whereby unacceptable tax avoidance was to be detected by looking at an arrangement to determine

---

[948] *Cridland v. FCT* (1977), 140 CLR 330 (High Court) at p. 339, per Mason J.

[949] *Supra* no. 947 at 132 (noting that the choice principle did not easily co-exist with the predication test, as the adoption of virtually any legal form was upheld under the choice principle, whereas under the predication test the inquiry was whether, having regard to the overt acts, the legal form was implemented in a particular way in order to avoid tax).

[950] Cashmere, *supra* no. 938 at 132 (noting that taxpayers often escaped liability for tax because of this limitation to section 260).

[951] Richard Krever and Anthony van der Westhuysen, "Government to Review Antiavoidance Provisions", *Tax Notes International* 731-732 (Dec 6, 2010), 731 (noting that Australia's antagonist final court of appeal – the High Court – had by the end of the 1970's read down section 260 to such a large extent that "it had almost no application").

[952] Explanatory Memorandum, Income Tax Laws Amendment Bill (No. 2) 1981, page 2.

[953] *Newton v. F.C.T.* (1958), 98 CLR 1 (P.C.).

whether it was implemented in a particular way for the purpose of avoiding tax.[954]

In pursuing this course, the government announced that its new general anti-avoidance measure called for an examination of all evidence relevant to the purposes for which a taxpayer entered into an arrangement, including changes in the financial position of the taxpayer and connected persons.[955] This step in 1981 was the first legislative manifestation in Australia of recognition that economic substance has a central role to play in detecting unacceptable tax avoidance.[956] We have not yet experienced any similar recognition in Canada, although three decades have passed since this occurred in Australia.

Part IVA

The new GAAR was introduced, under Part IVA of the ITAA36 in 1981, with rules designed to overcome the underwhelming performance of section 260. The new GAAR was also coupled with a legislative requirement that a purposive approach must be taken to the interpretation of all Commonwealth statutes, including tax statutes.[957] In this regard, the High Court held in *Federal Commission-*

---

[954] Explanatory Memorandum, Income Tax Laws Amendment Bill (No. 2) 1981, page 3; see also: Pagone, *supra* no. 180 at 772 (calling the *Newton* case an "important bridge" between old and new GAAR regimes)

[955] Explanatory Memorandum, Income Tax Laws Amendment Bill (No. 2) 1981, page 3

[956] The Australian attention to whether there have been changes in the financial position of the taxpayer and connected persons parallels the U.S. economic substance doctrine's focus on whether there has been a meaningful change in the taxpayer's position, apart from tax benefits.

[957] Section 15AA, *Acts Interpretation Act 1901*. This new legislation also provided that the courts can have regard to extrinsic aids when interpreting statutes, including reports made to Parliament when the provision was enacted, explanatory memoranda relating to the provision which were put before Parliament, Ministerial speeches made when the related Bill was introduced in Parliament for second reading, and other documents falling within the ambit of subsection 15AB(2); but see: Cashmere, *supra* no. 938 at 126-127 (arguing that despite the long existence of this requirement for a purposive approach in the interpretation of tax statutes, there has been very little evidence of departure by

er of Taxation v. Spotless Services Ltd.[958] that Lord Tomlin's famous dictum in the *Duke of Westminster* case is not relevant in Australia in the interpretation of Part IVA, which is to be interpreted on its own terms.[959]

Essential elements

The three elements specified for the application of Part IVA are (a) a tax benefit; (b) a scheme; and (c) a sole or dominant purpose of the taxpayer or any other participant in the scheme to obtain the tax benefit for the taxpayer.[960] Each element must exist for Part IVA to be applied.[961] Once Part IVA has been applied, the taxpayer bears the burden of proving its inapplicability.[962]

Australian courts from a literalist approach. Also suggesting that the Commissioner of Taxation has increasingly relied upon the GAAR in attempting to control tax avoidance because of the tendency of the courts to avoid purposive interpretation and to adhere to the legal form of transactions).

[958] (1996), 96 ATC 5201 (Aust. High Ct.); (1996), 186 C.L.R. 404 (Aust. High Ct.)

[959] William Thompson, "Applying Part IVA", vol. 10, no. 4 *The Tax Specialist* 187-200 (April 2007), 187 (suggesting that in Australia the *Duke of Westminster* case has been "consigned to the dustbin of history", noting that the High Court held in *FCT v Spotless* that Part IVA should not be interpreted with "muffled echoes of old arguments").

[960] Pickup, *supra* no. 846, c. 2, at 16 (noting that "Part IVA is a complex provision" which essentially has these three requirements); Cooper, *supra* no. 36 at 234 (noting these are the three principal concepts which are needed to trigger Part IVA's operation).

[961] Cassidy, *supra* no. 939 at 4 (noting that it is an error of law for a court not to consider each of the elements of Part IVA individually); see also: "Improving the operation of the anti-avoidance provisions in the income tax law", Discussion Paper (Nov18, 2010), Attorney General's Department, Government of Australia, p. 4 (suggesting that while the three elements of Part IVA are separate, the examination of one of the elements will generally also involve the conclusions reached in relation to the other two elements).

[962] Paragraph 144ZZO(b) *Taxation Administration Act* 1953 (cth); see also: Cassidy, *supra* no. 238 at 768 (suggesting that under the Australian GAAR the taxpayer must show that all persons who entered into or carried out the scheme did not have the dominant purpose of obtaining a tax benefit); Pagone, *supra* no. 180 at 778 (noting that the taxpayer's burden may include the difficult task of proving a negative in the context of an hypothesis); see also: Cooper, *supra* no. 463 at 101 (commenting that a common design element

Tax benefit

Section 177C initially provided that a "tax benefit" was the non-inclusion of an amount that would or might reasonably be expected to be included in the taxpayer's income or the allowance of a deduction that would or might not have been expected to be allowable, but for the scheme. The definition was exhaustive and it did not include other kinds of tax benefits such as rebates or credits. The definition has therefore been extended by subsequent amendments, although it is still not a comprehensive definition.[963]

In order to determine whether there has been a tax benefit, there must be an understanding as to what a reasonable expectation would have been if the scheme had not been entered into.[964] In this regard, there must be a factual basis upon which to reach this understanding, and it is incumbent on the taxpayer to lead evidence in court as to what course would have been adopted;[965] plus, it is not open to the Commissioner to rely upon "a hypothetical situation based on speculation."[966]

---

of GAARs is that once the rule has been applied the taxpayer will have the burden of disproving its applicability).

[963] Cassidy, *supra* no. 939 at 8 (noting that even post-amendments there are limitations to the "tax benefit" that can be addressed for purposes of Part IVA); Julie Cassidy, "'To GAAR or Not to GAAR – That is the Question:' Canadian and Australian Attempts to Combat Tax Avoidance", 36 *Ottawa Law Review* 259-313 (2004-2005), 286 (arguing that the more comprehensive concept of "tax benefit" under Canada's GAAR is more effective).

[964] Graeme S. Cooper, "Australia's GAAR Comes Alive in the Courts", *Tax Notes International* 559-566 (May 16, 2011), 563 (noting that the identification of the relevant counterfactual is a critical step under Australia's GAAR as "the existence of a tax benefit and the amount of the tax benefit is dictated by the counterfactual. However, this is obviously a very fraught process because it involves speculating about what the taxpayer might have done.").

[965] Graeme Cooper, "Predicting the Past – the Problem of Finding a Counterfactual in Part IVA", Legal Studies Research Paper No. 11/49, http:ssrn.com/abstract=1910990, University of Sydney Law School, (August 2011), p. 14-15 (also published in 40:3 *Australian Tax Review* 185-200 (2011)) (noting that it is the taxpayer's responsibility to prove what might have happened instead of the scheme that actually took place).

[966] Cashmere, *supra* no. 938 at 136 (citing the decision in *FCT v. Hart* (2004), 55 ATR 712 (High Court) as illustrating the point that there must be sufficient

The definition of "tax benefit" excludes benefits arising from the structuring of an arrangement that is consistent with the aims of the legislation, in that subsection 177C(2) provides that a tax benefit does not include the non-inclusion of income and the claiming of deductions attributable to a declaration, election or option, etc. expressly provided for by the Act.[967] This is said to be a narrow version of the "choice principle", which had its genesis under section 260, insofar as it does not exempt arrangements entered into for the purpose of obtaining a tax benefit; and, unlike in the case of section 260, it only exempts declarations, etc. where there is an express provision.[968]

In a Discussion Paper on tax avoidance released in November 2010, the Australian Government raises the matter of whether the present definition of "tax benefit" is broad enough and reviews possible avenues for expanding the concept.[969] One of the proposed avenues is the adoption of a comprehensive definition of "tax benefit" to be combined with a list of common tax benefits.[970]

---

evidence upon which to make a reasonable prediction as to the appropriate alternative).

[967] Tooma, "Assessment of Alternatives to General Anti-Avoidance Rules: The Judiciary, The Administration and the Legislature", *supra* no. 15, chapter 5, p. 212 (suggesting the Australian approach in this regard may be "less amorphous, and provide greater certainty for taxpayers" than the Canadian misuse or abuse provision).

[968] Cassidy, *supra* no. 939 at 10-11 (stating the exemption *prima facie* exempts schemes based on specific choices under the Act, such as the choice between alternative accounting methods); Nabil F Orow, "Part IVA – Seriously Flawed in Principle", *Journal of Australian Taxation* 57-78 (1998), 61 (suggesting that an expansive application of the choice principle would make Part IVA irrelevant because so much of taxation has to do with choices under the ITAA); see also: Cassidy, *supra* no. 963 at 309 (suggesting that confusion surrounding the meaning of the misuse and abuse concept in subsection 245(4) of the Canadian *Income Tax Act* indicates that the better approach is the exclusionary approach adopted in Australia in subsection 177C(2)).

[969] Improving the operation of the anti-avoidance provisions in the income tax law", Discussion Paper (Nov18, 2010), Attorney General's Department, Government of Australia.

[970] *Ibid.*

Scheme

Subsection 177A(1) provides a definition of "scheme":

(a) any agreement, arrangement, undertaking, promise or undertaking, whether express or implied and whether or not enforceable, or intended to be enforceable in legal proceedings; and

(b) any scheme, plan, proposal, action, course of action or course of conduct.

The Commissioner has been prevented by the courts from defining a scheme narrowly.[971] According to the decision in *FCT v. Peabody*:

> Part IVA does not provide that a scheme includes part of a scheme and it is possible, despite the very wide definition of a scheme, to conceive of a set of circumstances which constitutes only part of a scheme and not a scheme in itself. That will occur where the circumstances are incapable of standing on their own without being 'robbed of all practical meaning'.[972]

This requirement that a scheme must be capable of standing on its own feet, without being "robbed of all practical meaning", is said to have caused difficulty because of its uncertainty.[973] Professor Cassidy thinks, however, that given the exceptionally broad definition of "scheme" in subsection 177A(1), that in most cases its requirements will be easily met.[974] Furthermore, the Commissioner

---

[971] Tooma, "Assessment of Alternatives to General Anti-Avoidance Rules: The Judiciary, The Administration and the Legislature", *supra* no. 15, chapter 5, p. 230-231 (noting that if a scheme is cast broadly it is easier for a taxpayer to establish the non-tax purposes/effects of the scheme whereas it is in the Commissioner's interest to have the scheme defined narrowly).

[972] *FCT v. Peabody* (1994), 94 ATC 4663 (High Court) at p. 4670.

[973] Cashmere, *supra* no. 938 at 136 (noting, however, that two justices of the High Court established the necessity for an inter-connection between a scheme and the disputed tax benefit in *FCT v. Hart* (2004), 55 ATR 712 (High Court) at p. 716.

[974] Julie Cassidy, "Observations on the Application of Part IVA: Peabody v. Federal Commissioner of Taxation", vol. 21 *Australian Business Law Review* 424-439 (December 1993), 425 (suggesting the two issues arising from the definition are identifying the scheme and whether tax purposes must underlie

is not bound by the identification of the scheme that he made at the outset, and an alternative formulation of the scheme may be acted upon by a court or administrative tribunal.[975]

Dominant purpose

Professor Cooper has observed that tax avoidance is commonly understood to be a purpose-based notion;[976] and, that "[w]hether listing purportedly objective factors adds anything to the analysis that a court would likely undertake [re what purpose was extant] is doubtful. But having the list does confirm that the investigation is to be based on an objective assessment of purpose, rather than a subjective one ...."[977] He has also observed that determining the sole or dominant purpose is always the least predictable element in GAAR cases.[978] Eight criteria are specified under paragraph

---

the whole scheme or only steps in it); see also: Cooper, *supra* no. 36 at 236 (suggesting that because of the broad definition of "scheme", the existence of a scheme will rarely be disputed, although there are interpretational problems relating to the identification of the scheme).

[975] Cassidy, *supra* no. 939 at 7 (citing the case of *Spotless Services Ltd. v FCT* regarding this point).

[976] Cooper, *supra* no. 29 at 28 (arguing that a purpose-based test is always over-inclusive, so that while purpose may be a necessary ingredient for a GAAR, it will not be sufficient, i.e. the GAAR must only be triggered where the policy goals underlying the legislation are defeated).

[977] Cooper, *supra* no. 463 at 100 (a common design element of GAARs is a purpose element which triggers their application); Cooper, *supra* no. 36 at 241 ("purpose" is the objective purpose disclosed by analyzing the facts by reference to the eight factors); compare: Richard Krever, "ATO Releases New GAAR Guidance", *Tax Notes International* 1133-1134 (Dec 2005), 1133 (suggesting that although the GAAR legislation lists "apparently objective criteria ... [t]he test is nevertheless subjective because it turns on the taxpayer's purpose, a factor that ultimately rests with the taxpayer"); Peter Donovan, "The aftermath of Hart's case – a case for reform of Part IVA?", vol. 39, no. 5 *Taxation in Australia* 253-256 (Nov. 2004), 255 (arguing the test is in no small part subjective because the eight s. 177D factors "must be weighted and ultimately adjudged by a human").

[978] Cooper, *supra* no. 964 at 561 (suggesting that under the objective determination of sole or dominant purpose for Part IVA the correct question is: Why would someone else do what this taxpayer did rather than why did this taxpayer do what it did?)

177D(b) for examination in determining whether the dominant purpose of a scheme was of a non-tax nature:

- (i) the manner in which the scheme was entered into or carried out;
- (ii) the form and substance of the scheme;
- (iii) the time at which the scheme was entered into and the length of the period during which the scheme was carried out;
- (iv) the result in relation to the operation of the Act that, but for the operation of Part IVA, would be achieved by the scheme;
- (v) any change in the financial position of the taxpayer that has resulted, will result, or may reasonably be expected to result, from the scheme;
- (vi) any change in the financial position of any person who has, or has had, any connection (whether of a business, family or other nature) with the relevant taxpayer, being a change that has resulted, will result or may reasonably be expected to result, from the scheme;
- (vii) any other consequence for the relevant taxpayer, or for any person referred to in subparagraph (vi), of the scheme having been entered into or carried out; and
- (viii) the nature of any connection (whether of a business, family or other nature) between the relevant taxpayer and any person referred to in subparagraph (vi).

Cashmere says that the required consideration of these eight factors amounts to the application of a formula, and that they are the only factors which are relevant in determining the outcome. [979]

---

[979] Cashmere, *supra* no. 938 at 140-142 (arguing however that the High Court's approach has made the form and manner in which transactions have been carried out determinative of the outcome); but see: Cassidy, *supra* no. 974 at 436 (arguing Parliament intended the list in paragraph 177D(b) to be non-exhaustive).

Furthermore, each of the eight statutory criteria must be considered[980] although in a given case the weight of one factor alone may disclose the dominant purpose.[981] In any event, the test is "whether a reasonable person would conclude, having regard to the eight listed criteria, that the relevant parties in entering into, or carrying out, the particular scheme in its context, had as their dominant purpose the obtaining of a tax benefit."[982] Professor Cooper has noted a number of outstanding questions as to how the eight factors listed in paragraph 177D(b) are to be employed and analyzed; however, it is plain that the eight factors are to be considered when making an objective determination of purpose.[983] This again contrasts with the situation in Canada, where our GAAR does not presently specify any criteria that must be examined in determining purpose.

Utilizing this approach under paragraph 177D(b), the absence of any practical change in the financial position of the taxpayer and persons connected to the taxpayer has been held to suggest that the dominant purpose of entering into or carrying out a scheme was to

---

[980] See *Peabody v. FCT* (1993), 40 FCR 531 at p. 543 (holding that the Commissioner must have regard to each of the matters referred to in paragraph 177D(b)); see also: Cassidy, *supra* no. 974 at 436 (arguing that all of the factors listed in paragraph 177(D)(b) must be weighed against each other); but see: Cassidy, *supra* no. 939 at 24 (noting the High Court held in *FCT v Consolidated Press Holdings Ltd* that it is not necessary for a judge to refer to each factor individually and it is sufficient if reasons for judgment as a whole show a "global assessment of purpose")

[981] See *FCT v. Hart* (2004), 55 ATR 712 (High Court) at p. 92 per Callinan J; *FCT v. Consolidated Press Holdings (No. 1)* (1999), 99 ATC 4945 (Full Federal Court) at p. 4971 ("The section requires the decision-maker, be it the Commissioner or the Court, to have regard to each of these matters. It does not require that they be unbundled from a global consideration of purpose and slavishly ticked off. The relevant dominant purpose may be so apparent on the evidence taken as a whole that consideration of the statutory factors can be collapsed into a global assessment of purpose.")

[982] Cashmere, *supra* no. 946 at 247 (arguing that the principles to be followed in drawing an objective conclusion as to the dominant purpose remain uncertain after more than twenty five years)

[983] Cooper, *supra* no. 36 at 241-245 (noting the subjective assertions by a taxpayer as to purpose are not considered to be relevant)

obtain a tax benefit.[984] Similarly, in *Re: Clough Engineering and Deputy Commissioner of Taxation* the Administrative Appeals Tribunal also relied on a scheme's lack of economic substance, having regard to the circularity of the transaction, and the absence of a change in the taxpayer's financial position, in finding that the dominant purpose was obtaining the tax benefit.[985] This manner of approach does not presently exist in Canada, where our Supreme Court has held that a lack of substance has "no meaning in isolation from the proper interpretation of specific provisions of the *Income Tax Act*."[986] Thus, although the presence or absence of economic consequences is an obligatory factual reference point, in determining purpose under Australia's GAAR, it is not even an allowable reference point in Canada. This is a problematic difference that needs to be cured legislatively.

The conclusion drawn as to dominant purpose cannot be "merely fanciful and not based on reason"[987] and the "actual subjective purpose of any relevant person is not a matter to which regard may be had in drawing the conclusion."[988] With respect to the latter point, it has been suggested that the eight factors listed in paragraph 177D(b) "effectively constructs a tunnel of factors" which the Commissioner

---

[984] See Australian Taxation Office Practice Statement Law Administration 2005/24, para. 108 (referring to Sackville J's decision in *Pridecraft Pty Ltd v. Commissioner of Taxation*, 2005 ATC 4001 (High Court), in which he held that a tax benefit of several million dollars, enjoyed by a taxpayer who had to part with only a few hundred thousand dollars, suggested that the dominant purpose for entering into the scheme was obtaining the tax benefit).

[985] (1997), 35 ATR 1164 at para. 122.

[986] *Canada Trustco Mortgage Co. v. R.*, [2005] 2 S.C.R. 601 (S.C.C.) at para. 59. Although we do not have the "dominant purpose" test in Canada which exists under the Australian GAAR, the absence of economic substance should still be relevant as an objective fact in the determination of "*bona fide* purpose" under Canada's GAAR.

[987] *Hart v. FCT*, 2002 ATC 4608 (FCA) at p. 4621.

[988] *FCT v. Peabody* (1993), 93 ATC 4104 (FCA) at p. 4113; see also: Julie Cassidy, "Are tax schemes legitimate commercial transactions? Commissioner of Taxation v Spotless Services Ltd and Commissioner of Taxation v Spotless Finance Pty Ltd", http.//epublications.bond.edu.au/hcourt/7 (1996), page 8 (arguing that it is "nonsensical" not to consider evidence of subjective motivations and that such evidence should be tested against objective facts)

may consider, excluding factors which could operate in the taxpayer's favour.[989] Nevertheless, the High Court has spoken to the appropriateness of the emphasis in section 177D on only objective factors in *Consolidated Press Holdings*: "One of the reasons for making section 177D turn upon the objective matters listed in the Section, it may be inferred, was to avoid the consequence that the operation of Part IVA depends upon the fiscal awareness of the taxpayer."[990]

The dominant purpose means "that purpose which [is] the ruling, prevailing or most influential purpose,"[991] according to the High Court's decision in *FCT v. Spotless*. The statute does not require that it is the taxpayer's purpose which must be ascertained, and the intention of persons connected to the scheme can be attributed to the taxpayer.[992] Controversy has arisen as to how the dominant purpose is to be identified, as some court decisions call for speculation about what other kinds of schemes the taxpayer might have entered into or carried out, rather than an inquiry into the purpose of the taxpayer in entering into the scheme. Because of divergences of opinion amongst the courts regarding this issue, there is said to be no settled jurisprudence as to how Part IVA applies.[993]

---

[989] Nicole Wilson-Rogers, "Coming out of the Dark?: The Uncertainties that Remain in Respect of Part IVA: How does Recent Tax Office Guidance Help?", (2006) 4(1) *eJournal of Tax Research* 25 (noting that subjective purpose, for example, cannot be considered).

[990] 2001 ATC 4343 (High Court) at para. 95.

[991] (1996), 186 C.L.R. 404 (Aust. High Court) at p. 416.

[992] See *FCT v. Consolidated Press Holdings Ltd*, [2001] HCA 32 at para. 95 (which held that attributing the purpose of a professional advisor to the taxpayer is in some instances appropriate); Cassidy, *supra* no. 939 at 26 (also noting that under the terms of section 177D it is not necessary for the taxpayer to have had the requisite purpose and that the purpose of advisors may be attributed to the taxpayer); Tony Pagone, "Part IVA – The voyage continues", vol. 10, no. 1 *The Tax Specialist* 37-45 (August 2006), 35 (commenting that it is a necessary consequence of an objective standard that Part IVA may apply even where those who entered into or carried out the scheme did not do so for the purpose of obtaining a tax benefit"); see also: Cashmere, *supra* no. 938 at 155 (commenting that it is open to doubt re whether purpose should be capable of being attributed to the taxpayer from anyone involved in the transaction).

[993] Cashmere, *supra* no. 938 at 144 (explaining this has occurred because some judges have maintained that in order to ascertain the taxpayer's purpose, an inquiry must be made to find out whether there was another way of carrying

However, there is certainty that the eight specified criteria, including economic substance, must be examined.

Cashmere's further criticism of Part IVA is that the inquiry which has to be made regarding purpose "is constrained by the eight reference criteria", which omit reference to commercial context and make no reference to the artificiality, blatancy or contrived nature of transactions, although these features were identified by the government as describing the type of transactions at which Part IVA was aimed.[994] Nevertheless, section 177D is said to be an embodiment of Lord Denning's predication test, in that it requires the purpose of obtaining a tax benefit, rather than commercial or family reasons, to be the dominant reason for entering into the scheme.[995]

As set out above, there has been a judicially imposed requirement that a scheme must be capable of standing on its own[996] and Part IVA has been interpreted to require that the requisite purpose must exist in relation to the scheme as a whole, as opposed to in reference to any sub-scheme:[997] "Part IVA does not provide that a scheme includes part of a scheme and it is possible, despite the very wide definition of scheme, to conceive of a set of circumstances which constitutes only part of a scheme and not a scheme in

---

out the transaction, i.e. there must be identification of an "alternate postulate" or "hypothetical counter-factual situation")

[994] *Ibid.* at 158 (noting that the artificiality, blatancy and the contrived nature of transactions were what Parliament was primarily concerned about when Part IVA was announced as a general anti-avoidance measure); compare: Cassidy, *supra* no. 963 at 298 (suggesting that in practice the limit of eight factors for the objective determination made under paragraph 177D (b) is not a limitation given their breadth)

[995] Cassidy, *supra* no. 974 at 437 (noting that this point-of-view has been corroborated by various Australian government officials); see also: Explanatory Memorandum, Income Tax Laws Amendment Bill (No. 2) 1981, p. 3 (stating that the enactment of Part IVA was intended to restore the state-of-the law to that which existed following *Newton v. FCT*)

[996] But see: Cassidy, *supra* no. 238 at 748 (suggesting however that the authority of the "capable of standing alone" test has lately become unclear)

[997] Explanatory Memorandum, Income Tax Laws Amendment Bill (No. 2) 1981, 27 (stating that purpose is to be tested "having regard to the scheme as a whole")

itself."[998] This is a significant limitation on the scope of the application of the GAAR in Australia.[999]

Case law has established that the purpose must exist at the time the scheme was entered into;[1000] however, there is also authority that in some cases it may be tested when the scheme is still being carried out.[1001] A related question is if a scheme later turns out to be profitable is that relevant.[1002]

Reconstruction provision

Section 177F was included in Part IVA to enable the Commissioner to determine what tax adjustments should be made when the GAAR applies.[1003] The provision was designed to alleviate the problem which had existed under section 260 in regard to the inability of the Commissioner to impose appropriate taxation once a transaction had been declared void.[1004] Under the new GAAR provision the Commissioner is permitted to construct and substitute an alternative counterfactual arrangement that would most likely have occurred in the absence of the scheme that gave rise to the disputed tax benefits. Professor Cooper thinks, based on his reading of recent case law, that this will be "the new battleground" for Part IVA disputes.[1005]

---

[998] *FCT v. Peabody* (1993), 93 ATC 4104 (FCA) at p. 4111; But see: Cassidy, *supra* no. 238 at 751 (suggesting this point has also become unclear lately)
[999] Cassidy, *supra* no. 963 at 279 (suggesting that the deeming provision in subsection 248(10) of the Canadian *Income Tax Act* which provides that a series of transactions or events includes any related transactions or events completed in contemplation of the series overcomes the difficult Australian scheme versus sub-scheme issue)
[1000] *FCT v. Consolidated Press Holdings Ltd (No 1)* (1999), 99 ATC 4945 (Full Federal Court) at p. 4971
[1001] *Vincent v. Commissioner of Taxation*, 2002 ATC 4742 (Aust. Fed. Ct.) at p. 4760
[1002] Wilson-Rogers, *supra* no. 989 (also arguing that "attempting to define tax avoidance is a futile task" with the consequence that Part IVA is unworkable on account of uncertainty).
[1003] Explanatory Memorandum, Income Tax Laws Amendment Bill (No. 2) 1981, page 16.
[1004] Cassidy, *supra* no. 939 at 5 (noting that section 260 did not permit any reconstruction by the Commissioner as it only rendered the arrangement void).
[1005] Cooper, *supra* no. 965.

Notice provision

Under section 177F, the Commissioner may give notice of his determination to parties to the arrangement and need not issue a notice to the person who obtains the tax benefit.[1006]

Provision of last resort

According to the government's Explanatory Memorandum, released in 1981 with the new GAAR measures, the Part IVA provisions are those of last resort.[1007] That is to say that all of the other provisions of the *Income Tax Assessment Act 1936* are to be applied, before the GAAR is sought to be applied; and if, for example, a specific anti-avoidance provision takes away a tax advantage, the GAAR does not have application.[1008] Subsections 177B(3) and (4) reflect this understanding.[1009] Recently, the decision in *Futuris Corporation Ltd v. Federal Commissioner of Taxation* has indicated

---

[1006] Cassidy, *supra* no. 939 at footnote 22 (also noting proposed amendments permitting the Commissioner to issue a single determination that would apply to every person participating in the scheme); subsection 177F(2C) of the *Income Tax Act Assessment Act 1936* provides that notice of a determination must be given to the taxpayer; subsection 177F(2E) provides that failure to do so does not affect the validity of the determination)

[1007] See Explanatory Memorandum, Income Tax Laws Amendment Bill (No. 2) 1981, page 9, in reference to subsection 177B(3); see also: Thompson, *supra* no. 959 at 187 (arguing that the definition of "tax benefit" means Part IVA is a provision of last resort because a tax benefit can only exist if, relative to a tax benefit pertaining to a deduction, the deduction would, but for the operation of Part IVA, otherwise be allowable – *Vincent v. Commissioner of Taxation*, 2002 ATC 4742 (Aust. Fed. Ct.))

[1008] Explanatory Memorandum, Income Tax Laws Amendment Bill (No. 2) 1981, page 5; see also: Kendall, *supra* no. 241 (arguing that there must be a "linear progression" in considering the applicability of Part IVA, a provision of last resort. This involves first determining whether the transaction is a sham; and, if not, whether it is effective vis-à-vis the substantive tax legislation. If so, specific anti-avoidance rules must be considered next. If no specific anti-avoidance rule applies to render the arrangement ineffective, the last step is to consider whether Part IVA applies)

[1009] Wilson-Rogers, *supra* no. 989 (arguing that it is strange that Part IVA can still apply where Parliament has addressed its mind to a particular activity with specific anti-avoidance provisions that do not preclude the particular transaction)

that a tax benefit which was triggered by the operation of a specific anti-avoidance rule could be set aside under Part IVA.[1010] According to Professor Cooper, this suggests that there is an even stronger case that Part IVA must apply when a specific anti-avoidance rule that might have applied has not actually been triggered.[1011]

What has been accomplished

Part IVA has recently been described by Professor Evans as "a weapon of mass destruction that is not only perceived to be a potent threat, but which actually is powerful when used."[1012] He also notes, however, that after many years there is still uncertainty regarding the application of Part IVA, and that there are a large number of unresolved issues regarding Part IVA, which are at least partly owing to divergences between the views of the Federal Courts and the High Court.[1013]

Part IVA has been said to be superior to section 260, with the caveat that it has not put an end to the "smell test which, historically, has probably been a better predictor of outcomes than any quantity of logic."[1014] It has also been suggested, however, that the

---

[1010] [2010] FCA 935 (Aust. Fed. Ct.)
[1011] Cooper, *supra* no. 964 at 566 (submitting that specific and general anti-avoidance rules operate "cumulatively and sequentially")
[1012] Chris Evans, "The Battle Continues: Recent Australian Experience with Statutory Avoidance an Disclosure Rules", *Beyond Boundaries–Developing Approaches to Tax Avoidance and Tax Risk Management*, Oxford University Centre for Business Taxation (Judith Freedman ed. 2008), c. 5, p. 39 (noting High Court victories for the Commissioner in several court cases under Part IVA)
[1013] *Ibid.* at 41; see also: Cassidy, *supra* no. 238 at 779 (suggesting that unresolved questions include whether the capable of standing alone test still needs to be satisfied and whether Part IVA can be applied to a sub-scheme, leading to a great level of uncertainty); Pagone, *supra* no. 180 at 780 (suggesting the scope of the eight specified criteria is open to debate as is what it is about the eight criteria that provide indicia as to the dominant purpose)
[1014] Michael D'Ascenzo, Second Commissioner, Australian Tax Office at the Taxation Institute of Australia, 37th West Australia State Convention, Perth 2 May 2003, "Part IVA – The Steward's Inquiry – A Fair Tax System"; see also: Donovan, *supra* no. 977 at 255 (suggesting that in applying Part IVA the courts may be using a "smell test")

Commissioner has not restricted the application of Part IVA to transactions which are "artificial, blatant or contrived" contrary to the government's announced intention, and also that the High Court has not provided any clear principles to use in distinguishing between appropriate and inappropriate transactions.[1015]

The High Court has nevertheless accepted in *FCT v. Spotless Services Ltd.* that the mere existence of a "rational commercial decision" relative to entering into a transaction is not by itself determinative of the question of whether a person entered into or carried out a scheme for the dominant purpose of obtaining a tax benefit.[1016] This overcame a very significant pre-1981 weakness of the GAAR in section 260, as previously the courts had held that the existence of a commercial rationale for entering into or carrying out a transaction prevented its application.

Professor Burgess thinks that "the GAAR is poorly suited for complicated commercial transactions in which tax minimization is one of several purposes."[1017] The Administrative Appeals Tribunal complained in *Case V160* that section 260 has been replaced with a provision with greater complexity, which gives rise to greater problems than those which were confronting its predecessor.[1018] Professor Cassidy also thinks that "the complexity of Part IVA is such that it cannot be interpreted without difficulty."[1019] More pessimistically, Professor Dabner takes the position that given the level of

---

[1015] Cashmere, *supra* no. 938 at 135 (arguing Part IVA has been wrongly utilized by the Commissioner to attack "transactions that have been commonplace in the commercial world for decades" in spite of the government's assurances in its 1981 Explanatory Memorandum; but, accepting that Part IVA has been "a significant force in controlling tax avoidance")

[1016] (1996), 186 C.L.R. 404 (Aust. High Court); (1996), 96 ATC 5201

[1017] Philip Burgess, "2010 Year in Review (Australia)", *Tax Notes International* 900-901 (Dec. 20, 2010), 901

[1018] (1988), 88 ATC 1058

[1019] Cassidy, *supra* no. 974 at 428 (arguing that the decision of the Federal Court in *Peabody* was a significant victory for taxpayers as it provided reassurance that Part IVA does not catch legitimate business and family arrangements)

uncertainty that Part IVA generates, it is "clearly inadequate."[1020] Orow also argues that Part IVA does not provide a reasonably coherent standard and that its establishment effectively undermines fundamental taxation principles and even the rule of law.[1021] Justice Sackville thinks, however, that the enactment of Part IVA became necessary because of the literalist approach to interpreting tax legislation adopted by the High Court under Barwick.[1022]

In any event, there is not universal despair over the enactment of Part IVA, and Xynas thinks "[t]he system has been relatively successful in achieving clearer distinctions between acceptable tax planning [and] illegitimate tax avoidance" since the tax avoidance heydays in the 1970's.[1023]

In regard to the level of certainty that is now extant under the Australian GAAR, it is certainly notable that the 2011 New Zealand private sector report to government "Improving the Operation of

---

[1020] Dabner, *supra* no. 198 at 40 (arguing that the legalistic approach in interpreting tax statutes should be replaced with a policy orientated approach based on a legislative purposive rule, and several other measures)

[1021] Nabil F Orow, "The Future of Australia's General Anti-Avoidance Provision", vol. 1 *New Zealand Journal of Taxation Law and Policy* 225-246 (June 1995), 226 (arguing "the combined effect of the penalty provisions and the uncertainty surrounding the operation of Part IVA, is such that it makes it a gamble for taxpayers to legitimately seek to plan or organize their affairs in the most tax effective manner"); Orow, *supra* no. 968 (also arguing that an enforced purposive approach to statutory interpretation would render all GAAR provisions like Australia's Part IVA redundant)

[1022] Justice Ronald Sackville, "Avoiding Tax Avoidance: The Primacy of Part IVA", Victorian/Tasmanian State Convention, Sept 9-11, 2004, page 15 (also suggesting that a contextual and purposive construction of tax legislation is to be preferred, for rule of law and certainty reasons, over heavy reliance on a general anti avoidance provision)

[1023] Xynas, *supra* no. 935 at 37 (suggesting that there is more respect for the tax system since the ATO shifted from a "predominantly command-and-control regulatory framework" to a "responsive regulation and meta risk management" framework in its efforts to combat aggressive tax planning. "Command and control" involved the traditional audit system with the implementation of penalties and occasional inducements whereas "responsive regulation" involves an enforcement pyramid under which little enforcement is required at the base. "Meta risk management" involves monitoring the tax community and risk management)

New Zealand's Tax Avoidance Laws"[1024] commented that "[a]n outsider looking at the Australian provision would ... suggest that the eight indicia must be helpful guidance to all the concerned parties in a transaction which may potentially be subject to the GAAR."[1025]

Conclusion

Australia's GAAR, and the ATO, place economic substance front and centre amongst the factual considerations to examine in determining whether there has been unacceptable aggressive tax planning. While there are a number of interpretative difficulties which have emerged that are associated with applying Part IVA, none of the difficulties relate to its reliance upon economic substance as an objective reference point in determining purpose. Given the ongoing steady performance of economic substance as an objective criterion in the determination of purpose under Australia's GAAR, there is no reason to think that it would not serve as suitably for Canada's GAAR, in respect of which our Supreme Court has mistakenly ruled that a lack of substance "has no meaning in isolation from the proper interpretation of specific provisions of the *Income Tax Act*."[1026] Canada should amend its GAAR to overcome this patent shortcoming.

NEW ZEALAND

The courts in New Zealand have concluded, without requiring any legislative nudging, that economic substance is an essential

---

[1024] Report to the New Zealand Government prepared by representatives of New Zealand's three leading industry bodies representing taxpayers and tax advisors: the Taxation Committee of the New Zealand Law Society, the Corporate Taxpayers Group, and the Taxation Committee of the New Zealand Institute of Chartered Accountants: see http://email.business.auckland.ac.nz/2011/1121-tax-avoidance/

[1025] *Ibid*, para. 1.6

[1026] *Canada Trustco Mortgage Co. v. R.*, [2005] 2 S.C.R. 601 (S.C.C.) at para. 59

reference point in detecting unacceptable tax avoidance.[1027] Indeed, despite the absence of legislative direction in New Zealand as to any necessity for the examination of economic substance in tax avoidance cases, there has been a veritable torrent of jurisprudence and academic commentary that endorses such an examination.[1028]

[1027] This is so, although a report made to the New Zealand Government in 1992 by the Valabh Committee on tax avoidance had recommended that the GAAR be amended to specify a set of objective criteria for use in determining a taxpayer's objectives in relation to an arrangement: see Valabh Committee, Key Reforms to the Scheme of Tax Legislation, (Auckland, October 1991), and Valabh Committee, Final Report of the Consultative Committee on the Taxation of Income from Capital, (Wellington, October 1992). Note, however, that the Committee of Experts on Tax Compliance did not favour adopting the Valabh Committee recommendations on the GAAR (see Tax Compliance: Report to the Treasurer and Minster of Revenue by a Committee of Experts on Tax Compliance, (Wellington, December 1998), Part II: Robustness Against Avoidance and Evasion, Ch 6: Tax Mitigation, Avoidance and Evasion, p 129). The Committee of Experts considered that adopting the Valabh Committee recommendations would make the GAAR less effective (p 129); "Supreme Court lays down tax avoidance law for the first time", no. 1 *New Zealand Tax Planning Reports* 1-10 (CCH: 2009), 10 (noting that the Supreme Court's decisions have put taxpayers on notice that they can only expect to keep the resulting tax benefit when they have actually borne the economic cost); see also: Eugen Trombitas, "Trinity Exposed: Does the Emperor Really Have No Clothes or is He Wearing an Unusual Silver Rugby Jersey? – The Latest News from the GAAR Front", 13 *New Zealand Journal of Taxation Law and Policy* 583 (December 2007), 605 (arguing that adopting the Valabh Committee recommendation re specifying objective criteria would be a route to a more certain GAAR than whether the courts "like" an arrangement); Eugen Trombitas, "The Conceptual Approach to Tax Avoidance in the 21st Century: When the Statute Gives But the GAAR Can Take Away", 15 *New Zealand Journal of Taxation Law and Policy* 352 (December 2009), 389 (arguing that to remove uncertainty GAAR should be amended to specify objective criteria or signposts as to when it applies)

[1028] John Prebble, "Tax Avoidance, International Tax Arbitrage, and New Zealand as Haven for Foreign Capital and Income", vol. 16 *Revue Juridique Polynesienne* 169-182 (2010), 170 (suggesting that GAARS like section BG 1 "operate by going behind the legal form of a transaction and taxing it according to its economic substance"); Michael Littlewood, "*Ben Nevis Forestry Ventures Ltd v CIR; Glenharrow Ltd v CIR*: New Zealand's Supreme Court and tax avoidance", vol. 2 *British Tax Rev*iew 169-180 (2009), 178 (arguing that the Supreme Court's reliance on economic reality involves sound reasoning); Craig Elliffe, "Tax Avoidance and the Supreme Court – Waiting for Godot?", vol. 14, no. 3 *New Zealand Business Law Quarterly* 128-140 (September

In 1986, the Privy Council emphasized the importance of economic substance in tax avoidance cases in *Challenge Corporation Ltd. v. Commissioner of Inland Revenue*.[1029] In that case, Lord Templeman stated, in describing unacceptable tax avoidance, as previously set out in Part I, that "[i]ncome tax is avoided and a tax advantage is derived from an arrangement when the taxpayer reduces his liability to tax without involving him in the loss or expenditure which entitles him to that reduction. The taxpayer engaged in tax avoidance does not reduce his income or suffer a loss or incur an expenditure but nevertheless obtains a reduction in his liability to tax as if he had."[1030]

This analysis by Lord Templeman is said to have "stood the test of time" in New Zealand.[1031] Lord Nolan later made the same point

---

2008) (suggesting that one of the key questions in considering the GAAR in relation to specific tax rules is whether real economic consequences have been incurred); Trombitas, *supra* no. 1027 at 593 (arguing that it is a hallmark of tax avoidance that the taxpayer does not suffer the economic consequences that Parliament intended be suffered); Adrian J. Sawyer, "Blurring the distinction between avoidance and evasion – the abusive tax position", vol. 5 *British Tax Review* 483-504 (1996), 486 (suggesting that issues as to the economic realities and the artificiality of arrangements play significant roles in distinguishing between tax mitigation and unacceptable tax avoidance); John Tiley, "Tax Avoidance Jurisprudence as normal law", vol. 4 *British Tax Review* 304-331 (2004), section 10.1 (describing Lord Templeman's distinction between tax mitigation and tax avoidance as "superficially attractive" but noting that the test as to whether a party genuinely suffered the economic consequences is "a principle in its own right")

[1029] *Inland Revenue Commissioner v. Challenge Corp.*, [1987] A.C. 155 (N.Z. P.C.) at pp. 167-168; [1986] 2 NZLR 513 (P.C.); see also: *Ensign Tankers (Leasing Ltd) v Stokes*, [1992] 1 A.C. 655, per Lord Goff, at p. 681C

[1030] *Inland Revenue Commissioner v. Challenge Corp.*, [1986] 2 NZLR 513 (P.C.) at p. 561; see also: David Dunbar, "Judicial Techniques for Controlling the New Zealand General Anti-Avoidance Rule: The Scheme and Purpose Approach, from Challenge Corporation to Peterson", 12 *New Zealand Journal of Taxation Law and Policy* 324 (December 2006), 354, 380 (noting that Lord Templeman's test focused on the "actual financial consequences", i.e. under his analysis the taxpayer "did not truly bear the losses" because it "had nothing at risk and spent nothing")

[1031] Michael Lennard, "Two Tribes and an Elephant Called Ben Nevis", *Taxation Today* (September 2009) (suggesting that the New Zealand Supreme Court decision in *Ben Nevis* reinforces the test for objectionable tax avoidance from

in his judgment in *Inland Revenue Commissioners v. Willoughby*: "The hallmark of tax avoidance is that the taxpayer reduces his liability to tax without incurring the economic consequences that Parliament intended to be suffered by any taxpayer qualifying for such reduction in his tax liability."[1032]

According to Professor Elliffe and Jessica Cameron, the first two decisions concerning New Zealand's general anti-avoidance rules from the Supreme Court of New Zealand, in *Ben Nevis Forestry Ventures Ltd. & Ors v. Commissioner of Inland Revenue*; *Accent Management Ltd. & Ors v. Commissioner*[1033] (*Ben Nevis*) and *Glenharrow Holdings Ltd. v. Commissioner of Inland Revenue*[1034] (*Glenharrow*), both illustrate the point that when applying the GAAR, the courts in New Zealand find it necessary to "look through the legal form of the arrangements to the economic substance of the taxpayers arrangements. There is more and more emphasis by the court being placed on this factor. ... [W]hile the emphasis on the economic substance of the transaction in recent decision[s] is not new, the increasing importance placed on it seems to be indicative of a trend in judicial attitude toward tax avoidance. The judiciary appears to be less tolerant of diverging economic and legal effects of transactions and more likely to 'call a spade a spade'."[1035]

---

the Privy Council's decision in the *Challenge Corporation* case concerning whether a cost has been truly incurred). Note also that appeals from New Zealand to the Privy Council were eliminated by the *Supreme Court Act 2003*.

[1032] (1997), 70 TC 57 (H.L.) at p. 116

[1033] (2009), 24 NZTC 23, 188 (S.C.); see also: Mark Keating, "Problems Flowing from the Nil Depreciation of Buildings", 16 *New Zealand Journal of Taxation Law and Policy* 307 (Sept 2010), 301 (noting *Ben Nevis* involved attempts to immediately deduct and depreciate amounts that would not become payable until the future, if at all); Prebble, *supra* no. 1028 at172 (describing *Ben Nevis* as essentially a Son-of-Boss arrangement, under which taxpayers incur heavy obligations which in practical terms do not really exist)

[1034] (2009), 24 NZTC 23, 236 (S.C.)

[1035] Elliffe and Cameron, *supra* no. 22 at 446, 455 (arguing that the "judicial sea change" in New Zealand is that the GAAR is now to be given equal weight with technical rules and purposively interpreted with an additional Parliamentary contemplation test. Also commenting that the *Ben Nevis* scheme was "an especially egregious arrangement" which featured "a large disparity

The substantial importance attached to economic substance under the New Zealand GAAR has been emphasized again recently by the Supreme Court in its decision in *Penny and Hooper v. Commissioner of Inland Revenue*,[1036] where the Court adapted Lord Templeman's statement in the *Challenge Corporation* case,[1037] in holding that impermissible tax avoidance had occurred in a tax reduction scenario, where "the taxpayers suffered no actual loss of income but obtained a reduction in liability to tax as if they had."[1038]

The New Zealand courts are thus light years away from where Canadian courts presently are in regard to recognition of the essential role that economic substance plays in tax avoidance cases. Moreover, this has occurred by virtue of the courts in New Zealand doing their own analysis, to arrive at an understanding as to what factors are indicative of unacceptable tax avoidance.[1039] As the courts in Canada have not yet undertaken such an analysis, legislative nudging is required to bring us apace with New Zealand.

---

between the magnitude of the tax advantages claimed as compared to the economic burden borne"); see also: Craig Elliffe and John Prebble, "General Anti-Avoidance Rules and Double Tax Agreements: A New Zealand Perspective", vol. 19 no. 1 *Revenue Law Journal* 1-23 (2009), 4 (noting that the Supreme Court denied deductions which were in accordance with "the black letter law in each case" on the basis that the taxpayers had not truly suffered the economic burden required to warrant the tax benefits).

[1036] *Penny and Hooper v. Commissioner of Inland Revenue*, [2011] NZSC 95.

[1037] *Challenge Corporation Ltd v. Commissioner of Inland Revenue*, [1986] 2 NZLR 555 (P.C.) at p. 561.

[1038] *Penny and Hooper v. Commissioner of Inland Revenue*, [2011] NZSC 95 at para. 47.

[1039] In addition, although the New Zealand general anti-avoidance rule contains no statutory element which requires it to be applied only to arrangements that defeat, frustrate or undermine the policy behind the behind the legislative provisions relied upon by the taxpayer, the New Zealand courts have developed interpretative techniques to "read it down" – see Dunbar, *supra* no. 1030 at 345, 353-354 (noting a scheme and purpose approach was taken to s BG 1 by Richardson J in the Court of Appeal in the *Challenge case*, which the Privy Council did not overrule in its decision).

Historical GAAR

New Zealand's first general anti avoidance provision, said to be "the world's oldest GAAR",[1040] was enacted as part of the *Land Tax Act 1878*, to ensure that land tax would be borne by the owner of the lands and its burden not shifted to others, such as tenants.[1041] Subsequently, income taxation was introduced in New Zealand and section 40 of the *Land and Income Tax Assessment Act 1891* was a general anti-avoidance provision in that Act, relating to land and income tax. Section 40 was succeeded by section 82 of the *Land and Income Tax Assessment Act 1900*, which provided that a contract, agreement or arrangement made or entered into was absolutely void, insofar as it had the purpose or effect of in any way directly or indirectly altering the incidence of any tax, or relieving any person from liability to pay any tax or make any return, or defeating, evading or avoiding any duty or liability imposed on any person by the Act, or preventing the operation of the Act in any respect.[1042]

Section 82 was in turn succeeded by section 103 of the *Land and Income Tax Assessment Act of 1908*; and, then by section 162 of the *Land and Income Tax Act 1916*, except the reference to avoiding tax was omitted and it was provided that any affected arrangement was void as against the Commissioner for tax purposes.[1043] Section 162 was replaced by section 170 of the *Land and Income Tax Act 1923*; and, section 170 was replaced by section 108 of the *Land and Income*

[1040] Prebble and Prebble, *supra* no. 102 at 703 (suggesting that although the New Zealand GAAR has been amended many times "it retains its original thrust and constitutes a reasonably typical example of a GAAR." Also arguing that tax avoidance and tax evasion are not separable morally and that tax avoidance cannot be morally justified or defended in cases that are "clear")

[1041] *Land Tax Act 1878* (NZ), section 62; see also: Littlewood, *supra* no. 98 at footnote 13 (noting section 62 seemed to be directed to preventing landlords from passing on the tax burden to their tenants, referencing *Mangin v. CIR*, [1971] NZLR 591 (P.C.) at p. 610 per the dissenting judgment of Lord Wilberforce)

[1042] Dunbar, *supra* no. 1030 at 325 (noting that section 82 is the origin of and contains the same elements as present section BG 1. The occurrences of the rule in the *Land and Income Tax Act 1908*, *Income Tax Act 1917*, section 170 *Land and Income Tax Act 1923* and section 108 *Land and Income Tax Act 1954* were also all based on section 82)

[1043] *Ibid.* at 327-328

Tax Act 1954,[1044] which omitted reference to land tax. The section was then substantially amended in 1974, by expanding the definition of "arrangement"; providing that tax avoidance could be either the purpose or effect or one of the purposes or effects of the arrangement so long as it was more than merely incidental;[1045] providing that the section could apply to persons "whether or not a party thereto"; giving the Commissioner power to adjust income in a manner considered appropriate to counteract the tax advantage; and, changing the definition of tax avoidance to reintroduce "avoiding" tax and introduce the concept of "reducing" and "postponing" tax.[1046]

Section 108 was replaced by section 99 of the *Income Tax Act 1976*;[1047] and, section 99 was replaced by section BB9 of the *Income Tax Act 1994*,[1048] which subsequently became section BG1 of the *Income Tax Act 2004*. Finally, this section became section BG1 of the present *Income Tax Act 2007*, without any further changes in its wording.[1049] Professor Dabner suggests that the provisions in

---

[1044] This provision was described as "notoriously difficult" by McCarthy P. in *Commissioner of Inland Revenue v. Gerard*, [1974] 2 NZLR 279 at p. 280.

[1045] Dunbar, *supra* no. 1030 at 328 (explaining that this change was made to preclude Lord Denning's predication test, pronounced in the *Newton* case, from being an automatic defence, by providing that tax avoidance can exist whenever the tax advantages are more than an incidental effect, although they are business or family related)

[1046] Section 9 *Land and Income Tax Amendment Act (No 2) 1974*; see also: James Coleman, "Tax Avoidance Law in New Zealand", CCH New Zealand Limited (August 2009), c. 2, pp. 16-17; Littlewood, *supra* no. 98 at 197 (noting that section 99 reflected amendments regarding problems that had plagued earlier versions of the general anti-avoidance rule, including a reconstruction provision that overcame the earlier "annihilation" problem and the power to adjust the incomes of anyone affected)

[1047] J. G. Bassett, "Estate plans and arrangements to avoid income tax", 9 *Victoria U. Wellington Law Review* 217-253(1977-1978), 217 (describing section 99 of the *Income Tax Act 1996* as being "somewhat like the sword of Damocles" in potentially denying efficacy to every arrangement with the purpose or effect of avoiding taxes)

[1048] *Ben Nevis Forestry Ventures Ltd v. Commissioner of Inland Revenue*, [2008] NZSC 115 at fn. 31

[1049] Coleman, *supra* no. 1046, c. 2, at 24 (commenting that there were no meaningful changes to key parts of the general anti-avoidance provisions after section 99 of the *Income Tax Act 1976* in the re-enactments in the *Income*

the New Zealand GAAR draw heavily from the former Australian GAAR in section 260 of the *Income Tax Assessment Act 1936*,[1050] which Australian courts emasculated.[1051]

Section BG 1 – Essential Elements

According to the Supreme Court, the policy underlying section BG 1 is to negate any structuring of a taxpayer's affairs, whether or not done as a matter of ordinary business or family dealings, unless any tax advantage is just an incidental feature.[1052] The principal elements of section BG 1 are that a tax avoidance arrangement is one that has more than a merely incidental purpose or effect of tax avoidance; tax avoidance arrangements are void against the Commissioner for income tax purposes; and, the Commissioner has the power to reconstruct a tax avoidance arrangement so as to counteract the tax advantage obtained from or under the arrangement.[1053]

It is also noteworthy that Inland Revenue released a document in September 2004 outlining its approach, involving a six step process, to the application of section BG 1. The six steps are as follows: (1) determine if there is a tax avoidance arrangement and if so, its scope; (2) does the arrangement involve "tax avoidance" as defined in the *Income Tax Act*; (3) is there a purpose or effect of tax avoidance; (4) determine if any purpose or effect is more than merely incidental; (5) does the arrangement frustrate Parliament's intention for the

---

Tax Act 1994, 2004 and 2007); Adrian Sawyer, "Surgeons' Practices and Tax Avoidance: A Mutually Exclusive Relationship?", 15 *New Zealand Journal of Taxation Law and Policy* 97 (June 2009), 97 (stating that the provisions is section BG 1 have essentially remained the same throughout its occurrences in the ITA 1994, ITA 2004 and ITA 2007).

[1050] Dabner, *supra* no. 198 at 40-41 (suggesting that although the New Zealand GAAR is broadly worded the conservative approach to its application by Inland Revenue has helped it avoid the fate of Australia's section 260)

[1051] See the discussion of Australia's GAAR in this chapter.

[1052] *Penny and Hooper v. Commissioner of Inland Revenue*, [2011] NZSC 95 at para. 47.

[1053] "Improving the operation of the anti-avoidance provisions in the income tax law", Treasury Department Discussion Paper, Australian Government (Nov. 18, 2010), p. 38.

particular provision, regime or the *Income Tax Act* as a whole; and (6) consider the adjustment to the tax position under section BG 1.[1054]

Arrangement

"Arrangement" is defined in section YA 1 as "any contract, agreement, plan, or understanding, whether enforceable or unenforceable, including all steps and transactions by which it is carried into effect."[1055] Tax avoidance can be found in an individual step in a wider arrangement and that step can make the wider arrangement a tax avoidance arrangement.[1056]

Tax avoidance

New Zealand utilizes a comprehensive inclusive definition of the term "tax avoidance" rather than the Australian list-based definition of the term "tax benefit," to describe what its GAAR seeks to redress.[1057] Section YA 1 provides that:

tax avoidance includes–

(a) directly or indirectly altering the incidence of any income tax;

[1054] NZIRD: Public Rulings Unit Adjudication and Rulings, "BG 1 and BG1 of the *Income Tax Act 2004*: Exposure Draft for External Consultation Reference INA 0009", www.taxpolicy.ird.got.nz; see also: "Improving the Operation of New Zealand's Tax Avoidance Laws", the Taxation Committee of the New Zealand Law Society, the Corporate Taxpayers Group and the Taxation Committee of the New Zealand Institute of Chartered Accountants (2011) http://email.business.auckland.ac.nz/2011/1121-tax-avoidance/, para. 2.34 (stating that the draft has still not been finalized after 6 ½ years); Adrian J. Sawyer, "Tax Avoidance in New Zealand and Further Uncertainty for Business", Tax Analysts, Doc. 2010-13053 (indicating Inland Revenue hasn't released its guidance re section BG 1).

[1055] Section YA 1.

[1056] *Penny and Hooper v. Commissioner of Inland Revenue*, [2011] NZSC 95 at para. 34.

[1057] "Improving the operation of the anti-avoidance provisions in the income tax law", Treasury Department Discussion Paper, Australian Government (Nov. 18, 2010), page 7.

(b) directly or indirectly relieving a person from liability to pay income tax or from a potential or prospective liability to future income tax;

(c) directly or indirectly avoiding, postponing, or reducing any liability to income tax or any potential or prospective liability to future income tax.

This provision has been heavily criticized, because its literal application would make it applicable to well-nigh all transactions.[1058] In this regard, the Privy Council held in *Mangin v. Inland Revenue Commissioner* that, because of the absurdities to which a literal application of the section would lead, "judges have been compelled to search for an interpretation which would make the section both workable and just."[1059] In light of this, New Zealand courts accepted Lord Denning's predication test, from the Privy Council decision in *Newton (Lauri Joseph) v. Commissioner of Taxation of Australia*,[1060] in reference to the general anti-avoidance provision in section 108 of the *Land and Income Tax Act 1954*; however, the substantial amendments made to the section in 1974 put this position in doubt.[1061]

In any event, in *Ben Nevis* the Supreme Court has set out a list of factors to be considered in determining whether a tax avoidance arrangement exists.[1062] These factors include the manner in which the arrangement is carried out; the role of relevant parties and any

---

[1058] Michael Littlewood, "Tax Avoidance, the Rule of Law and the New Zealand Supreme Court", *New Zealand Law Review* 35-68 (2011), 41 (arguing that the definition is "worse than useless, because it is not merely nonsense, but misleading ... as nearly all transactions alter the potential incidence of tax."); compare: Freedman, *supra* no. 21, at 352 and footnote 105 (citing the New Zealand GAAR as an example of the usual combination of purpose tests and concepts of tax avoidance or tax benefit that are found in statutory anti-avoidance provisions).

[1059] [1971] A.C. 739 (P.C.) at p. 749.

[1060] [1958] 2 All E.R. 759 (England P.C.).

[1061] Bassett, *supra* no. 1047 at 220 (noting that the amendment to section 108 bringing ordinary family or business dealings potentially within the purview of the section places the applicability of Lord Denning's predication test in doubt)

[1062] Trombitas, *supra* no. 1027 at 386 (noting that the factors listed by the New Zealand Supreme Court are similar to those specified in Part IVA of the Australian GAAR provision, and suggesting that the factors "have been read into the New Zealand legislation as part of the judicial interpretation process").

relationship they may have with the taxpayer; the economic and commercial effect of documents and transactions; the duration of the arrangement; and, the nature and extent of the financial consequences that it will have for the taxpayer. The Court has also explained that the significance of these individual factors will depend upon the particular facts of a case, and that it will often be a combination of the various elements in the arrangement that will be significant. Furthermore, and importantly:

> In considering these matters, the courts are not limited to purely legal considerations. They should also consider the use made of the specific provision in the light of the commercial reality and the economic effect of that use. The ultimate question is whether the impugned arrangement, viewed in a commercially and economically realistic way, makes use of the specific provision in a manner that is consistent with Parliament's purpose. If that is so, the arrangement will not, by reason of that use, be a tax avoidance arrangement. If the use of the specific provision is beyond Parliamentary contemplation, its use in that way will result in the arrangement being a tax avoidance arrangement.[1063]

This position that the use made of specific provisions should be considered, "in light of the commercial reality and the economic effect of that use", contrasts sharply with the position of the Supreme Court of Canada, which has held that "economic substance ... has little meaning in isolation from the proper interpretation of specific provisions of the [Income Tax] Act."[1064] The New Zealand approach has the merit of recognizing that economic substance is an independent factual consideration, which sheds essential light on whether there is abusive tax avoidance.

Tax avoidance arrangement

Section YA 1 of the *Income Tax Act 2007* defines a "tax avoidance arrangement" as an arrangement, that either directly or indirectly has tax avoidance (a) "as its purpose or effect" or (b) "as one its purposes or effects, whether or not any other purpose or effect is referable to ordinary business or family dealings, if the tax avoidance

---

[1063] [2008] NZSC 115 at pp. 108-109.
[1064] *Canada Trustco Mortgage Co. v. R.*, [2005] 5 C.T.C. 215 (S.C.C.) at para. 76.

purpose or effect is not merely incidental."[1065] The Supreme Court held in *Ben Nevis* that the words "purpose or effect" in section YA 1 are to be interpreted objectively.[1066] Importantly, the Court also held that there is no restriction on the matters that may be taken into account in determining whether a tax avoidance arrangement exists:

> The general anti-avoidance provision does not confine the Court as to the matters which may be taken into account when considering whether a tax avoidance arrangement exists. Hence the Commissioner and the courts may address a number of relevant factors, the significance of which will depend on the particular facts. The manner in which the arrangement is carried out will often be an important consideration. So will the role of all relevant parties and any relationship they may have with the taxpayer. The economic and commercial effect of documents and transactions may also be significant. Other features that may be relevant include the duration of the arrangement and the nature and extent of the financial consequences that it will have for the taxpayer. As indicated, it will often be the combination of various elements in the arrangement which is significant. A classic indicator is the structuring of an arrangement so that the taxpayer gains the benefit of the specific provision in an artificial or contrived way. It is not within Parliament's purpose for specific provisions to be used in that manner.[1067]

The Supreme Court's finding in *Ben Nevis* was that the insurance premium sought to be deducted had not been paid "in any real sense" and that "[t]he purported payment did not give rise to any economic consequences on either side", so it was not deductible.[1068] Similarly, in the *Glenharrow* case, the Supreme Court held that an exchange of cheques had been "inserted into a 'pay as you go' transaction so as to produce an artificial effect with consequent tax advantage, contrary to all economic reality." The GST refund

---

[1065] The reference to not excluding "ordinary business or family dealings" from the scope of "tax avoidance arrangement" came as the result of a legislative amendment aimed at reversing the Privy Council's decision in *Mangin v. Inland Revenue Commissioner*, [1971] A.C. 739 (P.C.) at p. 749 which stated "judges have been compelled to search for an interpretation which would make the section both workable and just."
[1066] [2008] NZSC 115 at p. 107
[1067] (2009), 24 NZTC 23 at p. 188; [2008] NZSC 115, per Tipping, McGrath and Gault JJ, at pp. 108-109
[1068] [2008] NZSC 115 at p. 147

claimed was held "totally disproportionate to the economic burden undertaken by Glenharrow" and this "was a distortion which very plainly defeated the intent and application of the Act."[1069] If the Supreme Court of Canada had taken this manner of approach in *Canada Trustco*, the capital cost allowance deductions claimed in that case would have been denied, as the transactions did not involve real economic consequences.[1070]

The recent decision of the Supreme Court in *Penny and Hooper v. CIR*[1071] reinforces the Court's emphasis on the substantial importance of economic substance in tax avoidance cases. In the High Court, Mackenzie J had allowed the taxpayers' appeals on the basis that the arrangements entered into by the taxpayers did not have either the purpose or effect of tax avoidance; or, alternatively, if tax avoidance was a purpose, that purpose was incidental to the main purpose, being the adoption of a corporate form to conduct orthopaedic practices.[1072]

While commentary from tax practitioners was very enthusiastic about the High Court's decision, Professor Sawyer very astutely observed that upholding the decision could be problematic, because of the judge's failure to consider whether the taxpayers had "suffered the economic cost of the arrangements."[1073] As noted above, the Supreme Court set aside the taxpayers' arrangements on the ba-

---

[1069] [2008] NZSC 116 at pp. 51-54

[1070] Dunbar, *supra* no. 1030 at 324 (noting Revenue Canada denied the deductions in *Canada Trustco* because "under the complex series of commercial transactions and cash flows, the taxpayer assumed little or no economic risk."); Arnold, *supra* no. 8 at 199 ("Apart from the fees and transaction costs, the financial and commercial positions of all of the parties to the transactions remained unchanged."); Cassidy, *supra* no. 963 at 302 (arguing that "the circularity of the arrangements and the absence of any real capital costs to the taxpayer should have indicated that this was a misuse of the CCA provisions and an abuse of the Act as a whole.")

[1071] [2011] NZSC 95

[1072] (2009), 24 NZTC 23 (H.C.) at p. 406

[1073] Sawyer, *supra* no. 1049 at 107 (canvassing the enthusiastic reactions of tax practitioners to the High Court's decision, while also noting that nothing should be considered certain in the area of tax litigation); see also: Elliffe and Keating, *supra* no. 22 at 391 (also noting that McKenzie J failed to

sis that they "suffered no actual loss of income but obtained a reduction in liability to tax as if they had."[1074]

Although the taxpayer's appeal from the disallowance of depreciation deductions was allowed by the Privy Council in *Peterson v. Commissioner of Inland Revenue*,[1075] Professor Littlewood points out that three of the five panel members shared the view that the correct test was whether the "economic burden" had been borne by the taxpayer, although they did not agree in the result.[1076] Professor Freedman has suggested that the *Peterson* case illustrates the difficulties the judiciary has when it is not given guidance about the relationship between the GAAR and the specific legislation in question,[1077] although recent developments in New Zealand do not bear this out.

---

consider whether the taxpayers had truly suffered the economic cost of the arrangement)

[1074] *Penny and Hooper v. Commissioner of Inland Revenue*, [2011] NZSC 95 at para. 47

[1075] [2005] UKPC 5; see also: Pickup, *supra* no. 846, c. 2, at 16 (describing the Privy Council's decision as "deeply unsatisfactory" and pointing out that the New Zealand Supreme Court was established as the final court of appeal after the decision); David Dunbar, "Judicial Techniques for Controlling the New Zealand General Anti-Avoidance Rule: A Case of Old Wine in New Bottles, from Challenge Corporation to Peterson", Working Paper no. 38, School of Accounting and Commercial Law 1-47 (2005)(explaining that the Privy Council's decision enabled the taxpayer to write off his investment and make a financial profit from a film which was "a commercial failure" and "a financial disaster." The tax advantage was derived by utilizing a circular self-cancelling limited recourse loan to finance a film purchase)

[1076] Littlewood, *supra* no. 98 at 201 (also arguing that general anti-avoidance rules work in Australasia and that they would be just as effective in the U.K., notwithstanding that "it seems reasonable to conclude that the idea of tax avoidance is simply not susceptible to coherent explication"); also see: Nicola Williams, "Privy Council Delivers Final Tax Avoidance Decision: Peterson v. CIR", vol. 11 *New Zealand Journal of Taxation Law and Policy* 283-291 (September 2005) (suggesting that the majority intimated the result would have been different if the case had been argued differently)

[1077] Judith Freedman, "Interpreting Tax Statutes: Tax Avoidance and the Intention of Parliament", vol. 123 *Law Quarterly Review* 53-90 (2007), 80 (arguing that the New Zealand GAAR is problematic as it "does not attempt to spell out what amounts to tax avoidance in the sense used by the legislation." The recent cases suggest otherwise); see also: Prebble, *supra* no. 1028 at 173

Attendance to examination of the economic substance of arrangements has also been a key feature of the judicial analysis by lower courts in tax avoidance cases. In *BNZ Investments Limited & ORS v. Commissioner of Inland Revenue*, the High Court set aside a foreign tax credit generator arrangement upon the basis that, viewed in a commercially and economically realistic way, "tax was not paid in the US, at least not in the amount of the FTC claimed by the BNZ or anything remotely approaching it."[1078] Similarly, Harrison J held in *Westpac Banking Corporation v. Commissioner of Inland Revenue*, following the Supreme Court's decision in *Ben Nevis*, that constraints of a legalistic focus, "to the exclusion of economic realism, have gone."[1079]

These foreign tax credit generator cases involved an estimated NZ $2.4 billion in tax and interest, plus possible penalties.[1080] The egregiousness of such schemes, which to date have succeeded in the Tax Court of Canada because of its focus on the legal meaning of "paid" and its inattention to the underlying economic substance of the transactions, becomes apparent when one considers that the taxpayers who utilize them can essentially choose to pay whatever (or no) taxation level they consider desirable, assuming that they can find accommodating foreign counterparties.[1081]

(noting that the promoters were convicted of fraud in the *Peterson* case and that the House of Lords held that essentially the same scheme failed in *Ensign Tankers (Leasing) Ltd v. Stokes (Inspector of Taxes)*, [1992] 1 A.C. 655 (HL), albeit not under a GAAR)

[1078] (2009), 24 NZTC 23 at p. 582 per Wild J at p. 486. I review this decision at length in the case studies in chapter IX, emphasizing the difference between the New Zealand High Court's examination of the economic substance of the transactions and the Canadian Tax Court's reliance upon legal form when dealing with essentially the same foreign tax credit generator transaction. Note, however, in the Canadian case the Crown did not argue that GAAR applied.

[1079] (2009), 24 NZTC 23,834 at p. 194

[1080] Prebble, *supra* no. 1028 at 171-172 (noting that the "bank conduit" cases were settled on December 23, 2009 on the basis that the banks paid 80 percent of total tax and interest, without penalties)

[1081] Prebble and Prebble, *supra* no. 102 at 743 (noting the tax avoidance schemes were so successful that banks could choose a tax rate as low as they liked); see also: Greenaway, *supra* no. 239 at 637, footnote 44 (noting that foreign

The onus of proof is on the taxpayer vis-à-vis establishing the purpose or effect of an impugned arrangement and the matter is to be determined objectively.[1082] In this regard, when a court finds that "no change" in the taxpayer's position has been brought about by the arrangement, the only possible explanation for the arrangement is the intention to reduce taxation, unless some sound business motivation is shown.[1083] This state-of-affairs in New Zealand differs from our situation in Canada, where an absence of change in a taxpayer's position has typically meant nothing in a tax avoidance context, given our courts' super-emphasis on the right to take steps to minimize taxes, regardless of economic substance.[1084]

Reconstruction provision

Subsection BG 1(2) provides that the Commissioner can "counteract a tax advantage that a person has obtained from or under a tax avoidance arrangement." Subsection GA 1(2) further provides that the Commissioner "may adjust the taxable income of a person affected by the arrangement in a way the Commissioner thinks appropriate, in order to counteract a tax advantage obtained by the person from or under the arrangement."[1085] Subsection GA 1(4) provides that the Commissioner may identify the hypothetical situation which, in the Commissioner's opinion, would have existed but for the tax avoidance arrangement, for the purpose of determining what taxes are payable. These provisions have been criticized on the basis that they go further than giving the Commissioner the power to counteract the

---

tax credit generators "can be scaled up to wipe out almost any amount of ... tax liability, assuming a willing foreign counterparty")

[1082] Bassett, *supra* no. 1047 at 240-242 (suggesting however that New Zealand courts do not attach much significance to the statutory placement of the onus of proof; and, noting that it is not enough for a taxpayer to state his/her purpose)

[1083] *Ibid.* at 242 (citing N.Z. case examples where courts have relied upon business reality considerations)

[1084] See my discussion of this point in chapter V re the Supreme Court of Canada's treatment of economic substance.

[1085] Elliffe and Prebble, *supra* no. 1035 at 10 (noting that the Commissioner's reconstruction power is quite broad and would "clearly contemplate" the re-characterisation of a sale of shares as a dividend)

actual tax advantage gained.[1086] Nevertheless, the onus is on the taxpayer to demonstrate that the reconstruction was unreasonable or beyond the Commissioner's wide statutory powers.[1087]

Relationship of section BG 1 to other provisions

Relative to the relationship that the GAAR has with other provisions of the *Income Tax Act*, Trombitas describes the New Zealand GAAR as a "back stop" provision and takes the position that "there is much merit in the view that the rule should operate as a provision of last resort."[1088] One of the deficiencies that the 1992 Valabh Committee[1089] identified with section BG 1 of the *Income Tax Act 2004* was that it did not assist in identifying when the section should apply so as to displace other provisions of the Act which, for example, provide incentives to encourage certain types of economic activity.[1090] Sir Ivor Richardson later added, in commenting on the "formidable un-

---

[1086] "Improving the Operation of New Zealand's Tax Avoidance Laws", the Taxation Committee of the New Zealand Law Society, the Corporate Taxpayers Group, and the Taxation Committee of the New Zealand Institute of Chartered Accountants (2011), http://email.business.auckland.ac.nz/2011/1121-tax-avoidance/ paras. 4.7–4.17

[1087] Elliffe and Keating, *supra* no. 22 at 384 (suggesting the Commissioner's reconstruction will be hard to challenge)

[1088] Eugen Trombitas, "The Role for a General Anti-Avoidance Rule in a GST", 13 *New Zealand Journal of Taxation Law and Policy* 396 (September 2007), 405, 421 (arguing that under GAAR the legislative scheme can be used to prevent outcomes sought by taxpayers based on literal readings of legislation; plus, the GAAR acts as a signpost)

[1089] Consultative Committee on the Taxation of Income from Capital (Valabh Committee), Key Reforms to the Scheme of Tax Legislation, (Auckland, October 1991) and Consultative Committee on the Taxation of Income from Capital (Valabh Committee), Final Report, (Wellington, October 1992); see also: Trombitas, *ibid.* at 403 (discussing the Valabh Committee's findings and its conclusion that a GAAR is required for income tax)

[1090] Dunbar, *supra* no. 1030 at 394, 396 (suggesting that although Canada's general anti-avoidance provision did not accomplish anything that judges could not have achieved purely on the basis of statutory interpretation, statutory provisions such as section BG 1 support the rule of law because they provide statutory authority to judges, assist in judicial line-drawing, and provide greater certainty than judicial doctrines such as the principle of fiscal nullity, etc.)

certainties" with section 99 of the *Income Tax Act 1976* [now BG 1 of the *Income Tax Act 2007*], that the legislature could not have intended that the section would over-ride or be subordinate to all other provisions of the Act.[1091] In that respect, the Supreme Court has recently clarified that the existence of specific anti-avoidance provisions does not have the consequence that the general anti-avoidance provisions cannot operate where the tax avoidance arrangement employed by the taxpayer does not fall within those specific rules: "Unless the specific rules plainly are intended to cover the field in relation to the use of particular provisions by taxpayers or plainly exclude the use of the general anti-avoidance provision in a certain situation ... then the Commissioner can rely upon s. BG 1 to counter avoidance where that has occurred."[1092]

What has been accomplished

Trombitas argues that although tax avoidance is a very difficult concept to define, the New Zealand GAAR has a good overall deterrent effect by discouraging taxpayers from entering into aggressive schemes.[1093] The Keatings argue, however, that disputes concerning tax avoidance consume a disproportionate share of resources, accounting over the past decade for nearly 20 percent of all adjudication reports issued by Inland Revenue (where tax avoid-

---

[1091] Rt Hon Sir Ivor Richardson, "Reducing Tax Avoidance By Changing Structures, Processes and Drafting", Tax Avoidance and the Rule of Law, (Amsterdam: IBFD, 1997), Graham Cooper, ed., chapter 10, p. 329 (arguing that less emphasis should be put on anti-avoidance legislation than on the design of tax legislation and of the tax collection system)

[1092] *Penny and Hooper v Commissioner of Inland Revenue*, [2011] NZSC 95 at para. 48; see also: Arnold, *supra* no. 14 at 547 (citing *Inland Revenue Commissioner v. Challenge Corporation Ltd.*, [1986] S.T.C. 548 (P.C.) as an instance where the New Zealand GAAR was held to apply to deny a loss which was expressly permitted by other provisions of New Zealand tax legislation)

[1093] Trombitas, *supra* no. 1088 at 396, 404, 411 (suggesting that for every tax avoidance case that makes it to court there are many others that have been deterred by the GAAR. Also commenting that there is merit to the view that the judiciary has a role to play in tax avoidance cases as judges are responsible for the development and preservation of tax laws as a body of principle to ensure that the integrity of the tax system is upheld)

ance was one of the grounds of dispute), and 30 percent of all reported tax judgments. This, they suggest, shows that "the law on tax avoidance is far from what we should expect from a good tax system."[1094] Mark Keating has, nevertheless, credited the Supreme Court with providing a "clear sign-post regarding tax avoidance", by ruling that "the single most important indicia of tax avoidance is whether the tax consequences of the transaction are at odds with its economic effect."[1095]

According to Professor Littlewood, the Supreme Court's decision in *Ben Nevis* has contributed an important new principle to the interpretation of New Zealand's GAAR, by establishing that unprofitable transactions which are undertaken for no purpose other than to reduce tax liability amount to tax avoidance.[1096] In Professor Littlewood's words, "[i]t might seem obvious, to those unfamiliar with tax avoidance jurisprudence, that undertaking an unprofitable transaction for no purpose other than to reduce one's liability to tax on one's other income ought to be counted as tax avoidance."[1097]

Professor Elliffe and Cameron have also concluded that "in expenditure related cases, the test of whether the economic burden is actually shouldered by the taxpayer is fundamental to the tax avoidance test, regardless of the legal form."[1098] They consider that the

---

[1094] Mark Keating and Kirsty Keating, "Tax Avoidance in New Zealand: The Camel's Back That Refuses to Break!", 17 *New Zealand Journal of Taxation Law and Policy* 115 (March 2011), 136 (arguing that "the current system is failing us all", and that the lack of precision inherent in a GAAR, coupled with the Commissioner's inability to provide guidance on its application and the court's refusal to provide clear rules, is exacerbating the problem)

[1095] Mark Keating, "GST Tax Avoidance: A New Zealand Perspective on the Application of Div 165", vol. 8, no. 1 *eJournal of Tax Research* 64-89 (2009), 82 (pointing out that the Supreme Court has stressed that taxpayers must bear the true economic cost of any tax benefit they claim)

[1096] Littlewood, *supra* no. 1058 at 65 (noting that establishment of the principle that pre-tax negative transactions constitute impermissible avoidance is a desirable development)

[1097] *Ibid.* at 56 (suggesting that the Privy Council decision in *Peterson* is now "dubious authority at best" and that it is unlikely that the courts will hold pre-tax negative transactions to be the only form of avoidance)

[1098] Elliffe and Cameron, *supra* no. 22 at 451

Supreme Court has succeeded in establishing a link between the existence of hallmarks of tax avoidance and the likelihood that an arrangement falls outside Parliamentary contemplation: "In determining whether an arrangement is consistent or inconsistent with Parliament's purpose, a host of factors will be relevant including artificiality, pretence and circularity and all importantly, the underlying economic substance of the arrangement."[1099] As an illustration, they say that while the "cheque swap" in *Glenharrow* and the promissory notes in *Ben Nevis* could technically be viewed as "payment", the Supreme Court's focus on economic substance revealed the reality that the burden of payment was not actually born. This approach is obviously to be contrasted with what occurs with regularity in Canada, where adherence to legal form is usually paramount.[1100]

Lennard suggests that there are uncertainties attendant to the application of section BG 1, including how to determine the scheme and purpose of the tax legislation in question; identification of the scope of the arrangement; and, the extent of the reconstruction power. Nevertheless, he considers that there is a "coherent conceptual framework" to be utilized.[1101] In regard to certainty concerns, I have already noted that the 2011 New Zealand private sector report to government "Improving the Operation of New Zealand's Tax Avoidance Laws"[1102] commented that "[a]n outsider looking at the Australian provision would ... suggest that the eight indicia must be helpful guidance to all the concerned parties in a transaction which may potentially be subject to the GAAR."[1103] However, the oppos-

---

[1099] *Ibid.* at 451, 459 (commenting that the Supreme Court's reliance in *Ben Nevis* upon the hallmarks of tax avoidance arrangements is nothing new, but that the Court's emphasis on economic and commercial considerations portrays a focus on the substance of transactions rather than legal form)
[1100] See the discussion of this point in chapter V.
[1101] Lennard, *supra* no. 1031.
[1102] Report to the New Zealand Government prepared by representatives of New Zealand's three leading industry bodies representing taxpayers and tax advisors: the Taxation Committee of the New Zealand Law Society, the Corporate Taxpayers Group, and the Taxation Committee of the New Zealand Institute of Chartered Accountants, *supra* no. 1024.
[1103] *Ibid*, para. 1.6

ing viewpoint is that the adoption by Australia of a detailed general anti avoidance rule in Part IVA has been problematic, as it has made "each word or phrase a potential battle ground between taxpayers and the revenue."[1104]

Professor Littlewood argues that amending New Zealand's GAAR to include a list of factors which are thought to be indicative of avoidance "adds nothing other than an extra layer of complexity."[1105] Moreover, Professor Littlewood thinks that although the basic concept of tax avoidance still seems incoherent, complaints about uncertainty require little sympathy in New Zealand, as all of the instances where GAAR has been invoked have involved "plainly attempted unmeritorious raids on the Treasury. Those who sail too close to the wind should not complain if they get wet."[1106] This is highly reminiscent of the Supreme Court's comments re certainty:

> Parliament has left the general anti-avoidance provision deliberately general ... The courts should not strive to create greater certainty than Parliament has chosen to provide. We consider that the approach we have outlined gives as much conceptual clarity as can reasonably be achieved. As in many areas of the law, there are bound to be difficult cases at the margins.

[1104] G. T. Pagone, "Aspects of Tax Avoidance: Trans-Tasman Observations", International Fiscal Association Conference, Wellington, New Zealand, March 12, 2011, pages 12, 34 (arguing that uncertainty resulting through discretionary power is a means of combating tax avoidance)

[1105] Littlewood, *supra* no. 1058 at 68 (also noting that the Australian government has expressed doubts about its list-based approach in Improving *the Operation of the Anti-Avoidance Provisions in the Income Tax Law* (Discussion Paper, 18 November 2010)); see also: Littlewood, *supra* no. 98 at 175, 205 (conceding that it could be the case that the law reports only disclose the flagrant cases; and, arguing "the idea of tax avoidance is not susceptible to coherent explication and that rules against it are therefore inescapably problematic. ... [H]owever, having a general anti-avoidance rule might nonetheless be better than not having one" as they may be so effective because of their "mercurial unpredictability")

[1106] Littlewood, "Tax Avoidance, the Rule of Law and the New Zealand Supreme Court", *ibid.* at 65-66 (suggesting in any event that uncertainty may not be a feature "of the anti-avoidance rule, but of the rules defining the scope of the tax")

But in most cases we consider it will be possible, without undue difficulty, to decide on which side of the line a particular arrangement falls.[1107]

Professor Dabner thinks the fact that New Zealand's GAAR applies to arrangements that have either the purpose or effect of tax avoidance brings it "closer to the ideal", because this results in the predominant focus being on the purpose of the legislation.[1108] In any event, the Supreme Court's decisions are said to have "clearly put tax advisers and taxpayers on notice that only if they actually suffered the true economic cost expected to be paid under the black letter law can they keep the resulting tax benefit."[1109]

Conclusion

The courts in New Zealand have taken a dramatically different position than the courts in Canada have relative to the importance of the role of economic substance in tax avoidance cases. The jurisprudential focus in New Zealand on economic substance puts it in the same company as Australia, South Africa and the US, in terms of the end result, although the paths travelled by these countries have been along different routes. The universal point, however, at which all four countries have arrived, dramatically illustrates that Canada is definitely the "odd man out" in terms of its treatment of economic substance in tax avoidance cases. We need to rectify this problem by amending Canada's GAAR to require that our courts evaluate economic substance.

[1107] (2009), 24 NZTC 23,188 (SC) at p. 112
[1108] Dabner, *supra* no. 198 at 41-42 (arguing that a less legalistic and more policy orientated approach from the judiciary is required in dealing with tax avoidance)
[1109] Elliffe and Keating, *supra* no. 22 at 369, 392 (noting that the Supreme Court followed the existing Privy Council authority in *Challenge Corporation Ltd. v CIR* in holding that the economic realities of arrangements are relevant)

OTHER COUNTRIES

It is also notable that section 61A of the *Inland Revenue Ordinance* of Hong Kong is a GAAR provision to the same effect as in Australia;[1110] sections 811 and 811A of the *Taxes Consolidation Act, 1997* of Ireland call for regard to, *inter alia*, the substance and final result of a transaction in reaching a conclusion as to whether the transaction is an avoidance transaction;[1111] and, India is introducing a GAAR in April 2012 that is modelled on the South African GAAR legislation.[1112] These GAARS therefore also all have an economic substance component.

U.K. DRAFT GAAR

The U.K. has not, to date, enacted a general anti-avoidance rule, although the government initiated a study in 2010, as to whether one should be put in place.[1113] The study was undertaken because of concerns that the U.K.'s reliance upon targeted anti-

---

[1110] Jefferson VanderWolk, "The Stain of *Spotless Services* Spreads to Hong Kong: The Tai Hing Cotton Mill Case", vol. 12 no. 1 Asia-*Pacific Journal of Taxation* 20-30 (Spring/Summer 2008), 28 (noting Part IVA of the Australian general anti-avoidance statute is substantially similar to section 61A of the Hong Kong Inland Revenue Ordinance).

[1111] Connor Kennedy and Daragh O'Shaughnessy, "Anti-Avoidance – Restrictions in Tax Planning", *Taxation / Revenue Policy*, Feb. 21, 2006, www.cpaireland.ie/UserFiles/File/.../Taxation/.../Anti-Avoidance.pdf (stating that the introduction of this general anti-avoidance provision [in 1989] became necessary after it became clear that the judiciary could not be relied upon to assume as aggressive a stance towards tax avoidance as would be preferred by Revenue and the Government).

[1112] Freedman, *supra* no. 26 at 12-14; Revised Discussion Paper on the Direct Taxes Code, Chapter XI General Anti Avoidance Rule, para. 3.1, (an impermissible avoidance arrangement only exists where, in addition to the tax benefit for the assessee, one of four conditions exist. One of the four conditions is "lacks commercial substance" – http://ww.incometaxindia.gov.in)

[1113] HMRC Study of a General Anti-Avoidance Rule, Terms of Reference, December 1, 2010 http://www.hmrc.gov.U.K./budget-updates/gaar.pdf (stating that the Government asked Graham Aaronson QC to lead a study programme to establish whether a GAAR could be framed that would be effective in the U.K. tax system)

avoidance rules had caused its tax system to become too complex, so that the competiveness of the U.K. as a business location was being impaired.[1114] The ensuing GAAR Study Group Report released on November 11, 2011 strongly recommends the enactment of a "moderate [GAAR] which does not apply to responsible tax planning, and is instead targeted at abusive arrangements."[1115] The government has, however, undertaken not to introduce a GAAR, without formal public consultation.[1116]

Nonetheless, regardless of whether the government proceeds to enact a GAAR, it is fair to say that U.K. law puts economic substance at the front and centre of matters to be examined in determining whether there has been abusive tax avoidance.[1117] Professor Ulph, Head of the School of Economics and Finance at the University of St. Andrews, describes tax avoidance as "what happens when a taxpayer uses artificial or contrived methods of adjusting their social, economic or organizational affairs to reduce their tax liability in accordance with the law while not affecting the economic substance of the transactions."[1118] Professor Freedman of Oxford

---

[1114] Tracey Bowler, "Tackling Tax Avoidance in the U.K.", *Beyond Boundaries – Developing Approaches to Tax Avoidance and Tax Risk Management*, Oxford Centre for Business Taxation (ed. Judith Freedman: 2008), c. 8 at 63 (noting that more detailed tax rules create more "loopholes" which encourage more attempts at tax avoidance)

[1115] Report by Graham Aaronson QC, GAAR Study, November 11, 2011, p.4- 6 (stating that a number of benefits would accrue from a GAAR, including counteracting and deterring contrived and artificial tax avoidance schemes)

[1116] HMRC Study of a General Anti-Avoidance Rule, Terms of Reference, December 1, 2010 http://www.hmrc.gov.U.K./budget-updates/gaar.pdf

[1117] Karen B. Brown, "Tax Avoidance, Treaty Shopping and the Economic Substance Doctrine in the United States", vol. 2 *British Tax Review* 160 (2008), 164 (arguing that an economic substance test has been applied by both the US and U.K. courts in tax avoidance cases); compare: Professor Freedman saying that "In the United Kingdom we are very 'English'. We do not talk about economic substance, we do not mention it." – see Brian Arnold, Judith Freedman, Al Meghji, and Hon. Marshall Rothstein, "The Future of GAAR", *supra* no. 81 at. 4:11 (suggesting there was arguably no expenditure in the *Barclays Mercantile* case, but that the House of Lords found that a deduction was allowable because of the statutory scheme in place)

[1118] Richard Murphy, "The Missing Billions – The U.K. Tax Gap", located at www.tuc.org.U.K./touchstonepamphlets, p. 9 citing www.kpmg.co.U.K./

University argues that the enactment of a GAAR, which includes directions about the significance of economic substance, would be an asset in supporting the judiciary's handling of statutory interpretation in tax avoidance cases.[1119] She also suggests that the Supreme Court of Canada's decision, in allowing the capital cost deductions at issue in the *Canada Trustco* case, is the not-to-be-unexpected result of applying a GAAR which contains no direction as to economic substance.[1120] This latter point aligns with my own claim in this paper that Canada's GAAR needs to be amended, to provide the courts with direction regarding economic substance.

---

pubs/Tax_and _CSR_Final.pdf (suggesting tax revenues of £25 billion are lost to the U.K. government annually, due to tax avoidance by individuals and large corporations; and, also advocating the enactment of a statutory GAAR)

[1119] Freedman, *supra* no. 1077 at 55, 73-75 (arguing that a general anti-avoidance principle should set out economic substance and other objective factors to be reviewed in determining the motive for the transaction and also whether it was consistent with the legislation. Suggesting also that Australia is ahead of Canada in this respect. Acknowledging, however, that economic substance cannot be used as a reference in every case, e.g. if the basis of the specific tax legislation differs conceptually from economic reality. Capital cost allowances serve as an illustration of this); Freedman, *supra* no. 21 (arguing that "a legislative general anti-avoidance principle would provide the overlay needed to give legitimacy to judicial development and offer a framework in which the uncertainty inherent in any system capable of tackling tax avoidance can be fairly managed"; also, suggesting that there is a "culture of artificiality" encouraged by distinctions in the tax system, which helps to explain the large extent of tax avoidance); see also: Cashmere, *supra* no. 938 (arguing that a GAAR would also be valuable because purposive interpretation on its own "may not prove to be capable of controlling tax avoidance")

[1120] *Ibid*, *Law Quarterly Review*, p. 76-77 (arguing that an improved GAAR is needed in Canada, which sets out "an express policy on economic substance and other criteria"); see also: Lara Friedlander, "Canada Trustco Mortgage Co v. The Queen and Mathew v The Queen: the Supreme Court of Canada finally considers GAAR", vol. 1 *British Tax Review* 48-54 (2006), 50 (comparing the decisions in the *Canada Trustco* and *Barclays Mercantile* cases; and, also noting that the Supreme Court of Canada found in *Canada Trustco* that the taxpayer did not need to have a true economic cost, or even to be economically at risk, in order to obtain the capital cost allowance deductions in issue)

Historical anti-avoidance efforts

The U.K. has historically relied upon a combination of common law anti-avoidance doctrine, specific anti-avoidance rules, and targeted anti-avoidance rules, to counteract abusive tax avoidance.[1121] With respect to reliance upon specific and targeted anti-avoidance rules, as a part of the weaponry against abusive tax avoidance (a topic which I am not examining in this paper), there are serious short-comings. An important one of these is that specific and targeted anti-avoidance rules are typically only enacted after objectionable tax avoidance has taken place, i.e. "the legislature is forever reduced to shutting the door after the horses have gone."[1122] Other major objections to heavy reliance upon specific and targeted anti-avoidance rules have been that they add very substantially to the complexity of the tax legislation, and they also create more opportunities for tax avoidance.[1123] Nevertheless, in the context of

---

[1121] Glen Loutzenhiser, "Income splitting and settlements: further observations on Jones v Garnett", vol. 6 *British Tax Review* 693-716 (2007), 712 (explaining that targeted anti-avoidance rules "act like 'mini-GAARs', in that although they are narrower in scope than a GAAR, they are drafted using much broader language than would typically be found in a specific anti-avoidance provision"); Pickup, *supra* no. 846, c. 2, at 11 (noting that reliance on targeted anti-avoidance rules can be "highly complex" and has attracted much criticism); see also: Adrian Shipwright, "Finance Act notes: extension of restrictions on allowable capital losses – section 27", vol. 5 *British Tax Review* 456-458 (2007), 456 (noting that many would dispute the description of section 27 *Finance Act 2007* as a "targeted anti-avoidance rule", considering it instead to be a GAAR)

[1122] Littlewood, *supra* no. 98 at 178 (also arguing that although "the idea of tax avoidance is not susceptible to coherent explication and that rules against it are therefore inescapably problematic ... having a general anti-avoidance rule might nonetheless be better than not having one"); see also: Loutinsky, *supra* no. 181 at 102-103 (noting specific anti-avoidance rules "are targeted at narrow, exact areas where abuse has been previously identified or revenue leakage is suspected"; however, they "are easily avoided and incorporated into new avoidance activities")

[1123] Tax Law Review Committee Discussion Paper No. 7, The Institute for Fiscal Studies, February 2009, para. 2.1; Freedman, *supra* no. 21 at 353 (noting that increased reliance on specific anti-avoidance rules results in complexity "and the problem of creative compliance")

enacting specific and targeted anti-avoidance rule rules, the U.K. has also historically placed reliance on economic substance.[1124]

In the realm of common law, the House of Lords was at first widely credited with giving birth to a non-statutory anti-avoidance doctrine in *W.T. Ramsay Ltd. v. Inland Revenue Commissioners*,[1125] in which it held that where there was a preordained transaction, or series of transactions, which had steps inserted for no commercial purpose, those steps could be ignored for tax purposes.[1126] This approach has been roughly characterized as one which looks at a series of transactions to determine whether they have any economic purpose other than the avoidance of tax.[1127] Indeed, [now] Lord Mil-

---

[1124] See, for example, Ronald S. Nock, "Legislative change by Practice Statement", vol. 1 *British Tax Review* 21-31 (1999), 22 (noting that for over 70 years there have been provisions involving stamp duty which turn upon whether there has been a real change in the economic position of the parties)

[1125] *W.T. Ramsay Ltd. v. Inland Revenue Commissioners* (1981), [1982] A.C. 300 (U.K. H.L.); Edward G. Nugee, "The United Kingdom Experience: McGuckian – Formalism and Economic Substance", 1997 Conference Report (Toronto: Canadian Tax Foundation, 1998), 36:1-36:12 (noting that "in reality [the taxpayer] did not make any loss: the money purported to be involved went round in a circle, and the only payment in the real world was the payment of the fee to the tax consultant who provided the scheme"); see also: John Tiley, "The Avoidance Problem: Some U.K. Reflections", *Beyond Boundaries – Developing Approaches to Tax Avoidance and Tax Risk Management*, Oxford Centre for Business Taxation (ed. Judith Freedman: 2008), c. 9, p. 72-73 (suggesting the doctrine of composite transaction, which was successfully advanced by Inland Revenue, was "in the context of a particularly outrageous scheme"; and, also suggesting that allowing the taxpayer to succeed "would have created gross unfairness between those who paid their advisers and those who paid the Revenue")

[1126] T.E. McDonnell, "The House of Lords – Judicial Anti-avoidance Techniques Expanded?, Current Cases", (1992) vol. 40, no. 4 *Canadian Tax Journal* 929-938 (pointing out that the *Ramsay* case dealt with "a series of contrived and interconnected transactions designed to manufacture a loss for capital gains tax purposes in circumstances in which no real economic loss was sustained."); see also: Evans, *supra* no. 94 at 126-127 (noting that the "Ramsay doctrine", also known as "the principle of fiscal nullity", was thought to be a separate judicial doctrine; however, the *Barclays Mercantile* case later established that the "new approach" to tax avoidance in the U.K. is for courts to give statutory provisions a purposive construction)

[1127] Prebble and Prebble, *supra* no. 402 at 7 (suggesting a parallel between the U.K. decision in *WT Ramsay Ltd v. IRC* and the US decision in *Gregory v. Helvering*,

lett has argued that the *ratio decidendi* of *Ramsay* was that "where the taxpayer claims to have entered into a transaction which is incapable of appreciably affecting his financial position except to give rise to a reduction of his tax liability, it is to be disregarded."[1128] This is, of course, a rough proxy for the economic substance tests that are being used in other jurisdictions (but not in Canada).

The "*Ramsay* doctrine" is thought to have become conflated with a purposive approach to statutory interpretation, in the subsequent House of Lords decision in *Barclays Mercantile Business Finance Ltd v. Mawson (Inspector of Taxes)*.[1129] Professor Freedman has argued, however, that the *Ramsay* doctrine remains alive, as a way of dealing with composite transactions, and that "there is an element of seeking economic substance in this approach."[1130] However, regardless of whether any vestiges of the *Ramsay* doctrine remain part of the U.K. tax avoidance landscape, it is plain

---

in terms of their focus on economic substance); Morgan *supra* no 1 at 390 (noting that in the years following *Ramsay*, tax commentators have interpreted U.K. tax avoidance cases as importing the US economic substance doctrine into the common law); Lee A. Sheppard, "British Propose Toothless Antiavoidance Rule", *Tax Notes International* 764-768 (Dec 12, 2011), 765 (describing the decision in *Ramsay* as "an economic substance rule")

[1128] P. Millett (now the Rt Hon. Lord Millett), "A new Approach to Tax Avoidance Schemes", 98 *Law Quarterly Report* 209 (1982), 222

[1129] (2004), [2004] UKHL 51, [2005] 1 A.C. 684 (H.L.); Morgan, *supra* no. 1 at 390-391 (calling the *Barclays Mercantile* decision a clear departure from the view that the British judiciary can avail itself of common law anti-avoidance doctrines in tax avoidance cases; and, also noting claims that the *Ramsay* principle is now incorporated into a general principle of statutory interpretation); Judith Freedman, Geoffrey Loomer and John Vella, "Moving Beyond Avoidance? Task Risk and the Relationship between Large Business and HMRC", *Beyond Boundaries – Developing Approaches to Tax Avoidance and Tax Risk Management*, Oxford Centre for Business Taxation (ed. Judith Freedman: 2008), c. 10, p. 82 (arguing that the U.K. judiciary has "rejected a formulaic judicial anti-avoidance doctrine", instead favouring purposive statutory construction – citing *Barclays Mercantile Business Finance Ltd. v. Mawson*); see also: Freedman, *supra* no. 1077 at 53 (also arguing that the development of U.K. case law over 25 years has not been impressive, failing "to produce a clear framework for dealing with tax avoidance, with the result than an increasing amount of specific anti-avoidance legislation is necessary")

[1130] *Ibid, Law Quarterly Review*, p. 54

that economic substance has played a central role in the judiciary's decisions in tax avoidance cases. This is very different from the judiciary's treatment of economic substance in Canada.

Lord Nolan's test for tax avoidance was set out in *Inland Revenue Commissioners v. Willoughby*: "The hallmark of tax avoidance is that the taxpayer reduces his liability to tax without incurring the economic consequences that Parliament intended to be suffered by any taxpayer qualifying for such reduction in his tax liability."[1131] Previously, Lord Templeman offered a similar definition of tax avoidance in the *Challenge Corporation* case, which I have already recited in chapter I.[1132]

This manner of approach is said to work well in expenditure-related tax avoidance cases, but not to capture all forms of abusive tax avoidance.[1133] In any event, the approach is important, in that it helps to turn the tide against some of the most egregious forms of abusive tax avoidance.[1134] As noted recently by McCarthy in the *British Tax Review*, "[t]he exploitation of the tax code to achieve tax advantages at odds with economic reality can clearly be said to be contrary to the policy underlying the legislation."[1135]

[1131] [1997] S.T.C. 995 (H.L.) at pp. 1003-1004

[1132] *Challenge Corporation Ltd v. Commissioner of Inland Revenue*, [1987] A.C. 155

[1133] Heather Self, "Acceptable Tax Avoidance?", *Beyond Boundaries – Developing Approaches to Tax Avoidance and Tax Risk Management*, Oxford Centre for Business Taxation (ed. Judith Freedman: 2008), c. 17, p. 153-154 (noting that this test works well when there are expected economic consequences, but that it is difficult to apply when there is highly technical legislation, e.g. in the structured finance area, where it is not clear when economic benefits are expected to arise); Tax Law Review Committee Discussion Paper No. 7, "Countering Tax Avoidance in the U.K.: Which Way Forward?", February 2009, 11-12 (also suggesting that Lord Templeman's definition of tax avoidance does not catch all forms of tax avoidance, giving the example of tax avoidance through income-shifting)

[1134] Littlewood, *supra* no. 98 at 201 (noting that although the Privy Council found for the taxpayer in *Peterson v. CIR*, [2005] U.K.PC 17, three of the five member panel agreed that the test was whether the economic burden had been borne)

[1135] Hui Ling McCarthy, "HMRC: SHIPS that pass in the night – reconciling Mayes and Drummond", vol. 3 *British Tax Review* 279-299 (2011) (arguing that in such circumstances it is typically impossible to find a rational policy justification for the taxpayer's desired result)

This level of endorsement of economic reality, as a touchstone for the determination of whether transactions run against the policy underlying the relevant tax legislation, does not exist in Canada. That speaks of the need for our GAAR to be amended, in order to provide that tax-motivated transactions which do not substantially affect the economic position of the taxpayer in relation to their expected tax benefits, should be presumed to be a misuse of the provisions of the *Income Tax Act*, or an abuse of the *Income Tax Act* as a whole.

HMRC's administrative position

HMRC categorizes taxpayers who engage in transactions that have little or no economic substance as "high-risk" businesses.[1136] HMRC's Anti-Avoidance Group has also developed a list of risk factors, that it considers to be "signposts" of potentially abusive tax avoidance, including "[t]ransactions or arrangements which have little or no economic substance or which have consequences not commensurate with the change in a taxpayer's (or group of related taxpayers') economic position"; and, "[t]ransactions or arrangements bearing little or no pre-tax profit which rely wholly or substantially on anticipated tax reduction for significant post tax profit."[1137] These administrative stances are not unhelpful in the U.K., unlike they would be presently in Canada, as the judiciary in the UK has historically paid attention to the significance of economic substance in tax avoidance cases.

1997 Tax Law Review Committee Report

The U.K. Tax Law Review Committee published a report on Tax Avoidance in November 1997.[1138] It proposed adoption of a gen-

---

[1136] HMRC, "Approach to Compliance Risk Management for Large Businesses" (March 2007), http://www.hmrc.gov.U.K./budget2007/large-business-riskman.pdf, para. 5.12

[1137] HMRC, "Guidance from Anti-Avoidance Group", http://www.hmrc.gov.U.K./avoidance/aag-ris-assessing.htm

[1138] http://www.ifs.org.U.K./comms/comm64.pdf

eral anti-avoidance rule in the U.K., as preferable to, and providing more certainty than, the ongoing and unpredictable evolution of judicial anti-avoidance rules. While the Committee went to some lengths to explain that it was not suggesting the exact language of a general anti-avoidance rule for enactment by Parliament, it did also set out an illustrative statutory general anti-avoidance rule, in order to "stimulate constructive debate."[1139]

The basic rule in the illustrative example given by the Committee was, subject to exception for "protected transactions", that "[w]here a person carries out a tax driven transaction, he shall be taxed as if he had carried out the normal transaction." "Tax driven transaction" was in turn defined as "a transaction that has as its sole purpose, or as one of its main purposes, the avoidance of tax." The draft GAAR also provided:

> In determining whether a transaction is a tax driven transaction, the following shall be taken into account-
>
> Its legal form including the legal rights and obligations created by the transaction; *its economic and commercial substance*; the timing of any step; the expected duration of any step or any feature in the transaction; the change in the financial or other circumstances of the taxpayer or anyone connected with the taxpayer, as a result of the transaction; the expected tax consequences of the transaction on the assumption that this rule does not apply. (italics emphasis added)

The UK Committee's approach was motivated by its understanding that a taxpayer's assertion of purpose needs to be tested, by reference to *all* of the surrounding circumstances and evidence. It therefore suggested using criteria similar to those that are present in Australia's GAAR.[1140] Very prominent amongst the factors to be considered was the transaction's economic substance.[1141]

[1139] *Ibid*, c. 5
[1140] http://www.ifs.org.U.K./comms/comm64.pdf, chapter 5, p. 39
[1141] *Ibid.* at 38.

By comparison in Canada, because of the Supreme Court's ruling in *Canada Trustco* that economic substance "has little meaning in isolation from the proper interpretation of specific provisions of the Act",[1142] we do not enjoy this manner of approach in the determination of "purpose." There is, however, no reason for us to be so completely out-of-step with Australia, New Zealand, South Africa, the United States, and the thinking of the UK Tax Law Review Committee, as regards the important role that economic substance should have in detecting abusive tax avoidance; and, we therefore now need a curative amendment to our GAAR.

1998 Inland Revenue Consultation Document

The government published a Consultative Document regarding the introduction of a general anti-avoidance rule ("GAAR") in 1998,[1143] following the Tax Law Review Committee's paper which endorsed the drafting of such a provision. The Consultative Document also envisaged that a list of factors would be used to determine "purpose."[1144] Once again, one of the factors to be taken into account, in determining whether a transaction was a "tax driven transaction", was "its economic and commercial substance."[1145] However, the Government did not take any further steps towards drafting a general anti-avoidance rule at that time.[1146] This was at least partly because the robustness of the judiciary's response to tax

---

[1142] *Canada Trustco Mortgage Co. v. R.*, [2005] 5 C.T.C. 215 (S.C.C.) at para. 76
[1143] Inland Revenue, *A General Anti-Avoidance Rule for Direct Taxes: Consultative Document*, October 1988
[1144] Referred to by Tax Law Review Committee, "A General Anti-Avoidance Rule for Direct Taxes – A Response to the Inland Revenue's Consultative Document", February 1999 , chapter 3, p. 11 (noting that the main difference – and principal difficulty – with the Consultative Document, was its approach taken to multiple step transactions)
[1145] Inland Revenue, *A General Anti-Avoidance Rule for Direct Taxes: Consultative Document*, October 1988, p. 17, para. 6.6.4
[1146] Bowler, *supra* no. 1114, c. 8 at 63 (indicating the government did not take any further steps towards enacting a general anti-avoidance rule at the time); Phillip R. West. "Antiabuse Rules and Policy: Coherence or Tower of Babel?", *Tax Notes International* 1161-1180 (March 31, 2008), 1179 (noting that the U.K. considered and did not adopt a statutory anti-abuse rule in the 1990's)

avoidance in the U.K. encouraged tax commentators to take the position that a GAAR was not required, as the better alternative was to "leave the judges to do their work."[1147] We do not at present have this same option in Canada.[1148]

2009 Tax Law Review Committee Discussion Paper

The Tax Law Review Committee also issued a Discussion Paper in 2009: "Countering Tax Avoidance in the UK: Which Way Forward?"[1149] The Discussion Paper noted, among other matters, that "the most aggressive forms of [tax] avoidance" are those "where there is little economic substance behind the transactions."[1150] The Discussion Paper also noted that the forty (40) or so targeted anti-avoidance rules enacted in the U.K., subsequent to the recommendation of the Tax Law Review Committee in 1998 that a GAAR be enacted, may not have been necessary if the GAAR had been enacted, because of the economic substance component of the GAAR.[1151]

2011 Advisory Committee GAAR Study Group Report

As noted above, the Advisory Committee headed by Graham Aaronson QC issued the GAAR Study Group Report on November 11, 2011, in which it recommends the enactment of a "moderate

---

[1147] Tiley, *supra* no. 1125, c. 9 at 72 (adding, however, that tax rules must be "justiciable" in the sense that they are clear enough to be applied)

[1148] The Supreme Court of Canada has said repeatedly that the courts should not be quick to "embellish" the provisions of the *Income Tax Act* in response to concerns about tax avoidance, "when it is open to Parliament to be precise and specific with respect to any mischief to be prevented" – see *Entreprises Ludco ltée c. Canada* (2001), [2002] 1 C.T.C. 95 (S.C.C.) at para. 39, citing four more Supreme Court of Canada decisions and the *Duke of Westminster* principle

[1149] Tax Law Review Committee Discussion Paper No. 7, The Institute for Fiscal Studies

[1150] *Ibid.* at 40, para. 12.6

[1151] Bowler, *supra* no. 1114, c. 8 at 64. See, for example, Tax Law Review Committee Discussion Paper No. 7, The Institute for Fiscal Studies, p. 156 in relation to "manufactured payments" and the targeted anti-avoidance rule aimed at stopping deductions where there has not been a corresponding economic loss.

[GAAR] which does not apply to responsible tax planning, and is instead targeted at abusive arrangements." The benefits such a GAAR will bring are predicted by the Committee to include counteraction to, and deterrence of, "contrived and artificial schemes which are widely regarded as an intolerable attack on the integrity of the U.K.'s tax regime."[1152] The Committee makes the point in its report that "[i]n discussions with various representative bodies of the tax profession there has been unanimity of view that such schemes are wholly unacceptable."[1153]

Given this high level of disapprobation having been expressed by Committee members regarding such tax avoidance schemes, it is more than notable that the illustrative general anti-abuse rule included in the Report, as reflecting the views of the Committee members, includes the notions of "true economic income, profit or gain" and "true economic cost or loss", as the first two "features" to be taken into account in determining whether an arrangement is "abnormal."[1154] The quality of "abnormality", in turn, results in the arrangement being "short listed" as a potential target for the GAAR. From this field of arrangements, those excluded as not being abusive tax results are those "which can be regarded as a reasonable response to choices afforded by the legislation."[1155]

The GAAR Study Group's recommendation has already been characterized by Sheppard as proposing a "toothless antiavoidance rule"; however, the criticism does not extend to the illustrative GAAR's emphasis on economic profits and economic losses for the purpose of determining abnormality. This is because Sheppard thinks it is "a given" that "big discrepancies between economic profits or costs and tax reporting" are "abnormal."[1156]

[1152] Aaronson GAAR Study, *supra* no. 1115, p.4, para. 1.7.
[1153] *Ibid.*
[1154] Appendix I – Illustrative Draft GAAR, Part XY General Anti-Abuse Rule, p. 46-47, paras. 7(3)(a) and (b)
[1155] *Ibid.* at 31, para. 5.15 and 45, para 4.
[1156] Sheppard, *supra* no. 1127 at 767.

European Community concept of abusive practice or abuse of law

The concept of "abusive practice" or "abuse of law" has become part of U.K. law by reason of the European Court of Justice (ECJ) decision in *Halifax*.[1157] Under the abusive practice doctrine, EU law may be interpreted to deny a tax advantage, despite an express provision, if the advantage was wrongly or abusively obtained.[1158] The same anti-abuse principle has been articulated in both the *Halifax* and *Cadbury Schweppes*[1159] decisions. The ECJ has developed objective criteria for determining whether the general anti-abuse principle applies.[1160] The principle was applied in the *Ampliscientifica* decision, in which the ECJ held that "[t]he effect of [the] principle is therefore to prohibit wholly artificial arrangements which do not reflect economic reality and are set up with the sole aim of obtaining a tax advantage (see, to that effect ... *Cadbury Schweppes,* paragraph 55.)"[1161]

It is thus apparent that economic reality also has a central role under European Community ("EC") law. The fact the Supreme Court of Canada's view of the import of economic substance in tax avoidance cases is out-of-step with this legal state-of-affairs in the

---

[1157] *Halifax Plc, Leeds Permanent Development Services Ltd, County Wide Property Investments Ltd v. Commissioners of Customs and Excise* (Case C–255/02), [2006] S.T.C. 919 (preordained arrangements had been made that were intended to overcome the problem of input tax attributable to exempt suppliers being irrecoverable)

[1158] Greg Sinfield, "The Halifax principle as a universal GAAR for tax in the EU", vol. 3 *British Tax Review* 235-246 (2011), 236-237 (stating the defining characteristic of abuse is that it is contrary to the purpose of the relevant law)

[1159] *Cadbury Schweppes Plc v. IRC* (C-196/04), [2006] ECR I-7995, [2006] STC 1908; see also: West, *supra* no. 1146 at 1170 (observing that the ECJ restricted the U.K.'s ability to tax profits of European subsidiaries under its controlled foreign corporation ("CFC") rules unless there are wholly artificial arrangements intended to escape national tax normally payable)

[1160] Freedman, *supra* no. 1077 at 80-81 (noting that the objective criteria developed by the European Court of Justice are similar to the criteria listed in Australia's GAAR)

[1161] *Ampliscientifica Srl v. Ministero dell'Economia e delle Finanze* (C-162/07), [2008] ECR I-4019, [2011] STC 566 at p. 28

EC, as well as in Australia, New Zealand, South Africa, the United States and the U.K., speaks very loudly.

Observations

Academics, jurists, tax administrators, U.K. tax professionals including private sector accountants and lawyers, and even the European Court of Justice, have all recognized that economic substance is a central factor in determining whether there is abusive tax avoidance.

Conclusion

The set of factors, including economic substance, that are contained in the illustrative GAARs put forward in the U.K. in 1998, and again in 2011, reflect thinking that an informed judiciary should be able to come up with, without legislative direction, in considering whether a purpose of a transaction was the avoidance of tax. This has, after all, already happened in New Zealand. However, given that the Supreme Court of Canada has declined to recognize that economic substance has the role in Canada that it has abroad, in the detection of abusive tax avoidance, our GAAR needs to be amended.

VIII

Reporting Requirements and Penalties

Canada's most recent enterprise in the realm of enacting legislative measures for the purpose of deterring abusive tax avoidance focuses on strengthening information reporting requirements. While mandatory information reporting is undoubtedly one of the elements of a successful anti-avoidance regime, its stature is limited when viewed in the context of the other elements of a comprehensive anti-avoidance regime. In this chapter I review the anti-avoidance regimes that are in place in Australia, New Zealand, South Africa, the U.K. and the U.S., and I suggest that some additional steps could be taken in Canada to improve the government's anti-avoidance efforts.

Apart from the general anti-avoidance, and related legislative measures, which are in place in Canada and in many other jurisdictions, there are a variety of complementary anti-avoidance measures employed by governments, with a view to strengthening their anti-avoidance regimes. These other measures include reporting requirements, penalties for non-reporting, penalties for understatements of income attributable to participation in unacceptable tax avoidance schemes, and penalties for the promoters of such schemes. Different jurisdictions have taken different approaches in their degree of reliance upon these other types of anti-avoidance measures; and, there is no clear answer to an inquiry as to what combination of these measures works "best."[1162]

At the end of the day, however, while legislated reporting requirements and penalties do help tax administrations, by assisting them with the identification of unacceptable tax avoidance arrangements, and presumably also by providing some level of deterrence, these measures are of little avail, if the substantive anti-avoidance law is not interpreted by the courts in a manner which discourages aggressive tax avoidance. In the cases of Australia, New Zealand, South Africa and the United States, there is legislation in place, a judicial state-of-mind, or both, which helps to defend against this species of aggressive tax avoidance. Canada needs to join company with these four countries, by amending its GAAR to provide that economic substance must be considered to be a relevant factual circumstance in determining purpose, and in determining whether there has been misuse or abuse of statutory provisions of the *Income Tax Act* as a whole. Assuming this takes place, addressing the effectiveness of Canada's complementary anti-avoidance measures will be a sensible priority. Until this occurs, not a lot is to be gained.

This point appears to have been recognized by the Canada Revenue Agency, when it announced its intention to strengthen its focus on aggressive tax planning. At that time, it defined aggressive tax planning in this manner:

> *In Canada, it involves transactions, arrangements or events that are normally fully disclosed* but undertaken to achieve a tax result that is not supportable within specific anti-avoidance provisions or the overall scheme of the *Income Tax Act*, *Excise Tax Act*, or Income Tax Conventions. *Typically, the transactions, arrangements or events lack economic substance and*

[1162] Organisation for Economic Co-operation and Development, *Tackling Aggressive Tax Planning Through Improved Transparency and Disclosure: Report on Disclosure Initiatives* (Paris: OECD, February 2011), pp. 13-14 (www.oecd.org/dataoecd/13/55/48322860.pdf), (citing Canada as an example of a mandatory disclosure regime along with the U.K. and the US)

commercial reality and would not have materialized except for the tax result sought. The transactions, arrangements or events result in: sheltering income and capital gains that should be reported; creating or inflating tax deductions and losses, including capital losses, that would not otherwise exist; misusing treaty provisions; or accessing tax incentives, credits and exemptions in an offensive manner. ... Aggressive tax planning undermines the integrity of tax laws and the tax base.[1163]

This makes it apparent that the nub of the matter is that dealing with aggressive tax planning requires effective measures to combat transactions, arrangements or events that, although "normally fully disclosed", are lacking in "economic substance and commercial reality."

CANADA

There has been a tax shelter reporting regime in place in Canada for a considerable period, coupled with penalties for promoters who do not comply with the tax shelter identification legislation, or make false statements or omissions in their applications for tax shelter reference numbers. There is also a proposal presently outstanding for a more comprehensive regime.[1164]

Reporting requirements

In 1989 a requirement was introduced into the *Income Tax Act* in section 237.1, for promoters to obtain identification numbers for tax shelters, in order to assist Revenue Canada in the collection of

---

[1163] Canada Revenue Agency, Summary of the Corporate Business Plan 2005-2006 to 2007-2008 (Ottawa: CRA, 2005), 16 available at http://www.cra-arc.gc.ca/gncy/bsnss_plns/2005/ntr_sm-eng.html (italics emphasis added).

[1164] Backgrounder: 2010-043–*Government of Canada Seeks Public Input on Proposals To Require Information Reporting of Tax Avoidance Transactions*, Ottawa, May 7, 2010; see also: Paul Hickey, "Aggressive Tax Planning", (2010) vol. 18, no. 4 *Canadian Tax Highlights* 2-3 (noting the federal government's statement that the proposed new reporting regime is less strict than similar regimes in place in the United States, the United Kingdom and Québec).

information.[1165] A "tax shelter" was defined as any property in respect of which it is expected that the purchaser will be entitled to deductions and prescribed benefits in the first four years in excess of the cost to the purchaser of the property.[1166] According to Revenue Canada Circular 89-4 dated August 14, 1989, "[t]he definition of what constitutes a tax shelter depends entirely on the reasonable inferences to be drawn from representations made in connection with the property."[1167] However, the representations do not need to influence the decision to purchase the tax shelter.[1168]

[1165] Wertschek and Wilson, *supra* no. 57 (noting that the original administrative purpose for section 237.1 was "to ensure the more effective audit of certain tax-advantaged investments" by requiring a promoter of a tax shelter to obtain an identification number from the Canada Revenue Agency for the shelter before marketing it to potential investors)

[1166] Subsection 237.1(1); Technical Notes to Bill C-139, June 30, 1988; see also: Trevor McGowan, "Tax Shelters: An Overview and Update", 2006 *Conference Report* (Toronto: Canadian Tax Foundation, 2007), 37:1-14 ("At its most basic, a tax shelter is a transaction in which deductions are promoted as equaling or exceeding the true cost of the transaction." With respect to the promotion of tax-advantaged investments, the four year test applies prospectively. Also, "cost" is determined without reference to revenue arising from the property, so that it is not measured by reference to unrealistic revenue projections); Donald H. Watkins, "The Tax Shelter Rules: An Update", 1998 *Conference Report* (Toronto: Canadian Tax Foundation, 1999), 5:1-32 (A "prescribed benefit" is defined in *Income Tax Regulation* 231(6) as an amount that may reasonably be expected, having regard to statements or representations made in respect of the tax shelter, to be received or made available to a person who acquires an interest in the tax shelter and which has the effect of reducing the impact of any loss that the purchaser may sustain by acquiring, holding or disposing of the tax shelter)

[1167] Information Circular 89-4, August 14, 1989, para. 3; see also: Donald H. Watkins, "The Tax Shelter Rules: An Update", 1998 *Conference Report* (Toronto: Canadian Tax Foundation, 1999), 5:1-32 (commenting that the tax shelter definition contemplates the situation that could reasonably be expected to apply to a hypothetical purchaser. Also noting the test is not results-based, i.e. it looks to statements made in offering memoranda, prospectuses, etc. However, also noting Revenue Canada considers that representations may exist without active investor recruitment); see also: Wertschek and Wilson, *supra* no. 57 (suggesting that the reference in the definition of "tax shelter" to statements or representations that are "proposed to be made" was to ensure that an identification number would be issued to a tax shelter before any marketing of the shelter was done to investors)

[1168] *Baxter v. R.*, [2007] 3 C.T.C. 211 (F.C.A.) at para. 54, leave to appeal refused 2007 CarswellNat 3625 (S.C.C.) ("Because ... the person referred to in the definition of tax shelter [in section 237.1] is a prospective purchaser of the property, no consideration of the subjective knowledge of that person would be possible.")

A "promoter" is defined as any person who, in the course of a business, sells, issues or promotes the sale, issuance or acquisition of a tax shelter, or who acts as an agent or adviser in respect of such activities.[1169] Under this legislation, promoters are required to provide the identification number for tax shelters to purchasers,[1170] and to file information returns annually concerning such shelters providing the name, address and social insurance number of every person who acquired an interest, and the amount paid for the interest.[1171] Taxpayers are also required to provide the tax shelter identification number with tax returns, failing which deductions relating to the tax shelter are not available.[1172] There have been several cases where deductions were denied on this basis.[1173]

The number and value of shelters registered under section 237.1 were recorded as follows for the 2005 through 2012 taxation years:[1174]

Shelter Offerings and Sales

Year	Number of Tax Shelter Numbers Issued	Maximum Dollar Amount
2005	153	$5,558,943,777
2006	89	$2,985,470,200
2007	132	$4,646,704,200
2008	93	$1,688,041,200
2009	136	$2,545,922,543

[1169] Subsection 237.1(1); see also: Steven A. Yaphe, "Tax Shelters After Tax Reform", 1988 *Conference Report* (Toronto: Canadian Tax Foundation, 1989) 29:1-27 (1988), 29:26-29:27 (expressing concern that tax professionals giving advice to a client regarding the purchase of a tax shelter might be captured under the broad "promoter" definition); Trevor McGowan, "Tax Shelters: An Overview and Update", 2006 *Conference Report* (Toronto: Canadian Tax Foundation, 2007), 37:1-14 (arguing that the definition of "promoter" is very broad and potentially applies to persons who don't fall within its ordinary meaning); but see: CRA document no. 5-9372, April 23, 1990–"When the lawyer or accountant is merely giving advice to a client who proposes to invest in a tax shelter, the lawyer or client will not be affected by the reporting requirements of subsection 237.1(7)")
[1170] Subsection 237.1(2)
[1171] Subsection 237.1(7)
[1172] Subsection 237.1(6)
[1173] See, for example, *Haggarty c. R.*, [2003] 4 C.T.C. 2535 (T.C.C. [Informal Procedure]); *Clayton v. R.* (2003), [2004] 1 C.T.C. 2265 (T.C.C. [Informal Procedure])
[1174] Information provided by the Canada Revenue Agency from the Tax Shelter Database pursuant to the *Access to Information Act*.

Shelter Offerings and Sales

Year	Number of Tax Shelter Numbers Issued	Maximum Dollar Amount
2010	169	$3,076,361,889
2011	135	$2,943,738,775
2012	73	$1,485,965,789

Following a joint announcement by the Ministers of Finance and National Revenue of additional new measures aimed at abusive tax shelters on December 1, 1994,[1175] the definition of "tax shelter" was broadened by including "any outlay or expense" in addition to "any property."[1176] The definition of "promoter" was also broadened to include any person who, in the course of business, "accepts, whether as principal or agent, consideration in respect of the tax shelter." According to Revenue Canada, a lawyer or accountant merely giving advice to a client who proposes to invest in a tax shelter is not subject to the section 237.1 reporting requirements.[1177]

Promoter penalties

Failure to obtain an identification number before selling or accepting consideration in respect of a tax shelter results in a penalty of 25 percent of the total consideration received or receivable from purchasers in respect of the tax shelter, with a minimum penalty of $500.[1178] The penalty also applies if false or misleading information

---

[1175] Canada, Department of Finance, Release no. 94-112, December 1, 1994. The amendments were included in a technical bill that was ultimately enacted in 1998, applicable to outlays and expenses incurred after Nov. 1994.

[1176] Wayne Penny, "Tax Shelter Rules: Where Are We?", 1995 *Conference Report* (Toronto: Canadian Tax Foundation, 1996), 13:1-22 (suggesting that the legislative change was intended to capture tax shelters in which commissions are paid up front and the revenue follows in several years' time, or film deals structured as service agreements)

[1177] Revenue Canada Roundtable, 1988 *Conference Report* (Toronto: Canadian Tax Foundation, 1989), 53:1-188, question 4, p. 53:78

[1178] *Blier c. R.* (2003), [2004] 2 C.T.C. 2392 (T.C.C. [Informal Procedure]) at para. 74 (beginning on Dec. 2, 1994, the penalty under subsection 237.1(7.4) of the Act for selling an interest in a tax shelter without having obtained an identification number increased from 3 percent to 25 percent); see also:

has been given in the application for the shelter number.[1179] It has been suggested that if there is any doubt about whether an arrangement is a tax shelter, it is advantageous to register, as registration is accepted on a "without prejudice" basis; and, the promoter penalties under subsection 237.1(7.4) and the denial of deductions to investors because of non-registration can for that reason be avoided.[1180]

Further civil penalty provisions were enacted in 2000, in section 163.2 of the Act, which are aimed at tax promoters who devise schemes that result in unwarranted claims for deductions and at tax return preparers who manufacture deductions.[1181] According to the Canada Revenue Agency's Information Circular 01-1 re "Third Party Penalties," section 163.2 is only intended to be applicable to egregious situations.[1182]

Proposed additional reporting requirements

The Government of Canada has recently said, in soliciting comments on its proposals for strengthening information reporting

---

Wertschek and Wilson, *supra* no. 57 (suggesting that section 237.1 should be accorded a "strict construction" because it is a penal provision).

[1179] Subsection 237.1(7.4).

[1180] Donald H. Watkins, "The Tax Shelter Rules: An Update", 1998 *Conference Report* (Toronto: Canadian Tax Foundation, 1999), 5:1-32 (noting that registration as a tax shelter does not automatically result in a denial of tax deductions; and, also that there is no provision for de-registration after registration as a tax shelter has taken place).

[1181] The Auditor General made a recommendation in 1996 that legislation be enacted to impose civil penalties on promoters of abusive tax shelters. This initiated a series of events culminating in the third-party penalties – see Brian R. Carr and Grace Pereira, "The Defence Against Civil Penalties", (2000), vol. 48, no. 6 *Canadian Tax Journal* 1737-1792 (arguing that the third party penalties provisions in section 163.2 are broader than required to address the abuses at which the Auditor General and the Department of Finance were aiming; and, also arguing that the language of the provisions is vague and imprecise).

[1182] Information Circular 01-1, "Third-Party Penalties", September 18, 2001. Very few assessments have been made under section 163.2 and the Tax Court has held that the provision should be considered as creating a criminal offence because it is so far-reaching and broad in scope – see *Guindon v. the Queen*, [2013] 1 C.T.C. 2007 (T.C.C.) (under appeal). Also see the notes to section 163.2 in the *Practitioner's Income Tax Act*, ed. David Sherman, Carswell.

requirements in relation to tax avoidance transactions, that it is aware aggressive tax avoidance has an impact on the tax system.[1183] Although information reporting is already required for tax shelters, the March 4, 2010 budget proposals stated that a new reporting regime is required to assist in identifying aggressive and potentially abusive tax-planning arrangements.[1184] According to the Backgrounder released with the proposals, they are intended to address concerns about the impact of aggressive tax avoidance transactions on the fairness of the tax system. The Backgrounder notes that the United Kingdom,[1185] the United States[1186] and the Province of Québec[1187] now have similar reporting regimes, which identify aggressive tax avoidance planning by reference to typical "hallmarks" of such tax planning.

The hallmarks are said to reflect circumstances that commonly exist in the context of tax avoidance transactions. These are (1) promoters or tax advisors in respect of the transaction are entitled to fees that are to any extent attributable to the amount of the tax benefit from the transaction; contingent upon the obtaining of a tax benefit from the transaction; or attributable to the number of taxpayers who participate in the transaction or who have been provided advice by the promoter or advisor regarding the tax consequences from the transaction; (2) a promoter or tax advisor in respect of the transaction requires "confidential protection" with respect to the transaction; and (3) the taxpayer or the person who entered into the transaction for the benefit of the taxpayer

---

[1183] See Backgrounder: 2010-043–*Government of Canada Seeks Public Input on Proposals To Require Information Reporting of Tax Avoidance Transactions*, Ottawa, May 7, 2010.

[1184] Canada, Department of Finance, 2010 Budget, Budget Plan, March 4, 2010, 382-384; see also: Hickey, *supra* no. 1164 at 2-3 (noting the federal government's statement that the proposed regime is less strict than similar regimes in place in the United States, the United Kingdom and Québec)

[1185] HM Revenue & Customs, "Disclosure of Tax Avoidance Schemes", effective Nov. 1, 2008.

[1186] See Abusive Tax Avoidance Transactions", Highlights of GAO-11-493, a report to congressional requesters (May 2011), p. 4 (noting that the *American Jobs Creation Act 2004* put updated disclosure and list-maintenance rules and updated penalty provisions in place)

[1187] Information Bulletin 2009-5, *supra* no. 608.

obtains "contractual protection" in respect of the transaction (otherwise than as a result of a fee described in the first hallmark).

Under the proposed new regime, a "reportable transaction" will be a transaction entered into by or for the benefit of a taxpayer that is classified within the existing definition of an "avoidance transaction" under GAAR, and that bears at least two of the three hallmarks listed above. An information return would be required to be filed in respect of reportable transactions, unless they are also tax shelters or flow-through share arrangements, in which case the existing reporting regimes for those types of transactions would apply. The consequences of failing to file an information return would be that the tax benefits obtained would not be available until the transaction is reported and, if applicable, the penalty for failure to disclose the transaction is paid.

Proposed additional penalty

The proposed penalty for which the taxpayer will be liable is the total of all amounts each of which is a fee in respect of the transaction, described in a hallmark, to which a promoter or tax advisor is or would be entitled to receive. This is coupled with a provision for joint and several liability for the penalty in respect of all persons involved in the transaction for the benefit of the taxpayer, including the promoter or adviser. A due-diligence defence is proposed for where the person who failed to file the return has exercised the degree of care, diligence and skill to prevent the failure that a reasonably prudent person would have exercised in comparable circumstances.

Early commentary from the tax community concerning the proposed new reporting regime has been that, while there are uncertainties surrounding what is a "reportable transaction" and when penalties will be applicable, the existence of the "hallmarks" criteria, and the conservative state of the usual tax planning engaged in by most owner-managed businesses in Canada, may mean that the new regime will not have a very wide application.[1188] However, the Canadian Bar Association has also suggested that proposed subsection 237.3(2), which imposes a reporting obligation in respect of a "reportable transaction", would be an incursion into the realm of solicitor-client privilege.[1189] In this regard, the Minister of Finance has undertaken to consider amended rules.[1190]

Observations

Although even the existing section 237.1 tax shelter registration provisions have been described as giving rise to "draconian consequences",[1191] the legislative proposals that have been made recently, in order to assist the Canada Revenue Agency in identifying potentially abusive transactions, are substantially less vigorous than the reporting and penalty regime that has recently been strengthened in the U.S.[1192] For example, there is no understatement penalty in Canada,[1193] whereas there is a 20 percent to 40 percent understate-

---

[1188] Marc D. Léger, "Canada Proposes Disclosure of Aggressive Tax Planning", *Tax for the Owner-Manager*, Canadian Tax Foundation (July 2010); compare: Douglas J. Forer and Glen F. Thompson, "Recent Legislative and Administrative Developments in Federal and Provincial Law", 2011 *Prairie Provinces Tax Conference*, (Toronto: Canadian Tax Foundation, 2011), 2:1-53 (suggesting that although it is not surprising that an increased tax reporting regime is being introduced, especially given developments in Québec, the U.S. and U.K., that "it is not at all apparent that the Department of Finance, and the Minister, understand the scope of their proposed legislation")

[1189] Letter dated September 27, 2010 to Minister of Finance from Canadian Bar Association re August 27, 2010 Draft Legislation – Information Reporting of Tax Avoidance Transactions, http://www.cba.org/cba/submissions/pdf/10-65-eng.pdf

[1190] Letter dated January 11, 2011 from Minister of Finance to Canadian Bar Association – see Brian R. Carr, "Solicitor-Client Privilege", 2010 *Conference Report* (Toronto: Canadian Tax Foundation, 2011), 7:1-31

[1191] Wertschek and Wilson, *supra* no. 57 (arguing that the denial of deductions to investors in respect of tax shelters which have not been registered are "harsh and punitive" tax consequences)

[1192] Section 6662 *Internal Revenue Code*

[1193] "Abusive Tax Planning: The Problem and The Canadian Context", Library of Parliament Background Paper (Feb. 18, 2010), p. 6-7 (noting Canada does not impose penalties in respect of assessments that are revised because of aggressive tax planning, unlike some other tax authorities, and suggesting that consideration

ment penalty in the U.S, in respect of which it no longer even recognizes a due diligence defence.[1194] Larin and Duong, among others, have recommended that a system of penalties be implemented in Canada in respect of understatement that is attributable to abusive tax avoidance.[1195] The more serious problem, however, is that unless the courts in Canada begin considering economic substance, in the manner that U.S. courts have done for decades, and in the manner that the GAAR regimes in Australia, New Zealand and South Africa contemplate, it will matter little whether the Agency can identify abusive transactions, as abusive tax avoidance will continue to succeed in the courts. Reliance on the Government's proposed new information reporting requirements alone will not solve the quagmire the Supreme Court has created, with its limitations on economic substance.

QUÉBEC

In January 2009, the Government of Québec released a Working Paper on aggressive tax planning, following a 2008-2009 Budget Speech indicating that aggressive tax planning was a matter of serious concern for Québec's tax authorities, because of revenue loss and the related undermining of the integrity and fairness of the tax system.[1196] The Working Paper proposed steps to be taken against the proliferation of aggressive tax planning, including a mandatory early disclosure regime to be triggered by characteristics associated with tax avoidance transactions; penalties for failing to file mandatory early disclosure; extending the limitation period for assessing when the GAAR applies; and, penalties contingent on the application of the GAAR.

---

   be given to doing so); Arnold, *supra* no. 14 (suggesting that a reasonable penalty would signal that the GAAR is only to be applied in clear cases of abuse)
[1194] Section 6662(b)(6) *Internal Revenue Code*
[1195] Larin and Duong, *supra* no. 31, c. 2 at 9-10 (advocating a graduated set of understatement penalties relative to taxpayer behaviour); see also: Brian J. Arnold, "Why the General Anti-Avoidance Rule Needs A Penalty", *The Arnold Report*, Posting: 019, Canadian Tax Foundation, September 21, 2011
[1196] Aggressive Tax Planning Working Paper, *supra* no. 30.

The Working Paper also reviewed the concept of economic substance at some length, noting that Professors Li and Arnold have both concluded that economic substance should be taken into account in determining whether the GAAR is to be applied.[1197] Ultimately, however, on account of concerns about the potentially disruptive effects of disharmony between the provincial and federal tax systems, Québec concluded that a *unilateral* curative amendment is not desirable.[1198]

Mandatory disclosure regime/Understatement penalties

Following consultation with the public, on October 15, 2009 Finance Québec released Information Bulletin 2009-5 re Fighting Aggressive Tax Planning. This Bulletin announced measures to be adopted to combat aggressive tax planning, including a mandatory disclosure mechanism with a penalty regime; the introduction of a 25 percent understatement penalty where the GAAR applies; plus, a 12.5 percent penalty for the promoters of such avoidance transactions, that is calculated by reference to the consideration received or receivable in relation to the aggressive tax planning transaction.[1199]

The announced changes were introduced in the Québec legislature on May 11, 2010 as Bill 96 *An Act to amend the Taxation Act, the Act respecting the Québec sales tax and other legislative provisions*. The provisions were finally assented to and came into force on October 27, 2010.[1200]

Observations

The understatement penalties introduced in Québec increase the risk to taxpayers who enter into aggressive tax planning transactions. Canada should follow Québec's lead in this regard.

[1197] "The GAAR and the concept of economic substance", Aggressive Tax Planning Working Paper, *supra* no. 30 at 85-90
[1198] *Ibid.* at 89-90.
[1199] Information Bulletin 2009-5, *supra* no. 608.
[1200] Statutes of Québec 2010, chapter 25

UNITED STATES

Given that the mass-marketing of abusive tax shelters has been estimated to reduce U.S. tax revenues by several billions of dollars a year,[1201] it is not surprising that the U.S. has a wide range of measures in place that are aimed at combating abusive tax avoidance transactions,[1202] which are said to often involve little to no risk of economic loss and little to no possibility of profit.[1203]

Reporting requirements

Tax shelters are often designed to avoid detection.[1204] Taxpayers have often been successful in avoiding detection of tax shelters buried in corporate returns by relying on the "audit lottery":[1205] "[I]dentifying tax shelters in an audit is a bit like looking for a needle in a haystack. It is a game of roulette, with the taxpayer using a tax shelter having a good chance of non-detection."[1206]

In order to improve its odds of discovering tax shelter arrangements, the U.S. Government adopted regulations under *Internal Revenue Code* sections 6011 and 6112 in 2004,[1207] requiring tax-

---

[1201] Jared T. Meier, "Understanding the Statutory Tax Practitioner Privilege: What is Tax Shelter "Promotion"?, 78 *University of Chicago Law Review* 671-704 (2011), 675 (describing shelter-marketing practices by major accounting firms in the late 1900's / early 2000's); see also: Joseph Bankman, 83 *Tax Notes* 1775-1795 (June 21, 1999), 1781

[1202] Abusive Tax Avoidance Transactions", *supra* no. 1186 at 1 (describing abusive tax avoidance transactions as threatening the tax system's integrity and fairness)

[1203] Meier, *supra* no. 1201 at 674 (noting that abusive tax shelters can be created by long term advisers who develop customized plans; or, prepackaged and mass-marketed – very often by accounting firms)

[1204] "Discussion Paper on Tax Avoidance", *supra* no. 5 at 9.

[1205] Bankman, *supra* no. 2 at 931 (stating that the government "did not have good success in finding tax shelters that were hidden in complex corporate returns").

[1206] Owens, *supra* no. 575 at 875 (noting that some governments are moving away from a traditional audit approach to a more proactive approach by targeting tax shelter promoters)

[1207] Abusive Tax Avoidance Transactions", *supra* no. 1186 at 4 (noting that the *American Jobs Creation Act 2004* put updated disclosure and list-maintenance rules and updated penalty provisions in place)

payers and promoters to disclose transactions with shelter-like characteristics or effects.[1208] Prior to the adoption of these regulations, IRC 6111 required tax shelter organisers to register a tax shelter on or before the date the investment was offered for sale; however, the penalties in place prior to the 2004 amendments were not broad or severe enough to provide a deterrent.[1209]

Under the earlier regime, six categories of "reportable transactions" were established (1) listed transactions; (2) confidential transactions for which an adviser was paid a fee; (3) contractual transactions entitling the taxpayer to a refund of fees where the intended tax consequences were not available; (4) loss transactions exceeding specified thresholds; (5) transactions with significant book / tax differences,[1210] and (6) certain transactions with brief holding periods.[1211]

[1208] Bankman, *supra* no. 2 at 929 (noting taxpayers have been required to disclose transactions that produced a tax loss in a single year in excess of ten million dollars and stating that the enactment of sections 6011 and 6122 was the most important step the government has taken against tax shelters); see also: "GAO Urges Stiffer Tax Shelter Penalty", *Journal of Accountancy* 100 (October 1988) (reporting that the General Accounting Office recommended increasing penalties for abusive tax shelters because the penalty under *Internal Revenue Code* section 6700 for promoting abusive tax shelters was not a financial disincentive for tax shelter promoters)

[1209] Cong. Rec. S5215 (daily ed. May 11, 2004) (Treasury and IRS officials recognized in the context of the Enron scandal that the abusive shelter provisions are a "joke [that] provide no deterrent at all."); see also: Sandra K. Miller, "The Battle against Abusive Tax Shelters Continues", *Journal of Financial Service Professionals* 58-66 (November 2005), 59 (suggesting that increased disclosure obligations and harsher penalties applicable to promoters and investors enacted in the *Jobs Creation Act of 2004* should cause financial planners to alert their clients that "Transactions should have a viable economic purpose other than to reduce taxable income.")

[1210] The IRS announced the phasing out of this category in Notice 2006-46, because of the introduction of Schedule M-3, which calls for significant detail regarding book-tax differences.

[1211] Treasury Regulation I.6011-4; see also: Herbert N. Beller, "New Disclosure Rules Require Serious Attention", *Financial Executive* 59-61 (September 2003) (noting that the "reportable transaction concept" is the cornerstone of the new Treasury disclosure regulations and that various exceptions exist under Rev. Proc. 2003-24 and 2003-25); Alan Granwell and Sarah McGonigle, "US tax shelters: a U.K. reprise?", vol. 2 *British Tax Review* 170-208 (2006),

"Reportable" and "listed" transactions have had continued importance under the 2004 amendments; however, the tax shelter registration regime was replaced with an information return under IRC 6111. "Material advisers" are required to file information returns with respect to reportable transactions, including a description of the transaction, a description of the potential tax benefits expected, and any other prescribed information.[1212] "Material advisers" are defined in IRC 6111(b)(1) as any person who provides any material aid, assistance, or advice with respect to the organizing, managing, promoting, selling, implementing, insuring or carrying out any reportable transaction and who directly or indirectly derives gross income therefrom in excess of threshold amounts.[1213] Under IRC 6112, material advisers are also required to maintain lists identifying each person to whom the adviser has been a material adviser, and to provide the list when requested in writing.[1214] Twenty-three requests for investor lists were made during the period 2006 – 2009.[1215]

Promoter penalty

IRC 6700 imposes a penalty in relation to the promotion of abusive tax shelters. A penalty can apply to "any person" who, directly or indirectly, organizes or assists in the organization of an entity, plan or arrangement, or participates in the sale of any interests in the entity, plan or arrangement, so long as that person made or furnished, or caused another person to make or furnish, a statement with respect to the tax benefits that the person knew or had reason to know was false or fraudulent as to a material matter. The factors looked to by the courts as to whether a person had the degree of knowledge to justify a penalty are: (1) extent of reliance on

---

173-174 (the "reportable transaction" concept is one of the most powerful tools for identifying tax avoidance)

[1212] Material Advisor Disclosure Statement (Form 8918)
[1213] The IRS issued guidance in Notice 2005-12, 2007-7 IRB494 as to who is a "material advisor"
[1214] Treas. Reg. s. 301.6112-1(g)(1) requires that the list be provided within 20 days of a request
[1215] "Abusive Tax Avoidance Transactions", *supra* no. 1186 at 35-36.

knowledgeable professionals; (2) level of sophistication and education; and (3) familiarity with tax matters. Application of the penalty requires analysis of the facts and circumstances of each case.[1216] The *Jobs Creation Act 2004* changed the penalty from a maximum of $1,000 to 50 per cent of gross revenue from a promotion, typically resulting in penalties over $1 million.[1217]

Penalties for failure to file returns and failure to maintain investor lists

IRC 6707(b)(1) imposes a penalty upon any material adviser who fails to file a return for a reportable transaction or who reports false or incomplete information. Most penalty amounts have exceeded $1 million.[1218] IRC 6708 imposes a penalty for failure to maintain investor lists; maintaining incomplete lists; and, for failing to make the list available when it is requested.[1219] Most penalty assessments under this provision have ranged from $740,000 to $1.1 million.[1220]

Penalties for false statements and gross valuation overstatements

The 2004 amendments increased the penalty for statements by persons who knew or had reason to know that their statements were false to 50 percent of the gross income derived by the person from the activity.[1221] The purpose of these amendments was to help deter

---

[1216] "IRS Implements Promoter Penalty by Analogy to Corporate Tax Shelter Rules", 100 *Journal of Taxation* 247-248 (April 2004), 247 (suggesting the IRS has interpreted the section 6700 promoter penalty as casting a wide net)
[1217] "Abusive Tax Avoidance Transactions", *supra* no. 1186 at 24-25 (showing higher numbers and amounts for promoter penalty assessments in 2008 and 2009 years)
[1218] *Ibid.* at 26.
[1219] Miller, *supra* no. 1209 at 61 (pointing out that the sanctions for offences have been increased).
[1220] *Supra* no. 1217 at 26.
[1221] P.L. No. 108-357 s 818(a) Note, however, that the penalty for a gross valuation overstatement continued to be subject to a maximum penalty of $1,000.

the promotion of tax shelters.[1222] Net penalty assessments of $192 million were made under these provisions in 2004-2009.[1223]

Penalties for failure to disclose

IRC 6707A provides substantial penalties for taxpayers who fail to disclose reportable or listed transactions in their tax returns, irrespective of whether there has been an understatement of income.[1224] On January 19, 2005 the IRS issued Notice 2005-11, IRB 2005-7, to provide guidance to taxpayers with respect to these penalties. Most penalty assessments have been $100,000 or $200,000.[1225]

Penalties for understatement

IRC 6662A also imposes penalties for understatements concerning any listed transaction and any other reportable transaction, if a significant purpose is the avoidance or evasion of federal income tax. The penalty is 20 percent of the understatement in the case of a reportable transaction and 30 percent of the understatement in the case of a listed transaction in respect of which the relevant facts were not disclosed under IRC 6011. Penalty assessments totalled $3.5 million during 2005-2009.[1226]

Strict liability understatement penalty

As set out above, there was a 20 percent understatement penalty prior to the economic substance doctrine's codification. Tax shelter promoters would seek to avoid the penalty, by having a law firm opine that

---

[1222] House Report to Act Section 818, RIA para. 5138, p. 2,689.
[1223] *Supra* no. 1217 at 37-38.
[1224] The number of listed reportable transactions disclosed by taxpayers (on Form 8886) was approximately 6100 in 2007 and 1300 in each of 2008 and 2009 – see "Abusive Tax Avoidance Transactions", supra no. 1217 at 10, 18 (most of these disclosures related to loss transactions)
[1225] *Supra* no. 1217 at 25.
[1226] *Ibid.* at 37.

the transaction was "more likely than not" to hold up if challenged in court.[1227] This is because, under the former penalty regime, exceptions were permitted for "reasonable cause" and "good faith", if the taxpayer reasonably believed that that the treatment of the tax shelter on the taxpayer's return was "more likely than not" the proper treatment.[1228] The existence of these defences is said to have unfortunately given rise to the practice of some tax counsel issuing favourable tax opinions "concerning transactions that clearly lacked economic substance, relying on strained logic and tendentious interpretation of governing law":[1229]

> Like sellers of treasure maps, promoters of tax shelters promise that for a large fee one can navigate a secret route. What clinches these deals is not the chart itself but [an opinion letter] that appears to warrant that the map is as good as gold. ... Written by tax lawyers using the embossed stationery of their firms, the letters typically cost $50,000, $75,000 or more, and require a signed promise to keep the contents secret, like the treasure map, lest the Internal Revenue Service discover where untaxed fortunes lie.[1230]

In light of this phenomenon, a new strict liability 20 percent underpayment penalty was created in section 6662 for an underpayment attributable to any disallowance of claimed tax benefits by reason of a transaction lacking economic substance, as defined in new section 7701(o), or for failing to meet the requirements of any similar rule of law. The penalty is increased to 40 percent if the taxpayer does not adequately disclose the relevant facts affecting the tax treatment in the return or a statement attached to the return.[1231] According to the Technical Explanation, it is also intended that these penalties will

---

[1227] Bankman, *supra* no. 2 at 929-930 (stating that in most cases the strategy has worked in avoiding potential penalties)

[1228] Section 6664(d) *Internal Revenue Code*.

[1229] Karen C. Burke and Grayson M. P. McCouch, "COBRA Strikes Back: Anatomy of a Tax Shelter", vol. 62, no. 1 *Tax Lawyer* 59-93 (2008), 90 (arguing that the rise of contingent-liability tax shelters has "reaffirmed the importance of economic substance as a pervasive judicial doctrine and an essential backstop to the increasingly tangled web of tax statutes and regulations")

[1230] David Cay Johnston, "Costly Questions Arise on Legal Opinions for Tax Shelters", *New York Times*, Feb. 9, 2003, 25

[1231] Section 6664(i)(3) provides that an amended return filed after the taxpayer has been contacted for audit does not cure the omission. See also: McMahon Jr., *supra* no. 79 at 752 (suggesting that given the history of taxpayers and their advisers

apply to a transaction the tax benefits of which are disallowed as a result of the application of similar factors and analysis to that required under the provision for an economic substance analysis, even if a different term is used to describe the doctrine.[1232]

The new strict liability penalty has been described by U.S. tax practitioners as a "hammer" waiting to drop on taxpayers, despite their best efforts to follow technical tax rules.[1233] Many objections have been made to the enactment of the new strict liability penalty, including that it (1) results in substantial overlap with the existing valuation misstatement penalty; the substantial understatement penalty with respect to a tax shelter negligence penalty; and, also the reportable transaction understatement penalty, all of which the IRS says may apply to transactions that lack economic substance, thus complicating the penalty landscape immensely; (2) unfairly punishes taxpayers who have made good faith efforts to comply with the law; and (3) may lead courts to decide the economic substance doctrine does not apply when it should apply, because they do not wish to apply the penalty.[1234]

Outside opinions or in-house analysis will not protect a taxpayer from the penalty if it is determined that the transaction lacks economic substance, or fails to meet the requirements of any similar rule of law. Tax practitioners have said that the new penalty provisions are going to have a large impact because no exceptions to the penalty are available.[1235] In the words of one leading tax lawyer, "[o]ur

---

in hiding their transactions "even a 40 percent strict liability penalty might not be sufficient to deter the most die-hard participants of tax avoidance.")

[1232] Technical Explanation of the Revenue Provisions of the 'Reconciliation Act' of 2010, As Amended, in Combination With the 'Patient Protection and Affordable Care Act', *supra* no. 789 at 155-156 and footnote 359.

[1233] Coder, *supra* no. 797 at 1424 (citing remarks by conference co-chair Byran Skarlatos at a Tax Controversy Forum sponsored by the New York University School of Continuing and Professional Studies); Thomas, *supra* no. 682 at 448 (arguing the penalty "is redundant in light of the current accuracy-related penalties related to tax shelters, and cannot be justified when this standard has not been applied to other tax shelter penalties.")

[1234] Thomas, *supra* no. 682.

[1235] Crystal Tandon, "Treasury Planning Guidance on Economic Substance Penalties", 127 *Tax Notes* 965-966 (May 31, 2010), 965 (citing concern expressed

opinions are worth even less than they were before."[1236] According to Professor Abrams, if Congress hadn't enacted the new strict liability penalties, there would be much less interest in the Treasury issuing an "angel list": "This whole conversation is about the penalties. ... Nobody cares about the codification. They care about the penalties, and we need an angel list to avoid the penalties."[1237]

The IRS initially responded to concerns expressed about the new strict liability penalty by issuing a directive in September 2010 that required any examining agent, proposing to apply the penalty, to first obtain approval from the appropriate Director of Field Operations.[1238] Then on July 15, 2011, the Large Business and International Division issued a directive to field examiners providing guidance for analyzing transactions in determining whether the economic substance doctrine applies.[1239] This directive sets out a detailed set of steps that examiners must follow in determining whether it is appropriate to seek approval to impose the strict liability penalty; and, there are a number of safe harbours described. These include the choice to capitalize a business with debt or equity; the choice between using a foreign corporation and a domestic corporation for a foreign investment; the choice to undertake a

---

by panelists at a Practising Law Institute seminar in New York about the lack of a reasonable cause or good-faith defence).

[1236] Amy S. Elliott, "Economic Substance 'Angel List' Unlikely, Says Treasury Official, 127 *Tax Notes* 521-522 (May 3, 2010), 521 (quoting Robert H. Wellen, a partner at Ivins, Phillips & Barker).

[1237] Amy S. Elliott, "Economic Substance Guidance May Address Rules of Disclosure", 127 *Tax Notes* 1190-1191 (June 14, 2010), 1191 (quoting Professor Howard Abrams, Emory Law School).

[1238] Large and Midsize Business Division directive LMSB-20-0910-024

[1239] Large Business and International Division directive LB&I-4-0711-015 available at http://www.irs.gov/businesses/article/0,,id=242253,00.html (the directive prescribes four steps: (1) evaluate circumstances to determine whether application of economic substance doctrine is likely not appropriate; (2) evaluate circumstances to determine whether application of the doctrine may be appropriate; (3) if it appears the application of the doctrine may be appropriate, there are a series of steps for the examiner to follow before seeking approval to apply the doctrine; and (4) steps are prescribed re how to seek the Designated Field Office's approval. There is also a process prescribed for seeking approval to apply the doctrine to separate steps in a series of steps)

corporate organization or reorganization; and, the choice to use a related-party in a transaction, provided the section 482 arm's length standard "and other applicable concepts" are satisfied.[1240]

The commentary to date regarding the contents of this IRS directive has generally been quite positive, with a suggestion that the directive seems to leave the economic substance doctrine "confined to its proper role as a deterrent to transactions that have no business purpose and that achieve a truly inappropriate tax result, such as the creation of a tax loss that does not correspond to any true economic loss or that allows a taxpayer in effect to deduct the same loss twice."[1241]

The IRS directive is also said to have been well received by tax professionals "because it sets out factors for taxpayers to discuss with exam teams" and also because it "helps provide a framework for analyzing transactions."[1242] Notably, one of eighteen listed positive factors tending to indicate that the application of the economic substance doctrine is not appropriate is "[t]ransaction creates a meaningful economic change on a present value basis (pre-tax)"; and, one of seventeen listed negative factors tending to favour application of the doctrine is "[t]ransaction creates no meaningful economic change on a present value basis (pre-tax)." This is not at all surprising, given the understanding (not enjoyed by Canada's Supreme Court) that an absence of economic consequences (apart from tax benefits) is a primary signal of abusive tax avoidance.

However, until the GAAR is amended in Canada, to bring economic substance fully into the range of considerations that must be

---

[1240] David C. Garlock, Kevin M. Richards, Eric Solomon and Karen Gilbreath Sowell, "Analysis of the LB&I Directive on the Economic Substance Doctrine", *Tax Notes* 193-201 (October 10, 2011), 201 (providing an extensive analysis of the IRS directive, and describing it as "welcome and helpful guidance that provides a procedure for asserting the ESD, as well as significant substantive direction for examiners and taxpayers.")

[1241] *Ibid.*

[1242] Jeremiah Coder, "Economic Substance Guidance Should Reassure, Official Says", *Tax Notes* 1318-1319 (December 12, 2011), 1318 (citing statements by practitioners at an American Bar Association Taxation Section conference in Las Vegas)

explored, in determining whether there has been abusive tax avoidance, treating the presence or absence of economic substance as a "positive" or "negative" factor in assessing transactions is not helpful here.

Website advisories, standards of practice and settlement initiatives

The IRS website contains notices of listed abusive tax shelters and transactions; plus, advisories against typical abusive tax avoidance arrangements that taxpayers should avoid. There is also a referral form for reporting abusive promotions and/or promoters.[1243] The IRS has also issued regulations and Circular 230 describing standards for "best practices" for tax practitioners with respect to issuing tax shelter opinions and providing tax advice regarding federal tax issues.[1244] Professor Miller says that although the standards themselves do not contain sanctions, they are mandatory and failure to comply with them can result in professional disciplinary proceedings.[1245]

The IRS has also instigated settlement initiatives on a global basis and collected, for example, $3.78 billion in taxes, interest and penalties under its Son-of-Boss settlement initiative:[1246]

> Our settlement initiatives and increased audits have sent a signal: the playing field is no longer as lopsided as it once was. Taxpayers and promoters cannot afford to take an Alfred E. Neuman 'What, me worry?' approach to

---

[1243] http://www.irs.gov/pub/irs-ut/referralform_reportingabusiveschemes.pdf
[1244] Under section 10.37, for example, written advice from tax advisors may not be based on unreasonable factual or legal assumptions, must consider all relevant facts, and must not rely unreasonably upon representations of the taxpayer or any other person.
[1245] Miller, *supra* no. 1209 at 63-65 (suggesting all tax practitioners should review Circular 230 as the regulations prohibit the provision of written advice with specified content even outside the tax avoidance realm); see also: Granwell and McGonigle, *supra* no. 1211 at 189 (the IRS and Treasury have specified that only egregious departures from normal practices are targeted)
[1246] Announcement 2004-46, 2004-21 IRB 964 (Many 5, 2004); see also: Granwell and McGonigle, *supra* no. 1211 at footnote 120 (under the settlement, promoter fees could be deducted as capital losses or one-half of such losses as an ordinary loss. Failure to disclose a Son of Boss transaction resulted in a variety of penalties plus disqualification from Appeals Office consideration)

questionable tax shelters. They can no longer assume – 'All I'm putting at risk is the possible payment of the full tax with no penalty.' Now they might have to pay the entire tax, interest and a stiff penalty. A taxpayer might have to wrestle with questions like 'how much am I going to have to pay the lawyers and expert witnesses to litigate this thing?' And going to court is a public matter. Many wealthy individuals otherwise seen as community leaders may not want to be identified as paying less than their fair share in taxes.[1247]

Enjoined conduct

The *American Jobs Creation Act of 2004* also expanded the power to obtain injunctions under the *Internal Revenue Code*, to enable obtaining injunctions against material advisors in relation to specific conduct. The IRS obtained 430 injunctions during 2003-2009, although its data tracking does not enable it to say what percentage of injunctions related to material advisors.[1248]

Observations

The U.S. has the most comprehensive set of complementary measures in place with respect to the ongoing problem that all countries experience with the proliferation of abusive tax avoidance transactions. Although Canada is setting out to improve its complement of similar measures, there is obviously more that can be done here. This includes adopting understatement penalties.

AUSTRALIA

Australia has a civil penalty regime for understatement of income attributable to aggressive tax avoidance and for promoting tax exploitation schemes. The ATO also issues Tax Alerts which are designed to give taxpayers notice that certain tax avoidance schemes may offend Part IVA.

[1247] IRS News Release (IR-2005-30) Remarks of Commissioner Everson at National Press Club in Washington DC (March 30, 2005).

[1248] Abusive Tax Avoidance Transactions", *supra* no. 1186 at 26, 40-41.

No reporting requirement

There is no formal tax scheme disclosure regime to date in Australia, unlike in the U.K., U.S. and Canada; however, Professor Evans thinks it may just be a matter of time until such a scheme is enacted, as concern about aggressive tax avoidance remains high.[1249]

Shortfall penalties

Subsection 177F(2A) imposes a penalty of additional tax where a tax benefit has been cancelled under Part IVA and there has been an increase in the amount of tax assessable to the taxpayer.[1250] The tests for the application of the penalty are (a) whether the taxpayer would, apart from the application of the Part IVA adjustment provision, have obtained a benefit from a scheme; and (b) whether it is reasonable to conclude, having regard to any relevant matters, that the scheme was entered into or carried out with the sole or dominant purpose of obtaining the benefit.[1251]

The penalty is 50 percent of the tax attributable to the tax benefit or 25 percent of the amount if it is reasonably arguable that Part IVA might not have applied.[1252] Whether the matter is reasonably arguable is by reference to the standard of "as likely to be correct as incorrect"

[1249] Evans, *supra* no. 1012, c. 5, at 46; see also: Aggressive Tax Planning Working Paper, *supra* no. 30 at 70, 75 (noting the Australian tax system does not have disclosure rules for aggressive tax planning schemes, unlike the United States, United Kingdom and South Africa)

[1250] Explanatory Memorandum, Income Tax Laws Amendment Bill (No. 2) 1981, Clause 9: Additional tax in certain cases, page 20; see also: Larin and Duong, "Australia General Anti-Avoidance Rule", *supra* no. 31 at 52 (noting that the ATO has discretion to cancel the penalty and also arguing that a penalty for understating tax payable in relation to abusive tax planning is highly desirable)

[1251] Tooma, *supra* no. 15 at 156-158 (noting that if Part IVA applies to a scheme, the conclusion as to the purpose required for the application of the penalty should be able to be drawn)

[1252] Duff, *supra* no. 160 at 494 (citing the penalty as a measure that is implemented to discourage aggressive tax planning); see also: Tax Law Review Committee, "Tax Avoidance", The Institute for Fiscal Studies (Nov. 1997), p. 52 (noting that the Australian penalty regime is much less severe than the New Zealand regime and that Canada has no penalty)

or "more likely to be correct than incorrect" in the circumstances, having regard to the relevant authorities. The relevant authorities include explanatory memoranda associated with the introduction of the tax legislation, court decisions and public rulings.[1253] The existence of this penalty provision is to some extent ameliorated by the fact that taxpayers can obtain private rulings on transactions, including with respect to the application of Part IVA.[1254]

Promoter penalties

Legislation also came into force in 2006 aimed at penalizing the promoters of "tax exploitation schemes."[1255] Under this legislation, the Commissioner can seek the imposition of civil penalties on the promoters or implementers of such schemes; seek injunctions to stop their promotion or implementation; and, also obtain undertakings re how schemes are promoted or implemented.[1256]

To qualify as a "tax exploitation scheme", it must be reasonable at the time the scheme is promoted to conclude that an entity that entered into or carried out the scheme had the sole or dominant purpose of obtaining the scheme's benefit, and it must not be reasonably arguable that the scheme benefit is available under the tax laws. The

---

[1253] Rachel Tooma, "Tax Planning in Australia: When is Aggressive Too Aggressive?", *Tax Notes International* 427-442 (May 2, 2006), 431-432 (noting the Commissioner is obliged to give reasons for finding that a penalty applies)

[1254] An ATO Commissioner cites an example of this, as an effort to address certainty concerns, addressing the Taxation Institute of Australia: Michael D'Ascenzo, Second Commissioner, Australian Tax Office at the Taxation Institute of Australia, 37th West Australia State Convention, Perth 2 May 2003, "Part IVA – The Steward's Inquiry – A Fair Tax System"; see also: Cooper, *supra* no. 463 at 106 (commenting that the Commissioner routinely issues rulings that Part IVA does not apply); Tooma, *ibid.* at 442 (suggesting that requests for rulings should include an application regarding Part IVA); but see: Orow, *supra* no. 968 at 69 (arguing that rulings do not resolve the question of what the law actually is and that they undermine the rule of law)

[1255] Tooma, *supra* no. 1253 at 438-440 (noting that the maximum penalties for individuals and corporations are the greater of the set amounts of $550,000 or $2.75 million and twice the consideration received for the tax exploitation scheme)

[1256] Evans, *supra* no. 1012, c. 5 at 43.

Government's announced purpose in enacting this legislation was to enable the Commissioner to take "real time" steps against the promotion of tax avoidance and evasion schemes. The benefits of enacting a civil penalty regime aimed at promoters were said by the Government to include enhanced community confidence in the tax system and the production of a more efficient market for investment products, including tax effective investments. The Government specifically chose to enact the civil penalty regime vis-à-vis promoters, rather than introducing increased reporting and disclosure requirements, because it was a more targeted measure with low compliance costs.[1257]

Although the Explanatory Memorandum accompanying the draft legislation stated that the new civil penalty regime was not intended to interfere with the provision of independent advice in relation to tax planning, Australian tax commentators have nevertheless expressed fears that it will do that.[1258]

Tax alerts

The ATO issues Tax Alerts regarding avoidance schemes that it considers may offend Part IVA, as part of its overall strategy in combating aggressive tax avoidance.[1259] Taxpayer alerts are intended as an early warning to taxpayers and their advisers of significant tax planning issues or arrangements that the Tax Office has under risk assessment or about which it has concerns.[1260]

[1257] Chapter 3, Explanatory Memorandum to *Tax Laws Amendment (2006 Measures No. 1) Act 2006*.

[1258] Evans, *supra* no. 1012, c. 5, at 44; Tooma, *supra* no. 15 at 183-184 (arguing that the definition of "promoter" is broad, with the result that it has a potential to apply to tax advisers)

[1259] Richard Krever, "Tax Office Warns Miners About Avoidance Scheme", *Tax Notes International* 574 (Feb 16, 2009) (referring to the issuance of TA 2009/3 cautioning mining companies against using a scheme being circulated)

[1260] See Australian Taxation Office, *ATO Examining Takeover Arrangements*, located at: http://www.ato.gov.au/corporate/content.asp?doc=/content/003211795htm

Observations

Canada could potentially benefit from adopting Australia's tax shortfall penalties and tax alert strategy. These are two measures that could be easily added to our anti-tax avoidance arsenal.

NEW ZEALAND

New Zealand utilizes a combination of penalties as deterrents regarding income understatement and the promotion of arrangements which involve abusive tax positions, plus Revenue Alerts. To date there is no reporting requirement regime.

No reporting requirement

In January 2002, Inland Revenue published a paper entitled "Mass-marketed tax schemes", detailing its concerns about the harm being done to the New Zealand tax system by the proliferation of mass-market tax schemes. Its principal concerns were that the existence of such schemes has a negative effect on the integrity of the tax system and undermines taxpayer confidence in the system. One of the proposed solutions was the enactment of a scheme registration system, similar to those then in effect in Canada and the United States. The proposed registration criteria were aimed at the types of schemes that erode the tax base. The consequence of not registering would be that all tax deductions would be deferred until after registration of a scheme.[1261] In keeping with New Zealand's attention to the correspondence between the economic burden borne and the quantum of tax deductions allowed, the term "mass-marketed tax schemes" referred to schemes in which investors received more tax losses than the amount of money invested.[1262] Although no disclosure

---

[1261] Policy Advice Division, Inland Revenue, "Mass-marketed tax schemes: An officials' issues paper on suggested legislative amendments" (January 2002)
[1262] Policy Advice Division, Inland Revenue, "Summary of 'Mass-marketed tax schemes'" (January 2002)

regime has to date been enacted,[1263] Professor Evans has suggested that this development may occur in New Zealand given time.[1264]

Shortfall penalties

Section 141D of the *Tax Administration Act 1994* provides for a civil penalty of 100 percent of the tax shortfall in relation an "unacceptable tax position." Not all tax avoidance qualifies for the penalty, as it is only aimed at taxpayers who have taken an "unacceptable tax position" as defined in section 141B; however, in practice, it is said that this penalty is often imposed.[1265]

An "unacceptable tax position" is a position that "viewed objectively, fails to meet the standard of being about as likely as not to be correct," where the dominant purpose of the arrangement was avoiding tax.[1266] Although the test for tax avoidance looks to both the purpose and effects of arrangements, abusive tax positions only exist when the purpose was avoiding tax. This means that the section 141D penalty is not to be applied by the Commissioner when only the effect of the arrangement is tax avoidance.[1267] The Supreme Court upheld the imposition of a 100 percent section 141D tax shortfall

---

[1263] Keating, *supra* no. 1095 at 89 (pointing out that the proposed registration scheme was abandoned)

[1264] Evans, *supra* no. 94 at 122; Evans, *supra* no. 191 at 28 (pointing out such disclosure regimes in the US, Canada and the U.K.)

[1265] Keating and Keating, *supra* no. 1094 at 132 (noting that the Supreme Court agreed with the Commissioner in *Ben Nevis* that the 100 percent shortfall penalty should be imposed on the taxpayer)

[1266] Section 141D(7) TAA 1994; see also: Shelly Griffiths, "The Abusive Tax Position in the Tax Administration Act 1994: An Unstable Standard for a Penalty Provision?", 15 *New Zealand Journal of Taxation Law and Policy* 159 (June 2009), 170 (noting that interpretative issues have arisen in the courts regarding the standard of "about as likely as not" and whether the "dominant purpose" is that of the arrangement or must be the purpose of the taxpayer)

[1267] Sawyer, *supra* no. 1028 at 489 (arguing that introduction of the "abusive tax position" concept creates confusion and uncertainty by blurring the distinction between traditional tax evasion and tax avoidance concepts)

penalty in the *Ben Nevis* case, finding on the basis of an objective test that the arrangement involved an abusive tax position.[1268]

The 100 percent penalty is reduced to 20 percent if the tax shortfall is less than $50,000, the taxpayer has had independent advice stating that the position is not an abusive one, and the taxpayer is a party to a mass-marketed scheme.[1269] The penalty is also reduced for taxpayers who make voluntary disclosures and for those who have not been the subject of a penalty within the last four years.[1270] The penalty was introduced in 1996 as being consistent with the norm that "non-compliance is unacceptable,"[1271] following a report to the government by a committee that had been appointed to review the organization of the Inland Revenue Department.[1272]

The 1994 Government Discussion Document which introduced the abusive tax position penalties reasoned that the penalties were appropriate, as tax avoidance results in revenue loss and undermines the compliance of other taxpayers.[1273] It also proposed that the indicators of dominant or substantive purpose would be criteria, such as the presence of artificiality and the circularity of funding,

---

[1268] [2008] NZSC 115, at [209]; see also: Elliffe and Keating, *supra* no. 22 at 382 (noting that the penalty for an abusive tax position is based entirely on objective criteria, such that the subjective motive of an unknowledgeable / unsophisticated tax payer is not a material fact); Trombitas, *supra* no. 1027 at 597 (arguing that applying the dominant purpose test without regard to the taxpayer's subjective understanding is a "curious position" given the reason for the penalty).

[1269] Section 141D(3B) TAA 1994.

[1270] David G. Duff, "Tax Avoidance in the 21st Century", http://ssrn.com/abstract=1457453 (2009), 494-495 (suggesting that the enactment of such penalties is a reasonable reform vis-à-vis aggressive tax planning).

[1271] New Zealand Government, Taxpayer Compliance, Standards and Penalties: A Government Discussion Document (Wellington, August 1994), Part I: Introduction, Ch 1: Overview, para. 1.12.

[1272] Organisational Review Committee, Organisational Review of the Inland Review of the Inland Revenue Department: Report to the Minister of Revenue (and on Tax Policy, also to the Minister of Finance), (Welllington, April 2004)

[1273] New Zealand Government, Taxpayer Compliance, Standards and Penalties: A Government Discussion Document (Wellington, August 1994), Part III: Proposals, Ch. 5: Taxpayer Standards, para. 5.34; see also: Sawyer, *supra* no. 1029 at 488 (noting that the concept of abusive or blatant tax avoidance was first introduced in the August 1994 Discussion Document).

etc., from which the purpose could be reasonably concluded.[1274] A proposal that taxpayers should be able to recover from their advisors any tax shortfall and penalties, arising from tax advice found to be non-compliant, was eventually dropped.[1275]

The abusive tax position penalty fits within a civil penalty regime in which there are a variety of penalties with increasingly steep consequences depending upon the seriousness of the behaviour being targeted: not taking reasonable care – s. 141A – 20 percent; unacceptable tax position – s. 141B – 20 percent; gross carelessness – s. 141C – 40 percent; abusive tax position – s. 141D – 100 percent; and, civil evasion – s. 141E – 150 percent. The standard of proof is the civil standard of balance of probabilities and the onus is on the taxpayer, except with respect to the civil evasion penalty.[1276]

Professor Sawyer has criticized the abusive tax position penalty, on the basis that it adds intolerable complexity for taxpayers and blurs the usual distinction between tax avoidance and tax evasion.[1277] He also argues that the existence of the abusive tax avoidance penalty makes it more difficult for lawyers to provide their clients with legal advice re the boundary between tax avoidance and tax evasion, as some of the conventional classic indicators of tax evasion, e.g. concealment and non-disclosure of information, are now also being relied upon by Inland Revenue as indicators of unacceptable tax positions.[1278] Professor Freedman also thinks that the "fuzziness" around

---

[1274] New Zealand Government, Taxpayer Compliance, Standards and Penalties 2: Detailed Proposals and Draft Legislation, (Wellington, April 1995), Part I: Proposals—Tax Avoidance, para 7.9.
[1275] Sawyer, *supra* no. 1029 at 497-498 (noting however that the Government advised that it would monitor tax adviser's advice to determine if the offence of aiding and abetting tax evasion should extend to tax agents / advisers)
[1276] Griffiths, *supra* no. 1266 at 161 (arguing that the wording of the abusive penalty provision is "dense" and "ambiguous" such that Parliament should reconsider the standard in light of international human rights jurisprudence and the New Zealand *Bill of Rights Act* 1990)
[1277] Sawyer, *supra* no. 1029 at 490,496 (arguing that such complexity and uncertainty are harmful elements in a taxation system based on self-assessment and voluntariness, although "an increase and realignment of penalties for more blatant forms of tax avoidance was long overdue")
[1278] *Ibid.* at 498.

the concepts of "abusive tax position" and "unacceptable" interpretation "may represent a deficit in the law", notwithstanding that there is extensive guidance available from Inland Revenue.[1279]

Promoter penalties

The promoters of tax avoidance arrangements are also subject to penalties, where they offer, sell or promote an arrangement to ten or more people in a taxation year, and the arrangement also constitutes an abusive tax position.[1280] The penalty is effectively the sum of the tax shortfalls for an abusive tax position taken by the parties to the arrangement.[1281] Inland Revenue has issued a standard practice statement (SPS) INV-290 stating that for a person to be a "promoter" the person must have knowledge of the key features of the arrangement, or contractual or similar involvement. Persons who are only peripherally involved in the arrangement are not meant to be characterized as promoters.[1282] Furthermore, the matter of whether someone is a "promoter" is a question of fact in each case. It has been suggested that promoter penalties were adopted in New Zealand, rather than a

---

[1279] Freedman, *supra* no. 21 at 355-356 and footnote 120 (arguing that certainty may not be the right test at the tax avoidance / tax evasion boundary, so long as criminal penalties are not applicable to tax avoidance, as an entirely certain test would be subject to manipulation)

[1280] Sections 141EB, 141EC and 141EC *Tax Administration Act 1994*

[1281] Subsections 141EB(1) and (4) *Tax Administration Act 1994*; see also: Lindsay Ng, "Promoter penalties – tax agents beware!", *Chartered Accountants Journal* 26-27 (October 2010) (suggesting that Inland Revenue has been overstepping boundaries in its imposition of promoter penalties on tax agents who are not actually promoters); Graham Tubb, Inland Revenue Department "Promoter Penalties", *Chartered Accountants Journal* 4-5 (November 2010) (responding that the Inland Revenue Department targets only the most overt mass-marketed tax avoidance schemes and that its focus is only on tax agents and other advisors who actively market such schemes to others)

[1282] Report of the Finance and Expenditure Select Committee on Taxation (Annual Rates, Maori Organisations, Taxpayer Compliance and Miscellaneous Provisions), Bill 2002

registration scheme, because of strong opposition to the latter course by tax professionals and industry groups.[1283]

Revenue alerts

Inland Revenue issues "Revenue Alert" statements, which highlight key areas that are likely to be targeted by as tax avoidance arrangements.[1284] For example, following the decision of the Supreme Court in the *Penny* and *Hooper* cases, Inland Revenue issued a Revenue Alert on September 1, 2011, outlining the circumstances in which diverting personal income into other business structures or entities to take advantage of lower tax rates can be considered to be tax avoidance. According to the Alert, Inland Revenue is "focusing on cases where there are clear indicators that someone is deemed to be paying themselves an artificially low salary, and a substantial amount of their income is diverted into a structured arrangement delivering financial and tax benefits to themselves or their family."[1285]

Observations

Canada could benefit from adopting New Zealand's tax shortfall penalties and revenue alert strategy. These are measures that could both be easily added to our anti-tax avoidance arsenal.

[1283] Tooma, *supra* no. 15 at 5.2.1.3 Promoter Penalties in New Zealand, 202-203 (suggesting the New Zealand promoter penalties may be less effective than Australia's penalties as they can be circumvented by restricting the marketing of tax avoidance schemes to fewer than ten investors)

[1284] Elliffe and Cameron, *supra* no. 22 at 453; see also: Inland Revenue Department, Revenue Alert RA 10/01, 18 June 2010

[1285] See: Inland Revenue issues guidance on tax avoidance arrangements", Press Release: Inland Revenue Department (September 1, 2011) http://www.scoop.co.nz/stories/BU1109/S00023/inland-revenue-issues-guidance-on-tax-avoidance-arrangements.htm and http://www.ird.govt.nz/technical-tax/revenue-alerts/revenue-alert-ra1102.html. Note that the substantive tax law regarding this point differs from Canada's. Section 67 of the Canadian *Income Tax Act* denies the deduction of amounts as salary which exceed a "reasonable" amount; however, there is no requirement that an owner-manager be paid a salary which is at least equivalent to the value of services provided to the corporation. Moreover, it is commonplace for family shareholders to receive dividend payments – see, for example, *Aessie v. R.*, [2004] 4 C.T.C. 2159 (T.C.C. [Informal Procedure]) at paras. 7 and 8, per Mogan J. commenting that it was "a common and reasonable deal" for a corporation owned by family members to receive management fees)

SOUTH AFRICA

South Africa has a reporting requirements regime with associated penalties, but it does not have any shortfall or understatement penalties, unlike the case in Australia, New Zealand and the United States.

Reporting requirements

Simultaneously with the amendments to the GAAR enacted by the *Revenue Laws Amendment Act*, 2006, the existing reportable arrangements provisions in section 76A of the *Income Tax Act*[1286] were repealed and replaced by new reportable arrangements legislation enacted as Part IIB of Chapter III of the Act, comprising sections 80M to 80T which came into force on April 1, 2008.[1287] Although SARS had expressed dissatisfaction with the level of reporting that had been made under the provisions of section 76A, they may nevertheless have worked to a degree, as the SARS Commissioner issued a notice on January 10, 2007 advising that it had become aware of transactions, which were to be vigorously challenged, that had been elaborately structured to avoid the tax consequences that would normally flow from the associated transactions.[1288]

According to the Explanatory Memorandum released by the government with the 2006 GAAR amendments, "[t]he proposal of a new General Anti-Avoidance Rule (GAAR) also provides for the opportunity to link the reportable arrangements legislation to the

---

[1286] Anne Bennett and Nola Brown, "Revenue Service Completing Guidance on 'Reportable Arrangements'", 34 *Tax Notes International* 1400 (June 28, 2004) (noting that *Revenue Laws Amendment Act* 45 of 2003 introduced a reporting requirement under section 76A in the *Income Tax Act* designed to identify innovative tax products).

[1287] Kyle Mandy, "Reportable Arrangements", *Accountancy South Africa* (November 2008) (criticizing the new factors which cause a matter to be a reportable arrangement as largely subjective and likely to capture many legitimate transactions. Also predicting, because of the uncertainty as to what is a reportable arrangement and the potential penalty involved, that SARS is likely to be inundated with disclosure related to legitimate arrangements, with the result that the scheme will be frustrated in that it will take years to identify abusive tax arrangements).

[1288] Meyerowitz, *supra* no. 918 at 37.

factors that are indicative of a lack of commercial substance for GAAR purposes."[1289] The factors which cause a matter to be a reportable arrangement under subsection 80M(1) are:

(a) provisions exist whereby the calculation of "interest", finance costs, fees or any other charges are wholly or partly dependent on assumptions relating to the tax treatment;

(b) the arrangement has the characteristics of, or characteristics which are substantially similar to, the tests for lack of commercial substance in the new GAAR, including the inclusion or presence of round trip financing, an accommodating party, or offsetting or self-cancelling elements;[1290]

(c) the arrangement is treated as a financial liability under GAAP but not for the purposes of the Act;

(d) the arrangement does not result in a reasonable expectation of pre-tax profit for any participant; or

(e) the arrangement results in a reasonable expectation of a pre-tax profit which is less than the value of the tax benefit if both are discounted to a present value at the end of the first tax year the tax benefit is derived.

Interestingly, these conditions do not reflect an identical overlap with the conditions specified in the GAAR which indicate "lack of commercial substance"; however, they do focus on features of impermissible tax avoidance arrangements which are associated with no economic substance. These features include those stipulated above under paragraphs 80M(1)(d) and (e), which are variations of tests which have been developed by courts in the U.S. to test economic substance.

[1289] Mazansky, *supra* no. 857 at 159 (referring to the government's explanation that the number and nature of the transactions disclosed to SARS since the promulgation of section 76A had proven to be disappointing); see also: Explanatory Memorandum, Revenue Laws Amendment Act Bill 2006.

[1290] *Ibid.* at 163 (suggesting the latter point is "particularly controversial ... [as] it requires the taxpayer to be a witness against itself, so to speak, by identifying a major element of something that could lack commercial substance and then reporting it to the SARS").

A 41 page Draft Guide to Reportable Arrangements was released by SARS on March 31, 2010 which is intended to provide guidance for the interpretation and practical application of sections 80M to 80T – see the following "Decision Tree" that has been extracted from the SARS Draft Guide:

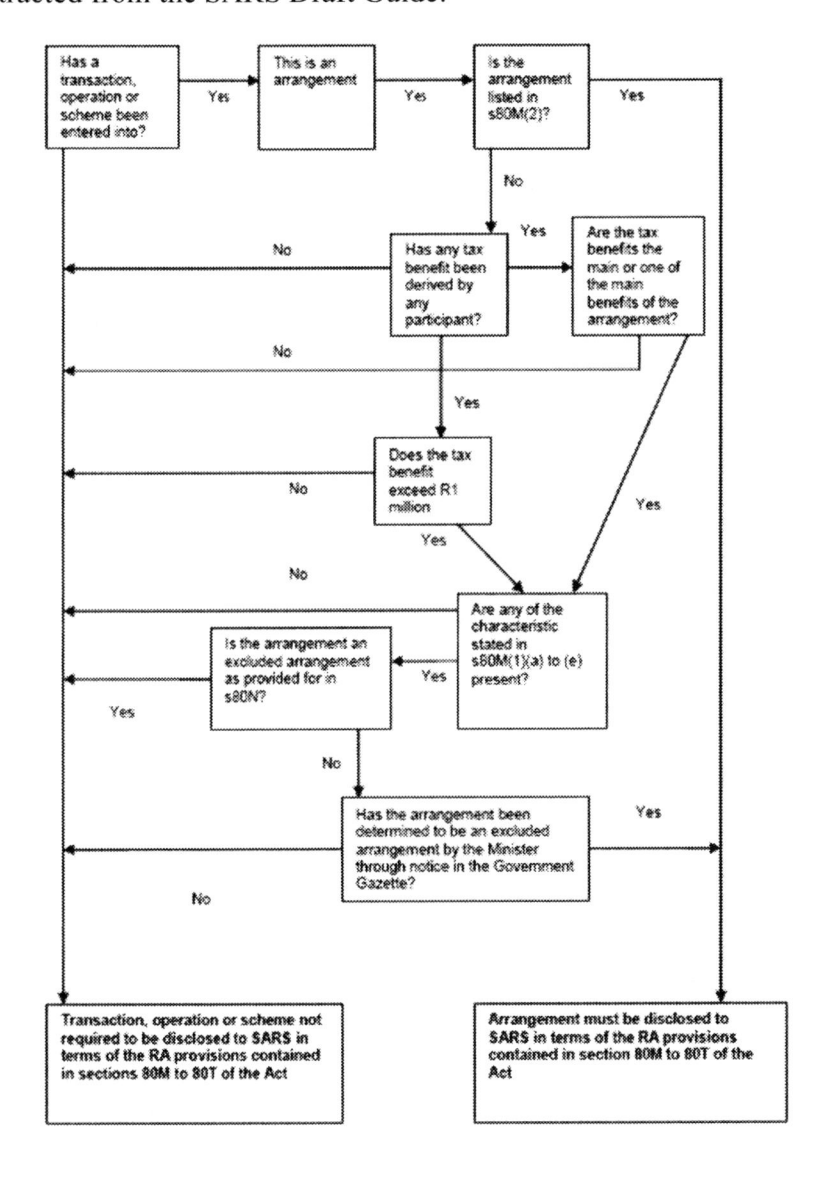

The contents of the Decision Tree box, dealing with paragraphs 80M(a) to (e), make it clear that arrangements without economic substance are reportable arrangements.

Reporting penalties

Under the final GAAR, SARS must be notified in the prescribed form and provided with the prescribed information, failing which the promoter or a participant may be subject to a penalty of up to ZAR 1 million, subject to reduction when there are certain extenuating circumstances.

No shortfall penalties

The SARS Discussion Paper proposed penalties for promoters of abusive avoidance schemes, as well as a penalty to be imposed in the event of a substantial understatement of income.[1291] This proposal is said to have caused much controversy and it did not survive in the final legislation.[1292] There is, however, provision in section 80K with respect to "compulsory interest," when the GAAR has been applied in determining a tax liability.[1293]

Observations

The absence of shortfall/understatement penalties in South Africa (and in Canada) is out-of-step with the state-of-affairs in several other jurisdictions including Québec, Australia, New Zealand and the United States.

[1291] "Discussion Paper on Tax Avoidance", *supra* no. 5 at 57; see also: Mazansky, *supra* no. 833 at 130 (suggesting that the application of penalties was the most controversial aspect of the changes to the GAAR proposed in the Discussion Paper)

[1292] Mazansky, *ibid.* at 160 (again suggesting this was the most controversial SARS proposal).

[1293] See Draft Comprehensive Guide to the General Anti-Avoidance Rule, *supra* no. 835 at 50.

U.K.

Given the U.K.'s heavy reliance on specific anti-avoidance legislation, it is essential that the government have accurate and timely knowledge of what taxpayers are doing. Provisions were therefore introduced in the *Finance Act 2004*, designed to elicit information about arrangements taxpayers are making which are designed to, or have the effect of, reducing their tax liabilities.[1294] As the U.K. does not have a GAAR, and shortfall or understatement penalties are usually imposed by reference to adjustments made under the relevant GAAR, there are presently no U.K. shortfall or understatement penalties.

Reporting requirements

The U.K. enacted U.S.-style shelter regulation rules in 2004, which were designed to provide HMRC with early information about avoidance transactions, with tax shelter registration and taxpayer disclosure requirements. Avoidance transactions are assigned reference numbers which are distributed to participants, and participants are obliged to report the reference numbers on their tax returns.[1295] A dedicated HMRC Anti-Avoidance group conducts tax shelter analysis and assists in drafting legislation to combat the avoidance schemes which have been detected.[1296]

Notifiable arrangements and notifiable proposals must be reported. A transaction is a notifiable arrangement if it (1) yields or is expected to yield a tax advantage; (2) a main benefit of the

---

[1294] Ross Fraser, "Tax scheme disclosure provisions", vol. 4 *British Tax Review* 282-296 (2004), 282 (noting that his article was written after the Report Stage of the Finance Bill based on drafts of the instruments published to date)

[1295] Lynne Oats and David Salter, "Finance Act notes: disclosure of tax avoidance schemes–section 116 and Schedule 38", vol. 5 *British Tax Review* 505-510 (2008) (noting significant amendments to the scheme reference number system after 2004. HMRC estimated that at April 2008 there were 12,500 known users of disclosed schemes and that only between 5,000 and 6,000 users had reported a scheme reference number in 2007)

[1296] Inland Revenue Impact Assessment, Tackling Tax Avoidance (April 2004).

transaction must be the achievement of such a tax advantage; and (3) the transaction must fall within certain regulatory descriptions (and not be excluded). A notifiable proposal is a proposed notifiable arrangement.[1297] In connection with the "main benefit" determination, the guidance provided suggests that where a transaction would not result in a net economic benefit but for the tax advantage, the tax advantage is a main benefit.[1298] Regarding whether the transaction falls within regulatory description, the determination calls for detailed analysis. The requirements for exclusion from disclosure include (1) a finding that a hypothetical experienced buyer would not pay a fee to invest in the transaction; (2) a determination of whether the transaction involves a "premium fee," i.e. whether the fee is chargeable by reference to the expected tax savings; and (3) a confidentiality test aimed at determining whether it might reasonably be expected that the promoter or another party to the transaction would wish to keep the transaction confidential.[1299]

The U.K. system imposes its initial reporting requirements on those persons who may be considered to be "promoters." Those who are involved in providing services related to taxation, banks and securities houses can be considered to be promoters, if they are also involved with designing, marketing, managing or organizing the scheme (subject to specific exclusions by regulation).[1300] The reporting obligation is to disclose "sufficient information as might reasonably be expected to enable an officer of the board to comprehend the manner in which the proposal is intended to operate."[1301] In the case where all promoters of a notifiable arrangement or notifiable proposal reside outside the U.K., the disclosure obligation falls on the person

---

[1297] *Finance Act 2004*, s. 206(1)-(2)
[1298] Granwell and McGonigle, *supra* no. 1211 at 195 (noting that more recent guidance states that whether obtaining a tax advantage is a main benefit is an objective question of fact that considers the value of the expected tax benefit compared to the value of any other benefits likely to be enjoyed)
[1299] *Ibid.* at 199-200 (noting these filter tests carve out transactions from a wide array of possible transactions).
[1300] *Ibid.* at 200-201 (noting there is a "reasonableness" criteria re an exclusion test based on ignorance regarding notifiability).
[1301] *Tax Avoidance Schemes (Information) Regulations* (SI 2004 no. 1863), reg. 3(1)

who enters the transaction.[1302] There is also a reporting obligation on taxpayers who devise their own tax avoidance schemes.[1303]

Investors are required to provide HMRC with the reference number assigned to the scheme in which they have participated and the period in which it is expected to yield its tax benefits.

Promoter penalties

Penalties of up to £5,000 may be imposed on those who fail to comply with the reporting obligation. The penalty may be increased by up to £600 per day for continuing failure.[1304] Failure to provide investors with reference numbers can also result in a penalty of up to £5,000.[1305]

Investor penalties

A person who fails to report a reference number for a shelter in which the person is participating is liable for a penalty of £100, subject to increased penalties for repeated failures to report.[1306]

Observations

Given the powers present in the *Taxes Management Act 1970* and the *Finance Act 1998* to require that information be produced, it was suggested at the outset of the new disclosure regime that "it was a little odd that a completely new body of legislation has been introduced."[1307] Nevertheless, there has been speculation that these rules are making a difference, in the sense that fewer people are in-

---

[1302] *Finance Act 2004*, section 309(1).
[1303] *Tax Avoidance Schemes (Information) Regulations*, regs. 3(4) and 4(5).
[1304] Tiley, *supra* no. 1125, c. 9 at 75 (contrasting the U.K. approach with Australia's in that the U.K. approach is designed to obtain compliance with a daily penalty until the failure to report is remedied).
[1305] *Finance Act 2004*, s. 315(1)-(2)
[1306] *Taxes Management Act 1970*, section 98C imposed by *Finance Act 2004*, s. 315.
[1307] Fraser, *supra* no. 1294 at 295-296 (although noting that one of the purposes of the new regime was to assist Inland Revenue in identifying the promoters of schemes)

volved in aggressive tax planning, as the number of disclosures has diminished since introduction.[1308] In any event, if the U.K. eventually introduces a GAAR, it will need to decide whether to also include understatement/shortfall penalties to act as a deterrent.[1309]

CONCLUSION

Canada should follow the lead of other jurisdictions including Québec, Australia, New Zealand and the United States, by adding shortfall/understatement penalties to its GAAR, in order to increase the risk for taxpayers who engage in aggressive tax planning.[1310] This step should be subsidiary, however, to doing what needs to be done to improve the chances that Canada's GAAR will be effective in future cases, i.e. by adding a requirement for consideration of economic substance.

In the next chapter I examine court decisions in tax avoidance cases, including the first post-GAAR decision of the Supreme Court of Canada in *Canada Trustco*, which also minimized the role of economic substance, and I argue that the amendments that I am proposing for GAAR will enhance the ability of the courts to deal with abusive tax avoidance in an effective manner.

[1308] Maria Italia, "Taxpayer Privilege and the Revenue Authorities' Obligation to Maintain Secrecy of Taxpayer Information: Recent Developments in Australia, and a Comparison with New Zealand, the United Kingdom and the United States", 17 *New Zealand Journal of Taxation Law and Policy* 151-177 (June 2011), 177 (noting that a GAAR has not been enacted in the U.K. and that its tax avoidance decisions involve interpretation of taxing statutes)

[1309] See Aaronson GAAR Study, *supra* no. 1115, sections 5.47 and 5.48 (recommending against the inclusion of such a provision, since although it would increase the deterrent effect and "might be regarded by a significant proportion of taxpayers as no more than just retribution for schemes designed to avoid paying a fair share of tax", including such a provision "would be seen as presenting an irresistible temptation to HMRC to wield the GAAR as a weapon rather than to use it, as intended, as a shield.")

[1310] Loutinksy, *supra* no. 181 at 121 (suggesting that generally tax avoidance is "a function of the size of the penalty and the likelihood that the penalty will be imposed"); see also: Graeme S. Cooper, "Business Purpose, Economic Substance, and Corporate Tax Shelters", vol. 54 SMULR 83 (2001), 108 (noting that amongst the four countries with a GAAR that were examined in his paper, "except in Canada, triggering the GAAR increases a taxpayer's culpability").

IX

Case Studies

In this chapter I examine reported tax avoidance cases with a view to assessing the impact that an amendment to GAAR relating to economic substance would have upon the outcomes of such cases. I also argue that the economic substance amendments I am proposing would be a substantial advance in strengthening Canada's present defences against abusive tax avoidance, while at the same time not being seriously disruptive; and, in fact, contributing to more certainty.

As noted previously, the Supreme Court of Canada has "refused to strike down several blatant tax-avoidance schemes."[1311] Also, as I set out in chapter V, the Supreme Court's decisions in tax avoidance cases have generally been made on the basis of it essentially ignoring economic substance. Assuming that GAAR had been in place, with the amendments that I am proposing, the outcomes in the cases where tax benefits have been allowed in respect of transactions without economic substance should have been different. In

---

[1311] Arnold, *supra* no. 130 at 2 (arguing that the Supreme Court's application of a literalist or plain meaning approach to statutory interpretation, despite its avowed adoption of the modern approach, informs its attitude to tax avoidance).

saying so, I am mindful that the economic substance doctrine has generally only been applied in the U.S. in a tax shelter context.[1312] Nevertheless, and as Sheppard has noted, the economic substance doctrine can also be applied to individual cases.[1313]

Analysis of these cases by reference to my proposed amendments is not meant to suggest that an economic substance analysis would have been the only viable way for the courts to approach the cases. In this regard I note that the courts can reach the same result in a particular case, e.g. uphold the Minister's assessment, through a variety of different avenues.[1314] I am also not suggesting that the proposed amendments will be a universal cure for all of the tax avoidance problems in the Canadian landscape.[1315] Rather, the

---

[1312] Thomas, *supra* no. 682 at 486 (suggesting that "It is difficult to determine if violations of the economic substance doctrine are a subset of tax shelters, if tax shelters are a subset of violations of the economic substance [doctrine], or if the two can be considered proxies for one another.")

[1313] Sheppard, *supra* no. 684 at 428 ("Economic substance, after all, was originally devised to apply to individual cases."); also see Swiderski and Manasuev, *supra* no. 15 at 18:1-31 (suggesting that the reach of the codified economic substance doctrine in the U.S. is not "limited to tax shelter and highly structured, marketed transactions.")

[1314] See, for example, *Boardman v. R.* (1985), [1986] 1 C.T.C. 103 (Fed. T.D.) where Strayer J. upheld the Minister's assessment under subsecs. 56(2) and 245(2) of *the Income Tax Act*, leaving open the possibility that it could also be upheld under subsec. 15(1) of the Act; See also *Antle v. R.* (2009), [2010] 4 C.T.C. 2327 (T.C.C. [General Procedure]), affirmed 2010 FCA 280 (F.C.A.), leave to appeal refused 2011 CarswellNat 5822 (S.C.C.), reconsideration / rehearing refused 2012 CarswellNat 172 (S.C.C.), leave to appeal refused 2011 CarswellNat 1491 (S.C.C.), reconsideration / rehearing refused 2012 CarswellNat 183 (S.C.C.), where the Tax Court upheld the Minister's assessment on the basis that a trust had not been validly constituted, or alternatively if the trust was valid, also because GAAR applied to the transactions.)

[1315] Edgar, "Some Lessons from the Saga of Weak-Currency Borrowings", *supra* no. 128 at 23-24 (suggesting, in response to suggestions from others that there be a moratorium on the promulgation of further technical tax rules, that in the context of tax avoidance via exploiting the differences in tax treatment of financial instruments (e.g. capital gain and loss treatment available for investors who hold instruments on capital account and not as traders; dividend treatment for instruments that are considered shares; interest treatment limited to debt financing charges within the restrictive legal definition of interest; gain or loss recognition when realized, etc.), "it is doubtful whether, in practice, the courts have the capabilities" for coming up with the appropriate responses).

proposed amendments are meant to move the yard sticks, so that Canadian courts are on the same playing field as the courts are in many other similar jurisdictions.

The Supreme Court's first GAAR decision in *Canada Trustco* is a good starting point for my analysis, in that it reflects the Court's continuing restrictive treatment of economic substance even after GAAR was enacted.[1316] The need for the amendments to GAAR that I am proposing is highlighted by the fact that similar sale and leaseback transactions that were undertaken in the U.S. have been ignored by U.S. courts for tax purposes, because they were found to be lacking in economic substance and would place an undue burden on the balance of the taxpaying public.[1317]

CANADA TRUSTCO MORTGAGE CO. v. R.[1318]

The taxpayer engaged in transactions involving the purchase of tractor-trailers for $120 million and their immediate albeit round-about leaseback to the vendor:

> In a single day, [Canada Trustco Mortgage Co. or "CTMC")] borrowed money, purchased a fleet of trailers, leased the trailers to a bank-controlled subsidiary which subleased them back to the original owner, the original owner repaid all amounts owing under the sublease to the bank-controlled subsidiary, and the subsidiary then deposited an amount equal to the loan in the bank. The trailers always remained with the original owner, but because CTMC became the legal owner of the trailers at a legal cost of $122.3 million, it claimed tax deductions even though it sustained no actual cost. ...

[1316] Cassidy, *supra* no. 963 at 301-302 (arguing that if the economic reality of the arrangements had been considered in the *Canadian Pacific* and *Shell* cases, the deduction of inflated interest payments would have been considered to be a misuse of subparagraph 20(1)(c)(i) of the *Income Tax Act*; and, that the Supreme Court took the same "legal rights / form approach" after GAAR in its decision in *Canada Trustco*)

[1317] See the review of the U.S. tax treatment of sale and leaseback ("SILO") transactions in chapter VI.

[1318] *Canada Trustco Mortgage Co. v. R.*, [2005] 2 S.C.R. 601 (S.C.C.).

Neither [the trial judge] nor the Court of Appeal was prepared to consider the economic realities of the arrangement." [1319]

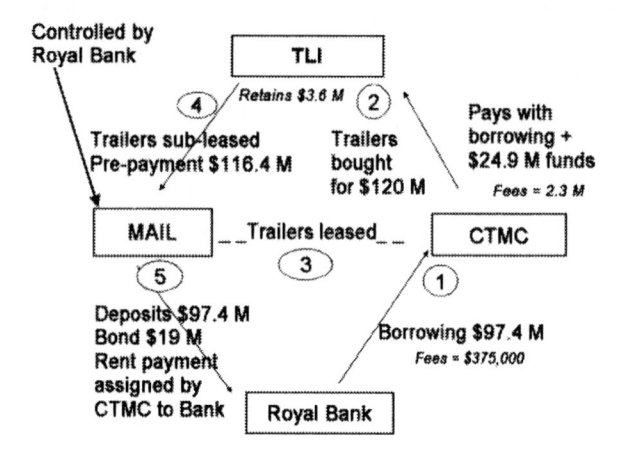

```
Controlled by
Royal Bank                TLI
        \        Retains $3.6 M  (2)      Pays with
         \       /                  \     borrowing +
    Trailers sub-leased    Trailers    \  $24.9 M funds
    Pre-payment $116.4 M   bought         Fees = 2.3 M
         |                 for $120 M
         |
        MAIL    _ _Trailers leased_ _    CTMC
         (5)              (3)           /  (1)
    Deposits $97.4 M                   / Borrowing $97.4 M
    Bond $19 M                        /  Fees = $375,000
    Rent payment                     /
    assigned by
    CTMC to Bank      Royal Bank
```

The steps in the transactions were as follows, according to the Factum filed by the Crown in the Supreme Court:

(1) CTMC obtained a loan of $97.4 million from the Royal Bank of Canada (which was returned to the bank on the same day). The Bank limited its recourse against CTMC to the payments due to CTMC under of a lease of the trailers that CTMC would purchase (described in point 3). CTMC then added $24.0 million of its own funds, for a total of $122.3 million;

(2) CTMC entered into an agreement to purchase the trailers from an American company, Transamerica Leasing Inc. ("TLI") for $120 million. It paid a fee of $2.3 million to Macquarie for arranging the transaction, including $375,000 paid to the Bank for facilitating it. Thus, CTMC's apparent cost totalled $122.3 million (although TLI continued to treat the property as its own and deduct depreciation in the U.S.);

[1319] Factum of the Appellant Her Majesty the Queen in the Supreme Court of Canada, No. 30290, paras. 4-5; see also: Cassidy, *supra* no. 963 at 301-302 (noting the Supreme Court's refusal to countenance the Crown's submission that there was "only a shuffling of paper" and no real money being invested).

(3) CTMC immediately leased the trailers back to TLI through a UK company, Maple Assets Investments Limited (MAIL), which was controlled by the Bank and was interposed to facilitate the transaction (TLI continued to earn income from the operating leases for the duration of the arrangement and was assured of the return of legal title);

(4) As required by the contracts, TLI immediately prepaid all of its obligations under the sub-lease ($116.4 million) to MAIL and kept $3.6 million as an accommodation fee;

(5) MAIL deposited $97.4 million of the prepayment with the Bank, thus returning exactly the amount of the loan to the Bank on the same day. MAIL then used the balance of the prepayment ($19 million) to acquire a Government of Ontario bond acceptable to CTMC and in which CTMC was granted a security interest. In addition, the payments due under the lease with MAIL were assigned by CTMC to the Bank. The bond was to mature at $33.5 million just in time to fund the exercise by MAIL of a purchase option under the lease that was to become available in December, 2005. The transaction documents provided that the deal could be unwound if there were changes to the tax regime which adversely affected CTMC.[1320]

McDonnell has summarized the transactions in *Canada Trustco* in these terms:

> The arrangement was carefully designed to provide the taxpayer with substantial CCA shelter at little or no economic cost. In terms of commercial reality, little changed as a result of the transaction. TLI, the owner of the trailers before the transaction commenced, had the possession, use, and risk of these assets afterward. Apart from transaction costs, TLI put no new money into the system, and it had no direct use of the purchase money paid for the trailers. Its equity investment was secured and expected to be returned on the first option exercise date. After the dust cleared, the practical

---

[1320] Factum of the Appellant Her Majesty the Queen in the Supreme Court of Canada, No. 30290, paras. 4-5.

result of the arrangement was that the taxpayer had a substantial pool of CCA available to shelter other lease income."[1321]

The purpose of the transactions was to obtain capital cost allowance deductions to be used to shelter income from leasing other assets. According to an internal taxpayer memorandum, "[t]he transaction provides very attractive returns by generating CCA deductions which can be used to shelter other taxable lease income generated by Canada Trust."[1322] The taxpayer had retained an "arranger" to locate a leasing transaction for $100 million, as it had previously entered into a similar arrangement and it knew that tractor-trailers yielded "good after-tax return."[1323] The facts of the case[1324] are similar to those in *Rice's Toyota* (see chapter VI – US tax shelter cases, Sale and leaseback ("SILO") shelters), which did not survive the U.S. economic substance doctrine.[1325]

[1321] Thomas E. McDonnell, "The GAAR: Limited-Recourse Defeased Lease Survives Review, Current Cases", (2003) vol. 51, no. 4 C.T.J. 1602-1629, 1628.

[1322] *Canada Trustco Mortgage Co. v. R.*, [2005] 2 S.C.R. 601 (S.C.C.) at para. 2.

[1323] *Canada Trustco Mortgage Co. v. R.*, [2003] 4 C.T.C. 2009 (T.C.C. [General Procedure]) at para. 5, affirmed 2004 CarswellNat 305 (F.C.A.), affirmed 2005 CarswellNat 3212 (S.C.C.).

[1324] Jack Bernstein, Barbara Worndl and Kay Leung, "Canadian Supreme Court's Pronouncement On GAAR: A Return to Uncertainty", *Tax Notes International* 437-447 (October 31, 2005), 439 (setting out that under the "numerous and factually complex" transactions, the result was that "Canada Trustco would not be at economic risk with respect to its purchase of the trailers, and that Canada Trustco would be entitled to claim a substantial capital cost allowance (CCA) for the full C $120 million paid for the trailers. In addition, Canada Trustco would be entitled, for tax purposes, to deduct the interest expense on the loan from the bank. As a result, Canada Trustco would be entitled to tax deductions in excess of its lease income, allowing it to shelter its other income from tax. From an economic point of view, Canada Trustco was not at risk regarding its cost of acquiring the trailers because of the various nonrecourse, pledge, support, and security arrangements."; Diagram and description of the facts taken from Factum of the Appellant Her Majesty the Queen in the Supreme Court of Canada, case No. 30290, para. 23)

[1325] 752 F.2d 89 (4th Cir. 1985); see also: Vitaly Timokhov, "Supreme Court Cases Test Canada's Antiavoidance Rules", *Tax Notes International* 415-421 (May 2, 2005), 415 (noting that in the *Rice's Toyota* and *Canada Trustco* cases the taxpayer "used a combination of recourse and nonrecourse debt to finance a purchase of equipment that was immediately leased back to accommodation party through an entity controlled by an arm's-length lender").

The Canada Revenue Agency disallowed the $31,196,700 deduction by the taxpayer for capital cost allowance in relation to the purchase price of the tractor-trailers. The sole ground relied upon by the Crown, in defending the reassessment at trial, was that the deduction for capital cost allowance was not allowable under GAAR. The taxpayer's transactions bore many of the hallmarks of classic tax avoidance schemes, in that an "arranger" was engaged to locate a tax reduction vehicle and structure the transactions, the costs and expenditures were effectively eliminated by engaging in offsetting circular transactions, and there was no possibility of any pre-tax profits. The trial judge found that the transactions amounted to an "ordinary sale-leaseback",[1326] but he still considered that they constituted an "avoidance transaction" within the meaning of subsection 245(3) of the Act, because they could not be viewed as having been undertaken primarily for *bona fide* purposes other than to obtain the tax benefits.[1327]

The trial judge did not do an analysis of the economic consequences of the transactions in relation to the expected tax benefits. However, given that there was no possibility of generating any pre-tax profit other than from the return on the investment in the government bond, which return would have been greater if the taxpayer had invested its own equity, the transactions did not result in a substantial change in the taxpayer's economic position, when considered in relation to the tax benefits obtained.[1328] According to Professor Li, "it is obvious that the

---

[1326] *Canada Trustco Mortgage Co. v. R.*, [2005] 2 S.C.R. 601 (S.C.C.) at para. 8.
[1327] *Canada Trustco Mortgage Co. v. R.*, [2003] 4 C.T.C. 2009 (T.C.C. [General Procedure]) at para. 54, affirmed 2004 CarswellNat 305 (F.C.A.), affirmed 2005 CarswellNat 3212 (S.C.C.).
[1328] Arnold, *supra* no. 8 at 199 ("Apart from the fees and transaction costs, the financial and commercial positions of all of the parties to the transactions remained unchanged."); see also: Lipton, *supra* no. 237 at 211 (noting that the Federal Claims Court in *Wells Fargo* evaluated objective economic substance by noting that the same return could have been earned by simply investing without entering into the various transactions; plus, "the net present value of these non-tax investments was less than the total cost ... of participating in the transactions. On a net present value basis, each SILO was a losing proposition without the tax benefits. This loss arose due to the significant transaction costs, the incentive payment ... and the cost of finds ... The court found that at the bottom line the SILOs provided [Wells Fargo] with no reasonable possibility of profit at all absent a claim for tax deductions.")

transactions had no economic substance", considering that the transactions were pre-ordained; the loan from the Royal Bank was effectively re-paid on the day that it was made when the taxpayer/borrower assigned the rent payments; there was no risk that the rent payments would not be made because the rent payments originally came from the taxpayer; and, the taxpayer's own contribution to the deal and its transaction costs were covered by the government bond.[1329]

As the taxpayer had no economic investment in the trailers and no risk in the leased assets, it is hard to fathom how it could be contemplated that the tax benefits arising from the transactions could have been intended by Parliament.[1330] Considering that the capital cost allowance regime is intended to recognize the diminishment in value over time of the economic cost of assets that are acquired for the purpose of earning income,[1331] it should have been apparent to the courts that the deduction of capital cost allowance, in the absence of any actual economic outlay, was not appropriate. The Supreme Court nevertheless upheld the taxpayer's position that it was

---

[1329] Li, *supra* no. 8 at 50 (arguing that where all of the economic risks associated with real business transactions have been hedged "then it is likely that there is no economic substance to the transaction.")

[1330] Cassidy, *supra* no. 963 at 302 (arguing that "the circularity of the arrangements and the absence of any real capital costs to the taxpayer should have indicated that this was a misuse of the CCA provisions and an abuse of the Act as a whole.")

[1331] *Duncan v. R.*, [2002] 4 C.T.C. 1 (Fed. C.A.) at para. 44, per Nöel J, leave to appeal refused 2003 CarswellNat 707 (S.C.C.) ("There can be no doubt that the object and spirit of the [capital cost allowance] provisions is to provide for the recognition of money spent to acquire qualifying assets to the extent that they are consumed in the income earning process under the Act."); see also: *Landrus v. R.* (2008), [2009] 1 C.T.C. 2009 (T.C.C. [General Procedure]), affirmed [2009] 4 C.T.C. 189 (F.C.A.) at para. 110, per Paris J ("The amount of the allowance is based on the cost of the assets to the taxpayer and is intended to allocate the cost of the assets over its [sic] economic life.") compare: Freedman, *supra* no. 21 at 351-352 ("the capital allowances legislation is quite deliberately *not* based on economic reality so the government cannot complain when the leasing industry uses the regime to the full, absent any indication in the legislation that it should not have the advantage of capital allowances in these circumstances. This takes us back to the test of construing legislation according to its parliamentary intention, which is apparently the only one we can apply.")

entitled to capital cost allowance, by settling upon a narrow legal definition of "cost" for capital cost allowance purposes.[1332]

Perhaps the Court was bamboozled into thinking that permitting the capital cost allowance deductions reflected an appropriate tax result;[1333] however, if the courts had been obliged to examine the economic substance of the transactions, as the U.S. courts have been doing for decades, and as the GAAR amendment that I am proposing requires, it should have understood the tax mischief being done. In Professor Duff's words, "the production of CCA deductions through a circular flow of funds that left the taxpayer at little or no economic risk with respect to the trailers in respect of which it claimed CCA could legitimately be regarded as an abuse having regard to the provisions of the ITA read as a whole."[1334]

Courts in other jurisdictions have not had difficulty with reaching such a conclusion: "If the commissioner had shown that the features on which he relied, singly or in combination, had the effect that the investors, while purporting to incur a liability to pay $x+y to acquire the film, had not suffered the economic burden of such expenditure before tax which Parliament intended to qualify them for a depreciation allowance, then he could invoke s 99 to disallow the deduction."[1335] In Canada, tax commentators have noted that "[t]he [*Canada Trustco*] transaction was both circuitous and

---

[1332] *Canada Trustco Mortgage Co. v. R.*, [2005] 2 S.C.R. 601 (S.C.C.) at paras. 74-76 (the Court stated that the applicable CCA provisions do not refer to economic risk and that if the government wanted to introduce the concept of economic risk into the provisions it could do so expressly)

[1333] See Lewis Carroll, "Alice's Adventures in Wonderland", chapter XII-Alice's Evidence, in which the White Rabbit confuses the King, who is presiding as the judge at the trial of the Knave of Hearts, by suggesting an interpretation of Alice's evidence "in a very respectful tone, but frowning and making faces at him as he spoke."

[1334] David G. Duff, *supra* no. 25 at 41-42.

[1335] *Ben Nevis Forestry v. CIR*, (2009) 24 NZTC 23, 188 (SC) at para. 98, quoting Lord Millett on behalf of the majority with approval in *Peterson v. Commissioner of Inland Revenue*, [2006] 3 NZLR 433 (PC) at paras. 36-37.

tax-motivated, but the apparent patina of commerciality was evidently sufficient to save it from the application of GAAR."[1336]

My point is that a "patina of commerciality" should not suffice, once the courts are obliged to consider the economic substance of the transactions before them – hence the amendments to GAAR that I am proposing – with a view to securing the appropriate result in SILO cases.

OSFC HOLDINGS LTD. v. R.

The *OFSC Holdings* case concerned what is colloquially known as "loss trading", which involves a corporation purchasing the accrued losses of another corporation, to be used as a deduction in reducing taxable income. It is generally well-understood that the *Income Tax Act* does not permit "loss trading" amongst arm's length parties, although the Act does allow access to another corporation's losses in limited circumstances.[1337] However, the general prohibition against arm's length "loss trading" does not stop enterprising tax planners from attempting to invent technical strategies which will overcome the rules in the Act regarding loss transfers.[1338]

OFSC Holdings involved such a scenario. The Standard Trust Company was in the business of lending money on the security of mortgages of real property. It became insolvent and a court ordered that it be wound up. During the course of the winding up, the

---

[1336] Bleiwas and Hutson, *supra* no. 17, c. 16, V. GAAR, Canada's Answer to Tax Avoidance, B. Analysis of Section 245, 7. Misuse or Abuse, h. Selected Supreme Court of Canada Cases

[1337] *OSFC Holdings Ltd. v. R.*, 2001 D.T.C. 5471 (Fed. C.A.) at para. 98, per Rothstein J, leave to appeal refused 2002 CarswellNat 1388 (S.C.C.): "I have no difficulty concluding that the general policy of the *Income Tax Act* is against the trading of non-capital losses by corporations, subject to specific limited circumstances."

[1338] Jack Bernstein and Kay Leung, "Loss Utilization Planning: An Update", 2003 *Ontario Tax Conference* (Toronto: Canadian Tax Foundation, 2003), 17:1-48 (noting that "taxpayers have been very creative in their tax planning and have devised structures to avoid the application of [avoidance provisions limiting the deductibility of losses]")

liquidators devised a plan to sell the mortgage portfolio, and also to sell the substantial accrued losses on properties in the portfolio, to third parties. The cost of the mortgages had been approximately $85 million and the value of the properties at the time was only approximately $33 million. Pursuant to the plan devised by the liquidators, Standard first incorporated a subsidiary. It next formed the STIL II Partnership with its subsidiary, and then transferred its portfolio on a tax-deferred basis to the partnership, in consideration for a 99 percent interest in the partnership. Pursuant to subsection 18(3) of the *Income Tax Act*, as it read at the time, Standard was unable to realize the accrued $52 million loss on the transfer; however, the cost to the partnership was recorded as Standard's original cost of $85 million (the cost to the partnership, plus the loss to Standard on the sale).

Six months later, OFSC Holdings Ltd purchased Standard's 99 percent interest in the STIL II Partnership for $17.7 million and an earn-out based on proceeds from the disposition of the portfolio; plus, up to $5 million for the losses contingent upon their successful deduction. OFSC Holdings Ltd then disposed of its 99 percent partnership interest to SRMP Partnership, in which it retained a 23 percent interest, for consideration of $3.5 million and 81 percent of the income of the partnership from the mortgages; plus, 25 percent of any losses realized. SRMP realized a tax loss in excess of $52 million in 1993, which it allocated to its various partnership unit holders. The CRA denied the deduction of OFSC Holdings Ltd.'s share of the SRMP losses, which were approximately $12.5 million. The transactions are represented in the following diagrams:[1339]

[1339] Peter E. McQuillan, "Some Important Issues in Partnerships in the Past Year", 2002 *Conference Report* (Toronto: Canadian Tax Foundation, 2003) 1:1-25 (noting that the facts of *OSFC Holdings Ltd.* and the case of *Mathew v. The Queen* heard by the Supreme Court are basically the same).

Before

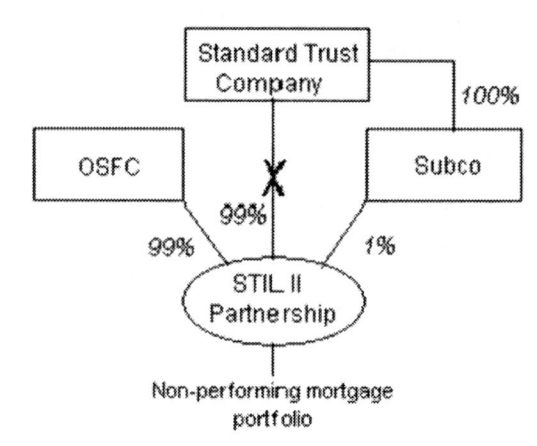

- Standard Trust Company
- OSFC
- Subco (100%)
- STIL II Partnership (OSFC 99%, Standard Trust 99% ✗, Subco 1%)
- Non-performing mortgage portfolio

After

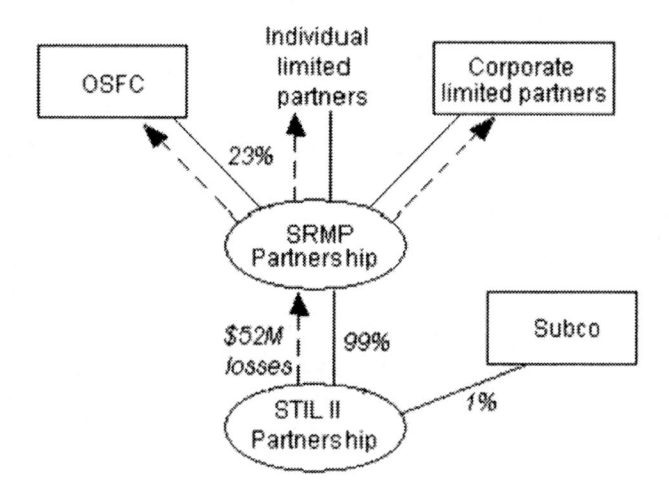

- OSFC
- Individual limited partners
- Corporate limited partners
- SRMP Partnership (23%)
- Subco
- STIL II Partnership ($52M losses, 99%, Subco 1%)

366 Economic Substance and Tax Avoidance

It is readily apparent that the series of transactions was only undertaken in this fashion in order that OSFC Holdings Limited, and other members of the SRMP Partnership, could access the accrued losses of $52 million from Standard. The sole purpose of the two partnerships was to facilitate the transfer of the losses. Neither OSFC Holdings Ltd, nor the other partnership members, were experienced in dealing in real property; and, the two partnerships carried on no activity, other than realizing the losses in question either by sale or writedown of mortgages.[1340]

First appellate GAAR decision

The Federal Court of Appeal upheld the Tax Court's decision that the non-capital losses claimed as deductions by OSFC Holdings Ltd. were barred under GAAR, in the first appellate decision rendered in a GAAR case in Canada. The main focal point of the Court of Appeal's decision, which is not relevant for the purposes of my analysis in this paper, was whether the acquisition by OSFC Holdings Ltd. of the 99 percent interest in the STIL II Partnership was part of a series of transactions, within the meaning of subsection 248(10) of the *Income Tax Act*. This point was concluded in the affirmative.[1341] Also, the fact that there was a "tax benefit" was not disputed.[1342]

[1340] Richard Thomas, "The Supreme Court of Canada – A Disciplined Approach to GAAR", vol. 54, no. 1 *Canadian Tax Journal* 221-240 (2006) (commenting on the facts of the *Mathew* case heard by the Supreme Court of Canada, which involved the same set of transactions; also suggesting GAAR may not have applied if "the partnerships had carried on a genuine commercial enterprise")

[1341] Michael Kandev, Brian Bloom and Oliver Fournier, "The Meaning of 'Series of Transactions' Disclosed by a Unified Textual, Contextual, and Purposive Analysis", (2010) vol. 58, no. 1 *Canadian Tax Journal* 277-330 (stating that the Court's decision that OSFC's purchase of the partnership interest was part of a series of transactions was reasonable given the facts of the case)

[1342] Sheldon Silver, QC and Glenn Ernst, "Recent Cases on GAAR", 2001 *Ontario Tax Conference* (Toronto: Canadian Tax Foundation, 2001), 1B:1-35 (stating that the fact there was a tax benefit did not appear to be debatable, as it was obvious that OSFC Holdings Ltd. benefited from a reduction of tax payable as a result of the transactions); see also: Robert Kopstein, Kristen Kjellander and Andrew McGuffin, "Current Cases", (2010) vol. 58, no. 1 *Canadian Tax Journal* 97-115 (noting that the party obtaining the tax benefit need not be the party undertaking the transaction).

Primary purpose issue

OSFC Holdings Ltd argued that its participation was not as part of an "avoidance transaction", as its acquisition of an interest in the STIL II Partnership was undertaken primarily for *bona fide* purposes other than obtaining a tax benefit. The Court found that although there was a *bona fide* non-tax commercial purpose for the series of transactions, as OFSC Holdings Ltd was in the business of buying distressed mortgages, and it was buying properties which could be sold, that could not be said for each of the transactions in the series. Rather, since the tax benefits of the losses far exceeded the earnings that could reasonably be predicted from the acquisition and disposition of the mortgages, the primary objective was held to be acquiring the tax losses.[1343]

The language of subsection 245(3) of the Act, i.e. whether the series of transactions "may reasonably be considered to have been undertaken or arranged primarily for *bona fide* purposes other than to obtain the tax benefit", requires an objective test which takes account of "the relevant facts and circumstances",[1344] assessed as of the time the transactions were undertaken. The facts and circumstances which the Court considered relevant did not *expressly* include economic substance; however, by weighing the potential benefit from the sale of the mortgage portfolio against the benefit expected to be obtained from deducting the tax losses, the Court was actually engaged in an analysis that courts in the U.S. employ under the economic substance doctrine.[1345]

[1343] McQuillan, *supra* no. 1339 (noting that the tax savings would be 62 times more than the after-tax profits, as the immediate tax savings would be $345,760 per unit versus after-tax profits of $5,500 per unit).

[1344] *OSFC Holdings Ltd. v. R.*, 2001 D.T.C. 5471 (Fed. C.A.) at para. 46, per Rothstein J, leave to appeal refused 2002 CarswellNat 1388 (S.C.C.).

[1345] See, for example, *A.S.A. Investerings Partnership v. C.I.R.*, 201 F.3d 505 (D.C. Cir., 2000), where losses generated by a CINS tax shelter were disallowed on economic substance grounds as although investment income of $3.6 million was earned after transaction costs the profit generated was insignificant in relation to claimed losses of $300 million) .

Given prior pronouncements by the Supreme Court, as to the subordinate role of economic substance in tax avoidance cases,[1346] it is not too surprising that the Court did not say that it was engaged in an economic substance analysis. This state-of-affairs does speak to the need, however, for an amendment to GAAR, to clarify the role that economic substance has in the determination of purpose. The amendment should stipulate that economic substance is one of the factors which must be taken into account in determining the taxpayer's primary purpose. This would bring Canada's position vis-à-vis the significance of economic substance in tax avoidance cases into harmony with its position in Australia, New Zealand, South Africa, the United States, the European Court of Justice, and in the proposed draft UK GAAR legislation.

Also, the further juncture in the GAAR analysis, where economic substance is relevant, is when the courts consider whether there has been a misuse of the provisions of the *Income Tax Act* or an abuse of the Act as a whole, within the meaning of subsection 245(4) of the Act. Although, as it happens, the Court found in *OSFC Holdings* that the series of transactions violated the policy of the Act re the prevention of loss transfers between unrelated corporations,[1347] and therefore was the subject of the GAAR, the Court's conclusion under subsection 245(4) was far from being a slam-dunk.[1348]

However, under the amendments to the GAAR that I am proposing transactions such as those in *OSFC Holdings*, which do not have substantial economic consequences in relation to their expected tax benefits, will be presumed not to give rise to any tax benefits. This presumption being rebuttable, it will remain open to the taxpayer to

---

[1346] *Canada Trustco Mortgage Co. v. R.*, [2005] 2 S.C.R. 601 (S.C.C.) at para. 59; *Shell Canada Ltd. v. R.*, (*sub nom.* Shell Canada Ltd. v. Canada) [1999] 3 S.C.R. 622 (S.C.C.) at paras. 39-40.
[1347] Subject to some specific exceptions that didn't apply.
[1348] Brian Arnold, Judith Freedman, Al Meghji, Mark Meredith, and Hon. Marshall Rothstein, "The Future of GAAR", *supra* no. 81 at 4:6 (Justice Rothstein stating that it was not intuitive that there was anything intrinsically bad about loss trading; and, that the *Income Tax Act* is "really complicated for those of us who aren't experts").

show that the benefits were legislatively intended, despite their lack of economic substance. This is not at all a radical proposition.[1349]

The courts are sometimes already relying upon economic substance in the misuse or abuse determination,[1350] and this approach will be standardized with a GAAR amendment. The Tax Court distinguished the *OSFC Holdings* case, in its decision in *Landrus v. R.*,[1351] in which a loss transfer via the allocation of terminal losses to limited partners was upheld, on the basis that in *Landrus* the taxpayer had "suffered a real economic loss."[1352] The case involved a condominium investment which had declined in value, where the investors restructured by transferring the assets of an existing partnership into a new partnership, so that partners in the first partnership were also partners in the second partnership.[1353] It has been

---

[1349] See Li, *supra* no. 8 at 53 ("As a general proposition, unless the relevant provisions of the Act are intended to permit the enjoyment of a tax benefit resulting from a transaction that lacks economic substance, such a transaction should be presumed to be abusive."); Duff, *supra* no. 25 at 36 (arguing that it follows from the Explanatory Notes to GAAR that transactions that lack economic substance might reasonably be considered to result in an abuse having regard to the provisions of the Act when read as a whole).

[1350] see also: Robert Kopstein and Jasmine Sidhu, "The Federal Court of Appeal – What Factors Motivate You?, Current Cases", (2009) vol. 57, no. 3 *Canadian Tax Journal* 563-585 (stating that, for "the first time" in *The Queen v. Landrus*, the Federal Court of Appeal found that the magnitude of the tax benefit derived by the taxpayer as compared with the costs to be saved by the taxpayer was relevant in determining the primary purpose of the transactions, and therefore whether it was an avoidance transaction. Also suggesting that this approach is contrary to the Supreme Court's *Canada Trustco* decision).

[1351] (2008), [2009] 1 C.T.C. 2009 (T.C.C. [General Procedure]), affirmed [2009] 4 C.T.C. 189 (F.C.A.).

[1352] Andrew Bateman and Michael Wolng, "GAAR: No Abuse of the Stop-Loss Rules in Landrus", (2008) vol. 8, no. 3 *Tax For the Owner-Manager* 8-9 (also pointing out that the Tax Court stated in *Landrus* that "this case does not involve a scheme whereby the [taxpayer] is trying to claim a loss incurred by some other taxpayer").

[1353] Amanda Stacey, Michael Colborne, Michael McLaren, Timothy Fitzsimmons, Michael Friedman and Ashley Palmer, "Mind the GAP – Landrus v. The Queen, Current Cases", (2008) vol. 56, no. 4 *Canadian Tax Journal* 923-956 (also noting that the Court found there was no general or overall policy in the Act of prohibiting loss transfers between related parties); see also: Joel Nitikman, "A Year's Worth of GAAR Cases", 2008 *British Columbia Tax*

suggested by tax commentators that the Federal Court of Appeal also factored "economic substance into" its determination of the misuse or abuse test in *Landrus*, and that it would also have found the transactions to be abusive, if "a tax benefit arose but there were no underlying changes to the taxpayer's economic interests, rights and legal obligations before and after the transactions."[1354] This line of thinking is essentially a reflection of the foundation for the now codified economic substance doctrine in the United States.[1355]

The Court of Appeal held in *Landrus* that there had been material changes in the risks and benefits to the taxpayer, by reason of acquiring an undivided interest in assets doubled in size, and sharing in an extended rental pool which accounted for revenues generated by two limited partnerships.[1356] This manner of analysis is, in effect, an approach to the determination of misuse or abuse under subsection 245(4), which relies upon an economic substance analysis. In order to ensure that the same approach is universally applied by the courts in Canada, including by the Supreme Court of Canada, it should be specifically mandated by amending GAAR. This will help to alleviate concerns re certainty by providing a boundary, beyond which it can be presumed that transactions will not be upheld.

Conference, (Vancouver: Canadian Tax Foundation, 2008), 7:1-23 (noting that "instinctively the transfer of the condominiums from one partnership to another with essentially the same partners might be viewed as not the type of transaction which should crystallize a terminal loss", but that the new partnership created a new rental pool in which all partners participated).

[1354] Mike Power, Harriet Man and Tony Tse, "Loss Utilization Strategies within a Related Group of Companies", 2009 *Atlantic Provinces Tax Conference* (Halifax: Canadian Tax Foundation, 2009), 4A:1-28 (noting that the terminal loss allocation would now be caught under the stop-loss provisions in subsection 13(21.2) of the Act).

[1355] Under section 7701(o) of the Internal Revenue Code, in the case of any transaction where the doctrine is found by a court to be relevant, the transaction shall be treated as having economic substance only if (A) the transaction changes in a meaningful way (apart from Federal income tax effects) the taxpayer's economic position, and (B) the taxpayer has a substantial purpose (apart from Federal income tax effects) for entering into such transaction.

[1356] Robert Carvalho and Tim Clarke, "Current Cases 2008-2009", 2009 *British Columbia Tax Conference*, (Vancouver: Canadian Tax Foundation, 2009), 2:1-30 (noting the Court found there was "a real economic loss").

PRODUITS FORESTIERS DONOHUE INC. c. R.

The *Donohue* case is an instance where the courts did not apply GAAR, as they did not find any misuse or abuse, within the meaning of subsection 245(4) of the Act.[1357] The result in the case would not be different, after the amendments to GAAR that I am recommending, as the transactions attacked by the Minister of Revenue under GAAR involved a real economic loss.[1358] The fact that a substantial economic loss was incurred means that the proposed presumption that no tax benefit was intended, in the absence of economic substance, would not apply in the case.

Donohue Group ("Donohue") and an arm's length Quebec government agency ("Rexfor") each owned 50 percent of Donohue Mantane Inc. ("DMI"), which operated paper mills in Quebec. As pulp prices collapsed, the value of the properties owned by DMI declined dramatically. At that point, Donohue's investment in DMI had a cost of approximately $62 million and a value of nil. In order to make the loss available to shelter income in a profitable subsidiary ("DSF"), Donahue undertook a reorganization to enable DSF to realize a loss on a subsequent sale to a third party.

[1357] (2001), [2003] 1 C.T.C. 2010 (T.C.C. [General Procedure]), affirmed (2002), [2003] 3 C.T.C. 160 (Fed. C.A.).

[1358] This implies that a specific legislative measure would be required to address the *Donohue* type of situation.

Prior to the reorganization, the corporate structure is illustrated in the following diagram:[1359]

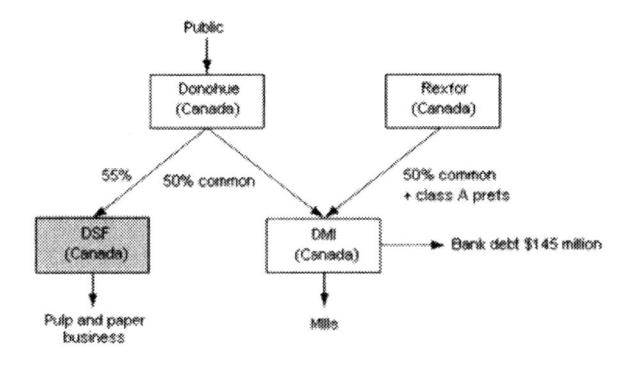

```
                    Public
                      |
         ┌────────────┴──────────┐
         |                       |
    Donohue                   Rexfor
    (Canada)                  (Canada)
       /   \                    |
     55%   50% common       50% common
      /       \              + class A prets
     /         \            /
    DSF         DMI
  (Canada)    (Canada) ────► Bank debt $145 million
     |           |
  Pulp and     Mills
   paper
  business
```

Pursuant to the reorganization, a series of transactions took place with a view to preserving the ACB of the assets and also producing an ABIL deduction for DSF. Amongst other steps (1) 98.5 percent of DMI's assets were sold to a sister corporation ("DMI 1993"), utilizing subsection 85(5.1) of the *Income Tax Act*, to transfer the cost of the assets of DMI to DMI 1993; (2) Donohue transferred all of the issued and outstanding shares of DSF to a newly incorporated wholly-owned subsidiary ("PDI"); (3) DSF acquired all of the shares of DMI from PDI for a nominal price, equal to their fair market value at the time; and, (4) DSF sold the shares of DMI to a third party for $2 in 1993, triggering a business investment loss equal to 100 percent of the accrued economic loss. DSF claimed an ABIL of $46.6 million (75 percent of $62.2 million) in its 1993 taxation year, which it carried back as a deduction from income in its 1990 taxation year.

The ABIL claimed by DSF was disallowed by the Minister on the basis that retention of indirect control over assets, which gave rise to the ABIL, was contrary to a "basic principle" under the Act, to the effect that there should be a matching between the value of a

---

[1359] Mark Meredith and Nancy Diep, 2010 *Conference Report* (Toronto: Canadian Tax Foundation, 2011), 10:1-32 (noting that the reorganization was undertaken to transfer the DMI shares to DSF, preserving the loss inherent in the shares, so it could be triggered to shelter DSF's income).

corporation's property and the value of the corporation's shares.[1360] The Minister's position was motivated by a concern about the potential for a "double dip", i.e. once by DSF as an ABIL and again on an asset sale.[1361]

DSF conceded at trial that the transactions produced a tax benefit, and that there was an avoidance transaction, arguing only that there was no misuse or abuse within the meaning of subsection 245(4) of the *Income Tax Act*. The Tax Court and the Federal Court of Appeal both found that the GAAR did not apply. Although tax attributes had been duplicated (albeit not exploited twice), both courts found that there was no misuse or abuse, as nothing in the Act prevents a taxpayer from realizing a loss on shares sold to an arm's length person, even though a substantial portion of the assets to which the loss on the shares relates remain within the corporate group. In this regard, the Tax Court noted that a person holding less than 90 percent of a corporation's shares can realize a loss on the shares when the corporation is wound up, while obtaining ownership of a portion of the corporation's underlying assets, in support of its conclusion that the transactions did not offend a scheme established by the *Income Tax Act*.

The result in *Donohue* is said to confirm the Minister's long-standing administrative position that loss utilization within a corporate group is acceptable.[1362] Furthermore, the Court of Appeal found that:

> ... the principle on which the Minister relied simply does not exist. ... Under corporate law, a business corporation's property belongs to the corporation and not to the shareholders. The Act recognizes this legal reality, as it recognizes the effects of private law. The entire system of taxation of

---

[1360] Bernstein and Leung, *supra* no. 1338 (noting that the Minister argued that "there should be some congruent relationship between the value of the assets of a corporation and the value of its shares).

[1361] Brian S. Nichols, "GAAR and More", 2002 *Ontario Tax Conference* (Toronto: Canadian Tax Foundation, 2002), 1:1-42 (noting the court's position that when a taxpayer holds shares of a corporation, which in turn holds underlying assets, there is no policy preventing the double taxation of a gain or the double deduction of a loss in respect of the corporation's shares and the underlying assets).

[1362] Bernstein and Leung, *supra* no. 1338 (noting that the loss was simply shifted to another member of the corporate group).

taxation of corporations and their shareholders is conceived in terms of this legal reality. This is what explains, as the trial judge notes, that a gain or loss may be realized at the same time by a shareholder in respect of his shares and by the corporation in respect of its own property. ... There is no principle that would allow the effect of these transactions to be consolidated by matching them. The principle underlying the Act, if there is one, is contrary to the one invoked by the Minster.[1363]

The existence of specific stop-loss rules that apply only in a non-arm's length context, which require the sort of "matching" called for by the Minster, was also considered to be supportive of the conclusion that there is no broader principle under the Act. However, the most telling findings by the trial judge, relative to my point regarding the relevance of economic substance in determining misuse or abuse under GAAR, were that Donohue actually lost the $62 million invested in DM, and that no attempt was made to increase the amount of the loss through transactions designed to artificially increase the adjusted cost base of DM's shares held by DSF.[1364]

In the trial judge's words, "DSF genuinely incurred a loss of [$62 million]."[1365] This emphasis on the existence of a "genuine loss", in determining that there was no misuse or abuse within the meaning of subsection 245(4) of the Act, corroborates my claim that economic substance should be formally added to GAAR, as a required consideration in the abuse or misuse determination, so that there is a common approach by the courts, including by the Supreme Court of Canada,[1366] and hence greater certainty. The

---

[1363] (2002), [2003] 3 C.T.C. 160 (Fed. C.A.) at para. 17 (reciting the finding to this effect by the trial judge with approval).

[1364] (2001), [2003] 1 C.T.C. 2010 (T.C.C. [General Procedure]) at para. 77, affirmed 2002 CarswellNat 3052 (Fed. C.A.); see also: Silver and Ernst, *supra* no. 1342 (noting that the transactions were structured so that the taxpayer could realize an ABIL from the sale of shares equal to the value of its investment).

[1365] *Ibid.* at para. 78.

[1366] Although the Supreme Court of Canada did suggest in *Canada Trustco* that economic substance may be relevant as part of the factual context in an inquiry under subsection 245(4), the Court's statement that a "lack of substance" has "no meaning in isolation from the proper interpretation of specific provisions of the *Income Tax Act*" confuses the matter and an amendment to GAAR is therefore required.

Donohue case also helps to illustrate the limitations of economic substance analysis in tax avoidance cases, i.e. if the type of potential tax avoidance that the series of transactions gives rise to is to be prohibited, a more specific legislative response is required.[1367]

FARAGGI c. R.

Faraggi c. R.[1368] involved the manufacture of capital dividend accounts in several corporations and the subsequent sale of the accounts to third parties for profit. Several million dollars were paid as capital dividends using subsection 83(2) elections, to participants who subscribed for shares in new corporations, which had been "seeded with synthetic CDA":[1369]

> The plan contemplated using newly formed corporations with nominal assets to subscribe for shares in other newly formed corporations and then create CDA through a combination of share subscriptions, redemption of shares, capital gains by sale of shares and purported elections under subsection 83(2) of the *Income Tax Act* ("Act"), among other things. Then, through another sequence of share subscriptions and share redemptions, third parties at arm's length to the appellants would receive capital dividends.
>
> In short, after the "creation" of capital gains several corporations would make elections under subsection 83(2) of the *Act* and declare tax-free dividends on classes of preferred shares. Near the end of the exercise the aggregate CDAs of these corporations would find their way to an appellant corporation. A third-party corporation would subscribe for shares in an appellant

---

[1367] Tim Edgar, "Designing and Implementing a Target-Effective General Anti-Avoidance Rule", *Tax Avoidance in Canada After Canada Trustco and Mathew*, David G. Duff and Harry Erhlichman, ed., (Toronto: Irwin Law Inc., 2007), c. 9, p. 224, footnote 9; p. 244 and p. 257, Appendix A (arguing that the *Donohue* case, amongst many others, can be categorized as involving "transactional substitution", which needs to be addressed with specific legislation).

[1368] (2007), [2008] 1 C.T.C. 2425 (T.C.C. [General Procedure]), affirmed (2008), [2009] 3 C.T.C. 77 (F.C.A.), leave to appeal refused 2009 CarswellNat 1152 (S.C.C.).

[1369] John Jakolev and Graham Turner, "Sham Capital Dividends", (2007) vo. 15, no. 9 *Canadian Tax Highlights* 7-8 (noting that the transactions occurred in 1987 before amendments to section 83 were introduced to curtail this type of plan and similar schemes).

corporation. These shares would have a nominal par value, say $0.01 per share, and a high redemption amount, say $1,000 per share. The third-party corporation would pay $1,210 per share and an appellant corporation would redeem the share for $1,000, electing under subsection 83(2) of the *Act* that the deemed dividend of $999.99 (subsection 84(1) of the *Act*) be paid out of the appellant company's capital dividend account. The third-party corporation would then have a capital dividend account and pay its shareholders, after making its own subsection 83(2) election, $1,000 tax-free. Before the transaction, the third-party corporation had no amount in a capital dividend account and could only pay its shareholders a taxable dividend of $1,210; the tax rate in Quebec for individual shareholders was 41.87 per cent. After the transaction the shareholders received $1,000 tax-free; the third-party corporation effectively paid $210 for the tax-free $1,000 dividend. The effective cost to the third-party corporation and its shareholders for the $1,000 dividend was 21 per cent, an economic saving of 20.87 per cent.[1370]

GAAR was not applicable as the transactions were completed in 1987. Nevertheless, the trial judge found that the appellants had "exploited provisions of the *Income Tax Act*" by carrying on "a business of creating dividends" and that "[t]he manner in which they wished to achieve their goal was not consistent with the object, spirit or purpose of, for example, section 89, subsections 52(3), 83(2) and 84(1) of the Act."[1371] However, in light of the Supreme Court's ruling in *Shell Canada Ltd. v. R.*, that economic realities cannot supplant *bona fide* legal relationships,[1372] the trial judge resorted to the doctrine of sham to set aside the transactions for tax purposes. In doing so, the trial judge is said to have extended the meaning of "sham" to include an abuse of the provisions of the *Income Tax Act*:[1373]

> The reasons can be read as saying that using statutory provisions in a way that is contrary to their object and spirit is abusive and that the result of the

---

[1370] (2007), [2008] 1 C.T.C. 2425 (T.C.C. [General Procedure]) at paras. 2-3, affirmed 2008 CarswellNat 4465 (F.C.A.), leave to appeal refused 2009 CarswellNat 1152 (S.C.C.).
[1371] *Ibid*, paras. 79-80.
[1372] (*sub nom.* Shell Canada Ltd. v. Canada) [1999] 3 S.C.R. 622 (S.C.C.) at para. 39.
[1373] Laura Stoddard, "Stretching the Sham Doctrine?, Current Cases," (2007) vol. 55, no. 4 *Canadian Tax Journal* 824-854 (suggesting that because the transactions predated GAAR, "the only general anti-avoidance weapon available to the CRA was the doctrine of sham").

abuse may be a sham where the arrangers knew that there was no underlying economic substance to their series of transactions. In such a case, filing tax returns on a basis that relies on the form instead of the (lack of) substance involves deceit, and this supports a finding of sham.[1374]

Although the Court of Appeal upheld the trial judge's decision on a different basis,[1375] rejecting the notion that the concepts of "sham" and "abuse" are the same, it did find that the subsection 83(2) elections were "shams".[1376] It has been suggested that this is "a loose usage of the term 'sham'– the elections were not capable of forming a legal relationship, misleading or otherwise."[1377]

In any event, the Court of Appeal did observe that, after the advent of GAAR, the Minister can "repudiate a transaction on the sole ground that it gives rise to an abuse of the Act or some of its provisions."[1378] In this respect, the amendment to GAAR that I am recommending, which will presume that transactions do not give rise to any tax benefits where they do not have substantial economic consequences in relation to their expected tax benefits, will be applicable in Faraggi-type circumstances, i.e. where everything done in the series of transactions was "artificial".[1379]

My only caveat regarding the application of GAAR in these circumstances is that it does not appear that resort to it should actually

---

[1374] Thomas E. McDonnell, "CDA Tax Scheme Voided-Sham Doctrine Expanded?" (2007) vol. 7, no. 4 *Tax for the Owner Manager*, 8-9 (arguing that where a series of transactions is engaged in based on an aggressive interpretation of the law, and a court subsequently disagrees with the interpretation, the series of transactions was not "deceitful" within the meaning of the sham doctrine unless there was no reasonable basis for the interpretation relied upon).

[1375] (2008), [2009] 3 C.T.C. 77 (F.C.A.) at para. 66, leave to appeal refused 2009 CarswellNat 1152 (S.C.C.) (the amounts collected by the corporate appellants were business income).

[1376] *Ibid*, para. 79.

[1377] Jim Cruickshank, "Trusts: Recent Developments", 2010 *Conference Report* (Toronto: Canadian Tax Foundation, 2011), 29:1-29:42 (noting that the case did not turn on a sham analysis and the elections were "simply invalid").

[1378] *Supra* no. 1375, para. 54.

[1379] (2007), [2008] 1 C.T.C. 2425 (T.C.C. [General Procedure]) at para. 80, affirmed 2008 CarswellNat 4465 (F.C.A.), leave to appeal refused 2009 CarswellNat 1152 (S.C.C.).

be required.[1380] However, given the history of Canadian courts vis-à-vis non-literalist interpretation in the realm of tax avoidance, it would be prudent to have the GAAR available. Given this, having the presumption enacted that I am recommending will contribute certainty to the treatment of aggressive transactions without economic substance.

4145356 CANADA LTD. v. THE QUEEN

According to the Department of Finance, foreign tax credit generator arrangements can potentially result in the loss of "billions" of dollars in lost tax revenues.[1381] This occurs when a complex set of transactions is entered into, which in substance amount to a Canadian corporation making a loan to a corporation in a foreign jurisdiction, where Canadian tax law and the law of the foreign jurisdiction treat the transaction differently.[1382] The transactions are structured to result in the creation of artificial foreign tax credits for the Canadian company, in respect of income earned by an accommodating third party financial institution in the foreign jurisdiction, in circumstances where no net foreign tax has been paid because of

---

[1380] Brian J. Arnold, "The Tax Court's Trilogy of GAAR Cases", *The Arnold Report*, posting 024, Canadian Tax Foundation, December 16, 2011 (arguing that on the basis of textual, contextual and purposive interpretation sections of the *Income Tax* Act can be interpreted as not recognizing losses where there is no underlying economic loss, without resorting to the GAAR).

[1381] Raj Junega and Geoffrey Turner, "Foreign Tax Credit Generator Proposals – An Inadvertent Attack on Hybrids?", no. 52 *International Tax* (CCH) 1-6 (July 2010), 3 (quoting a senior Department of Finance official at a 2010 IFA Conference in Montreal).

[1382] Because of a "repo" feature which requires a U.S. limited partnership member to buy back the shares in the limited partnership that were purchased by the taxpayer, the U.S. limited partner's investment is treated as a loan under U.S. law, which gives rise to an interest deduction. This is offset by interest earned on a different loan made to another member of the U.S. corporate group. This enables the limited partnership to have income and foreign tax credits for Canadian tax purposes, although the partnership does not actually bear any U.S. taxes as it elects to be treated as a corporation under U.S. law – see explanation by Genevieve Lille and Elizabeth Johnson in "Partnerships: An Update", 2010 *Conference Report* (Toronto: Canadian Tax Foundation, 2011).

the creation of offsetting interest income and deductions. The Canadian company uses the foreign tax credits to reduce the tax that is otherwise payable on the interest income arising from the loan and the Canadian tax savings are generally shared between the Canadian lender and the foreign borrower.[1383]

One of the Joint International Tax Shelter Information Center's ("JITSIC") projects has been attempting to identify these foreign tax credit generator transactions.[1384] A former counsel to JITSIC has reported that "FTC generators – if they work – can be scaled up to wipe out almost any amount of ... tax liability, assuming a willing foreign counterparty."[1385]

The amount of tax at stake in a few foreign tax credit generator cases in the U.S. has been reported at $3.5 billion and in cases involving New Zealand banks the number is reported as NZD 1.5 billion.[1386] Because of the "magnitude of this problem" in Canada, the Government announced legislative measures effective for foreign taxes incurred in respect of taxation years that end after March 4, 2010, aimed at denying foreign tax credits claimed under these schemes.[1387] Following receipt of comments regarding its proposals,

---

[1383] Department of Finance, Budget 2010, Annex 5: Tax Measures: Supplementary Information And Notices of Ways and Means Motions (March 4, 2010).

[1384] Lisa M. Nadal, "JITSIC Puts Antiabuse Effort on Fast Track, Says Former Director", 121 *Tax Notes* 396 (Oct. 27, 2008), 396 (quoting former Director Tamara Ashford).

[1385] Greenaway, *supra* no. 239 at footnote 44 (also stating that "the Service and the Treasury candidly admit that these structured financing transactions are too much of a drain on the fisc to tolerate. ... It is inconsistent with the purpose of the foreign tax credit to permit a credit for foreign taxes that result from intentionally structuring a transaction to generate foreign taxes in a manner that allows the parties to duplicate tax benefits and share the cost of the tax payments. The result in these structured transactions is that both parties as well as the foreign jurisdiction benefit at the expense of the U.S. fisc.")

[1386] "News Analysis: OECD Disclosure Initiatives on the Rise", 61 *Tax Notes International* 744-745 (Mar. 7, 2011), 744.

[1387] Department of Finance, Budget 2010, Annex 5: Tax Measures: Supplementary Information And Notices of Ways and Means Motions, International Taxation, Foreign Tax Credit Generators (March 4, 2010).

the Government announced amended legislative measures which were released on August 27, 2010.[1388]

The Explanatory Notes issued with the amended proposals contain an example of the structure being targeted[1389] (see below) which corresponds closely with the transactions described in *4145356 Canada Ltd. v. R.*,[1390] in which the taxpayer succeeded in obtaining the foreign tax credits, although no foreign tax was actually borne by the taxpayer.

The Tax Court's decision is reviewed in a US tax blog, which features the rather sardonic heading "Adverse Impact of FTC Generators on Canadian Treasury: Apparently Not to the Tax Court of Canada."[1391]

[1388] Legislative Proposals Relating to the Income Tax Act, The Air Travellers Security Charge Act, The Excise Act, 2001 and The Excise Tax Act, Part III, Department of Finance News Release 2010-074, ss. 126(4.11)-(4.13); Junega and Turner, *supra* no. 1381 at 2 (providing a diagram of the example given by the Department of Finance of a targeted foreign tax credit generator, which depicts the court case with some minor modifications)

[1389] Explanatory Notes in Respect of Legislative Proposals Relating to the Income Tax Act and Related Acts and Regulations, September 2010, 161-164, 173-174 (the new provisions "are intended to address tax schemes established by taxpayers with the intent of creating foreign tax credits and similar deductions for foreign tax the burden of which is not, in fact, borne by the taxpayer. The main thrust of all these schemes is to exploit asymmetry as between the tax laws of Canada and those of a relevant foreign jurisdiction in the characterization of equity and debt instruments. These schemes clearly offend the policy underlying the foreign tax credit, foreign accrual tax and underlying foreign tax rules in the Act. Although the Government believes that these schemes can be successfully challenged under existing rules in the Act, including the General Anti-Avoidance Rule in section 245, the magnitude of the potential problem warrants greater assurance through specific and immediate legislative action.")

[1390] *4145356 Canada Ltd. v. R.*, 2011 TCC 220 (T.C.C. [General Procedure]), Crown's appeal discontinued in the Federal Court of Appeal on May 25, 2012 (A-193-11).

[1391] Jerald David August, "Tax Court of Canada approves of foreign tax credit generator arrangements in *Canada Limited v. The Queen* (Case 4145358); cross border impacts" (June 13, 2010) http://fedtaxdevelopments.foxrothschild.com/2011/06/articles/federal-taxation-developments/tax-court-of-canada-approves-of-foreign-tax-credit-generator-arrangement-in-canada-limited-v-the-queen-case-4145358-cross-border-impacts/?utm_source=feedburner&utm_

Almost none of this context appears in the Tax Court's reasons for judgment,[1392] however, which contain a clinical description of the transactions; a recitation of the Supreme Court's statement in *Shell* that a caveat to the examination of "economic realities" is that "the taxpayer's legal relationship must be respected in tax cases", except in the case of a statutory provision to the contrary or a finding of sham; and, a legal definition of the word "paid" in subsection 126(2) of the *Income Tax Act* which does not require an associated liability for payment of the tax.[1393]

This latter point arose, because although the case had been referred to the CRA's GAAR Committee at the audit stage, it was determined that the assessment should be made on the narrow basis that subsection 126(2) did not permit the taxpayer to claim a foreign tax credit.[1394] This approach to the case by the Crown and the Tax Court of Canada is vastly different from the one taken in New Zealand, where the High Court observed that "[t]he ultimate question is: viewed in a commercially and economically realistic way, does the impugned arrangement make use of the specific provision in a manner consistent with Parliament's purpose?"[1395] In analyzing its foreign tax credit generator case in this different manner, the High Court was applying New Zealand's GAAR which, as set out earlier, has been interpreted by the New Zealand Supreme Court on the basis that the economic and commercial effect of documents and transactions are centrally relevant in determining whether there has been a "tax avoidance arrangement".[1396]

---

medium=feed&utm_campaign=Feed%3A+FederalTaxationDevelopmentsBlog+%28Federal+Taxation+Developments+Blog%29

[1392] Except for acknowledgement at the conclusion of the reasons for judgment that there are proposed amendments to section 126 effective for years ending after March 4, 2010 that might affect entitlement to foreign tax credits.

[1393] The limited partnership in which the Appellant invested was a separate legal entity under the laws of Delaware which was liable for the tax which the Appellant claimed a share of as a member of the limited partnership.

[1394] Lille and Johnson, *supra* no. 1382 at paras. 19-20.

[1395] *BNZ Investments Limited & ORS v. Commissioner of Inland Revenue* (2009), 24 NZTC 23 (H.C.) at para. 130.

[1396] *Ben Nevis Forestry v. CIR*, (2009) 24 NZTC 23, 188 (SC) interpreting ss. BG 1 and GB 1 of the *Income Tax Act* 1994; Elliffe and Cameron, *supra* no. 22 at

In the result, the appeals from the disallowance of the foreign tax credits in issue in New Zealand were dismissed. The High Court placed reliance on expert evidence that "in the absence of the taxation benefits, none of the transactions, taken either as a whole or in terms of the components, are reasonable or defensible from a commercial or economic point of view."[1397] The Court also found that "these transactions were, in economic substance, unsecured loans."[1398]

The import of this finding, from a Canadian tax law perspective, is that if the taxpayer had made direct loans to the U.S. borrower in *4145356 Canada Ltd. v. The Queen*, it would have paid Canadian tax on its interest income and no foreign tax would have been paid (hence no foreign tax credits).[1399] The Court also accepted the expert evidence of Professor Evans that "[e]ach of the six BNZ Group transactions that I analyzed utilised the BNZ Group's tax capacity and thereby the New Zealand tax base. They relied on reduction in the New Zealand base for their profitability. Taken as a whole the transactions were very profitable to the BNZ Group and imposed significant economic costs on New Zealand society. These costs are quite unusual for commercial transactions."[1400] The Court's finding on this point was that "[t]he transactions enhanced the value of the BNZ by $238.6 million, but imposed an economic cost on New Zealand society of $335.6 million, a significant part of

---

441, 460 (suggesting that in New Zealand "there has been an empowering of the judiciary to pursue a form of interpretation that is much less formalistic, and that necessarily involves even more of an enquiry into the commercial and business motivations of the taxpayer."; and, that the judiciary in New Zealand is now "prepared more than ever to focus on the economic consequences of a transaction, rather than its legalistic form.")

[1397] *BNZ Investments Limited & ORS v. Commissioner of Inland Revenue* (2009), 24 NZTC 23 (H.C.) at para. 467.
[1398] *Ibid*, para. 520.
[1399] Glenn Ernst, "Canadian FTC Generators Survive Court Challenge", *Tax Notes International* 838-840 (June 13, 2011), 838 (noting that "FTC generators typically consist of a series of transactions that are substantively equivalent to a loan by a Canadian resident corporation to a resident of a jurisdiction that taxes based on economic substance.")
[1400] *Supra* no. 1397, para. 477.

that being the dead weight cost of the monies transferred off shore and permanently lost to the New Zealand economy."[1401]

Needless to say, this manner of judicial approach will not find its way into Canada, so long as our courts remain wedded to the narrow view of the role of economic substance which the Supreme Court has articulated in *Shell* and *Canada Trustco*. The type of expert evidence which the High Court accepted in New Zealand would arguably not even be admissible in Canada, given the Supreme Court's insistence that economic realities / substance are generally not relevant. The remedy for this is to make the amendments to GAAR that I am proposing.

Foreign tax credit generator transactions are also "one of the most problematic" areas facing the IRS, according to Commissioner Douglas Shulman.[1402] IRS officials have said that they plan to take several different foreign tax credit generator fact pattern cases to court in order to obtain precedents which deny the foreign tax credits on the basis that the transactions are lacking in economic substance, amongst other deficiencies.[1403] One of these cases involves Sovereign Bancorp, which has filed suit in US District Court in respect of the denial of tax benefits claimed in relation to arrangements entered into with Barclays Bank of England.[1404] Hewlett-Packard Co., which has a financial services unit which recorded $2.7 billion in revenue in a recent fiscal year, is also contesting disallowed foreign tax credits in relation to transactions with a Dutch entity which the IRS says lacked economic substance, amongst other problems.[1405] Another prominent case involves American In-

---

[1401] *Ibid,* para. 524.
[1402] Michael Joe, "IRS Commissioner Talks Tough on Tax Avoidance", 121 *Tax Notes* 1215-1216 (Dec. 15, 2008), 1216 (quoting Commissioner Shulman at the 21st annual Institute on Current Issues in International Taxation).
[1403] Crystal Tandon, "IRS Honing Its Strategy as FTC Cases Head to Court", 123 *Tax Notes* 1179 (June 8, 2009).
[1404] "Sovereign bank sues the IRS", *The Boston Globe* (June 18, 2009); David D. Stewart, "Bank Challenges IRS Foreign Tax Credit Generator Determination", 123 *Tax Notes* 1527-1528 (June 29, 2009).
[1405] John Letzing, "H-P unlikely target in IRS crackdown on foreign tax deals", *MarketWatch* (Feb. 18, 2010).

ternational Group Inc., which the U.S. Government bailed out in 2008 during the financial collapse. The company has subsequently claimed in the U.S. District Court that the IRS improperly disallowed its claims for foreign tax credits.[1406]

None of these cases have resulted in U.S. court decisions yet;[1407] however, in criticizing a proposed U.S. foreign tax credit generator regulation, a senior U.S. attorney has opined that "[t]he problem with many, if not most, of the transactions that are intended to be targeted by the proposed regulation is that they lack economic substance."[1408] A subsequent analysis following the codification of the economic substance doctrine in the United States has concluded that "there may be foreign tax credit generator transactions that pass the economic substance test as codified in section 7701(o)."[1409]

These foreign tax credit generator cases in Canada, New Zealand and the U.S. illustrate that the Supreme Court of Canada's refusal to endorse the importance of the economic substance of transactions in tax avoidance cases, even after the enactment of GAAR,

---

[1406] Amy S. Elliott, "AIG Sues IRS for Refund While Accepting New Federal Bailout Funds", 122 *Tax Notes* 1192-1193 (Mar. 9, 2009), 1192 (noting the IRS claims that FTC generators exploit the foreign tax credit regime by enabling taxpayers to get the U.S. credit while incurring no foreign tax).

[1407] Thomas, *supra* no. 682 at 458 (noting that judicial decisions on the economic substance doctrine do not generally come out until many years after the transactions in issue, citing several recent court decisions on economic substance dealing with taxation years ranging from 1991 to 2002).

[1408] Kevin Dolan, "Foreign Tax Credit Generator Regs: The Purple People Eater Returns", *Tax Notes International* 251-258 (July 16, 2007), 253-256 (also noting re the proposed regulation that "The problem with rules-based guidance is that, while it may be designed to implement some underlying, unstated principle, it is invariably too narrow, too broad, or both, to accomplish its underlying purpose. As such, rules-based guidance is arbitrary and ineffectual in many cases because it can be easily avoided. ... A rules-based rule can be a rifle shot that hits only one piece of the logical target or hits the wrong target. Alternatively, it can be a scattershot, hitting many wrong targets and causing collateral damage. Rules-based rules are an inefficient and ineffective way to administer a tax system.")

[1409] Roberto P. Vasconcellos and H. David Rosenbloom, "Measuring a Foreign Tax Credit Generator Transaction Against the Codified Economic Substance Doctrine", *Tax Notes International* 119-125 (Oct. 11, 2010), 121.

leads to inappropriate tax results. Unless the courts in Canada are obliged to stop clinging to the conviction that the economic substance of transactions is not relevant in tax avoidance cases, except in the event of a statutory provision to the contrary or a sham, we will remain seriously short of where we should be in defending against abusive tax avoidance. Given this state-of-affairs, GAAR should be amended to require that economic substance be considered in tax cases, as it now is in other countries, either because of judicial stances taken there or statutory requirements. This can be accomplished by legislating that economic substance *must* be considered as a relevant factor in determining (1) whether a transaction is an avoidance transaction; and (2) whether the tax benefits claimed by taxpayers are the result of an abuse or misuse of the *Income Tax Act*.

X

Conclusion

My contribution in this book to the existing tax literature is that, while many others have also been alive to the problem that the Supreme Court of Canada has created with its restrictive view of the role of economic substance in tax avoidance cases, I have now undertaken the most fulsome analysis of the subject to date. In particular, I am covering previously untilled ground with my suggestion that the Supreme Court is operating with a double standard in terms of its treatment of economic substance in tax versus non-tax cases; and, in my detailed review of the position that economic substance occupies under GAAR in Canada relative to its position in the tax avoidance spheres in Australia, New Zealand, South Africa, the U.K. and the United States.

Professor Arnold has commented that the approach of the courts to tax avoidance cases raises important questions "that go to the heart of any income tax system and the underlying values of society."[1410] Professor Alarie speaks of what he views as "an enduring puzzle": the government's "deliberately half-hearted efforts at combating tax

---

[1410] Arnold, *supra* no. 8 at 190.

avoidance".[1411] Professor Li has argued that the concept of economic substance provides the best method of balancing conflicting policy concerns in Canadian income tax law.[1412] These points all support my claim that a legislative fix to the GAAR is required.

My conclusion is that the present GAAR should be amended to require that economic substance must be considered as a relevant circumstance in determining whether a transaction amounts to an "avoidance transaction" within the meaning of subsection 245(3) of the Act; and, also in considering whether a transaction constitutes a misuse of the relevant taxing provisions or an abuse of the provisions as a whole within the meaning of subsection 245(4) of the Act. My further conclusion is that GAAR should also be amended to provide that transactions which are primarily entered into in order to secure tax benefits, and which are found not to have substantial economic consequences for the taxpayer compared to their expected tax benefits, shall be presumed not to give rise to tax benefits. In this latter regard, the onus should be on the taxpayer to show that claimed tax benefits are within the realm of what Parliament intended.[1413]

To those who would resist these proposed changes to GAAR with reliance upon "muffled echoes of old arguments",[1414] the answer is that the case for legislating as to the essential role of

---

[1411] Alarie, *supra* no. 21 at 2-3 (suggesting that "many of [governments'] most effective anti-avoidance tools lie dormant most of the time" thus "countenancing ongoing and significant foregone tax revenues", this being "particularly puzzling when governments complain about tax avoidance.")

[1412] Li, *supra* no. 8 at 27 and 56 (arguing that economic substance analysis offers the best standard for drawing the line between legitimate tax planning and abusive tax avoidance).

[1413] Compare: Tooma, *supra* no. 15 at 294 (the conclusion in her PhD thesis, Australian School of Taxation, Faculty of Law, University of New South Wales is "there may be greater certainty where a statutory GAAR exists, with safeguards to ensure that it is appropriately administered.")

[1414] *Federal Commissioner of Taxation v. Spotless Services Ltd.* (1996), 186 C.L.R. 404 (Aust. High Ct.) at p. 414 (holding that Lord Tomlin's statement in the *Duke of Westminster* case has no significance in interpreting Part IVA of the *Income Tax Assessment Act 1936* of Australia dealing with schemes for reducing income taxes).

economic substance in evaluating tax avoidance transactions is really quite overwhelming:

(1) given the performance of the Supreme Court of Canada to date, in declining to set aside blatant tax avoidance schemes, even after GAAR was implemented, it would be fiscal insanity for the Government to expect much different results in future tax avoidance cases, without having made amendments pertaining to economic substance – recall that a definition of "insanity", which is often attributed to Albert Einstein, is "doing the same thing over and over again and expecting different results";

(2) the Supreme Court is already relying upon "economic realities" as an important reference point in non-tax cases, and there is nothing sacrosanct about transactions aimed at avoiding taxation which exempts them from this same manner of analysis;

(3) the general anti-avoidance legislation in tax jurisdictions not unlike Canada, e.g. Australia and South Africa, enumerate economic and commercial realities as objective factors to be considered in determining whether there has been unacceptable tax avoidance;

(4) the experience in the U.S. for decades, with its courts denying billions of dollars of claimed tax benefits in abusive tax avoidance cases under the common law economic substance doctrine, speaks loudly of the importance of economic substance in combating tax avoidance;

(5) the position of the European Court of Justice on economic realities and the role of economic substance in the proposed U.K. GAAR both highlight that Canada is out-of-step;

(6) the capacity of courts to make appropriate decisions, once economic substance has become part of the GAAR playing field, is well-demonstrated by judgments of the courts in New Zealand;

(7) the proposed amendments will send a signal to the courts, and to taxpayers, that transactions which comply with the literal requirements of tax legislation, but do not possess economic substance, may not be upheld for tax purposes; and

(8) allowing tax deductions and losses in circumstances where taxpayers have not made real economic outlays is *prima facie* unreasonable, as is well-understood elsewhere, and it should only occur when Parliament has clearly legislated in a fashion which enables the opposite result.

Furthermore, as the courts are now sometimes utilizing an economic substance analysis in GAAR cases, legislative amendments will standardize the practice and provide greater certainty.

XI

Select Bibliography

ARTICLES

Andreoni, James, Brian Erard, and Jonathan Feinstein, "Tax Compliance", vol. XXXVI *Journal of Economic Literature* 818-860 (June 1998).

Aprill, Ellen P. "Tax Shelters, Tax Law, and Morality: Codifying Judicial Doctrines", 54 *Southern Methodist University Law Review* 9-35 (2001).

Arnold, Brian J, "Confusion Worse Confounded – The Supreme Court's GAAR Decisions", (2006) vol. 54, no. 1 *Canadian Tax Journal* 167-209.

Arnold, Brian J, "Policy Forum: The Supreme Court and the Interpretation of Tax Statutes-Again", (2006), vol. 54, no. 3 *Canadian Tax Journal* 677-684.

Arnold, Brian J., "The Long, Slow, Steady Demise of the General Anti-Avoidance Rule", (2004) vol. 52, no. 2 *Canadian Tax Journal* 488-511.

Arnold, Brian J., "Reflections on the Relationship Between Statutory Interpretation and Tax Avoidance", (2001) vol. 49, no. 1 *Canadian Tax Journal* 1-39.

Arnold, Brian J, "Statutory Interpretation: Some Thoughts on Plain Meaning", 1998 *Conference Report* 6:1-36 (Toronto: Canadian Tax Foundation, 1999).

Arnold, Brian J, "Supreme Court of Canada Approves Blatant Tax-Avoidance Scheme", 19 *Tax Notes International* 1813-21 (Nov. 8, 1999).

Arnold, Brian J, "Canada's Supreme Court Rules on Duha Printers: The Triumph of Plain Meaning", 17 *Tax Notes International* 8 (July 6, 1998).

Arnold, Brian J, "Canada's Supreme Court Holds for Taxpayer in Hickman Motors", 15 *Tax Notes International* 337 (Aug. 4, 1997).

Arnold, Brian J, "The Canadian General Anti-Avoidance Rule", vol. 6 *British Tax Review* 541-556 (1995).

Arnold, Brian J., "Canada's Top Court Approves Income-Splitting Scheme", *International Tax News* 1829-1831 (June 15, 1988).

Avi-Yonah, Reuven S, "Globalization, Tax Competition, And the Fiscal Crisis of the Welfare State", 113 *Harvard Law Review* 1573-1676 (2000).

Bank, Steven A., "Codifying Judicial Doctrines: No Cure For Rules But More Rules", 54 *Southern Methodist Law Review* 37-45 (2001).

Bankman, Joseph, "The Tax Shelter Problem", 57 *National Tax Journal* 925-936 (2004).

Bankman, Joseph, "Modeling the Tax Shelter World", 55 *Tax Law Review* 455-464 (2002).

Bankman, Joseph, "The Business Purpose Doctrine and the Sociology of Tax", 54 *Southern Methodist University Law Review* 149-157 (2001).

Bankman, Joseph, "The Economic Substance Doctrine", 74 *Southern California Law Review* 5-30 (2000).

Bankman, Joseph, "The New Market in Corporate Tax Shelters", 83 *Tax Notes* 1775-1795 (June 21, 1999).

Barker, William B., "The Ideology of Tax Avoidance", vol. 40 Loyola *University Chicago Law Journal* 229-251 (2009).

Bateman, Andrew and Michael Wolng, "GAAR: No Abuse of the Stop-Loss Rules in Landrus", (2008) vol. 8, no. 3 *Tax For the Owner-Manager* 8-9.

Bassett, J. G., "Estate plans and arrangements to avoid income tax", 9 *Victoria University Wellington Law Review* 217-253 (1977-1978).

Beller, Herbert N., "New Disclosure Rules Require Serious Attention", *Financial Executive* 59-61 (September 2003).

Bennett, Anne and Nola Brown, "Revenue Service Completing Guidance on 'Reportable Arrangements'", 34 *Tax Notes International* 1400 (June 28, 2004).

Berg, Andrew N., "NYSBA Objects to Codification of Economic Substance Provisions", *Tax Notes* 1324 (June 2, 2003).

Bergin, Christopher, "Summers Delivers Sharp Words on Corporate Tax Shelters", 89 *Tax Notes* 991-994 (Nov. 20, 2000).

Bernstein, Jack, Barbara Worndl and Kay Leung, "Canadian Supreme Court's Pronouncement On GAAR: A Return to Uncertainty", *Tax Notes International* 437-447 (October 31, 2005).

Bernstein, Jack and Kay Leung, "Loss Utilization Planning: An Update", 2003 *Ontario Tax Conference* (Toronto: Canadian Tax Foundation, 2003).

Blank, Joshua D., "What's Wrong with Shaming Corporate Tax Abuse", vol. 62 *Tax Law Review* 539-589 (2009).

Blank, Joshua D., "Overcoming Overdisclosure: Toward Tax Shelter Detection" 56 *UCLA Law Review* 1629-1690 (2009).

Blum, Walter J., "Knetsch v. United States: A Pronouncement on Tax Avoidance", Taxes – *The Tax Magazine*, 296-312 (1962).

Boyce, Bret, "Obscenity and Community Standards", vol. 33, *Yale Journal of International Law* 299-368 (2008).

Bowman, Stephen W., "Interpretation of Tax Legislation: The Evolution of Purposive Analysis", (1995), vol. 43, no. 5 *Canadian Tax Journal* 1167-1189.

Brill, Alex, "Dear DAD: Southgate and the American Jobs Creation Act", 126 *Tax Notes* 505-511 (Jan. 25, 2010).

Brincker, Emil, "The Purpose Requirement of the General Anti-Avoidance Provision in South African Fiscal Law", vol. 2001, no. 1 *Journal of South African Law* 158-168.

Brooks, Neil, "The Responsibility of Judges in Interpreting Tax Legislation", *Tax Avoidance and the Rule of Law*, (Amsterdam: IBFD, 1997).

Broomberg, E.B., "The legacy of UK tax law in South Africa", vol. 3 *British Tax Review* 291-303 (2008).

Broomberg, E.B., "Then and now – VI", 22 *Tax Planning Corporate and Personal* 74-75 (2008).

Broomberg, E.B., "Then and now–V", 22 *Tax Planning Corporate and Personal* 52 (2008).

Broomberg, E.B., "Then and Now–II", 21 *Tax Planning Corporate and Personal* 131-133 (2007).

Brown, Karen B., "Tax Avoidance, Treaty Shopping and the Economic Substance Doctrine in the United States", vol. 2 *British Tax Review* 160 (2008).

Burke, Karen C. and Grayson M. P. McCouch, "COBRA Strikes Back: Anatomy of a Tax Shelter", vol. 62, no. 1 *Tax Lawyer* 59-93 (2008).

Burgess, Philip, "2010 Year in Review (Australia)", *Tax Notes International* 900-901 (Dec. 20, 2010).

Canellos, Peter C., "Tax Practitioner's Perspective on Substance, Form and Business Purpose in Structuring Business Transactions and in Tax Shelters", 54 *Southern Methodist University Law Review* 47-72 (2001).

Caplin, Mortimer, "Tax Shelter Disputes and Litigation With The Internal Revenue Service – 1987 Style", 6 *Virginia Tax Review* 709-759 (1986-1987).

Carr, Brian R., "Solicitor-Client Privilege", 2010 *Conference Report* 7:1-31 (Toronto: Canadian Tax Foundation, 2011).

Carr, Brian R. and Grace Pereira, "The Defence Against Civil Penalties", (2000), vol. 48, no. 6 *Canadian Tax Journal* 1737-1792.

Carvalho, Robert and Tim Clarke, "Current Cases 2008-2009", 2009 *British Columbia Tax Conference*, 2:1-30 (Vancouver: Canadian Tax Foundation, 2009).

Cashmere, Maurice, "A GAAR for the United Kingdom? The Australian Experience", no. 2 *British Tax Review* 125-159 (2008).

Cashmere, Maurice, "Towards an appropriate interpretative approach to Australia's general tax avoidance rule – Part IVA", 35 *Australian Tax Review* 231-247 (June 2006).

Cassidy, Julie, "The holy grail: The search for the optimal gaar", vol. 129, no. 4 *South African Law Journal* 740-779 (2009).

Cassidy, Julie, "'To GAAR or Not to GAAR – That is the Question:' Canadian and Australian Attempts to Combat Tax Avoidance", 36 *Ottawa Law Review* 259-313 (2004-2005).

Cassidy, Julie, "Part IVA – A Toothless Tiger?", vol. 11, issue 1 *Revenue Law Journal* 1-27 (2001).

Cassidy, Julie, "Observations on the Application of Part IVA: Peabody v. Federal Commissioner of Taxation", vol. 21 *Australian Business Law Review* 424-439 (December 1993).

CCH, "Supreme Court lays down tax avoidance law for the first time", no. 1 *New Zealand Tax Planning Reports* 1-10 (CCH: 2009).

Chirelstein, Marvin A., and Lawrence Zelenak, Lawrence, "Tax Shelters and the Search for a Silver Bullet", vol. 105, no. 6 *Columbia Law Review* 1939-1966 (2005).

Chirelstein, Marvin A., "Learned Hand's Contribution to the Law of Tax Avoidance", vol. 77, no. 3 *Yale Law Journal* 440-474 (1968).

Chodorow, Adam, "Economic Analysis in Judicial Decision Making – An Assessment Based on Judge Posner's Tax Decisions", vol. 25, no. 1 *Virginia Tax Review* 67-127 (2005).

Cilliers, Chris, "Thou shalt not peep at thy neighbour's wife: Section 80A(c)(ii) of the Income Tax Act and the Abuse of Rights", vol. 57 *The Taxpayer* 85-92 (May 2008).

Cilliers, Chris, "The Proposed Section 80A(c)(ii) of the Income Tax Act: Should It Be Enacted?", vol. 55, no. 10 *The Taxpayer* 182-187 (October 2006).

Clegg, David, "Use it or abuse it", 21 *Tax Planning* 38 (2007).

Coder, Jeremiah, "Economic Substance Guidance Should Reassure, Official Says", *Tax Notes* 1318-1319 (December 12, 2011).

Coder, Jeremiah, "Economic Substance Guidance Will Have Limited Scope", 127 *Tax Notes* 1423-1424 (June 28, 2010).

Coder, Jeremiah, "Living With GAAR Lite?", 127 *Tax Notes* 1187-1190 (June 14, 2010).

Coder, Jeremiah, "Alexander Addresses Determination of Economic Substance Relevance", 127 *Tax Notes* 1076-1077 (June 7, 2010).

Coder, Jeremiah, "Will Economic Substance Be Worth It?", 127 *Tax Notes* 16-19 (Apr. 5, 2010).

Coder, Jeremiah, "Federal Circuit Overturns Penalty Determination in Jade Trading", 126 *Tax Notes* 1568 (Mar. 29, 2010).

Coder, Jeremiah, "Wells Fargo Loses $115 Million SILO Refund Suit", 126 *Tax Notes* 293-295 (Jan. 18, 2010).

Coder, Jeremiah, "Fifth Circuit Adopts Majority View of Economic Substance Doctrine", 123 *Tax Notes* 969-971 (May 25, 2009).

Coder, Jeremiah, "IRS Wins Third Sale-Leaseback Case and Penalties", 119 *Tax Notes* 909-910 (June 2, 2008).

Cooper, Graeme S., "Australia's GAAR Comes Alive in the Courts", *Tax Notes International* 559-566 (May 16, 2011).

Cooper, Graeme S., "The Design and Structure of General Anti-Avoidance Regimes", *Bulletin for International Taxation* 26-32 (January 2009).

Cooper, Graeme S., "The emerging High Court jurisprudence on Part IVA", vol. 9, no. 5 *The Tax Specialist* 234-251 (June 2006).

Cooper, Graeme S., "International Experience with General Anti-Avoidance Rules", 54 *Southern Methodist University Law Review* 83-130 (2001).

Cooper, Graeme S. and Clare Cunliffe, "Skinning the Tax Avoidance Cat", vol. 30 *Australian Tax Review* 26-38 (2001).

Couzin, Robert, "Some Reflections on Corporate Control", (2005) vol. 53, no. 2 *Canadian Tax Journal* 305-332.

Cruickshank, Jim, "Trusts: Recent Developments", 2010 *Conference Report* 29:1-42 (Toronto: Canadian Tax Foundation, 2011).

Cullinan, Thomas A. and Shane A. Lord, "Economic Substance Doctrine: Unconstitutionally Vague?", 130 *Tax Notes* 700-705 (Feb. 7, 2011).

Cummings, Jr., Jasper L., "Economic Substance Doctrine Felonies", 131 *Tax Notes* 977-984 (May 30, 2011).

Cummings, Jr., Jasper L., "The New Normal: Economic Substance Doctrine First", 126 *Tax Notes* 521-530 (Jan. 25, 2010).

Cunningham, Nöel B. and James R. Repetti, "Textualism and Tax Shelters", 24 *Virginia Tax Review* 1-63 (2004).

Dabner, Justin, "There are Too Many Witchdoctors in Our Tax Courts: Is There a Better Way?", vol. 15, no. 1 *Revenue Law Journal* 36-49 (2005).

Dabner, Justin, Dr., "The Spin of a Coin – In Search of a Workable GAAR", 3 *Journal of Australian Taxation* 232 (2000).

Davison, Kent, "Avoidance, Evasion and the Problem Client", 1998 *Conference Report* 7:1-20 (Toronto: Canadian Tax Foundation, 1999),.

Debenham, David Bishop, "From the Revenue Rule to the Rule of the 'Revenuer': A Tale of Two Davids and Two Goliaths", (2008) vol. 56, no. 1 *Canadian Tax Journal* 1-66.

Diksic, Nik, "Some Reflections on the Roles of Legal and Economic Substance in Tax Law', 2010 *Conference Report* 25:1-34 (Toronto: Canadian Tax Foundation, 2011).

DiSciullo, Joseph, "Guidance Issued on Codification of Economic Substance Doctrine", 128 *Tax Notes* 1237-1239 (Sept. 20, 2010).

Dodge, David A., "A New and More Coherent Approach to Tax Avoidance", (1988) 36 *Canadian Tax Journal* 1-78.

Dolan, Kevin, "Foreign Tax Credit Generator Regs: The Purple People Eater Returns", *Tax Notes International* 251-258 (July 16, 2007).

Donmoyer, Ryan J., "Debate Over Tax Shelters Dominates Finance Hearing", *Tax Notes Today* (Mar. 8, 2000).

Donovan, Peter, "The aftermath of Hart's case – a case for reform of Part IVA?", vol. 39, no. 5 *Taxation in Australia* 253-256 (Nov. 2004).

Duff, David G., "Justice Iacobbuci and the 'Golden and Straight Metwand' of Canadian Tax Law", (2007) 57 *University of Toronto Law Journal* 525-579.

Duff, David G., "Weak-Currency Borrowings and the General Anti-Avoidance Rule in Canada: From Shell Canada to Canadian Pacific", *I.B.F.D. Bulletin* 233-240 (June 2001).

Duff, David G., "Interpreting the Income Tax Act–Chapter 1: Interpretive Doctrines" (1999), vol. 47, no. 3 *Canadian Tax Journal* 464-533.

Duff, David G., "Interpreting the Income Tax Act–Chapter 2: Towards a Pragmatic Approach", (1999) vol. 47, no. 4 *Canadian Tax Journal* 741-798.

Dunbar, David, "Judicial Techniques for Controlling the New Zealand General Anti-Avoidance Rule: The Scheme and Purpose Approach, from Challenge Corporation to Peterson", 12 *New Zealand Journal of Taxation Law and Policy* 324 (December 2006).

Edgar, Tim, "Building a Better GAAR", vol. 27 *Virginia Tax Review* 833-905 (2008).

Edgar, Tim, "Discussion Paper on Tax Avoidance and Section 103 of the Income Tax Act, 1962, (Act no. 58 of 1961), South African Revenue Service, Current Tax Reading,", (2006) vol. 54, no. 2 *Canadian Tax Journal* 551-553.

Edgar, Tim, "Financial Instruments and the Tax Avoidance Lottery: A View from North America", vol. 6 *New Zealand Journal of Taxation Law and Policy* 63-102 (2000).

Edgar, Tim, "Some Lessons from the Saga of Weak-Currency Borrowings", (2000) vol. 48, no. 1 *Canadian Tax Journal* 1-34.

Edgar, Tim, "Lisa Philipps, 'The Supreme Court of Canada's Tax Jurisprudence: What's Wrong with the Rule of Law', Current Tax Reading" (2000), vol. 48, no. 6 *Canadian Tax Journal* 1975-1976.

Elliffe, Craig, and Jess Cameron, "The Test for Tax Avoidance in New Zealand: A Judicial Sea Change", *New Zealand Business Law Quarterly* 440-460 (December 2010).

Elliffe, Craig and John Prebble, "General Anti-Avoidance Rules and Double Tax Agreements: A New Zealand Perspective", vol. 19, no. 1 *Revenue Law Journal* 1-23 (2009).

Elliffe, Craig, and Mark Keating, "Tax Avoidance – Still Waiting for Godot?", 23 *New Zealand Universities Law Review* 368-393 (June 2009).

Elliffe, Craig, "Tax Avoidance and the Supreme Court – Waiting for Godot?", vol. 14, no. 3 *New Zealand Business Law Quarterly* 128-140 (September 2008).

Elliott, Amy S., "Courts Will Interpret Economic Substance: McMahon Says", 129 *Tax Notes* 391-392 (Oct. 25, 2010).

Elliott, Amy S., "Economic Substance Guidance May Address Rules of Disclosure", 127 *Tax Notes* 1190-1191 (June 14, 2010).

Elliott, Amy S., "Economic Substance 'Angel List' Unlikely, Says Treasury Official, 127 *Tax Notes* 521-522 (May 3, 2010).

Elliott, Amy S., "Alexander Downplays Effect of Economic Substance Doctrine", 126 *Tax Notes* 1309-1311 (Mar. 15, 2010).

Elliott, Amy S., "AIG Sues IRS for Refund While Accepting New Federal Bailout Funds", 122 *Tax Notes* 1192-1193 (Mar. 9, 2009).

Ernst, Glenn, "Canadian FTC Generators Survive Court Challenge", *Tax Notes International* 838-840 (June 13, 2011).

Evans, Chris "Barriers to Tax Avoidance: Recent Legislative and Judicial Developments in Common Law Jurisdictions", vol. 37, no. 1 *Hong Kong Law Journal* 103-136 (2007).

Felesky, Brian A. and Sandra E. Jack, "Is There Substance to 'Substance Over Form' in Canada?", (1992) *Conference Report* 50:1-63 (Toronto: Canadian Tax Foundation, 1993).

Fitzsimmons, Timothy, "Mind the GAP – Landrus v. The Queen, Current Cases", (2008) vol. 56, no. 4 *Canadian Tax Journal* 923-956.

Forer, Douglas J. and Glen F. Thompson, "Recent Legislative and Administrative Developments in Federal and Provincial Law", 2011 *Prairie Provinces Tax Conference*, (Toronto: Canadian Tax Foundation, 2011).

Forer, Douglas J., "Recent Tax Cases and Legislative Proposals", 1998 *Prairie Provinces Tax Conference* 15:1-30 (Toronto: Canadian Tax Foundation, 1998).

Forst, David L. (ed.), "IRS Implements Promoter Penalty by Analogy to Corporate Tax Shelter Rules", 100 *Journal of Taxation* 247-248 (April 2004).

Fortin, Guy, "Economic Reality Versus Legal Reality", 1996 *Conference Report* 5:1-39 (Toronto: Canadian Tax Foundation, 1997).

Fraser, Ross, "Tax scheme disclosure provisions", vol. 4 *British Tax Review* 282-296 (2004).

Freedman, Judith, "Improving (Not Perfecting) Tax Legislation: Rules and Principles Revisited", vol. 6 *British Tax Review* 717-736 (2010).

Freedman, Judith "A GANTIP: Was it really such a bad idea?", *The Tax Journal* 8-10 (April 2009).

Freedman, Judith, Geoffrey Loomer and John Vella, "Corporate Tax Risk and Tax Avoidance: New Approaches", no. 1 *British Tax Review* 74-116 (2009).

Freedman, Judith, "Interpreting Tax Statutes: Tax Avoidance and the Intention of Parliament", vol. 123 *Law Quarterly Review* 53-90 (2007).

Freedman, Judith, "Converging Tracks? Recent Developments in Canadian and UK Approaches to Tax Avoidance", (2005) vol. 53, no. 4 *Canadian Tax Journal* 1038-1046.

Freedman, Judith, "Defining Taxpayer Responsibility: In Support of a General Anti-Avoidance Principle", no. 4 *British Tax Review* 332-357 (2004).

Frieberg, A., "Ripples from the Bottom of the Harbour: Some Social Ramifications of Taxation Fraud", 12 *Criminal Law Journal* 136-192 (1998).

Friedlander, Lara, "Canada Trustco Mortgage Co v. The Queen and Mathew v The Queen: the Supreme Court of Canada finally considers GAAR", vol. 1 *British Tax Review* 48-54 (2006).

Gardner, Leland I., "An Elephant in the Room: Double Deductions and the Economic Substance Doctrine in Coltec Industries, Inc. v. United States", vol. 60 no. 2 *Tax Lawyer* 519-532 (2007).

Garlock, David C., Kevin M. Richards, Eric Solomon and Karen Gilbreath Sowell, "Analysis of the LB&I Directive on the Economic Substance Doctrine", *Tax Notes* 193-201 (October 10, 2011).

Gergen, Mark P., "The Common Knowledge of Tax Abuse", 54 *Southern Methodist Law Review* 131-147 (2001).

Gibbs, Lawrence B., "Constancy and Change in Our Federal Tax System", vol. 61, no. 3 *Tax Lawyer* 673-703 (2008).

Ginsburg, Martin D., "Making Tax Law Through the Judicial Process", 70 *Anerican Bar Association Journal* 74 (March 1984).

Glassman, Daniel J., "'It's Not A Lie If You Believe It': Tax Shelters and the Economic Substance Doctrine", 58 *Florida Law Review* 665-711 (2006).

Glicklich, Peter and Angela M. Eiref, "New US International Tax Legislation May be the Most Significant Since 1986", Selected US Tax Developments, (2004) vol. 52 no. 4 *Canadian Tax Journal* 1259-1284.

Granwell, Alan and Sarah McGonigle, "US tax shelters: a UK reprise?", vol. 2 *British Tax Review* 170-208 (2006).

Shelly Griffiths, "The Abusive Tax Position in the Tax Administration Act 1994: An Unstable Standard for a Penalty Provision?", 15 *New Zealand Journal of Taxation Law and Policy* 159 (June 2009).

Greenaway, Thomas D., "International Tax Arbitrage: A Frozen Debate Thaws", 126 *Tax Notes* 631-639 (Feb. 1, 2010).

Grewal, Amandeep S., "Economic Substance and the Supreme Court", *Tax Notes* 969 (Sept. 10, 2007).

Gunn, Alan, "The Use and Misuse of Anti-Abuse Rules: Lessons from The Partnership Abuse Regulations", 54 *Southern Methodist University Law Review* 159-176 (2001).

Gunn, Alan, "Tax Avoidance", 76 *Michigan Law Review* 733-767 (1978).

Halpern, James S., "Putting The Cart Before The Horse: Determining Economic Substance Independent of the Language of the Code", 30 *Virginia Tax Review* 327-338 (2010).

Hariton, David P., "When and How Should the Economic Substance Doctrine be Applied?", 60 *Tax Law Review* 29-56 (2006).

Hariton, David P., "Sorting Out The Tangle of Economic Substance", 52 *Tax Lawyer* 235-273 (1999).

Harnish, Kerry, "Interpreting the Income Tax Act: Purpose v. Plain Meaning and the Effect of Uncertainty in the Tax Law", (1996) 35 *Alberta Law Review* 687-725.

Hayward, Paul D., "Monetization, Realization, and Statutory Interpretation", (2003) vol. 51, no. 5 *Canadian Tax Journal* 1761-1824.

Hayward, Paul D. "Income Trusts: A 'Tax-Efficient' Product or the Product of Tax Inefficiency?", (2002) vol. 5 *Canadian Tax Journal* 1529-1569.

Hickey, Paul, "Aggressive Tax Planning", (2010) vol. 18, no. 4 *Canadian Tax Highlights* 2.

Hicks, Timothy R., "Government Victories Using The Economic Substance Doctrine: A Changing of the Tide in Tax Practice?", 38 *Cumberland Law Review* 101-138 (2007).

Italia, Maria, "Taxpayer Privilege and the Revenue Authorities' Obligation to Maintain Secrecy of Taxpayer Information: Recent Developments in Australia, and a Comparison with New Zealand, the United Kingdom and the United States", 17 *New Zealand Journal of Taxation Law and Policy* 151-177 (June 2011).

Isenbergh, Joseph, "Musings on Form and Substance in Taxation", 49 *University of Chicago Law Review* 859-884 (1982).

Jackel, Monte A., "Jackel Urges Comment on Economic Substance Doctrine", 127 *Tax Notes* 1398 (June 21, 2010).

Jackel, Monte A., "Dawn of a New Era: Congress Codifies Economic Substance", 127 *Tax Notes* 289-308 (Apr. 19, 2010).

Jackel, Monte A. and Robert J. Crnkovich, "Son-of-BOSS Revisited", 123 *Tax Notes* 1481-1485 (June 22, 2009).

Jakolev, John and Graham Turner, "Sham Capital Dividends", (2007) vo. 15, no. 9 *Canadian Tax Highlights* 7-8.

Jennings, Gray, "Economic Substance and the Taxpayer's Purpose", 127 *Tax Notes* 535-545 (May 3, 2010).

Joe, Michael, "IRS Commissioner Talks Tough on Tax Avoidance", 121 *Tax Notes* 1215-1216 (Dec. 15, 2008).

Johnson, Calvin H.,"H.R. ___, The Anti-skunk Works Corporate Tax Shelter Act of 1999", 84 *Tax Notes* 443-461 (July 19, 1999).

Johnson, Calvin H., "What's a Tax Shelter?", 68 *Tax Notes* 879-883 (Aug. 15, 1995).

Joubert, Billy, "Legislative Restraint and The Problem of Over-Compensation", *Accountancy South Africa* (May 2010).

Junega, Raj and Geoffrey Turner, "Foreign Tax Credit Generator Proposals – An Inadvertent Attack on Hybrids?", no. 52 *International Tax* 1-6 (CCH) (July 2010).

Kahan, Dan M., "The Logic of Reciprocity: Trust, Collective Action, and Law", 102 *Michigan Law Review* 71-103 (2003).

Kandev, Michael, Brian Bloom and Oliver Fournier, "The Meaning of 'Series of Transactions' Disclosed by a Unified Textual, Contextual, and Purposive Analysis", (2010) vol. 58, no. 1 *Canadian Tax Journal* 277-330.

Kaplow, Louis, "Rules Versus Standards: An Economic Analysis", vol. 42 *Duke Law Journal* 557-629 (1992).

Keating, Mark and Kirsty Keating, "Tax Avoidance in New Zealand: The Camel's Back That Refuses to Break!", 17 *New Zealand Journal of Taxation Law and Policy* 115 (March 2011).

Keating, Mark, "Problems Flowing from the Nil Depreciation of Buildings", 16 *New Zealand Journal of Taxation Law and Policy* 307 (Sept. 2010).

Keating, Mark, "GST Tax Avoidance: A New Zealand Perspective on the Application of Div 165", vol. 8, no. 1 *eJournal of Tax Research* 64-89 (2009).

Keinan, Yoram, "It is Time for The Supreme Court to Voice its Opinion on Economic Substance", 7 *Houston Business and Tax Law Journal* 93-137 (2006).

Keinan, Yoram, "The Many Faces of the Economic Substance's Two-Prong Test: Time for Reconciliation?", 1 *NYU Journal of Law and Business* 371-456 (2005).

Kendall, Keith, "The Structural Approach to Tax Avoidance in Australia", vol. 9, no. 5 *The Tax Specialist* 290-298 (2006).

Kenney, Allen, "Korb Speculates on Codification of Economic Substance Doctrine", 105 *Tax Notes* 932 (Nov. 15, 2004).

Knight, Ray and Lee Knight, "Substance Over Form: The Cornerstone of Our Tax System or a Lethal Weapon in the IRS'S Aresenal?", 8 *Akron Tax Journal* 91 (1991).

Kopstein, Robert and Jasmine Sidhu, "The Federal Court of Appeal – What Factors Motivate You?, Current Cases", (2009) vol. 57, no. 3 *Canadian Tax Journal* 563-585.

Krever, Richard and Anthony van der Westhuysen, "Government to Review Antiavoidance Provisions", *Tax Notes International* 731-732 (Dec 6, 2010).

Krever, Richard, "Tax Office Warns Miners About Avoidance Scheme", *Tax Notes International* 574 (Feb 16, 2009).

Krever, Richard "ATO Releases New GAAR Guidance", *Tax Notes International* 1133-1134 (Dec. 2005).

Lederman, Leandra, "W(h)ither Economic Substance?", 95 *Iowa Law Review* 389-444 (2010).

Lederman, Leandra, "The Interplay Between Norms and Enforcement in Tax Compliance", vol. 64, no. 6 *Ohio State Law Journal* 1453-1514 (2003).

Léger, Marc D., "Canada Proposes Disclosure of Aggressive Tax Planning", *Tax for the Owner-Manger*, Canadian Tax Foundation (July 2010).

Lennard, Michael, "Two Tribes and an Elephant Called Ben Nevis", *Taxation Today* (September 2009).

Li, Jinyan, "'Economic Substance': Legitimate Tax Minimization vs. Abusive Tax Avoidance", (2006) vol. 54, no. 1 *Canadian Tax Journal* 23-56.

Libin, Jerome B., "Congress Should Address Tax Avoidance Head-On: The Internal Revenue Code Needs A GAAR", 30 *Virginia Tax Review* 339-353 (2010).

Liebenberg, Justin, "General anti-avoidance rule", vol. 1 *the tax line* 1-10 (May 2007).

Likhovski, Assaf, "The Duke and The Lady: Helvering v. Gregory and The History of Tax Avoidance Adjudication", 25 *Cardozo Law Review* 953-1018 (2004).

Lille, Genevieve and Elizabeth Johnson in "Partnerships: An Update", 2010 *Conference Report* 36:1-62 (Toronto: Canadian Tax Foundation, 2011).

Lipton, Richard M., "Going to Trial is No Guarantee of Success in A Silo Case if Non-Tax Purpose is Lacking", *Journal of Taxation* 205-212 (April 2010).

Lipton, Richard M., "What Will Be The Long-Term Impact of the Sixth Circuit's Divided Decision in Dow Chemical?", 104 *Journal of Taxation* 332-337 (2006).

Littlewood, Michael, "Tax Avoidance, the Rule of Law and the New Zealand Supreme Court", *New Zealand Law Review* 35-68 (2011).

Littlewood, Michael, "*Ben Nevis Forestry Ventures Ltd. v. CIR; Glenharrow Ltd. v. CIR*: New Zealand's Supreme Court and tax avoidance", vol. 2 *British Tax Rev*iew 169-180 (2009).

Littlewood, Michael "The Privy Council and the Austalasian anti-avoidance rules", vol. 2 *British Tax Review* 175-205 (2007).

Livingston, Michael, "Practical Reason, 'Purposivism', and the Interpretation of Tax Statutes", 51 *Tax Law Review* 677-724 (1996).

Loutinsky, Genevieve, "Gladwellian Taxation: Deterring Tax Abuse Through General Anti-Avoidance Rules", vol. 19, no. 2 *Temple Political & Civil Rights Law Review* 101-135 (Spring 2010).

Loutzenhiser, Glen, "Income splitting and settlements: further observations on Jones v Garnett", vol. 6 *British Tax Review* 693-716 (2007).

Loveland, Norman, "Recent Cases of Interest", 1997 *Conference Report* (Toronto: Canadian Tax Foundation, 1998).

Luke, Charlene D., "What Would Simons, Henry Do: Using An Ideal To Shape And Explain The Economic Substance Doctrine", 10 *Houston Business and Tax Law Journal* (forthcoming) (2010).

Luke, Charlene D., "Risk, Return, and Objective Economic Substance", 27 *Virginia Tax Review* 783-832 (2008).

Lurie, Alvin D., "I Know Crane and BOSS isn't Crane (An Historical Perspective)", 86 *Tax Notes* 1932-1941 (Mar. 27, 2000).

MacKnight, Robin J., "Prophecies and Soda: Evolving and Surviving Tax Shelters", 95 *Conference Report* 14:1-17 (Toronto: Canadian Tax Foundation, 1996).

MacKnight, Robin J., "Cabbages and Soda: A Skeptic's Review of Tax Shelters", 1993 *Conference Report* 50:1-50 (Toronto: Canadian Tax Foundation, 1994).

Madison, Allen D., "Rationalizing Tax Law By Breaking The Addiction to Economic Substance", 47 *Idaho Law Review* 1-37 (2011).

Mandy, Kyle, "Reportable Arrangements", *Accountancy South Africa* (November 2008).

Mattingly, David, "Empty Forms: Applying the Assignment-of-Income Doctrine to Contingent Liability Tax Shelters", 94 *Georgetown Law Journal* 1993-2027 (2006).

Mazansky, Ernest, "South Africa's New General Anti-Avoidance Rule – The Final GAAR", 31 *Bulletin for International Taxation* 159-167 (2007).

Mazansky, Ernest, "A New GAAR for South Africa – The Duke of Westminster is Struck a Blow", 60 *Bulletin for International Taxation* 124-132 (2006).

Mazansky, Ernest, "The Duke of Westminster Still Lives in South Africa (But is Very Careful When He Crosses the Road)", 59 *Bulletin for International Fiscal Documentation* 116-120 (March 2005).

McCarthy, Hui Ling, "HMRC: SHIPS that pass in the night – reconciling Mayes and Drummond", vol. 3 *British Tax Review* 279-299 (2011).

McDonnell, Thomas E., "CDA Tax Scheme Voided-Sham Doctrine Expanded?" (2007) vol. 7, no. 4 *Tax for the Owner Manager*, 8-9.

McDonnell, Thomas E., "The GAAR: Limited-Recourse Defeased Lease Survives Review, Current Cases", (2003) vol. 51, no. 4 *Canadian Tax Journal* 1602-1629.

McDonnell, Thomas E., "Who's in control here?, Current Cases" (1997), vol. 45, no. 1 *Canadian Tax Journal* 114.

McDonnell, Thomas E. "The House of Lords – Judicial Anti-avoidance Techniques Expanded?, Current Cases", (1992) vol. 40, no. 4 *Canadian Tax Journal* 929-938.

McDonnell, Thomas E. "Business Purpose Test – Whither the Duke's Case?", (1981) vol. 29, no. 2 *Canadian Tax Journal* 184-192.

McGowan, Trevor, "Tax Shelters: An Overview and Update", 2006 *Conference Report* 37:1-14 (Toronto: Canadian Tax Foundation, 2007).

McGuffin, Andrew, "The Interaction of GAAR and Withholding Tax, Current Cases", (2010) vol. 58, no. 1 *Canadian Tax Journal* 97-115.

McMahon Jr., Martin J., "Living With the Codified Economic Substance Doctrine", 128 *Tax Notes* 731-754 (Aug. 16, 2010).

McMahon, Jr., Martin J., "Economic Substance, Purposive Activity, and Corporate Tax Shelters", 94 *Tax Notes* 1017-1026 (Feb. 25, 2002).

McMahon, Jr., Martin J., "Random Thoughts On Applying Judicial Doctrines To Interpret The Internal Revenue Code", 54 *Southern Methodist University Law Review* 195-208 (2001).

McQuillan, Peter E., "Some Important Issues in Partnerships in the Past Year", 2002 *Conference Report* 1:1-25 (Toronto: Canadian Tax Foundation, 2003).

Meghji, Al and Gerald Grenon, "An Analysis of Recent Avoidance Cases", 1996 *Conference Report* 66:1-54 (Toronto: Canadian Tax Foundation, 1997).

Meier, Jared T., "Understanding the Statutory Tax Practitioner Privilege: What is Tax Shelter "Promotion"?, 78 *University of Chicago Law Review* 671-704 (2011).

Meredith, Mark and Nancy Diep, "Duplication of Tax Attributes", 2010 *Conference Report* 10:1-32 (Toronto: Canadian Tax Foundation, 2011).

Meyerowitz, Dave, "What Does The New Section 80A Add To Our Law", vol. 57 *The Taxpayer* 64-67 (2008).

Meyerowitz, Dave, "General Anti-Avoidance Rule", vol. 56, no. 3 *The Taxpayer* 41-42 (Mar. 2007).

Meyerowitz, Dave, "Aggressive Tax Planning", vol. 56, no. 2 *The Taxpayer* 37-38 (Feb. 2007).

Meyerowitz, Dave, "Tax Avoidance Editorial", vol. 55, no. 10 *The Taxpayer* 181 (October 2006).

Meyerowitz, Dave, "Tax Avoidance", vol. 55, no. 3 *The Taxpayer* 49-52 (Mar. 2006).

Meyerowitz, Dave, "Some Musings on the Meaning of Tax Avoidance", vol. 55, no. 4 *The Taxpayer* 62-64 (April 2006).

Meyerowitz, Dave, "What Is Tax Avoidance?", vol. 54, no. 11 *The Taxpayer* 201-206 (Nov. 2005).

Meyerowitz, Dave, "Tax Avoidance Legislation", vol. 54, no. 4 *The Taxpayer* 61-64 (April 2005).

Milet, Matias, "Permanent Establishments Through Related Corporations Under the OECD Model Treaty", (2007) vol. 55, no. 2 *Canadian Tax Journal* 289-330.

Millett. P., "A new Approach to Tax Avoidance Schemes", 98 *Law Quarterly Report* 209 (1982).

Miller, David S., "An Alternative to Codification of the Economic Substance Doctrine", 123 *Tax Notes* 747-753 (May 11, 2009).

Miller, Jr., Gerald W., "Corporate Tax Shelters and Economic Substance: An Analysis of the Problem and its Common Law Solution", 34 *Texas Tech Law Review* 1015-1069 (2003).

Miller, John A., "Indeterminacy, Complexity, and Fairness: Justifying Rule Simplification in the Law of Taxation", 69 *Washington Law Review* 1-78 (1993).

Miller, Sandra K., "The Battle against Abusive Tax Shelters Continues", *Journal of Financial Service Professionals* 58-66 (November 2005).

Millet, QC, P., "Artificial Tax Avoidance: The English and American Approach", 6 *British Tax Review* 327-339 (1986).

Mogle, James R., "The Future of International Transfer Pricing: Practical and Policy Opportunities Unique to Intellectual Property, Economic Substance, and Entrepreneurial Risk in the Allocation of Intangible Income", 10 *George Mason Law Review* 925-950 (2002).

Morgan, James, "Cross-Border Regulation of Tax Shelters: The Implied Economic Substance Doctrine", *Tax Notes International* 387-395 (Oct. 22, 2007).

K. Murphy, "An examination of taxpayers' attitudes towards the Australian tax system: Findings from a survey of tax scheme avoiders", *Australian Tax Forum* 18(2), 209-242 (2003).

Nadal, Lisa M., "JITSIC Puts Antiabuse Effort on Fast Track, Says Former Director", 121 *Tax Notes* 396 (Oct. 27, 2008).

Nahass, Zachary, "Codifying the Economic Substance Doctrine: A Proposal on the Doorstep of Usefulness", 58 *Administrative Law Review* 247-268 (2006).

Ng, Lindsay, "Promoter penalties – tax agents beware!", *Chartered Accountants Journal* 26-27 (October 2010).

Nichols, Brian S., "GAAR and More", 2002 *Ontario Tax Conference* 1:1-42 (Toronto: Canadian Tax Foundation, 2002).

Nitikman, Joel, "A Year's Worth of GAAR Cases", 2008 *British Columbia Tax Conference* 7:1-23, (Vancouver: Canadian Tax Foundation, 2008).

Nock, Ronald S., "Legislative change by Practice Statement", vol. 1 *British Tax Review* 21-31 (1999).

Nugee, Edward G., "The United Kingdom Experience: McGuckian – Formalism and Economic Substance", 1997 *Conference Report* 36:1-12 (Toronto: Canadian Tax Foundation, 1998).

Oats, Lynne and David Salter, "Finance Act notes: disclosure of tax avoidance schemes–section 116 and Schedule 38", vol. 5 *British Tax Review* 505-510 (2008).

O'Neill, Sandra "Let's Try Again: Reformulating the Economic Substance Doctrine", *Tax Notes* 1053-1062 (Dec. 1, 2008).

O' Reilly, Terrance, "Economics and Economic Substance", 9 *Florida Tax Review* 725-792 (2010).

Orow, Nabil F., "Part IVA – Seriously Flawed in Principle", *Journal of Australian Taxation* 57-78 (1998).

Orow, Nabil F., "The Future of Australia's General Anti-Avoidance Provision", vol. 1 *New Zealand Journal of Taxation Law and Policy* 225-246 (June 1995).

Owens, Jeffrey, "Abusive Tax Shelters: Weapons of Tax Destruction?", 40 *Tax Notes International* 873-876 (Dec. 5, 2005).

Pagone, Tony, "Part IVA – The voyage continues", vol. 10, no. 1 *The Tax Specialist* 37-45 (August 2006).

Pagone, GT, "Part IVA: The General Anti-Avoidance Provisions in Australian Law", vol. 27, no. 3 *Melbourne University Law Review* 770-779 (2003).

Pederick, Willard, "Fair and Square Taxation for Australia", *Taxation in Australia* 570 (Dec 1984).

Peaslee, James M., "Creditable Foreign Taxes and the Economic Substance Profit Test", 114 *Tax Notes* 443-451 (Jan. 29, 2007).

Penny, Wayne, "Tax Shelter Rules: Where Are We?", 1995 *Conference Report* 13:1-22 (Toronto: Canadian Tax Foundation, 1996).

Philipps, Lisa, "The Supreme Court of Canada's Tax Jurisprudence: What's Wrong with the Rule of Law?", 79 *Canadian Bar Review* 120-144 (2000).

Pichhadze, Aviv and Amir Pichhadze, "Economic Substance Doctrine: Time for a Legislative Response", 48 *Tax Notes International* 61 (Oct. 1, 2007).

Power, Mike, Harriet Man and Tony Tse, "Loss Utilization Strategies within a Related Group of Companies", 2009 *Atlantic Provinces Tax Conference* 4A:1-28 (Halifax: Canadian Tax Foundation, 2009).

Prebble , Zoe and John Prebble, "The Morality of Tax Avoidance", 43 *Creighton Law Review* 693-746 (2010).

Prebble, John, "Tax Avoidance, International Tax Arbitrage, and New Zealand as Haven for Foreign Capital and Income", vol. 16 *Revue Juridique Polynesienne* 169-182 (2010).

Pross, Achim and Raffaele Russo, "News Analysis: OECD Disclosure Initiatives on the Rise", 61 *Tax Notes International* 744-745 (Mar. 7, 2011).

Quinn, Jason, "Being Punished for Obeying the Rules: Corporate Tax Planning and the Overly Broad Economic Substance Doctrine", 15 *George Mason Law Review* 1041-1080 (2008).

Raby, Burgess J.W., and William L. Raby, "Practitioner Advice as a Defense Against Penalties", 109 *Tax Notes* 329-334 (Oct. 17, 2005).

Rector, Jeff, "A Review of the Economic Substance Doctrine", 10 *Stanford Journal of Law, Business & Finance*, 173-190 (2004).

Rickman, Johnathan, "Government Revises Proposed Antiavoidance Legislation", 43 *Tax Notes International* 1049 (Sept. 25, 2006).

Sandler, Daniel, "The Minister's Burden of Proof Under GAAR", (2006) vol. 54, no. 1 Canadian Tax Journal 3-22.

Saparie, Marie, "Codified Economic Substance Doctrine Still an Uncertain Area", 129 *Tax Notes* 30-31 (Oct. 4, 2010).

Sawyer, Adrian J., "Surgeons' Practices and Tax Avoidance: A Mutually Exclusive Relationship?", 15 *New Zealand Journal of Taxation Law and Policy* 97 (June 2009).

Sawyer, Adrian J., "Blurring the distinction between avoidance and evasion – the abusive tax position", vol. 5 *British Tax Review* 483-504 (1996).

Scarborough, Robert H., "NYSB Tax Section Concerned About Codifying Substance Doctrine", 88 *Tax Notes* 752-753 (Aug. 7, 2000).

Scarborough, Robert H., "Different Rules for Different Layers and Products: The Patchwork Taxation of Derivatives", 72 *Taxes* 1031-1049 (1994).

Schneider, Daniel M., "Use of Judicial Doctrines in Federal Tax Cases Decided By Trial Courts, 1993-2006: A Quantitative Assessment", 57 *Cleveland State Law Review* 35-75 (2009).

Scott, Larry R., "Sale-Leaseback v. Mere Financing: *Lyon*'s Roar And The Aftermath", no. 4 *University of Illinois Law Review* 1075-1104 (1982).

Shakow, David J., "Consolidated Edison Turns on the Lights", 126 *Tax Notes* 625-630 (Feb. 1, 2010).

Sharlow, Karen R., "Recent Developments – Deductibility of Fines and Penalties", 1998 *British Columbia Tax Conference* 18A:1-11, (Vancouver: Canadian Tax Foundation, 1998).

Shaviro, Daniel N. and David A. Weisbach, "The Fifth Circuit Gets it Wrong in Compaq v. Commissioner", 94 *Tax Notes* 511-518, (Jan. 28, 2002).

Shaviro, Daniel N., "Economic Substance, Corporate Tax Shelters and the Compaq Case", 88 *Tax Notes* 221-244 (July 10, 2000).

Sheppard, Lee A., "British Propose Toothless Antiavoidance Rule", *Tax Notes International* 764-768 (Dec 12, 2011).

Sheppard, Lee A., "Recent Shelter Cases: The Right Result for the Wrong Reasons", 126 *Tax Notes* 421-428 (Jan. 25, 2010).

Sheppard, Lee A., "Behind the Economic Substance Codification Provision", 117 *Tax Notes* 205-206 (Oct. 15, 2007).

Sheppard, Lee A., "KPMG: Has the Prosecution Overcharged the Crime?", 112 *Tax Notes* 405-416 (July 31, 2006).

Sheppard, Lee A., "LTCM Case: What They Won't Do For Money, Chapter 2", 104 *Tax Notes* 1006 -1013 (Sept. 6, 2004).

Sheppard, Lee A., "Economic Substance Abuse", 89 *Tax Notes* 1095-1100 (Nov. 27, 2000).

Shipwright, Adrian, "Finance Act notes: extension of restrictions on allowable capital losses – section 27", vol. 5 *British Tax Review* 456-458 (2007).

Sikka, Prem and Mark P. Hampton, "The Role of Accountancy Firms in Tax Avoidance: Some Evidence and Issues", 29 *Accounting Forum* 325 (2009).

Silver, QC, Sheldon and Glenn Ernst, "Recent Cases on GAAR", 2001 *Ontario Tax Conference* 1B:1-35 (Toronto: Canadian Tax Foundation, 2001).

Sinfield, Greg, "The Halifax principle as a universal GAAR for tax in the EU", vol. 3 *British Tax Review* 235-246 (2011).

Smith, Robert Thornton, "Business Purpose: The Assault Upon The Citadel", 53 *Tax Lawyer* 1-34 (1999).

Stewart, David D., "Bank Challenges IRS Foreign Tax Credit Generator Determination", 123 *Tax Notes* 1527-1528 (June 29, 2009).

Stoddard, Laura, "Stretching the Sham Doctrine?, Current Cases," (2007) vol. 55, no. 4 *Canadian Tax Journal* 824-854.

Stratton, Sheryl, "IRS, Tax Bar Urge Congress to Leave Economic Substance Alone", 114 *Tax Notes* 814-815 (Feb. 26, 2007).

Stratton, Sheryl, "DOJ Alleges Fraud in Design, Marketing of KPMG Tax Shelters", 111 *Tax Notes* 541-542 (May 1, 2006).

Stratton, Sheryl, "KPMG Shelter Civil and Criminal Proceedings – Parallel No More?", 109 *Tax Notes* 297-298 (Oct. 17, 2005).

Surtees, Peter, "South Africa", 44 *Tax Notes International* 1106 (Dec. 25, 2006).

Surtees, Peter, "South Africa", 41 *Tax Notes International* 99 (Jan. 9, 2006).

Swiderski, Tony and Alexey Manasuev, "The New US Statutory Economic Substance Doctrine: They Forgot the Important Parts – Has Everything or Nothing Changed?", 2010 *Conference Report* 18:1-31 (Toronto: Canadian Tax Foundation, 2011).

Tandon, Crystal, "Treasury Planning Guidance on Economic Substance Penalties", 127 *Tax Notes* 965-966 (May 31, 2010).

Tandon, Crystal, "IRS Honing Its Strategy as FTC Cases Head to Court", 123 *Tax Notes* 1179 (June 8, 2009).

Thomas, Kathleen DeLaney, "The Case Against A Strict Liability Economic Substance Penalty", vol. 13:2 *University of Pennsylvania Journal of Business Law* 445-496 (2011).

Thomas, Richard. "The Supreme Court of Canada – A Disciplined Approach to GAAR", vol. 54, no. 1 *Canadian Tax Journal* 221-240 (2006).

Thomas, Richard B., "Shellshocked! The Queen v. Shell Canada Limited, Current Cases", (1998) vol. 46, no. 2 *Canadian Tax Journal* 357-376.

Thomas, Richard B., "Tax Avoidance with a Little Help from Downunder – Shell Canada Limited v. The Queen", *Current Cases*, (1997) vol. 45, no. 2 *Canadian Tax Journal* 295-96.

Thomas, Richard B., "Management Companies – Business Purpose Test", (1983) vol. 31, no. 2 *Canadian Tax Journal* 236-238.

Thompson Jr., Samuel C., "Despite Widespread Opposition, Congress Should Codify the ESD", *Tax Notes* 781 (Feb. 13, 2006).

Thompson, William, "Applying Part IVA", vol. 10, no. 4 *The Tax Specialist* 187-200 (April 2007).

Tiley, John, "Tax Avoidance Jurisprudence as normal law", vol. 4 *British Tax Review* 304-331 (2004).

Tiley, John, "Judicial Anti-Avoidance Doctrines: The US Alternatives", *British Tax Review* 180-197 (1987).

Timokhov, Vitaly, "Supreme Court Cases Test Canada's Antiavoidance Rules", *Tax Notes International* 415-421 (May 2, 2005).

Tooma, Rachel, "Tax Planning in Australia: When is Aggressive Too Aggressive?", *Tax Notes International* 427-442 (May 2, 2006).

Trombitas, Eugen, "The Conceptual Approach to Tax Avoidance in the 21st Century: When the Statute Gives But the GAAR Can Take Away", 15 *New Zealand Journal of Taxation Law and Policy* 352 (December 2009).

Trombitas, Eugen, "Trinity Exposed: Does the Emperor Really Have No Clothes or is He Wearing an Unusual Silver Rugby Jersey? – The Latest News from the GAAR Front", 13 *New Zealand Journal of Taxation Law and Policy* 583 (December 2007).

Trombitas, Eugen, "The Role for a General Anti-Avoidance Rule in a GST", 13 *New Zealand Journal of Taxation Law and Policy* 396 (September 2007).

Tubb, Graham, "Promoter Penalties", *Chartered Accountants Journal* 4-5 (November 2010).

U.S. Government, "GAO Urges Stiffer Tax Shelter Penalty", *Journal of Accountancy* 100 (October 1988).

VanderWolk, Jefferson, "The Stain of *Spotless Services* Spreads to Hong Kong: The Tai Hing Cotton Mill Case", vol. 12 no. 1 *Asia-Pacific Journal of Taxation* 20-30 (Spring/Summer 2008).

van Schalkwyk, Linda and Bernard Geldennuys, "Section 80A(c)(ii) of the Income Tax Act and the scope of Part IIA: the big boom – Part II", *Accountancy South Africa* (October 2009).

van Schalkwyk, Linda and Bernard Geldenhuys, "Section 80A(c)(ii) of the Income Tax Act and the scope of Part II A: the big boom part I", *Accountancy South Africa* 30-31 (October 2009).

Vasconcellos, Roberto P. and H. David Rosenbloom, "Measuring a Foreign Tax Credit Generator Transaction Against the Codified Economic Substance Doctrine", *Tax Notes International* 119-125 (Oct. 11, 2010).

Ventry Jr., Dennis J., "Save the Economic Substance Doctrine from Congress", 118 *Tax Notes* 1405-1412 (Mar. 31, 2008).

Walton, Robert S. and Jenny A. Austin, "Jade Trading and Cemco Investors: Economic Substance Governs in Son-of-Boss", 108 *Journal of Taxation* 300-306 (2008).

Ward, David A. and Maurice C. Cullity, "Abuse of Rights and the Business Purpose Test as Applied to Taxing Statutes", (1981) vol. 29, no. 4 *Canadian Tax Journal* 451-475.

Warren, Jr., Alvin C., "Understanding Long Term Capital", 106 *Tax Notes* 681-696 (Feb. 7, 2005).

Warren, Jr., Alvin C., "Financial Contract Innovation and Income Tax Policy", 107 *Harvard Law Review* 460-492 (1993).

Warren, Jr., Alvin C., "The Requirement of Economic Profit in Tax Motivated Transactions", 59 *Taxes – The Magazine* 985-992 (1981).

Watkins, Donald H., "The Tax Shelter Rules: An Update", 1998 *Conference Report* 5:1-32 (Toronto: Canadian Tax Foundation, 1999).

Weisbach, David A., "Ten Truths About Tax Shelters", vol. 55 *Tax Law Review* 215-254 (2001-2002).

Weisbach, David A., "The Failure to Disclose as an Approach to Tax Shelters", 54 *SMU Law Review* 73-82 (2001).

Wells, Bret, "Economic Substance Doctrine: How Codification Changes Decided Cases", vol. 10, no. 6 *Florida Tax Review* 416-457 (2010).

Wertschek, Rosmarie and James R. Wilson, "Shelter from the Storm: The Current State of the Tax Shelter Rules in Section 237.1", (2008) vol. 56, no. 2 *Canadian Tax Journal* 285-236.

West, Phillip R., "Antiabuse Rules and Policy: Coherence or Tower of Babel?", *Tax Notes International* 1161-1180 (March 31, 2008).

Willens, Robert, "'Economic Substance' Doctrine Denies Tax Benefits", 118 *Tax Notes* 537-540 (Jan. 28, 2008).

Wilkie, J. Scott, and Heather Kerr, "Common Links Among Jurisdictions: Informing The GAAR Through Comparative Analysis", 1997 *Conference Report* (Toronto: Canadian Tax Foundation, 1998).

Williams, Nicola, "Privy Council Delivers Final Tax Avoidance Decision: Peterson v. CIR", vol. 11 *New Zealand Journal of Taxation Law and Policy* 283-291 (September 2005).

Wilson-Rogers, Nicole,"Coming out of the Dark?: The Uncertainties that Remain in Respect of Part IVA: How does Recent Tax Office Guidance Help?", 4(1) *eJournal of Tax Research* 25 (2006).

Wolfman, Bernard, "Why Economic Substance is Better Left Uncodified", 104 *Tax Notes* 445 (Jul. 26, 2004).

Wolfman, Bernard, "The Supreme Court in the Lyon's Den: A Failure of Judicial Process", 66 *Cornell Law Review* 1075-1102 (1981).

Wood, Robert W., "What Wells Fargo Brings to the SILO/LILO Debate", 131 *Tax Notes* 1389-1393 (June 27, 2011).

Wood, Robert W. and Steven E. Hollingworth, "SILOs and LILOs Demystified", 129 *Tax Notes* 195-205 (Oct. 11, 2010).

Woods, Judith M., "Recent Jurisprudence", 1993 *Conference Report* 48:1-22 (Toronto: Canadian Tax Foundation, 1994).

Wong, Lisa T., "Goodbye 'Economic Realities', Hello 'Legal Substance'", (2001) vol. 49 no. 6 *Canadian Tax Journal* 1571-1575.

Xynas, Lidia, "Tax Planning, Avoidance and Evasion in Australia 1970-2010: The Regulatory Responses and Taxpayer Compliance", vol. 20, issue 1 *Revenue Law Journal* 1-37 (2010).

Yaphe, Steven A., "Tax Shelters After Tax Reform", 1988 *Conference Report* 29:1-7 (Toronto: Canadian Tax Foundation, 1989).

Yin, George K., "The Problem of Corporate Tax Shelters: Uncertain Dimensions, Unwise Approaches", 55 *Tax Law Review* 405-426 (2002).

Yin, George K., "Getting Serious About Corporate Tax Shelters: Taking A Lesson From History", 54 *Southern Methodist University Law Review* 209-237 (2001).

Young, Sam, "Son-of-BOSS Ruling May Be Only a Temporary Setback for IRS", 124 *Tax Notes* 518-520 (Aug. 10, 2009).

Zelenak, Lawrence, "Codifying Anti-Avoidance Doctrines and Controlling Corporate Tax Shelters", 54 *Southern Methodist University Law Review* 177-193 (2001).

BOOKS

Bleiwas, Paul and John Hutson (eds.), *Taxation of Private Corporations and Their Shareholders,* 4th ed. (Toronto: Canadian Tax Foundation, 2010).

Braithwaite, John, *Markets in Vice: Markets in Virtue,* (Oxford University Press: Sydney, 2005).

Carroll, Lewis G., "Alice's Adventures in Wonderland", (Random House: New York, 2006).

Coleman, James, "Tax Avoidance Law in New Zealand", CCH New Zealand Limited (August 2009).

Cooper, Graeme (ed.), *Tax Avoidance and the Rule of Law,* (Amsterdam: IBFD Publications, 1997).

Duff, David G. and Harry Erlichman (eds.), *Tax Avoidance in Canada After Canada Trustco and Mathew,* (Irwin Law: Toronto, 2007).

Eisenstein, Louis, *The Ideologies of Taxation,* (New York: Ronald Press Company, 1961).

Freedman, Judith, (ed.), *Beyond Boundaries,* Oxford University, Centre for Business Taxation (2008).

George, Peter, *Dr. Strangelove Or, How I Learned to Stop Worrying and Love the Bomb* (Oxford: Oxford University Press, 1963).

Harley, Geoff, "Collecting Taxes", *Roles and Perspectives in the Law* (Victoria University Press, Wellington, N.Z.: 2002).

Hayek, F.A., "Law, Legislation and Liberty: Volume I – Rules and Order", (University of Chicago Press, 1983).

Jones, John Avery, Peter Harris and David Oliver (ed.), *Comparative Perspectives on Revenue Law: Essays in Honour of John Tiley,* (Cambridge University Press, 2008).

Kafka, Franz, *The Trial* (Schocken Books: New York, 1925).

Krishna, Vern, *Tax Avoidance: The General Anti-Avoidance Rule*, (Toronto: Carswell, 1990).

Larin, Gilles, and Robert Duong, *Effective Responses to Aggressive Tax Planning: What Canada Can Learn From Other Jurisdictions*, Canadian Tax Paper No. 112 (2009).

McMechan, Robert and Gordon Bourgard, *Tax Court Practice* (Toronto: Carswell, 2012).

Orow, Nabil, "Policy Considerations", *General Anti-Avoidance Rules – A Comparative International Analysis* (Bristol: Jordan Publishing, 2000).

Shaw, Jonathan, Joel Slemrod, and John Whiting, *Dimensions of Tax Design: The Mirrlees Review*, Oxford University Press (2010).

Swift, Jonathan, *Gulliver's Travels*, (New York: Oxford University Press, 1986)

Thuronyi, Victor (ed.), *Tax Law Design and Drafting*, Vol. 1 (Washington: IMF, 1996).

Tooma, Rachel Anne, "Legislating Against Tax Avoidance", (Amsterdam: IBFD, 2008).

CONFERENCE PAPERS/RESEARCH PAPERS

Braithwaite, John, "Making Tax Law More Certain: A Theory", Working Paper No. 44, Centre for Tax System Integrity, The Australian National University (December 2002).

Calvert, Theresa, "An analysis of the 2006 amendments to the General Anti-Avoidance Rules: A case law approach", unpublished dissertation (North-West University: 2011).

Cooper, Graeme S., "Predicting the Past – the Problem of Finding a Counterfactual in Part IVA", Legal Studies Research Paper No. 11/49, http:ssrn.com/abstract=1910990, University of Sydney Law School, (August 2011).

Cooper, Graeme, "The Emerging High Court Jurisprudence on Part IVA", Legal Studies Research Paper no. 06/09, University of Sidney Law School 1-36 (2006).

Cummings, Jr., Jasper L., "Enforcement Responses to Intentional Tax Reduction, Including the Economic Substance Doctrine", *The Supreme Court's Federal Tax Jurisprudence*, American Bar Association Section of Taxation, 145-241 (2010).

D'Ascenzo, Michael, Second Commissioner, Australian Tax Office, "Part IVA – The Steward's Inquiry – A Fair Tax System", Taxation Institute of Australia, 37th West Australia State Convention, Perth (May 2, 2003).

Evans, Chris, "Containing Tax Avoidance: Anti-Avoidance Strategies", University of New South Wales Faculty of Law Research Series 40, (2008).

McKenny, Paul L.B., "Economic Substance Doctrine – Not Just for Shelters Anymore", ABATAX-CLE 0913048 (2008).

Murphy, K. "Procedural Justice and the Australian Tax Office: A study of scheme investors", *Centre for Tax Integrity Working Paper No. 35* Canberra (2002).

Neville, J.W., "Macro-Economic Effects of Tax Avoidance", Working Paper No. 44, Centre for Applied Economic Research, University of New South Wales 1-11(March 1983).

Pagone, G. T., "Aspects of Tax Avoidance: Trans-Tasman Observations", International Fiscal Association Conference, Wellington, New Zealand (March 12, 2011).

Paravano, Jeffrey H. and Melinda L. Reynolds, "Tax Shelters: Evaluating Recent Developments", 895 Practising Law Institute Tax Law and Estate Planning Course Handbook Series, *Tax Law and Practice* (2005).

Prebble, Rebecca and John Prebble, "Does the Use of General Anti-Avoidance Rules to Combat Tax Avoidance Breach Principles of the Rule of Law?", *Critical Tax Conference*, Saint Louis University School of Law Center for International and Comparative Law 1-25 (April 9-10, 2010).

Sackville, Justice Ronald, "Avoiding Tax Avoidance: The Primacy of Part IVA", Victorian/Tasmanian State Convention (Sept 9-11, 2004).

Slemrod, Joel, "The Economics of Corporate Tax Selfishness", Working Paper 10858, National Bureau of Economic Research, 1-37 (2004).

Slemrod, Joel, and Shlomo Yitzhaki, "Tax Avoidance, Evasion, and Administration", Working Paper 7473, National Bureau of Economic Research, 1-76 (2000).

Uph, David, "Avoidance Policies – A New Conceptual Framework", Working Paper 09/22, Oxford Centre University Centre for Business Taxation 1-31 (2009).

Waldron, Jeremy, "Thoughtfulness and the Rule of Law", British Academy Lecture 1-20 (Feb. 1, 2011).

Weisbach, David A. "Corporate Tax Avoidance", John M. Olin Program in Law and Economics Working Paper no. 202 (Chicago: University of Chicago Law School, January 2004).

Weisbach, David A., "An Economic Analysis of Anti-Tax Avoidance Doctrines", John M. Olin Law & Economics Working Paper No. 99 (2d series), 1-41 (2002).

MAGAZINE AND NEWSPAPER ARTICLES

Cameron, Stevie, "Offshore Billions: Canadians are finding new ways to hide their money from the tax man", *Maclean's* (Oct. 9, 1995).

Canada Revenue Agency News Release, "Abusive tax schemes tackled by international tax administrations", Ottawa, Ontario (May 23, 2007).

"Deutsche Bank Settles Tax Shelter Case for $553 Million", *New York Times*, (Dec. 21, 2010).

Donnoyer, Ryan J., "Andrew Beal Denied $1.1 Billion Tax-Shelter Loss by U.S. Judge", *Bloomberg* (Aug. 21, 2009).

Greene, Bob, "And you thought the IRS was heartless", *Chicago Tribune*, Oct. 24, 1999.

Johnston, David Cay, "Costly Questions Arise on Legal Opinions for Tax Shelters", *New York Times* (Feb. 9, 2003).

Krishna, Vern, "Please report your aggressive tax avoidance plans", *Financial Post* (Apr. 15, 2010).

Letzing, John, "H-P unlikely target in IRS crackdown on foreign tax deals", *MarketWatch* (Feb. 18, 2010).

MacLeod, Ian, "Push Canadian population to 100 million, scholar argues", *Ottawa Citizen* (June 12, 2010).

Novack, Janet, "Are You A Chump?", *Forbes* 122 (Mar. 5, 2001).

Novack, Janet and Laura Saunders, "The Hustling of X Rated Shelters", *Forbes* 203 (Dec. 14, 1998).

O'Neill, Juliet, "G8 countries fall $10B short of aid commitments: report", Canwest News Service (June 20, 2010).

"Revenue Canada seeks $2 billion from Merck Frosst", *Globe & Mail* (Oct. 19, 2006).

Simpson, Glenn R., "A New Twist in Tax Avoidance: Firms Send Best Ideas Abroad", *Wall Street Journal* (June 24, 2002).

"Sovereign bank sues the IRS", *The Boston Globe* (June 18, 2009).

"U.S. files anticipated tax case against Deutsche Bank", *Thomson Reuters News & Insight* (June 15, 2011).

REPORTS

Alarie, Benjamin, Sanjana Bhatia, and David G. Duff, "Symposium on Tax Avoidance After Canada Trustco and Mathew: Summary of Proceedings" (2005) vol. 53, no. 4 *Canadian Tax Journal* 1010.

Arnold, Brian, Judith Freedman, Al Meghji, Mark Meredith, and Hon. Marshall Rothstein, "The Future of GAAR", 2005 *Conference Report* 4:1-16 (Toronto: Canadian Tax Foundation, 2006).

Canada Revenue Agency Annual Report (2006-2007).

"Comparison of the Reported Tax Liabilities of Foreign and U.S. Controlled Corporations", 1996-2000 (Washington, D.C.: U.S. General Accounting Office, 2004).

Department of the Treasury, General Explanations of the Administration's Revenue Proposals (February 1999).

Department of Finance Canada, *Tax Reform 1987*.

Duff, David G, "Tax Avoidance in the 21st Century", Australian Business Tax Reform in Retrospect and Prospect 477-501 (2009).

"Executive Summary, Request for Guidance on Implementation of Economic Substance Legislation", American Bar Association Tax Section (January 18, 2011).

"Explanatory Notes to Legislation Relating to Income Tax", (Ottawa: Department of Finance, June 1988).

"Final Report of the Review of Business Taxation, A Tax System Redesigned", (Canberra: Australian Government Printing Service, July 1999).

Finances Québec, "Aggressive Tax Planning", (Québec: Finances Québec, January 2009).

Fitzpatrick, Kevin, "The Australian Taxation Office's approaches to Aggressive Tax Planning", Centre for Tax System Integrity, Third International Research Conference Responsive Regulation: International Perspectives in Taxation: Canberra (July 24-25, 2003).

GAO-11-493, "Abusive Tax Avoidance Transactions", 1-55 (May 2011).

GAO, Internal Revenue Service: Challenges Remain in Combating Abusive Tax Schemes, GAO-04-50 (Washington D.C.: Nov. 19, 2003) and GAO-04-10T (Washington, D.C.: Oct. 21, 2003).

Government of Australia, "Improving the operation of the anti-avoidance provisions in the income tax law", Discussion Paper, Attorney General's Department, (Nov.18, 2010).

Government of Canada, Backgrounder: 2010-043–Government of Canada Seeks Public Input on Proposals To Require Information Reporting of Tax Avoidance Transactions (Ottawa, May 7, 2010).

Government of Canada, "Abusive Tax Planning: The Problem and The Canadian Context", Library of Parliament Background Paper (Feb. 18, 2010).

Government of New Zealand, Inland Revenue, "Impact Assessment, Tackling Tax Avoidance" (April 2004).

Government of New Zealand, Inland Revenue, "Mass-marketed tax schemes: An officials' issues paper on suggested legislative amendments" (January 2002).

Government of New Zealand, Inland Revenue, "A General Anti-Avoidance Rule for Direct Taxes: Consultative Document" (October 1988).

Internal Revenue Service, "Forecasting Potential Abusive Tax Avoidance Transaction Promoters and Participants", (June 2006).

Government of South Africa, Draft Comprehensive Guide to the General Anti-Avoidance Rule, Legal and Policy Division, South African Revenue Service (December 2010).

Joint Committee on Taxation, "Study of Present-Law Penalty and Interest Provisions as Required by Section 3801 of the Internal Revenue Service Restructuring and Reform Act of 1998 (including Provisions Relating to Corporate Tax Shelters)", JCS-3-99.

Korb, Donald, "The Economic Substance Doctrine in the Current Tax Shelter Environment", *Doc. 2005-1540, 2005 TNT 16-22* (Jan. 25, 2005).

Miniority Staff of Senate Permanent Subcommittee On Investigations for the Committee on Government Affairs, 108th Congress, U.S. Tax Shelter Industry: The Role of Accountants, Lawyers and Financial Professionals 1-129 (2003).

New Zealand Government, "Organisational Review of the Inland Revenue Department: Report to the Minister of Revenue" (Wellington, April 2004).

New Zealand Government, "Taxpayer Compliance, Standards and Penalties 2: Detailed Proposals and Draft Legislation" (Wellington, April 1995).

New Zealand Government, "Taxpayer Compliance, Standards and Penalties: A Government Discussion Document" (Wellington, August 1994).

Organisation for Economic Co-operation and Development, "Harmful Tax Competition: An Emerging Global Issue", (Paris: OECD, 1998).

Report by Graham Aaronson QC, GAAR Study, UK (November 11, 2011).

Report of Investigation of Enron Corporation and Related Entities Regarding Federal Tax and Compensation Issues, and Policy Recommendations, Staff of the Joint Committee on Taxation (February 2003).

Report of the Auditor General of Canada, (December 2002).

Report of the Committee of Experts on Tax Compliance, "Tax Mitigation, Avoidance and Evasion", (Wellington: NZ Government Printer, 1999).

Report on the White Paper on Tax Reform (Stage 1), House of Commons Standing Committee on Finance and Economic Affairs (Ottawa: Queen's Printer, November 1987).

Report of the Royal Commission on Taxation (Ottawa: Queen's Printer, 1966).

Report to the Treasurer and Minster of Revenue by a Committee of Experts on Tax Compliance, (Wellington, December 1998).

"Request for Guidance on Implementation of Economic Substance Legislation", American Bar Association Tax Section (January 18, 2011).

Slemrod Joel, and Varsha Venkatesh, "The Income Tax Compliance Costs of Large and Mid-Sized Businesses", *Report to the Internal Revenue Service Large and Mid-Size Business Division*, Washington, D.C. (September 2002).

South African Revenue Service, "Discussion Paper on Tax Avoidance", Law Administration, (November 2005).

Staff of Joint Committee on Taxation, "Technical Explanation of the Revenue Provisions of the Reconciliation Act of 2010, As Amended, In Combination with the Patient Protection and Affordable Care Act", JCX-18-10 (Mar. 21, 2010).

Staff of Joint Committee on Internal Revenue Taxation, 94th Cong., "Overview of Tax Shelters", (1975).

Tanzi, Vito, "Globalization, Technological Developments, and the Work of Fiscal Termites", vol. 38, no. 1 Finance & Development (Washington DC: IMF, March 2001).

Tax Law Review Committee Discussion Paper No. 7, The Institute for Fiscal Studies, (Feb. 2009).

Tax Law Review Committee, "A General Anti-Avoidance Rule for Direct Taxes – A Response to the Inland Revenue's Consultative Document" (Feb. 1999).

"Technical Explanation of the Revenue Provisions of the 'Reconciliation Act' of 2010, As Amended, in Combination With the 'Patient Protection and Affordable Care Act'", JCX-18-10, (Mar. 21, 2010).

"The Problem of Corporate Tax Shelters – Discussion, Analysis and Legislative Proposals", (Washington, D.C.: United States Treasury Department, 1999).

U.S. Government, "U.S. Tax Shelter Industry: The Role of Accountants, Lawyers and Financial Professionals – Four KPMG Case Studies: FLIP, OPIS, BLIPS and SC2", Report by the Minority Staff of the Permanent Subcommittee on Investigations, Committee on Government Affairs, US Senate 1-129 (2003).

Valabh Committee, "Final Report of the Consultative Committee on the Taxation of Income from Capital", (Wellington, October 1992).

Valabh Committee, "Key Reforms to the Scheme of Tax Legislation" (Auckland, October 1991).

WEBSITES

Alarie, Benjamin, "Price Discrimination in Income Taxation: Defending Half-Hearted Anti-Avoidance", http://ssrn.com/abstract=1796284, 1-34 (Mar. 26, 2011).

Arnold, Brian J, "The Tax Court's Trilogy of GAAR Cases", *The Arnold Report*, Posting: 024, Canadian Tax Foundation, http://www.ctf.ca/ctfweb/en/ (Dec. 16, 2011).

Arnold, Brian J, "Why the General Anti-Avoidance Rule Needs A Penalty", *The Arnold Report*, Posting: 019, Canadian Tax Foundation, http://www.ctf.ca/ctfweb/en/ (Sept. 21, 2011).

Arnold, Brian J., "The Land of the Free, the Home of the Brave, and the Economic Substance Doctrine", *The Arnold Report*, Posting: 007, Canadian Tax Foundation http://www.ctf.ca/ctfweb/en/ (Jan. 17, 2011).

August, Jerald David, "Tax Court of Canada approves of foreign tax credit generator arrangements in *Canada Limited v. The Queen* (Case 4145358); cross border impacts" http://fedtaxdevelopments.foxrothschild.com/2011/06/articles/federal-taxation-developments/tax-court-of-canada-approves-of-foreign-tax-credit-generator-arrangement-in-canada-limited-v-the-queen-case-4145358-cross-border impacts/?utm_source=feedburner&utm_medium=feed&utm_campaign=Feed%3A+FederalTaxationDevelopmentsBlog+%28Federal+Taxation+Developments+Blog%29 (June 13, 2010).

Canada Revenue Agency, Summary of the Corporate Business Plan 2005-2006 to 2007-2008, http://www.cra-arc.gc.ca/gncy/bsnss_plns/2005/ntr_sm-eng.html (Ottawa: CRA, 2005).

Canadian Bar Association, "Draft Legislation – Information Reporting of Tax Avoidance Transactions", http://www.cba.org/cba/submissions/pdf/10-65-eng.pdf (Sept. 27, 2010).

Cassidy, Julie, "Are tax schemes legitimate commercial transactions? Commissioner of Taxation v Spotless Services Ltd and Commissioner of Taxation v Spotless Finance Pty Ltd", http.//epublications.bond.edu.au/hcourt/7 (1996).

Christian Aid, "The shirts off their backs: How tax policies fleece the poor", *Christian Aid Briefing Paper*, http://www.christina-aid.org.UK.indepth/509tax/ (2005).

Deloitte, "Codification of the Economic Substance Doctrine: What Does It Mean for Your Company?", webcast (April 27, 2010).

Duff, David G., "Tax Avoidance in the 21st Century", http://ssrn.com/abstract=1457453 (2009).

Freedman, Judith, "Analysis GAAR: challenging assumptions", www.taxjournal.com (Sept. 27, 2010).

Government of Australia, "ATO Examining Takeover Arrangements", http://www.ato.gov.au/corporate/content.asp?doc=/content/003211795htm (Feb. 18, 2010)

Government of Canada, "General Explanations of the Administration's Fiscal Year 2001 Revenue Proposals", Department of the Treasury, http://www.treas.gov/offices/tax-policy/library/gfnbk00.pdf (Feb.2000)

Government of Québec, "Fighting Aggressive Tax Planning", Information Bulletin 2009-5, http://www.finances.gouv.qc.ca/documents/bulletins/en/BULEN_2009-5-a-b.pdf (Oct. 15, 2009).

Government of Québec, "Aggressive Tax Planning Working Paper", http://www.finances.gouv.qc.ca/en/page.asp?sectn=2&contn=276 (2009).

HMRC, "Study of a General Anti-Avoidance Rule, Terms of Reference", http://www.hmrc.gov.UK/budget-updates/gaar.pdf (Dec. 1, 2010).

HMRC, "Disclosure of Tax Avoidance Schemes", http://www.hmrc.gov.UK/aiu/guidance.htm (Nov. 1, 2008).

HMRC, "Approach to Compliance Risk Management for Large Businesses", http://www.hmrc.gov.UK/budget2007/large-business-riskman.pdf (Mar. 2007).

HMRC, "Guidance from Anti-Avoidance Group", http://www.hmrc.gov.UK/avoidance/aag-ris-assessing.htm

"Improving the Operation of New Zealand's Tax Avoidance Laws", the Taxation Committee of the New Zealand Law Society, the Corporate Taxpayers Group and the Taxation Committee of the New Zealand Institute of Chartered Accountants http://email.business.auckland.ac.nz/2011/1121-tax-avoidance/ (2011).

Kennedy, Connor and Daragh O'Shaughnessy, "Anti-Avoidance – Restrictions in Tax Planning", *Taxation / Revenue Policy*, Feb. 21, 2006, www.cpaireland.ie/UserFiles/File/.../Taxation/.../Anti-Avoidance.pdf

Kroft, Ed and Deborah Toaze, "Copthorne: Supreme Court of Canada's Latest Views on Statutory Interpretation and GAAR", CBA PracticeLink, http://www.cba.org/CBA/PracticeLin k/02-12-BC/03.aspx

Murphy, Richard, "The Missing Billions – The UK Tax Gap", www.tuc.org.UK/touchstonepamphlets

New Zealand Inland Revenue Department, "Guidance on tax avoidance arrangements", http://www.scoop.co.nz/stories/BU1109/S00023/inland-revenue-issues-guidance-on-tax-avoidance-arrangements.htm (September 1, 2011).

New Zealand Inland Revenue Department: Public Rulings Unit Adjudication and Rulings, "BG 1 and BG1 of the *Income Tax Act 2004*: Exposure Draft for External Consultation Reference INA 0009", www.taxpolicy.ird.got.nz

Organisation for Economic Co-operation and Development, "Tackling Aggressive Tax Planning Through Improved Transparency and Disclosure: Report on Disclosure Initiatives", www.oecd.org/dataoecd/13/55/48322860.pdf (Paris: OECD, February 2011).

Organisation for Economic Co-operation and Development, "Study into the Role of Tax Intermediaries", http://www.oecd.org/28/34/39882938.pdf (Paris: OECD, 2008).

"Organisation for Economic Co-operation and Development, "The Global Forum on Transparency and Exchange of Information for Tax Purposes: A Background Information Brief", http://www.oecd.org/dataoecd/32/43757434.pdf (March 16, 2001).

Organisation for Economic Co-operation and Development, Centre for Tax Policy and Administration, "Glossary of Tax Terms", http://www.oecd.org/document/29/0.3343en_2649_33933853_1_1_1_1.00html

Prebble, John, "The US GAAR", Victoria University, Wellington NZ TaxProfBlog (May 25, 2010).

Report re Tax Avoidance by the Taxation Committee of the New Zealand Law Society, the Corporate Taxpayers Group, and the Taxation Committee of the New Zealand Institute of Chartered Accountants: http://email.business.auckland.ac.nz/2011/1121-tax-avoidance/

Revised Discussion Paper on the Direct Taxes Code, http://ww.incometaxindia.gov.in

Tax Law Review Committee, Tax Avoidance, IFS Commentary no. 64, (http://www.ifs.org.UK/comms/comm64.pdf)

U.S. Department of the Treasury, "The Problem of Corporate Tax Shelters: Discussion, Analysis and Legislative Proposals", http://www.treas.gov/press/releases/reports/ctswhite.pdf (1999).

Appendix A

Economic and Commercial Realities in Tax Cases

RELIANCE ON ECONOMIC REALITIES IN TAX CASES

There are many different genres of tax cases where courts look to economic realities in order to make legal determinations.

Computation of Profit

Judges make findings as to economic realities or substance in considering matters relative to the computation of profits. The courts have held:

(a) there was no *economic reality* to support the position that book entries related to liabilities incurred for bonus accruals to managers–*Prosperous Investments Ltd. v. Minister of National Revenue*, [1992] 1 C.T.C. 2218 (T.C.C.) at para. 26;

(b) an unpaid balance of sale shown in a financial statement had no *economic substance*, and was not a proper entry–*Lipper v. R.*, [1979] C.T.C. 316 (Fed. T.D.) at para. 47;

(c) the timing of the inclusion of amounts in income was in accordance with the *economic reality* of the use of the sums received, and complied with the *Income Tax Act*–*Archambault v. Minister of National Revenue*, [1988] 2 C.T.C. 2391 (T.C.C.) at para. 69; and

(d) an accounting method was "*out of whack with economic reality*", and did not meet fundamental criterion of accuracy in reporting income–*Bernick v. R.*, [2004] 3 C.T.C. 191 (F.C.A.) at para. 23.

Employees versus Independent Contractors

The matter of whether an individual is an employee or an independent contractor is often litigated and the courts have fashioned a number of tests to be applied in making this distinction. The tests include (a) the degree of control that is exercised over the worker and the manner in which the work is performed; (b) the ownership of the tools utilized in the work; (c) the opportunity of the worker to profit and the accompanying risk of loss; and (d) the degree to which the work being done is an integral part of the payor's business–*671122 Ontario Ltd. v. Sagaz Industries Canada Inc.*, [2001] 2 S.C.R. 983 (S.C.C.) at para. 46, reconsideration / rehearing refused 2001 CarswellOnt 4155 (S.C.C.). It is said that none of these tests are individually determinative: "The most that can profitably be done is to examine all the possible factors which have been referred to in ... cases as bearing on the relationship between the parties concerned. Clearly not all of these factors will be relevant in all cases, or have the same weight in all cases. Equally clearly no magic formula can be propounded for determining which factors should, in any given case, be treated as the determining ones."–*Wiebe Door Services Ltd. v. Minister of National Revenue*, [1986] 2 C.T.C. 200 (Fed. C.A.) at para. 15, quoting Professor P.S. Atiyah, "Vicarious Liability in the Law of Torts", London, Butterworths, 1967, 38.

The Federal Court has said it uses *economic reality* as a test in making the employee versus independent contractor legal distinction–*Marotta v. R.*, [1986] 1 C.T.C. 393 (Fed. T.D.) at para. 19. The Exchequer Court has also concluded that a contract was one of employment "... as a matter of business and *economic reality*"–*Alexander v. Minister of National Revenue*, [1969] C.T.C. 715 (Can. Ex. Ct.) at p. 724.

The Tax Court has similarly relied upon its view of the economic realities in such cases:

(a) physicians who worked for other physicians were independent contractors, as the *economic reality* was that they carried on business on their own account–*Chernesky v. Minister of National Revenue*, 2000 CarswellNat 4324, [2000] T.C.J. No. 704 (T.C.C. [Employment Insurance]) at para. 40.

(b) the provision of accounting and bookkeeping services amounted to employment, having regard to, *inter alia*, the *economic reality* test, which was said to be essentially similar to the chance of profit and risk of loss test–*Nelson v. R.* (1997), [1998] 1 C.T.C. 2008 (T.C.C.) at para. 15, affirmed 1998 CarswellNat 618 (Fed. C.A.), leave to appeal refused (1999), (*sub nom.* Nelson v. Canada) 237 N.R. 398 (note) (S.C.C.); and

(c) an individual who provided construction cost appraisal services could reasonably be regarded as an employee, under the "decisive chance of profit and risk of loss [test] or the test of *economic reality*"–*Placements Marcel Lapointe Inc. c. Ministre du Revenu national* (1992), (*sub nom.* Placements Marcel Lapointe Inc. v. Minister of National Revenue) [1993] 1 C.T.C. 2506 (T.C.C.) at para. 109.

This focus on economic reality by the lower courts parallels the approach taken by the U.S. Supreme Court in the same genre of cases, where it has held that deciding the legal question of employee vs. independent contractor is "a matter of *economic reality.*"–United States v. Silk, 331 U.S. 704 (1947) at p. 713.

Whether Business Exists

Similarly, in finding whether a business exists as a source of income, the lower courts resort to economic reality determinations:

(a) no rental business existed, where the element of *economic reality* was missing, and there were insufficient indicia of commerciality to justify the conclusion that a real commercial enterprise was being conducted–*Cheesemond v. R.*, [1995] 2 C.T.C. 2567 (T.C.C.) at para. 12.

(b) cattle breeding activities did not amount to a business, where they were said to be based more on the appellant's aspirations, than on *economic reality*–*Roy v. Minister of National Revenue* (1987), (*sub nom.* Roy v. M.N.R.) [1988] 1 C.T.C. 2361 (T.C.C.) at para. 13.

(c) a purported partnership created for the purpose of developing a computer language was found to have no *economic reality*–*Côté (Succession de) c. R.* (1995), (*sub nom.* Coté (Succession de) v. R.) [1996] 1 C.T.C. 2862 (T.C.C.) at para. 30; and

(d) in rejecting appeals from the disallowance of expenses purportedly incurred in connection with a business of marketing speed-reading courses, Joyal J. referred to the reasons of the Supreme Court in the *Bronfman* decision: "They underline an objective and common sense approach to statute interpretation and bring added respect for the *commercial and economic realities* of transactions which have tax connotations."–*Moloney v. R.* (1989), 89 D.T.C. 5099 (Fed. T.D.) at para. 156, affirmed 1992 CarswellNat 328 (Fed. C.A.), leave to appeal refused 1993 CarswellNat 2467 (S.C.C.).

Fair Market Value Determinations

Economic realities also play a role in determinations by the courts involving fair market value:

(a) the hypothetical buyer and seller involved in the determination of fair market value must have "their feet firmly planted on the bedrock of *economic reality*"–*Western Securities Ltd. v. R.* (1997), 97 D.T.C. 977 (T.C.C.) at para. 12; and

(b) the value of an asset acquired by a corporation is not necessarily reflected in the value of shares issued as consideration for the asset; and, the mere fact that the asset acquired may have a value in excess of the increase in stated capital of the shares does not, as a matter of *economic reality*, result in a cost to the corporation in excess of the value of the asset–*Teleglobe Canada Inc. v. R.*, [2000] 4 C.T.C. 2448 (T.C.C. [General Procedure]) at para. 96, affirmed 2002 CarswellNat 3053 (Fed. C.A.).

Miscellaneous Instances

Besides the above occasions where courts have relied upon economic realities in making legal determinations in tax cases, there are also various other instances:

(a) the assessment of a benefit was not in accordance with *economic reality* or fundamental fairness, where all that occurred was the exercise of options to facilitate a corporate line of credit–*Del Grande v. R.* (1992), (*sub nom.* Del Grande v. Canada) [1993] 1 C.T.C. 2096 (T.C.C.) at para. 29.

(b) share options were required to be included in computing capital for the purposes of the large corporations tax, because the *economic reality* was that the transactions by which the options were exchanged resulted in an excess of net assets over share capital–*Inco Ltd. v. R.*, [2007] 2 C.T.C. 2347 (T.C.C. [General Procedure]) at para. 50.

(c) the adjusted income of the appellant's *de facto* spouse, for the purpose of the child tax benefit, was held not to represent the *economic reality* of the family–*Dionne c. R.* (2001), [2003] 3 C.T.C. 2503 (T.C.C. [Informal Procedure]) at para. 7.

(d) the respondent's suggestion that a director should have "killed a deal" to sell properties did not accord with practical *economic reality–Jeffs v. R., (sub nom.* Jeffs v. Canada) [1999] G.S.T.C. 48 (T.C.C. [Informal Procedure]) at para. 21.

(e) the *economic substance* of a transaction was held to include its tax consequences, in a case where a loss from a currency conversion was not allowed as a deduction in computing the amount of a capital gain–*Avis Immobilien GmbH v. R.*, 1996 CarswellNat 2529 (Fed. C.A.) at para. 14, leave to appeal refused (May 22, 1997), Doc. 25749 (S.C.C.).

(f) the existence of a $1 million loss on the sale of shares was not consistent with *economic reality*, and subsec. 55(1) of the *Income Tax Act* applied to deny the loss–*Industries S.L.M. Inc. c. Ministre du Revenu national* (1995), (*sub nom.* Industries S.L.M. Inc. v. Minister of National Revenue) [1996] 2 C.T.C. 2572 (T.C.C.) at para. 77, reversed in part 2000 CarswellNat 2416 (Fed. T.D.).

(g) *economic reality* did not support the argument that the services of a mandatary, in receiving sums of money, were not remunerated–*Gravel v. Minister of National Revenue*, [1992] 1 C.T.C. 2521 (T.C.C.) at para. 44.

(h) the *economic reality* is that the decision makers who form an intention preceding a decision must deal with changing or constantly evolving realities dictated by the speed of technological developments and by the modern economy– *Bois Daaquam Inc. c. R.* (2000), [2002] 1 C.T.C. 2650 (T.C.C. [General Procedure]) at para. 24; and

(i) the practical, *commercial and economic reality* of transactions was that the real purpose of making payments of interest and guarantee fees was to achieve tax savings through the utilization of losses of a non-related party–*Canwest Broadcasting Ltd. v. R.*, (*sub nom.* Canwest Broadcasting Ltd. v. Canada) [1995] 2 C.T.C. 2780 (T.C.C.) at para. 44.

The point is not that the lower courts are relying upon economic realities in a consistent manner in making tax decisions. Indeed, economic realities findings in these cases appear to serve as a catch-all justification for judge's decisions. However, the readiness with which the lower courts rely upon their findings as to economic realities in tax cases goes to show, at a minimum, that there is nothing prohibitively daunting about the economic realities inquiry.

RELIANCE ON COMMERCIAL REALITIES IN TAX CASES

As previously noted in chapter V, "commercial realities" and "economic realities" share common ground. Moreover, just as there is no common law doctrine of "economic realities" or "economic substance" in Canada, there is no common law doctrine of "commercial realities" or "commercial substance", yet courts routinely pronounce upon their assessments of "commercial realities" as justification for tax decisions:

(a) the Federal Court of Appeal held that benefits were properly taxable to employees under s. 7 of the *Income Tax Act* as the *commercial reality* of the employer's plan was that it put shares into the hands of employees at a discounted price–*Placer Dome Inc. v. R.*, (*sub nom.* Placer Dome Inc. v. Canada) [1992] 2 C.T.C. 99 (Fed. C.A.) at para. 26, leave to appeal refused 1993 CarswellNat 2484 (S.C.C.).

(b) the Tax Court held that statutorily prescribed interest rates can be used as a reasonable yardstick in calculating the value of the benefit from an interest free loan, in the absence of deeming legislation, so long as they relate to *commercial reality*–*Cooper v. Minister of National Revenue,*

[1987] 1 C.T.C. 2287 (T.C.C.) at para. 20, reversed 1988 CarswellNat 478 (Fed. T.D.).

(c) the Tax Court held that there was no benefit to a shareholder considering the *commercial reality* of the transaction in issue, as the redemption of shares was for the same amount paid for the shares, in the same currency–*MacMillan Bloedel Ltd. v. R.*, [1997] 3 C.T.C. 3012 (T.C.C.) at para. 14, affirmed 1999 CarswellNat 1183 (Fed. C.A.).

(d) the Tax Court rejected an argument that legal expenses could not be deducted as current expense, on the basis that the result would not be consistent with *commercial reality*–*Continental Lime Ltd. v. R.*, [1999] 3 C.T.C. 2525 (T.C.C. [General Procedure]) at para. 16.

(e) the Tax Court characterized the cost of fishing licences as capital, as the *commercial reality* was that the appellant did not expect to only fish the licences in the short run–*F.A.S. Seafood Producers Ltd. v. R.*, [1998] 4 C.T.C. 2794 (T.C.C.) at para. 15.

(f) the Tax Court has held on more than one occasion that the *commercial reality* was that an expense relating to the acquisition of a customer list was a capital outlay–*Rigid Box Co. v. Minister of National Revenue*, [1991] 2 C.T.C. 2374 (T.C.C.) at para. 18; *R. Bruce Graham Ltd. v. Minister of National Revenue*, [1986] 1 C.T.C. 2326 (T.C.C.) at para. 42.

(g) the Federal Court has held, in finding that the costs of engineering studies regarding a potential hydroelectric development were deductible as current expenses, that *commercial realities* must always be taken into account–*Bowater Power Co. v. Minister of National Revenue*, [1971] C.T.C. 818 (Fed. C.A.) at para. 57.

(h) the Federal Court has held that payments related to the termination of a distributorship were, in the context of *commercial reality*, current expenses made in the course of an income-earning enterprise–*Angostura International Ltd. v. R.*, [1985] 2 C.T.C. 170 (Fed. T.D.) at para. 38.

(i) the Federal Court of Appeal relied upon *commercial reality* in concluding that monies spent in an unsuccessful attempt to get into a propane and butane marketing business were current expenditures–*Minister of National Revenue v. M.P. Drilling Ltd.*, [1976] C.T.C. 58 (Fed. C.A.) at para. 17.

(j) the Tax Court held that the *commercial reality* was that transactions concerned an attempt to purchase a third party's non-capital losses, although the appellants purportedly purchased partnership interests with the intent of earning income–*Makuz v. R.*, [2006] 5 C.T.C. 2332 (T.C.C. [General Procedure]) at para. 44, additional reasons 2006 CarswellNat 3375 (T.C.C. [General Procedure]).

(k) the Federal Court held that the underlying *commercial reality* gave no substance to the characterization where a claim for investment tax credits depended upon the appellant establishing the relationship of lender and borrower under a contract–*Ticketnet Corp. v. R.*, [1999] 3 C.T.C. 564 (Fed. T.D.) at para. 54, additional reasons 1999 CarswellNat 1298 (Fed. T.D.).

(l) the Tax Court held that the *commercial reality* was that the sub-trades were paid for their labour only, in a case involving whether there was a taxable supply of property by the appellant to the sub-trades–*Imperial Drywall Contracting Ltd. v. R.*, (*sub nom.* Imperial Drywall Contracting Inc. v. Canada) [1997] G.S.T.C. 81 (T.C.C.) at para. 19.

(m) the Tax Court held that the *commercial reality* was that the true nature of an amount was that it was a component of the purchase price for a product where the issue was whether a payment under a franchise agreement was one to which para. 212(1)(d) of the *Income Tax Act* applied–*Entré Computer Centers Inc. v. R.* (1996), [1997] 1 C.T.C. 2291 (T.C.C.) at para. 31.

(n) the Tax Court held that the *commercial reality* of a rental agreement was that a portion of the payments made under it were consideration for a service, rather than rent or penalty–*On-Guard Self-Storage Ltd. v. R.*, (*sub nom.* On-Guard Self-Storage Ltd. v. Canada) [1996] G.S.T.C. 9 (T.C.C.) at para. 13, reversed 1996 CarswellNat 1999 (Fed. C.A.), leave to appeal refused (1997), (*sub nom.* Minister of National Revenue v. Sentinel Self-Storage Corp.) 222 N.R. 399 (S.C.C.).

(o) the Tax Court held that although Her Majesty was mentioned in a contract that did not change the *commercial reality* of the relationship between the parties–*Com Dev Ltd. v. R.*, [1999] 2 C.T.C. 2566 (T.C.C.) at para. 37.

(p) the Tax Court held that the *commercial reality* of a transaction was that payments identified as maintenance fees were for the supply of services, and not for land–*Hidden Valley Golf Resort Assn. v. R.*, (*sub nom.* Hidden Valley Golf Resort Assn. v. Canada) [1998] G.S.T.C. 95 (T.C.C.) at para. 37, reversed 2000 CarswellNat 1162 (Fed. C.A.).

(q) the Tax Court looked to *commercial reality* in considering whether a director had exercised the degree of care that a reasonably prudent person would have exercised in comparable circumstances–*Parfeniuk v. R.*, (*sub nom.* Parfeniuk v. Canada) [1996] G.S.T.C. 22 (T.C.C.) at para. 18; *McGowen v. R.*, [2005] G.S.T.C. 109 (T.C.C. [General Procedure]) at para. 22.

(r) the Tax Court held that an individual who provided technology consulting services to her own company was an independent contractor, in part because it is an accepted fact of *commercial reality* that a sole shareholder can enter into contractual relations with his or her own company–*Zupet v. Minister of National Revenue*, 2005 TCC 89 (T.C.C. [Employment Insurance]) at para. 13.

(s) the Tax Court held that a series of transactions which had no purpose other than to reduce taxes payable was not in accordance with normal business practice, and could best be described as "fiscal manipulation not *commercial reality*"–*722540 Ontario Inc. v. R.* (2001), [2002] 1 C.T.C.

2872 (T.C.C. [General Procedure]) at para. 59, affirmed 2003 CarswellNat 1350 (Fed. C.A.), leave to appeal refused 2003 CarswellNat 4612 (S.C.C.), quoting McArthur J. in *Canwest Broadcasting Ltd. v. R., (sub nom.* Canwest Broadcasting Ltd. v. Canada) [1995] 2 C.T.C. 2780 (T.C.C.) at para. 55.

(t) the Federal Court of Appeal held that a corporation was carrying on business where the *commercial reality* of the situation was that efforts were made to bring products it expected to be able to acquire through negotiation to the attention of potential purchasers–*Minister of National Revenue v. M.P. Drilling Ltd.* (1976), 76 D.T.C. 6028 (Fed. C.A.) at para. 10.

(u) the Federal Court of Appeal agreed with the trial judge's finding that a purported record production, marketing, promotion and distribution business did not exist, as the arrangements were *commercially unrealistic–King v. R.*, [2001] 1 C.T.C. 295 (Fed. C.A.) at para. 7.

(v) the Tax Court held that no rental business existed, where the element of economic reality was missing, and there were insufficient indicia of *commerciality* to justify the conclusion that a real commercial enterprise was being conducted–*Cheesemond v. R.*, [1995] 2 C.T.C. 2567 (T.C.C.) at para. 12.

(w) the Tax Court held that no business of operating a health care centre existed, at a time when it could not be said, as a matter of *commercial reality*, that the process had commenced of operating a profit making entity–*Goren v. R.*, [1997] 3 C.T.C. 2025 (T.C.C.) at para. 9.

(x) the Tax Court held that no farming business existed, where the circumstances showed that the operation lacked any air of *commercial reality–Schimmens v. R.*, [1996] 3 C.T.C. 2132 (T.C.C.) at para. 9.

(y) the Tax Court held that claims for tax credits for charitable donations, which were based upon mark-ups on the cost of prints of several hundred per cent over a period of days from the time of their purchase, were out of touch with *commercial reality*–*Klotz v. R.*, [2004] 2 C.T.C. 2892 (T.C.C. [General Procedure]) at para. 46, affirmed [2005] 3 C.T.C. 78 (F.C.A.), leave to appeal refused 2006 CarswellNat 930 (S.C.C.).

(z) the Tax Court held that determining under a pooling approach what a prospective purchaser would pay for eleven computer game engines was a method of valuation that was simply a *commercial reality*–*Brown v. R.* (2001), [2002] 1 C.T.C. 2451 (T.C.C. [General Procedure]) at para. 126, additional reasons 2001 CarswellNat 2824 (T.C.C. [General Procedure]), additional reasons 2002 CarswellNat 402 (T.C.C. [General Procedure]), additional reasons 2002 CarswellNat 5531 (T.C.C. [General Procedure]), affirmed on other grounds [2003] 3 C.T.C. 351 (Fed. C.A.), leave to appeal refused 2004 CarswellNat 84 (S.C.C.).

(aa) the Tax Court held that valuation "is a relatively mundane task in which common sense and *commercial reality* necessarily pay a large part"–*Hallatt v. R.* (2000), [2001] 1 C.T.C. 2626 (T.C.C. [General Procedure]) at para. 30, affirmed 2004 CarswellNat 613 (F.C.A.).

(bb) the Tax Court held that although subsection 110.1(3) of the *Income Tax Act* permits a corporate donor to designate a figure between the adjusted cost base and the fair market value of an asset, the designated amount has nothing to do with the *commercial reality* of the matter–*Jabs Construction Ltd. v. R.*, [1999] 3 C.T.C. 2556 (T.C.C. [General Procedure]) at para. 35.

(cc) the Tax Court held that a purchase/leaseback scenario appeared to be at odds with *commercial realities* in deciding whether lease payments were properly treated as income–*On-Line Finance & Leasing Corp. v. R.* (2010), [2011] 1 C.T.C. 2068 (T.C.C. [General Procedure]) at para. 38.

(dd) the Federal Court of Appeal held that a proper interpretation of the word "acquired", in relation to a tax credit program, required that the *commercial reality* applicable to the dealers and producers of farming equipment, as well as that of the farmers, be taken into account–*Kowdrysh v. R.*, [2001] 2 C.T.C. 156 (Fed. C.A.) at para. 7.

(ee) the Federal Court held that it would not reflect *commercial or economic reality* to hold that the word "immediately" under the replacement property rules requires a meaning equivalent to "instantly"–*Macklin v. R.* (1992), (*sub nom.* Macklin v. Canada) [1993] 1 C.T.C. 21 (Fed. T.D.) at para. 42.

(ff) the Federal Court of Appeal held that no partnership existed where arrangements were *commercially unrealistic*– *King v. R.*, [2001] 1 C.T.C. 295 (Fed. C.A.) at para. 7.

(gg) the Tax Court held that *commercial reality* compelled the conclusion that the appropriate time to consider whether there was an income earning purpose was at the time a guarantee was given–*Gordon v. R.*, [1996] 3 C.T.C. 2229 (T.C.C.) at para. 29.

(hh) the Federal Court held that the *commercial reality* of a situation was that there was a series of transactions, the net result of which was to enable the taxpayer to borrow money in order to earn income from business, although the interest was paid on the mortgage on a home–*Shore v. Minister of National Revenue*, [1992] 1 C.T.C. 34 (Fed. T.D.) at para. 4.

(ii) the Federal Court of Appeal held that the *commercial reality* is that corporate borrowing is as integral to the income-earning process as is the provision of third-party security granted by related corporations or shareholders to lenders–*74712 Alberta Ltd. v. Minister of National Revenue*, [1997] 2 C.T.C. 30 (Fed. C.A.) at para. 64.

(jj) the Tax Court held that the *commercial reality* was that the appellant had loans under his guarantee, although he did not make payments directly to the creditor–*Gordon v. R.*, [1996] 3 C.T.C. 2229 (T.C.C.) at para. 28.

(kk) the Tax Court held that the *commercial, practical and economic reality* of transactions was that the real purpose of making payments of interest and guarantee fees was to achieve tax savings through the utilization of losses of a non-related party–*Canwest Broadcasting Ltd. v. R.*, (*sub nom.* Canwest Broadcasting Ltd. v. Canada) [1995] 2 C.T.C. 2780 (T.C.C.) at para. 44.

(ll) the Tax Court held that there was no *commercial reality* to transactions as structured other than to benefit the children of the owner/operator of a company through the distribution of profits to them–*W.F. Botkin Construction Ltd. v. R.*, (*sub nom.* W.F. Botkin Construction Ltd. v. Canada) [1993] 1 C.T.C. 2765 (T.C.C.) at para. 22.

(mm) the Tax Court held that it would be a distortion of *commercial reality* to say that the purpose of payments for the maintenance of a rental property was not to earn income, simply because they were made after the tenants who had occasioned the expenses had moved out–*Reid v. R.*, (*sub nom.* Reid v. Canada) [1993] 2 C.T.C. 3145 (T.C.C.) at paras. 12-13.

(nn) the Tax Court held that *commercial reality* supported the view that a co-chairman of the board and the major shareholder of a company would have exchanged shares for shares, rather than taking cash, to avoid giving a negative signal to the stock market and in light of securities legislation re insider trading–*MIL (Investments) S.A. v. R.*, [2006] 5 C.T.C. 2552 (T.C.C. [General Procedure]) at para. 47, affirmed 2007 FCA 236 (F.C.A.).

(oo) the Tax Court held that the *commercial reality* of the modern world enabled finding that an individual, who was not a professional engineer, was employed in connection with an engineering activity, for the purpose of the overseas employment tax credit–*Gabie v. R.* (1998), [1999] 1 C.T.C. 2352 (T.C.C.) at para. 23.

(pp) the Tax Court held that it is *commercial reality* that taxpayers take into consideration the tax implications of transactions, and the *commercial reality* was that the appellant had a substantial potential benefit of being able to use non-capital losses–*Gibson Petroleum Co. v. R.*, [1997] 3 C.T.C. 2453 (T.C.C.) at para. 39.

(qq) the Federal Court of Appeal held that under today's *commercial reality*, with international corporations doing business across the world through affiliates, Canadian companies should be obliged to answer proper questions on examination for discovery that require answers from foreign affiliates–*Crestbrook Forest Industries Ltd. v. R.*, [1992] 2 C.T.C. 81 (Fed. T.D.) at para. 39, reversed 1993 Carswell-Nat 914 (Fed. C.A.), leave to appeal refused (1993), (*sub nom.* Crestbrook Forest Industries Ltd. v. Minister of National Revenue) 163 N.R. 320 (note) (S.C.C.), approving *Monarch Marking Systems Inc. v. Esselte Meto Ltd.* (1983), [1984] 1 F.C. 641 (Fed. T.D.) per Mahoney, J.

(rr) the Federal Court of Appeal held that maintaining the fiction of an impenetrable corporate veil inhibiting the flow of authentic information for the purpose of evaluating the admissibility of answers given by the appellant's nominee for examination for discovery would be to ignore *commercial reality–R. v. Capitol Life Insurance Co.*, [1986] 1 C.T.C. 388 (Fed. C.A.) at para. 7.

(ss) the Federal Court of Appeal held that the trial judge correctly attributed no tax consequences to a "release agreement" and was entitled to look at the "*true commercial and practical nature*" of the transactions–*Dundas v. Minister of National Revenue*, (*sub nom.* Dundas v. Canada) [1995] 1 C.T.C. 184 (Fed. C.A.) at para. 26, leave to appeal refused (1995), 8 C.C.P.B. 224 (note) (S.C.C.).

(tt) the Federal Court drew inferences as to the *commercial realities* of what had taken place to conclude that there was a sale of scrap or waste material from a printing process–*Web Press Graphics Ltd. v. Minister of National Revenue*, 2006 G.T.C. 1151 (F.C.) at para. 13.

(uu) the Federal Court held that industry practice in hedging the price to be received under contracts of sale was relevant to the *commercial and economic reality* of the taxpayer's operations, in an appeal concerning whether income from the settlement of forward sales contracts should be included as resource profits–*Echo Bay Mines Ltd. v. R.*, (*sub nom.* Echo Bay Mines Ltd. v. Canada) [1992] 2 C.T.C. 182 (Fed. T.D.) at para. 17.

(vv) the Federal Court of Appeal held that *commercial reality* is to be considered in interpreting provisions like subparagraph 40(2)(g)(ii) of the *Income Tax Act*, which limits deduction of the capital loss on a debt, so long as *commercial reality* is consistent with the text and purpose of the provision–*Byram v. R.*, [1999] 2 C.T.C. 149 (Fed. C.A.) at para. 17.

(ww) the Tax Court held that that it is important to approach matters in a common sense way, with an eye for the *reality* of the transactions involved, when considering the application of legislation–*Maritime Life Assurance Co. v. R.* (1999), 99 G.T.C. 3055 (T.C.C.) at para. 18, affirmed 2000 G.T.C. 4157 (Fed. C.A.).

(xx) the Tax Court held that a warranty agreement which the Minister did not regard as a sham was bereft of *commerciality*–*Sherman v. R.*, 2008 D.T.C. 3069 (Eng.) (T.C.C. [General Procedure]) at para. 120, affirmed 2009 CarswellNat 2110 (F.C.A.).

(yy) the Tax Court found that a net worth statement ignored some *commercial realities*–*Jewett v. R.*, 2009 CarswellNat 4836, 2010 TCC 4, 2010 D.T.C. 1052 (Eng.), [2010] 4 C.T.C. 2062 (T.C.C.) [General Procedure] at para. 32; and (zz) the Tax Court held that the supply of President's Choice financial products and the supply of points connected to that supply could not, as a matter of *commercial reality*, be sensibly separated into two separate supplies–*President's Choice Bank v. R.*, [2009] G.S.T.C. 60 (T.C.C. [General Procedure]) at para. 53.

Appendix B

Tax Court GAAR Cases

Tax Court of Canada Case	GAAR Applied	Impact of Proposed GAAR Amendments
Husky Oil Ltd. v. R. (1998), [1999] 4 C.T.C. 2691 (T.C.C.)	No	N/A: transactions involved transfer of an existing accrued loss and were found to have been undertaken primarily for a genuine non-tax commercial purpose
Jabs Construction Ltd. v. R., [1999] 3 C.T.C. 2556 (T.C.C. [General Procedure])	No	N/A: transactions involving corporate gift now governed by subsec. 118.1(16) and (17) ITA anti-avoidance loanback rules
Canadian Pacific Ltd. v. R. (2000), [2001] 1 C.T.C. 2190 (T.C.C. [General Procedure]), affirmed 2001 CarswellNat 2916 (Fed. C.A.), reconsideration / rehearing refused 2002 CarswellNat 555 (Fed. C.A.)	No	N/A: transactions involving weak currency borrowing now governed by s. 20.3 ITA
Rousseau-Houle c. R., 2001 CarswellNat 1126 (T.C.C. [General Procedure])	No	N/A: GAAR amended effective Sept. 1988 to apply to federal ITA Regulations

Tax Court of Canada Case	GAAR Applied	Impact of Proposed GAAR Amendments
Produits Forestiers Donohue Inc. c. R. (2001), [2003] 1 C.T.C. 2010 (T.C.C. [General Procedure]), affirmed 2002 CarswellNat 3052 (Fed. C.A.)	No	See case study in chapter IX
Geransky v. R., [2001] 2 C.T.C. 2147 (T.C.C. [General Procedure])	No	N/A: trial judge found transactions were real commercial transactions that were carried out tax-efficiently
Jabin Investments Ltd. v. R., [2002] 1 C.T.C. 2315 (T.C.C. [General Procedure]), affirmed 2002 CarswellNat 4346 (Fed. C.A.)	No	N/A: transactions re debt parking now governed by subsecs. 80.01(6) to (8) ITA
Hill v. R. (2002), [2003] 4 C.T.C. 2548 (T.C.C. [General Procedure])	No	N/A: transactions involved liability for payment of real non-contingent interest
Imperial Oil Ltd. v. R. (2002), [2003] 2 C.T.C. 2754 (T.C.C. [General Procedure]), affirmed 2004 CarswellNat 104 (F.C.A.)	No	N/A: transactions were found to involve the investment of real surplus cash in a tax-efficient manner by taking advantage of an existing statutory "loophole" with respect to the large corporations tax
CIT Financial Ltd. v. R. (2003), [2004] 1 C.T.C. 2232 (T.C.C. [General Procedure]), reconsideration / rehearing refused 2003 CarswellNat 3670 (T.C.C. [General Procedure]), affirmed 2004 CarswellNat 2845 (F.C.A.), leave to appeal refused 2004 CarswellNat 4370 (S.C.C.)	No	N/A: GAAR not applicable as deduction of artificially-high CCA denied under s. 69 ITA
Loyens v. R., [2003] 3 C.T.C. 2381 (T.C.C. [General Procedure])	No	N/A: transactions involving transfer of profits via two step rollover through partnership to a corporation with real existing losses held not to be abusive of subsec. 85(1) or 97(2) ITA policy

Tax Court of Canada Case	GAAR Applied	Impact of Proposed GAAR Amendments
Canada Trustco Mortgage Co. v. R., [2003] 4 C.T.C. 2009 (T.C.C. [General Procedure]), affirmed 2004 CarswellNat 305 (F.C.A.), affirmed 2005 CarswellNat 3212 (S.C.C.)	No	See case study in chapter IX
Howe v. R. (2004), [2005] 1 C.T.C. 2243 (T.C.C. [General Procedure])	No	N/A: trial judge found no "avoidance transaction" as transactions primarily undertaken for non-tax commercial purposes
Univar Canada Ltd. v. R. (2005), [2006] 1 C.T.C. 2308 (T.C.C. [General Procedure])	No	N/A: trial judge found that transactions did not give rise to a "tax benefit"
Evans v. R. (2005), [2006] 2 C.T.C. 2009 (T.C.C. [General Procedure])	No	N/A: trial judge found the transactions did not lack economic substance; and, also there is no overall scheme in ITA against surplus stripping
Brouillette c. R., [2005] 4 C.T.C. 2013 (T.C.C. [General Procedure])	No	N/A: trial judge found the transactions were fundamentally entered into for a non-tax business or commercial purpose
MIL (Investments) S.A. v. R., [2006] 5 C.T.C. 2552 (T.C.C. [General Procedure]), affirmed 2007 CarswellNat 1719 (F.C.A.)	No	N/A: Court of Appeal found no abuse or misuse by virtue of treaty exemption. Also, LOB clause in treaty will cure this problem on a going-forward basis
Overs v. R., [2006] 3 C.T.C. 2255 (T.C.C. [General Procedure])	No	N/A: Transactions similar to those in *Lipson* involving reverse attribution were held by trial judge to have been primarily undertaken for non-tax purposes. In *Lipson*, Bowman C.J. distinguished decision in *Overs* on the basis of its "underpinning of estate planning"

Tax Court of Canada Case	GAAR Applied	Impact of Proposed GAAR Amendments
MacKay v. R., [2007] 3 C.T.C. 2051 (T.C.C. [General Procedure]), reversed 2008 CarswellNat 677 (F.C.A.), leave to appeal refused (2009), 2009 CarswellNat 41 (S.C.C.)	No	See *OSFC Holdings Ltd* case study
McMullen v. R., [2007] 2 C.T.C. 2463 (T.C.C. [General Procedure])	No	N/A: trial judge found the transactions did not lack economic substance. Also, the court held that there is no general anti-surplus stripping scheme in the ITA
Landrus v. R. (2008), [2009] 1 C.T.C. 2009 (T.C.C. [General Procedure]), affirmed 2009 CarswellNat 919 (F.C.A.)	No	N/A: trial judge found that the transactions involved a "real economic loss"
Remai Estate v. R. (2008), [2009] 3 C.T.C. 2024 (T.C.C. [General Procedure]), affirmed 2009 CarswellNat 5570 (F.C.A.)	No	N/A: courts found no misuse or abuse of statutory scheme re gifting of "qualified securities" under subsec. 118.1(13) ITA
Collins & Aikman Products Co. v. R., 2009 CarswellNat 1510 (T.C.C. [General Procedure]), affirmed 2010 CarswellNat 3613 (F.C.A.)	No	N/A: transactions involving cross-border reorganization of a foreign corporation held by Court of Appeal not to be subject to GAAR as the result of a "deliberate policy choice" made by Parliament
Garron Family Trust (Trustee of) v. R. (2009), [2010] 2 C.T.C. 2346 (T.C.C. [General Procedure]), affirmed 2010 CarswellNat 5521 (F.C.A.), affirmed 2012 CarswellNat 953 (S.C.C.)	No	N/A: trusts held to be subject to tax as residents of Canada; however, if trusts were resident in Barbados, they would be eligible for an exemption under Treaty
Triad Gestco Ltd. v. R., [2011] 6 C.T.C. 2302 (T.C.C. [General Procedure]), affirmed 2012 CarswellNat 3853 (F.C.A.)	Yes	GAAR applied as artificial capital loss created without any economic loss

Tax Court of Canada Case	GAAR Applied	Impact of Proposed GAAR Amendments
1207192 Ontario Ltd. v. R. (2011), [2012] 1 C.T.C. 2085 (T.C.C. [General Procedure]), affirmed 2012 CarswellNat 3894 (F.C.A.)	Yes	Artificial capital loss transactions created without economic substance
Global Equity Fund Ltd. v. R. (2011), [2012] 1 C.T.C. 2224 (T.C.C. [General Procedure]), reversed 2012 CarswellNat 4117 (F.C.A.)	No	Loss created from a shuffle of paper; no real economic loss was suffered; proposed amendments are applicable

Index

A

Abusive tax avoidance
    defence against
        judicial doctrines, 65–70, *see also* Judicial doctrines
        technical rules and laws, 58–65
    ill-effects of, 80–81
        competition distortion, 54
        effect on taxpayer compliance, 42–44
        inequitable allocation of tax liabilities, 45–47
        interference with government social and economic policies, 48–54
        wasting resources on uneconomic activity, 47–48
Australia's economic substance doctrine
    GAAR, historical, 259–262
    GAAR, new Part IVA, 262–278
        dominant purpose, 267–273
        notice provision, 274
        provision of last resort, 274–275
        reconstruction provision, 273
        scheme, 266–267
        tax benefit, 264–265
        what has been accomplished, 275–278

reporting requirements and penalties, *see* Reporting requirements and penalties
Author's conclusion, 387–390

B

Bond and option sales strategy (BOSS) and son-of-BOSS (SOB), 195–200
Business purpose test, 79–81, 94, 96, 102, 148, 152, 159

C

Canada Trustco Mortgage Co., 104, 119, 179
    case study, 357–364
Case studies, see *Canada Trustco Mortgage Co., OSFC Holdings Ltd., Produits Forestiers Donohue Inc., Faraggi, 4145356 Canada Ltd.*
Commercial and economic reality, 131–135
Concluding remarks by author, 387–390
Contingent instalment sales (CINS) U.S. tax cases, 185–191
Corporate-owned-life insurance (COLI) U.S. tax cases, 192–193

D

Distressed asset debt (DAD) U.S. tax cases, 200–202
Duha Printers (Western) Ltd., 95–98

E

Economic substance doctrine
    academic consideration, 38–39
    Australia's doctrine, *see* Australia's economic substance doctrine
    author's conclusion, 387–390
    codification of, U.S., 202–228
    doctrine of, 78

GAAR, and, 3–9
international consideration, 1–2, 37–38
introduction, 1–28
New Zealand's doctrine, *see* New Zealand's economic substance doctrine
other countries' doctrine (Hong Kong, Ireland, India), 300
South Africa's doctrine, *see* South Africa's economic substance doctrine
Supreme Court's treatment of, 83–127, see also *Mara Properties Ltd., Duha Printers (Western) Ltd., Shell Canada Ltd.*
    non-tax cases treatment of, 127–137
U.K., *see* U.K. draft GAAR
U.S. doctrine, *see* U.S. economic substance doctrine

F

Faraggi, case study, 376–379
Frank Lyon v. United States, 157–160

G

GAAR in Canada
    proposed amendments to, 5–12, 26
    Technical Notes, 105
Goldstein v. Commissioner, 155–157
Gregory v. Helvering, 15, 94, 97, 142, 149–154

H

Haig-Simons income concept, 38
High-basis, low-value tax shelters, U.S. tax cases, 193–195

J

Judicial doctrines, 65–70
    business purpose test, 79–81
    economic substance, 78
    legal ineffectiveness, 72–73
    present day application of, 71–77
    sham, 77–78
    substance over form, 73–76, 78

K

Knetsch v. United States, 131, 154–155

L

Legal ineffectiveness, 72–73

M

Mara Properties Ltd., 92–94

N

New Zealand's economic substance doctrine
    GAAR, historical, 283–285
    GAAR, current provisions
        arrangement, defined, 286
        reconstruction provision, 293–294
        section BG 1 essential elements, 285–286
            relationship to other provisions of Act, 294–294
        tax avoidance, defined, 286–288
        tax avoidance arrangement, defined, 288–293
    reporting requirements and penalties, *see* Reporting requirements and penalties
    what has been accomplished, 295–299

O

OSFC Holdings Ltd., case study, 364–371
Ordinary course of business exception, U.S., 160–168

P

Produits Forestiers Donohue Inc., case study, 372–376

Q

Quebec reporting requirements and penalties, 325–326

R

Ramsay doctrine, 304–306
Reporting requirements and penalties
    Australia
        no reporting requirement, 338
        promoter penalties, 339–340
        shortfall penalties, 338–339
        tax alerts from ATO, 340
    Canada
        promoter penalties, 320–321
        proposed new reporting regime, 321–324
        tax shelter reporting requirements, 317–320
        generally, 315–317
New Zealand
    no reporting requirement, 341–342
    promoter penalties, 345–346
    revenue alerts, 346
    shortfall penalties, 342–345
Quebec, 325–326
South Africa
    reporting penalties, 349
    reporting requirements, 347–349

United Kingdom
    investor penalties, 353
    promoter penalties, 353
    reporting requirements, 351–353
United States
    enjoined conduct, 337
    failure to disclose, 331
    failure to file returns, 330
    failure to maintain investor lists, 330
    false statements and gross valuation overstatements, 330–331
    IRS website advisories and settlement initiatives, 336–337
    promoter penalty, 329–330
    reporting requirements, 327–329
    strict liability understatement, 331–336
    understatements, 331

S

Sale and leaseback (SILO) U.S. tax cases, 180–185
SARS (South African Revenue Service) Discussion Paper on Tax Avoidance, 34, 37, 230, 236, 242, 251, 350
Sham transactions, 77–78, 91
Shell Canada Ltd., 90–92, 98–103
South Africa's economic substance doctrine
    Discussion Paper on Tax Avoidance, 2005, 236
    GAAR amendments, 2006, 237–256
        abnormality requirement, 242–243
        application in the alternative, 252
        application to avoidance scheme in whole or any part, 252
        arrangement, defined, 237–238
        avoidance arrangement/tax benefit, defined, 238
        determination of purpose, subjective vs. objective, 241–242
        impermissible avoidance arrangement, 238–239
        lack of commercial substance, 245–248

misuse or abuse of provisions of the Act, 248–251
normality factors, 243–245
notice requirements, 253
purpose of avoiding taxes, 239–241
remedies under GAAR, 253
what has been accomplished, 253–256
GAAR, historical, 231–235
reporting requirements and penalties, *see* Reporting requirements and penalties

Stubart Investments Limited guidelines, 60–61, 79, 88

Supreme Court of Canada cases
Canada Trustco Mortgage Co., 104, 119, 179
Duha Printers (Western) Ltd., 95–98
Mara Properties Ltd., 92–94
non-tax cases treatment of, 127–137
rationale of re economic substance of tax transactions, 107–127
certainty and predictability, 119–124
prohibition against "judicial re-drafting", 108–119
right to minimize taxes, 125–127
Shell Canada Ltd., 90–92, 98–103
Stubart Investments Limited, 60–61, 79, 88

T

Tax arbitrage, 38
Tax avoidance
abusive, 33, *see also* Abusive tax avoidance
defined, 31–32
tax mitigation, 33
Tax minimization *vs* abusive tax avoidance
difference between, 35–40
Tax mitigation, 33–34
Tax shelters
Canadian experience, 176–177
Quebec's efforts to curb ATP (aggressive tax planning), 178

defined, 171–172, 175
OECD pronouncements, 177–178
U.S. experience, 169–176
U.S. tax shelter cases
    bond and option sales strategy (BOSS) and son-of-BOSS (SOB), 195–200
    contingent instalment sales (CINS), 185–191
    corporate-owned-life insurance (COLI), 192–193
    distressed asset debt (DAD), 200–202
    high-basis, low-value, 193–195
    sale and leaseback (SILO), 180–185
value billing in, 175–176

U

U.K. draft GAAR
    European Community concept of abusive practice, 312–313
    GAAR Study Group Report, 2011, 310–311
    historical anti-avoidance, 303–307
    HMRC's administrative position, 307
    Inland Revenue Consultation Document, 1998, 309–310
    reporting requirements and penalties, *see* Reporting requirements and penalties
    Tax Law Review Committee Discussion Paper, 2009, 310
    Tax Law Review Committee Report, 1997, 307–309
U.S. economic substance doctrine
    application by courts, 139–142, 146
    bona fide legal relationships, 169
    codification of, 202–228
        budget proposal for fiscal year 2000, 211
        budget proposal for fiscal year 2001, 213
        budget proposal for fiscal year 2010, 216–217
        codification in 2010, 217–218
        debate for and against, 203–210
        Joint Committee study/White Paper 1999, 212
        key provisions of, 218–223

criticism of, 142–145, 147–149
flexibility advantage, 145–146
leading court cases
    Frank Lyon v. United States, 157–160
    Goldstein v. Commissioner, 155–157
    Gregory v. Helvering, 149–154
    Knetsch v. United States, 154–155
legislative intent, 168–169
ordinary course of business exception, 160–168
reporting requirements and penalties, *see* Reporting requirements and penalties
subjective business purpose, 147–149
tax shelter cases, *see under* Tax shelters

Numbered

4145356 Canada Ltd., case study, 379–386